ROYAL HORTICULTURAL SOCIETY

GARDENING
THROUGH THE YEAR

ROYAL HORTICULTURAL SOCIETY

GARDENING
THROUGH THE YEAR

IAN SPENCE

A Dorling Kindersley Book

For Mum & Dad, in loving memory

Dorling **DK** Kindersley

LONDON, NEW YORK, SYDNEY, DELHI, PARIS,
MUNICH AND JOHANNESBURG

Project Editor Louise Abbott
Art Editor Alison Lotinga

Managing Editor Anna Kruger
Managing Art Editor Lee Griffiths

DTP Designer Louise Waller
Media Resources Charlotte Oster, Romaine Werblow
Picture Research Sharon Southren
Production Controller Elizabeth Cherry

First published in Great Britain in 2001 by
Dorling Kindersley Limited,
9 Henrietta Street, Covent Garden, London WC2E 8PS

A CIP catalogue record for this book is
available from the British Library

ISBN 0751 313114

Colour reproduced by Colourscan, Singapore
Printed and bound by Mohndruck GmbH, Gütersloh Germany

see our complete catalogue at
www.dk.com

contents

Introduction

Gardeners are born optimists, always looking forward to the year ahead, convinced that they will achieve much more than in the previous year. But to get better results, gardeners need to plan ahead and have a good sense of timing. We must get sowing and planting times right so the young plants we have nurtured in a warm environment are not put outside and then promptly killed by frost. And if a shrub is pruned at the wrong time, we may discover too late that we have cut off all this year's flowers. It is quite easily done, by any one of us, no matter how expert we like to think we are, especially in the mad spring rush when our enthusiasm is fired by the cheering sight of the first snowdrops and daffodils, or the first seedlings germinating in a seed tray.

It is often recommended that you keep a notebook handy and write down jobs as you do them, so you can refer to your notes at a later date. But if your memory is anything like mine, you'll often forget to note down the jobs you have already done. This book will make it easier to plan your time, not by

dictating exactly what should be done when, but by giving general guidelines and realistic advice. Climatic conditions can vary widely – there can be a difference of up to four weeks from a plant flowering in the south compared to the north of the country – so you can't give hard and fast rules on the timing of operations in the garden. Another consideration to take into account will be the weather conditions at the time a particular job has to be done. If there is a foot of snow on the ground in late April then you cannot sow seeds outside! This actually

happened to me in my native Scotland in the mid-1980s. So the timing of operations in the garden will vary from month to month and from year to year and you must always remain flexible.

In recent years there has been a notable change in our weather patterns, with one season now seeming to merge into the next. This appears to be the result of global warming, caused by excessive emissions of so-called greenhouse gases such as carbon dioxide. Owing to milder conditions, plants tend to come into flower much earlier than in previous years. And plants that are considered tender are surviving our increasingly mild winters, while pests and diseases once killed off by snow and frost are now on the increase. We also seem to be experiencing extremes of weather, with parts of the country receiving considerable rainfall in short periods of time. This has led to widespread flooding, and the year 2000 has seen some of the worst floods for centuries. Patterns of work in the garden are changing, and we must adapt to change when planning which plants to grow and where to plant them.

This book is not only a guide to the gardening year; it also offers practical suggestions for improving your garden, in the form of straightforward projects that will take no more than a day or, at most, a weekend – projects such as creating themed borders, or building a potting bench. I always get tremendous satisfaction from making things myself rather than buying them (perhaps it's in my Scottish blood!).

Despite what I have said about climate changes earlier, try not to worry too much about the timing of jobs in the garden. Nature always seems to have a way of balancing things out, and even if you think you're very late sowing those hardy annuals or planting out the summer bedding plants, they can still surprise you by growing and flowering beautifully, just at the right time. Enjoy your garden and don't let it become a chore. Indeed, gardening may become a passion that lasts a lifetime, and this guide to the gardening year will hopefully inspire you to be as dedicated as I am. Happy gardening!

IAN SPENCE

JANUARY

The garden in J a n u a r y

Think that there is nothing to do and that the garden looks boring at this time of year? Then think again! However harsh the weather, there are plants to enjoy, and plenty of jobs to be getting on with.

COLD WINDS, FROST AND HEAVY RAINS can often make it seem as if nothing can be done in the garden now. But even though it is usually the coldest time of the year, January can be regarded as the most optimistic month. Those few plants that do dare to flower really are to be marvelled at, and without the distraction of a riot of colourful blooms, it's a time to admire the beautiful silhouettes of bare branches, the colours and textures of bark, and the reassuring solid forms of evergreens. And a garden covered in snow always looks so good too.

Warm winter glow ▷
Although deciduous, beech hedges retain their dead leaves over the winter.

Watch the weather forecasts

A blanket of snow can actually be good for the garden, killing off unwanted pests and protecting plants from severe frost. Do, however, keep an eye on the weather forecasts and look out for warnings of heavy falls of snow and sharp frosts, as action will have to be taken to prevent damage to some plants in the garden. Conifers in particular are prone to damage from heavy snowfalls, as the weight of the snow can bring branches down and out of place. Fruit cages can also suffer badly under heavy snow.

Strong winds are also a regular January feature. This is why it is important to make sure young trees and shrubs are well staked, especially in exposed parts of the country. It's also why newly planted shrubs, especially evergreens, need a wind barrier. Cold winds can cause severe damage, particularly to evergreen leaves. These biting winds will scorch young foliage, and it rarely recovers, so temporary shelter will certainly help preserve the investment you have made in new plants.

You may find that some parts of your garden seem to get much more heavily frosted than others, especially if the garden includes a slope or other change in level. Cold air is heavier than warm air and always finds the lowest level. This is an important point to bear in mind when siting slightly tender plants in the garden. You should also beware of planting fruit trees in low parts of the garden where there is a frost pocket, as the flowers may be damaged in the spring.

Time for some exercise

With the days just beginning to lengthen even shortly after New Year celebrations, it's a good time to work off the excesses of the holiday period. If you want to get warmed up on a cold winter's day, continue with winter digging of borders and in the vegetable garden, as long as the soil is not

△ **Winter treats**

Most winter-blooming shrubs, like this hamamelis, or witch hazel, have the most intensely sweet-scented flowers.

waterlogged or frozen. If the ground is frozen, it is still a good time to barrow out manure or garden compost and spread it on the ground.

Lawns will also benefit from some attention, even though it's still the middle of winter. Work done at this time of year will pay handsome dividends in creating a smooth green sward in the summer. But do keep off the grass when it is frosted over.

This is also a good month to go round the garden and catch up with repairs to fences and trellises, and other tidying jobs which may not be very exciting but will make all the difference to the appearance of the garden in the summer months. Keep a notebook handy and take this with you when pottering around the garden in winter. This is a great help if you're planning any changes to the garden, especially to remind you of all the plants you want to buy later!

Plants to admire

Less strenuously, a walk round the garden on a January day can reveal surprises, with snowdrops and also carpets of the yellow winter aconite coming into

WEATHER WATCH

Winter temperatures in the United Kingdom are largely governed by the temperature of the sea, with January and February being the coldest months. Coastal areas are colder in February. The coldest nights occur when there is no wind, the skies are clear and there is snow on the ground. The coldest air will be found on low ground. Our lowest ever temperature – -26°C – was recorded in a Shropshire valley on 10 January 1982. Average daily temperatures in January will be 6–8°C in the south and 2–4°C in the north.

January is a month of gale force winds associated with deep depressions crossing near or over the British Isles, with high ground experiencing the worst of all. The number of days with gales and their strength varies considerably between north and south. Northern parts of the country, especially those on exposed western coasts, experience the strongest winds, with on average 7.5 days of gales, whereas the south has on average 0.2 days.

Southern regions get the most sunshine now mainly because they are flatter. In the north, eastern parts get more sun than the west for the same reason. Southern regions get on average 57.2 hours of bright sunshine whereas, say, in Shetland they will get only 22 hours this month.

The amount of rain falling on different parts of the country also varies according to its topography (how hilly or flat it is), southern and eastern regions being the driest. In some parts of the north-west Highlands of Scotland 236mm of rain may fall this month; on the south coast of England, 81mm.

Snow is rare in coastal areas, more frequent over high ground inland. The amount varies hugely from almost none at all in many areas to heavy falls which last all winter. North-east Scotland fares worst, averaging 16 days of snow, with the south coast of England having only on average 0.8 days.

◁ **Bark and stem interest**
Several species of dogwood (*Cornus*) and willow (*Salix*) can be pruned hard to send up these clumps of narrow stems, with brightly coloured bark in many shades.

Planning ahead

If the weather is just too cold and wet to venture outside, then there is plenty to be getting on with indoors. It's a good month for planning the rest of the gardening year. One job to do at this time, if you haven't already done so, is to put your feet up by the fireside with a glass of something to keep out the cold, and browse through the seed catalogues. Or, you can go down to the local garden centre and pick the seeds you require. And although the first spring bulbs may have yet to open in the garden, it's time to choose summer-flowering bulbs too.

Raising plants

It's not too soon to start thinking about sowing some early crops, always the most welcome, and of course the ones which will save you most money. Summer bedding plants that need an especially long growing season, such as pelargoniums and snapdragons (*Antirrhinum*), can also be started off towards the end of the month. If you have a greenhouse or conservatory which can be heated sufficiently to keep out the frost then you're off to a flying start, but even without a glasshouse there is still plenty that can be done raising plants on a windowsill.

Raising your own plants from seed is a thrill which never leaves you, no matter how long you have been gardening. It's very easy to do, but there are a few items you will need, especially at this time of year, to provide a little extra heat. To heat a whole greenhouse is very expensive nowadays, and many plants can be started off instead in a propagator. Plants such as tomatoes and the tender summer bedding plants all need that bit more heat, preferably

flower. Another must for January is the Christmas rose, *Helleborus niger*, which despite its name usually hangs back until this month – but the stunning white flowers are worth waiting for. For the purest flowers, protect the plants as the buds begin to open, to prevent rain and snow spoiling the blooms.

We mustn't forget the tremendous amount of interest that can be created in the winter garden by using plants with attractive bark and colourful stems. Plants such as dogwoods (*Cornus*) can be pruned back in spring to eye-catching bright winter stems in shades of red, green, yellow and even black. Evergreen shrubs and conifers in all shades from dark green to golden yellow also add life and lustre to the winter scene. Scent is another bonus of many winter-flowering plants – chimonanthus (wintersweet), *Viburnum × bodnantense* and sarcococca, another shrub which despite its festive common name, Christmas box, will continue to pour out its stunning fragrance into the air through the New Year.

◁ **Build a potting tray**
This high-sided tray (see p.30) will be invaluable in spring when it comes to filling pots and trays, and potting up cuttings and seedlings.

▽ **Bold shapes**
The strong outlines of conifers look even more dramatic when lit by low, slanting winter sunshine. Here they are underplanted with heathers.

from below the soil, to get the seeds to germinate, and this is where a propagator is so very useful, gently warming the compost from the base. There are many on the market these days; your choice will be based on cost, the space available and the amount of seed you want to raise. Even the cheapest and simplest do a great job.

Always be careful with electrical appliances, especially where they will come into contact with moisture, and follow the manufacturer's instructions to the letter. If you have any doubts contact the manufacturer or a qualified electrician.

A building project for January

Another piece of equipment to help with raising plants, useful on a greenhouse bench and invaluable if you have to do your seed-sowing on the kitchen table, is a potting tray or "tidy", with back and sides to stop compost mixes getting everywhere. Our practical project this month (see p.30) shows how to make one simply and inexpensively.

So there you have it – almost as busy a month as in the summer. Bet you can't wait to get going now!

J A N U A R Y
AT A GLANCE

- Make sure that birds have food and water.
- Keep on top of winter-germinating weeds.
- Clear the crowns of plants of damp leaves.
- Continue with winter digging as soil conditions allow. Cover ground to keep out the wet.
- Order seeds and summer-flowering bulbs.
- Check newly planted trees and shrubs and refirm if lifted by frost.
- Brush snow off heavily laden trees, shrubs and hedges before the weight breaks branches.
- Check supports of trees and shrubs.
- Protect plants vulnerable to wind and cold.
- Plant deciduous hedging.
- Prune trees and shrubs to shape.
- Prune wisteria and other vigorous climbers.
- Take hardwood cuttings of trees and shrubs.
- Take root cuttings from perennials.
- Check forced bulbs for growth.
- Sow sweet peas under cover.
- Aerate lawns to improve drainage.
- Keep a small area of ponds free from ice.
- Sow early vegetable crops under cover.
- Chit early potatoes.
- Protect fruit trees from bird damage.
- Continue planting and winter-pruning of fruit.
- Force rhubarb.
- Sow some summer bedding under cover.

! LAST CHANCE
- Prune grape vines before the sap starts rising.
- Protect container plants from freezing spells and insulate outside taps.

★ GET AHEAD
- Warm up some soil with cloches for early seed-sowing outdoors.
- Clean pots and seed trays for spring sowing.
- Send the lawnmower off for servicing.

Rhododendron '**Vuyk's Scarlet**' ☆ • Small azalea suitable for a pot or tub under cover *(see p.346)*

Betula papyrifera • The paper birch, with brilliant white peeling bark *(see p.301)*

Freesia '**Imperial Red**' • Delicate bulb to force for indoor display *(see p.320)*

Hamamelis x intermedia '**Arnold Promise**' ☆ • Scented flowers on bare branches *(see p.322)*

Galanthus plicatus subsp. *byzantinus* ☆ • Classic snowdrop with nodding, green-marked flowers *(see p.321)*

Garrya elliptica • Evergeen shrub that makes a good hedge in sheltered areas *(see p.321)*

Lonicera x *purpusii* • Shrubby honeysuckle with intensely fragrant flowers *(see p.331)*

Prunus x *subhirtella* 'Autumnalis Rosea' ♀ • Winter-flowering cherry tree *(see p.344)*

Acer pensylvanicum 'Erythrocladum' ♀ • Tall maple with warm-toned patterned bark *(see p.295)*

Skimmia japonica • Tough evergreen shrub that does best in shade *(see p.353)*

Lachenalia aloides 'Nelsonii' • Tender bulb to grow in pots indoors *(see p.328)*

Sarcococca hookeriana var. *humilis* • Small but powerfully scented evergreen shrub *(see p.352)*

Chimonanthus praecox • Twiggy shrub with strongly scented flowers *(see p.304)*

Iris unguicularis ♀ • Clump-forming perennial with fragrant flowers *(see p.327)*

Eranthis hyemalis ♀ • Woodland perennial forming mats of yellow stars *(see p.317)*

Erica carnea 'Springwood White' ♀ • One of the many winter-flowering heathers *(see p.317)*

Prunus serrula ♀ • Flowering cherry, bare in winter, but with glossy ornamental bark *(see p.344)*

Helleborus niger 'Potter's Wheel' • Small perennial for dappled shade *(see p.324)*

TOP ROW: *Cornus sanguinea* 'Winter Beauty' • *Cornus alba* 'Aurea' ♥ • *Cornus stolonifera* 'Kelseyi'
BOTTOM ROW: *Cornus alba* 'Sibirica' ♥ • *Cornus alba* 'Elegantissima' ♥ • *Cornus stolonifera* 'Flaviramea' *(see p.310)*

WHAT TO DO IN JANUARY

AROUND THE GARDEN

SHRED THE OLD CHRISTMAS TREE. Once Christmas is over there is always the problem of what to do with the tree, if you bought a real one. The best way of dealing with it is to take it to your local waste tip, where many local authorities now run recycling schemes; the tree will be shredded and used for compost and mulching. If you have your own shredder (or have been bought one for Christmas) do it yourself, and you will be able to use the material in the garden.

MAKE SURE GARDEN BIRDS HAVE FOOD AND WATER. Birds need most help in finding food and drink when the ground is frozen solid or covered in a thick blanket of snow.

IT'S AMAZING HOW WEED SEEDLINGS germinate during mild spells even in the depths of winter. On any winter rambles round the garden, take a hoe with you so that these weed seedlings can be knocked out before they get too big. This will save an

Clear weeds *Chickweed may germinate and flourish all through the winter months.*

enormous amount of time and effort when spring comes around. Collect up annual weeds and put them on the compost heap. Any perennial weeds should be dug up with as much of the roots as possible, putting these in the bin. Pieces of root left in the soil or put on the compost heap often start to grow again, actually increasing the weed problem.

THERE ARE FEW PESTS AND DISEASES around at this time of year, but many are lurking in nooks and crannies just waiting for the warmer spring weather. So it is worth practising good garden hygiene and clearing up any rubbish left lying around. Weeding (see above) is also a good idea. Fresh green weeds often attract pests such as whitefly even at this time of year, and groundsel is notorious for harbouring rust disease.

ANY DECAYING LEAVES should be collected and put on the compost or leafmould heap. Pay particular attention to clearing the crowns of herbaceous perennials and alpines, as these are vulnerable, especially the latter, to rot in prolonged damp conditions under fallen leaves. Leaves are best composted, not burned, as they can then contribute to the goodness of the soil. Be careful when disturbing large piles of leaves in which a hedgehog may be hibernating. The garden grippers or "big hands" one sees advertised in magazines are safer tools to use than forks or rakes.

ORDER SEEDS FROM CATALOGUES. There is a bewildering array of seeds and young plants available from all the seed companies. It can sometimes be

daunting, even for experts, trying to decide which seeds to choose. But it's a pleasant job leafing through catalogues and planning what to grow in the year to come. Stick to older, tried and tested varieties and you won't go wrong, but it can be great fun trying some of the new ones that are brought out every year.

When seeds start arriving from the seedsmen, store the packets in a cool spot. The ideal place is in a plastic container with a sealable lid; just pop it in the bottom of the fridge.

GET TO KNOW YOUR SOIL BETTER. It can be disheartening to see plants, especially expensive ones, struggle because the soil in your garden does not suit them. If you're not sure which plants and seeds to choose, testing your soil for its type and pH – its acidity or alkalinity – is always a good idea. Feel some soil in your hands to get to know

FEEL YOUR SOIL'S TEXTURE

Good soil holds together yet also crumbles easily.

Clay forms a solid ball.   Sand feels dry and gritty.

Spread manure over the ground and the weather should help incorporate it into the soil.

its structure: whether it contains a high proportion of clay, making it heavy and wet, or sand, making it light and dry – or something between the two, the perfect balance being known as "loam".

The pH of soil can be tested with kits stocked by garden centres. There are plenty available, costing anything up to to several pounds. The cheaper ones with colour-coded charts are perfectly adequate for most purposes.

Knowing more about your soil will help you to choose plants that will really do well in your garden, either by scrutinising labels when you buy, or, if you prefer to plan at home, getting yourself a good "plants for places" guide.

Regularly adding bulky organic matter to your soil – for example, digging in compost or well-rotted manure, or mulching with leafmould – can do wonders to improve extreme soil types, stopping plants drowning in heavy clay or drying out in free-draining sand. But it's better and easier not to try to change the pH of your soil in beds and borders, and just choose plants that like it instead – you can always grow other plants in containers filled with tailor-made soil mixes.

BARROW ORGANIC MATTER ONTO FROZEN GROUND. There isn't much to do outside when the soil is rock-hard, but an ideal job that will save you time later is spreading out well-rotted manure or garden compost. It's quite alright to walk on the soil if it is frozen hard. Barrowing muck or compost about can be a messy job, but in these conditions the barrow can be wheeled over the ground with little effort and without getting caked with soil. Don't, however, take the barrow over a frozen lawn; if you can't avoid going over the lawn put down planks to protect it.

Spread the load evenly over the surface and the ground will soon thaw out when the weather improves. It's a job to keep you warm on a cold day. No need to sit huddled indoors by the fire!

CHECK TOOLS and equipment when the weather is too bad to work outside. Non-stainless steel spades, forks and hoes will benefit from a rub over with an oily rag to prevent them rusting. Most tools wear out more from neglect than from use; if you look after good tools well, they will last a lifetime.

WRAP INSULATION AROUND OUTSIDE TAPS. If this was not done earlier, do it now, as we often get the coldest weather of the year in February.

COLLECT AS MUCH RAIN AS YOU CAN in water butts to save on water use in the summer.

CHECK THAT PROTECTIVE MULCHES AND BLANKETS over frost-tender plants and pots (see November) have not been disturbed by winter weather.

TREES & SHRUBS

MOVE DECIDUOUS SHRUBS OR TREES IN THE WRONG POSITION. No matter how expert we like to think we are, we can all make mistakes in placing plants. Now there is still time to move deciduous trees and shrubs if they are in the wrong place, or have outgrown their allotted space. You may need a friend to help with moving larger ones. Never underestimate the effort needed to move large plants (see p.64 for illustrations), because you want to take as much of the root system and the heavy soil around it as you can for the plant to survive and grow well.

CHECK TREE TIES AND STAKES. Young trees and bushes which are being blown about by strong winds will never last long. It is therefore essential to check ties and stakes regularly. When trees and bushes are planted loosely, a sunken area will develop around the base of the main stem, caused by the continual rocking back and forth. This is where water can collect, and it is here that the plant will begin to rot and die off.

Ties should be secure, but not so tight that they restrict the growth of the plant. Check them regularly, and if they are constricting the main stem, loosen them a little to allow for expansion.

TO PROTECT NEWLY-PLANTED TREES AND SHRUBS, especially evergreens, from wind damage erect a windbreak to shelter the plant. The windbreak can be in the form of hessian, horticultural fleece, bubble plastic or strong polythene, tied securely to a framework around the plants. To increase the level of protection, some straw can be placed inside the windbreak framework, but make sure air can circulate and light can get in, particularly for evergreens.

HEAVY FALLS OF SNOW seem to be getting rarer these days, but when we do get snow storms they can cause a lot of damage, particularly to trees and shrubs. The weight of even a little snow on branches can be considerable, so to prevent any damage brush the snow off as soon as you can. It's quite a pleasant job on a winter's day.

PLANTING

PLANT BARE-ROOT TREES AND SHRUBS (see November), but only if soil conditions allow. If the soil is frozen or very wet, heel in the plants temporarily in a corner of the garden until conditions are suitable. Take out a trench big enough to hold the root system, and cover the roots with soil, firming gently. The plants will survive like this for quite some time.

If the soil is too frozen even to heel in the plants, then provided that their roots are wrapped in hessian or sacking, they can be kept in a porch, shed or garage with some light. Unwrap the top growth if packed in straw to let it get some light, and never let the roots dry out, so keep the wrapping around the roots moist. As long as you look after them, plants can last in this situation for a few weeks.

PRUNING AND TRAINING

THIS IS A GOOD TIME OF YEAR TO PRUNE TREES TO SHAPE (see also December). Young trees often grow out in all directions into other plants in the

TREES & SHRUBS *continued*

CLEARING A TREE TRUNK

First year   *Second year*

Using loppers
When pruning off thicker stubs in the third year, leave the slightly swollen ring, or "branch collar", intact when you remove branches. Use loppers, rather than straining and damaging secateurs.

border, throwing out shoots along the whole length of the trunk. You can prune out misplaced stems this month, cutting always to a junction or the main stem, and if you want to make a standard tree with a length of bare trunk, then cut back some of the side growths now too. Don't do it all at once, but over two or three seasons, shortening some this year and removing them completely next year (see above). The extra leaves left on the main stem over the summer will help to encourage the vigour of the tree; cutting side branches off all at once would severely affect the tree's growth.

SOWING SEEDS FROM BERRIES

1 The best way of separating the seed from the flesh of the berries is to wash them under the tap in a fine mesh sieve. If necessary, wrap the berries in a teatowel first and crush the pulp under running water.

2 Tap out the remains onto kitchen paper, pick out the seeds and rinse them again.

3 Sow the seeds in trays or pots of peat-free compost, and cover them lightly with coarse grit.

4 Place in a cold frame or at the foot of a sheltered wall outside, covering with a sheet of glass to keep off excessive rain and prevent mice getting at the seeds. Some seeds may take a long time to germinate, so don't be too quick to throw out the pot.

PROPAGATION

SOW SEEDS OF BERRYING SHRUBS AND TREES (see above) such as cotoneaster, pernettya and sorbus. Like alpines, seeds of these shrubs need a period of cold to break their dormancy.

THERE IS STILL PLENTY OF TIME TO TAKE HARDWOOD CUTTINGS (see October) from deciduous shrubs such as dogwoods (*Cornus*), willows, roses, forsythia, flowering currant (*Ribes*)

and chaenomeles. Even if your garden is well stocked, it costs nothing to grow on a few favourites in case plants are lost in the future. And if do you end up with a surplus, young rooted shrubs are always a welcome contribution to plant stalls at fairs and fetes.

HEDGES

BRUSH SNOW OFF EVERGREEN HEDGES before the weight of it splays out branches.

OVERGROWN DECIDUOUS HEDGES can be cut back into shape at this time of year (see December).

DECIDUOUS HEDGING PLANTS such as beech, hawthorn and hornbeam can be planted now in well-prepared ground, if weather conditions permit. The cheapest way to buy hedging is as young, bare-rooted plants known as "whips", sold in bundles. If the soil is frozen or waterlogged, heel in the plants (see previous page) temporarily.

To prepare the ground, mark out a strip at least two spade-blades wide along the length of the proposed hedge. Start taking out a trench to one spade's depth at one end and barrow the first load of soil to the other end. If the soil in the bottom of the trench is heavy, compacted clay it can be loosened up with a garden fork, but don't bring the poorer subsoil to the surface.

Incorporate as much organic matter as you can get into the soil at the bottom of the trench, and then cover this with soil by digging the next section of the trench, repeating the process until you reach the end of the line, when the last part can be filled with the soil in your

barrow. Space the young plants out along the trench, fill in and firm with your boot. In exposed sites, a windbreak of, for example, plastic mesh stapled between posts, on the windward side of the hedge, will help the plants establish.

PREPARING TO PLANT A HEDGE

Even if the plants are small and slender, digging a trench for them is better than individual holes.

Well-rotted farmyard manure worked into the bottom of the trench will give plants a good start.

CLIMBERS

BRUSH SNOW OFF dense evergreen climbers and wall shrubs; when snow accumulates on these it can break stems and put strain on ties and supports.

CLIMBERS TO PRUNE NOW include wisteria (see below), ornamental vines (see also December), ivies, Virginia creeper and Boston ivy, and climbing hydrangea. These plants have a habit of working their way into window frames and doors, so cut them back as needed to prevent any expensive damage being done. And don't forget to prune them away from gutters on house walls.

WISTERIAS REQUIRE PRUNING twice during the year. In summer (see July) they need all the long new shoots cut back to 5–6 buds from the main stems. Now these same shoots should be shortened even more, to two or three buds from the main stems. You can do the same to any new sideshoots that have grown since summer. The advantage of doing this pruning now is that with no leaves on the plant, you can see exactly what you are doing. It encourages the formation of flower buds to give a terrific show of colour in late spring and early summer.

Pruning wisteria In winter, shorten all of the sideshoots from the main framework of stems.

PERENNIALS

THERE AREN'T MANY PERENNIALS flowering this month, so hellebores are particularly welcome. The flowers can easily be damaged by winter rains splashing soil onto them, so it is a good idea to cover the plants with a cloche to protect them. This way you will have perfect flowers in the garden or to cut and take into the house.

CONTINUE TO CLEAR WEEDS from around plants, and cut down any dead stems left for winter interest that are looking tatty or diseased.

ORDER HERBACEOUS PERENNIALS from nursery catalogues now for delivery and planting in the spring. Now is the time to look through bits of paper to find all those notes you made of "must-have" plants seen at shows and gardens last year. There is a bewildering array of plants to choose from these days, and you can have plants in flower, if you choose them carefully, almost all the year. For interest all season, and a foil for the flowering plants, choose from some of the beautiful foliage plants on offer, especially the increasingly popular grasses, sedges and ferns.

CONTINUE TO LIFT AND DIVIDE OVERGROWN CLUMPS of herbaceous perennials (see March) when soil conditions allow – in other words, when the soil is not frozen or so wet that it sticks to your boots.

INSPECT DAHLIA TUBERS IN STORE. Take a close look from time to time to see if there is any disease present. Any that are showing signs of rotting off should be removed from the rest, or the disease may spread through the lot. Any individual tubers infected can be cut from the main crown of the plant, retaining the rest. Early stages of rotting can be controlled by cutting out the infected area and dusting with flowers of sulphur.

TAKING ROOT CUTTINGS from perennials is an easy way of increasing your plants and it doesn't need a lot of special equipment. Plants that are ideal for this method of propagation are those with long fleshy roots, such as Japanese anemones, Oriental poppies, verbascums and acanthus. Dig up the plant and wash off as much soil as you can to expose the roots. When taking cuttings (see right), make a diagonal cut across the "bottom" (the end that was furthest from the plant) so you remember which way up to plant them.

Plants with finer roots can also be used, for example phlox, nepeta and primulas. Prepare the cuttings in the same way, but lay them flat on a tray of the same "cuttings compost" mixture and cover lightly with compost.

Provided that you haven't denuded it of roots, the parent should grow away again if carefully replanted and fed.

ALPINES

ALPINE PLANTS NEED PROTECTION not from the cold, but from winter rains. If you haven't already done so (see October), make them a shelter to keep off the worst of the wet.

SOW ALPINE SEEDS THIS MONTH (see December). By sowing now you can give the seeds the period of cold that they experience in the wild, which is essential for germination in spring.

TAKING ROOT CUTTINGS

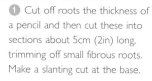

❶ Cut off roots the thickness of a pencil and then cut these into sections about 5cm (2in) long, trimming off small fibrous roots. Make a slanting cut at the base.

❷ Insert the cuttings, upright, in compost mixed with vermiculite. Cover with grit, and water well.

❸ Put in a frost-free cold frame. You can put them in a heated propagator for faster rooting, but it is not essential.

❹ New growth should appear in the spring, when you can separate the cuttings and put each in its own small pot of compost.

❺ Grow on the young plants over the spring and summer, watering regularly, until they are large enough to plant out (autumn is a good time).

BULBS

ORDER SUMMER-FLOWERING BULBS now in good time for planting in spring. Leafing through colourful catalogues at this time of year is a pleasant occupation, allowing you to dream of the summer to come. Ordering early and by mail will give you the best choice of varieties, especially useful if your local garden centre usually only stocks a limited selection. Lilies are the most popular, but why not try some of the more unusual bulbs (see below), such as *Galtonia candicans* (wood hyacinth) and *Ornithogalum* (star of Bethlehem). Even the frost-tender bulbs such as tigridias, which, like dahlias and gladioli, need lifting and storing in a dry frost-free place over winter, are easy to grow.

FORCED BULBS. Bring bulbs planted in pots and bowls last autumn (see August and September) into the house in batches to give a prolonged flowering display. The time to bring them inside is when they have made about an inch of growth, so watch them carefully. It's best to bring them into a cool room or greenhouse for a week or two first; if it is too warm too quickly, they will grow fast, becoming leggy, and produce poor flowers. Water bulbs in bowls without drainage holes carefully or you may overwater them.

FIND A SHELTERED SPOT outdoors, out of sight but in the light, where you can put pots of bulbs as they finish flowering for you indoors. Remove the spent flowerheads to prevent the plants' energy going into producing seeds. Feed them with a high-potash fertiliser to build up flower buds for next year. Continue feeding regularly until the foliage dies back, and then in spring, the bulbs can be planted in the garden. It is not a good idea to force the same bulbs year after year. Forcing takes a lot of energy out of the plants, and they rarely flower well if forced more than once.

REGULARLY CHECK BULBS BEING STORED over the winter to see if there is any disease present. Any bulbs which have rotted should be removed immediately, otherwise the disease will spread to other bulbs.

POT UP HIPPEASTRUM BULBS (see December) and start into growth.

Galtonia candicans

Ornithogalum umbellatum

Tigridia pavonia

ANNUALS & BEDDING

SOW SUMMER-FLOWERING BEDDING PLANTS THAT NEED A LONG SEASON TO GROW: begonias (tuberous, fibrous-rooted and semperflorens kinds), snapdragons, lobelias, pelargoniums and gazanias. To raise bedding in any quantity you will, unless you commandeer an entire spare bedroom, need a greenhouse or conservatory – especially when, like these, the young plants will be taking up space for months. See Under Glass.

IF YOU ORDER SEEDS AND PLUG PLANTS BY MAIL, choose now, especially plug plants, to ensure that the varieties you want are reserved for you. See also February, Under Glass.

SOW SWEET PEAS now unless you got ahead by sowing them in the autumn. They like a good root run, so it is best to sow them in long sweet pea tubes, which can be bought from garden centres. Or, make your own with newspaper rolled into tubes and held together with sticky tape – or keep the cardboard centres from rolls of toilet or kitchen paper. Place the tubes side by side in a seed tray and fill with peat-free compost. Some seeds, depending on the variety (check the packet), need soaking overnight to soften the seed coat. Another method is to "chit" the seed – to remove a sliver of the seed coat carefully with a garden or craft knife at the opposite end from the "eye", where the root will start growing. This allows water to penetrate the seeds more easily, hastening germination. Sweet peas don't need very high temperatures to germinate so there is no need for a propagator – a cool light room or even a sheltered cold frame is sufficient.

AUTUMN-SOWN SWEET PEAS sown several to a pot (see October) need potting on to make strong healthy plants for putting out in May. Soak the compost and gently knock the plants out of the pot, and separate carefully. Put each into a 9cm (3½in) pot of peat-free compost and gently firm in. Water in gently to settle the compost, and put in a light place. A high shelf in a greenhouse or conservatory is ideal; failing that, the sunniest windowsill you've got. You should also pinch out the tip of the young shoots, either now or next month (see February).

SOWING SWEET PEAS

❶ If necessary, soak the seeds overnight to soften the seed coat, or chit (nick) the tough coating to help the seeds germinate.

❷ Push a couple of seeds into the compost in each tube to a depth of about 2.5cm (1in). Water well, and keep in full light.

CONTAINERS

DEADHEAD POTS OF WINTER-FLOWERING PANSIES to keep the display going into spring, and check whether they need water (see below).

EVEN IN WINTER, CONTAINER PLANTS MAY NEED WATERING, especially those that are growing at the base of house walls. Here they can be sheltered from rain by the overhang of the eaves of the house. It is surprising how dry plants can get when they are in this position.

ALL POT-GROWN SHRUBS may need some protection as we enter the coldest part of the winter. It is not the hardiness of the plant that is the point here; during very frosty weather plants in pots are more vulnerable to damage from freezing because the roots in the pots are above ground. If you haven't already protected them, there are several ways to do it. The pots can be wrapped in bubble plastic, or use hessian sacking if you can get it (see November). Extra protection can be given by wrapping straw or bracken around the pot and holding this in place with bubble polythene, hessian or old compost sacks. Grouping the pots together will also give them some mutual protection.

Alternatively, if you've got the space, take the plants indoors during bad weather. Even a cold greenhouse, or a shed with windows, will provide enough protection from all but the severest frost. You can wrap the pots too to be on the safe side.

Remember that empty pots used for ornament in the garden, especially glazed pots and old terracotta, are also vulnerable to cracking by frost, and may need protection too.

PONDS

THERE IS LITTLE to do with ponds this month, but do keep a watch on the weather forecasts for freezing temperatures. If there are fish in the pond and it is left frozen over for long periods the fish will die from lack of oxygen. Every morning, check the pond, and if it is frozen over, melt a small area of ice with a pan of hot water. Just sit the pan or a kettle on the ice for a few seconds and it will melt. Don't whatever you do try to break the ice with a hammer or stick, as the shock waves could kill the fish and any other wildlife in the pond, and also possibly damage the pond liner.

Another precaution is to float a small plastic or rubber ball on the pond. This is important in ponds with rigid sides, such as those made from cement or preformed fibreglass liners. The ball will absorb the pressure of the sheet of ice (water expands when frozen) so that strain is not put on the pool sides. You can pop the ball out to create an airhole in the ice, but you must replace it at night, which may involve enlarging the hole again if temperatures have stayed low.

For large ponds, or if you have trouble bending, a handy alternative to a ball is one of the plastic milk or juice containers with a handle, part-filled with water. You can tie a cord round the handle and peg it at the side of the pond, then you will be able to pull it out without leaning over too far.

LAWNS

Spike lawns *Use a garden fork to aerate grass. You can hire mechanical spikers for large areas.*

KEEP OFF ICY GRASS. Don't walk or work on the grass at all when it is frozen or frosted, otherwise later, when it thaws out, your footprints will show up as yellow patches on the lawn where the grass has been damaged.

IMPROVE DRAINAGE. If you did not do so in the autumn (see September), improve the drainage of the lawn using a garden fork. Badly drained parts of the lawn will be easily recognisable as lower patches where the water tends to collect and takes longer to drain away. Wait until the surface of the lawn dries out a bit, and then push a garden fork 15cm (6in) into the ground and wiggle it about to open up the holes, at about 15cm (6in) intervals over the affected area. Immediately after aerating the lawn spread some sharp or horticultural sand (not builder's sand), or a sand and soil mixture, over the area and work this into the holes with a stiff broom. This prevents the holes closing up too quickly and further improves the drainage. It is a tedious job, but well worth doing. If you have a large lawn you can hire a mechanical aerator to make the job easier.

REPAIR HOLLOWS AND BUMPS. Even out bumpy lawns this month if the weather is mild and dry. Hollow areas where water tends to collect can be raised level with the rest of the lawn quite easily. First make 'H'-shaped cuts in the lawn with a spade or lawn edging iron, and then carefully push a spade under the turf and roll each half back (see below). Add soil to the exposed area, firm it well and carefully roll back the turf. You may have to add more soil to get the turf very slightly higher than the surrounding lawn to allow for settling. After rolling back the turf, tamp down firmly with the back of a rake and the job's done.

To repair bumps in the lawn do exactly as for repairing hollows, but when the turf is rolled back, scrape some soil from underneath to lower the level of the turf.

GET THE LAWN MOWER SERVICED. Send it off now to avoid the servicing agents' busiest time and get the mower back quickly – because, believe it or not, the lawn can be given a light trim occasionally even through the winter. It only needs a light topping with the blades set at their highest setting. Don't do it if the lawn is very wet or frozen as

Bumps and hollows *Lift a flap of turf and either scoop out or fill in with soil to even them out.*

LAWNS *continued*

this will ruin the grass. An occasional trim during winter keeps the lawn looking healthier, because the less grass you take off every time you mow the lawn (and this applies in summer as well) the better it is for the grass plants.

Don't forget to send your garden and edging shears off with the mower for a professional sharpening.

DISPERSE WORM CASTS. Worms are quite active in lawns at this time and are most noticeable by the casts they leave on the surface of the lawn. These should be brushed off regularly; if they are left, they will be trodden into the surface of the lawn, looking unsightly and encouraging weed seeds to grow in these small patches. However, worms do a lot of good in other parts of the garden and should be encouraged. It doesn't take long to clear even a large lawn if you use a long, flexible cane and swish it back and forth over the lawn to scatter the casts. On smaller lawns you can use a stiff broom. Try to do the job when the surface of the lawn is dry and the worm casts will spread more easily.

NEW LAWNS

LAY TURF. Turf can be laid (see October) on prepared ground only if the soil is not frozen or so wet that it sticks to your boots. Work from planks laid on the ground so that you do not make compacted dents in the levelled soil. While seed is economical, making a lawn from turf is more or less instant; you will have to keep off it for only a few weeks until it settles in. Turf costs more than seed, but if you can, buy the best quality turf, guaranteed weed-free.

VEGETABLES & HERBS

Maintaining deep beds *Each year, spread organic matter over the beds, rather than digging it in. The level will fall over the season.*

COMPLETE WINTER DIGGING of empty beds and new vegetable plots as soon as the weather allows. The sooner cultivation is completed the better, to allow the winter weather to play its part in breaking down large clods of earth, improving the soil structure and making it easier to work in the spring.

If you cannot dig at all this month, you can at least, if the ground is frozen hard, barrow out manure or compost and spread it on top of the soil (see Around the Garden). When the soil is very wet it is best to keep off it completely, or it will compact down and become a sea of mud that dries to a hard crust, and you will have great difficulty working it later on trying to make seed beds.

One way of avoiding having to walk on the soil is to use the deep bed method of growing vegetables (see November). With this, beds only four feet wide can be tended by reaching over from paths each side; you never need to tread on the soil. Initially double-dig the beds (see October) incorporating plenty of organic matter. Once this is done, you need never dig

them again. Every winter, you simply add organic matter as a surface layer, and the healthy worm population that should exist in the beds will take it down into the soil for you. Crops can be grown much closer together because you don't need to leave extra space between rows to get at the plants. The soil is not compacted in any way, and you'll get higher yields than on a conventional arrangement of rows.

PLAN YOUR CROP ROTATION. In order to avoid the buildup of certain pests and diseases, and to make the best use of manures and fertilisers, it is best to practice crop rotation. Vegetable crops can be divided into three main groups

that share some vulnerability to the same plant problems, and also prefer different soil treatments before they are planted or sown. Vegetables within these groups should never be grown in the same place again until at least two years have gone by. The table below shows a simple crop rotation, meant as a guide only. You may not grow all the crops listed or you may grow more, but the principles remain the same.

There are some vegetables that do not lend themselves to rotation, and don't need it – the perennial crops, such as asparagus, globe artichokes and sea kale. Asparagus needs its own bed, as it will be in place for many years, but the others are beautiful plants in their own

THREE-YEAR CROP ROTATION

YEAR ONE

GROUP ONE	GROUP TWO	GROUP THREE
Add compost over winter, and fertiliser before sowing	Rotted manure in winter, and fertiliser before sowing	Add compost, lime (see February) and fertiliser
Grow:	*Grow:*	*Grow:*
Beetroot	Beans	Cabbage
Carrots	Peas	Cauliflower
Kohl Rabi	Leeks	Brussels Sprouts
Potatoes	Lettuces	Broccoli
Turnips	Onions	Kale
Swedes	Shallots	Savoy
Celeriac	Radish	Spinach

YEAR TWO

GROUP TWO	GROUP THREE	GROUP ONE

YEAR THREE

GROUP THREE	GROUP ONE	GROUP TWO

YEAR FOUR

GROUP ONE	GROUP TWO	GROUP THREE

Cover the ground where your earliest sowings and plantings will go, to dry and warm the soil.

right that make handsome additions to ornamental plantings. Sweetcorn is an annual crop that does not fall into any particular group, so it can move around from year to year as a gap-filler.

COVER GROUND WITH POLYTHENE. When you have dug over an area, cover the ground with a large sheet of polythene, anchored round the edges or tucked firmly into the soil, or with cloches. This will keep off the worst of the winter weather so that the soil can easily be raked down into seedbeds next month, and also helps to warm up the soil for early setting out of young plants sown now indoors, and also for earlier sowing outdoors. This way you'll get the earliest vegetables when they are at their most expensive in the shops.

HARVESTING

CONTINUE TO HARVEST Brussels sprouts (from the base of the stem upwards), leeks, parsnips, swedes and turnips. If you haven't grown any winter greens, remember that turnip tops can be cooked and eaten as a green vegetable.

SOWING OUTDOORS

IN VERY SHELTERED SOUTHERN PARTS of the country seeds may be sown under cloches on land which has already been covered for a few weeks. In most of the country, however, it is better to wait until February to sow under cloches, or March to sow direct. Seeds to sow (see also February) include lettuce, salad onions, radishes, peas, broad beans and spinach. Sow small amounts at 10 to 14-day intervals, and these crops will follow on from any sown under glass (see below).

SOWING INDOORS

SOW A FEW EARLY CROPS, either in seed trays or in modules (large trays with individual cells). The advantage of growing in modules is that you need not disturb these young plants until it is time to plant them out, when the little rootballs can be transplanted intact, so the plants get off to a flying start without any check to their growth. The plants will be ready to be put out under cloches or blankets of horticultural fleece from late February, depending on where you live.

Sow small quantities of lettuce, summer cabbages and cauliflowers, radishes, carrots (choose round varieties for module sowing), spinach, salad onions, turnips, peas and broad beans. None of these seeds requires high temperatures to germinate – about 13°C (55°F) is adequate, so a windowsill in a warm room will do, or, for faster results, use a propagator. Then grow them on in good light. If you sow in seed trays rather than modules you will need to prick them out (this means lifting them very carefully by the seed leaves and spacing them out in new trays of compost) once the seedlings are large enough to handle.

SOW ONION SEED THIS MONTH. To get the best onions they need a fairly long growing season, and if you're thinking of entering some in a local flower show later in the year, then to see off the opposition, the sooner they are sown the better. To grow for exhibition quality, onions are sown in seed trays and potted on carefully as required, but for us ordinary mortals, or just for ordinary onions, the easiest way to start off is to sow them in clusters in modules. Fill the modules with peat-free compost and water to settle it. Sow five or six seeds per cell and cover them with vermiculite. Put in a heated propagator or on a warm windowsill until the seeds germinate.

The onions will be ready to plant out in late March. There's no need to thin, just plant out the whole cluster. As the onions grow they push each other apart

Protect cauliflower curds You can use the plant's own leaves, bending or tying them over the top.

and produce fine bulbs of an ideal size for use in the kitchen.

There is another way to grow onions without raising seedlings, and that is to plant small onion bulbs known as "sets" in spring, just as one plants cloves of garlic. They can be put straight into the ground (see March).

LOOKING AFTER CROPS

BEND LEAVES OVER CAULIFLOWERS to protect the developing curds, which actually are the plants' undeveloped flowerheads. When exposed to a prolonged period of light the curds tend to turn green and, after a while, the flower buds develop, making them inedible. By bending a few leaves over the curd this process is slowed down, making the crops last a bit longer. It's very easy to do: just snap leaves near the base of the midrib and tuck them in around the curd. You can tie the leaves up to keep the curds covered in windy weather.

PLANNING AHEAD

START EARLY POTATOES. Freshly dug potatoes are in a class of their own when it comes to flavour, better than anything in the supermarket. It's time to look out for seed potatoes as they need to be chitted (started into growth) before planting in March. As well as advancing the date on which the potatoes will be harvested, chitting them will also increase the overall yield.

To start them off, lay the tubers in a tray with the "rose" end uppermost (the end with most buds on it). Put them in a light, cool but frost-free place – a spare room, porch or utility room –

VEGETABLES *contd*

Sprouting seed potatoes *An egg tray is ideal, but they can rest against each other in a shallow box.*

and after two or three weeks, shoots will begin to sprout. To get the best crop thin the shoots to two or three per tuber. Plant out from March.

BEAT THE SEASONS

FORCE CHICORY Chicory forced for tightly packed, blanched leaves is a good alternative when other salad crops are scarce in winter, but it can be eaten cooked as well. You need to have sown the seeds and raised plants outside over the summer (see May). Now, lift the large tap roots and pot them up. A 20cm (8in) pot will take about five roots. Any old potting compost will do for forcing. Once potted, invert another pot over the planted-up one, and make sure you cover any drainage holes to keep out the light. Keep in a temperature of 10–13°C (50–55°F). Keep the roots moist, but not wet. If the compost was well watered to begin with, then little or no watering should be needed, provided that the pot is not in too warm a place. The chicory should be ready three or four weeks after potting up.

FRUIT

PROTECT FRUIT CAGES FROM DAMAGE by heavy snowfalls. Either roll the roof netting to the centre supports and tie it in, or remove the roof netting entirely and drape it over trees and bushes vulnerable to bird damage (see below).

PICKING AND STORING

INSPECT FRUITS IN STORE and remove any showing signs of rotting off. Disease can spread rapidly through fruits in store, so the sooner it is detected, the less likely it is that other fruits will be affected. A place which is cool and dark is the ideal place for storage. Fruits that have been wrapped in paper (see September) are less likely to spread rots. If you have a surplus in store, or are feeling kind-hearted, throw some older fruits outside on the vegetable garden or somewhere similar for the birds.

LOOKING AFTER CROPS

PROTECT FRUIT TREES AND GOOSEBERRIES WITH NETTING. Birds can cause a lot of damage in the fruit garden, even in winter. Bullfinches in particular love to eat plump, developing fruit buds. Larger free-standing trees can be difficult to protect, so you may just have to accept some loss, but restricted forms of trees such as cordons and fans grown against a wall or fence are easily protected with netting draped over them. Make sure the netting is well secured so birds don't get themselves trapped in it. Plastic mesh or fleecy web are safer for birds.

TOWARDS THE END OF THE MONTH is a good time to apply an

Check ties *Look at all stakes and ties, especially on the growing stems of young trees*

organic fertiliser to all fruit in the garden. Although you may not notice it, even in late January things are beginning to stir; sap is beginning to rise and trees are awakening after their winter rest. An organic fertiliser such as blood, fish and bone or seaweed meal is ideal, because organic fertilisers release their nutrients slowly over a long period; the plants don't get the sudden boost to growth as they would get with inorganic, or chemical, fertilisers. Too much soft growth early in the season is more susceptible to damage from frosts and pests and diseases. Pull away any mulch around the bases of trees and bushes if necessary before feeding; water the ground, and renew the mulch.

CHECK ALL FRUIT TREE TIES AND STAKES ARE SOUND. Older ties can break, so it is as well to check them regularly. Also, do bear in mind that as a tree grows the stem expands, so on winter inspection tours, however brief, check ties are not too tight on young trees or they will be strangled.

EXAMINE APPLE TREES FOR SIGNS OF CANKER. The symptoms to look for are flattened areas of bark which show signs of splitting, causing the bark to flake off. The branch may also become swollen around the affected

area. During the winter, red fungal fruiting bodies can also be seen. Canker is caused by a fungus called *Nectria galligena*; it is spread by wind-borne spores and attacks the tree through open wounds or pruning cuts. To control canker you may have to cut out whole branches or fruiting spurs. Make sure you remove all damaged bark and wood back to healthy tissue. Cut to a healthy-looking bud, a branch junction, or the main trunk. Look at the pruning cut: if the wood is white, you have pruned back to healthy wood and the cut should heal well. If it still shows brown staining, you should prune further back.

SPRAY FRUIT TREES AND BUSHES with a tar oil winter wash unless you did so last month (see December). Many pests like to hibernate in little cracks and crevices in the bark. It is important to spray really thoroughly with the wash to make sure any pests lurking there are killed. Be careful when using winter wash because it can damage evergreen plants, including grass. If fruit trees are growing in grass, put large sheets of polythene down to protect it. Protect other plants nearby by covering them with polythene. Black plastic bin bags are ideal for plants that

If canker attacks an apple tree, the whole branch must come off

are not too large. Do any spraying on a frost-free, calm day, so that spray does not drift on the breeze onto other plants.

SPRAY PEACHES AGAINST PEACH LEAF CURL. This disease is quite noticeable in spring and summer. The foliage of the tree becomes puckered and turns red and purple, dropping off prematurely. It is not fatal for the tree; leaves produced later in the season usually remain healthy. But year on year it will weaken it, and it is certainly unsightly and distressing.

Trees grown under glass are usually immune as the disease is spread by spores carried by wind and rain. Dwarf varieties are now available and these are easily grown in large pots for the patio; they can be taken inside for the winter if you have the space.

A way of protecting outdoor fan-trained trees is to erect a temporary open-ended polythene shelter. Put the shelter in position from mid-winter until mid-spring. This prevents the spores of the disease reaching the tree. Spray with a copper fungicide or mancozeb at intervals from mid- to late winter, following the instructions carefully. Stop spraying as flower buds begin to open.

RENEW GREASE BANDS on fruit trees (see September) if these have been in place for a long time. These prevent insects crawling up the tree trunk to lay their eggs.

Symptoms of peach leaf curl

PRUNING AND TRAINING

CONTINUE TO WINTER-PRUNE apples, pears, red and white currants, gooseberries and blackcurrants.

• **WINTER PRUNING OF APPLES AND PEARS** (see November for illustration) consists mainly of pruning back the leaders of trained fruit trees, whether they be fan-trained, espaliers, cordons or bush trees. The main, or leading, shoots of main branches should be cut back by about one-third to half, depending on the vigour of the tree. The one basic rule to remember about pruning is that the harder you prune, the stronger will be the subsequent growth from the point of pruning. Also, thin out overcrowded fruiting spurs on trained trees. This allows better air circulation, reducing the risk of disease.

• **PRUNING OF RED AND WHITE CURRANTS AND GOOSEBERRIES** is similar. If fruiting shoots were summer-pruned (see July), they can now be pruned further to a couple of buds from the main branches.

• **BLACKCURRANTS ARE PRUNED** in a slightly different way (see right). Some people prune blackcurrants just after the fruit has been picked, but in winter you can see better what you are doing without a lot of foliage on the plants. Blackcurrants fruit on new and old wood and they are grown as a stool plant (that is, branches grow in a clump from or just under ground level). Pruning is all about maintaining a balance between old and new wood. Around one-third of the bush should be removed each year to maintain the vigour of the plant. Wherever possible cut out older stems to the ground, leaving younger wood to fruit in the summer. It is inevitable that you will cut out some young growth. When finished, you should have a balance between old and new branches on a fairly open bush. Mulch, ideally with well-rotted farmyard manure, after pruning. Do not let it actually touch the stems.

PRUNE AND TRAIN SUMMER-FRUITING RASPBERRIES if this was not done in the autumn (see September). This is quite a good time of year to do the job, as it's easier to see what you are doing. The old canes that bore the fruit last year need to be cut from the wires to which they were tied last year, and cut to ground level. Tie in the new canes that grew last year, but did not fruit, about 10cm (4in) apart. Any stems taller than the support wires can be cut back to the top wire, or the tip of the shoot can be brought down and tied to the top wire (see February for illustration). Either way, this will encourage the formation of fruit-bearing sideshoots in the summer.

PRUNE OUTDOOR GRAPE VINES (SEE DECEMBER). Finish off this job this month if you haven't already done it, as the sap will soon begin to rise, and if vines are pruned any later it will cause "bleeding": the sap will seep badly out of the pruning cuts. All laterals (sideshoots made last season) should be pruned back to two or three buds and leading shoots pruned back to within the allotted space.

PLANTING

CONTINUE TO PLANT fruit trees and bushes (see November), but only when the soil conditions are right. If trees are planted when the soil is too wet, firstly the soil will get compacted with walking on it. Secondly, even if only the surface of the soil is frozen, it is not good practice to put frozen lumps of soil around plant roots. The ideal condition for soil to be in for planting is moist, but not sticking to your boots.

PRUNING AN ESTABLISHED BLACKCURRANT BUSH

Before pruning *Blackcurrant stems grow from the base of the plant, eventually forming a crowded clump which must be thinned.*

After pruning *Taking out around one in three of the stems, always choosing the oldest ones, leaves a more open bush that will fruit better.*

FRUIT *continued*

If conditions are not right for planting, heel in the plants in a sheltered corner (see Trees & Shrubs) or put them in the shed for a day or two. They will be fine if you keep the roots moist.

BEAT THE SEASONS

BEGIN TO FORCE STRAWBERRIES which were potted up last August, taking them into the greenhouse or conservatory (see Under Glass).

FORCE RHUBARB for tender young stems in the spring. Clear away all dead foliage from the crown. If the winter has been mild, you may see fresh growth already starting at ground level; be careful not to damage it. Cover the plant with an old dustbin or large pot. Alternatively you can buy terracotta rhubarb forcers. These are upturned clay pots with a lid to check on the forced rhubarb, usually decorative. Place one of these over the crown of the plant, and if you can get it, cover the forcer with a pile of fresh horse manure. The heat generated by the manure as it rots will force the rhubarb on even quicker.

Forcing rhubarb *The shaped terracotta covers, with a lid for checking progress, are attractive too.*

UNDER COVER

CHECK GREENHOUSE HEATERS are working properly. Electric heaters that are not working properly will waste electricity and cost more to run. With paraffin heaters make sure the wick is trimmed regularly; if the flame does not burn properly, toxic fumes will be given off and these will harm the plants. Gas heaters should also be checked regularly by a qualified engineer. Don't tinker with any appliance if you're not sure about what you are doing; call in a professional to do the job safely.

CHECK GREENHOUSE INSULATION put up earlier to make sure it is sound and is in place. Any gaps will cause a loss of heat, and bigger heating bills.

CLEAN THE GREENHOUSE OR CONSERVATORY inside and out. If this job wasn't done in the autumn, now is a good time to do it before the onslaught of seed-sowing begins. You may have to move plants about, or put them outside for a while if the weather is not too cold. Cleaning the glass thoroughly, inside and out, is the most important job, as plants need all the light they can get at this time of year with short days. The inside should be scrubbed down with a garden disinfectant – floors, walls and benches. Pay particular attention to all the little corners where glass meets frame and the roof meets the sides of the structure; these are the places where pests lurk and hibernate through winter.

VENTILATE ON MILD DAYS. Even in January, on the occasional sunny day, temperatures inside can rise dramatically in a short time. Open the ventilators for a few hours on such days, but close them well before sundown.

KEEP AN EYE OUT FOR FUNGAL DISEASES like botrytis, commonly called grey mould after its appearance on the surfaces of stems and leaves. It is difficult to control, as the spores are carried in the air. It attacks plants through wounds and on decaying stems, leaves and flowers. The best way to try to control it when cold weather makes ventilation difficult is by practising good hygiene. Remove any yellowing leaves or stems from plants before the fungus gets a chance to invade. Clear any fallen leaves away promptly and put them in the bin, not on the compost heap where the spores may survive. If there is a bad attack of botrytis, spray with a fungicide containing carbendazim.

WATCH OUT FOR VINE WEEVIL in heated greenhouses and conservatories, where the larvae of this pest may be active all year. Symptoms are a general lack of vigour or wilting, caused by damage to the roots by the grubs of the weevil: legless, creamy-white larvae, about 10mm (⅜in) long, with curved bodies and a brown head. A wide variety of plants grown in pots can be affected. In a heated house, you can use a biological control to combat vine weevil (see April), even at this time of year.

CLEAN POTS AND SEED TRAYS, ready for seed sowing in the months ahead. Using clean containers, especially for seed sowing and rooting cuttings, will help to cut down on the incidence of pests and diseases, reducing the need for chemicals to control problems. Use a garden disinfectant and rinse thoroughly. Make sure children cannot get near these solutions.

INSPECT ANY BULBS, CORMS AND TUBERS stored in the greenhouse and throw away any that show signs of rot.

WATERING AT THIS TIME OF YEAR needs to be done with some care. Only water plants when they absolutely need it. The best way to gauge whether a plant needs water is to regularly lift the pot and feel the weight; the lighter the pot the more water it will need, and the heavier it is the less water it will need. Plants which are almost dormant this month, such as overwintering fuchsias and pelargoniums resting in frost-free greenhouses, should be watered very sparingly, just enough to keep them alive. Too much water and they will put on too much growth, long and drawn because of the lack of light in winter. Actively growing plants like winter-flowering azaleas, poinsettias and bulbs will need more watering. It's best, if you can, to do any watering early in the day in winter. This gives the greenhouse or conservatory time to dry out a bit before the cold night sets in.

PRUNE ESTABLISHED FUCHSIAS in heated greenhouses and conservatories. Fuchsias can be started into growth now by watering more often and moving them into the lightest position; indeed, they may already have started, with buds beginning to burst. To keep the plants bushy and healthy prune them quite hard, pruning all the side shoots back to one or two buds from the main framework of stems. The plants also need repotting at this time. Remove the plants from the pots and tease out as much of the old compost as you can. Then repot the plant into the same size pot with fresh peat-free potting compost, and water in well to settle the compost around the roots. Spray the plants occasionally with a fine mist of clear water to encourage buds to swell.

RAISING PLANTS FOR OUTDOORS

SOW SEED OF THOSE SUMMER-FLOWERING BEDDING PLANTS that need a long growing season to produce

SOWING TENDER PERENNIALS

❶ Fill a pot or tray to overflowing with peat-free compost, and give it a tap on the bench to settle it. Strike off the surplus and press lightly.

❷ Water the compost with a fine rose or from below before sowing the seeds thinly over the surface of the compost.

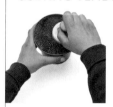

❸ Larger seeds like those of pelargoniums can be covered with sieved compost or vermiculite – just enough to cover the seeds.

❹ Place a sheet of glass over the pot and place in a propagator until the seeds germinate. Shade against strong sunlight to prevent drying out and scorching of the young seedlings.

flowers in time for summer – all kinds of begonias, and antirrhinums, pelargoniums, lobelias and gazanias. To germinate successfully these seeds need to be grown in a propagator which can be maintained at a constant temperature of 21–22°C (68–70°C). Most propagators give a lift of about 10°C (20°F) above the ambient temperature, so on very cold nights, some extra heating may be needed. At this time of year light is at a premium, so place the propagator on a south-facing bench.

To sow, see left. The fine seeds of antirrhinums and begonias do not need covering. Even the lightest covering of compost is likely to be too deep for these very fine seeds. More information on sowing can be found on the back of seed packets. When the seeds are large enough they can be pricked out into trays or potted up separately. Seeds sown in the warm moist conditions in a propagator are particularly prone to a disease called damping off. Avoid this by sowing thinly, to avoid overcrowding, and use only clean trays and pots. If you regularly have problems with damping off, it is worth using Cheshunt compound, a fungicide, as a preventative.

SOW SWEET PEAS if you didn't get this done in the autumn, and pot on and pinch out the tips of any sown in autumn. See Annuals and Bedding.

START OFF SOME VEGETABLES AND SOW ONIONS (see Vegetables and Herbs).

GLASSHOUSE AND HOUSE PLANTS

KEEP WINTER-FLOWERING POT PLANTS such as azaleas and poinsettias

Pot up lilies for summer, for example Lilium duchartei *(left) and* Lilium martagon *(right)*

in a cool place in good light. If the room or conservatory is too warm the flowers will go over much more quickly. A light windowsill facing south, if you haven't got a greenhouse or conservatory, is the ideal place. The plants will have to be turned every two or three days to prevent them growing one-sided towards the light.

FORCED BULBS Bring in pots of spring bulbs that were plunged outside in autumn. A greenhouse or conservatory makes a good staging post on their way into the house, to get them used to warmer temperatures gradually. Pots of bulbs that have finished flowering can be put outside now (see Bulbs).

POT UP SOME LILY BULBS FOR EARLY FLOWERS INDOORS. Lily bulbs are available in the garden centres now and will be spectacular grown in containers indoors. Not only do you get the beautiful flowers, but the scent is terrific too. Put three or four bulbs into a 17cm (7in) pot containing peat-free multi-purpose compost. Cover the bulbs with 7–10cm (3–4in) of compost and put in a light place. After a few weeks the bulbs will come through and in late spring, the flowers will fill your home

with colour and with many, wonderful scent. The bulbs can be planted in the garden when the flowers are over.

CROPS UNDER GLASS

PRUNE VINES UNDER GLASS as soon as possible, because even in winter, the temperature under glass can rise considerably, and the vines will start into growth very quickly. If they are pruned when the sap is rising they will 'bleed': sap will ooze out from the pruning cuts, weakening the plant. To prune them, untie the fruited stems from the supports and cut back to one or two buds from the main stem, or rod, as it is called. Prune back the rod if it is growing beyond its allotted space. Check for pests by gently removing any flaking bark, and spray with a tar oil winter wash, as used on fruit trees (see Fruit). Don't spray if you see green buds starting to swell or they will be damaged; wait until next winter.

BRING IN STRAWBERRIES which were potted up last August to be forced. If you have enough plants, bring half in now and the rest next month, then the fruiting season will be extended. Remove any old, dead and diseased foliage and place the pot in as much light as possible, a high shelf being ideal.

Forced strawberries
An underplanting of spring salad complements these pretty plants.

MAKE A POTTING TRAY

A HIGH-SIDED POTTING TRAY (basically, a potting bench without legs) is a very useful piece of equipment to have when taking cuttings, sowing seeds and repotting plants, keeping compost in one place and preventing mess. It can be used in the house or in the greenhouse. You can adjust the measurements to make whatever size you require. Buy slightly larger pieces of timber to allow for waste when sawing.

YOU WILL NEED: Quarter-inch plywood cut into 4 pieces: one 850 × 675mm for the base, one 850 × 210mm for the back, and two 700 × 210mm for the sides • 6 lengths of roofing lath for the supports: two pieces 850mm long and two 625mm long for the base, and two 235mm long for the sides • Panel pins • Non-toxic wood preservative

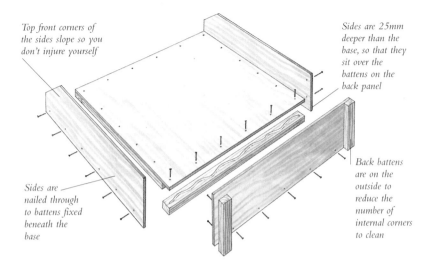

Top front corners of the sides slope so you don't injure yourself

Sides are 25mm deeper than the base, so that they sit over the battens on the back panel

Sides are nailed through to battens fixed beneath the base

Back battens are on the outside to reduce the number of internal corners to clean

① Mark a diagonal across one corner of the each of the sides and saw it off.

② Sand down any rough edges.

③ Put the base on the floor and place the 4 battens for the base on it to check the fit. Adjust as necessary.

④ Glue the battens on to the base and allow to dry.

⑤ Turn the base over, and nail through to the base battens with panel pins.

⑥ Glue and nail the remaining 2 battens on each end of the back section, then turn the base up on its end and nail the back to the base, through to the batten underneath, with panel pins.

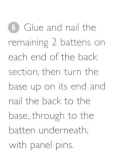

7 Nail the sides into the base battens, sawn corners uppermost at the front. The sides overlap the base to sit over the back battens, so you can nail through to fix the sides to the back.

8 Now coat the tray inside and out with a non-toxic timber preservative.

9 The tray being put to good use in late spring.

FEBRUARY

The garden in February

This month sees the sap beginning to rise, not only in plants but in the gardener too. It can actually be a colder month than January, but it's rare that there aren't a few days of watery sunshine to tempt us outside.

Winter landscape ▷
Sumach trees are dramatic in snow, with chunky, felted, rust-coloured seedheads.

THERE IS NOW A NOTICEABLE DIFFERENCE in the length of daylight and a feeling of anticipation, too, as a new season is just around the corner. It's a lovely month to just wander around the garden and look at the buds beginning to swell. Many buds are attractively coloured at this time, and they're packed with youthful energy, ready to burst forth. Towards the end of the month, early spring-flowering bulbs such as *Narcissus* 'February Gold' are in flower, and the earliest primroses are also appearing. And in many parts of the country, early-flowering shrubs such as chaenomeles and daphnes will start to bloom.

Winter wet

Weatherwise, however, February can be very cold, with heavy snow, severe frosts and a lot of rain. Try to keep off the soil when it is excessively wet as you will do more harm than good. Tramping over very wet soil compacts it, pushing out all the air and damaging the structure. Once this has happened, raking the soil down into a fine, crumbly tilth that will give seeds a good start becomes much more difficult. If you really must tread on soil in these conditions, work from a plank that will spread your weight evenly over the soil and reduce compaction.

△ **On the lookout**
Even though buds are breaking and insect life is stirring, food is still very scarce for garden birds in February. Don't forget them, even if weather conditions seem to be improving.

Towards the end of the month, a fairly mild spell may often delude us into thinking that spring has sprung. But beware; winter can often return with a vengeance. Always be guided by your local weather conditions when considering planting or sowing or doing any other work in the garden. You will find that from year to year the timings of sowing and planting will vary quite considerably, depending on the weather conditions at the time. Don't get too frustrated if you are stuck indoors – do some planning instead. A little bit of thought now about where plants should go in the garden will save you a lot of time in the busy spring season ahead.

Beat the blues

But it's not all doom and gloom outdoors, and February can often be a good month for working off the winter blues. There is plenty to do as the garden begins to come to life. Check on any newly planted trees and shrubs to see if they have been loosened by frost and refirm gently where necessary, but don't be too heavy-handed (or should I say heavy-booted) about doing this, because if the soil is very wet you will drive out all the air from around the roots. It's also an ideal time for planting bare-rooted

WEATHER WATCH

As far as temperatures are concerned, January and February are very similar, with February being on average the colder of the two. The temperature over land is largely governed by the temperature of the sea, which is at its lowest in February. Average daily temperatures in the south will be around 6–8°C, and in the north 4–6°C. Hard frosts are still common, so continue to protect vulnerable plants outdoors.

February can still be windy, but less so than January. The north of the country will have on average 3–4 days of gales this month, the south only 0.1 day on average. These figures do vary according to the height above sea level and the local topography. Coastal areas are always windier than inland.

Generally there is more sunshine in February compared to January, with southern parts of the country getting around 7.6 days, and northern parts around 5.2 days of bright sun. The days are now getting appreciably longer, too. Sunny days make you want to get on with jobs such as seed-sowing, but don't be in too much of a hurry as there can still be a lot of bad weather to come.

The amount of rainfall varies considerably from one part of the country to another, south-eastern parts generally getting the least rain with on average 35–38mm. In Scotland this month, the north-east coast is the driest area, with around 36mm of rain falling, but the south west is one of the wettest parts of the country, with on average 110mm of rain, due mainly to the high ground, some of which is 242m above sea level.

A thick layer of snow can persist in high areas for most of the winter, but on lower ground the amount of snow will vary a lot. Western coastal areas, kept milder by the warm air from the Gulf Stream, or more correctly the North Atlantic Drift, have very little snow and extremely mild temperatures. This is why there are many gardens on the west coasts of Scotland and Ireland growing plants usually found in much warmer regions of the world. In the north, on high ground above 100m there will be on average 2–3 days of snow, increasing to around 15 days over 300m. In southern parts 1–2 days is the average snowfall for the month.

△ **Icy waters**

Ice on ponds can persist after frosts have thawed, so check water features and make an air hole for aquatic life if necessary.

deciduous trees and shrubs. The conventional wisdom on planting bare-rooted stock is that it can be planted at any time in the dormant season, from November until March. This still holds true, but current thinking now leans toward planting in February rather than in the autumn. The reasoning for this is that often with autumn planting, the trees and shrubs will just sit through winter in the cold, wet soil doing nothing, and they may be killed off in very cold spells. But if they are planted in February, then with spring just around the corner, they will get off to a much better start.

Recycling prunings

This is a month for pruning woody plants. Hardy shrubs that flower on new wood later in the summer, such as the butterfly bush (*Buddleja davidii*), can be cut right down, generating piles of twiggy prunings.

You can recycle the sturdiest of these to make plant supports, but the rest of the debris is still too useful to burn. If shredded, it can be added to the compost heap or used as a mulch. There are many different types of shredder on the market these days, and if you buy, your choice will depend on personal preference and how deep your pockets are. But if you think you will only need a shredder once or twice a year, then remember that they can also be hired from the local hire shop.

Shredded prunings make a good home-grown mulch, but don't lay it now – wait until next month, when the soil has warmed up a little, then you will lock some of that warmth in under the mulch blanket. What you can do now is give the soil a dressing of an organic-based fertiliser, so that the nutrients it contains will be available to plants just when they need it – as they start into growth. Although this book is not specifically about organic gardening, organic fertilisers, such as blood, fish and bone, hoof and horn, fish and seaweed meals and pelletted chicken manure, deserve a few words. The

synthetic or chemical fertilisers available today normally act as a quick tonic or quick fix to get plants off to a good start. But with these fertilisers plants often produce soft, sappy growth which is much more susceptible to attack from pests and diseases. The nutrients are used up more quickly and so they have to be applied more often. They also do little to improve the soil, whereas some organic fertilisers, especially those based on seaweed meal, do have some soil-conditioning properties.

With organic fertilisers, the nutrients are released more slowly and are available to plants over a longer period. So instead of a rapid boost to growth, the plants grow more steadily and sturdily. They are also easier to use, because quantities don't need to be as precise as when using artificial fertilisers. Because the nutrients of organic fertilisers are released slowly they are best applied two or three weeks before sowing or planting, so they are available to the plants.

Under cover

If you have a greenhouse or a conservatory it will be a busy time, but don't be in too much of a hurry to sow a lot of summer bedding plants yet. Better to start them off next month to reduce heating costs. If sowings are made too early, the plants will become leggy due to poorer light conditions, and they also risk becoming starved from being in seed trays or pots for too long before planting out. Later sowings will produce much better quality plants for planting out at the end of May and beginning of June. For now, be sure you have a good supply of seed-sowing compost, pots and seed trays on hand for the busy sowing season ahead. You can also plan container colour schemes using books and catalogues – a satisfying job when it's too wet for anything else.

If you do have a few young plants growing up on a windowsill – perhaps some of the bedding plants sown last month that really need the longest growing season you can give them – then the lightbox we show you how to make this month (see p.52) will really make a difference to their progress. There are no special materials involved, nor a single nail or screw – it couldn't be simpler to help your seedlings to grow up sturdy and straight.

Sowing for early crops

This is a good time to sow some early vegetables for planting out under cloches next month: lettuce, radish, beetroot, salad onions, peas and broad beans. The easiest way of doing this is to sow the seeds in plastic modules (large trays divided into individual cells). These seeds don't need heat, but they do need the lightest spot you can give them. Once you've sown seeds inside, cover the piece of ground outdoors where the young vegetable plants are to be put out, using a cloche or a sheet of polythene to protect the soil from further rain and snow and to warm it up. Then you will have the tastiest, freshest and most welcome vegetables in the neighbourhood.

△ **Planting snowdrops in the green**
Once snowdrops finish flowering, large clumps can be lifted and divided. They should also be on sale to plant out now.

△ **Changing crops**
The tight florets of sprouting broccoli make a welcome change from leafy winter greens.

△ **Pruning back**
Many shrubs that have splayed out with age or under the weight of snow, like this santolina, can be pruned hard back now.

FEBRUARY AT A GLANCE

- Make sure garden birds have food and water.
- Apply organic-based fertilisers.
- Continue planting trees, shrubs, and fruit trees and bushes as the weather allows.
- Firm newly planted trees and shrubs if lifted by frost.
- Prune winter-flowering shrubs that have finished flowering, including winter heathers.
- Prune summer-flowering shrubs that flower on new wood.
- Prune hardy evergreen trees and shrubs.
- Prune jasmines and late-summer-flowering clematis.
- Prune off old stems of herbaceous perennials.
- Start dahlia tubers into growth.
- Divide and plant snowdrops.
- Repot or top-dress shrubs in containers.
- Bring in the last of spring bulbs being forced.
- Prepare seedbeds for vegetables.
- Lime vegetable plots if necessary.
- Mulch fruit trees after feeding.
- Protect gooseberry bushes from bird damage.
- Prick out or pot up seedlings sown last month.
- Start tender perennials under cover into growth.

! LAST CHANCE

- Cut back overgrown shrubs and hedges before the nesting season starts.
- Finish pruning fruit.

★ GET AHEAD

- Check tools, equipment and plant supports are sound well before you need to use them.
- Make sure all pots and seed trays are clean.
- Check on stocks of pots, compost and labels.
- Prune roses in southern regions.
- Prepare ground for making new lawns in spring.
- Sow annuals under cover.

Helleborus orientalis • Evergreen perennial with variably coloured flowers *(see p.324)*

Iris 'Harmony' • Dwarf bulb ideal for an alpine trough or raised bed *(see p.326)*

Narcissus cyclamineus ♥ • Short-stemmed, flowering earlier than larger daffodils *(see p.334)*

Cyclamen coum Pewter Group ♥ • Low, clump-forming perennial with marbled leaves *(see p.314)*

Euonymus fortunei 'Silver Queen' ♥ • Brightly variegated evergreen shrub *(see p.318)*

Erica x darleyensis 'Arthur Johnson' ♥ • Low-growing heather ideal for ground cover *(see p.317)*

Clematis cirrhosa **'Freckles'** ♀ • Small-flowered evergreen climber for very early spring *(see p.306)*

Viburnum tinus • Bushy evergreen shrub with perfumed flowers and black berries *(see p.358)*

Camellia x williamsii **'Anticipation'** ♀ • Evergreen, glossy-leaved shrub for acid soil *(see p.302)*

Chaenomeles speciosa **'Phylis Moore'** • One of the first flowering quinces to come into bloom *(see p.304)*

Cornus mas ♀ • Deciduous shrub or small tree; the leaves colour well in autumn *(see p.311)*

Crocus tommasinianus ♀ • Carpeting bulb that naturalizes well in grass *(see p.313)*

AROUND THE GARDEN

Have a clear-out Spring-clean sheds and cupboards to be rid of old and obsolete products.

IF YOU USE CHEMICALS in the garden, even "organic" kinds, it is a good idea to go through them and see which have been lying around for a long time and can be discarded. There may be bags that have split open, and the contents spilt on the floor or shelves, or bottles with only a few drops left in them, or some that have been in the shed unused for years. Don't just pour them down the drain or scatter old fertiliser over the garden as you may cause a lot of harm. Take this sort of stuff to your local authority waste site, and let them deal with it. Numbers will be in your local phone book.

MAKE SURE GARDEN BIRDS HAVE FOOD AND WATER. It's a very hungry month for wildlife, and putting food out may distract birds and small mammals from taking buds and bulbs.

PUT UP BIRD BOXES. Birds need a little time to get used to new boxes before they will select them to nest in.

CHECK ALL TOOLS AND MACHINES ARE IN WORKING ORDER. Once the busy gardening season really gets under way, it is maddening to go to the shed, and only then remember that your favourite spade has a broken handle – just when you need to get on with digging or planting a newly bought plant. Wiring of all electrical appliances should be checked for cuts too, and if you are not sure what to do, contact a qualified electrician, or take it to your nearest stockist for advice.

APPLY ORGANIC-BASED FERTILISER TO ALL BORDERS. This is a good time of year to do this, as organic fertilisers release their nutrients more slowly than inorganic ones, so they will be available to the plants just as they start into growth in the spring. A sprinkling of organic fertiliser like seaweed meal, blood, fish and bone, or pelleted chicken manure around the plants will do them the world of good after the long winter. Spread the fertiliser according to the maker's instructions and lightly stir it into the surface of the soil with a hoe or garden fork.

ORDER PLENTY OF COMPOST, POTS AND SEED TRAYS for the busy season ahead. Having a good supply on hand saves a lot of unnecessary trips to the garden centre – time that could be spent gardening. Buying in bulk in partnership with your neighbours or as part of a gardening society could save you a lot of money. The use of coir compost (which comes from coconut husks and is a renewable resource) and other peat substitutes is becoming more popular as we all become more environmentally aware. The less peat we use, the more we help to conserve the fast-disappearing peat bogs where precious native flora and fauna exists.

TREES & SHRUBS

PLANTING

BARE-ROOTED TREES AND SHRUBS, including roses, can be planted (see also November) at any time during the dormant season from November to March, but recent research has shown that February can be the ideal time. Provided that the soil is not frozen, or so wet that it sticks to your boots, plants put in this month get off to a really good start. The main reason is that the plants are not stuck in cold, wet soil all winter, when new roots will not grow much at all, especially so soon after they

PLANTING BARE-ROOTED TREES

1 Dig a generous hole that won't cramp the root system. If you haven't had time to prepare the soil beforehand, incorporate plenty of organic matter into the hole now.

2 Put a stake in first for trees and tall shrubs, on the windward side so the plant is blown away from the stake (this prevents rubbing).

3 Set the plant in to the same depth it was planted on the nursery (easily seen by the darker part of the stem near the roots). Fill in the hole and firm in gently with your boot.

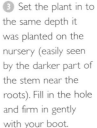

have been lifted from the nursery. But by planting this month it is not long before the soil begins to warm up and those new roots will get growing, quickly establishing the plant. Remember to look after new plants well and water thoroughly during dry spells, especially as they are getting established in their first year.

DECIDUOUS SHRUBS in the wrong place can be moved (see January).

PRUNING AND TRAINING

THERE MAY BE QUITE A LOT OF PRUNING to be done this month, especially if you haven't been able to brave the winter weather so far. Birds will soon be looking for nesting sites, so you should get pruning out of the way this month to avoid disturbing them later. Overgrown or misshapen deciduous trees and shrubs can all be pruned to improve their health and shape (see December for details). You can probably also start pruning roses this month in sheltered parts of the country. Many people start pruning roses in November, but in colder parts of the country, as in my native Scotland, the winters can sometimes be harsh, causing dieback, and if the roses have already been pruned this means you will have to go over them again in spring. For details of how to prune see March, the traditional time to tackle roses and the safest in the north and cold regions.

EVERGREENS that have become overgrown can be pruned now, provided that they are completely hardy plants like *Prunus laurocerasus*; more tender shrubs such as *Choisya ternata* (Mexican

Pruning evergreens Cutting back to well within the plant's outline often gives the best results.

orange blossom) should be left until later in the year. Shoots that have become overcrowded or grown out awkwardly can be pruned back, to the main stems if necessary, to maintain the shape of the plant. Cutting back to ground level may be an option if the plant is one that tolerates drastic pruning – for example, *Prunus laurocerasus*, spotted laurel (*Aucuba japonica*) and *Viburnum tinus*. This will encourage strong growth from the base of the shrub. Feed after pruning, preferably with an organic fertiliser, and mulch with organic matter.

TRIM WINTER-FLOWERING HEATHERS as they finish flowering. This job has to be done, otherwise the plants will become straggly and the centre of the plant will become bare. The easiest way is to go over the plants with a pair of garden shears. Trim back to the base of the flower stalks: this will encourage sideshoots to grow, keeping the plant bushy and compact. Mulching

the plants with a peat substitute and feeding in a few weeks' time will do a lot to encourage strong growth.

LARGER WINTER-FLOWERING SHRUBS such as witch hazel (*Hamamelis*) don't as a rule need regular pruning, but at this time of year, once the flowers are over, you can remove any stems that are rubbing or spoiling the shape of the plant.

LATE-FLOWERING SHRUBS CAN BE PRUNED this month. These include *Buddleja davidii* (the butterfly bush), *Caryopteris clandonensis*, *Ceanothus burkwoodii* (the deciduous ceanothus), hardy fuchsias, santolina, ceratostigma, lavatera and leycesteria (the nutmeg bush). These shrubs flower best on growth made since the spring. It's a terrific job if you've had a bad day, as you can be quite brutal with them! Cut them back almost to the ground (see right), leaving one or two buds or shoots on each stem. You may feel you're cutting off far too much, but it is the right thing to do to get the best show of flowers. Where you want to increase the size of the shrubs, leave a few stems on and prune these lightly. After pruning, give a feed of organic fertiliser and mulch with garden compost or farmyard manure to get them off to a flying start.

HEDGES

BRUSH SNOW OFF evergreen hedges before the weight splays out branches.

OVERGROWN OR MISSHAPEN HEDGES can be pruned now to improve their health and shape. Most

deciduous hedges can be pruned back hard (see December), as can broadleaved evergreens such as *Prunus laurocerasus* and laurel, but you must never cut conifers back into bare wood, with the exception of yew. Yew is thought of as slow-growing, but it is surprising how quickly it does grow, and even if regularly trimmed, it can gradually creep outwards if it is not trimmed hard enough. Unlike other conifers like Leyland cypress, yew will take very hard pruning: cut it back as much as you like and it will grow away again from the stumps. Other conifers must be lightly but regularly trimmed from the word go to keep them compact; never let them become overgrown.

PRUNING SUMMER SHRUBS

Pruning Buddleja davidii Use loppers to cut the thick stems back to a stubby framework.

Pruning caryopteris Cut back all of the whippy stems, and a new crop will grow and flower.

TREES & SHRUBS *contd*

CONIFERS MAY NEED SOME ATTENTION. If you didn't tie them in as a precaution (see December), wind or snow may have bent branches down, spoiling the shape. If these branches are pruned off it can leave an unsightly gap. So the thing to do is to tie them up again. Plastic-coated wire is fine as long as it is cushioned against the trunk with a piece of hessian or similar – a rag cut into strips and folded, for example – otherwise the wire will cut into the trunk eventually killing the tree.

DISPLACED CONIFER BRANCH

① Conifer branches are pliable, and if bent down will often splay out but rarely break.

② Tie them back in place with soft twine, a strip of fabric or cushioned wire.

CLIMBERS

BRUSH SNOW OFF dense evergreen climbers and wall shrubs; when snow accumulates on these it can not only break stems but also puts strain on ties and supports.

PRUNE LATE-FLOWERING CLEMATIS. Towards the end of the month, you can prune *Clematis orientalis*, *C. texensis*, *C. viticella* and its many varieties, such as 'Madame Julia Correvon' and 'Gravetye Beauty', and also the late large-flowered hybrids such as 'Ville de Lyon' and 'Jackmannii'. In some books these are all classed together as the "Group 3" clematis. In sheltered parts of the country they may already be starting to produce shoots. These can be rather brittle, so be careful when pruning and pulling away the old growth from last year. Apart from this, they are the easiest of all clematis to prune. All you have to do is cut down all of the growth to 23–45cm (9-18in) from the ground, cutting each stem back to just above a healthy bud. These clematis are ideal for growing through other shrubs, because as they start afresh each year, they never become so overgrown that they swamp their host. After pruning, feed with an organic fertiliser and mulch with organic matter, or put a large stone at the base of the plant. Clematis like their heads in the sun but their roots shaded and cool.

WINTER-FLOWERING JASMINE CAN BE PRUNED now that the flowers have gone over. This lanky plant needs some attention to stop it becoming very untidy. First prune out any dead or damaged wood. Then tie in any stems that you need to extend the framework or coverage of the plant, and then shorten all the side growths from this main framework to 5cm (2in) from the main stems. This will encourage plenty of new shoots for flowering next winter. Feed and mulch as for clematis.

SUMMER-FLOWERING JASMINES can also be pruned, but you must tackle this type by taking out an entire main stem or two to the ground. If you prune back all the side growths as with winter jasmine, they produce a mass of tangled leafy growth that is no good to anyone.

PLANT NEW CLIMBERS exactly as you would trees and shrubs (although they are more likely to be container-grown rather than bare-rooted), digging holes at least 9in (22cm) away from walls and fences so that the plant is not in a dry "rain shadow" and leaning the plants into the support.

Pruning late-flowering clematis Once buds break, cut the plant down close to the ground.

PERENNIALS

FINISH WEEDING AND DIGGING over borders and new planting areas, incorporating organic matter if you can. Cut down any old dead growth from plants such as sedums and acanthus which was left on for effect over winter. The sooner this is done the better, as new shoots will already be emerging from some plants towards the end of the month and they are easily damaged.

TOWARDS THE END OF THE MONTH herbaceous perennials will be starting into growth; it's a good time to feed them with an organic-based fertiliser (see Around the Garden).

CONTINUE TAKING ROOT CUTTINGS from perennials. For choice of plants and method see January.

CHECK STAKES AND SUPPORTS removed in autumn, and stock up if you will not have enough for your plants later in the spring. One cheap way of doing this is to keep the best of the prunings from shrubs pruned this and next month (see Trees & Shrubs).

BOX UP DAHLIA TUBERS stored during the winter and they will produce shoots that make good cuttings (see March). The tubers can be potted up singly, or several can be put into large trays. Place the tubers in good light, and spray them occasionally with clear water to encourage the buds to grow.

New tubers bought from the garden centre can be treated in exactly the same way. There are many different dahlias available (see right) from the smallest pompon blooms to blowsy decorative ones like the large cactus-flowered types.

Starting dahlia tubers Set them in a shallow tray filled with multipurpose compost.

CHOOSING DAHLIAS

'Zorro'

'Jescot Julie'

'Hamari Gold'

'Barberry Carousel'

'Kathryn's Cupid'

'Preston Park'

BULBS

Planting snowdrops Unlike most other bulbs, snowdrops are planted while in leaf.

PLANT AND DIVIDE SNOWDROPS AND WINTER ACONITES after flowering, but while the foliage is still green. Both of these bulbs should be bought "in the green" as it is known. They often do not grow well when they are planted as dry bulbs in the autumn. Look through the gardening press now and you will see plenty advertised by specialist nurseries, who will supply them in the green by mail order. Many garden centres also sell them in pots. It's as well to buy snowdrops in particular from a reputable supplier, then you can be sure that they haven't been uprooted from the wild, an illegal practice which is causing great conservation worries.

Work in some compost or leafmould to enrich the soil before planting; a little bonemeal won't go amiss either. Put the plants in a little deeper than they were previously and water them in if the soil is dry. Overcrowded clumps in the garden can be also be lifted carefully with a fork after flowering, and separated out. Replant them singly in informal drifts at the same depth as they were growing.

POT LILIES FOR PLANTING LATER. Lilies are normally planted in autumn (see October) in borders and patio tubs, but if you didn't manage to do it then, you can still have lilies in flower this summer. Even if the soil is too wet for planting outside you can pot up some lily bulbs and either move them or plant them out later in the spring. There should be plenty of lily bulbs in the garden centres to choose from now. Look for good plump bulbs, avoiding those which have become shrivelled and dry in the sun.

Plant the bulbs three or four to a 18cm (7in) pot and keep them in a cool greenhouse or cold frame. Grow on inside, watering whenever the compost feels dry, to plant out later.

PROTECT EMERGING BULBS IN THE ROCK GARDEN. Delightful dwarf bulbs like *Iris reticulata*, *I. histrioides* and *I. danfordiae* will all be coming into flower this month. If they are growing outside they will benefit from some overhead protection. Use a sheet of glass or perspex on bricks or a cloche to prevent the flowers being spoiled by rain and snow. Covering with a cloche brings them into flower a bit earlier too.

An ideal way of growing these wonderful bulbs is in pots or shallow pans. The containers can then be stood on a table or on a low wall, and the flowers can be appreciated without having to get on your knees.

ANNUALS & BEDDING

KEEP A WATCHFUL EYE ON GERMINATING SEEDLINGS sown last month to ensure they get enough light (see Under Glass).

SOW HARDY ANNUALS IN MODULES. These cheap and cheerful plants are ideal to give a splash of colour if you are starting a garden from scratch on a limited budget. And they are the perfect way to get children interested in gardening. It's very easy to sow hardy annuals outside next month, but if you want to get a head start and have earlier flowers, or if you want some young plants to fill containers, then the way to sow them is in modular trays. These trays come in all sizes and are available at garden centres. Basically they are just seed trays divided into individual cells. The advantage of using them is that the plants can be planted out without disturbing the root systems and so they get off to a flying start. Fill the trays with compost, give a sharp tap

Sowing in modules These cell trays can save on all the bother of pricking out and potting on.

ANNUALS *continued*

on the bench to settle the compost, strike off any surplus and gently firm with the bottom of another tray (some module trays come with a firming board which can also be used as a "pusher-out" when it comes to planting). Water the trays and then sow the seeds. Sow a small pinch of seed in each cell and cover with vermiculite. Place in a cold frame or sheltered part of the garden and they will germinate in a few days. Plant out when they are big enough to handle.

CONTINUE DEADHEADING WINTER PANSIES. By doing this the display will be prolonged. Although they are called winter-flowering, they will in fact continue to flower into early summer if you are assiduous about deadheading.

SWEET PEAS CAN BE SOWN OUTSIDE (see March) in sheltered southern parts of the country. Sow the seeds 1cm (½in) deep, and to speed up germination and protect the seedlings at this early time, cover each with an improvised cloche, using the top half of a plastic bottle.

POT UP SWEET PEAS SOWN IN AUTUMN UNDER COVER if you didn't do it last month. These plants will be growing well now, and if you want plenty of flowers the growing tip needs to be pinched out to encourage sideshoots to grow. If left unpinched the leading shoot often grows "blind": it will grow on without producing any flower buds and growth often stops. Plenty of sideshoots will give a mass of flowers throughout the summer.

CONTAINERS

CHECK TUBS, TROUGHS AND POTS OUTSIDE FOR WATER. Evergreen shrubs are particularly at risk of drying out, as their foliage prevents rain from getting into the pot. Do any watering in the morning, but don't water if there is frost forecast, or the water in the exposed pots may freeze and damage the roots of the plant.

TOP-DRESS POT-GROWN SHRUBS. Shrubs that have been growing in large pots for many years benefit from top-dressing with fresh compost each year. Scrape away as much of the old compost from the surface as you can, about 2.5cm (1in) is ideal. Then add fresh potting compost with some slow-release fertiliser added to it. This will

Plan container planting schemes Books and magazines are always good sources of inspiration.

feed the plants over several months, doing away with the chore of feeding them every week or month through the spring and summer.

PLAN NOW FOR SUMMER PLANTING SCHEMES IN CONTAINERS. Some time spent now planning what plants and how many to grow in containers is well spent. It's great fun browsing through seed catalogues, dreaming up various plant and colour combinations, from tasteful pastel shades to bright colours that will knock your eye out. It's all a matter of personal choice and deciding which plants will suit a particular situation, for example sunny or shady positions. If you have space, grow the plants from seed (see March) or if you haven't the time for this, all the seed firms sell young plants now, and if you can bring these on under cover you get a much wider choice by buying early.

Top-dressing *Carefully scrape off the top layer of soil and replace it with fresh multipurpose compost.*

PONDS

AS IN JANUARY, make sure the water is never completely frozen over.

DIG A NEW POND. It's a good time to dig and line a new pond; with any luck, spring rains will help to fill it, and the water will have settled and become more balanced before the time comes to stock the pond (see April). The extent of the surface area of a pond is not too critical, unless you are intending to keep fish, but the deeper you can make a pond the better. The minimum depth for the deepest area should be 60cm (2ft). The pond will then be very unlikely ever to freeze to its whole depth, so any aquatic creatures will be safe in the lower regions (although you should still always melt a hole in surface ice). Contouring the hole so that you have both a deep zone and a shallow marginal area will give you more scope for using different types of plants, and making a gently sloping area on one side will form a "beach" where birds can drink and bathe in safety, and small animals, especially hedgehogs, will be able to escape should they fall in.

Visit a local aquatic centre or a garden centre with a good water garden department, and they will be able to advise you on the choice of lining material and the quantity you will need. Generally, the more you are prepared to spend now, the longer the liner will last you, but of course it's up to you.

It cannot be said often enough that garden ponds are a very real danger for small children, and you must consider this very carefully if you have a young family. A rigid security grille can be installed across a pond to protect children; again your local aquatic centre should be able to advise about these.

LAWNS

KEEP OFF THE GRASS when it is frozen or frosted, otherwise later, when it thaws out, your footprints will show up as yellow patches on the lawn where the grass has been damaged.

DISPERSE WORM CASTS Brush away worm casts on the lawn regularly (see January). There are no chemicals currently available to amateur gardeners that can be watered onto the lawn to kill worms, but in any case, it is far better to preserve these creatures, which do so much good in the soil by breaking down organic matter and aerating the earth as they move through it. A few worm casts are a small price to pay for having a healthy population of worms in your garden. Brushing the casts to disperse them is the best option.

IN MILDER AREAS, MOW (see also March). It may seem early to start cutting the lawn, but in warm areas and mild spells, even in winter, the grass will continue to grow, albeit not a lot. So it does no harm at all to give the lawn an occasional light trim, setting the blades of the mower at their highest setting. Don't do this if the lawn is soaking wet or frozen, or you'll do more harm than good. In more exposed, colder parts of the country, don't mow until next month.

DIG OUT LAWN WEEDS. If you have only a few weeds in the lawn, then the ideal way of removing them is individually. You can buy tools for the job, but an old kitchen knife is just as good. Weeds with fibrous root systems like daisies and plantains are quite easy to deal with; dandelions, which have long tap roots, are trickier. You have to make sure all of the root is removed as any portion of the root left in the soil will grow again. If dandelions are too big to remove with a knife, or weeds are too extensive, use a selective lawn weedkiller or a spot-weeding treatment in the spring (see May). You need to wait until weeds are growing really strongly for these to work at their best.

MAKING NEW LAWNS

LAY TURF. Turf can be laid (see October) during this month on ground prepared earlier, provided that the soil is not frozen or so wet that it sticks to your boots.

PREPARE GROUND FOR SOWING GRASS SEED. If you haven't dug over the ground where a new lawn is to be made over the winter, now is about the latest time to get the work done for making a new lawn in the spring. By the end of March the soil will have warmed up enough to give grass seed a flying start.

The ground should be dug over, incorporating organic matter to help retain moisture and removing all perennial weeds. Remove large stones as you see them too. Now leave the ground to settle for a few weeks. To continue preparations, see March.

VEGETABLES & HERBS

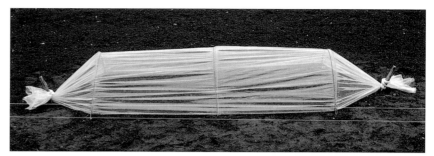

Polythene sheeting stretched over strong wire hoops makes a cloche to warm soil and protect young plants.

Wind and knot the polythene around pegs at each end, and plunge these firmly into the soil

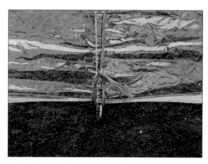

Make loops in the wire to mark soil level and to tie twine to, to secure the polythene over the top.

START PREPARING SEEDBEDS AND COVER THEM WITH CLOCHES. Soil that has already been covered with polythene for a while should be dry enough to make a start on preparing seedbeds ready for sowing next month. Rake down the soil until it is reasonably level, removing any large stones. Apply an organic fertiliser now (see Around the Garden), about two weeks before sowing, and its nutrients will be available for the young seedlings as they germinate.

Put cloches or polythene over the prepared soil. This will not only keep off the worst of the winter rain and snow, but also help to warm up the soil, enabling earlier sowing and planting outdoors. By using cloches you can gain about three weeks, therefore harvesting early crops when they are at their most expensive in the shops.

Kits to build cloches and of course ready-made cloches are available from garden centres. There are many types to choose from, the more decorative ones usually tending to be more expensive. I think it's more satisfying to make them yourself (see above). The easiest way to make cloches is to put wire hoops in the soil at regular intervals and stretch a long sheet of clear polythene between them, burying or pegging the ends of the polythene in the ground at each end to anchor it in place. You'll find most garden centres sell the polythene off the roll, so you can buy whatever length you want.

VEGETABLES & HERBS *continued*

FINISH PREPARING DEEP BEDS. Digging of new deep beds (see January) and top-dressing of established ones should be finished now before the busy seed sowing time gets under way.

LIME IF NECESSARY. If you follow the crop rotation plan shown in January, about one-third of the vegetable plot probably needs to be limed every year, generally where the brassicas – Brussels sprouts, cabbages and cauliflowers – are to be grown, as these all like alkaline soil. Lime should be added at least two

SOWING PEAS IN GUTTERING

Space out all the peas before pushing them in, so you don't lose track of where you've got to.

Once the seedlings have a few pairs of leaves the whole lot can simply be "shunted" into a trench.

months before planting, so if you do it now, the beds will be ready when you move transplants into them (see May). But before applying any lime always first check the existing pH of the soil – its acidity or alkalinity – with a soil-testing kit, as this will determine the amount of lime you put on. It may be that if you naturally have a very alkaline soil, you do not need to add lime at all.

The pH of the soil is a scale of 1–14 by which the alkalinity or acidity of the soil is determined. Around seven is neutral; values less than 7 are acid, and higher than 7, alkaline. Soil-testing kits are easy to use; most come with a numbered chart to which you match the colour of your soil sample, after mixing it with the solutions provided.

Once you know your soil's pH, the instructions on the packet will help you add the correct quantity of lime. Wear gloves, goggles and a face mask, and choose a still day. It's safest to use the ordinary sort of garden lime, calcium carbonate – or the organic alternative, dolomitic limestone – rather than quicklime or slaked lime, as although more effective these are highly caustic.

HARVESTING

CONTINUE TO HARVEST WINTER CROPS and check on any chicory being forced (see January).

SOWING INDOORS

KEEP SOWING EARLY CROPS (see January) and take care of those sown earlier (see Under Cover).

SOW PEAS IN GUTTERING (SEE LEFT). An ideal way of sowing peas is

to sow them in a piece of plastic guttering, choosing an early variety such as 'Douce Provence'. You will have to drill drainage holes in the bottom of the guttering, then fill with a peat-free seed compost. Sow the seeds evenly in two rows 2.5-5cm (1-2in) apart and about 2.5cm (1in) deep, and water. Keep them on a windowsill or in a greenhouse; it does not need to be heated, although bottom heat will speed up germination. When the seedlings have a few leaves they can be planted out under a cloche by carefully sliding them out of the guttering into a shallow trench already made in the soil.

SOWING AND PLANTING OUTDOORS

SOW SEEDS UNDER CLOCHES – towards the end of the month in colder areas – provided that the soil has been covered for a few weeks to warm it up. Seeds to sow include lettuce, radish, salad onions, peas, broad beans, beetroot, summer cabbage and spinach.

To sow the seeds, rake the soil to a fine tilth, which should be easy if the soil has dried out under cover. Then take out shallow drills with a cane to the depth required and space the drills at the distance given on the seed packet. Water along the drills first, before sowing. If you water after sowing the seeds may be washed deeper into the soil, making germination more difficult or even impossible. After watering, sow the seeds as thinly as possible and cover over carefully with dry soil. Firm down with your hand and the job's done. Put a cloche on top and wait for the seeds to germinate. Thin out the seedlings when they are large enough to handle;

the spacing to thin to will be on the back of the seed packets too, so keep them somewhere safe.

PLANT SHALLOTS. It may seem early to do this, but now is the time. Prepare the ground thoroughly, if not done earlier, incorporating plenty of organic matter. Add an organic fertiliser, following the instructions on the packet, and rake the soil to a fine tilth. Plant the shallots 15-18cm (6-7in) apart, in rows the same distance apart. Don't just push them into the soil, or the new roots, as they form, will push the bulbs up and out again. Birds love to pull them out too if they see them. The best way to plant the shallots is with a trowel, with the bulb tips just beneath the surface of the soil.

PLANT JERUSALEM ARTICHOKES. Jerusalem artichokes are difficult to site within a traditional vegetable plot because they grow enormously tall and cast a lot of shade. But they are ideal plants if you want a productive summer screen for a garden shed or the compost heap. Do be aware, though, that they will spread rapidly, so keep an eye on them before they take over the garden. The tubers, which look like long knobbly potatoes, should be planted in a single row 15cm (6in) deep and 30cm (1ft) apart. They will grow quite tall in their first year, perhaps to 2m (6ft), and may need some staking as the tall stems can be battered to the ground in wet weather. One way of supporting them is to drive four stakes into the ground, two at each end of the row and run string or thin wire around them. The tubers are harvested from autumn through winter.

PLANNING AHEAD

PREPARE A BED FOR PLANTING ASPARAGUS. This delicious vegetable, expensive to buy, is quite easy to grow in the garden, but it is a long-term crop, and will occupy a place of its own for several years. For planting the crowns, see April. This month, prepare the soil by digging thoroughly, removing perennial weeds completely and incorporating plenty of organic matter. If you garden on heavy clay, dig in lots of coarse grit to improve the drainage.

PREPARE TRENCHES FOR RUNNER BEANS. If you want a delicious and heavy crop of runner beans, now is the time to prepare a bean trench. The better the preparation now, the better the crop later on. Take out a trench, to the depth of a spade and 45cm (18in) wide (or double if you want to plant either side of a support), and heap the soil up on either side. It need not be a straight trench – it could be a ring shape if you are planning to grow the beans up wigwams. These are often easier to site than rows in a small garden, because they only cast a slim pointer of shade that moves around with the sun. Put as much organic matter as you can get into the bottom of the trench and fork it well in. If you are short of organic matter, even old newspapers torn up into strips will do. After digging in the organic matter leave the trench open, just as it is, to allow the weather to break down the soil, improving its structure right up until it's time to sow (see May) or plant (see June).

SPROUT EARLY SEED POTATOES if not done last month. See January.

LOOKING AFTER CROPS

FEED SPRING CABBAGES. Cabbages that have been standing all winter will benefit from a feed now. Use a general organic fertiliser to boost growth. As you harvest, cut every alternate plant in the row leaving the others to grow on and form a heart in late spring. It is possible to get a second crop from cabbages that have already been cut. Leave the stem and root in the soil and make a cross-cut on the top of the stump. Feed the plant and in a few weeks "mini-cabbages" will grow from the cuts. Use these as spring greens.

HERBS

COVER PARSLEY AND OTHER OVERWINTERING HERBS with horticultural fleece or cloches. This will protect the plants from pests and bring them into growth a little bit earlier.

MINT IS AN EXCELLENT HERB with the first of the early potatoes dug fresh from the garden. A few roots dug and potted up now (see right) will provide sprigs in the kitchen ready for the first vegetables of the new season. In fact this is quite a good way to grow mint outside, as it can be very invasive, easily taking over parts of the garden. Grow it in a large pot and stand this on the terrace, or plunge the pot into the ground, leaving the top 5-10cm (2-4in) of the pot proud of the soil surface. This will usually prevent the mint from creeping over the rim into the soil, but keep an eye on it anyway.

TOP-DRESS SHRUBBY HERBS IN POTS such as bay and rosemary (see Containers).

POTTING UP MINT

① Clumps of mint in the garden will now be looking tatty and are probably overgrown, and slugs may well be eating any shoots that there are. Dig a section up and separate out the healthiest looking parts.

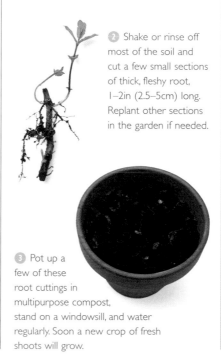

② Shake or rinse off most of the soil and cut a few small sections of thick, fleshy root, 1–2in (2.5–5cm) long. Replant other sections in the garden if needed.

③ Pot up a few of these root cuttings in multipurpose compost, stand on a windowsill, and water regularly. Soon a new crop of fresh shoots will grow.

FRUIT

PICKING AND STORING

CONTINUE TO CHECK FRUIT IN STORE. Any fruit showing signs of rotting should be removed immediately. If left, rot will quickly spread through the rest of the fruits. Any fruits not too badly rotten can be put out on the ground for hungry birds to feed on. This is a welcome addition to their diet if the ground is frozen hard and it is difficult for them to get food.

LOOKING AFTER CROPS

FEED ALL FRUIT unless you did so towards the end of last month (see January).

SPRINKLE SULPHATE OF POTASH around fruit trees – or, if you want to be organic, use rock potash. To get good quality crops, fruit trees need a high-potash fertiliser. Normal organic fertiliser, while good for them, is not especially high in any one nutrient, so supplementing it with a little extra potash will go a long way to helping you produce good quality fruit. Spread it below the trees or bushes in an area

Feeding fruit trees Mark out and calculate the area beneath the full spread of the crown of branches

FRUIT *continued*

equal to the spread of the branches. Use fertilisers strictly according to the manufacturer's instructions. There is no point in putting on a little extra for luck. It's just wasteful.

MULCH ALL FRUIT WITH WELL-ROTTED MANURE or garden compost. It is well worth doing this after all the pruning and feeding has been done. Not only will a mulch help to keep down weeds, it will also hold in moisture. This cuts down the amount of watering you will have to do in the warm summer months, and will give you better quality fruit to enjoy. If by some strange circumstance the soil happens to be dry, soak the ground first before applying the mulch. Mulch is as good at keeping water out as retaining it in the soil. You can lay seep- or tricklehose beneath the mulch to make watering in the summer simple.

Mulching an apple bush A thick layer of organic matter will not, as grass does, compete with the tree.

Check tree ties and stakes This young tree needs a tall stake to support the pendent branches.

COMPLETE SPRAYING WITH TAR OIL WINTER WASH (see January). This month is the last until next winter to use these washes, which can help avoid pest and disease problems later on. Winter washes can only be used on trees and bushes that are fully dormant.

CHECK THAT NEWLY PLANTED FRUIT IS NOT LIFTED BY FROST. February can often bring the most severe weather of the winter, with hard, penetrating frosts. When soil freezes the water in the soil expands, and this can ease newly planted trees and shrubs slightly out of the soil. This loosens the plant's grip on the soil, and if left like this, it will be rocked about in windy conditions, eventually killing it. So it is a good idea to go round and check newly planted fruit when the frost has thawed out and firm in any that have been affected.

CHECK TREE TIES AND STAKES (see also January). Loosen any ties that are too tight or they will strangle the tree.

CHECK FRUIT TREES FOR SIGNS OF CANKER. For details of symptoms and what to do, see January.

CONTINUE TO PROTECT FRUIT TREES AND BUSHES FROM BIRDS using netting, mesh or webbing (see January). Bullfinches in particular are especially fond of gooseberry buds. If you didn't net the plants last month, do it now. Make sure coverings are supported off the plants, yet taut and held down firmly on the ground, otherwise the birds may get caught up and be injured. An ideal way of growing gooseberries, if you can, is to train them as cordons (one single stem) or as fans against a wall or fence. This way netting them against birds is a much easier task. If you have a lot of gooseberries and other fruits it may be worth investing in a fruit cage, or making one yourself.

PROTECT PEACHES AND NECTARINES against peach leaf curl if this was not done last month. This disease's symptoms (see January) show up as puckering and blistering of the leaves later in the year. The disease is spread when spores in the air are splashed onto the leaves by rain. The ideal way to prevent it is by covering the plants through the winter (see January) or by taking pot-grown trees under cover. You will need to hand-pollinate the flowers (see also April) if you are doing this – using a soft artists's brush, brush pollen from flower to flower all over the plant, at least twice while the flowers are open.

PRUNING AND TRAINING

FINISH WINTER-PRUNING FRUIT TREES, which will be starting into growth soon, so the sooner all the pruning is done the better. If pruning is done as the trees come into growth, the rising sap will ooze out from any large cuts, weakening the tree. This may also encourage disease to invade the wound. For details of pruning see January and November.

PRUNE AUTUMN-FRUITING RASPBERRIES. There is a distinction to be made between the pruning times and methods for summer- and autumn-fruiting raspberries. If you get it wrong then you lose a crop for the year. Autumn-fruiting raspberries, which are pruned now, produce their fruit from August or September onwards on long stems – canes – that grew during that summer. The best variety in my view is called 'September'. Summer-fruiting raspberries will fruit on the canes that grew the previous year. So the new canes they will produce this summer will fruit the following summer.

Autumn-fruiting raspberries Prune now, very simply, by cutting all canes down to the ground.

Autumn-fruiting raspberries should now have all their growth pruned to the ground. Sprinkle a high-potash organic fertiliser around the plants, and you should get strong canes growing that will produce a good crop of fruit. The stems of autumn-fruiting raspberries are quite sturdy and they don't need the tying in and training of their summer-fruiting cousins. You can wind twine along the rows and round posts at each end to keep them neat, but don't restrict them too much to allow sun to reach all of the ripening fruits.

SUMMER-FRUITING RASPBERRY canes that have grown taller than their support frame can have the tips of the canes pruned back to one or two buds from the top wire. Alternatively, they can be arched over and tied down to the top wire. Either option encourages the formation of sideshoots along the length of the cane, so you will get a heavier crop of fruit.

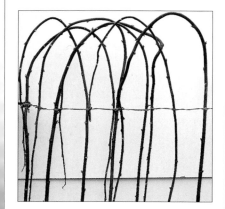

***Summer-fruiting raspberries** You can bend over and tie in long canes for more fruiting sideshoots.*

PLANTING

IT'S A GOOD MONTH TO PLANT bare-rooted fruit trees and bushes. If the soil was not prepared during the winter, be sure to incorporate plenty of organic matter before planting. The best way to do this is to put muck in the bottom of the planting hole, but only use well-rotted farmyard manure. Fresh stuff will scorch the roots. A feed of general fertiliser will also help the trees get off to a good start. Always plant to the depth to which the plants were planted in the nursery. This is easily seen by the darker mark on the main stem. Insert a stake for trees, tying the tree to it with a proper tree tie, before refilling the hole and you won't cut through any roots. Mulch with organic matter after planting, and keep the young trees or bushes well watered in their first year until they get established.

PLANT RASPBERRY, BLACKBERRY AND HYBRID BERRY CANES. Towards the end of the month is the latest time for planting bare-rooted cane fruits, usually sold in bundles. Have the soil thoroughly prepared by digging a trench all along the proposed row and working in plenty of organic matter, if not done during the winter. All except the autumn-fruiting raspberries will need support for the fruiting canes. This is usually given by a system of posts at either end of the row with at least three horizontal wires strained between the posts. Freestanding rows should be at least 1.5m (5ft) apart. If you are using a wall or fence for blackberries and hybrid berries (raspberries prefer to be in the open), then you may be able to attach the wires to vine eyes screwed into the wall. Plant raspberries about

PLANTING RASPBERRIES

① To give the plants a really good start, plant them in a trench to which plenty of organic matter has been added.

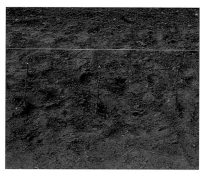

② Erect a sytem of support for the canes - for example, a post at each end of the row with three wires stretched between.

③ In spring, when new canes have grown, you can cut the original one back to ground level.

45cm (18in) apart in the row. Blackberries and hybrid berries need to be at least 1.5m (5ft) apart, and some vigorous cultivars may need even more space: ask the nursery for advice. Prune the newly-planted canes to about 22cm (9in) from the ground. It takes a bit of courage to do this, but it is essential to encourage the production of good, strong fruiting canes from the base of the plant. Later in the summer you can cut it right out. Tie the canes to the wires as they grow through the season, but don't take a crop this year. The odd fruit is alright, but remove flowers if there are a lot of them. At this time you are trying to get the plants established. They will then give a good crop next year.

BEAT THE SEASONS

CONTINUE TO FORCE RHUBARB. If you didn't cover rhubarb last month do it now, because it will soon be starting to grow. See January.

COVER STRAWBERRIES WITH CLOCHES for an early crop. As well as forcing strawberries in pots in the greenhouse (see Under Glass), a succession of fruits can be obtained by covering some plants outside with cloches. Any cloche will do, whether rigid plastic or polythene, but once the strawberries are in flower, open the sides during the day so that pollinating insects can get in. Keep an eye out for pests, especially greenfly, which will be attracted to the warm atmosphere under the cloches. If there aren't too many plants, greenfly can be squashed between your fingers – or use an organic spray.

UNDER COVER

CLEAN OUT GUTTERS of greenhouses and conservatories, as these will no doubt be full of leaves if there are large trees in the vicinity.

VENTILATE ON GOOD DAYS. With the lengthening days in February we often get warmish sunny spells that can send temperatures under glass soaring in a very short time. Open ventilators when you can to maintain more even temperatures, but not so much that you let in cold draughts, which can affect plants' growth. You must remember to close the ventilators well before sundown.

The aim is to keep the temperature as even as possible. The less difference between day and night temperatures the better for plants, otherwise they may produce a lot of spindly growth, because of the warmth and the relative lack of light during the short days of winter. Keeping air circulating will also cut down on the incidence of diseases.

BOX OR POT UP STORED DAHLIA TUBERS (see Perennials).

FUCHSIAS IN HEATED GREENHOUSES AND CONSERVATORIES can be sprayed with water to encourage growth. Those fuchsias that were started into growth and repotted last month will be showing signs of growing. Spraying with clear water occasionally helps buds to break and also keeps a humid atmosphere around the immediate vicinity of the plants, which is ideal. Plants which were pruned early last month should now be producing many new shoots and some of these can be used for making cuttings to increase your stock. Taking tip cuttings from a

CUTTINGS FROM FUCHSIAS

① The tips of shoots at least 2.5cm (1in) long can be rooted successfully. Remove the cutting by cutting just above a bud.

② Trim the base of the cutting just below a bud and remove the lower leaves, making sure there are at least two leaves left at the tip.

③ Dip the base of each cutting in hormone rooting solution and put each in a module cell containing a mixture of equal parts peat-free compost and vermiculite.

④ Water the cuttings and put in a propagator at 18–21°C (65–70°F). The cuttings will root in three to four weeks, and can then be moved onto a bench or windowsill.

stock plant will also have the effect of encouraging more sideshoots to grow, and therefore more flowers.

PRUNE TENDER PERENNIALS that have been overwintering, dormant, in cool greenhouses, such as pelargoniums (geraniums), fuchsias, argyranthemums, lantana and salvias. These older plants can now be taken out of the pots or boxes they were kept in. If they are not pruned now, they become very tall, with all the flowers produced at the top of the plant while the lower part becomes bare. Prune all the main stems back to two or three buds, or 5–8cm (2–3in) from their point of origin. Prune any sideshoots quite hard to one or two buds from the main stems. Any prunings about 8cm (3in) long can be made into cuttings (see August, Annuals & Bedding), increasing your stock. At the same time prune out any dead or diseased material and any shoots crossing each other to open up the centre of the plant. Repot the plants into pots of fresh compost, gently firming around the roots, and water them in. After a few weeks new shoots will grow to give a stunning display of flowers over summer, either out in the garden or inside.

MAKE SURE SEEDLINGS GET ENOUGH LIGHT, otherwise they will grow tall and leggy trying to reach the light – and then, being weak, they will be more susceptible to attack from diseases such as botrytis and damping off. Once they have germinated, move them to a high shelf if you can, to get the maximum amount of light. If they are growing on a windowsill, turn them at least once a day or they will lean over towards the light.

WATCH FOR DAMPING OFF IN SEEDLINGS. Warm moist conditions encourage damping-off disease, causing rotting-off and collapse. A fungicide called Cheshunt compound can be used to prevent this, but the best prevention is always to sow seeds thinly so they have room to develop. And don't keep seedlings too wet either.

PRICK OUT SEEDLINGS. If you sowed seed in small pots or trays in order to fit more into your propagator, then once they have developed two leaves then you must move them into more spacious surroundings to give them room to develop and reduce the risk of damping off. This is called "pricking out". Replant the seedlings either 2.5cm (1in) apart in larger trays, or into the individual cells of a module tray to grow on. Hold them by the leaves but do not pull – lever them out from below with something thin, like a pencil. Drop them into holes dibbled in the compost and just nudge some compost into the hole to fill – never firm or press it.

RAISING PLANTS FOR OUTDOORS

ORDER PLUG PLANTS With a greenhouse, you have the luxury of being able to have the first choice of young bedding plants to raise yourself under glass, so make the most of it by placing orders now with seed firms.

SOW HARDY ANNUALS IN MODULES (see Annuals and Bedding).

SOW SEEDS OF IMPATIENS (busy Lizzies). This is a difficult plant to grow from seed, so if you're a beginner, it's probably not worth trying yet. But if you have a knack for raising seedlings, it will save you some money. The seed can be difficult because it needs light to germinate, so it can't be covered, and it also needs a constant warm temperature with a humid atmosphere. The easiest way to get them to germinate is to draw shallow drills with a label across the compost in a seed tray, sow the seeds in these little drills and lightly cover with vermiculite. The vermiculite holds moisture and still lets light through. Place the tray in a propagator, put a sheet of glass over the tray to hold in the moisture and keep at a temperature of 21°C (70°F). The seeds should germinate in two to three weeks.

SOW SWEET PEAS if not done last month, and pot up those sown in autumn (see Annuals & Bedding, January).

SOW EARLY CROPS in succession to those sown in January: for example, peas in guttering and broad beans in modules. See Vegetables & Herbs.

GLASSHOUSE AND HOUSE PLANTS

FREESIAS AND LACHENALIAS that have finished flowering can be rested. Bulbs planted last August will be coming to the end of their flowering period and will have to be fed to build up their reserves before resting for the summer. Feed them every week now for three or four weeks with a high-potash liquid feed to build up the bulbs for next year, and then gradually reduce the amount of watering until the foliage begins to die back. The best way of resting the bulbs is to lay the pots on

their sides under a bench. They can be restarted into growth next autumn.

START OFF BEGONIA, GLOXINIA AND ACHIMENES TUBERS. All can be started into growth this month and through to March. Begonia and gloxinia tubers can be placed several to a seed tray, or potted individually into small pots and then potted into larger pots as they grow. The tubers of both are slightly hollow on one side, and it is this hollow side which should be uppermost when the tubers are planted. Plant the tubers so they are just covered with compost, as they form roots all over the surface of the tuber. Achimenes have small tubers about 2.5cm (1in) long, and these can be laid on their side several to a pot and potted on as necessary. None of these need very high temperatures to get started; normal room temperature is quite sufficient. It is an easy way of growing these plants if you cannot maintain high enough temperatures to germinate their seed.

PRUNE INDOOR CLIMBERS such as plumbago and passion flowers. These two popular climbers for heated greenhouses and conservatories are pruned in similar ways. The passion flower is a vigorous climbing plant and can be trained against a wall. Prune all the shoots to within two or three buds from where the previous year's growth started. Plumbago is actually a lanky shrub best tied to a support. To prune it, again shorten all sideshoots to 1–2 buds of the previous year's growth.

POT UP A FEW MORE LILY BULBS to give a succession of flowers following those potted last month (see January).

REPOT OR TOP-DRESS CITRUS TREES. These will be putting on new growth from now on, so they will need either potting on into larger pots – or, larger more mature plants can be top-dressed with fresh potting compost. To top-dress (see also Containers), scrape away as much of the old compost as you can without exposing and damaging roots, and replace it with fresh loam-based compost such as John Innes No 3.

PLANT OUT LILY-OF-THE-VALLEY that was lifted and potted in the autumn (see Perennials, November), to flower indoors over winter. Plant in fertile, humus-rich soil in full or partial shade. To make them feel really at home, top-dress with leafmould in the autumn.

CROPS UNDER GLASS

CONTINUE TO FORCE STRAWBERRIES. The first batch brought in in January will be starting to grow now, so a second batch brought in now will provide a succession of succulent fruits much earlier than outside. If you cover a few plants outdoors with cloches (see Fruit) this will in turn continue the succession from those in the greenhouse, until uncovered plants begin to fruit naturally.

Water and feed the indoor plants with a high-potash feed to ensure good quality fruits. Once the plants begin to grow, be vigilant and watch for aphids which can become quite active even at this time of year in warm conditions. Once any flowers appear, they will need hand-pollination in the sheltered conditions under glass (see March).

Potted citrus A solid pot and soil-based compost will prevent standard trees becoming top-heavy and toppling over.

MAKE A LIGHT BOX FOR SEEDLINGS

WINDOWSILLS ARE CRUCIAL propagating environments for those of us without a greenhouse. This simple and very cheap idea allows you to grow seedlings and cuttings by a window without them becoming drawn to one side towards the light. The lining of reflective foil makes sure that the plants get even light from all directions. A piece of capillary matting should only cost a matter of pence from a garden centre.

YOU WILL NEED: A cardboard box that fits your windowsill, or a small table placed by the window • A pen and ruler • Scissors or a craft knife • A small amount of gloss paint • Glue • Kitchen foil • A square of capillary matting to fit the bottom of the box

❸ Paint the box, inside and out, with gloss paint to waterproof it. Brilliant white gloss also has light-reflective properties.

❹ Leave the paint to dry completely overnight before using the glue that will hold the foil in place.

❶ Mark the sides of the box with matching diagonal lines as above and cut down them, then across the front: the aim is to create a tray shape rather like the ones ice creams are sold from at the theatre (see right).

❷ Cut off the last flap, and glue the bottom flaps down securely if necessary.

❺ Spread glue in a thin layer over the whole inner surface of the box, bottom and sides. An offcut of cardboard makes a spreader.

❻ Unroll the foil and press it down, starting at the front, covering the base and the back. Handle the foil carefully as it tears easily.

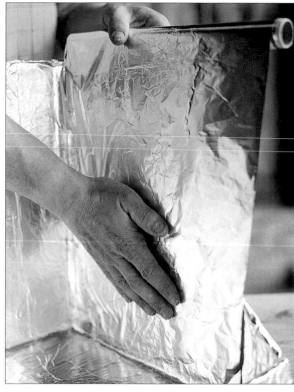

7 Now apply the foil to each side of the box, making sure it comes over the edges. Any overlaps can be held down with a spot of glue if you wish, and any surplus can be trimmed or folded over.

8 Fit the capillary matting into the base. This will act as a moisture reservoir; the plants will be able to draw up the water they need as they need it. It's simpler than using watering trays for each pot or tray, and takes up less space. Water will also evaporate from the matting to create a good, humid growing atmosphere around the plants.

9 Wet the matting, and fill the box with your young plants.

10 Place on a sunny windowsill for perfectly straight growth. Water the matting whenever it feels dry to the touch.

MARCH

The garden in March

The first month of spring at last, and the garden really begins to come alive after a long dreary winter. But it can be a tricky month weatherwise, with mild sunshine one day and hard frost the next.

Staking ▷
Now plants are really starting to grow, it's time to give perennials support. You're less likely to damage growth if you do this job early.

A PROFUSION OF SPRING FLOWERS should now be brightening up the garden. Spring-flowering bulbs are coming into their own, and towards the end of the month, those stalwart spring-flowering shrubs, the forsythias, bring forth their stunning show of bright yellow flowers. Some early-flowering cherry trees herald the spectacular display of blossom to come next month.

Later in the month the clocks go forward, lengthening daylight hours, so there is no excuse for not using that extra time in the garden. Even at this time of year you'll find there aren't enough hours in the day for all the gardening you want to do.

Take it easy at first

If you've been slumbering in an armchair all winter, and have a sudden urge to get out and put the garden to rights now that it's spring, then do take it gently at first. But don't let me put you off! Gardening is great exercise, and there is nothing better for clearing out the cobwebs than working in the garden on a clear, warm spring day. Just take it easy to begin with. Before starting any strenuous jobs such as digging, do some warm-up stretching exercises to ease yourself into the work. And jobs

such as digging should be done in short spells – a whole day doing one job with repetitive movements may harm your back. So do about half an hour's digging at first, then switch to another job which does not involve bending. You could try this month's practical project, for example (see p.78) – a smart obelisk to add height and elegance to any border, festooned with flowering plants. These garden features can be expensive to buy, but with only a few simple carpentry skills and tools you can make one, or even a pair, yourself at home. Having all the wood pre-cut to length when you buy will make the job even simpler, almost like assembling a kit.

Changeable weather

The weather can be fickle at this time of year, with one day having clear blue skies and the next wintry showers. Make the best of good weather and crack on with tasks such as making seed beds for sowing hardy annuals outside and in the vegetable garden, on the soil which was covered with polythene sheets or cloches earlier in the year. Do always bear in mind that we can still get sharp frosts, so don't be tempted to buy bedding plants starting to appear at garden centres unless you have a greenhouse or frost-free

place in which to keep them until all danger of frost has passed. And don't be in a hurry to remove protection from those frost-tender plants which were covered or wrapped up over winter. Plants can be uncovered during the day, but keep the protective material to hand in case frost is forecast at night.

Deciding when to sow outside

Sowing seeds of hardy vegetables and annual flowers outside can begin in earnest this month in most parts of the country, but in northerly parts wait until the end of the month or until early April before making

WEATHER WATCH

Although March can be a cold month, on the whole temperatures are rising. However, sharp frosts may descend on the land on clear nights, turning the ground hard, so don't put out tender plants yet. Cloud cover and wind will also have a direct effect on temperatures throughout each day.

March winds can be bitterly cold, but they do help to dry out the soil after winter rains and snow. High ground above 100m and exposed coastal areas, especially the west coast, can still be subject to gales for 0.6 to 4.3 days. In the south gales will occur on an average of 0.2–1.5 days in the month. All coastal areas, whichever way they face, are windier than inland, and the winds carry salt spray which can damage plants.

The longer days of spring bring more chance of more hours of bright sunshine each day. The north will still have less, on average, than the south. Clouds will, however, cut down the amount of direct sunshine everywhere on most days. On average the north can expect 85–105 hours, and the south 100–120 hours of sun this month.

The amount of rain falling around the country depends on how hilly or flat it is. Areas like the Lake District and the Western Highlands of Scotland have similar amounts of rain, with a March average of 228mm. But in the south-east of England the average is 41mm. Low-lying areas may be prone to floods as snow on hills begins to thaw.

Heavy snowfalls are rare this month, but in north-eastern areas especially, snow can still be thick on the ground, making spring very much later than other parts of the country. At Braemar in north-east Scotland, one of the coldest places in the country, even in March there will be 10 or more days of snow. In the south of England 0.9 to 1.4 days of snowfall is an average figure. It's very rare that snow will lie on the ground at sea level.

---

a start. And if you have a heavy clay soil, then you too may have to delay sowing, unless you've had the ground covered during part of the winter. Remember that while books such as this one can give general advice about when to do certain jobs, you should always be guided by local weather conditions before deciding to sow seeds or plant out young plants.

This year, try planting vegetables among flowers if your garden is small. Most modern gardens are too small to accommodate a separate kitchen garden, but fruit, vegetables, herbs and ornamentals

△ **Carpet of flowers**

Crocus and cyclamen make a good underplanting for deciduous trees and shrubs. Colour is so welcome at this time of year that even unlikely combinations somehow seem to work well.

can be grown together very successfully. Many vegetables are attractive plants in their own right, and they can make wonderful contrasts to other ornamental plants in the borders. The fine, feathery foliage of carrots contrasts well, for instance, with the bold leaves of hostas. Bright-coloured bedding plants can be set against the rich foliage of beetroot and

◁ **Willow wall**
Most trees will now be putting on a lovely display of bright, unfurling leaves. These woven willow wands look particularly effective against the dark backdrop of a conifer hedge.

ruby chards. Globe artichokes and cardoons are striking architectural plants and stand out in any border. You can have great fun mixing and matching plants, and as well as the garden looking attractive it will be productive too. Sow or plant the vegetables in groups rather than the conventional rows, and they will blend in perfectly.

Watch out for weeds

Remember that many little jobs that go to help keep the garden looking good can be done at the gentlest of paces. While having constitutional walks around the garden, keep a watch out for germinating weed seedlings and have them out with a hoe. The best time to do this is on a dry, sunny day, so that the weeds can be left on the surface of the soil to dry off and shrivel up in the warmth of the sun. Dig out any perennial weeds while they too are small, and they will be easier to control.

Weeding can become a bit of a chore, so to cut down on the time spent weeding, it is a good idea to mulch borders with a thick layer of organic matter after beds and borders have been tidied. An effective way to prevent weeds growing, mulching is also the perfect way to help conserve soil moisture, cutting down on the need to water as frequently during dry summer spells. Although it may seem hard to believe, water is becoming a scarce commodity, owing to adverse changes in weather patterns worldwide caused by global warming and we must all do our best to conserve it.

The best time for applying a mulch is early in spring while the soil is still moist; this way the moisture will not evaporate from the soil surface so rapidly. Water first if the weather has been dry. If a layer of mulch is applied to dry soil then it will make it difficult for water to penetrate the soil at all.

Rose pruning

It's a traditional time of year for pruning bush and shrub roses. Some people prefer to prune them in the autumn, but there's a lot to be said for waiting until spring. Firstly, the more growth in general you can leave intact in the garden over winter, the more possibilities for shelter you give to hibernating wildlife. Secondly, if your roses have taken a battering over winter – and pruned roses are certainly not immune to this – then you can tailor your pruning to leave you with the best-shaped plants after removing the damage. Don't be shy about pruning bush roses hard. Modern bush roses tend to be grafted onto the roots of much more vigorous rose

species, and are thus tremendously strong growers – they rise to the challenge of being pruned hard by producing really good growth and flowers.

Pest patrol

Pests and diseases begin to make their presence felt in earnest from this month onwards, particularly in the greenhouse, conservatory or the home (on houseplants, not the family!). Consider using biological controls this year, such as bacteria or tiny nematode worms that kill specific pests. These are regularly advertised in the gardening press, and you can order them by mail. Most are for use in the greenhouse, but there is one that can be watered onto open ground to control slugs. The sooner you can get on top of a slug or snail problem the better – at this time of year, they're just as eager as we are to see all that tender new growth emerging from the soil!

△ **Putting out young vegetable plants**
Salads and other crops sown earlier under cover can be put out now, under cloches or a blanket of horticultural fleece.

△ **Care for container plants**
Large plants that have overwintered outdoors in pots now need a top-dressing of new compost and a feed.

MARCH
AT A GLANCE

- Mulch bare soil in beds and borders.
- Move evergreen shrubs.
- Prune bush and shrub roses.
- Prune shrubs with colourful winter stems.
- Propagate shrubs by layering.
- Increase stocks of perennials by taking basal stem cuttings from the new shoots.
- Lift and divide overgrown clumps of perennials.
- Split polyanthus after flowering.
- Take cuttings from dahlia tubers.
- Plant summer-flowering bulbs.
- Sow sweet peas outdoors, or plant out young plants raised under cover. Pinch out growing tips of young sweet peas to encourage sideshoots.
- Sow hardy annuals where they are to flower.
- Reseed bare patches in the lawn.
- Start mowing lawns regularly.
- Take pumps out of store and put them back in the pond, and begin feeding fish.
- Sow vegetables outside, and harden off young plants to put outside.
- Plant early potatoes and asparagus.
- Protect fruit blossom against late frosts.
- Sow half-hardy annuals and other frost-tender bedding plants under cover.
- Water indoor plants regularly now the weather is warming up.

! LAST CHANCE

- Finish planting bare-root trees and shrubs and new fruit trees and bushes.
- This is the latest time to plant snowdrops and winter aconites.

★ GET AHEAD

- Put grow bags in the greenhouse to warm up before planting.
- Put stakes and other plant supports in to support new growth before it really needs it.

Doronicum x excelsum 'Harpur Crewe' • One of the earliest flowering perennials *(see p.316)*

Fritillaria imperialis • Striking bulb with clusters of bellflowers on tall stems *(see p.320)*

Pulmonaria angustifolia subsp. azurea • Herbaceous ground-cover perennial for sun or shade *(see p.344)*

Muscari armeniacum ♥ • The grape hyacinth, with small but intensely coloured flowers *(see p.333)*

Salix caprea 'Kilmarnock' • Small tree with drooping branches festooned with catkins *(see p.351)*

Iris danfordiae • Dwarf bulb ideal for an alpine trough or raised bed *(see p.326)*

Corylus avellana 'Contorta' ♀ • Hazel bearing long catkins on contorted branches (see p.312)

Chionodoxa forbesii 'Pink Giant' • Small bulb, lovely planted under deciduous shrubs (see p.304)

Hyacinthus orientalis 'City of Haarlem' • Bulb for indoor forcing or spring bedding (see p.325)

Daphne mezereum • Exquisitely perfumed pink flowers clustered on bare branches (see p.315)

Narcissus 'Dutch Master' ♀ • Classic golden-yellow daffodil with trumpet flowers (see p.334)

Anemone blanda 'Violet Star' • Plant tubers in autumn for a starry spring display (see p.298)

Lysichiton americanus ♀ • Perennial for damp ground or shallow water *(see p.331)*

Iris **'Katharine Hodgkin'** ♀ • Dwarf bulb, ideal for an alpine trough or raised bed *(see p.327)*

Primula **'Miss Indigo'** • Small but showy perennial for early spring display *(see p.342)*

Prunus sargentii ♀ • Flowering cherry tree with red-tinged young leaves, to 20m (60ft) tall *(see p.343)*

Caltha palustris ♀ • Water-loving perennial for pond margins and boggy ground *(see p.302)*

Narcissus **'Cheerfulness'** ♀ • Double-flowered narcissus with a powerful scent *(see p.334)*

Chaenomeles x superba 'Knap Hill Scarlet' ♀ • Stiff-branched shrub perfect for wall-training *(see p.304)*

Scilla siberica 'Spring Beauty' • Bulb, similar to but less invasive than bluebells *(see p.353)*

Primula Gold-laced Group • Showy, unusual polyanthus-type primula *(see p.342)*

Forsythia x intermedia • Cheerful shrub tolerant of most soils and positions *(see p.319)*

Tulipa tarda ♀ • Small species tulip, short-stemmed, pretty in a rock garden *(see p.356)*

Crocus vernus 'Pickwick' • A spring favourite with attractively striped petals *(see p.314)*

WHAT TO DO IN **MARCH**

AROUND THE GARDEN

WITH WARMER WEATHER PESTS are now on the increase, so keep an eye open for signs of infestation. If you pick or rub pests off as soon as they appear (or prune out badly infested shoots) you can stop them multiplying and causing more trouble later on.

MULCH BARE SOIL, having weeded and tidied it first, with organic matter – well-rotted farmyard manure, garden compost, cocoa shells, chipped bark or spent mushroom compost (don't use the last around acid-loving plants like rhododendrons, because it contains lime). Soil in borders left bare will very quickly lose water in dry spells. Covering with a thick layer of organic matter will cut down the rate at which water evaporates from the soil, reducing the need to water. This is especially important for young trees, shrubs and perennials that have been recently planted. After spending hard-earned cash on plants, never let them go short of water in their first year. A mulch will also suppress weeds, and it looks good too. Never put a mulch on top of dry soil. If the soil is dry, water it first. A layer of compost is just as good at keeping water out as sealing it in.

Mulching Always spread a generous layer for a mulch to do its best, at least 5cm (2in) deep.

TREES & SHRUBS

MOVING A SHRUB

① Dig a trench around the shrub, following a circle around the outermost extent of the shrub's branches.

② Start to work inwards, teasing soil out from between the roots with a fork, to reduce the weight of the rootball. Try not to damage roots as far as you can.

③ Use a spade to undercut the rootball, working from all sides until the shrub is completely free.

④ Half-roll up a sheet of sacking or polythene and ease the rolled half under the rootball by tipping the shrub.

⑤ Tip the shrub the other way to unroll the sheeting, then gather it up and secure to enclose the rootball.

MOVE EVERGREEN SHRUBS. This is a good time of year to do it. Evergreens moved in winter are unable to replace water lost from their leaves through the action of frost and strong cold winds. Plants generally do not take up water from the soil until the temperature rises above 4–5°C (around 40°F). Now the soil is beginning to warm up and the shrubs will shortly begin to grow; they will therefore lose less water, helping them re-establish. When moving shrubs, take as large a rootball as you can manage; if it is a large shrub, get a friend to help. Provide protection at first from cold winds with a screen of hessian or similar material, keep the shrub well watered and it should grow away well.

FEED WINTER-FLOWERING HEATHERS pruned in February with a high-nitrogen feed. Organic options are dried blood, fishmeal, and pelleted poultry manure from organic sources.

PLANTING

FINISH PLANTING BARE-ROOT TREES AND SHRUBS (see February). This really is the last month, until autumn, to get these plants in. With the leaves opening up they find it much more difficult to establish, because they are losing water rapidly from the foliage. Plants grown in containers can be planted year-round, although spring and autumn, the traditional times, are best.

PRUNING AND TRAINING

PRUNING BUSH ROSES

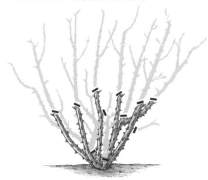

First remove any dead and diseased stems, and any crossing in the centre of the bush to open it up.
Hybrid teas, floribundas and patio roses *Cut out any weak shoots. Then prune last year's shoots to within 5–8cm (2–3in) of the previous year's growth (as above). Floribundas can be pruned more lightly for a larger plant.*
Standards *Treat the head exactly as above.*
Miniatures *Cut back hard only if the bush has become leggy and badly shaped.*

PRUNING SHRUB ROSES

Prune out any dead, damaged or diseased stems, cutting to stem junctions or healthy buds. Little more is needed in the first years. Once growth becomes crowded, thin shoots in the centre and cut one or two main stems to the base. This will encourage the plant to produce new growths from the base, keeping it young. Trim off any dead heads or hips left from last year (as above).

PRUNE ROSES NOW UNLESS YOU GOT A HEAD START LAST MONTH. Prune bush and shrub roses now. Climbers are usually pruned in the autumn (see September), so that they can be tidied up and tied in before winter winds blow them about. Never prune ramblers in the spring unless you need to drastically renovate them, as you will lose this year's flowers. Prune them after flowering (see August).

The main reason for pruning roses is to build a healthy framework of shoots that will produce a good display of flowers. Thinning overcrowded growth allows in light and air, so there will be less chance of problems with pests and diseases, and also encourages strong healthy growth. Cuts must be clean, not ragged or bruised, so equip yourself with a good pair of strong, sharp secateurs. You may also need a pair of loppers for thicker shoots.

The first thing to do on any type of rose is to remove any dead or unhealthy wood. Leaving this on the plant can encourage diseases to invade. The next is to cut out any shoots that are crossing and rubbing against another. Now, the flowering wood can be pruned, and here the method varies depending on the rose type (see left). Always prune to outward-facing buds. The main rule to remember is that the harder you prune, the more vigorous the subsequent growth will be.

Clear up rose prunings carefully, or they will ambush you later. It's best to dispose of or burn them, rather than shredding them for composting, as they can harbour disease. Then mulch around the roses, ideally with well-rotted farmyard manure, or a bagged product such as shredded bark.

Juvenile foliage *Eucalyptus cut hard back each year will produce attractive rounded leaves.*

PRUNE SHRUBBY EUCALYPTUS. Not all of us have room to grow eucalyptus as a tree, but it responds well to hard pruning, making a lovely foliage shrub (above). Just prune all last year's growth to 15cm (6in) from the ground, and you will be rewarded with the attractive round juvenile leaves on a small bushy plant.

PRUNE DOGWOODS AND SHRUBBY WILLOWS GROWN FOR THEIR ORNAMENTAL COLOURED STEMS. The best stem colour from *Cornus* and *Salix* is produced by one-year-old shoots, and this is the reason for pruning them in spring. Ornamental *Rubus* with their white stems should be pruned now too. Be careful when pruning these, as the stems have very sharp thorns on them. Prune all these shrubs very hard, to about one or two buds of last year's growth, to leave a stubby framework (see right).

FINISH PRUNING LATE-FLOWERING SHRUBS such as *Buddleja davidii* (see February).

PLANNING AHEAD

PREPARE FOR MOVING LARGE DECIDUOUS SHRUBS. You can at a pinch still move them (see January), but better by far now is to start preparing them for moving after the summer. Trees and shrubs often transplant more successfully when they have a good fibrous root system (that is, with plenty of small finer roots). These smaller roots allow the plant to take up water from the soil much more effectively and the plant gets off to a good start.

Many shrubs and trees don't make very fibrous root systems, but this can be encouraged. At this time of year dig a narrow trench around the plant to be moved, to at least a spade's depth (see Moving a Shrub, Step 1, facing page). This will cut through some of the roots, and this in turn encourages the formation of new, fine roots within the circle. The trench can either be refilled with the soil taken out or with a

Coloured stems *In spring, prune back dogwoods and willows grown for winter stems.*

TREES & SHRUBS *continued*

LAYERING A SHRUB

1 First select a shoot that is growing near the ground, and mark the spot where you are going to peg it down.

2 Dig a small hole with a trowel and fill with some potting compost. Push in a short cane.

3 Wound the stem by cutting part-way through it, or by twisting the stem until you just hear it crack.

4 Peg the wounded area into the soil. A large stone placed on top will help keep it in place and hold in moisture.

5 Very gently tie the stem beyond the peg to the cane. This will help the new young plant to grow upright.

compost mixture. Old potting compost is quite good, or fine, well-rotted garden compost mixed with the soil. In autumn, when you dig around the shrub to move it, you will find that plenty of the all-important finer roots have formed and the shrub will have a much better chance of re-establishing well when it is replanted.

PROPAGATION

LAYER SHRUBS TO MAKE NEW PLANTS. This is a good month to increase some of the shrubs in your garden by layering. It's a great way of propagating them, as it doesn't need any special equipment. In fact, many shrubs, like hydrangeas, forsythias and philadelphus (the mock orange), will layer themselves, forming roots on any shoots that are touching the ground. The technique of layering is quite easy (see left). Usually, wounding the stem is enough to stimulate roots to grow, but if you want to encourage the process, you can also dust the wound with hormone rooting powder before pegging it down. The layered shoot will have formed roots by the following spring, when it can be cut from the parent plant and planted elsewhere.

HEDGES

LAST CHANCE TO PLANT bare-root hedging plants (see January). From now until autumn only container-grown plants will generally be available, which can make buying in bulk for hedges expensive.

CLIMBERS

Wire stretched between vine eyes forms one of the simplest and most popular supports for climbers.

PLANT NEW CLIMBERS (see also February). Make sure supports such as wires and trellis are fixed up before you buy and plant. Wires may stand out at first but are soon hidden by the plants.

FINISH PRUNING LATE-FLOWERING CLEMATIS (see February).

PRUNE CLIMBING ROSES now if you didn't do so in autumn (see September).

RENOVATE CLIMBERS. This is a good time to tackle overgrown climbers: before they start fully into growth, yet with breaking buds so that you will be able to see where stems are dead. Climbers that can be cut hard back include honeysuckles, ivies, rambling roses and winter jasmine.

Renovation pruning Many climbers that have got out of hand can be pruned drastically.

PERENNIALS

CUT DOWN ALL GROWTH LEFT OVER WINTER. Even if seedheads and stems are still managing to look good, you need to get rid of them now to make way for new growth.

After a good tidy up, if you didn't feed plants last month, you can dress the soil with a fertiliser now so that it is ready for a layer of mulch (see Around the Garden).

IN THE SOUTH AND IN MILD AREAS, remove any cloches or protective blankets from plants susceptible to frost (see November), or new shoots may be damaged. In colder regions it may be safer to wait until April. Give the plants a feed to get them going. You can also divide overgrown clumps.

NEW SHOOTS SHOULD NOW BE GROWING STRONGLY from the crowns of plants, and it is an ideal time to increase plants such as achillea, anthemis, delphiniums, gypsophila and lupins by a type of cutting called a basal stem cutting. They are very easy to take, when the shoots are about 8-10cm (3-4in) high. Remove the shoots from as close to the plant as possible using a sharp knife. It's very like taking dahlia cuttings (see above right), except that the parent plant is in the ground. Insert the cuttings into a pot containing a mix of equal parts peat-free compost and perlite or vermiculite, cover with a polythene bag, and put on a shady windowsill or in a cold frame until they root in a few weeks' time.

Sometimes, you can take root cuttings with a small piece of root attached – especially from asters, and also campanulas, lupins, chrysanthemums and

CUTTINGS FROM DAHLIAS

Using a sharp knife, cut young shoots cleanly from the tubers, and trim them below a leaf joint.

Dip in fungicide and hormone rooting compound before firming gently into free-draining compost.

sedums. These are known as "Irishman's cuttings", and hardly ever fail.

TAKE CUTTINGS FROM DAHLIA TUBERS (see above). Cuttings should be taken when the shoots have reached 8–10cm (3-4in) long but before the stems become hollow (this is normal for dahlias as the stems mature). Trim the cuttings below a leaf joint and remove the lower leaves. Dip the cuttings into fungicide (wear gloves for this) and then dip the bases into hormone rooting solution. Dibble the cuttings into pots containing equal parts peat-free compost and perlite or vermiculite. Put the pots in a propagator set at 10-13°C (50-55°F), with a polythene bag over them, to encourage a good root system.

More shoots will grow from where the cuttings were taken, so you can take more later.

PLANT NEW PLANTS. Hardy perennials will grow away quickly if planted now (see September). Feed and mulch after planting, and keep well watered until they establish.

TOWARDS THE END OF THE MONTH SPLIT UP POLYANTHUS-TYPE PRIMULAS as the flowers go over. To divide them, dig up each clump with a fork. With very large clumps you will have to push two forks back to back into the centre of the clump and push the fork handles apart. The sections can then be divided by hand. Trim off most of the old foliage, leaving about 5cm (2in). Apart from making the plants tidier, this reduces loss of water from the leaves: the plants establish quicker and new leaves soon grow. Either plant the divisions back *in situ*, after revitalizing the soil with garden compost or manure, or plant them in rows in a corner of the vegetable garden to grow through the summer and plant out again in the borders in the autumn. The plants will then give a terrific splash of colour in the spring.

LIFT AND DIVIDE OVERGROWN CLUMPS of summer-flowering herbaceous perennials. Most can be lifted and divided in spring just as growth gets under way, and if the divisions are reasonably sized, they should flower later in the year. Plants which need dividing are usually quite easy to see. As perennials age the clumps push outwards, with fresh young growth to the edge of the clump, and the centre

dies out. This is the stage at which they should be divided. Lift each clump with a fork, and insert two forks back to back and prise them apart; smaller pieces can then be pulled apart by hand. Add organic matter and fertiliser to revitalize the soil, and plant the young divisions in groups of three, five or more, depending on the space you have. Water them in well if the soil is dry.

DIVIDING PERENNIALS

① Use a fork to loosen the clump all the way around the edges so it can be lifted clear of the soil.

② A mature clump can be hard to pull apart, but you can use a spade or a garden knife to cut it roughly into sections.

③ Tease out small, chunky pieces to replant. The best bits are often toward the outside of the clump.

④ Fork and water the soil where the plants are to grow. Scoop out small holes and firm the plants in. Water them regularly at first.

Protect hostas *For flawless foliage, you may need to protect the leaves from damage by slugs.*

PROTECT THE YOUNG, TENDER SHOOTS OF DELPHINIUMS AND HOSTAS from slug damage. Slugs and snails can do a lot of damage to young buds before they've barely emerged from the soil, and you may not be aware of the damage until the leaves begin to open up. The tiny holes, at this stage perhaps the size of pinheads, expand with the leaves, and by the summer there may be a great hole or series of holes ruining the foliage. There are general measures you can take to combat slugs and snails (see April, Around the Garden), but it's worth taking extra precautions to protect individual plants. The best way to prevent slugs getting to your (and their!) favourites is to use a physical barrier that the pests will not want to negotiate to get to the plants. The easiest barrier of all is coarse grit; slugs and snails really dislike moving over its rough surface. Put down a thick layer around the plants, the sooner the better.

SUPPORT HERBACEOUS PERENNIALS. Towards the end of the month many herbaceous perennials will be making plenty of growth, and at the

PERENNIALS *continued*

SUPPORT PERENNIALS

Get stakes and supports in early so that the plants grow up naturally around them.

first sign of rain or a strong breeze the shoots will be flattened. There is a wide variety of supports available today, and what you choose depends on the depth of your pocket. The easiest and cheapest are twiggy sticks (known as pea sticks) pushed in around each clump; the plants soon grow up between them. Prunings from other shrubs, provided that they are straight and strong enough, for example buddleja stems with the old flowers removed, are excellent. They look rather unsightly to begin with, but the plants soon hide them completely. Supports you can buy include canes, plastic-coated stakes that link together and round mesh supports which the plants grow through, some of which can be raised as the plant grows. The most important point about staking is to get it done early and the plants will then look natural as they grow. Don't leave it until the plants flop or are blown about; trying to stake stems that are growing in all directions never looks good.

ALPINES

IN THE ROCK GARDEN weed seedlings will be growing in grit or gravel between the plants. Although a covering of gravel is fairly good at suppressing weeds, seeds of annual weeds like groundsel and annual grasses can germinate in the moist soil beneath and push through. They are easy to control by pulling them out or digging them up with a small hand fork or an old kitchen knife. Never use a sprayer in the rock garden to apply weedkiller; the plants are too close together for this and would undoubtedly be damaged. The best way to deal with any perennial weeds that get in is by spot-treating them with a weedkiller painted onto the foliage of the weeds with a brush, usually built into the lid of the product. If the weed is growing up through the centre of a plant, place a piece of wood or cardboard under the foliage of the weed to protect the plant, then carefully paint on the weedkiller.

After weeding, top up any bare patches where the gravel may have been washed away. This will give the rock garden a neat and tidy finish as the alpines come into their main flowering period in spring.

Among alpines *A small weeding tool or an old kitchen knife or fork is handy for the rock garden.*

BULBS

Deadheading daffodils *Pinch off the head just behind the bulbous part, but leave the stem intact.*

DEADHEAD DAFFODILS as the flowers fade, but leave the foliage alone. If the old flowers are left on, the plant's energy will be used for the production of seed. At this time the important thing is to build up the the bulb's reserves so that a new flower bud forms inside it for flowering next spring.

PLANT SNOWDROPS IN THE GREEN if this was not done last month (see February). Snowdrops very rarely grow well from dry bulbs, so the best time to divide them or buy new ones is now while they are still green. Overgrown clumps can be lifted and divided now, or new plants can be bought from specialist mail order nurseries.

PLANT SUMMER-FLOWERING BULBS this month and next month for a succession of flowers. They all enjoy a sunny position in well-drained soil. All summer-flowering bulbs, if planted at intervals over a period of a few weeks, will give a succession of flowers throughout the summer and into autumn. However, in northern parts of

the country wait until next month before planting the frost-tender bulbs such as gladioli, eucomis and tigridias.

Gladioli can be grown in several ways: in rows for cutting, in tubs and in groups in borders. For the best effect in ornamental borders plant gladiolus bulbs (or more correctly corms) in groups of five or more. Plant the corms 10–15cm (4–6in) apart and 7–10cm (3–4in) deep. The deeper the corms are planted the

CHOOSING GLADIOLI

'Stardust' 'Stromboli' 'Esta Bonita'

'Parade' 'Sweet Dreams' 'Green Woodpecker'

ANNUALS & BEDDING

less likely will be the need to stake the plants. On heavy clay, dig the hole a little deeper and place the corms on a layer of coarse grit. Plant tigridias 5–8cm (2–3in) deep and 10–15cm (4–6in) apart. Plant galtonias 10–15cm (4–6in) deep and 22–30cm (9–12in) apart, and eucomis 15cm (6in) deep and 15–22cm (6–9in) apart.

Other bulbs to consider planting over the next few weeks include lilies and the de Caen anemones. Lilies can be planted outside in well-prepared soil in groups in any mixed border. Plant the bulbs to three times their own depth and 7–10cm (3–4in) apart. On heavy clay soils, plant the bulbs on a layer of coarse grit to aid drainage. Lilies don't like to sit in damp soil. Plant de Caen anemones about 2.5cm (1in) deep and 10–15cm (4–6in) apart.

CANNAS for setting out in June can be started into growth now. See Under Cover for details.

BULBS THAT WERE FORCED INTO FLOWER INSIDE can be planted out when the flowers are over, if this was not done earlier. Bulbs like narcissus, hyacinths and dwarf irises will have finished flowering by now so the best place for them is in the garden. Remove them from their containers and plant them just as they are, without disturbing the roots. This will help the bulbs get established. Feed them with a fertiliser high in potash to encourage the formation of next year's flower bud within the bulb. Don't try to force the same bulbs for a second year as they rarely flower as well. It's best to buy new ones in the autumn.

SWEET PEAS ON A WIGWAM

Make a wigwam of 2m (6ft) canes, tied together at the top. Sow two sweet pea seeds at the base of each cane.

Mixed colours and scented varieties are the best for a cottagey effect. Pick the flowers regularly and more will be formed.

SOW AND PLANT SWEET PEAS OUTSIDE IN SOUTHERN PARTS. The easiest way to grow sweet peas is to sow them where they are to flower. There

are many different ways of growing sweet peas, and they have many uses in the garden. The scented varieties are the best to grow. A sweet pea without scent is like a rose without thorns, useless. Erect a support, if necessary, first. There are many different ways of supporting sweet peas, from making wigwams from canes or bean poles to letting them scramble up through shrubs.

Germination will be improved by soaking the seeds overnight to soften the seed coat. Then plant two seeds at 30cm (1ft) intervals and 1cm (⅓in) deep. When the seeds have germinated, the weaker of the two can be removed or moved to fill in any gaps. The young plants may need to be attached to the support with sweet pea rings initially, just to get them started. Soon the tendrils will twine themselves around the support.

In sheltered parts of the country, you can also plant out sweet peas sown last autumn, in well-prepared soil.

SOW HARDY ANNUALS OUTSIDE. Now that spring has arrived, it is safe to begin sowing hardy annuals outside in most parts of the country. In northern parts you may have to wait until the end of the month or into early April. Hardy annuals look best grown in informal drifts. If the soil has not been prepared lightly fork it over, but don't add any manure or garden compost. If the soil is too rich, the plants will produce a lot of soft growth and very few flowers. All that needs to be done after forking over the soil is to apply a light dressing of a general fertiliser and rake the soil to a fine tilth. Now comes the fun part: marking out the informal drifts and sowing (see right). The only

SOW HARDY ANNUALS

① Get some dry silver sand, put it in an empty wine bottle and make irregular shapes by pouring out the sand.

② Sow the seeds thinly in shallow drills made with a stick. Check the back of the packet for distances between drills.

③ Lightly cover, water, and label each area with what you have sown. Keep the seed packets. Then you'll have advice on thinning distances to hand when the seedlings come up.

ANNUALS *continued*

rule to remember when planning an annual planting is that the taller plants, like larkspur (*Consolida*) and cosmos, go to the back and the shortest, such as nemophila (or baby-blue-eyes), lobularia and the poached egg flower (*Limnanthes douglasii*) at the front. You can, if you want to, spend time making elaborate colour-coordinated schemes, or theme borders around a particular colour. But from these plants all we really want is a good splash of colour, so don't worry too much about colours clashing.

By sowing in drills rather than broadcasting the seed over each drift area, the young seedlings will be more easy to tell apart from weeds. Once they grow together, you won't be able to tell that they are in rows. Varying the direction in which the drills cross neighbouring drifts also helps avoid a regimented look. When the seedlings are large enough to handle, they will have to be thinned out (see May).

ANY HARDY ANNUALS WHICH WERE SOWN UNDER COVER can be hardened off now to acclimatize them to outdoor conditions. To do this put the plants in a cold frame with the top closed for a few days. Then, gradually increase the ventilation until the lid can be left off or up. This is usually done over a week or 10 days. Keep some insulation like horticultural fleece or old bits of carpet to put over the frame at night if a sharp frost is forecast.

SOW SEED UNDER COVER of half-hardy annuals and tender perennials for summer bedding (see Under Glass).

CONTAINERS

PLANT UP ROSES IN POTS. Roses, particularly the "flowering carpet" varieties, miniature roses and elegant standards, look excellent on the patio, in containers filled with a soil-based compost such as John Innes No.3. Soil-based composts are far better for shrubs in containers; they hold a supply of nutrients more easily than soilless ones, and also retain moisture better, cutting down the need for watering. After planting, prune the roses hard to encourage plenty of new growth. After a couple of months, feed regularly with a high-potash feed to encourage a profusion of flowers, and you will be rewarded with a smashing display for weeks on end. Remember, though, that in dry weather watering may have to be done once if not twice a day. The roses may fare better if they are moved into the shade in fiercely sunny weather.

MANY OTHER PLANTS can be grown in containers, as above: small trees, shrubs and climbers, herbaceous perennials, annuals, alpines and ground cover plants. Let your imagination run riot. The only real rule is to look after the plants well, watering, feeding and deadheading regularly. Using slow-release fertilisers and the water-retentive crystals now available can save some work through the year.

PONDS

TAKE NETTING OFF THE POND or, if the pond was not netted in the autumn, remove as many leaves that have fallen into the pond as you can, together with any other winter debris. If too many leaves are left in the pond the water will become stagnant and stifle aquatic life. At the same time, remove any old foliage from pond plants. Remove pond heaters put in for winter to prevent the pond from freezing.

SUBMERSIBLE PUMPS and lighting systems can be taken out of store and put back in the pond. Circulating water will help to keep the water oxygenated for fish and other creatures – and the sound of water is so very relaxing. If anything doesn't work, let an electrician look at it – don't tinker.

IF YOU HAVE FISH in the pond, begin feeding them now. Little and often is the watchword at this time of year. Too much food in the pond left over by the fish will encourage the growth of algae.

Back in action *It's time to take pumps out of store, check them and put them back in the pond.*

LAWNS

GET THE MOWER SERVICED if you haven't already done it. This is usually a busy time of year for servicing agents. There is nothing worse than trying to mow a lawn with a blunt mower. The grass, rather than being cut cleanly, is more likely to be torn at with a blunt machine. It doesn't look good and harms the grass.

START MOWING REGULARLY. By this time in most parts of the country grass will be growing steadily now, and needs to be cut regularly to keep it in good condition. A lawn will be much healthier and stay greener the less grass you remove every time it is cut. Now, for the first few cuts, set the blades at the highest setting. Even if you tend to leave clippings on the lawn in summer, keep the box on the mower in spring, so that air, rain and fertiliser can penetrate the turf.

FEED THE LAWN (see April) towards the end of the month in southern parts. In the north or in cold springs, wait until next month: the grass needs to be actively growing to make the best use of the fertiliser.

REMOVE THATCH. If you did not scarify the lawn last autumn (see September), rake out the moss and

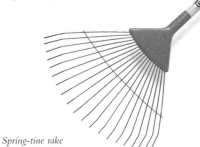

Spring-tine rake

dead grass which inevitably accumulates in the grass over the course of a season. If moss is a problem, scarify after applying any moss killer to the lawn, later in the month. Don't rake out moss before applying a moss killer, as you will just spread the moss all over the lawn. Moss in a lawn is a sign that all is not well. The application of a moss killer is a short-term answer, but to eradicate moss permanently you have to tackle the underlying likely causes; compaction, poor drainage, shade, the grass being cut too short, or combinations of any of

REPAIRING DAMAGE TO EDGES

① Cut out a square of turf surrounding the damage to the edge, undercut it with a spade, lift it, and rotate it by 180°.

② The "good" side of the turf will form a perfect edge, with no dip. Fill the hole with soil and reseed it to cover the gap.

these. Raking out thatch can be a backbreaking job if you're using the traditional tool, a spring-tine rake. On a small lawn it's fine, but on a larger area it may be best to use an electric scarifier; these can be bought from most garden centres, or you can hire one from a local hire shop. Petrol-driven scarifiers are available if you have a very large lawn, and these too can be hired.

It's amazing how much stuff will be taken out of the lawn, and it will look truly awful for a time; you may well wonder what you've done. But take heart: it will soon recover and look better than ever.

REPAIR DAMAGE TO LAWN EDGES. Over the summer lawn edges can be easily be damaged and often, especially with light sandy soils, edges can crumble away in places. To repair a broken edge, cut out the entire damaged portion of turf and turn it around (see left). Fill in any hollow with soil and sow grass seed onto this. Water, and peg polythene over the top to encourage the grass seed to grow and then you will have a perfect repair.

You can reseed other bare patches in the middle of the lawn like this all through the summer, by scarifying the bare patch to roughen the surface and spreading on a mix of potting compost and grass seed mixed together in equal proportions.

NEW LAWNS

FINISH PREPARATIONS for sowing a new lawn or laying turf. Soil which was dug over during the winter (see February) can now be levelled off and raked down to a fine tilth (a fine

PREPARING SOIL FOR GRASS SEED

Roughly level the soil to break down the lumps. Then tread the ground with your weight on your heels and keeping your feet together.

Rake over the soil again and then tread it again at right-angles to the previous time. Rake again. Stand back and squat down to check for any hollows and bumps to even.

crumbly surface for sowing seeds; see above). Seed sowing (see April for details) can be done at any time from the end of this month through until autumn, although sowing during the hot, dry summer months is less advisable.

Although turf can be laid any time, it is better to do it between autumn and this month, so that it can benefit from seasonal rain. When laying turf (see October for illustrations), always work outwards from the turf that is laid, using boards on the turf already laid to spread your weight. Turf is laid with the joints staggered, in a similar pattern to that of house bricks. The joints are never in line. It is absolutely crucial to keep newly laid turves well watered. If they dry out at this stage, even slightly, they will shrink and leave persistent unsightly gaps in the lawn.

VEGETABLES & HERBS

PREPARE SEEDBEDS FOR DIRECT SOWING. Even if it's been left exposed, soil should be beginning to dry out now, and will be in a better state for the making of good seedbeds for sowing. Getting the timing of this job right can be tricky sometimes. The soil doesn't want to be so wet that it sticks to your boots, nor so dry that it takes a lot of effort to break it up, but hopefully nature has given a helping hand and broken down the worst of the clods. If the soil is rather too moist for treading on but you feel you must get on, then use planks to stand on. These will distribute your weight and prevent localised areas becoming too compacted.

Break larger lumps of soil down by bashing them with a fork, then use a rake to smooth out smaller lumps and create a fine tilth, pushing and pulling the rake back and forth over the surface of the soil to a depth of about 2.5cm (1in). Tread the soil to firm it, and apply an organic fertiliser, such as one based on seaweed, about two weeks before sowing. Rake that in and the seedbed is ready for the seed (see overleaf).

SOWING INDOORS

HARDEN OFF EARLY SOWINGS OF VEGETABLES. Those vegetables sown under cover in late January or February can be hardened off (put in a cooler environment, such as a cold frame) to acclimatize to cooler conditions. A week or 10 days should be enough to acclimatize them before planting them out, under cloches that have ideally already been in place for a few weeks to warm up the soil (see Sowing and Planting Outdoors, overleaf).

VEGETABLES & HERBS *continued*

SOW GLOBE ARTICHOKES for planting out in May. These are quite large seeds, and can be spaced out easily. Sow two seeds each in small pots, watering the compost first, and cover with sieved compost. Place in a propagator at a temperature of around 18°C (65°F). When they germinate, move to a sunny bench or windowsill. Remove the weaker of the two young plants, or transplant it to its own pot.

LETTUCE, CABBAGE AND CAULIFLOWERS can still be sown indoors to give a succession of crops from those sown earlier. The plants will get off to a better start if they are grown in modules. With no disturbance to the plants' roots when they are transplanted, there is less chance of growth being checked, and there will therefore be less risk of the crops bolting, or running to seed prematurely. Cauliflowers are particularly prone to bolting, or the heads not forming properly, if they receive the slightest check.

SOWING AND PLANTING OUTDOORS

PLANT OUT YOUNG VEGETABLE PLANTS hardening off in cold frames (see Sowing Indoors, previous page). Prepare the ground by raking it down to a tilth and spreading on an organic fertiliser before planting. Plant at the distances recommended for final spacing after thinning on the seed packets. Water in well after planting, and ideally, cover with a cloche. A good tip is to plant up one half of a cloche with young plants, and sow seeds in the other; this way you get a succession of crops. On deep beds, the plants can go in much closer than

Planting out A plank marked at intervals makes an excellent guide when spacing young plants.

would normally be the case. Because the soil is never compacted by being trodden on, plant roots tend to grow downwards into the soil, rather than spreading out, so crops can be grown more closely together.

START SOWING OUTSIDE REGULARLY. This month seed-sowing outside can get under way in earnest. In northern parts, wait until late in the month or early next month before sowing outside. Sowings of lettuce, other salads such as endive, radish, salad onions, peas, broad beans, spinach, cabbage, turnips and beetroot can all be made now. Sow short rows at a time, at weekly or 10-day intervals; this way a succession of vegetables will become ready throughout the summer and autumn. Many seeds are now sold in small vacuum-packed foil sachets within the main packet. When the foil pack is opened the vacuum is broken and air gets in, so it's important to store the seeds between sowings in a cool, dry place – the fridge is ideal. Seeds not packed in foil sachets are also better kept in the fridge. These cool conditions ensure the seeds remain viable (capable

of germinating) for longer periods. To sow all of the fine-seeded vegetables, take out shallow drills with a cane. Water the drills before sowing if the soil is dry. Sow the seeds thinly along the drill and cover lightly with dry soil. Once the seedlings are large enough to handle it is important to thin them.

With peas and broad beans the technique is a little different. Take out a trench about 2.5cm (1in) deep with a spade and sow the seeds of peas about 2.5cm (1in) apart in the bottom of the trench and cover over. With broad beans, space the seeds about 15cm (6in) apart in rows and cover over with soil. Peas and broad beans will have to be protected with netting or horticultural fleece to prevent mice and wood pigeons digging them up.

SOW PARSNIPS OUTSIDE. Sowing parsnips requires yet another, slightly different technique, because parsnips are notoriously erratic at germinating. Take out a narrow drill as described above, but instead of sowing the seeds thinly along the drill, sow them in clusters of three or four seeds at 15cm (6in) intervals along the drill. This way, if some of the seeds don't germinate, there won't be any gaps in the row. Because germination can be slow and erratic, it's a good idea to sow a quick-maturing crop like radishes along the drill between the parsnip seeds; this way the row can be easily identified.

PLANT EARLY POTATOES. Early potatoes can go in now. There are several ways in which to do this. In 1.2m (4ft)-wide deep beds, potatoes are easily planted with a trowel. Plant about 30cm (1ft) apart and as deep as you can

SOWING OUTSIDE

Narrow drills Suitable for all fine seeds. Use a cane to draw out shallow, V-shaped trenches. A string guide will help you get them straight.

Wide drills Good for peas and beans grown in rows either side of supports. Provided that soil is dry and crumbly, you can use a draw or onion hoe, or a spade, to make the shallow trenches.

Station sowing Another option for large seeds such as broad beans. Traditional dibbers like these were made from broken spade and fork handles.

get with the trowel. In these deep beds, another way to get a really good crop is to mound up the soil into ridges about 60cm (2ft) apart across the beds. Plant the tubers on the ridges, again as deep as you can get with a trowel, spacing tubers about 30cm (12in) apart in the rows. After planting, cover the ridges with clear polythene, holding it in place between the ridges with planks of wood. After a few weeks, watch carefully to see the shoots growing, and when you see them through the polythene cut slits in the sheets to let them grow through. Keep some fleece handy in case frost is forecast, as the young shoots are very prone to frost damage. The polythene helps to retain heat in the soil so the potatoes can be harvested earlier, when they are at their most expensive in the shops.

The traditional way of planting on allotment-style beds is to take out planting trenches about a spade's depth and 60cm (2ft) apart. Put some organic matter in the trench and scatter an organic fertiliser either along the bottom of the trench, or on the soil removed in making the trench. Plant the tubers in the trench about 30cm (12in) apart, and cover with the soil taken out.

PLANT ONION SETS from now onwards. Prepare the ground as for

Early potatoes Plant the chitted seed potatoes with the "rose" end (the one with most shoots) uppermost.

Asparagus crowns The spidery roots need to sit on a ridge within a trench.

preparing seedbeds – although the soil doesn't have to be as fine for onion sets – and apply an organic fertiliser. Plant the sets about 10-15cm (4-6in) apart in rows the same distance apart. Plant each set with a trowel: don't just push them into the soil, because as the roots form they will push the set up and out again. It is also worth trimming off the dry skin at the tip of the onion set, cutting straight across with a sharp knife, as birds use this to get a hold on the sets and pull them out of the soil.

If growing onion sets on deep beds plant them about 8cm (3in) apart. The eventual onions may be smaller but you will achieve a higher overall yield.

PLANT ASPARAGUS CROWNS. This is a good time to plant asparagus. If you haven't already prepared a bed (see October), dig the soil deeply now, incorporating plenty of organic matter. If your soil is a heavy clay, add pea shingle to improve the drainage. The beds should be about 1.2m (4ft) wide and as long as you like. Make the bed slightly higher than the surrounding soil

to improve drainage. This should automatically happen if you are adding plenty of organic matter. Many firms sell asparagus crowns by post. All male varieties of asparagus, such as 'Franklim', 'Lucullus' and 'Dariana', produce the heaviest crops. When the crowns arrive they may have to be soaked for a couple of hours. To plant them, dig out shallow trenches about 15cm (6in) deep and 45cm (18in) apart, mounding up the bottom of each trench to make a slight ridge. Place the crowns on top of the ridges 45cm (18in) apart, with the roots spread down each side of the ridge, and replace the soil. Keep well watered. Don't cut any asparagus the first year to allow the plants to get established. Your patience will be rewarded next year.

LOOKING AFTER CROPS

FEED WINTER LETTUCES Plants sown to overwinter (see September) will benefit from an application of a general organic fertiliser after the long dark days. Sprinkle it between the plants according to the manufacturer's

Globe artichokes Sow these statuesque perennials now for one of the most beautiful edible plants.

instructions. Water it in well if the soil is dry. Cut every other lettuce when required and leave the others to grow on and heart up.

WATCH OUT FOR PESTS AND DISEASES. Always try to prevent pests and diseases getting to the point where they become serious by taking preventive measures. If you want to use chemical sprays, do so in the evenings when bees have gone for the day.

Even so-called safe organic sprays contain substances that are harmful to a wide range of predators that do a lot of good controlling pests. From experience, it has been shown that by building up a diversity of plants and flowers in the garden and making beneficial predators, such as ladybirds, welcome, the need for most spraying against pests is eliminated.

KEEP THE HOE GOING TO KEEP WEEDS DOWN. Now that spring is here, weeds seem to grow more vigorously than anything else in the garden. This is why it is important to keep the hoe going between rows of vegetables. Not only do weeds take valuable moisture and nutrients from the soil, they also act as host plants to pests and diseases. So the more you can keep on top of them, the better for the garden as a whole.

Hoeing is best done on a dry day when the weeds can be left on the soil surface to dry out in the sun. A Dutch hoe is the tool to use for this job, walking backwards with a pushing and pulling motion, slicing off the tops of the weeds. Perennial weeds will have to be dug out, because if any piece of root is left in the soil it will grow again.

VEGETABLES & HERBS *continued*

Winter crops *Brassicas such as sprouting broccoli and cabbages provide welcome winter greens.*

HARVESTING

HARVEST THE LAST OF THE WINTER CROPS. Put all of the debris on the compost heap, if not diseased. Spring greens should be cropping now.

AFTER HARVESTING FORCED CHICORY put all of the remains on the compost heap, and sow new plants for next winter later in the year (see May).

PLANNING AHEAD

MAKE A SEEDBED FOR SOWING WINTER CROPS. Towards the end of the month prepare an area, perhaps a corner of the vegetable garden, for sowing crops such as Brussels sprouts, winter cauliflower, winter cabbage, broccoli and kale. Prepare the soil in the usual way, raking it to a fine tilth, and apply a general fertiliser. Again, sowing the crops at intervals over a few weeks will ensure that they mature at different times, giving a succession of vegetables over winter when they are at their most scarce and expensive in the shops. Take out shallow drills with a cane about 15cm (6in) apart and sow each variety thinly in each row, watering the drills beforehand if the soil is dry. Cover the seeds with dry soil and label each row. Cover the seedbed with horticultural fleece to prevent damage from flea beetle. These tiny insects eat holes in the leaves. When the seedlings have made two or three true leaves they can be transplanted to their permanent growing area (see May).

MAKE RUNNER BEAN TRENCHES. If this was not done at the end of winter (see February) do it now. Take out a trench to a spade's depth, about 90cm (3ft) wide and the length of the proposed row. Break up the bottom of the trench with a fork, but don't bring the poorer subsoil to the surface. Put plenty of organic matter in the trench. Almost anything will do – even shredded newspapers put in a layer in the bottom of the trench are good at holding moisture, and they will have rotted down by the end of the summer. Just before planting the beans in early June, replace the soil taken out after mixing with a dose of general fertiliser.

ADD MANURE TO CELERY TRENCHES. Celery is a crop that requires plenty of water through the growing season, and to grow it well good soil preparation is essential. Take out a trench to a spade's depth, about 60cm (2ft) wide and the length of the row. Put plenty of organic matter in the trench and lightly fork it into the soil, being careful not to bring the poorer subsoil to the surface. Then partly fill the trench with some of the soil taken out, and the job's done for now. Celery plants are not planted until early June, but the sooner preparation is done the better.

HERBS

SOW HERBS OUTSIDE AND BUY YOUNG PLANTS. Herbs that are hardy can be sown outside now. These include chervil, chives, dill, fennel, marjoram, coriander and parsley. Sow the seeds in exactly the same way as for vegetables, in drills, and plant them out when they are large enough to handle. Young plants of herbs that are more difficult to raise from seed can be bought now from garden centres or specialist herb nurseries. These include mint, tarragon and shrubby herbs such as thymes and rosemary. Choose French tarragon rather than Russian, which has a coarser taste and is a very invasive plant. So is mint in nearly all its forms: plant it in a pot and partially sink the pot in the ground to stop it taking over the whole garden.

A dedicated herb garden (see our project in June) is undoubtedly one of the most attractive ways to grow these plants, but they also look wonderful growing in borders along with other plants, so if your garden is too small for a separate herb feature, grow them in with other plants, or in pots on the patio by the house.

DIVIDE CHIVES now that they are starting to grow. Lift each clump with a fork and divide them up, being quite ruthless with them. Small clumps can be replanted in soil that has been revitalized with organic matter. Water well after replanting. They make pretty edging for beds.

FRUIT

Protected peach *When the flowers are open, this polythene shelter keeps off rain and frost.*

LOOKING AFTER CROPS

CHECK THAT FRUITS HAVE WATER IN DRY SEASONS. Fruits of all description need plenty of water to develop properly. Fruits growing in containers and trained against walls and fences should be checked from time to time, should we happen to have a dry spring. Trees trained against house walls are especially vulnerable, as the eaves often keep off a lot of rain.

PROTECT OPEN FLOWERS FROM FROST DAMAGE. The buds and flowers of peaches, nectarines and cherries open up early and are therefore prone to frost damage. Wall-trained trees can easily be protected using polythene sheets or horticultural fleece. The sheet can be fixed to two poles, which can then be leaned against the trees at night and taken off during the day. Free-standing trees are a bit trickier to protect, but draping horticultural fleece over small trees or bushes will give some protection from all but the most severe frost. Large trees just have to take their chances.

CONTINUE TO PROTECT PEACHES, NECTARINES AND ALMONDS against peach leaf curl. The symptoms of this disease (see February) show as puckering of the leaves during summer. It is spread by spores which are carried in rain water. Sprays are not all that effective, but you can use a copper fungicide. Protecting the trees with a physical barrier in winter, as described above, is the best option. If you are plagued by this disease, grow dwarf varieties of peach and nectarine in large pots and keep them indoors until late spring or early summer.

HAND-POLLINATE PEACH AND NECTARINE TREES. During cooler spells in spring there are few pollinating insects around, and if you cover your trees (see above), or have pot-grown trees under cover at the moment, you also reduce the chances of insects

Hand-pollinating a peach *Imitate a pollinating insect by brushing gently from flower to flower.*

getting at them, so it is advisable to pollinate these trees by hand. Use a small, soft artist's paint brush and transfer the pollen from one flower to another, going over the whole tree. Do it two or three times over the course of a few days to ensure that all the flowers are pollinated. The best time of day to pollinate flowers is around midday, if you can, as the pollen is running freely at this time.

FEED ALL FRUIT WITH POTASH if you didn't do so last month (see February). Most general fertilisers contain some potash, but it is a good idea to give a little extra to get really luscious fruits. Always follow manufacturers' application rates. Draw back any mulch before applying the potash and watering it in. Water in really well if the weather is dry. If the fertiliser is not watered in properly, it will not go into solution in the soil and therefore will not be available for the plants to take up. Renew the mulch.

SPRAY APPLES AND PEARS TO PREVENT SCAB. If you use chemicals, then this is the time to use a preventative spray against scab. Most garden centres supply a range of chemical controls. Look at the labels and follow the instructions carefully. Spray firstly while the flower buds are tightly closed and again when they begin to burst and show colour.

PEARS THAT HAVE BEEN ATTACKED BY PEAR MIDGE can be sprayed with a preventative spray containing bifenthrin or permethrin. Spray when the buds are white, but still closed. Don't use sprays when flowers

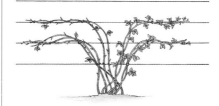

Tie in briar fruits *Old canes to one side and new canes to the other is the simplest system.*

are open or you will kill off pollinating insects such as bees. Do any spraying in the evening when these insects are not around.

PRUNING AND TRAINING

TIE IN BRIAR FRUITS like blackberries and loganberries. These plants grow at a terrific rate from early spring, and if you don't tie them in at regular intervals you will end up in a mess. Briars produce fruit on the stems that grew the previous year, and the easiest way to train them is to tie in last year's canes on the supporting wires to one side of the plant, and the new growth made this year, which will produce next year's fruit, to the other side. This makes pruning them later on very straightforward and less painful.

PRUNE AUTUMN-FRUITING RASPBERRIES if you have not already done so (see February). All of the old fruited canes from last year should be cut down to ground level. Be careful now not to damage any emerging new shoot tips.

PRUNE GOOSEBERRIES NOW if they were left unpruned over winter (see above right). If birds are a problem

PRUNING GOOSEBERRIES

1 Prune all sideshoots from the main upright stems to three healthy buds, cutting just above the third bud.

2 Prune back the main stems by about one-third of last year's growth. Again, make the cuts just above buds.

3 This combination of "tip" and "spur" pruning should encourage plenty of fruiting sideshoots, and also opens up the bush – crowded growth prevents fruits ripening.

eating the gooseberry buds you can sometimes gain some protection by leaving the bushes unpruned until spring. This makes it more difficult for the birds to get at the buds. But now is the latest time to prune gooseberries to have any hope of getting fruit. All the

FRUIT *continued*

sideshoots can be pruned to two or three buds from the main stems and the leading shoots pruned by one-third to half, depending on the vigour of the shoot (prune weaker shoots harder). Treat the head of a trained standard gooseberry exactly as if it were a bush. Gooseberry cordons are also pruned similarly, shortening all of last year's shoots to only 1-2 buds. Occasionally, when a really knobbly "spur system" has got very crowded, you can saw a portion of it off completely.

After pruning the gooseberries, feed with a general fertiliser and mulch with organic matter.

PLANTING

COMPLETE PLANTING OF bare-rooted fruit trees and bushes this month (see February). This is the last month when these plants will be in a near-dormant state and the sooner they are planted the better. If you have missed out on bare-rooted stock (certainly the cheapest) there will be container-grown fruit on offer at garden centres that can be planted through the spring (see also April). Older plants may be in flower, and you may get a small crop of fruits this year. But if you plant young trees and bushes, it's best to pinch any flowers out this year, so that the plants' energies are concentrated into establishing a good root system over the summer.

BEAT THE SEASONS

COVER SOME MORE STRAWBERRIES with a cloche (see February), to give a succession of early fruits.

UNDER COVER

KEEP THE GLASS OF GREENHOUSES and conservatories clean to give seedlings maximum light. Long, thin straggly seedlings rarely make good plants, and the cleaner the glass the sturdier they will grow. It is surprising how much dust and dirt accumulates on glass even in dry weather.

VENTILATE WHENEVER THE WEATHER IS GOOD. It is surprising how quickly the temperature rises even when the sun is out for a short time. Plants grow best when there are not extremes of hot and cold, and ventilation is important in regulating the temperature inside. It can be a nuisance if you leave for work on a fine sunny morning and later on it cools down, or vice versa, but there are many different types of automatic vent openers on the market. These can be set to open when the temperature reaches a certain level, closing again when it falls.

WATCH FOR PEST DAMAGE. Now the temperatures are rising all sorts of pests are on the move, enjoying the warm, still, humid atmosphere in the greenhouse and conservatory. By far the

Open windows *Ventilate whenever the weather is good, to give greenhouse plants some fresh air.*

best way to control pests under glass is by using what are called biological controls, very small living creatures that prey on or otherwise destroy pests. They can be bought by mail order. Most of the firms producing them advertise in the gardening press, giving details of which are appropriate for which pests. These tiny organisms need a warm atmosphere to thrive. If you have a heated glasshouse, you can introduce them now. If your greenhouse is unheated, then order controls now for delivery next month when temperatures have risen. If you are not sure which pests you have, or want an early warning system for pest attacks, hang yellow sticky traps in the greenhouse. You will be able to examine what you catch and identify it more easily, and be alerted early to any problems.

FEED PLANTS AND WATER THEM REGULARLY. By this time of year most plants are growing actively and we all have to keep up with the watering and feeding. On warm sunny days watering may have to be done several times as the temperature inside rises. Plants that have been growing in their pots for a few months will need regular feeding as most of the food reservoir in the compost will have been used up.

CONTINUE TO TAKE CUTTINGS from fuchsias (see February).

PRUNE AND REPOT PELARGONIUMS and other tender perennials kept over winter if you didn't do so last month (see February).

TAKE CUTTINGS from overwintered tender perennials that started into

growth last month. Take cuttings about 8cm (3in) long, making a clean cut above a leaf joint with a sharp knife. Remove the lower leaves and trim the cutting just below a leaf joint and dip the base of the cutting into hormone rooting solution. There is no need to use hormone rooting solution on fuchsias, heliotrope and pelargoniums as they all root very easily.

Put into a pot containing cuttings compost (most multipurpose composts, or any peat-free compost mixed with perlite, will do) and water in. Put a polythene bag or propagator cover over the pot and leave in a shaded area until the cuttings root in three or four weeks.

PRICK OUT AND POT ON CUTTINGS, SEEDLINGS AND YOUNG PLANTS. Seeds sown last month will need pricking out now, unless you used module trays (see February). Seedlings pricked out last month may be being planted out now, but those that have to stay indoors until all danger of frost has passed will be needing some more room, as will growing cuttings, and these can be potted up into their own small pots of multipurpose compost.

Watch out for damping-off on your seedlings. This disease causes seedlings to rot off and die. It is caused by a fungus, but can be largely prevented by sowing seeds thinly and not over-watering them. If it does become a problem water the seedlings with a solution containing Cheshunt compound. It is difficult to control once it gets going, so prevention is the best course of action.

SHADE YOUNG SEEDLINGS AND CUTTINGS ON BRIGHT DAYS. Plants lose water in the form of water vapour from their leaves and on sunny, warm days this transpiration, as it is called, increases. Young seedlings and cuttings are less able to cope with this, and so it is important to shade them on sunny days. There are several ways of providing shading, one being roller blinds fitted in the greenhouse or conservatory. But these can be rather expensive; the cheapest way to shade is to cover the young plants with sheets of newspaper.

RAISING PLANTS FOR OUTDOORS

Sow half-hardy annuals. Most half-hardy annuals can be sown now, and with even a modest greenhouse you may find you have enough space to raise all the bedding and container plants you need – far more economical than buying in young plants. If they are sown too early the plants will become leggy and no good for planting out in June.

Seeds to sow now include ageratum, alyssum, stocks, nicotiana and marigolds. Don't forget to include "everlasting" flowers such as statice and strawflowers if you like to make dried arrangements – botanical names to look for include *Rhodanthe*, *Limonium* and *Bracteantha*. Keep in a propagator at 16–18°C (61–65°F), at least until the seedlings have two true leaves, then if you need the space in the propagator you can move them to a bench, covered with a seed tray cover for extra warmth. Plants needing a minimum of 18°C (65°F) include lobelia, nemesia, phlox and zinnias.

Sow seeds of tender bedding like salvias and gazanias. Sow the seeds thinly (see p.29 for illustrations) and cover lightly with vermiculite as some of them need light to germinate. They need a minimum temperature of around 18°C (65°F). These plants can also be bought in as mini-plants or plugs for potting on. This is an easy way to grow them as it cuts down on the costs of providing heating to germinate the seeds. They will need at least frost-free conditions to grow on until the threat of frost is past, generally around the beginning of June.

Plants that need longer growing times as well as high germinating temperatures, like semperflorens begonias and busy Lizzies, are from now also better bought as young plug plants, as there isn't time for them to grow. You can, however, still sow seed of pelargoniums and have plants in flower this year provided that you buy specially "primed" seed. It is a little more expensive, but has been pre-treated to germinate rapidly so that the seedlings will eventually catch up with plants sown earlier.

Lettuce, cabbage and cauliflowers can still be sown indoors to give a succession of crops from those sown earlier (see Vegetables & Herbs).

Start cannas into growth The fat rhizomes of these showy plants can now be brought out of store (see October) and started into growth, for planting out in June. Split them up into short sections, each with a bud. Pot these up each to its own small pot of peat-free compost, and keep in a light place at 16°C (61°F). Water them very sparingly at first. Once the roots fill the small pot, move each into a bigger pot and grow on in good light, watering more regularly.

GLASSHOUSE AND HOUSE PLANTS

Continue to plant begonia and gloxinia tubers. These plants give a terrific show throughout the summer and it's not too late to plant up a few tubers. See February.

Feed and water hippeastrums (amaryllis) as the flowers go over. As the flowers fade it is important to feed the bulb to build up next year's flower bud which forms inside the bulb. Continue watering and feeding with a high-potash liquid fertiliser until the foliage begins to go yellow and dies down. Then watering can be stopped and the plants allowed to rest for the summer.

Sow seed of *Solanum capsicastrum* (winter cherry), exactly as for tomatoes (see right) These plants with their bright ornamental fruits are a cheerful sight in winter.

Fruiting vegetables *Sow aubergines, tomatoes and peppers this month to grow under glass.*

CROPS UNDER GLASS

Sow aubergines, peppers and tomatoes for the greenhouse. There is no point in sowing these too early: towards the end of the month is quite soon enough. Sow seed in small pots or trays of seed compost. Water the compost before sowing, sow the seeds thinly on the surface and cover with vermiculite or sieved compost until the seeds just disappear. Cover with a sheet of glass and paper to exclude the light and place in a propagator at 21°C (70°F). Germination takes two or three weeks. When you see the first signs of them coming through remove the paper and glass. When the seedlings are large enough to handle (usually when the seed leaves, or cotyledons, are fully expanded and you can just see the first true leaves developing in the centre), they need transplanting into individual pots.

Lay out growbags to warm up before planting. Plants can sometimes receive a check to their growth if planted into a cold growing medium. Think how you'd feel plunging your feet into a bucket of cold water at this time of year!

When forced strawberry plants start coming into flower you will have to pollinate the flowers for the fruits to set. This is easily done using a small paintbrush, such as those used for painting model aeroplanes – or a piece of cotton wool on the end of a cane or held with tweezers. Dab pollen from one flower to the next, doing this a couple of times at intervals of a couple of days to ensure pollination. Water and feed with a high-potash fertiliser and wait for luscious, mouth-watering fruits.

MAKE AN OBELISK

AN OBELISK is an attractive feature to have, allowing you to grow climbing plants such as clematis and sweet peas on a freestanding support to add height to borders. You do need to be handy with basic carpentry tools to get this just right, but it's well worth the effort. It costs a fraction of the price of similar bought wooden features.

YOU WILL NEED: Four 2.5-metre lengths of 34mm × 34mm timber for the uprights, and two smaller offcuts to make jigs, or templates *(see below)* • 25 metres of 34mm × 9mm battening, roughly cut into short lengths for the horizontal struts • Offcuts of 75mm x 25mm timber for the top plinth • 1 acorn or other decorative finial • 100 galvanized 34mm screws • Drill with countersinking bit • Non-toxic wood stain that doubles as a timber preservative

USING JIGS

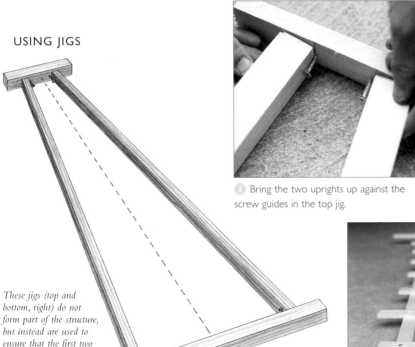

These jigs (top and bottom, right) do not form part of the structure, but instead are used to ensure that the first two sides of the obelisk match exactly. They consist of screws partially fixed into lengths of batten at the correct distances top and bottom. A guide line laid between the central point of each pair of screws should meet both jigs at right-angles to ensure the two uprights slope evenly about a common centre.

FOR THE FIRST TWO OPPOSITE SIDES

① Half-insert screws into batten offcuts to make the jigs, 125mm apart for the top one and 500mm apart for the base. Lay, or better fix, the jigs on the floor, 2.4m apart, parallel and about a common centre (see diagram, below left). Position two uprights at the base.

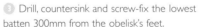

② Bring the two uprights up against the screw guides in the top jig.

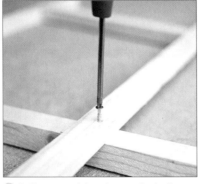

③ Drill, countersink and screw-fix the lowest batten 300mm from the obelisk's feet.

④ Similarly screw-fix a small offcut at the top to begin forming the plinth.

⑤ Screw-fix battens at 150mm intervals from the plinth to the lowest batten.

⑥ Trim the battens and top plinth flush to the uprights. Make a second side, and paint them both.

FOR THE REMAINING TWO SIDES

7 Fit the two completed opposite sides in your jigs, and screw-fix the lowest batten of the third side in line with its partners.

8 Work your way up the third side, and then repeat the process for the fourth side, before trimming all battens flush.

9 Cut and finish off the plinth and cap.

10 Attach the ornament (many styles are available) in the centre of the cap.

11 With the first two sides already stained, there is little to do to finish the feature.

12 Set in the border, ensuring it is level. Here it is planted with early- and late-flowering clematis.

APRIL

Amelanchier lamarckii ♀ • Shrubby tree with pinky-bronze young leaves (*see p.297*)

***Erythronium* 'Pagoda'** ♀ • Low-growing, clump-forming perennial for shade (*see p.318*)

Berberis darwinii ♀ • Spiny shrub whose flowers are followed in autumn by blue-black fruits (*see p.301*)

Dicentra spectabilis ♀ • Tall, arching perennial with pretty foliage (*see p.315*)

***Clematis alpina* 'Frances Rivis'** ♀ • Bell-flowered climber needing little pruning (*see p.306*)

***Bergenia* 'Sunningdale'** • Tough, leathery-leaved perennial, good ground cover (*see p.301*)

Magnolia stellata ♡ • Compact, to 3m (9ft) tall, an ideal magnolia for a small garden *(see p.331)*

Vinca minor • Creeping stems that are studded with flowers through spring and summer *(see p.359)*

Epimedium x warleyense • Clump-forming perennial making good ground cover *(see p.317)*

Euphorbia polychroma ♡ • Neat mound-forming perennial, very bright even in part shade *(see p.319)*

Fritillaria meleagris ♡ • The snakeshead fritillary, a small bulbous perennial that naturalizes well in grass *(see p.320)*

Corylopsis glabrescens • Large deciduous shrub that prefers acid soil *(see p.311)*

TOP ROW: *Prunus* 'Spire' ♀ · *Prunus avium* 'Plena' ♀ · *Prunus* 'Kanzan' ♀
BOTTOM ROW: *Prunus* 'Ukon' ♀ · *Prunus* 'Kiku-shidare-zakura' ♀ · *Prunus* 'Shirotae' ♀ *(see pp.342–3)*

TOP ROW: *Malus x hartwigii* 'Katherine' ♀ • *Malus x moerlandsii* 'Liset' ♀ • *Malus transitoria* ♀
BOTTOM ROW: *Malus toringo* ♀ • *Malus* 'Royalty' • *Malus* 'Evereste' ♀ (see p.332)

Pieris **'Flamingo'** • Large but rounded, compact evergreen shrub for acid soil *(see p.341)*

Pyrus salicifolia **'Pendula'** ♀ • Weeping ornamental pear tree with willow-like leaves *(see p.345)*

Pulsatilla vulgaris ♀ • Small perennial ideal for a rock garden, raised bed or paving *(see p.344)*

Convallaria majalis ♀ • Lily-of-the-valley, a sweet-smelling perennial that can be invasive *(see p.310)*

Erysimum cheiri **Bedder Series** • Plant wallflowers in autumn for bright spring bedding *(see p.318)*

Ribes sanguineum • Pinky-white flowering currant, a rounded upright shrub *(see p.347)*

Cytisus x *praecox* 'Warminster' ♀ • Drought-tolerant shrub with arching branches (see p.314)

Viburnum x *juddii* ♀ • Bushy deciduous shrub that often has good autumn leaf colour (see p.358)

Bellis perennis Tasso Series • Cheerful pompon daisy for spring bedding (see p.300)

Aubrieta 'J. S. Baker' • Creeping perennial, perfect tumbling over rocks or low walls (see p.300)

Jasminum mesnyi ♀ • The primrose jasmine, a twining climber with sweetly scented flowers (see p.327)

Rhododendron yakushimanum • Small mound-forming azalea covered in flowers (see p.346)

AROUND THE GARDEN

PESTS ARE ON THE MOVE NOW with warmer weather. Get on top of any problems as soon as you spot them, and nine times out of ten you can stop them getting a hold.

PROTECT PLANTS. The warmth and spring rains now will see huge increases in the populations of slugs and snails, which can cause enormous damage to plants. If you're not organic, spread slug pellets in amongst the plants affected. There is no need to put down a lot of pellets; it doesn't take many to kill off slugs. There are several organic ways to control slugs, including a biological control, a tiny nematode that attacks them that can be watered onto the soil. Traps are also effective. One of the oldest and best known is the beer trap: a jar sunk into the ground with the lip just proud of the surface, filled with beer, which will attract the slugs.

Hedgehogs, frogs, toads and thrushes all prey on these pests, so encourage these creatures. Lay a flat stone in a border, and you will soon notice whether a thrush is using it as a handy "anvil" on which to smash snail shells.

GIVE BORDERS A TIDY UP. Set aside a morning or afternoon to go round the garden doing those small jobs that make all the difference to its appearance. Lightly fork over the soil, pulling out any weeds you see. Any plants taking up too much space and growing into other plants can be lightly pruned into shape to keep them looking tidy. Don't be too hard with the pruning, or you may cut off all this year's flowers. Put in plant supports as you go, then you don't have to keep treading over the borders to do different jobs.

WATCH OUT FOR SELF-SOWN SEEDLINGS when working on the borders. It is amazing just how many plants seed themselves freely around the garden. A lot of hardy annuals seed quite prolifically, and many shrubs and herbaceous perennials can at times almost become weeds. One group of plants particularly good at self-seeding are the foxgloves (see right). They are quite happy to be moved at this time of year, and will flower later, so it's a good time to "edit" the foxglove population in your garden. Sadly, seedlings from white foxgloves often turn out to be purple in flower – but beautiful nevertheless. Remember to water any seedlings you move.

APPLY SYNTHETIC FERTILISERS NOW. If you didn't give plants an organic fertiliser earlier in the spring (see February), a chemical fertiliser will give them an instant boost now, when they need it. Pull back any mulch, lightly fluff up the soil with a rake and apply according to the maker's instructions. Replace the mulch.

Like us, all plants need nutrients to survive, but there is no need to feed absolutely everything every year. Trees and shrubs, for example, will on the whole grow quite happily for years provided that the initial preparation before planting has been done thoroughly. With these, all that may be necessary is to apply some fertiliser in the first two or three years after planting. After that, unless there is any obvious deficiency, they will cope well on their own. But do remember to water them well in dry weather in the early stages of getting established. The areas of the garden most in need of

SELF-SOWN SEEDLINGS

1 Foxglove seedlings form a flat rosette of slightly coarse leaves, oval in shape, coming to a point.

2 Water the soil first if it is dry, then lift the seedlings gently with a trowel, taking a good ball of soil up around the fragile roots.

3 Plant the seedling in its new position, firming gently with your fingerips – do not press too hard. Water the young plant in very gently.

fertilisers every year are the vegetable and fruit garden, annual borders and plants in containers, where the plants are taking more out of the soil. The more we deplete the soil, the more we have a duty to put more back in to keep the soil in a healthy state.

With all fertilisers, whether organic or artificial, wash your hands well after using them.

TREES & SHRUBS

REMOVE FROST-DAMAGED SHOOTS from any slightly tender evergreen shrubs like *Choisya ternata* (Mexican orange blossom). At the same time you can, if necessary, prune back any misplaced stems. In colder parts of the country pruning these shrubs is best left until next month, in case a late hard frost causes more damage. Stems should always be cut back to a healthy leaf lower down the shoot, or to a stem junction.

SPRAY ROSES WITH A RECOMMENDED FUNGICIDE to control blackspot, which looks exactly as you might expect – black spots, or blotches, on the leaves. This will have to be done at regular intervals, as blackspot is difficult to control. Follow the manufacturer's instructions for dosages and intervals between spraying.

Better still, try to grow only those varieties of roses that are resistant to blackspot, such as 'Graham Thomas', 'François Juranville' or *Rosa mundi* – more correctly called *Rosa gallica* var. *officinalis* 'Versicolor'. Catalogues will highlight many more. Rose breeders are constantly bringing out new varieties of roses which are more resistant to disease, therefore cutting down on the need to spray. A visit to a rose nursery's fields in summer is well worth the trip just to let

Watering pots *Give all plants grown in containers a good soak before planting.*

you see for yourself which roses are more disease-resistant.

CHECK ROSES FOR APHIDS. Rub or hose greenfly off to avoid using sprays, or use one of the hand-held sprays to direct the pesticide accurately. By doing this as soon as you spot them, you can help prevent colonies building up.

PLANTING

PLANT CONTAINER-GROWN TREES AND SHRUBS. Bare-rooted deciduous stock will no longer be available, but all plants are now sold as container-grown specimens to plant at any time of year, although spring and autumn are best for the plants. Water the plant well in its pot an hour or two beforehand, then ease the rootball out of the pot. Set it firmly in a generously-sized hole so that the top of the compost is level with the ground around it. Work soil down around the sides of the rootball with your fingers, water well again, and mulch around the plant to lock in that precious moisture. For advice on sheltering evergreens in exposed sites, see Hedges, overleaf.

PRUNING AND TRAINING

TRIM WINTER-FLOWERING HEATHERS with shears (see February) if you didn't do it earlier. The spent flowering stems will now be looking quite tatty, so remove them to show off the more attractive new growth.

PRUNE SHRUBS GROWN FOR THEIR COLOURFUL FOLIAGE, such as elder (*Sambucus*) and cotinus (the smoke bush). The best coloured foliage is produced by new stems hence the reason for pruning hard now. If you want to increase the size of the plants it is worthwhile leaving two or three shoots unpruned and these can grow on making the plant larger without compromising on the colourful foliage. As always after pruning feed with a general fertiliser and water it in if the weather is dry.

PRUNE FORSYTHIAS AND CHAENOMELES AFTER FLOWERING. These two shrubs put on a terrific show of colour in the spring, on wood made the previous summer, and now is the time to prune them for flowers next spring. Pruning for both shrubs is the same. When the flowers are over cut back the flowered shoots to two or three buds from their base. On more established shrubs cut out about a third of the older growth to the base of the plant. This will encourage new shoots from the base.

These shrubs can also be trained against walls or fences, and very attractive they look too. Pruning in this situation is slightly different. After you have tied in any stems you need to fill gaps, prune all flowered shoots to one or two buds from their point of

PRUNING EARLY FLOWERERS

Pruning forsythias *Cut the flowered stems back to strong new leafy sideshoots, pointing upwards and outwards.*

Pruning chaenomeles *Cutting sideshoots back to one or two buds encourages flowers. The shoot on the left was left unpruned.*

growing. You can do the same in summer to keep chaenomeles, and also pyracanthas, flat where space is limited. Leading shoots can be pruned to keep the shrubs within their allocated place.

CUT BACK LAVENDER once the plants approach the size you want them to grow to. If lavender plants are left unpruned the centre of the shrub grows sparse and the plant looks unattractive and they don't like being pruned into older wood. So it is a good idea to prune them every spring to keep them bushy and compact. Other silver-leaved shrubs to prune in the same way are

TREES & SHRUBS *continued*

Trim lavender *In spring, prune the tips of all the shoots with secateurs or shears.*

Helichrysum serotinum (curry plant) and santolina (cotton lavender). Go over the whole plant, trimming off 2.5–5cm (1–2in) of growth. Use shears for speed if you have a lot of lavender, for example a low hedge. It may seem a bit harsh, but by doing it the plants stay compact and the centre does not open up.

PROPAGATION

INCREASE CONIFERS BY TAKING CUTTINGS. This is a good time of year to propagate your favourite conifers. It's very easy to do (see right).

HEDGES

PLANT EVERGREEN HEDGING PLANTS. This is a good time to plant evergreens, not only conifers but the many broad-leaved plants that make excellent hedging. Most can be clipped to shape or grown informally, only being trimmed when they become overgrown. By planting evergreens at

this time of year there is less chance of them being damaged by cold winter winds, but they may still need some protection. It's not just winter winds that cause problems. Even in spring and summer, high winds can be just as damaging. The speed of the wind going over the surface of the leaf draws water from it more quickly than the plant can replace it from the soil, especially in summer if the ground is dry, and this causes withering.

If your plants are regularly scorched in this way, consider erecting more screens and windbreaks to shelter your garden – or research some more wind- and drought-tolerant shrubs to replace casualties.

CONIFER CUTTINGS

1 Pull off sideshoots about 7.5–10cm (3–4in) long. Trim off the tail or "heel" of older wood, and the lower leaves.

2 Dip the base in hormone rooting solution. Put the cuttings into small pots containing equal parts peat-free compost and perlite.

3 Water them in and place in a shady cold frame or under a sheltered wall. Rooting will take about eight weeks, when they can be potted up or planted in the garden.

CLIMBERS

Training climbing roses *Tie in shoots horizontally for more flowering sideshoots.*

CLIMBING AND RAMBLING ROSES should be tied in, training the shoots as near to horizontal as possible. By doing this the flow of sap is restricted; this causes more sideshoots to develop along the whole length of the main stems, and therefore more flowers are produced. If left to grow vertically, all the flowers are produced at the tips of the stems where they are difficult to see. If you are growing roses on a stout post, wind the stems around the post in a spiral fashion and tie in, and this will have the same effect of restricting the flow of sap.

TIE IN SHOOTS OF TWINERS such as clematis as they are growing fast now. With clematis, once they get a hold of their support they can usually be left to get on with it, especially if growing through other shrubs, but they may need some guidance if encroaching too much on other plants.

PLANT CONTAINER-GROWN CLIMBERS as for Trees and Shrubs.

PRUNE WALL-TRAINED forsythias and chaenomeles (see Trees & Shrubs).

PERENNIALS

CONTINUE PLANTING NEW PLANTS. Getting plants in by the end of the month will give the plants time to establish while the weather is still mild and wet, and put on good growth during the season.

FINISH DIVIDING AND REPLANTING SUMMER-FLOWERING PERENNIALS. This is the latest month for lifting and dividing if you want these to flower in the summer and autumn. Whenever possible, always revitalize the soil with well-rotted farmyard manure or garden compost before replanting perennials. Water in well after planting if the weather is dry.

WATER NEWLY PLANTED PLANTS AND DIVISIONS regularly, as spring winds can be drying.

DAHLIA TUBERS CAN BE PLANTED in milder parts of the country. In other areas, wait until next month. Make sure the ground has been prepared well as dahlias are gross, or greedy, feeders; add plenty of organic matter and a good dressing of organic fertiliser before planting, and also, insert a stake into the ground to support the plants before you plant – then you will not damage the tubers. The tubers should be planted so that the crown of the tuber is at least 7.5cm (3in) deep.

CONTINUE TAKING BASAL CUTTINGS (see March).

REMOVE WINTER PROTECTION from borderline hardy plants.

TOP UP GRIT AND GRAVEL around plants growing in a Mediterranean or scree bed setting if it has been lost or shifted by winter weather. This will really smarten the area up before plants get going, to set them off perfectly when at their best.

THIN SHOOTS ON PERENNIALS. To get top quality flowers from border plants it is sometimes necessary to thin out overcrowded shoots. Plants most likely to need thinning include delphiniums and lupins, especially if you are growing these for showing at your local flower show. Phlox will also put on a bolder show if thinned. Remove about one in three or four of the shoots, depending on how crowded they are.

ALPINES

REMOVE ALL WINTER PROTECTION from alpine plants and beds.

PLANT NEW ALPINES now that the cold rains they dislike so much should be tailing off.

Thinning shoots Some perennials flower better if you reduce the number of shoots at the base.

BULBS

DEADHEAD THE LAST OF THE DAFFODILS now that the flowers are going over. Snap the flowerhead off behind the swollen part; you can leave the stalk intact. If the spent flowers are left on, the plant's energy will be diverted into the production of seeds. By removing the old flowers, the plant's energy is instead diverted into the formation of next year's flower bud within the bulb. For this to happen, the foliage must be left on the plant. For many years the practice was to allow the foliage of the bulbs to die back completely, to give the plants the longest time to build up that flower bud for next year. But recent research has shown that the foliage can be cut down six weeks after the flowers are over. You can choose which ever method you like. The old foliage of daffodils can look rather messy, but do not tie it up with raffia or elastic bands. The best way to hide it is to grow daffodils in amongst other plants like hostas which have large, bold leaves.

PLANT OUT ALL SUMMER FLOWERING BULBS (see March). They should all be planted by the end of the month in time to flower during the summer. Tender bulbs like gladioli can go out now wherever you live. These like a sunny spot in well-drained soil, so if you garden on heavy clay, put a layer of coarse grit in the bottom of the hole and plant the corms on this to improve drainage.

DIVIDE NERINES Overcrowded clumps of these beautiful autumn-flowering bulbs can be split and replanted now. As when lifting all bulbs, put the spade or fork in the ground a little way out from the clump, or you risk slicing through or spearing the bulbs. Do not replant any damaged bulbs, as they attract rots that may spread through the rest.

DIVIDING NERINES

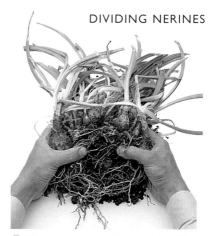

① Lift the clumps carefully and shake off as much soil as possible, then separate out the individual bulbs. Retain as much root on each as you can.

② Clean the bulbs up before replanting singly at the same depth as before, about 5cm (2in) apart. Peel off brown flaky debris, but leave a layer of white papery skin, or tunic, intact.

ANNUALS & BEDDING

CONTINUE SOWING HARDY ANNUALS OUTSIDE (see March). In colder parts of the country it is perhaps best to wait until this month before sowing outside, to give the soil more of a chance to warm up. Heavy clay soils in particular take longer to warm up than light sandy soils.

PLANT OUT hardy annuals raised in modules (see February). Prepare the soil in the same way as for direct sowing (see March), and mark out drifts in the same way. Plant the young plants in the drifts and that's it. There is no need to thin out the plants and they will flower a little earlier than those sown outside.

SOW HALF-HARDY SUMMER BEDDING PLANTS See Under Cover.

BUY PLUG PLANTS OF BEDDING if you have the room to grow them on in frost-free surroundings until it is safe to plant them out (see Under Cover).

POT UP CUTTINGS of tender perennials that you took last year (see August). Keep them under cover until next month, when you can start hardening them off for planting out.

BY THE END OF THE MONTH spring bedding may start to look past its best, but summer bedding cannot be planted out safely for a few weeks yet. So do what you can to keep plants neat, rather than pulling them out too early to leave bare ground that weeds will colonize.

SWEET PEAS should really have been sown earlier, but a late sowing now will still give some flowers in late summer and autumn.

ANNUALS & BEDDING *continued*

Asarina procumbens

Ipomoea tricolor

Tropaeolum peregrinum

PLANT OUT SWEET PEAS SOWN IN AUTUMN. Even in cold areas, towards the end of the month and into next month these sweet peas can be planted out, as long as they have been hardened off for a couple of weeks. Plant out in soil that has been well prepared, and sprinkle a little general fertiliser on the soil before planting – not too much, or you will get a lot of growth and few flowers.

SOW MORE UNUSUAL ANNUAL CLIMBING PLANTS. Climbing plants have many uses: adding height to a border, or hiding ugly buildings or other unsightly places like the compost heap. To use permanent perennial climbing plants like roses and clematis can be expensive, and many do take some time to get established and cover a given area. For a cheap and quick way to cover an eyesore, or to add height to a planting, annual climbers are ideal. Another way to use annual climbers is to let them scramble through evergreen shrubs or through trees, extending their period of interest.

Sweet peas and of course nasturtiums (*Tropaeolum majus*), in all shades from brilliant reds to yellows, can both be sown directly into the soil now, but other more unusual climbers can be raised in pots and planted out in June. Many are tender perennials grown in our climate as annuals.

Lovely plants to try include *Ipomoea* (morning glory), with large blue or pink flowers (see left, centre); *Cobaea scandens*, with violet and purple flowers; *Canarina canariensis*, the Canary bellflower, with almost courgette-like orangey flowers; *Eccremocarpus scaber*, or Chilean glory vine, with funnel-shaped red and yellow flowers; purple rhodochitons (see p.198); black-eyed Susan, or *Thunbergia alata* (see p.166); *Tropaeolum peregrinum* (see left, bottom), and in small spaces, *Asarina procumbens* (see left, top), which

Briza maxima

Lagurus ovatus

Hordeum jubatum

makes an effective trailing plant in a raised rock garden. Sow the seeds thinly and cover lightly with vermiculite as some of them need light to germinate. They will all need a temperature of around 18°C (65°F). These plants can also be bought in as mini-plants or plugs for potting on. This is an easy way to grow them, as it cuts down on the cost of providing heating to germinate the seeds. They will need at least frost-free conditions to grow on until the threat of frost is passed, generally around the beginning of June.

SOW ANNUAL GRASSES. Their delicate foliage and attractive seedheads contrast well with broad-leaved plants in the borders. It's an excellent, inexpensive way to try out the new way of growing perennials among grasses for a more "naturalistic" border look, and all of the seedheads can be dried and used in flower arrangements.

Annual grasses to look out on the seed packet shelves include *Briza maxima*, the quaking grass (left, top); *Lagurus ovatus*, hare's tail grass (left, centre), and *Hordeum jubatum* or squirrel tail grass (left, bottom). They can be sown outside from now onwards. You can sow *in situ* in drifts (see March for illustrations) as with annual flowers – in drills, so you can tell them from weed grasses when they germinate – or in drills on a spare piece of ground, to transplant in among plants in the border when big enough. Sow the seeds in shallow drills scratched out with a stick and water the drills if the soil is dry. Cover the seeds lightly and label them. Thin out the young seedlings, and transplant if necessary when they are large enough to handle.

CONTAINERS

CLEAN CONTAINERS AND POTS that are to be used for summer bedding displays. All pots should be cleaned using a weak solution of household bleach. This will reduce trouble from pests and diseases. You could also spruce up older, scruffy containers with some of the multi-surface garden paints now on offer, perhaps experimenting with some more unusual shades to enhance summer colour schemes.

PLANT UP ALPINE TROUGHS. Whether you buy a trough or sink, or make your own (see p.106), this is an ideal month for doing this job as many alpines are coming into flower now and you can get an instant effect when the job's done. The most important point to bear in mind when growing alpines is they like good drainage, so make sure any container used for growing these plants has plenty of drainage holes. Before filling the container with compost put a 5cm (2in) layer of broken pots or coarse gravel in the bottom to aid drainage. The compost used for filling the container should be what is called an alpine mix, consisting of equal parts garden soil, garden compost or coir compost and coarse grit.

After planting spread a layer of coarse grit over the surface of the compost between the plants. This not only sets off the plants well, but also keeps down weeds and prevents the plants being splashed with soil in rainy weather.

PONDS

CLEANING OUT A POND

① Lift all plants in their baskets, or scoop them out with your hands, and put them in trays of water before removing any fish.

② Bail or pump out the water, then scoop out mud in the bottom, using plastic implements gently so that you do not damage the liner.

③ Hose and wash down the liner using a soft brush or broom, and then clean out the resulting murky water.

④ Refill the pond, and then tidy up and divide the plants and put them back in. Finally, put fish back in together with the water they have been sitting in.

CLEAN OUT ESTABLISHED PONDS. This isn't a job that has to be done every year, only when the plants get overcrowded – usually after five or six years. If you have fish in the pond, they will have to be put into a temporary container – filled with pond water, not tap water – and if the pond is lined with a butyl liner, do be careful not to puncture it. Once any fish are out the pond can be emptied and the plants divided up and replanted. Larger clumps of waterlilies and other plants can be divided up in exactly the same ways as for dividing herbaceous perennials. After the pond is refilled the water may go green for a while, but it will soon sort itself out when the plants re-establish.

Dividing water lilies
Gently hose or rinse the soil from the clump of roots, then, using a sharp knife, divide up the thick fleshy rhizome into sections, each with a shoot. Discard any old, lifeless pieces. Replant the new sections in fresh aquatic compost (see overleaf).

Buying aquatics
When you get aquatic plants home, stand them in a tray of water or pop floating plants and water weeds in a bucket.

PLANT AQUATIC PLANTS IN PONDS. Now the water in ponds is warming up it's the ideal time to plant new aquatic plants, giving them the whole season to get established. When you get the plants home, if there is any delay before planting, make sure they do not dry up (see above).

Special containers are available for aquatic plants from most garden centres. The modern containers are made of fine mesh and don't need lining with sacking, as in the past. Fill with garden soil or special aquatic compost – don't use ordinary potting compost, as this has fertilisers added to it, and it will encourage the growth of algae in the pond. Place the plant in the container and fill around it with compost to about 2.5cm (1in) from the rim of the container. Then put a layer of coarse grit on the surface of the soil. This prevents the soil from floating out (see also overleaf). Don't forget to add some oxygenating plants. Water in a pond turning green with algae is a constant problem, and the smaller the pond the more of a problem it is. Most algae grow in water that is low in oxygen, so adding plants that increase the amount

PONDS *continued*

Darmera peltata

PLANTS FOR A NEW POND

BOGGY SOIL
Darmera peltata
Lysichiton americanus (see p.62)
Primula vialii

SHALLOW WATER (15CM/6IN)
Calla palustris
Caltha palustris (see p.62)
Houttuynia cordata

Calla palustris

Iris laevigata
Menyanthes trifoliata
Sagittaria latifolia

MARGINAL SHELVES (30CM/12IN)
Acorus calamus
Butomus umbellatus
Iris pseudacorus
Orontium aquaticum
Pontederia cordata
Ranunculus lingua 'Grandiflora'

Butomus umbellatus

Typha angustifolia, T. minima
Zantedeschia aethiopica

DEEP WATER
Aponogeton distachyos
Hottonia palustris
Nymphaea (see p.167)
Nymphoides indica

FLOATING PLANTS
Azolla filiculoides

Ranunculus lingua 'Grandiflora'

Hydrocharis morsus-ranae
Pistia stratiotes (frost-tender; see May)
Stratiotes aloides
Urticaria minor

OXYGENATING PLANTS
Ceratophyllum hermaphroditica
Hydrocleys parviflora
Myriophyllum aquaticum
Potamogeton crispa

Aponogeton distachyos

Azolla filiculoides

Hydrocharis morsus-ranae

Pistia stratiotes

LAWNS

PLANTING AQUATIC PLANTS

① Small plants or divisions can be held down with a galvanized hoop – useful when waterlily roots consist mostly of a chunk of rhizome.

② A layer of coarse grit over the surface of the soil or aquatic compost will stop it drifting, or being nosed out by fish.

of oxygen in the water will suppress them. Most algae problems occur in small, shallow ponds where the volume of water is relatively small and the water heats up fairly quickly in warm weather. You could as a last resort renovate the pond and dig it deeper, as this will help to keep the temperature of the water down. Installing a fountain or building a waterfall feature would also help, by increasing oxygen levels in the water.

FEED FISH REGULARLY as they get more lively, but only as they need it.

MOW REGULARLY. If grass is left to grow long and then cut short it will turn yellow and look unsightly, and it will also be weakened, so regular mowing – by summer once a week, or if you're really fussy twice a week – is the order of the day. Blades should be at their highest setting when you start mowing in spring – by the end of this month, start gradually lowering them each time you mow (see also May).

CONTINUE TO REPAIR AND RENOVATE ESTABLISHED LAWNS, as described in January and February. It is especially important to level off lumps and bumps, as these cause the mower to scalp the grass, weakening it and encouraging weeds and moss. Continue to remove weeds individually (see February). Coarse grasses, which are extremely vigorous and look out of place on a finer lawn, can be removed by criss-crossing the clump with an old knife, then pulling the tufts of grass out. After this regular mowing will discourage coarser grasses.

FEED ESTABLISHED LAWNS unless you did so late last month (see March). Always use fertilisers according to the manufacturer's instructions. There is no point in putting on a little extra to speed things up. Plants will only take up a certain amount, and the excess leaches into the water table and into streams and rivers, contributing to pollution.

There are several methods of applying lawn fertiliser. One is to mark out the lawn into square metres or yards with string and canes, and measure out and scatter the fertiliser by hand, wearing gloves, in measured doses, as when sowing seed (see top right). This can be

laborious if you have a large lawn, so use a fertiliser spreader. There are many types available, and they can be bought or hired.

YOU CAN TREAT MOSS with a mosskiller now, but do bear in mind that this only treats the symptoms rather than the cause. The main causes of moss in lawns are poor drainage, weak grass and compacted soil. The best way to remedy these faults is to aerate the lawn each year using a machine or fork to spike the lawn, and to rake out "thatch": the dead grass and moss that accumulates. By doing this and feeding the lawn regularly, the grass will be much healthier and moss and weeds will be less able to establish in it.

NEW LAWNS

SOW NEW LAWNS on prepared ground if this was not done last month. With the weather warming up grass seed will germinate quickly now. The area for a new lawn should have been dug over during the winter incorporating organic matter to retain moisture. You can still get away with this preparation now if you have a light sandy soil. After digging, the ground will have to be levelled off and the soil raked down to a fine tilth. Firm the soil well by treading it with your weight on your heels, rake the soil again, tread it at right angles to the previous direction and finally rake it level. To sow the seed, first mark out the area in metre squares, as when spreading fertiliser (see above right), using canes and string. Weigh out the quantity of seed required per square metre recommended on the packet once on kitchen scales, and then put it into a

SOWING GRASS SEED

① Broadcast the seed evenly over measured square metres. Scatter half one way, and the rest the other until you get confident.

② Rake very gently to just cover the seed, using short strokes so that you do not redistribute it unevenly.

cup, and mark its level on the side. Now you can either use the cup to measure out all the subsequent "doses" of seed, or tip a measure into your hand, see how it feels, and then take up similar-sized handfuls each time. This saves a lot of weighing. Scatter, or broadcast, the seed evenly over each area; rake in and water with a fine spray or sprinkler.

A quick alternative for a large area is to use a fertiliser spreader set at the seed-sowing setting.

Most grass seed nowadays is treated with a bird repellent, so there is no need to protect it. This may not be the most "organic" option, but it is certainly kinder than risking birds becoming entangled in netting or thread.

FINISH MAKING NEW LAWNS FROM TURF (see October) before the weather becomes too dry. Newly turfed lawns should grow away quite quickly now, and you may find that those laid earlier in the year already need a trim.

VEGETABLES & HERBS

SOWING UNDER COVER

SOW TOMATOES for planting outdoors in early June. Although you may have sown tomatoes for the greenhouse last month (see March, Under Glass), there is no point in sowing tomatoes to grow outdoors much more than six to eight weeks before you can plant them out.

Sow the seeds in trays or small pots containing seed compost. Overfill the container, give a sharp tap on the bench to settle the compost, strike off the surplus and firm gently with the base of a pot to level off. Water the container before sowing. Sow the seeds thinly and cover with vermiculite until the seeds just disappear.

Place in a propagator at a temperature of 22°C (70°F). Cover with a sheet of glass and paper, removing this when the seeds germinate in a couple of weeks. When the seedlings are large enough to handle them either prick out into trays or pot up into small pots.

There are many tomato varieties to choose from, and which you grow is a matter of taste, from the small cherry tomatoes to the large, beefy slicing types. However, they do grow in different ways. Cordon varieties of tomatoes are the tall kind with a single central stem, which need support, but there are bush varieties, many of which are relatively hardy, that do not need training and look very decorative, especially in containers on the patio. There are even trailing tomatoes for hanging baskets.

Cordons are the traditional choice for glasshouse growing, because you can use the full height of the greenhouse to ripen a good crop, but the bush and trailing varieties look equally good on greenhouse benches and conservatories.

SOW CELERY AND CELERIAC for planting outdoors in early June, exactly as you would tomatoes (see left).

SOW SWEETCORN, MARROWS AND COURGETTES, AND PUMPKINS AND SQUASHES towards the end of the month. If they are sown any earlier, they will get drawn and starved before it is safe to plant them out, at the beginning of June. Sow these two seeds per 8cm (3in) pot, pushing them into the compost on their edge. They don't need quite as high a temperature as tomatoes to germinate: 16°C (61°F) is sufficient. When the seeds have germinated, remove the weaker one and grow on the other one. Pot up into larger pots if necessary before planting out in June.

SOW LEEKS IN MODULES. You can sow leeks outside this month (see Sowing and Planting Outdoors), but if you're growing vegetables on deep beds the ideal way of growing leeks is to multi-sow them in modules. Fill a modular tray with seed compost and firm gently. Put some leek seeds onto a piece of card or paper and with the point of a knife, sow five or six seeds per cell. Cover the seeds with compost or vermiculite. When the seedlings are about 10cm (4in) high they can be planted out in their clusters, 30cm (1ft) apart each way. Although each leek will be smaller you get more crop per square metre than when growing in conventional rows.

SOWING AND PLANTING OUTDOORS

CONTINUE TO PLANT ASPARAGUS CROWNS (see March for details).

CARROTS SOWN LATE THIS MONTH may need carrot fly protection (see May).

PLANT MAINCROP POTATOES. This is the latest month for maincrops if you want to get a decent crop. To plant them (see also March), take out trenches 60cm (2ft) apart to the depth of the spade, heaping the soil to one side. If no organic matter was dug in earlier in the year, put some well-rotted manure or garden compost in the trench, and set the tubers on this. Space the tubers about 38cm (15in) apart. Sprinkle fertiliser in the gaps along the row before filling in. Cover the tubers with soil, leaving it slightly mounded up.

KEEP UP WITH SUCCESSIONAL SOWINGS of vegetables like lettuce, radish, beetroot, peas, broad beans, salad onions and turnips. By sowing little and often you will avoid having a glut of produce all at one time. Sow in shallow drills made with a stick, watering the drills before sowing if the soil is dry. Sow the seeds thinly and cover with soil and label them. Thin out when the seedlings are large enough to handle.

PLANT OUT ONIONS SOWN EARLIER IN THE YEAR. Rake in a general fertiliser before planting, and don't grow on soil that had onions on it the previous year. Onions being grown as single plants can be planted in rows 22cm (9in) apart, in rows 30cm (12in) apart. Those that were sown in modules and grown as multiple plants can be planted out in their clusters on deep beds, 15cm (6in) apart each way. As these onions grow they push each other apart. The individual onions may be smaller than when plants are grown singly, but the overall crop yield per square metre is greater because there are more plants.

SOW DWARF FRENCH BEANS under cloches in milder parts of the country. Take out a wide drill (see March) about 2.5cm (1in) deep, and space the seeds 15cm (6in) apart in staggered rows. Water if the soil is dry, and put cloches over the rows to protect from frost, and they should be up in a few days.

SOW LEEKS. It is now safe to sow leeks outside, in a nursery bed (a spare piece of ground used to raise plants before transplanting them to their final cropping positions). Sow them in short rows by taking out narrow drills in the usual manner. Water the drills if the weather is dry, and sow the seeds thinly along the drill. Cover with dry soil and label the row. When they are 10cm (4in) high they can be transplanted (see also May). The way to plant them is to make a hole with a large dibber, made from an old spade handle or buy one, and drop one plant into each hole. Water in, and some soil will be carried into the hole, anchoring the plant.

PLANT SEAKALE. This unusual vegetable is normally blanched for harvesting stems in winter and spring. It can be grown from seed, but for crops within the year, it is far better to buy it as roots or "crowns". Plant them about 30cm (12in) apart, with the top of the root just below the surface of the soil. When the young shoots begin to grow, remove the weakest ones leaving just one shoot on each root. By the autumn the plants will have formed good crowns for forcing (see October).

Kohl rabi *Harvest the curious, swollen stem bases while they are small and tender.*

SOW KOHL RABI (above) at intervals from now until August. It is the swollen part of the stem that is eaten; it has a turnip-like flavour. Sow the seeds in narrow drills in the usual way, and thin the resulting seedlings, leaving them 22cm (9in) apart each way.

SOW FLORENCE FENNEL in drills 60cm (2ft) apart, and thin the seedlings to 38cm (15in) when they are large enough to handle. These are quite decorative plants with feathery foliage, and grow to a height of around 1.25–2m (4–6ft). It's the swollen stem bases (see right), with an aniseed flavour, that are eaten.

SOW SEEDS OF SALSIFY AND SCORZONERA. These are two unusual root vegetables, little grown here because they are not quick to prepare, the roots being very long and thin. In countries such as France where food preparation is seen as an art, not a chore, they are very popular. Salsify tastes rather like oysters, and scorzonera has a nutty flavour that, though difficult to describe, is delicious. Grow both in soil that has been manured for a previous

crop applying a general fertiliser before sowing. Rake the soil level and to a fine tilth, and sow the seeds in narrow drills 30cm (1ft) apart, watering the drills before sowing if the weather is dry. Thin the seedlings to 30cm (12in) apart. The roots can be used in the autumn or stored in boxes over winter.

WINTER BRASSICAS – broccoli, cabbages, cauliflowers and Brussels sprouts – can all be sown outside on a prepared seedbed early in the month, if not done last month. Those sown last month and ready for transplanting should be moved to their permanent bed before the plants get too large, the ideal time being when the plants have made two or three true leaves. Spacing varies tremendously with the type and variety of crop, but will be given on the seed packets. Water well after transplanting, and place brassica collars (see May) round the young plants to ward off cabbage root fly. Adult flies lay their eggs at the base of the plant, and the resulting white larvae eat the plant's roots. Collars that fit snugly around the base of the stem prevent the adult flies

Florence fennel *Stem bases can be cooked as a vegetable; leaves can be used in garnishes and salads.*

laying the eggs in the soil and they fail to hatch. There are chemical controls available, but prevention is the easiest, and of course the organic way. Planting through mulching sheets and membranes also does the same job. You can even use old carpet, cut into 15cm (6in) squares.

LOOKING AFTER CROPS

WATER REGULARLY IN DRY WEATHER. All young vegetable plants need water to develop well.

THIN OUT ROWS OF SEEDLINGS SOWN EARLIER. If seedlings are not thinned out the plants will become straggly and not crop well at all. The distances to thin each type of vegetable will vary and it is best to check the back of the seed packet for details of individual plants.

The thinnings of most vegetables, except root vegetables such as carrots, beetroots and turnips, can be transplanted. The advantage of this is that these thinnings, having been disturbed, will mature that little bit later than the seedlings left in the row, therefore extending the succession of cropping. Water seedlings before and after thinning in dry weather. Seedlings being transplanted should also be watered gently but well after planting.

IF ANY SHOOTS OF EARLY POTATOES are starting to show through the soil, keep a sheet of horticultural fleece handy and cover them if any sharp frosts are forecast. They are vulnerable to cold damage. If you have planted the potatoes under sheets of clear polythene (see March), cut slits in

it as soon as you see the shoots, to allow them to grow through.

WATCH OUT FOR FLEA BEETLE. These small insects attack brassicas, turnips and radishes, nibbling small holes in the foliage. They are so-called because when they are disturbed, they jump. You can spray with an insecticide to control them, but one way you could try to keep the numbers down, or indeed if you want to confirm that flea beetles are the problem, is to make use of the fact that they do hop up when disturbed. Get a small, square piece of wood or cardboard and smear one side of it with grease or petroleum jelly. Run this over the tops of the leaves of the plants and the beetles will jump up and stick to the card.

SUPPORT PEAS SOWN EARLIER. Peas have rather straggly growth, and if they are not supported some of the crop will be lost, because it will become spoiled lying on the soil. There are several ways to support peas. Plastic green support mesh specially made for the purpose can be bought from the

Thinning seedlings *Be careful not to damage the remaining plants as you thin along the row.*

VEGETABLES & HERBS *continued*

Pea sticks *Twiggy prunings are ideal to give a backbone of support to rows of peas.*

garden centre, or use twiggy sticks. One method that is useful is to use the prunings from other shrubs in the garden provided they are strong enough and are reasonably straight. An ideal shrub for this is buddleja (the butterfly bush). It produces large purple or white flowers on long shoots made through the summer, and these shoots make ideal supports for peas, but any other shrubs with reasonably straight stems will do. Keep them to one side after you have pruned them from the shrub in spring. The tips with the old flower heads may have to be removed to make them look more presentable.

HERBS

DIVIDE CHIVES if not done last month. With larger clumps, you may have to use two forks back to back to prise the clump apart, but otherwise they can be pulled apart by hand. Water well after replanting in soil that has been revitalised with garden compost.

PROPAGATE THYME BY LAYERING. This method of propagation is very similar to that used on strawberry runners. Fill small pots with a mixture of equal parts of peat-free compost and sharp sand, and sink the pots into the soil beneath the vigorous outer stems to be layered. Peg the stems into the pots, and in a few weeks, roots will have formed. The new plants can be cut from the parent and planted out into their permanent positions. Thymes require a well-drained soil in a sunny spot.

CONTINUE SOWING AND PLANTING HERBS. By this time of year most herbs can be sown outside, and any sown earlier inside can be planted out from the end of the month, after hardening off in a cold frame. Many varieties of young herb plants are available from garden centres and by mail order from specialist herb nurseries. But it's a real treat to make a trip to a herb nursery, to see, and most enjoyably smell, all the different herbs on offer.

Planting herbs *Water young plants regularly, even the drought-tolerant types like thymes.*

FRUIT

HARVESTING

CHECK UNDER RHUBARB FORCERS regularly until the crop of young, pale stems is ready. When you have cut them all, leave the forcer off and feed the plants. Do not take a crop from the regrowth.

LOOKING AFTER CROPS

FEED BLACKCURRANTS, BLACKBERRIES AND HYBRID BERRIES with a high-nitrogen feed. These plants make a lot of growth during the season, and an extra dose of a high nitrogen feed will give them a welcome boost. Don't use too much – follow the directions on the package. Too much nitrogen will result in very soft growth, which is more susceptible to attack from pests and diseases.

CONTROL WEEDS AROUND CANE FRUIT. Weeds take valuable moisture and nutrients from the soil, and also act as hosts to pests and diseases. The easiest way to keep down weeds around fruit is to mulch with a thick layer of farmyard manure, garden compost or straw.

KEEP FROST PROTECTION ON EARLY-FLOWERING FRUITS (see March); however mild the weather appears now compared to earlier months, night frosts are still common. Remember that this will also involve hand-pollinating flowers (see March).

KEEP AN EYE OUT FOR PESTS AND DISEASES by inspecting fruits regularly. If you feel you must use chemical sprays then spray in the evenings when there are few pollinating insects around. Don't spray during the period when the flowers of any fruits are fully open – not even in the evenings – as you will harm pollinating insects. We have to do all we can to encourage a wide range of insects and mammals into the garden as their habitats in the countryside in general gradually disappear. Even so-called safe organic sprays kill a wide variety of insects and will harm the beneficial ones. By building up a diversity of plants in the garden you will attract beneficial insects, birds and mammals and these will keep the pest problem to a minimum so you may not have to spray at all. Sow or plant some annual flowers in the fruit garden, such as phacelia, to attract friendly pest predators such as hoverflies that will do the work of pest control for you.

WATCH OUT FOR AMERICAN GOOSEBERRY MILDEW on gooseberries. This shows as a white powdery coating on the leaves. If you want to spray, use a fungicide recommended for the purpose, bought from the garden centre. Read the instructions carefully. But it's better to grow varieties like 'Invicta' which are resistant to mildew, removing the need to spray at all. Winter pruning, watering and feeding well also helps plants grow strong and more resistant to attack.

BLACKCURRANTS are often affected by a mite that spreads a virus on its mouthparts: watch out for swollen buds in late winter and virus symptoms now. If the bush is affected by virus, the flowers will be red instead of grey. There is no choice but to dig it up and burn it. There is no effective cure. Replace lost bushes with mite-resistant cultivars, such as 'Farleigh' and 'Foxendown'.

Fan-trained stone fruits *Pruning shoots in spring and summer maintains the form.*

PRUNING AND TRAINING

PRUNE FAN-TRAINED STONE FRUITS like cherries, plums and nectarines. First prune out any shoots growing either into the wall and directly away from the tree. Then thin out any overcrowded and crossing shoots, while at the same time removing any dead, diseased or damaged shoots. The remaining shoots can be tied to the training wires.

The reason for pruning these trees now and not in winter is that they are prone to the fungal diseases silverleaf and bacterial canker. These enter the plant through open wounds; by pruning now when the plant is in growth, the pruning cuts heal over quickly, reducing the risk of disease getting in.

TIE IN VINES. Outdoor vines will be growing fast soon and the shoots will need tying in if they are not to get out of control. Vines grow extremely fast and can put on more than 3m (10ft) of growth in a season. So tying in, thinning and stopping the shoots (see also June) are important to encourage a good crop of grapes instead of a mass of leafy growth. The easiest way to train grapes is with a central, vertical main stem, or rod, that is kept pruned back to the height of the supporting system of wires. Each year, train selected sideshoots out sideways, in an espalier shape. These shoots will carry the fruits, then in winter, are cut back to within two or three buds of the main rod.

PLANTING

PLANT CONTAINER-GROWN TRAINED FRUIT TREES. By this month it is too late to plant bare-root fruit trees and bushes, but there are many different kinds, trained in attractive ways, available in containers. The advantage of container-grown plants is they can be planted at any time of the year, because the root system is not disturbed. You can even buy them in flower and may get some fruit from them in the first year after planting, but don't be too greedy and take a lot of fruit in the first year. It's better to let the plants get established now, and they'll fruit all the better in subsequent years. Lay seephose when you plant new fruit and mulch on top of it to water efficiently and conserve soil moisture.

Apples, pears, plums, red and white currants and gooseberries can all be trained in several different ways; espaliers (tiers of horizontal branches), cordons (single-stemmed trees grown at an angle to save space) and fans (branches are trained as in the spokes of a fan). These are all both attractive and productive, and with modern dwarfing rootstocks they can be fitted into the smallest of spaces, so no garden need be without some fruit.

UNDER COVER

VENTILATE WELL ON SUNNY DAYS. It may be necessary to leave vents and doors open all day in warm weather, as the temperature can climb dramatically in a short time when the sun is out.

DAMP DOWN ON WARM DAYS. On hot days the atmosphere indoors can become very dry – not the best conditions for plants. Damping down simply means splashing water on the floor to increase the humidity of the atmosphere, which is much more conducive to plant growth. Another advantage is that it reduces the incidence of red spider mite. This pest attacks the leaves of plants, causing them to become mottled and die off. It thrives in warm dry conditions, so damping down can reduce the problem without using sprays.

SHADE YOUNG PLANTS during sunny weather. As with newly pricked-out seedlings, cuttings will need to be shaded from strong sunlight too. Until new roots develop, the cuttings are continually losing water from their leaves, but in the meantime have no roots to replace the water lost. Shading them will reduce water loss from the leaves in hot weather. Temporary shading for young plants is easily provided with sheets of newspaper.

WATCH OUT FOR VINE WEEVIL. This pest has become a serious problem in recent years, and it is difficult to control. The little creamy white grubs live in the compost and eat roots, easily going unnoticed until you see the plants wilting. There is a biological predator available to control them: a microscopic nematode worm that attacks the grubs. It is bought by mail order and watered into the pots. The other organic way to control them is to squash them between your fingers when you see them!

INTRODUCE OTHER BIOLOGICAL CONTROLS if this was not done earlier (see March). In fact this is perhaps a better time to introduce them, especially in unheated greenhouses, as they do not work in temperatures below 10°C (50°F). These controls are usually in the form of nematodes or small predatory insects or mites, and there are specific ones for specific pests – for example, the tiny wasp *Encarsia formosa*, which kills young whitefly. Under cover, they do the job of friendly garden insects such as hoverflies and ladybirds, encouraged by all good gardeners.

WHITEFLY CAN BE A PROBLEM especially if you are growing tomatoes, which seem to attract every specimen in the neighbourhood. Put up yellow sticky cards to catch them. Hang the cards on string near the tops of plants and raise them as the plants grow. It's

Vine weevil and damage *The adults nibble the edges of leaves.*

Signs of greenhouse pests *Watch out for mottling of the leaves, especially underneath.*

UNDER COVER *continued*

amazing just how many will be caught on these traps. Whitefly seem to be strongly attracted to the colour yellow. Before an infestation becomes severe, use a biological control as well. Growing French marigolds in the greenhouse or conservatory is also believed to deter whitefly.

RAISING PLANTS FOR OUTDOORS

BUY BEDDING PLANTS AS PLUGS from the garden centre; in the south and in sheltered areas, they will grow on happily in an unheated greenhouse now. Buying bedding this way instead of growing from seed is growing in popularity among those gardeners who have space under glass to bring on the young plants. Many people simply don't have the time to sow seeds early on, then look after them until it's time for them to be planted out. Buying young plants also cuts out the time when seeds require the most heat to germinate, so saving on costs at home. It's also easier than sowing tricky seed such as impatiens.

Most types of bedding plants are now available in this way. They come in small modular trays, with one plant per cell. The advantage of this system is the plants can be potted up with no disturbance to the root system, so they grow away better without a check to their growth. When the young plants arrive, unpack them and pot them up into 9cm (3½in) pots containing peat-free compost and grow them on in a cool greenhouse or conservatory. Don't give too much heat as the plants will grow too fast and become drawn. Harden off for a week or two before planting out.

Plug plants *There are nurseries that specialize in raising these tiny, self-contained bedding plants.*

TOWARDS THE END OF THE MONTH, PLANT UP HANGING BASKETS. Although these cannot be hung outside until the threat of frost has passed, in early June, now or early next month is a good time to get them planted up. This will allow the plants to grow and fill out before being put outside. The choice of plants and colour schemes is almost limitless and it is worth paying a visit to a local garden centre where you will see a wide variety of plants on sale. See June for planting.

COMPLETE SOWING OF HALF-HARDY ANNUALS by the end of the month. Fast-growing half-hardy annuals like French marigolds can be sown as late as this, but others requiring a longer growing season to flower should have been sown by now. Check the back of seed packets for growing times.

CONTINUE PRICKING OUT SEEDLINGS of half-hardy annuals sown earlier. Pricking out means spacing the seedlings about 2.5cm (1in) apart in trays so they have more space to develop. Water seedlings in well after pricking them out. On warm sunny days they will benefit from shading from strong sunshine until they get established in the trays.

GIVE YOUNG PLANTS MORE GROWING SPACE. Continue to pot on growing young plants and cuttings. The ideal time to put plants into larger pots is just as the roots have filled the available compost, without becoming pot-bound – when you can see a mass of roots in the pot or tray, or the roots are growing out through the drainage holes. Generally pot on to pots one or two sizes larger than the one the plant is growing in.

IN MILD AREAS, BEGIN TO HARDEN OFF BEDDING PLANTS towards the end of the month (see May).

SOW WINTER-FLOWERING PANSIES. These can be sown outside, but you will get better plants by sowing them in gentle heat now. Sow the seeds thinly in trays or small pots, cover with a thin layer of compost and put a sheet of glass and paper over the tray. Prick out the seedlings when they are large enough to handle, then pot up into module trays with large cells or small pots. They can sit outside in a sheltered, shady spot through the summer, provided that you remember to water regularly. Planted in autumn, they will produce a terrific display right through the winter.

CONTINUE TO TAKE CUTTINGS from tender perennials like fuchsias and pelargoniums, as described last month.

Those which were taken earlier and have rooted can be potted up if not done already. To encourage the plants to bush out pinch out the growing tips. Fuchsias and pelargoniums being trained as standards (see p.185 for illustrations) should not have the growing tips removed. Instead, let the main stem grow to the height you want, tying it to a cane as it grows to keep the stem straight. Pinch out any sideshoots that form. When the stem reaches the required height, pinch out the tip and then sideshoots will grow to form the head. Pinch out the resulting sideshoots to make a dense bushy head full of flowers.

SOW TOMATOES, CELERY AND CELERIAC for planting outdoors in early June (see Vegetables & Herbs).

SOW SWEETCORN, MARROWS AND COURGETTES towards the end of the month (see Vegetables & Herbs).

SOW LEEKS (see Vegetables & Herbs).

GLASSHOUSE AND HOUSE PLANTS

TAKE HYDRANGEA CUTTINGS from pot-grown plants. Mophead hydrangeas are increasingly popular as pot plants, but they are difficult to keep going year after year. Remove stem-tip cuttings about 8-10cm (3-4in) long. Cut off the lower leaves and trim the base of the cutting. There is no need to trim immediately below a leaf joint as is normal practice with cuttings, as hydrangeas root perfectly well without. To reduce water loss from the large leaves, however, cut them in half. It may seem rather brutal, but it works. Put the cuttings into pots of cuttings compost and place on a shady windowsill or on the greenhouse bench. No extra heat is needed. Pot up when they have rooted.

REST AMARYLLIS AFTER FLOWERING. Give the bulbs several feeds of high potash fertiliser to build up the flower bud inside the bulb for flowering next time. When the foliage begins to turn yellow reduce the watering and dry off. Put the pots on their sides under a bench.

REST CYCLAMEN which have flowered in pots over the winter. This is done by gradually reducing the amount of watering until the foliage begins to die down. Place the pots on their sides under the greenhouse bench or in a cold frame until they are started into growth again later in the summer.

TAKE LEAF CUTTINGS OF STREPTOCARPUS (CAPE PRIMROSE). Remove a mature leaf from the plant, and cut it into 2.5cm

Rest cyclamen Laying cyclamen on their sides prevents overwatering as they go dormant.

POT HYDRANGEA CUTTINGS

1 Take stem-tip cuttings by removing the top 8–10cm (3–4in) of young, healthy, non-flowering shoots.

2 Remove leaves at the base and tip, and cut the remaining leaves cleanly across in half.

3 Dibble the cuttings into a mixture of peat-free compost and perlite or vermiculite, at the edges of the pot.

4 Either pot up three rooted cuttings together for a fast-growing bushy plant, or plant them up individually.

(1in) sections. Bury the base of each section in a pot, or put several in a tray, of equal parts peat-free compost and perlite or vermiculite. The part of the leaf that was nearest the plant should always face downwards. Put in a warm shady place, and after a few months new plantlets will emerge from the base of each leaf section. These can be potted up individually. Another method is to take a mature leaf, and cut it along the length of the mid-rib. Put in a tray with the midrib in the compost and plantlets will develop along the length of the midrib.

POT UP BEGONIA AND GLOXINIA TUBERS that were started off last month, into 12.5cm (5in) pots. Water them well after potting on.

CROPS UNDER GLASS

TIE IN VINE RODS. Vines growing inside will be galloping away now, and it is essential to keep up with tying in and pinching out growths, otherwise you will end up in the most awful mess. Fruiting stems should be pinched back to one or two buds beyond each flower truss, and all sideshoots from these stems removed.

POT UP TOMATO SEEDLINGS sown last month. Tomato seedlings should be transplanted when you can see the first true leaves beginning to emerge from between the two first, or seed, leaves (the cotyledons). Watering the seedlings an hour or two beforehand makes it easier to ease them out of the tray or pot. Pot up into 9cm (3½in) pots, with the seed leaves almost level with the compost. Water in well, and stand on

the greenhouse bench, or on a warm windowsill. If they are on a windowsill, turn them every day otherwise they will grow towards the light and bend over.

REMOVE SIDESHOOTS FROM OLDER TOMATO PLANTS. Those sown earlier will be growing strongly now, and cordon varieties (those grown as a single stem) need to have any sideshoots growing from the leaf axils removed. If these are not removed you will end up with a mass of growth and poor quality fruits. The best time to remove sideshoots is when they are small, just large enough to handle. Take the shoot between your thumb and forefinger and push or pull the shoot to one side, and it should snap off cleanly. If the shoots have been left on and grown quite large, use a knife or secateurs.

PLANT TOMATOES IN GROWBAGS. When earlier-sown tomatoes are potted up they grow away quickly, and towards the end of the month they can go into growbags, or be potted into 20cm (8in) pots, for cropping. Place the growbags in the greenhouse for a few days to warm up the compost before planting. Similarly, if you're potting them up, warm up the bag of compost in the greenhouse. You can plant either two or three plants per growbag. Tie cordon plants to canes or support wires attached to the framework of the glasshouse. There are also support frames made specially for growbags and these can be purchased from garden centres.

KEEP HAND-POLLINATING any forced strawberry plants in flower (see March).

MAKE AN ALPINE TROUGH

THIS LITTLE SINK-STYLE TROUGH is easily made and will fit into a corner of the tiniest garden. At least half the price of even the cheaper shop-bought ones, it will look attractive for many months of the year.

YOU WILL NEED: Two cardboard boxes, the same shape but with one about 5cm (2in) bigger than the other all round • A "hypertufa" mix of one part cement, 1 part sharp sand, and 2 parts sieved peat-free compost: you need enough, roughly, to fill the smaller box, but overestimate to avoid running short • Wire netting and wirecutters • Wooden pegs or corks to create drainage holes • Bricks to support the mould

PLANTS USED HERE: *Juniperus communis* 'Compressa'; *Sedum spathulifolium* 'Cape Blanco' and 'Purpureum'; *Lithodora diffusa* 'Heavenly Blue'; *Thymus pulegioides* 'Aureus' (all ♈)

① Mix the hypertufa: here 2 shovelfuls each of cement and sand to 4 of sieved compost.

② Add water until you have quite a wet mix, about the consistency of porridge. Mix well.

③ Cover the base of the larger box with a layer of the mix. Cut a sheet of netting to fit the base, snip out four or five holes (see above), and lay it over the hypertufa.

④ Here, we cut small lengths of roofing lath to make pegs. Insert them firmly through the mix; they will keep holes through the base clear to provide drainage for the trough.

⑤ Spread another layer of hypertufa mix over the base to sandwich the netting. The more rigid "grille"-type netting is easier to use than chicken wire, as it stays flatter.

⑥ Roughly pat down and smooth the base, brushing away any hypertufa that might impede removal of the pegs later on.

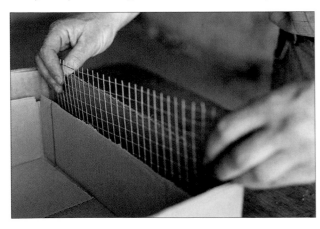

⑦ Place the smaller box inside the larger one. Cut four more oblongs of netting to fit the sides of the box, making them 2.5–5cm (1–2in) smaller each way. It is important that any sharp edges will be completely covered at the top. Set them in the gaps.

⑧ Start to fill the sides with hypertufa mix, putting equal amounts each side of the netting.

⑨ As you go, tamp the mix well down, again evenly on the inner and outer sides.

⑩ Once the mould is filled, support it on both sides with bricks, as the hypertufa makes the cardboard damp. Leave it overnight.

⑪ The next day, remove the bricks and peel away the cardboard, but don't try to move the trough. It needs at least a week to fully harden. Only then should you remove the cardboard from the base.

⑫ Before the hypertufa sets completely, scrape away the corners to give a distressed look, using an old chisel. You can also scrape away any obvious lines left by the cardboard.

⑬ Brush off the worst of the dust with a soft brush, and then go over the whole trough with a wire brush. This gives the trough the appearance of weathered stone.

⑭ Leave to harden completely for about a week and then, using another peg, knock out the pegs to leave the drainage holes open.

⑮ Set the trough up on bricks to ensure good drainage. Place crocks in the bottom to cover the drainage holes, preventing them getting clogged with compost. Fill with an alpine compost mix of equal parts soil, peat-free compost and coarse grit.

⑯ Plant up with plants of your choice. Spread grit or gravel over the surface to retain soil moisture and to prevent the plants being splashed with soil.

⑰ The finished feature, planted with a selection of spreading rock plants and a dwarf conifer.

MAY

The garden in May

Many gardeners regard May as one of the best months in the garden, with the freshness of spring and the promise of summer. It's also the month of the most famous flower show of all, the Chelsea Flower Show.

T HERE ARE SIGNS OF SUMMER EVERYWHERE, yet many spring-flowering bulbs, especially the tulips, are still at their best. Trees are in full leaf, and shrubs like rhododendrons are in full flower in most parts of the country during this month. There is a huge range of rhododendrons available, from dwarf shrubs only a few inches tall, which can be grown in pots and tubs, to great tree-like shrubs usually covered in large clusters of flowers. They are well worth growing if you have an acid soil. If your soil is alkaline then grow the smaller-growing rhododendrons in pots or raised beds filled with ericaceous compost. With quite mature container-grown shrubs now available year-round, you could buy a rhododendron in flower and have it installed in a tub on the patio the same afternoon.

Rhododendrons in bloom ▷

There are many gardens open to the public famed for their magnificent displays of rhododendrons. Even if you don't have acid soil, you can recreate the show in miniature in tubs and pots.

Change your bedding

While many plants are gearing themselves up for their summer display, the spring bedding plants will soon be over, and it's time to think about their replacements. A wide selection of summer bedding plants will be on show at nurseries and garden centres but, as in April, resist the temptation to buy these too early in the month unless you have a frost-free greenhouse, conservatory or cold frame to keep them in. The majority of these plants are still quite tender, and in northern parts of the country it may not be safe to plant them out until the end of the month or into June. In more southern, sheltered parts of the country you may get away with planting summer bedding around the middle of the month, but do keep an eye on weather forecasts.

If you are new to an area, then a visit to a local park, or just a stroll around the area having a look at some local gardens, will tell you a lot about when to plant out summer bedding safely in your area. Talk to local gardeners – there may be a local gardening club you can join, too – and find out as much as you can about the local weather conditions. You'll most likely find that they are quite a friendly bunch and will be glad to give out hints and tips on how to grow all manner of plants – and they often swap plants between themselves, so you might get a few plants for nothing as well as good advice!

Plants to protect

The weather in May is usually quite settled, but it can be changeable and there may still be the

◁ **Spring bedding**
Bright tulips planted amid misty forget-me-nots is a classic combination.

▽ **The plot thickens**
Plantings of vegetables start to bulk up and fill out the vegetable beds, and should reduce the need for weeding.

occasional sharp frost. So any tender plants being hardened off should be watched carefully and given protection with fleece or sheets of polythene, or put into a cold frame whenever required. The tell-tale signs of a night frost coming are a clear blue sky at the end of a warm, sunny day.

Start of the shows

This is also the month when the flower show season starts, with the greatest flower show of them all, Chelsea. Held in the grounds of the Royal Hospital Chelsea, under the auspices of the Royal Horticultural Society, it is without doubt the highlight of the gardening year. Here you will see millions of blooms and hundreds of innovative ideas for your own garden. There are, of course, many other flower shows throughout the summer, from large-scale national events down to small local shows, and all of them are worth visiting. Here you will meet like-minded people who are fascinated by plants, and undoubtedly, lifelong friendships are forged at these events.

WEATHER WATCH

The days are really warming up now, but do be aware that the nights can be cold and we can still get sudden sharp frosts at any time this month. These late frosts are the scourge of fruit growers. Most varieties of fruit trees will be in flower now and it only takes one sharp frost to destroy a potential crop for the whole year.

It's not a month for frequent gales, but there may be quite windy days. Exposed north-western coastal areas still get 0.5–0.7 days of gale-force winds, but it's rare for sheltered south-eastern parts to get any high winds at all.

The amount of direct sunshine will depend on the cloud cover, but generally southern parts of the country get the lion's share of sunshine, although some north-eastern parts compare favourably with the south-east. The western half of the country is more prone to cloud because weather fronts are driven over the Atlantic ocean, and because of the topography of that part of the country.

Although in general rainfall decreases in all parts by now, some parts are inevitably wetter than others. The north-west Highland region of Scotland averages 107mm of rain this month, and the south-west Borders region, and the Lake District in England, are not far behind with 95mm. It's not until you get to East Anglia that there is a considerable drop in rainfall: this region will get only around 44mm over the month.

The only places you are likely to find snow this month are in the hills above 100m, as at Cape Wrath in the northern Highlands of Scotland. Here snow can persist for most of the year. It is very rare indeed for snow to fall on other parts of the country, but there can still be hailstorms from time to time, which can be quite destructive.

△ **Lift cloches in daytime**
Temperatures can rise rapidly under glass and plastic, so do take care that plants are not stifled and scorched.

Spring is also a good time of year to visit other gardens opening to the public for the season, and to plan trips to those which are open for charity for a few days each summer. Here again there are many ideas to be gleaned which can be adapted to suit your own garden. Look out for the "Yellow Book" (*Gardens of England and Wales Open For Charity*, published by the National Gardens Scheme) listing gardens open to the public in aid of good causes. This is a mine of information on many small delightful gardens where you will find treasures of plants, often with cuttings or seedlings for sale – not to mention, in many cases, a welcome cup of tea.

Back to work

However, there is plenty to do in your own garden in between visiting flower shows and other people's gardens. In the vegetable plot you should now be harvesting delicious early vegetables planted out under cloches earlier in the year. To guarantee a succession of young vegetables throughout the summer, continue with regular sowing of all vegetables at seven- or ten-day intervals. Hoeing also becomes a very regular chore among vegetables now, as weeds burgeon in the milder conditions.

With the warmer, drier weather, watering may now become necessary, but don't use water indiscriminately, especially at this early stage in the season. Water only those plants that really need it – your precious young vegetables, developing fruits, and newly-planted trees, shrubs and perennials.

The pace hots up

Under glass, temperatures can get very high and it's vital from now on to shade young plants, open ventilators, windows and doors whenever possible, and damp down to prevent the air becoming too dry. Towards the end of the month it should be safe in all but the coldest regions to move pots containing tender shrubs and succulents such as agaves outdoors for the summer. Reducing crowding in the greenhouse will also help to increase good air circulation in the hot months to come.

Outside, ornamental borders will be brimming with colourful displays of late spring flowers and fresh foliage, the sound of birdsong will fill the garden and beneficial insects will be pollinating flowers. Herbaceous perennials are now growing fast and need to be staked, if this has not already been done. This is a job which often gets forgotten until it is too late, and the plants begin to flop all over the place and look unsightly. By this stage trying to tie up the stems is a hopeless task, and it is often better to cut the plants back hard and let them grow away again. The flowers may be later, but the plant will look much better for cutting back.

Waterside perennials ▷
Plants such as ferns, hostas, and the lovely candelabra primulas thrive in moist soil on the banks of streams and ponds. At this time of year, plantings really begin to look beautiful, with burgeoning new foliage that still retains all the freshness of spring.

A word about water

One aspect of Chelsea that never fails to inspire most visitors is the wealth of water features on show. Water in the garden not only cools and refreshes the air around it, but is also a real treat for wildlife - not only your regular garden friends, but new visitors such as dragonflies and frogs will be drawn to even the smallest feature. It's not too late to create your own – our practical project this month (see p.106) is a half-barrel pond, and although it may not be as grand as those in the show gardens, it's quick and easy to make, and will have instant impact. And once you've seen the beauty of water and water plants in your garden, not to mention the wildlife they attract, who knows what it will lead on to next year!

△ **Plant a half-barrel pond**
A small water feature planted now can look as good as this by high summer. Nearly all garden centres now have good aquatic departments where advice on suitable plants can be obtained.

MAY
AT A GLANCE

- Take action to protect plants if night frosts are forecast.
- Water plants that need it regularly.
- Prune spring-flowering shrubs that have finished flowering.
- Take softwood cuttings of shrubs.
- Lightly trim box and other formal hedging.
- Prune *Clematis montana* after flowering.
- Take cuttings from herbaceous perennials.
- Cut back and divide spring-flowering perennials.
- Plant out dahlias at the end of the month.
- Protect young plants from slugs.
- Clear out spring bedding, and begin hardening off summer bedding plants.
- Thin out annuals and vegetables sown outdoors earlier.
- Feed fish regularly, and also give a special aquatic fertiliser to water plants.
- Feed and weed lawns to encourage good growth, as well as mowing regularly.
- Sow and plant out tender vegetables at the end of the month.
- Protect crops from carrot fly.
- Continue successional sowing of vegetables.
- Remove all frost protection from fruit trees, and start pruning trained plums and cherries.
- Move tender shrubs in pots outside for summer.
- Ventilate greenhouses and conservatories, and think about permanent shading for summer.

! LAST CHANCE
- Sow or turf new lawns before it gets too dry.
- Finish planting evergreen shrubs.

★ GET AHEAD
- Sow biennials for next year's spring bedding plants.
- Inspect plants regularly for signs of pests and diseases, and nip potential problems in the bud.

Clematis montana f. *grandiflora* ♀ • A vigorous climber for quick cover *(see p.307)*

Laburnum x *watereri* 'Vossii' ♀ • Good small-to-medium garden tree with cascading yellow flowers *(see p.328)*

Papaver orientale 'Cedric Morris' ♀ • Showy perennial poppy with dark-centred flowers *(see p.338)*

Primula denticulata ♀ • The drumstick primula, a perennial that enjoys moist soil *(see p.342)*

Digitalis x *mertonensis* ♀ • Perennial foxglove that readily self-seeds *(see p.316)*

Exochorda x *macrantha* 'The Bride' ♀ • Notably free-flowering deciduous shrub *(see p.319)*

TOP ROW: 'Strawberry Ice' ♔ • 'Beauty of Littleworth' ♔ • 'Golden Torch' ♔
BOTTOM ROW: 'Freya' • 'Halfdan Lem' • *R. cinnabarinum* subsp. *xanthocodon* (see pp.345–6)

Tulipa **'Spring Green'** ♀ • One of the green-flecked viridiflora tulips *(see p.356)*

Trollius x *cultorum* **'Earliest of All'** • A lovely poolside perennial *(see p.356)*

Wisteria floribunda **'Multijuga'** ♀ • Woody-stemmed climber that needs twice-yearly pruning *(see p.359)*

Camassia cusickii **'Zwanenburg'** • Bulb with tall conical spires of vivid flowers *(see p.302)*

Choisya **'Aztec Pearl'** ♀ • Evergreen shrub with sweet-scented flowers *(see p.305)*

Clematis macropetala **'Markham's Pink'** ♀ • Looks good climbing through trees and large shrubs *(see p.306)*

Viburnum sargentii '**Onondaga**' ♀ • Deciduous shrub with lacecap clusters of flowers *(see p.358)*

Crataegus laevigata '**Rosea Flore Pleno**' • Plant hawthorn as a tree or informal hedging *(see p.313)*

Prunus padus '**Watereri**' ♀ • Flowering cherry popular with garden birds *(see p.343)*

Kerria japonica '**Picta**' • Clump-forming shrub with variegated foliage *(see p.328)*

Spiraea '**Arguta**' • Tall shrub with elegantly arching branches *(see p.354)*

Hyacinthoides non-scripta • The English bluebell, spreads vigorously once established *(see p.325)*

TOP ROW: *Syringa vulgaris* 'Charles Joly' ♀ • *Syringa vulgaris* 'Mme Lemoine' ♀ • *Syringa vulgaris* 'Président Grévy'
BOTTOM ROW: *Syringa vulgaris* 'Katherine Havemeyer' ♀ • *Syringa vulgaris* 'Charles X' • *Syringa vulgaris* 'Primrose' *(see pp.354–5)*

Corydalis flexuosa • Low-growing perennial with ferny leaves *(see p.311)*

Prunus 'Amanogawa' ♀ • Very slender flowering cherry tree for small gardens *(see p.342)*

Allium hollandicum ♀ • Drumstick seedheads look good long after the flowers fade *(see p.296)*

uphorbia x martinii ♀ • Bushy clump-forming perennial for a sunny site *(see p.319)*

Paeonia mlokosewitschii ♀ • Herbaceous peony with lemon-yellow flowers *(see p.338)*

Aquilegia vulgaris 'Nora Barlow' ♀ • Cottagey perennial that will self-seed *(see p.298)*

WHAT TO DO IN

MAY

AROUND THE GARDEN

PESTS AND DISEASES

Now the weather is warming up, you will have to watch for pests and diseases regularly. It may be necessary to use chemical controls in severe cases, but be aware that long-term use of synthetic chemicals can actually cause problems to build up. These chemicals kill off not only the pests, but also the beneficial insects that prey on them, such as ladybird and hoverfly larvae. If you feel it necessary to spray, do it on a still day, as late in the evening as possible when there are fewer beneficial insects around.

Ladybirds are gardeners' friends

Keep plants in the garden growing strongly and they will be less susceptible to attack. Prepare the ground well to get them off to a good start. Keep new plants well-watered during dry spells, so they don't suffer stress. Mulch newly planted plants to retain valuable moisture in the soil. The mulch will slow the rate of evaporation from the surface of the ground.

Keep the garden tidy, especially now it's time to clear spring bedding away (see Bulbs and Annuals & Bedding this month), and keep weeds, which often act as hosts to pests and diseases, under control. The most organic way of all to control pests is by using your fingers to squash them, but you have to be vigilant to keep on top of them this way. The memory of two days spent squashing cabbage white butterfly caterpillars on brassicas in a large garden remains with me.

HOE BARE GROUND TO KEEP DOWN WEEDS as they germinate. Weeds are more easily killed off at this stage, rather than leaving them until they get bigger. Then there is also no chance that they will be left too long, and will set seeds which will be spread around the garden. Hoe on dry, sunny days and the weed seedlings can be left on the surface of the ground to dry out and shrivel up in the sun. A mulch with organic matter will help to prevent the growth of further weeds. Water the soil first if it is dry before applying the mulch. Alternatively, put some plants in the gap to add colour to the border.

NIGHT FROSTS Even though daytime temperatures should now be mild, night frosts are not uncommon this month, especially after clear, bright days. Keep a sheet of horticultural fleece or even some old newspapers handy to cover any plants vulnerable to frost if night temperatures are forecast to fall.

Water new plants *Give newly planted plants a good soak regularly to help them establish.*

TREES & SHRUBS

WATER NEWLY PLANTED TREES AND SHRUBS regularly if the weather is dry. A few days of sunny weather accompanied by drying winds now will dry out the soil surprisingly quickly. Watering may have to be done on a daily basis. It is important to water new woody plants well until they get established and their roots develop enough to be able to seek out moisture deep down. Any organic matter, such as rotted manure or garden compost, either dug into the soil or applied as a mulch, has good water-holding potential which will help new, growing roots. Even grass clippings spread in a layer about 5–8cm (2–3in) thick around the plant (not touching the stems) will help to retain moisture. Try to water in the evenings when there is less chance of the water evaporating from the soil, as it will in the heat of the day.

KEEP CHECKING ROSES FOR APHIDS (see April).

IN MILDER REGIONS, tender shrubs in pots can be moved outside for the summer (see Containers).

PRUNING AND TRAINING

PRUNE EVERGREENS to remove any frost damage and tidy wayward shoots unless you did so last month (see April).

PRUNE PYRACANTHAS trained against a wall or fence. Prune out shoots growing directly into the wall and any growing directly away from it too. Shorten the others to about 8cm (3in). This encourages the formation of short spurs which bear the flower buds, and then the beautiful berries in autumn.

PRUNE EARLY-FLOWERING SHRUBS like *Kerria japonica* and *Spiraea* 'Arguta', which will finish flowering about now on wood produced the previous year. For kerria, prune all the shoots that have produced flowers back to young sideshoots lower down. This shrub tends to spread out by underground suckers, and these can also be removed if the plant is encroaching on other plants. *Spiraea* 'Arguta' should similarly have its flowered shoots pruned back to buds or shoots lower down on the shrub, and on older plants, in addition, cut out about one in three of the older stems completely to the ground. This will encourage young growth from the base of the plant, keeping it vigorous and healthy.

TAKE SOFTWOOD CUTTINGS FROM SHRUBS. Most shrubs in the garden will now be producing plenty of young, fresh shoots and these are excellent for making softwood cuttings through until July, when the wood begins to ripen. Take a few shoots from any part of the shrub where they will not be missed. About half-a-dozen should ensure you get at least one new shrub. It's always best to take more than you need as an insurance policy. Have a polythene bag to hand when you take the cuttings. Cut shoots about 8-10cm (3-4in) long from the plant, cutting just above a bud or leaf. Pop the cuttings into the bag straight away, and keep the bag out of the sun. This prevents the cuttings from wilting.

Trim the cuttings below a leaf joint with a sharp knife and remove the lower leaves, leaving them about 5-8cm (2-3in) long. Immerse the cuttings in a fungicide solution, wearing gloves, and then dip the cut ends into hormone rooting solution. Five or six cuttings per 12cm (5in) pot, containing a 50:50 mix of peat-free compost and vermiculite, will be sufficient. Cover with polythene, making sure it is held off the foliage of the cuttings (you can use short sticks to support it), and hold it in place with a rubber band. Place the pots in a shady part of the greenhouse or in a cold frame, and the cuttings should root in 6–8 weeks. They can then be potted up to be grown on.

HEDGES

LIGHTLY TRIM FORMAL EVERGREEN HEDGING such as box (*Buxus sempervirens*), even if it has not yet grown to the desired size. Box hedging does not take to being cut back hard, so the sooner it starts being trimmed to keep it in shape the better. This is best done with hand shears rather than with a mechanical hedge trimmer, which can bruise rather than cut leaves, making them turn brown and unsightly. It may take more time using shears, but the overall appearance of the hedge will be much better.

You can make cuttings from any shoots about 7.5cm (3in) long. Trim each cutting below a leaf joint, put into pots containing cuttings compost, cover with a polythene bag and stand the pot in a shady part of the garden, and in a few weeks the cuttings will root (see also Taking Softwood Cuttings, above). You can then pot them into their own pots, or space them out on a spare piece of ground until autumn or next spring, when they can be put in their final positions.

CLIMBERS

PRUNE *CLEMATIS MONTANA* after it has flowered. The amount of pruning will depend on where it is growing. This is a very vigorous climber, and it's best to allow it to scramble up through other trees and large shrubs or up a large area of fence or wall. In these situations, little pruning will be needed unless it is outgrowing its space. However, in more confined spaces some pruning will be necessary to prevent it taking over the whole garden. Pruning is easy, although the untangling can be tricky; all you have to do is prune out any dead or diseased wood, and prune the remaining stems back as far as you need to. This encourages young growth to grow and flower next spring.

TIE IN CLIMBERS REGULARLY. Vigorous climbers such as clematis, roses and vines need their shoots tied in at regular intervals, otherwise they may smother other plants in the border. Trying to untangle climbers from other plants is a tedious job, to be avoided if possible. Fixing wide-mesh wire netting to walls and fences is the easiest way to provide support for vigorous climbers. Trellis is more decorative, so choose lighter climbers for this so that the plants' growth does not hide it.

Tying in *Make figures-of-eight with twine so that stems do not rub directly on supports.*

PERENNIALS

Staking delphiniums *Tall plants need tall stakes. You must top them with corks or some other type of protector to prevent accidental eye injury when working in borders.*

CONTINUE STAKING AND TYING IN PERENNIALS, particularly tall-stemmed kinds like delphiniums. These will need several bamboo canes placed around each plant with string tied around the canes. Alternatively, tie each stem to an individual cane.

CUT BACK AND DIVIDE clump-forming spring-flowering perennials like doronicums and pulmonarias. Doronicum just needs the old flower spikes cut off to neaten up the plant. But pulmonarias should have all the old foliage cut to the ground, as it will usually be covered in mildew by now and look dreadfully shabby. It may seem a drastic thing to do, but new, fresh foliage soon grows, transforming the appearance of the plants. At the same time, lift, divide and replant overgrown clumps (see March). After pruning and dividing, feed with an organic fertiliser, watering it in if the soil is dry.

CUT BACK ALYSSUM, ARABIS AND AUBRIETA These spreading and trailing plants all tend to become bare and tatty, especially in the centre of the plant, when the flowers have gone over. Trim them back hard, almost to the ground, and fresh new growth will soon appear,

PERENNIALS *continued*

producing a mass of flowers on a neat compact plant next year. If you don't do this every year, then as the plant ages it will be more reluctant to grow from the base when cut hard back. After pruning, feed with an organic fertiliser. Mulch with fresh gravel or grit if the plants are growing in an alpine setting.

DIVIDE EARLY PRIMULAS AFTER FLOWERING. With larger clumps you may have to use two forks back to back to prise them apart initially, but after that the clumps can generally be pulled apart by hand. Cut off most of the old foliage, leaving about 5cm (2in) on each division, and replant in the original position after revitalizing the soil with garden compost or manure. Water in well if the soil is dry. Alternatively, line out the small divisions in a corner of the vegetable garden and replant them in the border in the autumn.

SOW SEED OF PERENNIALS OUTSIDE. There is no cheaper and more satisfying way to grow perennials than from seed, especially collected from plants growing in the garden rather than from a packet. Most perennials can be grown this way: achilleas, alstroemerias and hardy geraniums are especially easy examples. Take out shallow drills in the soil after raking it to a fine tilth. Water the drills if the soil is dry, allowing it to soak away before sowing the seeds as thinly as possible, then cover lightly with dry soil. Label each row. After a few weeks, when the seedlings are large enough to handle, they can be transplanted to a nursery area to grow on and bulk up. You can also sow the seed in pots to plant out in autumn, just as for ornamental cabbages (see facing page).

BULBS

CONTINUE DEADHEADING spring-flowering bulbs that are still going. Snap off tulip heads and leave the stalks. You must leave the foliage intact for at least six weeks after the last flower. If you must move them before this (for example if they have been grown in amongst wallflowers and forget-me-nots for a spring display), you can move them temporarily, heeling them in in a corner of a border or in the vegetable garden. Lift the bulbs carefully with a fork. Dig a shallow trench where they are to be heeled in, and place the bulbs in the trench with the foliage above ground. Cover the bulbs with some soil, and lift them when the foliage has died down. Don't forget to label the row or if you have a memory like mine you'll forget where they are.

FEED SPRING-FLOWERING BULBS now, whether still in place or heeled in, to encourage the development of the new flower bud in the bulb for next spring. A general organic fertiliser sprinkled around the bulbs according to the manufacturer's instructions is ideal. Water it in if the weather is dry.

Lifting bulbs These tulips can be uprooted carefully and heeled in in a corner to die down.

ANNUALS & BEDDING

Frost protection If you can't resist buying frost-tender bedding, shelter it until the end of May.

CLEAR SPRING-FLOWERING BEDDING PLANTS and prepare the ground for summer bedding. Now that spring-flowering plants like wallflowers, forget-me-nots and winter-flowering pansies are coming to the end of their flowering time they need to be cleared away and the ground prepared for summer bedding to go in. The old spring-flowering plants can be consigned to the compost heap to ensure a supply of valuable organic matter next year.

After the old plants have been removed, lightly fork over the soil, removing any weeds. At this time you can add a little organic fertiliser, as it breaks down slowly in the soil and will therefore be available to the plants when they are planted out. But don't apply too much, or you will get a lot of soft growth at the expense of flowers. A light sprinkling is sufficient. Also, don't dig in organic matter at this time for the same reason. The time for digging in organic matter is in the autumn. Most of the tender summer bedding plants we grow come from the warmer parts of the world like South Africa, where the soil is baked, and very poor

as far as the availability of nutrients is concerned, and this is why they don't require a lot of fertiliser to grow well.

HARDEN OFF SUMMER BEDDING PLANTS. Plants like petunias and French and African marigolds – whether bought now or raised from seed (see Under Glass) – need to be acclimatized to outdoor conditions before planting out at the end of the month and into early June. Do this by putting them into a cold frame and gradually opening the tops of the frames more each day until they can be left off altogether. Close the frame at night, and keep something like some fleece handy to throw over the frames, just in case a sharp frost is forecast. If you are bringing a lot of plants out in batches then in mild areas, the plants can be moved under a plastic cloche after a few days – but still be ready to give them extra protection at night.

TAKE CUTTINGS FROM TENDER PERENNIALS like argyranthemums, pelargoniums and fuchsias. You may have overwintered such plants from last year especially for the purpose of taking cuttings (see Under Glass in previous months). Or, you may have some that have miraculously survived in sheltered spots, and taking cuttings from these will produce stronger, fresher plants that will flower better than the parent (as well as increasing your stock). Alternatively, you can now buy quite good-sized plants from garden centres, from which you can harvest several young shoots for cuttings without harming the parent unduly. Cuttings taken now will provide plants for flowering well into autumn, but you must have somewhere frost-free to raise them until all danger of frost has passed. Shoots from all these plants can be removed when they are about 7.5–10cm (3–4in) long. Trim the cutting immediately below a leaf joint, and dip the end in hormone rooting solution. Put the cuttings into pots containing cuttings compost and water in well. Place a polythene bag over the pot and place on a shady windowsill if you have not got a greenhouse. They will root in about three to four weeks when they can be potted up ready to plant out in June.

THIN OUT HARDY ANNUALS SOWN EARLIER. If they are not thinned, the plants will become leggy and will not flower well. Thin out to leave one seedling at least every 15cm (6in). The taller the plants, the more space they require. Check seed packets for more precise details on spacing.

The easiest way to thin out the seedlings is to choose the one you want to keep, hold it in position with a finger on the soil each side of the stem, and pull or pinch out the others around it. Measure the gap to the next one and do the same until the job's done. Most hardy annuals don't transplant well when they grow taller, so if you thin out promptly as soon as the seedlings can be handled, they can be transplanted to fill any gaps in the rows, or put in other parts of the garden. Some of the very tall annuals – for example, cleome – need some support with twiggy sticks to prevent them flopping over. After that is done, all you have to do is enjoy the show.

Support for annuals *Twiggy sticks make informal supports for cottage-style annual flowers.*

TRAIN SWEET PEAS. Sweet peas planted out earlier will be growing vigorously towards the end of the month, and they may need a little steering in the right direction. If the plants are being grown for general display in the garden, tying them to the support initially will be all the help they need as the tendrils will then twine themselves around whatever they touch.

SOW SPRING-FLOWERING BIENNIALS. These are the wallflowers, *Bellis perennis*, forget-me-nots, sweet Williams and winter-flowering pansies that have just been cleared to make way for the summer bedding. The easiest way to remember the time for sowing these to flower next spring is to do it when the old ones are beginning to fade. Find a corner in the vegetable plot or other corner of a border to sow the seeds. One point to bear in mind is to try not to grow wallflowers in the same piece of ground year after year. They belong to the same family as cabbages and cauliflowers (brassicas) and are subject to the same diseases such as clubroot (swelling of the roots), which is incurable and persists in the soil for many years. The preparation for sowing is the same for other seeds. Rake the soil to a fine tilth and level it off. Take out shallow drills with a stick or cane about 15cm (6in) apart, and water them before sowing if the soil is dry. Sow the seeds thinly along the row and cover over lightly with dry soil, and firm gently with your hand. Label each row so you don't forget what is what. In a few weeks (see July) the seedlings will need to be thinned or transplanted to grow on with more space between them, before being planted in their final positions in autumn.

SOW ORNAMENTAL CABBAGES AND KALES. These handsome ornamental plants are grown for winter bedding displays. Their coloured foliage comes in shades of red, green and white. The colours are more intense when temperatures drop during autumn. Sow the seeds in 8cm (3in) pots of seed compost at a temperature of 18°C (65°F). Pot on when the plants are large enough to handle. They can be kept outside until planting time in autumn.

Ornamental cabbages *Sow plants such as these for winter colour and spring bedding now.*

CONTAINERS

CLEAR OUT SPRING BEDDING FROM CONTAINERS to make way for summer bedding plants. It is worthwhile removing some of the old compost if it has been in the container since last year. Some new compost will give the plants a fresh start. For containers, John Innes potting compost is best as it contains soil, and does not dry out as quickly as soilless composts do. Another advantage is that it is heavier than soilless composts, so containers are less likely to become top-heavy and be blown over in windy conditions.

IN MILD AREAS PLANT UP CONTAINERS with frost-tender plants towards the end of the month (see also June). If you haven't grown any plants, then pop down to the garden centre where you will find plenty. But do bear in mind not to plant out tender plants until at least the end of the month or early next month in more northerly parts of the country. Keep some fleece handy to drape over them at night if frosts are forecast.

IF YOU BUY READY-PLANTED HANGING BASKETS this month (and you may be tempted to do so in order to get the ones you want), you must harden them off to get them used to outdoor conditions (see also Under Glass). Leave them out for increasingly long periods until they can be left out at night as long as frost is not forecast.

WATER AND FEED ALL CONTAINERS REGULARLY. As the weather warms up, watering containers can become a daily or twice-daily task. Hanging baskets in particular are prone

CONTAINERS *continued*

to drying out quickly, being exposed to the sun and wind. Mixing up a feed solution every time plants need feeding can be very time-consuming; the easiest way to feed lots of plants in containers is to make up a feed solution in bulk. Fill a large tank such as a plastic water butt with water, mixing in plant food according to the manufacturer's instructions. This can be fed to the plants at every watering, so cutting down on the work. A high-potash feed is best for the production of flowers and a prolonged display. High-nitrogen fertilisers will result in a lot of leafy growth at the expense of flowers.

WATCH OUT FOR VINE WEEVIL.
Make sure you don't introduce vine weevil into containers along with new plants. They can wreak havoc when they multiply within the closed confines of a tub or windowbox. Knock new plants out of their pots and look for the small white grubs, which eat at the roots. The adult weevils are rarely seen as they only come out at night; notched foliage is a giveaway sign. However, it is the grubs that do the most damage. There are several products on the

Vine weevil grubs These larvae eat the roots of plants and can easily kill them.

market now for controlling vine weevil. The most effective organic control is a biological nematode which can be bought by mail order. There are also composts that have been treated with an insecticide that controls vine weevil, and these are useful for containers.

TENDER PERENNIALS IN POTS AND TENDER SHRUBS PUT INSIDE FOR THE WINTER can be put out towards the end of the month in most parts of the country. In northern parts wait until early June. Generally, the sooner these plants can be put outside the better. They will benefit from the fresh air and a shower of rain after their prolonged period indoors will do them the world of good. Larger-leaved shrubs, such as bay, can have their leaves wiped with a damp cloth. This will remove any dust and dirt accumulated indoors. Be sure to keep up with watering and feeding because during warm weather pots can dry out very quickly. During very hot spells you may have to water once or twice a day.

Potted bay Be careful of your back when moving heavy plants in pots outdoors for the summer.

PONDS

Duckweed Before floating leaves such as lilypads unfurl fully to suppress it, duckweed may multiply.

FEED FISH REGULARLY now the weather is warming up and the fish are becoming more active. Give them just enough food to be eaten in a short time otherwise the leftovers rot in the water, encouraging algae to grow. Feeding once a day will be sufficient. On the whole fish tend to fend for themselves so don't worry if you miss a day or two.

REMOVE DUCKWEED AND BLANKET WEED FROM THE POND. Duckweed is a floating plant which, if it gets established, is almost impossible to get rid of. It is easily removed using a net like the ones sold for children at the seaside, or an old kitchen sieve strapped to a broom handle. Blanket weed is a type of algae which resembles wet, bright green candy floss. It too can be easily removed, by twisting it around a or cane. It's quite a pleasant job for a Sunday morning.

To discourage the growth of duckweed and other algae, grow plants with floating leaves like waterlilies, which help to cover the surface of the water. Once they are in full leaf in the

summer, you should see the problem lessen. Oxygenating plants also help reduce the possibility of algae growing. Keeping the water moving, either by having a small waterfall feature or a fountain, is another good way to prevent the growth of algae.

THIN OUT EXCESSIVE GROWTH ON AQUATIC PLANTS, and generally tidy up the pond before summer. The early part of the month is a good time to do this as the plants really start into growth. Aquatic plants that have been in place for three or four years and are rather overgrown can be lifted out and divided now if you have not already done so (see April). Doing all this work may cause the water to turn a bit murky, but it will soon settle after a few days and become clear again.

FEED AQUATIC PLANTS using special aquatic plant fertiliser. You must buy this rather than using garden fertilisers, which will cause an explosion of algal growth. It needs to be placed in the containers holding the plants (it is available as pellets that can be pushed into the compost) and not just sprinkled on the surface of the pond.

CONTINUE TO PLANT NEW AQUATIC PLANTS, as last month. The water in the pond is beginning to warm up so in the south, towards the end of the month when danger of frost is passed is an ideal time to plant unusual tender floating plants like water hyacinth (*Eichhornia crassipes*) and the water chestnut (*Trapa natans*). In cold areas it is safer to wait until next month.

MAKING A HALF-BARREL POND

IF YOU HAVEN'T ROOM for a large pond, this is the ideal way to introduce water into the garden. It's easy to plant and easy to look after. It will look good on a patio – or, you could put one in a heated conservatory and grow more exotic water plants.

YOU WILL NEED: A half-barrel from an aquatic department or specialist, which will have been pre-treated against rot • Mesh baskets for planting • A little coarse grit • A couple of half bricks to stand marginal plants on. Tiny *Nymphaea tetragona* 'Helvola' is the waterlily to look for; we also used tall, slender *Typha minima*, and the feathery *Myriophyllum aquaticum* as an oxygenating plant; this will need regular thinning. Ask for advice on other plants suitable for such a small feature at your aquatic centre.

④ Place the marginal plants in carefully so as not to disturb the soil in the baskets.

⑤ Waterlilies and other deeper water plants can go in placed on the bottom of the barrel.

① If you can soak the barrel in a large container of water to make the wood swell and make it waterproof. Otherwise keep filling it until the wood is sealed. Plant the plants in special aquatic baskets using ordinary garden soil.

② Top off with a mulch of coarse grit to prevent the soil seeping into the water.

③ Place a half brick in the pond for marginal plants.

⑥ The mature pond will attract wildlife into the garden for a drink as well as looking beautiful.

LAWNS

MOW ESTABLISHED LAWNS ONCE A WEEK now that the grass is growing well. Each time you mow, lower the blades of the mower slightly, cutting the grass a little closer each time. Try not to lower the blades too much or the lawn will be "scalped". This makes the grass turn yellow, and causes bare patches to develop, allowing in weeds and moss – and it looks horrible too.

FEED ESTABLISHED LAWNS if you haven't already done so (see April). Follow the manufacturer's instructions carefully. Some modern fertilisers have anti-scorch properties, so it doesn't matter if you are a little heavy-handed when applying them, within reason of course. But it is also wasteful to apply too much.

TREAT WEEDS IN THE LAWN with a selective weedkiller. This is a good month to do this, as weeds are now growing vigorously and the weedkiller will act more effectively on them. It is important always to use a selective lawn weedkiller on a lawn. This only affects broad-leaved weeds in the lawn. Any other sort of weedkiller will kill off the grass too. Again follow instructions to the letter. Don't put on a bit extra for luck, as this may harm the grass. If your lawn has only a few weeds, such as dandelions, then you could use one of the "spot-treatment" weedkillers. These are painted or dabbed onto the leaves of individual weeds.

Grass clippings taken from the lawn just after applying weedkiller should not be put on the compost heap, as traces of the herbicide will be in the clippings, and could harm other plants in the garden. If you haven't the time to apply fertiliser and selective weedkiller separately, there are several products on the market that combine a fertiliser, weedkiller and moss killer all in one.

RENOVATE DAMAGED EDGES AND BARE PATCHES all through the summer until autumn, as needed. See January and February for details.

NEW LAWNS

FINISH SOWING NEW LAWNS before the weather becomes too warm (see April for details). The best times to sow grass seed are spring and autumn, when the soil is warm and generally moist.

ROLL NEWLY SOWN LAWNS, if you can, when the seed has germinated and the new grass is about 2.5cm (1in) high. The roller on the back of a cylinder mower is perfect for the job. Rolling encourages the grass shoots to grow from the base of the plant, ensuring a close-knit sward.

NEWLY SOWN LAWNS can have their first cut when the grass is about 5cm (2in) high. Set mower blades at their highest setting. Gradually reduce the height of cut each time you mow, but don't cut new lawns from seed too close in their first year.

New grass
Newly sown lawns may need their first cut this month.

VEGETABLES & HERBS

HARVESTING

HARVEST EARLY CROPS such as radishes and salad leaves as they mature. Established beds of asparagus will become ready to cut this month: cut spears by slicing cleanly through them at ground level.

SOWING INDOORS

VEGETABLES CAN STILL BE SOWN INDOORS to shorten the growing period. Crops to sow now include courgettes, marrows, runner beans, French beans, squashes and sweetcorn. This month, you can sow both indoors and outside at the same time. The plants sown indoors will grow a little quicker than those outside, giving a continuity of crops and not a glut all at once.

SOW CARDOONS. These relatives of globe artichokes are tall, handsome plants in their own right, and are often grown for their ornamental value alone. But the stems can be blanched in the summer for cooking later. Sow two seeds to each small pot and cover lightly with compost. They don't need especially high temperatures to germinate: putting the pots on a warm windowsill is sufficient, but placing them in a heated propagator will hasten germination. Pull out the weakest seedling when they are large enough to handle and plant out the one left in the pot in early to mid-June.

SOW RIDGE CUCUMBERS. These can be sown early in the month for planting out at the beginning of June. Sow these in small pots containing a compost suitable for seed-sowing, placing two seeds in each pot. Push the seeds into

Wetting drills
Especially now that the soil is drier, water along drills before you sow seeds.

the compost to about 2cm (1in) deep, and cover with compost. For quick germination, place the pots in a propagator, but this is not entirely necessary at this time of year.

SOWING AND PLANTING OUTDOORS

CONTINUE SUCCESSIONAL SOWING of beetroot, cabbage, carrots, salad onions, lettuce, peas, broad beans, radishes and turnips. Sow in short rows to prevent a glut of crops at one time. Take out shallow drills and water before sowing the seeds if the soil is dry. Sow the seeds thinly and cover with dry soil. When the seedlings are large enough, thin them out according to the spacing given on the seed packet. Large seeds like peas and broad beans can be space-sown, and won't need thinning out.

PLANT OUT SELF-BLANCHING CELERY towards the end of the month. Make sure the ground has been prepared thoroughly, incorporating plenty of organic matter to retain moisture – celery needs plenty of water through the growing season. Unlike blanching celery, there is no need to grow this type in a trench to blanch the stems. It is best, though, to grow it in blocks rather than in straight rows. Growing in blocks will aid the blanching process for most of the plants; for those around the outside of the block, a strip of plastic supported on canes around the edge of the block will improve blanching of the outer stems.

SOW WITLOOF CHICORY for forcing in winter. This vegetable is not eaten during the summer, but grown in order that during winter, its roots can be forced for tightly packed hearts or 'chicons' which are blanched and then cooked or eaten raw. Sow the seeds in drills in the usual manner, watering the drills before sowing if the soil is dry. Space the rows and thin out the seedlings when they are large enough according to the instructions on the seed packet. Keep well watered through the growing season, and they will form good roots for forcing in winter.

GLOBE ARTICHOKES SOWN EARLIER under cover can be planted out towards the end of the month. Traditionally globe artichokes are grown

Planting out celery *Planted in blocks, the plants will shade each other, aiding blanching.*

PLANTING OUT LEEKS

For leeks sown several seeds to a module, plant out the entire cluster without disturbing the rootball.

Drop single leek plants into a deep hole made with a cane or dibber. Do not firm them in, but water gently.

as perennials and planted at a distance of 90cm (3ft). You can grow them as biennials and plant them much closer together, 45cm (18in) apart. This year, pinch out flower buds from every other plant. After taking crops from the others this summer, remove them. The pinched-out plants will provide good crops next year, when you can also plant new plants between them, setting up a year-on-year cycle. Growing young plants each year also gives a continuity of crop throughout each season.

LEEKS SOWN EARLIER CAN BE PLANTED OUT if not done last month. The method of planting will depend on the way the young plants were raised, but with all planting, apply a general organic fertiliser a few days beforehand.

If the seeds were sown in seed trays and the plants left to grow on in the trays until 10–12cm (4–5in) high, they can be planted in individual holes. Make a hole about 15cm (6in) deep with a dibber and put one plant in each hole. Complete the row and water in. The plants should be about 30cm (1ft)

apart each way. Do not firm: watering them in will automatically wash some soil down the hole to cover the roots.

If seeds were multiple-sown in modular trays for deep beds, the small clumps of five or six plants can be planted in their clusters, 15–22cm (6–9in) apart each way. This way you get more weight of crop per square metre than if they are grown in conventional straight rows.

PLANT OUT MARROWS AND COURGETTES at the end of the month. These plants are tender and prone to damage from frosts. Plant into soil that has been enriched with plenty of organic matter, as marrows and courgettes require a lot of water during the growing season. They do take up quite a bit of room, so space them at 90cm (3ft) each way. Keep the plants well watered through the summer. If you do not have room on the vegetable garden to grow these plants, why not grow one or two in ornamental borders? The large leaves are bold and attractive and will provide a good contrast to other foliage plants in the garden, and the edible parts are a bonus. Trailing varieties can be grown up strong canes, bean poles or other forms of support to make an attractive feature, which also saves space at ground level.

DIRECT-SOW runner beans, French beans and sweetcorn. Although these plants are all tender, by sowing outside this month the seeds will germinate when the threat of frost has largely passed in most parts of the country. Seeds of runner beans can be sown two to the base of each bean pole or bamboo cane. The weaker seedling can

be removed when the seeds have germinated. Sowing two seeds per "station" also acts as an insurance policy in case one seed fails to germinate.

Sow sweetcorn in blocks (see also June), 60cm (1ft) apart each way, again with two seeds in each hole. French beans can be sown in rows 60cm (1ft) apart with the seeds 15–22cm (6–9in) apart in the rows.

Seedlings of all of these plants can be damaged by slugs as they germinate. To avoid this problem, after sowing the seeds cover them with plastic lemonade or water bottles that have had the bottom cut out, pushing them into the ground. To get the bottle round a cane, cut it lengthwise. These improvised cloches will also act like mini-greenhouses, hastening germination and giving some protection should a late frost occur.

TRANSPLANT BRUSSELS SPROUTS and other winter brassicas sown earlier. These plants can now be transplanted to their cropping positions. They do take up a fair amount of space over a long

TRANSPLANTING BRASSICAS

Planting through porous membrane (here a paper mulching sheet) will protect the plants from cabbage root fly.

Alternatively, individual collars can be bought or made and fitted around the stem of each plant.

VEGETABLES & HERBS *continued*

period of time. But other short-term crops such as lettuce, radishes and turnips can be grown between the brassicas to use the space efficiently. This method of double cropping is known as intercropping, and it makes the best use of the land available.

All the brassicas to be planted out should be well watered beforehand, as they wilt very quickly, especially in warm weather. One point to bear in mind is that cauliflowers will not produce a proper curd if they receive even the slightest check to their growth. So watering before planting out and afterwards is very important. The ideal stage at which to transplant the seedlings is when they have made two or three true leaves. The plants should be set out at a minimum of 60cm (2ft) each way.

If not planting through a membrane (see previous page), then after planting all your plants put a brassica collar round the base of each to prevent the cabbage root fly from laying its eggs at the base of the stem. These brassica collars can be bought from a garden centre; alternatively, 15cm (6in) squares of old carpet work just as well.

SOW CHARD AND LEAF BEET. Swiss chard has large leaves and pure white stems, both of which can be eaten, the leaves being used in a similar way to spinach. There are also ruby and "rainbow" chards, with deep red and multicoloured midribs respectively, which look good among ornamentals. Leaf beet or perpetual spinach is also a good substitute for spinach as it, like chard, is less susceptible to bolting (running to seed) than spinach is. Often spinach will start bolting just a few

weeks after the seeds germinate. Sow the seeds in drills according to the directions on the seed packets, watering the drills first if the soil is dry. Thin out the seedlings when they are large enough to handle and keep them well watered during the summer.

IT'S NOW TOO LATE to sow tomato seeds, but garden centres will have a choice of plants on sale. Try bush varieties like 'Red Alert' and 'Tornado', and you won't have to stake them or pinch out sideshoots. Plant them about 60cm (2ft) apart and mulch them with straw to prevent the fruits rotting on the soil. Alternatively plant them through a weed-suppressing membrane, which will allow moisture through whilst keeping weeds under control and helping to retain moisture in the soil.

LOOKING AFTER CROPS

PINCH OUT THE TOPS OF BROAD BEANS when they flower to discourage

Pinching broad beans *By removing the tender tip you take away the part blackfly like best.*

Carrot fly barrier *Fence carrots with fine mesh around canes to keep this pest away.*

blackfly, which love the young, succulent tips of the plants. By removing the young tips when several trusses of flowers have developed, there should be less need to spray to control these aphids. Provide some support for broad beans with string stretched between canes at either end of the row. The plants tend to flop over when the pods develop.

PROTECT CARROTS FROM CARROT FLY. The female of this pest flies around just above soil level seeking out juicy carrots by their smell, and laying her eggs at the base of the foliage. The small larvae of the fly burrow into the root of the carrot making holes in it, causing rot to set in; the carrots are then unappealing to eat and certainly useless for storing over winter. This pest also attacks parsnips and parsley. The easiest way to protect the plants is to cover them with horticultural fleece, leaving it over the crop permanently as there is another generation of carrot fly later in August. Or, you can erect a barrier made from horticultural fleece, fine mesh or polythene supported on a wooden framework, preventing the

carrot fly from getting to the crops.

To minimise the threat of carrot fly, sow seeds as thinly as possible to reduce the need for thinning the seedlings. Don't leave thinnings lying around, as the smell of the bruised leaves will attract any carrot fly which are around. You could also try growing alternate rows of onions and carrots, the theory being that the strong pungent aroma from the onions will mask the smell of the carrots, so confusing the carrot fly. There are some varieties of carrots, 'Flyaway' and 'Sytan', which are less susceptible to attack from carrot fly.

THIN FLORENCE FENNEL SOWN LAST MONTH. Thin the seedlings to 20cm (8in) apart in the row. The rows should be 45cm (1½ft) apart. The swollen stems at the base of this plant have a pleasant taste of aniseed. More can be sown through the summer. If sown in late summer, cover the plants with cloches for winter use.

KEEP YOUNG VEGETABLE PLANTS WELL WATERED, especially if the weather is dry.

HOE REGULARLY TO KEEP DOWN WEEDS. This job is well worth doing regularly, as it will save a lot of back-breaking work if the weeds are left to grow. Catch weed seedlings when they are small, and they can be left on the surface of the soil to dry out on a warm sunny day.

Not only are weeds kept under control by hoeing, but a tilth of crumbly soil is maintained on the surface of the soil. This helps to retain some moisture in the soil, reducing the need for watering.

FRUIT

EARTH UP EARLY POTATOES, drawing a little soil up over the emerging shoots. This not only protects them from any late frost, but also encourages the development of roots further up the stems, therefore increasing the yield. Keep earthing up potatoes at intervals as it covers any developing potatoes in the soil, preventing them turning green in the light. When potatoes turn green they become poisonous.

TOMATOES SOWN LAST MONTH need potting on now (see Under Glass, April). Those being grown as cordons should have the sideshoots which form at the leaf axils (where the leaf stalk joins the main stem) removed. Do this when they are quite small by rubbing them out with your forefinger and thumb, and it won't be such a shock to the plant. Once the first truss of flowers has faded and fruits are setting, feed the plants weekly with a high-potash fertiliser.

HERBS

LIFT AND DIVIDE MINT. Mint is always welcome in many dishes but in the garden it can become invasive so it is wise to lift and divide it before it becomes too large and takes over the garden. Be sure to remove as much of the roots spreading out from the plant as possible, because if these are left in they will continue to grow. New, small divisions can be replanted in the same place. To prevent mint becoming too invasive, grow it in pots. By growing it in containers you can have it by the back door, so the mint is to hand whenever you want it.

LOOKING AFTER CROPS

CONTROL PESTS BY PUTTING UP PHEROMONE TRAPS. Many pests are difficult to control nowadays because they are becoming immune to the chemicals we use to control them. Also, insects often fly in and away again very quickly, often not staying long enough to be hit with a spray. An alternative way to control some pests is by using traps. Codling moth is a good example. During May and June the moths mate and lay eggs on apples, and the eggs hatch into maggots which tunnel into the fruits. Male codling moths are attracted to the females by a pheromone, or hormonal scent, that the females give off to attract the male when they are ready to mate. This pheromone is now produced artificially, and can be bought in a small container which is placed in a small plastic housing, rather like a bird house. In the house is a piece of sticky paper impregnated with this substance to capture males attracted by the scent. This reduces the mating success of the moths and so fewer viable eggs are laid. You will need one trap for every three to five trees.

TUCK STRAW UNDER STRAWBERRIES to protect the fruits from rotting because they are resting on wet ground. This also prevents the fruits being spoiled by rain-splashed soil and slugs. Few things are more annoying to town gardeners than being told to use materials such as straw that are common enough in the countryside, but impossible to obtain in the city. But don't despair: garden centres stock special strawberry mats as an alternative to straw. As the fruits develop, cover the plants with netting to keep the birds from getting them. Make sure the netting is properly secured to prevent birds getting tangled up in it. If you are concerned about birds being caught in netting, use horticultural fleece to cover the plants instead.

REMOVE RUNNERS FROM STRAWBERRIES (the long stems that creep along the soil, developing plantlets along their length) if they are not

PROTECTING STRAWBERRIES

Tuck straw under strawberries and the fruits will not be damaged by splashes of mud.

Strawberry mats are an alternative to straw. They should be stocked by any garden centre selling fruit plants.

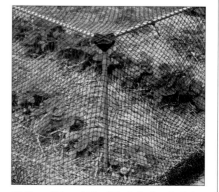

Netting will keep birds off the fruits, but check it every day to ensure that birds are not caught up.

required for propagating new plants. If runners are allowed to develop then a great deal of the plants' energy will go into producing them. The crop of fruit will be poorer, and the strawberry bed will end up as a mass of tangled plants which will be difficult to weed. Putting straw or strawberry mats down to protect the fruits from being splashed with soil will also be next to impossible. If you want to let a few plants develop runners for new plants (see Propagation, below), pick the flowers off these plants and sacrifice their crop so that you get really strong young plantlets.

TAKE OFF ALL COVERS AND PROTECTION from peach, nectarine and cherry trees. But continue to protect late blossoms on fruit trees and bushes from late frosts. Sharp frosts can still occur at any time this month, especially in northern parts of the country. The easiest way to give protection in a hurry is to use horticultural fleece. This can be thrown over small trees or draped over trees trained against walls and fences, and will help keep off a few degrees of frost. You might get fed up with hearing gardeners going on about late frosts at this time of year when it seems so mild, but they do happen often, so it is always better to be aware of them and not allow them to ruin your crop of hard-earned fruit later in the summer.

KEEP NEWLY PLANTED FRUIT PLANTS well watered. Young plants need tender loving care to help them get established in their first year after planting. If they suffer stress due to lack of water at any time, it makes them

FRUIT *continued*

more vulnerable to attack from pests and diseases, and reduces the amount of growth and subsequently the amount of fruit produced. It is far better to give them a good soak once a week rather than give smaller amounts every day during dry spells. Scant watering encourages the roots to come nearer the surface of the soil in search of moisture, making them even more vulnerable in drought conditions. And they will be more easily damaged when weeding amongst the plants.

MULCH ALL FRUIT if you have not done so before to retain moisture in the soil. Use well-rotted farmyard manure, garden compost, spent mushroom compost or any other organic matter you can get hold of. If the soil is dry, make sure it is watered well before applying a mulch, as mulches are just as good at keeping moisture out of the soil as keeping it in. If you have the luxury of a sprinkler, leave it on one area at a time for at least two hours to give the area a good soaking, and then mulch. There is no point in giving small amounts of water every day. Instead, concentrate on watering small areas really well in turn, otherwise the water is just wasted. Be sure to check there are no hose restrictions in your area before using a sprinkler.

PRUNING AND TRAINING

PRUNE OUT UNWANTED SHOOTS ON ALL RASPBERRIES. If too many new canes are allowed to develop then, as with strawberry runners, more energy will be put into developing these new canes than into fruit production. Thick, crowded rows are difficult to care for,

and the fruits will receive less ripening sunshine. Another important point is that the more congested the shoots are, the less air will be circulating through the plants and they will therefore be more susceptible to fungal diseases like botrytis. This fungal disease will attack the fruits, causing them to turn brown and rot off. The more air that can circulate around the plants, the less likelihood there is of them being attacked by disease. The canes which are left will also be all the more sturdy, because they have more light and room to develop.

PRUNE PLUMS AND CHERRIES trained against walls and fences (see April). The pruning of these trees is done in spring and summer because they are vulnerable to silverleaf disease, the spores of which enter through wounds. By pruning at this time wounds heal quickly, and there is less chance of the disease getting into the tree. When this year's young shoots have made six leaves, pinch out the growing tip. Once the fruit has been picked, prune back these shoots to about half

Unwanted raspberry canes *If grown too thick to hoe off, cut through the roots with secateurs.*

their length, taking out any overcrowded and unhealthy-looking stems at the same time.

Trained acid cherries like 'Morello' are pruned slightly differently. These produce fruit on two-year-old wood and so you have to think about this when pruning. To start what is an ongoing process, tie in one shoot made last year to fruit this year and tie in a new one alongside it for fruiting the following year. Don't prune these shoots, but remove any surplus ones. When the fruit has been picked, prune out the fruited shoot altogether and the other one tied in alongside will be its fruiting replacement next year, when it in turn will have a new shoot tied in alongside it.

PROPAGATION

IF STRAWBERRY RUNNERS ARE REQUIRED to make new strawberry plants, reduce the runners to about five or six per plant and peg them into small pots of peat-free compost which have been sunk into the ground around the parent.

BEAT THE SEASONS

STRAWBERRY PLANTS that were covered with cloches to hasten fruiting should have the cloches opened up for part of the day now, to allow pollinating insects in to pollinate the flowers – otherwise, no fruits will develop. It may be worth going over a few plants with a small, soft paintbrush transferring pollen from one flower to another to ensure pollination has taken place.

UNDER COVER

Greenhouse blinds *Shading is critical as temperatures rise, especially for young plants*

DAMP DOWN REGULARLY in the greenhouse and conservatory, splashing water on the floor and under staging to increase the humidity levels, ideally 2–3 times a day by mid-summer. Not only is this beneficial to plant growth, it also helps in the control of red spider mite. This microscopic pest can be detected by the mottled appearance it gives the foliage of affected plants. It can also be controlled chemically; alternatively, there is a tiny predatory mite that can be used as a biological control.

SHADE THE GREENHOUSE OR CONSERVATORY. It is best to try to avoid great fluctuations of temperatures under glass, and the best way to reduce the temperature is by using shading.

The cheapest form of shading is a wash for the glass; it comes as a powder (available at most garden centres) which is mixed with water and painted or sprayed on. It can be wiped off with a duster at the end of the summer.

The one problem with this type of shading is that it is there even on dull days, reducing light inside on cloudy days. The alternative is to fit roller blinds. Ideally they should be fitted to the outside of the greenhouse or conservatory when built, and you may have to move fast to find a firm with time to fit them now. A compromise is to use fine mesh netting which can be thrown over the structure on sunny days and taken off on dull days. Staple it to something like roofing laths to weight it down and hold it in place.

CONTINUE TO PRICK OUT AND POT ON seedlings, cuttings and young plants as they need it (see April).

CHECK ALL PLANTS REGULARLY for signs of pests and diseases, which become more prevalent as the weather becomes warmer; you must be vigilant to stop them building up into serious problems. Look on the undersides of leaves for whitefly, and the tips of shoots for greenfly. Small infestations of pests can be picked off, or may be caught on yellow sticky cards. Don't use these traps if you have plenty of predatory insects around, as these will be caught too. Another way to keep pests at bay is with biological controls (see April).

RAISING PLANTS FOR OUTDOORS

PLANT UP HANGING BASKETS AND OTHER CONTAINERS, provided that you can keep them frost-free in the greenhouse or conservatory to grow on, giving them a head start before putting them outside early next month. Pack in as many plants as you can – the more plants, the better will be the display.

HARDEN OFF HANGING BASKETS that were planted up last month to get them used to outdoor conditions. Leave them out for increasingly long periods until they can be left out at night so long as frost is not forecast.

HARDEN OFF BEDDING PLANTS for planting out at the end of the month and early next month. This means getting the plants used to growing in cooler conditions, without checking their growth. The usual way of doing this is to put the plants in cold frames and keep the lids (or lights, as they are known) closed for a few days. Then gradually open them, increasing the ventilation over a period of about a week until the lids can be left off – except on nights when frost is forecast. If you haven't got a cold frame, stand the plants outside for short periods during the day, increasing the amount of time they are left out each day.

Don't be in too much of a hurry to plant out, even though space in the greenhouse and cold frame will be at a premium at this time of year. If the plants have been in their pots or trays longer than they should have and are looking starved, give them a feed with a liquid fertiliser. Follow the manufacturer's instructions carefully.

SOW HALF-HARDY AND HARDY ANNUALS now for autumn colour. Some half-hardy annuals such as clarkia, calendula and candytuft (*Iberis*) can still be sown early in the month to produce flowers in late summer and autumn.

SOW ORNAMENTAL CABBAGES AND KALES (see Annuals and Bedding).

VEGETABLES CAN STILL BE SOWN INDOORS to shorten the growing period (see Vegetables and Herbs).

GLASSHOUSE AND HOUSE PLANTS

POT ON BEGONIAS AND GLOXINIAS which were potted into small pots earlier. Be sure to water the plants well beforehand, otherwise the root ball will remain dry and the roots will not grow into the new compost very well. 12–15cm (5 or 6in) pots are a perfectly adequate size for normal pot plants. If you are growing them for exhibiting they will have to be potted on again into larger pots later in the summer. Leave a gap of about 2.5cm (1in) between the surface of the compost and the rim of the pot to allow room for watering. Water them in after potting to settle the compost around the roots.

SOW HALF-HARDY AND HARDY ANNUALS now for winter-flowering pot plants. Some half-hardy annuals make excellent pot plants in the winter – for example, browallia, calceolarias, cinerarias and schizanthus. Sow them thinly in small pots or trays in a temperature of 18°C (65°F). Prick out the seedlings into small pots when they are large enough to handle. Pot on into larger pots when the roots have filled the smaller pots, and you will have a glorious mix of colour through the winter and spring.

Browallia 'White Troll' This makes a lovely winter pot plant if you can grow it under cover.

CROPS UNDER GLASS

AS FORCED STRAWBERRIES IN POTS FINISH CROPPING, discard the plants. They will not crop well a second time. Pot up some runners from plants in the garden (see Fruit) for next year.

PLANT UP TOMATOES, PEPPERS AND AUBERGINES SOWN EARLIER. Young plants can be potted on into large pots to crop, or put into growbags, or planted in the soil in the greenhouse border. Don't overcrowd them, as they will become drawn and leggy if planted too close together. Cordon tomatoes have weak stems and they will need supporting all season. An alternative to canes or frames is to run baler twine under the plant's rootball when planting, tying the other end of the twine to wire supports strung across the greenhouse roof. The plants are wound round the string as they grow.

CONTINUE TO REMOVE SIDESHOOTS from cordon tomatoes. The smaller the shoots when this is done the better. The best way to do it is to bend them to one side with your thumb and forefinger; they should snap off cleanly. If the shoots have grown too large to snap off, use a sharp knife, but have a weak solution of a garden disinfectant in a container with you and dip the knife into it each time a shoot is cut off. This sterilizes the knife and prevents the spread of virus diseases between the plants.

FEED ALL TOMATOES, PEPPERS AND AUBERGINES with a high-potash fertiliser every week from now on through the season for good crops.

JUNE

The garden in **June**

Summer is here at last. This is a time of year when the gardener can begin to enjoy the fruits of his or her labours. Above all else, do take time to appreciate the garden, and don't let it become a chore.

Ornamental borders will soon be at the peak of perfection, and there are plenty of early summer vegetables to be savoured now. Towards the end of the month soft fruit will also be ripening, to provide a mouthwatering selection of currants and berries during the rest of the summer. Again towards the end of the month, roses begin to flower in earnest. With most the scent is wonderful, and there is a terrific selection of flower colours and shapes available. Climbing and rambler roses look particularly good around doors and scrambling up through trees and large shrubs. At your local garden centre there will be wonderful displays of roses in bloom grown in containers; take some home and plant them for instant colour in the garden.

Most of the sowing, pricking out and potting on will have been done so you can now spend a little time relaxing in the garden. The long summer evenings are pure joy, and there is nothing better in the cool of a summer's evening than to sit quietly in the garden with a glass of something refreshing. Listen to the birds and insects and take in the scents (which are often stronger in the evening), and enjoy the sights and sounds of your own private piece of paradise. Pure bliss!

Wildlife hedge ▷
Exuberant informal hedges of native plants such as wild roses, elder and hawthorn do need space, but nothing brings the countryside into the garden more effectively.

The start of dry spells

The weather in June is usually quite warm, with few days of rain. There are often occasional thunderstorms followed by hot, dry spells, so keep a watchful eye on all newly planted plants and water them as and when required. With the sun now quite strong it is time to shade greenhouses and conservatories throughout the day to prevent plants being scorched in oven-like temperatures. Good ventilation is also vital, and the ventilators can usually be left open day and night through the summer. Thankfully, all tender plants can now be put outside as there should be little fear of night frosts. Now is the time to plant up all those container, basket and bedding schemes you have been dreaming about. Cluttered greenhouse benches, conservatories and windowsills can be cleared of all the young and tender plants sheltering indoors. If you haven't been growing on your own summer bedding, then get down to your garden centre or nursery as soon as possible, before all the best plants are snapped up. Even if you don't think you're a "bedding person", just take a look. You're bound to be tempted by some of the lovely new selections that have appeared in the last few years. Don't be afraid to plant up closely, leaving much less space than when setting out hardy

◁ **Damask roses**
The old garden roses usually choose this month to give their single, stunning show of evocatively scented flowers.

Water wildlife ▷
Even newly made garden ponds and water features should by now be attracting fascinating new visitors.

garden plants. After all, the plants only have to last a season. It's no bad idea to overestimate your needs when raising or buying bedding plants, as you'll always find gaps for any spares to fill.

Pests on the march

Pests and diseases are now on the attack in full force in the warm conditions both inside and outside. Biological controls are the way forward, especially in the greenhouse. Conditions indoors are more favourable to biological controls because most need warm temperatures to be effective.

Wherever possible, try to use organic means to control pests and diseases, rather than resorting instinctively to an arsenal of chemicals. Most problems with pests and diseases can be controlled by good garden hygiene and by good growing and gardening practices: not allowing plants to grow too closely together, and feeding them to encourage strong growth – but not lush, soft growth which is more susceptible to attack. By following these simple steps the plants will not only be healthier but also more able to shrug off attacks from pests and

△ **Meadow mood**
Grasses and wildflowers will attract bees and butterflies, but are also rich food resources for many other less conspicuous creatures.

WEATHER WATCH

At last we can look forward to warm sunny days: very warm at times, with temperatures reaching 20–22°C in places. In the north, average temperatures will be slightly cooler, but still a respectable 16–18°C. Don't let young plants suffer through lack of water during hot spells. Getting them well established in their first year is the most important consideration.

June is usually calm, with the exception of the south-western approaches, other coastal areas and the north-west coast of Scotland. As the height above sea level increases, so does the strength of the winds; this is often why wind farms with their huge windmills are seen on high ground and near coasts.

Thankfully there are usually more sunny days than dull, overcast ones this month. The north of the country gets less sunshine, with the Highlands of Scotland averaging 157 hrs this month and the Home Counties of England around 204 hrs. The north-west of England usually gets around 180 hrs and East Anglia about 190 hrs of direct sunshine.

This is usually one of the driest months of the year. There are occasional thunderstorms, but they tend to pass quickly and do little to replenish water in the soil. But the weather does vary from year to year and sometimes June can be quite wet, especially, and predictably perhaps, in northern and north-western parts. Average rainfall for the month falls sharply from 114mm in north-west Scotland down to 50mm in the north of England and 47mm in the south-east. On average it will rain on one day in every three in England, so you can never be guaranteed several dry days in succession.

Although it has been known for freak weather conditions to produce a sudden fall of snow in June, this is an extremely rare occurrence. Certainly no snow will lie on the ground anywhere except on the very highest peaks.

Clearing the greenhouse ▷
By now, most keen propagators will barely be able to move in their greenhouses, but thankfully, June nights should be reliably warm, and all the plants here can be put outside.

diseases, thereby reducing the need for chemical controls which do so much damage to our precious environment.

The way ahead for the weather

There is considerable debate these days about climate change and how this will affect us in the future, but it is difficult to predict what may happen in the longer term. The consensus of opinion seems to be that the south and east will become drier and warmer, while the north gets wetter and cooler. There will also be a tendency towards more extreme weather, and we have already witnessed severe droughts and dramatic floods in some countries.

Conserving water

With the effects of climate change becoming more apparent, we must do our best to conserve the natural resources of the planet. If you have not already done so earlier in the year, spread a mulch of organic matter over any bare soil after rain or watering to conserve moisture. Another way to conserve moisture and to keep weeds at bay is to use ground cover plants. There is a very wide choice of plants available from garden centres and nurseries that form a very effective green cover over the soil.

If you haven't already got one, install a water butt outside the greenhouse or conservatory to catch valuable rain water. Plants always grow much better when watered with rain water than with tap water, especially if you live in an area with hard water, which is alkaline. You can tell if you've got hard water if you see lime deposits on the inside of your kettle. Plants like rhododendrons and azaleas growing in pots prefer acid conditions, and hard water doesn't do them much good. Keeping a water butt for rain water for these plants is very worthwhile.

The reason plants in general prefer rain water is that it lacks the chemicals routinely added to tap water to eradicate any harmful bacteria for human consumption. Plants don't have kidneys, as we do, to filter out these harsh chemicals.

Keeping the garden looking good

Don't get too depressed about the climate, because nature always seems to balance things out. There will be plenty of opportunities to enjoy the garden on warm, sunny June days. There are plenty of jobs, too, to be getting on with. Spring-flowering plants may need some attention now their main season of display is over. Pruning shrubs and trimming and dividing perennials will ensure that they give a good show next year, and their neat appearance will set off your summer-flowering plants, rather than being a tatty, overgrown distraction.

One task which is important but is often regarded as being rather tedious is deadheading – removing fading flowers to encourage a fresh crop of blooms. Some plants such as pansies may have a very short flowering period if not deadheaded. All of the repeat-flowering roses also benefit from being deadheaded as the flowers fade; it is the best way to encourage a further flush of blooms throughout the summer and into the autumn.

◁ **Deadheading**

Whether you pick or snip off faded blooms, deadheading will become a regular job from now on, especially if you want to keep displays of bedding in containers looking their best.

▽ **Herb plantings**

Aromatic herbs such as rosemary, thymes and sages will flourish in a sunny spot yet survive really cold winters. Bay is best grown in a pot, as here, so that it can be brought under cover in autumn.

Plants that beat the heat

A group of plants that positively thrives in hotter, drier conditions are the Mediterranean herbs – thymes and oregano, sages and rosemary. There are so many pretty varieties of herbs now on sale, many with coloured or variegated foliage, that it's tempting to make a feature of them, which is exactly what we do in our practical project this month (see p.156) – a simple geometric herb bed that's not too strenuous to make, and will look good from the moment you finish planting it up. Site the feature near the kitchen door if you can, to make gathering herbs for cooking easy – or, you could make it the centrepiece of a bed system for growing vegetables, as we do in November, for a decorative, potager-style look.

JUNE
AT A GLANCE

- Keep weeding and deadheading to maintain beds, borders and container displays.
- Water new and young plants as necessary.
- Look out for pests and suckers on roses.
- Prune spring-flowering shrubs.
- Propagate climbers by layering.
- Cut back and tidy up spring-flowering perennials.
- Take cuttings from pinks.
- Sow seed of perennials.
- Cut down the faded foliage of bulbs, and lift and divide overgrown clumps.
- Plant out summer bedding in borders and containers, including hanging baskets.
- Sow plants for winter and spring colour, such as polyanthus and pansies.
- Introduce new fish into the pond.
- Remove blanket weed and duckweed to prevent them clogging up water features.
- Mow the lawn and trim edges regularly.
- Give tired lawns a boost with a liquid feed.
- Water new lawns made in the spring.
- Harvest vegetables as they mature.
- Plant winter brassicas, and protect them from pests.
- Keep fruit and vegetables well watered in dry spells.
- Shade and ventilate plants in the greenhouse.

! **LAST CHANCE**
- Plant new plants before the summer heats up.
- Sow hardy annuals outside to flower this year.
- Plant out tender vegetables such as tomatoes and runner beans to get good crops this year.

★ **GET AHEAD**
- Sow chicory to force in winter for salads.
- Peg down strawberry runners to make new plants.
- Sow seed for pot plants to flower in winter.

Santolina chamaecyparissus **'Lemon Queen'** • Low-growing grey-leaved shrub (see p.352)

Cistus x *cyprius* ♀ • Sun-loving shrub that flowers over a long period (see p.305)

Achillea **'Fanal'** • Perennial with flowers popular with beneficial insects (see p.295)

Astilbe **'Bronce Elegans'** ♀ • Perennial, good for a shady spot that is not too dry (see p.299)

Iris germanica ♀ • Bearded iris often with several flowers on each stem (see p.326)

Genista aetnensis ♀ • The Mount Etna broom, a large, drought-tolerant shrub (see p.321)

Tamarix tetrandra ♡ • Arching shrub that grows well in coastal districts *(see p.355)*

Potentilla fruticosa **Princess** • Small, bushy shrub that enjoys sun and dry soil *(see p.341)*

Crambe cordifolia ♡ • Statuesque perennial with huge sprays of flowers *(see p.313)*

***Dianthus* 'Little Jock'** • Small perennial forming flower-covered mounds *(see p.315)*

Nepeta* x *faassenii • Spreading perennial with a pungent scent *(see p.335)*

Lonicera* x *heckrottii • Vividly coloured honeysuckle for a sunny wall *(see p.330)*

TOP ROW: 'Duchess of Edinburgh' • 'Multi Blue' • 'Niobe' ♀ • 'Vyvyan Pennell' ♀ **MIDDLE ROW:** 'Fireworks' ♀ • 'Proteus' • 'Nelly Moser' ♀ • 'Marie Boisselot' ♀ **BOTTOM ROW:** 'The President' ♀ • 'Guernsey Cream' • 'Vino' • 'Lasurstern' ♀ *(see pp.307–8)*

Lupinus **'The Page'** • Clump-forming perennial with carmine-red flower spikes *(see p.331)*

Alchemilla mollis ♀ • Spreading perennial, good along path edges and as ground cover *(see p.296)*

Polemonium carneum • Jacob's ladder, a clump-forming perennial with pretty leaves *(see p.341)*

Philadelphus microphyllus • Free-flowering shrub with orange-blossom fragrance *(see p.340)*

Geranium himalayense • Perennial that gives its best display in early to mid-summer *(see p.321)*

Weigela **'Looymansii Aurea'** • Golden-leaved shrub to brighten shade *(see p.359)*

Veronica gentianoides ♥ • Perennial with palest blue to white flower spikes (see *p.357*)

Abelia 'Edward Goucher' ♥ • Sun-loving shrub that enjoys the shelter of a wall (see *p.294*)

Geum 'Borisii' • Perennial that flowers over a long period over summer (see *p.322*)

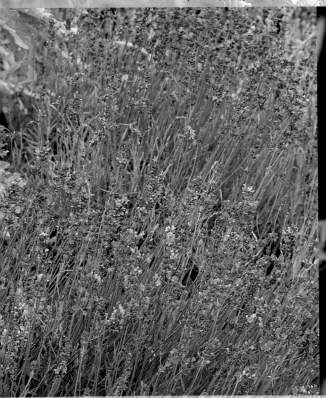

Lavandula angustifolia 'Munstead' • Compact, bushy lavender ideal for edging (see *p.329*)

Buddleja globosa ♥ • Large shrub with honey-scented flowers (see *p.302*)

Viburnum plicatum 'Mariesii' ♥ • Large deciduous shrub with tiered branches (see *p.358*)

TOP ROW: *Paeonia lactiflora* 'Sarah Bernhardt' ♀ • *Paeonia lactiflora* 'Laura Dessert' ♀ • *Paeonia lactiflora* 'Bowl of Beauty' ♀
BOTTOM ROW: *Paeonia lactiflora* 'Kelway's Supreme' • *Paeonia officinalis* 'Rubra Plena' ♀ • *Paeonia lactiflora* 'Ballerina' (see pp.337–8)

WHAT TO DO IN JUNE

GENERAL WORK

IN CASE NIGHT FROST IS FORECAST, as it may still be in some northern parts, keep some horticultural fleece or old newspapers to hand to give some protection to bedding and vulnerable young vegetables, including the shoots of late-planted potatoes. It's amazing how much frost a few sheets of newspaper will keep off.

APPLY AND RENEW MULCHES over the soil, a good idea at any time of year, but especially now, to reduce water loss from the soil and suppress weeds. More time enjoying your garden and less spent watering and weeding has got to be good news during summer. The most important point to bear in mind when putting down a mulch is to make sure the soil is moist beforehand. If the soil is dry the mulch is just as good at keeping water out as it is at retaining it in the soil. Don't forget that you can also "mulch" newly planted containers; there is a wide range of decorative chippings now on offer that will complement stone, terracotta and glazed pots.

WATER PLANTS THOROUGHLY during hot spells, concentrating on newly planted plants, young vegetables and plants in containers, which need it most. If there's a lot to do, it is no good going out every night and splashing a little water everywhere. In drought periods, divide the garden into areas, and every evening give a different one a good soaking, which should last for up to a week. This is more beneficial to the plants, because the roots will go deeper into the soil in search of water. Smaller amounts of water encourage the roots to come to the surface of the soil, causing more harm in the long run; roots near the surface make the plants even more vulnerable in drier conditions.

HOE OR HAND-PULL ANNUAL WEEDS while they are still small, to save a lot of work during the rest of the summer. Choose a dry day, and leave the weeds on the surface of the soil where they will wither in the sun. Perennial weeds will have to be dug out completely, leaving no trace of the roots in the soil. If any piece of root is left it will start to grow again, effectively propagating the weed.

ANY GAPS IN BORDERS are better filled with bedding plants for the summer now, and then more permanent plants can be put in in the autumn. These gap-fillers will give instant colour to what may have been a bare patch of earth. Any annuals will do, whether hardy or half-hardy. If you need height among medium-sized plants, you can even drop in a whole pot or tub full of summer display plants (remembering that it will need extra watering). Looking ahead, hardy annuals sown now will flower in late summer and autumn, so extending the flowering display in the borders.

DEADHEADING is a regular task in all parts of the garden as some flowers go over. With many plants – perennials, repeat-flowering roses, and hardy and half-hardy annuals – the flowering period can be extended considerably if old flowers are removed as soon as they fade. This will prevent the plants' energy going into the production of seeds, and channel it instead into new growth and

Deadheading *This phlox is among many plants that will produce more flowers if deadheaded.*

flowers later in the summer and autumn. Most deadheading can be done with secateurs, cutting back to just above strong buds lower down the stems of the plant. Some plants, like the hardy geraniums, can be quickly trimmed back hard with a pair of garden shears when the flowers fade. It may seem rather drastic action, but new foliage soon appears.

TREES & SHRUBS

CONTROL GREENFLY ON ROSES with an insecticide containing pirimicarb. If you have to spray a heavy infestation of aphids, always use an insecticide that is specific to them. Spray either early in the morning or, preferably, in late evening when there are fewer beneficial insects around.

WATCH OUT FOR LEAF-ROLLING SAWFLY on roses. As its name suggests, the symptoms of this pest are easy to identify, because it causes the leaf edges to roll up tightly downwards and inwards. There is little detrimental effect to the plant other than it looking rather unsightly. Minor infestations can be treated by picking off affected leaves and putting them in the bin. There are sprays that can be used, but by the time you see rolled-up leaves, it is too late. Much better to be vigilant and remove leaves as soon as the problem is noticed.

DISBUD HYBRID TEA ROSES IF LARGER BLOOMS ARE REQUIRED, either for cut flowers or for showing. These roses often produce several buds at the tip of each stem, making perfectly adequate blooms, albeit fairly small in size. If one, show-stopping bloom per stem is needed, remove all the smaller buds, leaving the central, larger bud to open up. This will also give a longer stem, ideal for arrangements.

REMOVE FADING FLOWERS from rhododendrons, camellias and lilacs. By removing the fading blooms the plant's energy is diverted from producing seeds into building up buds for next year's flowers. Be careful when removing the spent flowers from rhododendrons (see right) and camellias, as the new shoots

develop immediately below the old flowerheads. With lilacs, cut back the flowered stem to just above a pair of leaves or buds, or even small shoots, lower down the stem, in a similar way to deadheading roses.

REMOVE SUCKERS FROM ROSES. Most modern bush roses are grafted, or budded, onto a rootstock which gives the plant the vigour it needs to produce all those beautiful blooms. (Also, growers get a saleable, well-shaped plant much more quickly when roses are budded.) One slight drawback with budded roses is that every so often the rootstock itself throws out the odd shoot. It is clearly identifiable because the foliage is generally lighter in colour. It is better if suckers can be pulled off the plant at their point of origin on the roots rather than cut off. If they are cut off the sucker is more likely to grow again. If it is pulled off a little of the

DEADHEAD RHODODENDRONS

Remove the faded flowers very carefully between finger and thumb.

With the flower removed, you will see why care is needed: new leaf buds lie just behind it.

Pruning shrubs Shrubs like this deutzia benefit from having old main stems cut low down.

root is damaged and it is therefore less likely to be able to regrow.

PRUNING AND TRAINING

PRUNE MATURE DECIDUOUS SHRUBS THAT FINISH FLOWERING. These include deutzia, kolkwitzia, philadelphus and weigela. First, look over the whole plant and remove any dead or damaged growth, cutting to a stem joint or leaf. Then take a worm's eye view through the thicket of stems at the base of the plant, and cut out one in three quite low down (see above), selecting the oldest and thickest for removal. Larger stems can be cut with loppers. Really tough old wood will need a pruning saw. Be careful as you pull the whole stem away through the plant, so you don't cause too much damage. Prune away any that does occur. After pruning, feed with a general organic fertiliser and mulch with organic matter. The new growth produced over summer will flower next year.

IF LILACS HAVE BECOME OVERGROWN and leggy, now is the

Renovated lilac When new shoots regrow, thin them to make a few good branches.

best time for drastic action, just after you have enjoyed the flowers but early enough to let the shrub make some new growth over the summer. Saw them right down to about 45cm (18in) from the base. A mass of new shoots will regrow, and you should thin those growing inwards across the centre of the plant. You may be lucky and get some flowers next year, or have to wait – but the result will be a much bushier, better-shaped shrub.

PLANTING

YOU MAY STILL PLANT CONTAINER-GROWN PLANTS, but it isn't advisable now the weather has (hopefully!) started to heat up. A woody plant needs a lot of care and watering to get established in summer – far better to use a stop-gap such as a pot of tall lilies to fill any gaps, and plant something more permanent in autumn.

PROPAGATION

CONTINUE TAKING SOFTWOOD CUTTINGS from shrubs (see May).

CLIMBERS

KEEP ON TOP OF TRAINING CLIMBING AND RAMBLER ROSES. These produce so much growth at such a rate that if you don't tie them in regularly they end up in a mess, trailing over other plants, catching your clothing as you go by and generally getting in the way. Whenever possible tie in the stems as close to the horizontal as possible (see April).

PROPAGATE CLIMBERS BY LAYERING. Growing your own new plants is one of the most fascinating aspects of gardening and it can save you a lot of money. An easy way to propagate many climbers, including clematis, *Akebia quinata*, wisteria and honeysuckle, is by layering. Many plants will layer themselves when a branch or shoot touches the ground, forming roots at that point. If you spot any of these shoots with roots already forming, peg them either directly into the soil (see below) or into a pot full of compost sunk into the ground as you would with strawberry runners. The young plants can been severed from their parent either in autumn, over-wintering in a cold frame, or next spring.

PRUNE *CLEMATIS MONTANA* if you didn't do so last month (see May). This is a vigorous clematis, but only really needs pruning if it is getting out of control and smothering other plants. Thin out the growth and trim back to its allotted space.

LAYERING A CLIMBER

Peg down a stem still attached to the plant at intervals along the ground. Roots should grow into the soil below the pegs (see below).

❶ In autumn, or next spring, carefully uproot the stem and separate each rooted section.

❷ Pot each up individually in a mixture of peat-free compost and vermiculite. Water, and place in a cold frame.

HERBACEOUS PERENNIALS

Hellebore seeds Wear gloves to collect the ripe capsules, which can irritate some skins.

REMOVE OLD LEAVES AND FLOWER STEMS OF HELLEBORES. The old foliage does look very tatty now, and is often infected with blackspot and other diseases. Remove the leaves at ground level and discard them. The new young foliage can often be seen growing from the centre of the plant. A feed with a general fertiliser and a mulch with organic matter will also do no harm at all.

Hellebore seeds can be collected from the plants as you tidy them up, and sown straight away. If the seeds are left on the plants to ripen this will inhibit germination. They don't require any special conditions to germinate. Sow the seeds in a tray or small pot, cover them lightly with some compost and stand the container in a shady cold frame or at the base of a sheltered wall. When the seeds germinate, pot them on once they are large enough to handle.

You may find if you have never collected seeds from hellebores that every year a crop of seedlings appears around the plants. These seedlings can be potted up and grown on as new plants. They will never come true to type – that is to say if the seeds come from a pink flower, you may not necessarily get pink flowers from the new plants. But you never know – you may come across a stunning variation!

CUT BACK ORIENTAL POPPIES when they finish flowering. Once the flowers go over these plants tend to look a mess. It's one good reason for siting them in the middle or near the back of a border, so that when the flowers are finished other plants will hide them. To make them look better, cut the foliage to near ground level. It may seem a bit drastic, but it is the thing to do. Once cut back, sprinkle a little organic fertiliser around the plants and water it in thoroughly. This will encourage new growth to come and if you are lucky, a few more flowers later in the summer.

EUPHORBIA ROBBIAE and *E. characias* will look a lot tidier if the old flower heads are removed when they are going over. Always wear gloves when you are pruning euphorbias, as the milky white sap can irritate sensitive skin. Remove the old growths to ground level. This will encourage new growth from the base of the plant, keeping it bushy and healthy.

CUT BACK AND DIVIDE spring-flowering perennials, if you did not do so last month (see May).

CONTINUE TO STAKE TALL-GROWING PERENNIALS. Nothing looks more unsightly than plants that have been battered about by rain and wind lying all over other, smaller plants in the borders. Try to stake before this happens. The earlier it is done the better, but it is still not too late to continue doing this task. There are many ways of supporting plants, and many products available from garden centres. The types you use will largely depend on the depth of your pockets. Bamboo canes and string are cheap, but have to be used carefully if they are not to look too rigid and prominent in the border, and you must fit eye protectors on top of the canes. Twiggy sticks are another easy means of support. The advantage of these is that the plants can grow through and hide them.

DEADHEAD LUPINS AND DELPHINIUMS AS THEY FINISH FLOWERING. If this is done as the flowers fade there is a good chance of further blooms being produced later in the summer, and although they will not be as spectacular as the first flush, they are no less welcome. Cut the faded flower spires off at ground level or back to strong new shoots.

TAKE CUTTINGS FROM PINKS. The cuttings taken from pinks (*Dianthus*) are called "pipings" and they are very easy to root. Look for healthy, young, non-flowering shoots. Hold the stem about four pairs of leaves from the tip, and pull the cutting off. The cutting should come away cleanly from the point you are holding. Put several cuttings round the edge of a 10cm (4in) pot in a mixture of peat-free compost and perlite, water them in and place in a shady cold frame. The cuttings will start to root in three or four weeks when they can be potted up individually into 8cm (3in) pots.

CONTINUE TO POT UP CUTTINGS of perennials taken earlier in the spring. As soon as the plants have made a good root system, pot them up. Otherwise, if there are several cuttings to a pot, the roots will become entangled and you will damage them as you try to separate them. This makes it more difficult for the plants to get established in their new pot. Water the cuttings before and after potting them up. A shady, sheltered corner will be suitable over the summer, provided that you remember to water them regularly; they can be planted out in autumn.

SOW SEEDS OF HARDY HERBACEOUS PERENNIALS OUTSIDE. Perennials like lupins, delphiniums and hollyhocks can be sown in shallow drills now in a corner of the garden (see May). If space in your garden is limited, then sow perennials in trays or small pots, and place in a cold frame or at the base of a sheltered wall. When the seedlings are large enough, pot them on into individual pots and grow on during the summer. Plant them out into their flowering positions in the autumn.

Pruning flower spires *Cut back finished flower spires of delphiniums right to the ground.*

BULBS

Bulbs in grass *Wait until at least six weeks after flowering before shearing off the leaves.*

CUT DOWN THE FOLIAGE OF BULBS NATURALIZED IN GRASS. By now at least six weeks should have elapsed since flowering, and the bulb foliage and the grass can be trimmed. If you cut the leaves down too soon, the bulbs will be "blind" next year. Don't be too concerned about the grass turning yellow after it has been cut where the bulbs are planted. It will soon recover with a good watering and a feed.

LIFT AND DIVIDE BULBS WHICH HAVE FINISHED FLOWERING. Bulbs can be lifted, dried and stored when the foliage has died down, but if you tend to leave yours *in situ* year after year, lift overcrowded clumps now and divide them so that they can spend the summer re-establishing.

PLANT OUT CANNAS, AND ALSO LILY BULBS THAT WERE POTTED UP earlier in the year. Cannas started into growth in March, and lily bulbs potted up when the weather was too cold

outside to plant (see January) can be planted out in the borders. Or, simply put the whole pot in a gap in the border, either sinking it into the ground or, if the surrounding plants are tall enough to hide it, just setting it on the soil surface. Left in pots, they will need extra watering, so be vigilant.

PLANT ANEMONES TO FLOWER IN AUTUMN. Anemones generally flower about three months after planting, so timing the flowering can be quite accurate. By planting some now the small tubers will give a delightful show of flowers just when other plants are beginning to go over. Plant some in pots at the same time to enjoy these wonderful flowers on the windowsill. The ones to look for are *Anemone coronaria* and the de Caen types, which make flowers up to 8cm (3in) across in glowing colours. When planting late like this, it is best to soak the tubers overnight to get them off to a good start. Plant them 5cm (2in) deep and 8–10cm (3–4in) apart. Incorporate plenty of organic matter, and the plants will repay you with a glorious display.

***Anemone coronaria* 'Lord Lieutenant'** *Soak and plant corms now to flower in autumn.*

ANNUALS & BEDDING

Felicia amelloides   *Brachyscome iberidifolia*

PLANT OUT SUMMER BEDDING PLANTS. By this time of year it is safe to plant out all bedding plants, including tender kinds like begonias, without fear of frost damage. Plenty will be available from garden centres if you have not grown your own: look out for plants like bidens, felicia and brachyscome as well as old favourites such as pelargoniums, salvias and lobelia. Make sure any old spring bedding is removed, if this was not done last month, and lightly fork over the soil. Spread a little general fertiliser before planting, but not too much, otherwise the plants will produce a lot of lush growth at the expense of flowers. Water the plants well an hour or so before planting them out. This is particularly important where young plants are growing together in a seed tray and the roots will be disturbed when they are planted out. And don't forget to give the plants a thorough watering after planting too.

WATER BEDDING PLANTS REGULARLY after planting. The plants will have to be watered at regular intervals during dry spells and for a few weeks after planting. The best way to do this and conserve water at the same time is by using seephose. This is a permeable rubber hose which allows water to seep through its walls along its entire length. The advantage of this is that the water is concentrated where it is needed, at the plants' roots, instead of being sprayed through the air with a sprinkler, where it can drift in windy conditions – very wasteful of water. The seephose can be buried slightly under the soil surface, or just snaked between the plants. It will soon be hidden when the plants grow together.

If you do have to water with a sprinkler, do so in the early morning or in the evening or the plants will be scorched in hot sunshine.

THIN OUT SEEDLINGS OF HARDY ANNUALS sown earlier (see also May). They should be thinned out as soon as they are large enough to handle, otherwise the plants will become tall and leggy and will topple over – they never look good again once this happens. Some of the taller-growing annuals may also benefit from a little support from thin twiggy sticks, nothing too heavy, or they will look obvious in the display.

SOME HARDY ANNUALS SOWN DIRECTLY now will still have time to flower in late summer and autumn, extending the flowering display in beds and borders. Choose fast-growing annuals such as clarkia, godetia, candytuft and calendula. Sow them in the normal way, in shallow drills according to the directions on the seed packets. Thin them out when they are large enough to handle and they will flower their hearts out for you later.

CONTINUE TO SOW SEEDS OF BIENNIALS TO FLOWER NEXT SPRING (see May). Seedlings sown last month can be transplanted to a spare piece of ground to grow on during the summer until planted in their flowering positions in the autumn. If space in your garden is limited and you don't have any spare ground, then sow biennials in trays or small pots, and place in a cold frame or at the base of a sheltered wall. When the seedlings are large enough, pot them on into individual pots and grow on during the summer. Plant them out into their flowering positions in the autumn.

SOW POLYANTHUS FOR FLOWERING NEXT SPRING. Unlike other biennials like wallflowers and myosotis, polyanthus primulas need a little heat to germinate, 15°C (60°F) being about right. A sheltered cold frame should keep the temperature at the right level. Sow the seeds in trays on moist compost without covering them afterwards. The seed is very fine, and it is all too easy to cover fine seed too deeply, inhibiting germination. Cover the container with clear polythene and place in a light cold frame. When the seedlings are large enough to handle, pot them up and grow on through the summer. Plant out into their flowering positions in the autumn.

SOW WINTER PANSIES. These are sown in a similar way to polyanthus (see above) except that the seeds are covered to exclude the light. Some seeds need light to germinate, and others need darkness. After a couple of weeks, check to see if the seeds have germinated and uncover them if they have. Grow them on in exactly the same way as for polyanthus.

CONTAINERS

WATER ALL PLANTS in containers regularly during dry spells.

CONTAINERS AND HANGING BASKETS WHICH WERE PLANTED UP EARLIER and kept indoors to keep them from the threat of frost can now be placed outside for the summer.

PLANT UP HALF-HARDY ANNUALS AND TENDER PERENNIALS in tubs, troughs and other containers outdoors now that any danger of night frosts has passed. If you have been raising half-hardy annuals and tender perennials indoors, either from seeds or cuttings, you can plant them out in safety from now on. If you haven't raised any plants yourself then most garden centres will have a bewildering selection of plants for sale now. Put as many plants as you can get into each container to get the best effect. Upright plants will give some height, and trailing and semi-trailing plants look most effective tumbling over the sides and softening the hard edges.

HANGING BASKETS are an effective way to show off bedding plants and they are very easy to plant up (see facing page). Use one of the many types of liner available from garden centres. Don't use sphagnum moss, as its collection can endanger rare wildlife habitats. You can put a disk of polythene in the bottom of the basket to help retain moisture. Use taller plants in the centre to give height to the display and tuck in plenty of trailing plants around them. When the plants grow the basket will be completely hidden, and you will have a mass of flowers all summer long.

PLANTING UP A HANGING BASKET

1 Make a light, free-draining compost mixture with peat-free compost and perlite, and add some slow-release fertiliser.

2 Sit the basket on a large pot or basket, line it, and fill with a 5–8cm (2–3in) layer of the compost mixture.

3 To make planting through the sides easier, roll up the top growth of the plants in strips of plastic, using sticky tape to secure it.

4 Cut crosses in the liner, and ease the plastic tubes through these from within the basket. Remove the pots and unwrap the plants.

5 Once plants have been added all around the sides, add more compost mixture and firm it well around the root balls.

6 Add trailing plants around the sides of the baskets to spill over the edges – here fuchsias and ivy-leaved pelargoniums.

7 Add more compost mixture, and plant up the top of the basket. Fit in as many plants as you can for the best show.

8 Finally, give the basket a good soak, and top up compost where any sunken areas appear.

PONDS

THIS IS A GOOD MONTH TO INTRODUCE FISH into the pond. With the water in the pond warming up in spring and summer, fish will get acclimatized to new conditions quickly. It's best to get them home from the garden centre, or wherever they were bought, as quickly as possible because of the limited amount of oxygen in the bag they are usually transported in. Tip the fish into the pond gently.

INTRODUCING FISH

① Take a cardboard box with you to support the bag on the way home. The fish will have a smoother ride and be less stressed.

② Float the bag in the pond for an hour or two until the water temperature inside and outside are the same.

③ Cut the bag under water and let the fish swim out; don't force them.

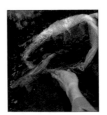

EVEN IN COLD AREAS, TENDER FLOATING PLANTS like the water hyacinth (*Eichhornia crassipes*) can be put in the pond now that the threat of frost has passed. It's also a good time to throw in extra new floating plants for the pond if you notice that this year they seem a little sparse. They will establish quickly with the warmer weather.

BLANKET WEED AND DUCKWEED are persistent problems in many ponds, and they have to be removed regularly if they are not to take over. Duckweed can be skimmed off the surface with a net or cane. And it's a really satisfying job to get a stick and twist blanket weed around it. When you lift it from the pond, leave it on the bank with an end trailing in the water for the rest of the day so that any aquatic creatures in it can escape back into the water. After that, it makes a superb ingredient for the compost heap, high in nutrients.

Remove blanket weed *Wind it round a stick like spaghetti, then lift it out.*

LAWNS

MOW REGULARLY. By this time of year the lawn should be cut at least once a week, and preferably twice a week if possible, the reason being that the less grass taken off at each cut, the healthier the grass will remain. Mow in a different direction each time, because if you mow in the same direction several times, the grass begins to grow in that direction and the mower blades, especially those on a cylinder mower, will not cut it as well. By this time the mower blades should be at the lowest setting required; for most lawns, about 1.25cm (½in), or a little higher for a lawn that takes a lot of use. If there are dry spells when the grass goes a bit brown, reduce the frequency of mowing and raise the blades a little so as not to cut it too close.

Now that grass is generating a lot of clippings, don't dump them in a mass on the compost heap or they will clump together and rot down into a slimy mess, rather than good compost. This is because they are too close-textured to admit air. Keep the clippings separate until you have some looser material to mix in with them. Torn and

Long-handled shears make edging the lawn less backbreaking.

crumpled newspaper will do if the garden is not generating much suitable debris at the moment.

DON'T FORGET EDGING. Another job to bear in mind is to trim the lawn edges at the same time as the grass is cut. It makes all the difference to the appearance of the garden if the edges are cut regularly. And it's less work doing the edges once a week as the trimmings are few and don't have to be cleared up.

FEED LAWNS WITH A LIQUID FERTILISER. These fast-acting feeds are the perfect thing to give a tired-looking lawn a quick tonic. Diluted in water, following the instructions on the bottle, they are easily applied with a watering can or sprayer. One advantage they have over dry fertilisers is they don't have to be watered in if the weather remains dry.

NEW LAWNS

WATER NEW LAWNS made in spring either from seed or turf. It is vitally important not to let newly laid turf dry out: it shrinks when it dries and it's almost impossible to get it back to how it was when this happens. One way to ensure that a sprinkler is watering the ground evenly is to place a number of empty jars around the lawn. You'll soon see by the level of water collected whether any areas are going short.

VEGETABLES & HERBS

HARVESTING

CONTINUE TO HARVEST ALL CROPS as they mature. Early peas will be ready to pick now. Cut down the top growth of the plants (known as the "haulm") after harvesting, but leave the roots of the peas in the soil, as these will return valuable nitrogen to it. Nodules on the roots of peas and beans are able to fix and store atmospheric nitrogen in the soil. Follow peas with a leafy crop, such as cabbages, which requires a higher nitrogen content in the soil. This is one way, by practising good crop rotation, of reducing the amount of artificial fertiliser we put on the soil.

JAPANESE ONIONS which were sown last year (see August) will now be ready to harvest. The tops should have begun to fall over and the skins to harden. Lift them to break the roots in the soil and let them dry out in the sun. If it rains, put them in a greenhouse or cold frame to dry out.

YOU MAY BE ABLE TO START HARVESTING EARLY POTATOES towards the end of the month. There is nothing like digging the first potatoes and taking them straight to the kitchen to be cooked. To harvest them, push a fork into the ground a little way from the base of the plant to reduce the chance of piercing any potatoes. Root around a bit to make sure you've got all the potatoes, as any left in the ground will grow again next year. They always seem to grow slap bang in the middle of a row of seedlings, making it difficult to get them out.

SOWING AND PLANTING OUTDOORS

PLANT CELERY in trenches prepared during winter or spring (see March). Apply a general fertiliser before planting, and put the plants in rows 30cm (1ft) apart. Water the plants well after planting, and keep them well watered throughout the growing season. Celery requires a lot of water to produce a good crop in the autumn. The soil which was heaped up on either side of the trench and will be used for blanching the celery in the autumn and winter, can be used in the summer for fast-maturing salad crops like lettuce, radish and salad onions. The technique of growing quick-maturing crops on spare ground like this is called catch cropping. Self-blanching celery (see May) does not have to be planted in trenches but is better planted in blocks 23cm (9in) apart, rather than rows, so each plant blanches its neighbour.

PLANTS OF CELERIAC raised earlier can also be planted out now.

CONTINUE TO SOW PEAS for maincrops later in the year.

SOW RADICCHIO (RED CHICORY) in rows 23cm (9in) apart. Sow in the usual manner, watering the seed drill if the weather is dry before sowing the seeds. This is a leafy chicory, unlike the forcing type: the leaves are eaten fresh and it is a useful vegetable

Radicchio

for autumn and winter salads, being able to stand through cold weather in the garden. Cloches will protect the heads from weather damage. There are several varieties available with attractively coloured foliage. They certainly add a touch of colour to any winter salad.

PLANT OUT RUNNER BEANS. Now that the threat of frost has passed these plants can go out into ground that was prepared during the winter. Put up whatever supports you require before planting, either making wigwams or parallel avenues of canes with 60cm (2ft) between the rows. Slugs love young runner bean plants; the plants can be protected by surrounding them with a collar made from an old plastic drinks bottle. To ensure runner bean flowers set and produce pods, spray the flowers with water regularly and make sure they don't dry out at the roots.

Dwarf runner beans can also go out now. These don't require much support. It may be worth inserting a few twiggy sticks around the plants, as they do often flop over even though they are dwarf. This will prevent the pods being splashed with soil when it rains.

Dwarf and climbing French beans can be treated in exactly the same way as runner beans.

KEEP SOWING SALAD VEGETABLES in small quantities at regular intervals of two or three weeks. This will provide a continuous supply of fresh salad stuff over a long period, rather than a glut at one time. One point to bear in mind now is that lettuce seed will not germinate in high temperatures, so if the weather is hot and dry, sow the seeds in a shady part of the garden, or

sow them in seed trays and put these in a shady part of the garden. Transplant the seedlings when they are large enough to handle.

PLANT TOMATOES OUTSIDE. Tomatoes can be planted in the soil at intervals of 45cm (18in), or planted two or three to a growbag. Tomatoes prefer a sunny spot against a south-facing wall if possible. Cordon plants will need staking with 1.2m (4ft) canes. When planting tomatoes outside, leave a slight depression in the soil. This helps retain water around the roots of the plants when watering them in. It can be difficult to push canes into growbags as there is insufficient compost to hold the canes upright. There are frames you can buy from the garden centre which hold canes for use in growbags.

Feed all tomatoes with a high-potash fertiliser every week from now on through the season to get a good crop. Be careful not to let tomatoes, especially those growing in growbags, go short of water. If they are neglected or watered irregularly, going dry in between times, they will be prone to blossom end rot. This appears as a sunken brown area at the end of the fruit furthest from the plant. It is due to calcium deficiency, brought about by a lack of water, even for a very short period. Regular watering is the key to preventing this problem. Another problem which may be caused by irregular watering is splitting of the fruits.

PLANT AND SOW MARROWS AND COURGETTES, AND PUMPKINS AND SQUASHES, OUTSIDE. Young plants should be spaced about 60cm (2ft) apart in soil that has been enriched with

VEGETABLES & HERBS *continued*

Plant ridge cucumbers The young plants will thrive in soil enriched with lots of organic matter.

plenty of organic matter to retain moisture (see also May). If plants were not raised earlier under glass, all is not lost. They can be sown directly outside now. Sow two seeds together in the place they are to crop. Pull out the weaker of the seedlings when they germinate, leaving the stronger one to grow on.

PLANT OUT RIDGE CUCUMBERS. Although called ridge cucumbers, they do not have to be grown on ridges of soil. Plant out the young plants in early June, in soil that has been enriched with plenty of organic matter to retain as much moisture as possible. Pinch out the growing tips of the plants when they have made six pairs of leaves, to encourage sideshoots to form and produce the cucumbers. Feed and water regularly with a high-potash fertiliser through the summer and you'll get delicious cucumbers all summer long.

SOW TURNIPS FOR AN AUTUMN CROP. Sow the seeds in rows 15cm (6in) apart. Thin the seedlings as soon as you can handle them without damaging the young plants. Thin them to leave

one plant every 10cm (4in). The turnips are best harvested when they are young, before they get to the size of a tennis ball. You can leave some roots in for longer, as their leafy tops can be cooked for winter greens.

SOW WITLOOF CHICORY FOR FORCING (see also May). Sow the seeds in rich, fertile soil to fatten up the roots for forcing in winter. Give a good dressing of a general organic fertiliser and sow the seeds in rows 30cm (12in) apart. Thin the seedlings to 15cm (6in) apart when they are large enough to handle. Keep them well watered in dry weather. For forcing, see January.

SOW CHINESE CABBAGE and other Oriental vegetables. These vegetables can be sown now at regular intervals until August. One way to get quick results is to sow the seeds under cloches. This way some of them will germinate in two or three days. These leafy vegetables are all excellent for stir-frying, making delicious meals fresh from the garden in a matter of minutes.

Sow pak choi This Chinese leaf vegetable can be picked fresh from the garden for crunchy stir-frys.

Planting out sweetcorn Use a marked plank to plant in blocks, the same distance each way.

Sweetcorn flowering Planted in blocks, wind will blow the pollen onto other sweetcorn flowers.

Some are prone to attack from flea beetle, and it may be worth growing them permanently under cloches or covered with horticultural fleece to stop the beetles getting at the plants.

PLANT OUT SWEETCORN. Plant sweetcorn in blocks, 30cm (1ft) apart each way, rather than in rows. The reason for this is that sweetcorn is pollinated by wind. The male flowers appear as the tassels at the tip of the plant and the pollen falls onto the

female parts lower down the plants. By growing the plants in blocks there is more chance of pollination being successful than if the plants are growing in conventional rows.

PLANT OUT ALL WINTER BRASSICAS SOWN EARLIER. The young plants will need protection against cabbage root fly (see May). These crops generally need plenty of room to grow – at least 60cm (2ft) apart each way. But other, quicker-growing crops can be grown between the brassicas until they reach their maximum size. Salad crops like lettuce, radish, and spinach can all be grown between the brassicas. This is known as intercropping and utilizes the space, fertilisers and organic matter added to the soil to the best advantage.

LOOKING AFTER CROPS

KEEP WATERING YOUNG VEGETABLE PLANTS and hoe off weeds regularly.

PROTECT YOUNG BRASSICAS AGAINST BIRDS. Birds love to eat young brassicas as soon as they are planted out. In fact wood pigeons often seem to sit and watch me planting, ready to pounce as soon as my back is turned. There are many bird scarer products on the market, with varying degrees of effectiveness. Whichever you use, the birds sooner or later come to realise that it poses no actual danger. The only foolproof way of stopping birds eating the plants is to grow them under cover. Support either netting or fine-weave mesh sheeting on stakes with strong twine or wire strung between them, so it is is held above the plants like a tent. If it is left resting on the plants, the birds will peck through it. Always make sure netting is well anchored at ground level so that small garden birds do not get tangled in it. It's not a very pleasant job trying to untangle a bird from netting.

CABBAGE WHITE BUTTERFLY CATERPILLARS will be hatching out now. A lot of damage can be prevented by going around inspecting the undersides of the leaves on all brassicas. You will usually find small clusters of yellow eggs here. The eggs can be squashed, but if you can't face doing that use a bacterial spray called *Bacillus thuringiensis*. This will kill off any young caterpillars. If you don't grow many brassicas, it is worth covering them with fleece as a physical barrier to prevent the butterflies laying their eggs in the first place.

CARROT FLY ARE STILL AROUND, so protect carrots with a barrier that the pest cannot penetrate (see May).

FEED ASPARAGUS AFTER FLOWERING. You won't be cutting spears from young crowns, but once they are established and giving you a crop, stop cutting in late June to allow the crowns to build up strength for next year's crop. Apply a general organic fertiliser then to all plants, young and old, and let the foliage grow until it turns brown later in the summer when it can be cut to the ground.

Asparagus doesn't attract many pests, but asparagus beetle can be damaging, so keep on the look out for it: it has an orange body and black and yellow wings. To control it, spray with derris, or

pick off the adults and their greyish-cream grubs by hand.

HERBS

IF YOU DON'T HAVE ROOM for our herb feature project this month (see p.156), plant herbs in containers for the patio or by the back door close to the kitchen. Most herbs are extremely effective grown in containers, but some are not very suitable; tall herbs like angelica and lovage can become top-heavy and also may look out of place in a pot – better to grow these in a border. All other herbs are suitable for containers, and with many of them, particularly the sages, having attractively coloured foliage, you can make stunning plant combinations by grouping pots together, or planting several different herbs in one large container.

Herbs in containers
For a space-saving alternative to a herb garden, plant up a selection of herbs in a traditional strawberry jar, here planted with a strawberry plant as well. Choose spreading plants such as thymes and oreganos for the side pockets.

FRUIT

HARVESTING

REMOVE CLOCHES FROM STRAWBERRIES and the fruits should ripen for picking.

HARVEST RHUBARB until the end of the month.

LOOKING AFTER CROPS

PUT UP PHEROMONE TRAPS FOR CODLING MOTH (SEE MAY). One trap will protect up to five apple trees.

CONTINUE PRUNING AND PINCHING OUT SHOOTS ON WALL-TRAINED FRUIT (see May). Get all pruning of peaches, plums and nectarines done through the summer. The sooner any wounds heal the less chance there is that the trees will be affected by silverleaf disease. Remove unwanted shoots as soon as possible and tie in those which will be used to replace the current year's fruiting wood. Select two new shoots at the base of the fruiting shoot and retain these for tying in. One is just for insurance purposes in case the other is damaged. Cut out any other new shoots. Any sideshoots from the fruiting shoots can be pinched out to 5–6 leaves.

HEAVY CROPS OF PLUMS can be thinned early in the month to prevent the brittle branches of plum trees from breaking under the weight of the crop. Thin in two stages, removing only any damaged or diseased fruit first. Don't remove too many fruits to begin with as the trees will naturally shed some fruit around now. This is called the "June drop". Wait until this has happened, then a second thinning out can be done

FRUIT *continued*

if the fruits are still overcrowded. You can also support heavy branches (see July) if you fear they will be damaged by the weight of fruit, especially on young trees.

DON'T BE TEMPTED TO THIN OUT APPLES AND PEARS until the "June drop" (see previous entry) has happened. It is all too easy to plough ahead thinning out the fruits, only to see the ones you have left all falling off, leaving you with none.

GOOSEBERRIES CAN ALSO BE THINNED for larger fruits. The thinnings can be cooked. One pest to look out for is gooseberry sawfly caterpillar. They can attack right through the summer, and a bad infestation can completely defoliate a plant. The caterpillars are up to 2cm (¾in) long, yellow-fawn in colour and marked with black spots. They rear up when disturbed. Spray with derris, or inspect the plants regularly from spring onwards, paying particular notice to the undersides of the leaves, and squash any eggs and caterpillars you see.

Plentiful plums *Heavy crops can break branches – thin now, and support branches if necessary.*

CONTROL GREY MOULD ON STRAWBERRIES. Spells of wet weather encourage the spread of grey mould (botrytis). Inspect fruits regularly and remove infected ones. Don't compost these, as they may spread the disease to other plants in the garden. If you need to spray, use a fungicide, but removing infected fruits early enough should keep the problem under control. Ensure plenty of air circulates around the plants and keep developing fruits off the soil by putting straw or mats under them. This stops soil being splashed on the fruits by rain, which can spread mould.

BLACKCURRANTS can often suffer from a viral disease called reversion. This distorts the leaves and usually makes them smaller than normal. Any badly infected plants should be dug up and burned. If you want to replace them, buy only certified stock that is free of the virus. The virus is spread by the blackcurrant big bud mite, which lives in the buds and gives them a distinctive enlarged appearance. Buds like this should always be picked off.

KEEP ALL FRUIT WELL WATERED in dry spells to ensure a good crop of quality fruits throughout the summer. Mulching with organic matter will help in retaining moisture and reducing the need to water. Mulching will also keep down weeds, which compete for water and nutrients in the soil; many weeds also act as hosts to pests and diseases.

PRUNING AND TRAINING

CONTINUE TYING IN NEW CANES of blackberries and hybrid berries. Methods of training are many and

Tie in blackberries *The long canes need to be secured regularly, or the thorns can be dangerous.*

varied and some are unnecessarily complicated. The easiest is to train the shoots in the form of a fan, with the current year's fruiting canes spaced out to one side of the plant on the framework of wires, and new canes tied in on the other side, completing the fan shape (see March for illustration). After fruiting, the old canes are cut out and the process repeated next year.

PRUNE EXCESS GROWTH ON VINES. "Stop" (pinch out the tip) of the fruiting shoots to a leaf beyond three or four developing fruit clusters. Pinch back any sideshoots from these stems to one or two leaves. Vines grown outdoors in our climate will only ripen a few decent bunches of grapes on each sideshoot from the main stem or rod, so it is counter-productive to allow any more to develop.

PROPAGATION

STRAWBERRIES will now be producing lots of runners. These can either be removed or pegged down to make new plants, depending on your needs (see May).

UNDER COVER

DAMP DOWN REGULARLY to keep the atmosphere in the greenhouse or the conservatory humid. This will benefit plants enormously, especially if you can close the ventilators and doors for a short time after damping down, to allow the temperature and the humidity to rise and create a wonderful growing atmosphere. Damping down just means splashing or spraying water around. It will also help to keep down the incidence of glasshouse red spider mite (see also May).

WATER AND FEED ALL PLANTS REGULARLY now they are all growing fast. If soilless or peat-free composts become dry it is almost impossible to re-wet them properly, so never let them dry out completely between waterings. If pot plants have become dry at the roots, give them a good soaking by sitting them in water overnight before feeding with fertiliser. If the fertiliser is applied to dry compost it may scorch roots. Feeding flowering pot plants and bedding plants with a fertiliser high in potash will ensure a continued display of good quality flowers through the summer until the first frosts of autumn. Be careful not to splash water on the foliage of plants in bright sunny weather. The water droplets on the leaves act like small magnifying glasses, scorching the leaves. Watering is best done in the evenings, if possible, then there is less chance of the water evaporating than in the heat of the day.

SHADE THE GREENHOUSE or conservatory with paint-on shading or blinds as described last month. Ventilate whenever you can by opening windows, doors and vents. Warm sunshine on a glasshouse can cause the temperatures to rise to dramatic levels. It is best for the plants if temperatures can be kept as even as possible. Big fluctuations in temperature will not encourage good sturdy growth in the plants.

There are many different automatic ventilator openers on the market which take the guesswork out of whether to leave the vents open or shut when you leave for work in the morning. They can be set to open and close at a set temperature, and so give you peace of mind. Working in conjunction with shading, these should help to control the temperature on the hottest of days.

POT ON ALL YOUNG PLANTS AND SEEDLINGS as necessary. Plants that become pot-bound over a period of time rarely recover and grow well. The ideal time to pot on any plant is when, having knocked the plant from its pot, you can see a good tracery of roots around the sides of the root ball, without it looking congested with roots. Another good indication that plants really need potting on is roots growing out through the drainage holes in the bottom of the pot. Keep young plants well watered, and shade them from the sun if the roots have been disturbed when the plants were potted up (for example, when separating a pot full of cuttings). It takes a few days for the roots to take up water after being disturbed.

GLASSHOUSE AND HOUSE PLANTS

HOUSEPLANTS WHICH HAVE BEEN STUCK IN STUFFY ROOMS can be moved to the greenhouse for a holiday. Even if houseplants are sitting on a sunny windowsill, they never really get all the light they need, and the dry atmosphere in most houses is far from ideal for plant growth. So a spell in the greenhouse will be like a well-earned holiday for your plants. The foliage of large-leaved plants like rubber plants will benefit from a sponge over. The leaves will be shiny again and look a lot better, and the plants will be healthier too; when that layer of dust has been removed, air can pass through the pores in the leaves much more easily.

SOW SEEDS OF *Primula malacoides, P. sinensis,* cinerarias and calceolarias (*Pericallis*) for pot plants to flower in the winter and spring. Sow small batches of the seeds in small pots of seed compost and place near a window. They don't need a lot of heat to germinate at this time of year. Pot on the seedlings, holding them by the seed leaves, when they are large enough to handle. Do be aware, though, that people with sensitive skin should handle primulas with gloves, as they can irritate some skins. If you are a sufferer, you may find it almost impossible to grasp the little seed leaves to transplant wearing gardening gloves. You either need the thin surgical-type gloves, or a kind friend to do you a favour. Grow the plants on in a cool place – a shady cold frame is ideal – to get good sturdy plants to take into the house in the autumn and winter. Whitefly and greenfly can be a problem, particularly with cinerarias. Inspect the plants regularly and squash the aphids before they get out of control.

POT ON CUTTINGS TAKEN EARLIER FROM POTTED HYDRANGEAS. Water the cuttings well before potting them on to larger pots. Knock the cuttings out of the pot and carefully tease the roots apart. Pot each cutting into a small 8cm (3in) pot, or for a really dramatic display pot three cuttings into a 12.5cm (5in) pot and pot these together into a larger pot when the roots have filled this one. This way you get three plants bushing out in place of one, making a spectacular show later in the year. Grow the plants on outside and feed them regularly with a high-potash fertiliser to build up the flower buds. Bring the plants inside in the autumn.

SOLANUM CAPSICASTRUM **PLANTS SOWN EARLIER IN THE SPRING** (see March) will also benefit from being put outside for the summer. The plants will produce fine sturdy growth which will ripen over summer. Putting the plants outside also allows pollinating insects to get at the plants easily to pollinate the flowers, ensuring that a good crop of the attractive fruits appears in early autumn.

CROPS UNDER GLASS

FRUITING CROPS – tomatoes, peppers and aubergines – need watering regularly, and a high-potash feed every week, to help the fruits swell and develop.

CHECK THE BASE OF GRAPE VINES to make sure they are not drying out. Traditionally, grape vines are planted outside the glasshouse, and their stems trained in through a low hole in the wall. That way, the roots benefit from

Wiping leaves *Some people like to use milk to give houseplant foliage a glossy sheen.*

rainfall. Grape vines are completely hardy – improved ripening of the fruits is why we, with our short summers, grow them under glass. At this time when the bunches are developing, check around roots whether outside or in and give the plants a regular soak if necessary.

CONTINUE REMOVING SIDESHOOTS FROM TOMATOES. The sooner the sideshoots are removed the less of a shock it is to the plant. They are easily removed by bending them to one side with your thumb and forefinger. Larger sideshoots can be cut off with secateurs. Dip the secateurs in a weak solution of a garden disinfectant after each cut to avoid spreading virus among the plants. Tomatoes are very prone to picking up viruses – one reason why tomatoes are often used in plant research work.

MAKE A HERB GARDEN

Herbs, as well as being useful for culinary purposes, are very decorative. This small feature consists of a 1.2m (4ft) square, slightly raised bed, divided into four planting areas by diagonal rows of bricks, set simply into the soil. The cost depends largely on the size of plants you use.

YOU WILL NEED: 4 pieces of 75mm x 25mm (3 x 1in) timber, 1.2m (4ft) in length • Eight wooden pegs, approx 30cm (12in) long • 40mm (1½in) nails • A spirit level, and a long lath or similar to rest it on across the bed • Weather-resistant bricks, such as engineering bricks • A barrowload of equal parts garden compost and good topsoil, or use a John Innes or other soil-based compost.

PLANTS USED: Greek basil; lavender 'Seal'; oregano 'Acorn Bank'; rosemary 'Tuscan Blue'; white-flowered chives; purple and gold-variegated sages; golden thyme; small bay (in pot).

① Nail pegs a little way from each end of the four edging timbers for the bed.

② Drive the wooden edging into the ground, pegs on the inside, to make a square.

③ Check each piece is level, and adjust by knocking in the higher ends if necessary.

④ Check diagonally to make sure one side isn't higher than the others, and adjust.

⑤ Fill the raised bed with the soil and garden compost mixture, or proprietary loam-based compost.

⑥ Level the compost to just below the height of the edging.

⑦ Wrap string around a couple of bricks and stretch this diagonally across the square both ways, slightly off-centre so that you can align the edge of the bricks with it.

⑧ First lay the bricks diagonally across the bed in both directions, so you can adjust the spacing easily to make them meet neatly in the centre. Then scoop out pockets in the compost to set them in.

⑨ Tap down the bricks with the handle of a club hammer to level them.

🔟 The bricks not only make a decorative pattern, but allow you to put a foot on the bed to reach the herbs in the centre.

⓫ Plant up the herbs, and water them in.

⓬ We used a small bay in an attractive pot as a centrepiece.

⓭ The finished herb garden will look better and better as the plants grow, and provide a supply of fresh herbs throughout the season.

JULY

The garden in **July**

The garden should be at its peak, with borders filled with colour and the vegetable garden producing fine crops. Long summer evenings in the garden can be enjoyed to the full, relaxing and entertaining friends.

THE GARDEN SHOULD NOW be looking its best. It's high summer; the borders are full of colour and the scent from flowers such as roses and sweet peas fills the air, especially on warm summer evenings. It's a month for taking time to enjoy the garden, having relaxing meals *al fresco*, appreciating the flowers and watching the abundance of wildlife in the garden.

Beat the heat

There is still plenty of routine work to be done, but by this time the work can be done at a more leisurely pace than in the hectic spring period. Care must be taken when working in the sun for long periods, even if you are taking it easy. Take breaks, wear a hat and do use sun cream to protect your skin from the harmful effects of sunlight. It's best to try not to work during the hottest part of the day. Wait until evening to do any strenuous work, if you won't be too busy with the barbecue. Hot days are often followed by thunderstorms and it's often a relief to do the gardening either in the cool of the evening or in the early morning.

If the weather is very hot you will have to pay careful attention to watering, especially trees and

Pick of the crop ▷
Keep picking courgettes when they are young and tender and make the best eating, and more flowers and fruits will be encouraged to form.

shrubs which were planted in the autumn and winter. The most beneficial times to water are also early morning or in the evenings when it is cooler. By watering at these times, the precious moisture will not evaporate from the surface of the soil nearly as rapidly as in the heat of the day. Do be aware, however, that in exceptionally dry periods there may be watering restrictions in your area, and the use of hosepipes – even the seephose variety – may be banned. Check with your local authority in these situations.

Use water wisely

During hot spells the lawn may begin to look rather brown and worn. It is tempting to water the lawn at times, but it really is not necessary, as grass has a remarkable ability to regenerate. Whenever rain does fall, the grass will, as if by magic, turn back into a lush green sward again. Better to use the water for plants that really need it: newly planted trees and shrubs, thirsty vegetables, and other precious plants in the borders and in containers, especially hanging baskets, which need water daily in high summer.

Perfect your plantings

During evening rambles around the garden, take a notebook and look at your planting schemes carefully to see which combinations of plants and colours have worked this year, and which are a disappointment. You can then plan to make changes in the autumn or in the spring.

If you feel your garden lacks a little sparkle this summer, on p.187 we suggest a grouping of plants that can be bought right now, either in flower or just about to be, and put straight in to give instant impact. Do remember, though, that new plantings need plenty of water at the moment, so mulch the plants well with a thick layer of organic matter.

Earlier-flowering plants will now have to be deadheaded if you don't want to save seed from them. Many perennials will, if deadheaded regularly, produce a further flush of blooms throughout the summer and into the autumn. It's quite a pleasant, relaxing job to do on a warm summer's evening.

◁ **Spent flower heads**
Carry a pair of secateurs with you whenever you wander around the garden, and you will be able to deadhead as you go. You will be rewarded in many cases by a second flush of flowers.

▽ **Summer stunners**
For intensity of colour and perfume in the garden, roses and lavenders are hard to match right now.

WEATHER WATCH

🌡 **July and August are generally the hottest months** of the year, with the highest temperatures occurring inland away from the cooling influence of the sea. One of the highest temperatures ever recorded in the United Kingdom was at Cheltenham in Gloucestershire: 37.1°C.

❀ **It's not really a month** for gales or high winds except in parts of north-west England and coastal areas, where sea breezes can be very welcome on hot, sultry days. North-west areas of England average 0.2 days of gales this month, rising to 0.3 days in the north of Scotland, especially on the west coast and western islands.

☀ **The sunniest parts of the United Kingdom** are along the south coast of England: owing to the formation of cumulus clouds over land, the skies over the sea remain cloud-free. Northern parts of the country are generally the cloudiest, due to the hillier nature of the terrain, and on western coasts the close proximity of low-pressure weather systems over the Atlantic may also bring in cloud cover. However, some parts of the north-east and south-west areas of Scotland compare favourably with Ireland and north-west England for hours of direct sunshine. The far northern coasts of Britain usually receive around 133 hours of sun in July, while the south of England averages 213 hours this month.

🌧 **July can be a dry month**, but we don't escape rain altogether. The trouble is that the sudden but short spells of summer rain do little to add to soil reserves of moisture. So it makes sense to save water when we can, especially in areas more prone to drier weather.

🌧 **There is no snow on the ground** in July except in small isolated pockets on the highest peaks. But there are times when a freak shower of hail can make for a temporary wintry scene, even in July.

△ Beat the heat
Make the most of shady areas in the garden, which will become welcome refuges in the heat of summer. Areas shaded from full sun will not get so dry, suiting many plants better.

Summer symptoms

In the warm moist weather which can be characteristic of this month, pests and diseases may spread rapidly. Keep a careful watch for them as many pests and diseases can be controlled easily if caught early enough. Aphids, for instance, can be easily killed simply by squashing if they are not present in large numbers. If you have a heavy infestation of one particular pest and you feel you must use an insecticide, then use one specific to that pest where at all possible so that it does not harm other, beneficial insects. And do any spraying in the

◁ **Vegetables on show**
Designing colour schemes with differently-coloured vegetable, herb and salad plants can be as satisfying as carpet bedding – and of course, you can eat the results too.

▽ **Strawberries ripening**
Pick strawberries regularly, as damaged and deteriorating fruits left on the plant can attract moulds that spoil sound fruits too.

evening when the bees have gone for the night. As for diseases, any parts of a plant showing signs of disease should be removed and either burned or put in the bin. Never compost diseased material or leave it lying around, as this will only risk spreading the disease to other plants in the garden. Under glass, scorch and heat stress are other dangers to plants. Pay particular attention to watering and ventilation. Another way of cooling the atmosphere is to damp down several times during the day, splashing water onto the floor to increase the humidity.

Flavours to savour

There is still time to continue making regular sowings of salad crops to see you into autumn. Regular hoeing and weeding still has to be done in the vegetable garden, and crops will also benefit from a mulch of organic matter to retain moisture in the soil. But above all, vegetable gardens should be providing plenty of food for the kitchen, not forgetting the lovely, summery flavours of fresh-picked bunches of herbs.

J U L Y
AT A GLANCE

- Make sure birds have water in dry weather.
- Keep new and young plants well watered during the summer, but use water wisely.
- Watch out for pests and diseases.
- Feed and water all plants in containers regularly.
- Continue deadheading flowers as they fade.
- Prune shrubs that flowered in early summer.
- Take semi-ripe cuttings from shrubs.
- Trim conifer hedges and take cuttings.
- Summer-prune wisteria.
- Divide bearded irises.
- Layer and take cuttings of carnations and pinks.
- Disbud dahlias to get larger blooms.
- Plant autumn-flowering bulbs.
- Transplant seedlings of biennials sown earlier.
- Water vegetables regularly.
- Lift new potatoes, onions and garlic.
- Pinch out runner beans when they reach the top of their canes.
- Pinch out outdoor tomatoes when four trusses have formed, and remove sideshoots.
- Pick raspberries and currants.
- Harvest herbs for drying.
- Keep greenhouses well ventilated, and damp down regularly.

! LAST CHANCE
- Fill any gaps in beds and borders with bedding.
- Sow the last vegetables for harvesting in autumn.
- Plant out all winter brassicas.

★ GET AHEAD
- Make plans to have plants cared for if you are taking your holidays in August.
- Order spring-flowering bulbs.
- Prepare ground for making new lawns in autumn.
- Sow salads under cover for autumn and winter.
- Prepare new strawberry beds.

***Centaurea hypoleuca* 'John Coutts'** • Pink cornflower, a nostalgic perennial *(see p.303)*

***Alstroemeria* 'Orange Glory'** ♡ • Perennial that forms tall clumps; lovely for cutting *(see p.297)*

***Hebe* 'Gauntlettii'** • Neat, bushy evergreen shrub that needs little pruning *(see p.353)*

***Oenothera fruticosa* 'Fyrverkeri'** ♡ • Perennial evening primrose *(see p.337)*

***Diascia barberae* 'Blackthorn Apricot'** ♡ • Slightly tender perennial that may need winter shelter *(see p.315)*

***Gunnera manicata* ♡** • Perennial; by high summer the huge leaves are at their best *(see p.322)*

***Verbascum* 'Cotswold Queen'** • Perennial bearing tall flower spires *(see p.357)*

Nicotiana sylvestris ♔ • Very tall, elegant perennial tobacco plant, strongly fragrant *(see p.335)*

***Phlox paniculata* 'Eva Cullum'** • Hardy perennial that will flower into autumn *(see p.340)*

Campanula lactiflora • The milky bellflower, a tall perennial that may need support *(see p.302)*

***Artemisia alba* 'Canescens'** ♔ • Foliage plant that makes a lovely foil for summer flowers *(see p.299)*

***Helianthemum* 'Raspberry Ripple'** • Sun-loving shrub with greyish leaves *(see p.323)*

Arctotis x *hybrida* '**Red Devil**' • Perennial grown in cool climates as a half-hardy annual *(see p.298)*

Solanum crispum '**Glasnevin**' ♡ • Sprawling shrub best trained on a warm wall *(see p.353)*

Hemerocallis '**Gentle Shepherd**' • Perennial: flowers last only a day, but keep on coming *(see p.324)*

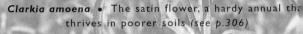

Cleome hassleriana '**Colour Fountain**' • Imposing annual, to 1.5m (5ft) tall *(see p.310)*

Thunbergia alata • Black-eyed Susan, a distinctive climber grown as an annual *(see p.355)*

Clarkia amoena • The satin flower, a hardy annual that thrives in poorer soils *(see p.306)*

TOP ROW: 'Vésuve' • 'Firecrest' • 'Marliacea Chromatella' ♀ • *N. tetragona* 'Helvola' MIDDLE ROW: 'Laydekeri Fulgens' • 'René Gérard' • *N. alba* • 'Marliacea Albida' BOTTOM ROW: Pearl of the Pool • 'Rose Arey' • *N. capensis* • 'Odorata Sulphurea Grandiflora' *(see p.336)*

Nicotiana x sanderae **Starship Series** • Annual for evening fragrance *(see p.335)*

Borago officinalis • Borage, an annual herb with flowers in steel blue *(see p.301)*

Zinnia elegans **'Dasher Scarlet'** • Bold-flowered half-hardy annual *(see p.359)*

Verbena bonariensis • Tall, airy perennial with stiff, slender stems *(see p.357)*

Delphinium **Black Knight Group** • Classic perennial in a beautiful deep indigo *(see p.315)*

Fremontodendron **'California Glory'** ♀ • Lanky shrub to train on a sunny wall *(see p.320)*

Nemesia strumosa **'KLM'** • Bedding plant with unusual bicoloured flowers *(see p.334)*

Lilium **'Sun Ray'** • Summer bulb that makes an elegant container plant *(see p.330)*

Petunia **Million Bells Pink** • Trailing petunia with small but abundant flowers *(see p.340)*

Papaver rhoeas **Shirley Series** • Papery poppy that self-seeds freely in the garden *(see p.338)*

Antirrhinum majus **'Trumpet Serenade'** • Cheery, cottage-style perennial grown as an annual *(see p.298)*

Ipomoea tricolor **'Heavenly Blue'** • Aptly named cultivar of the morning glory *(see p.326)*

TOP ROW: Hannah Gordon • 'Crimson Glory' • Blue Moon • Chinatown ♈ **MIDDLE ROW:** Eglantyne • Graham Thomas • 'Königin von Danemark' ♈ 'Anna Ford' ♈ **BOTTOM ROW:** Amber Queen • 'William Lobb' ♈ • William Shakespeare 2000 • *Rosa gallica* 'Versicolor' ♈ *(see pp.347–9)*

TOP ROW: 'Climbing Iceberg' ♀ • 'American Pillar' • Handel • High Hopes **MIDDLE ROW:** Danse du Feu • 'Albertine' ♀ • Compassion ♀ • 'Goldfinch' ♀ **BOTTOM ROW:** 'Noisette Carnée' • 'Francois Juranville' ♀ • Golden Showers ♀ • 'Bobbie James' ♀ *(see pp.349–50)*

Lychnis chalcedonica ♀ • Perennial popular with beneficial insects (see p.331)

Alcea rosea **Chater's Double Group** • Hollyhock with pompon flowers (see p.296)

Nigella damascena 'Miss Jekyll' ♀ • Love-in-a-mist, an old-fashioned hardy annual (see p.335)

Cosmos bipinnatus **Sensation Series** • Annual with flowers in pink and white (see p.312)

Eschscholzia californica ♀ • California poppies, annuals that will reappear every year (see p.318)

Impatiens **Super Elfin Series** • Frost-tender annuals to brighten shade (see p.325)

Matthiola Brompton Group • Strongly scented annuals, ideal for cutting (see p.333)

Tropaeolum majus 'Empress of India' • Annual with edible flowers and blue-green leaves (see p.356)

Tagetes 'Naughty Marietta' • Small but striking plants for summer display (see p.355)

Helianthus annuus 'Teddy Bear' • Double sunflower with fluffy blooms (see p.323)

Lobelia erinus 'Crystal Palace' • Half-hardy annual, a container classic (see p.330)

Astrantia major • Cottage-garden style perennial; the flowers dry well (see p.300)

WHAT TO DO IN JULY

AROUND THE GARDEN

WITH WARM WEATHER, PESTS AND DISEASES can multiply rapidly. Greenfly and blackfly breed especially fast, and it can be a job to keep on top of the problem.

If you can build up diversity in the garden by growing a great variety of plants, you will attract a lot of beneficial insects and other wildlife, and a healthy balance should develop between pests and predators. It does take time, and you will have to have the courage of your convictions in the early stages, but it is well worth it in the end. There may be a little bit of damage to some plants and the occasional casualty, but that is a small price to pay for the enjoyment of having so many different creatures making a home in your garden.

There are many biological controls available now for pests and these are widely available by mail order direct from the manufacturers. Try to use cultural (that is, good gardening) and biological methods of control whenever you can, even if you do not consider yourself an organic gardener.

Sweet pea 'Geoff Hamilton' If you are going away, ask someone to pick your sweet peas.

PLAN FOR HOLIDAYS. July and August are generally the holiday months, and it is better to prepare the garden before going away so that you don't come back to a jungle or a sea of dead plants. Now is the time to "book up" a neighbour, another member of the family or a friend to call in periodically to attend to the routine tasks of watering and feeding plants and mowing the lawn if necessary. Most people are only too willing to help out, though a little bribery may not be a bad idea. Ask someone to pick vegetables like beans and courgettes, which all seem to come at once, and use them. If beans, and also cutting flowers like dahlias, chrysanthemums and sweet peas are picked regularly, they will continue to produce crops and blooms well into autumn. Mow the lawn, but don't mow it too close or you'll just encourage it to grow even faster. Most houseplants can be moved outside for a summer break; you can plunge the pots in the soil to lessen water loss. Automatic trickle irrigation systems are inexpensive and easy to install. They can be connected to a small computer control and set to come on whenever you want them to.

BIRDS AND OTHER WILDLIFE need a drink, especially during dry spells – just as much as plants and we gardeners do. Regularly top up any containers left out for the birds to ensure they get water. If you build a garden pond, make sure the sides slope gently to allow birds and other animals to drink and bathe in the shallow water. A decorative way of achieving this is to form a beach area with pebbles set around the edge of the pond.

SAVE WATER. It is inevitable that if we have a few weeks of dry weather, water will be in short supply and more than likely hosepipe bans will be brought into force. So it is wise to conserve as much water as we can.

• Water can be collected from guttering along the roof of the house in a water butt. There are many types available, from plastic to genuine wooden casks; the latter are an attractive addition to the garden.

• Mulch borders with any organic matter you can get your hands on, making sure the soil is moist before applying the mulch. Even old newspapers will reduce water loss from the surface of the soil.

• Only water plants that really need it: newly planted trees, shrubs and other plants. Newly sown or turfed lawns should be kept watered, established lawns will recover if they have gone brown.

• Most importantly, give plants a good soaking when you do water them. It is better to water a few at a time, giving them a thorough soak, than to give everything a little water each day.

• The ideal, water-efficient way of watering plants in the border is to use the leaky pipe or seephose system. This porous pipe lets the water seep out around the roots of the plant, just where it's wanted, avoiding waste.

PLANT AN "INSTANT" SUMMER SHOW. If you're feeling energetic, on page 187 we suggest a grouping of hardy perennials and tender plants that are looking good right now.

TREES & SHRUBS

Deadheading roses Cut through the stem well below the faded flowers, just above a leaf.

DEADHEAD ROSES TO PROLONG THE DISPLAY. Many people, when deadheading roses, just snap the old flowerheads off. But if you want to continue the display into autumn you have to prune back to a bud in a leaf axil lower down the stem to encourage strong new shoots. Prune to an outward-facing leaf to keep the centre of the rose bush open. Wild roses should not be deadheaded as they produce attractive hips in the autumn.

After deadheading, give the roses a feed to boost growth and encourage more flowers later in the summer. Use a fertiliser specific to roses, or one high in potash to encourage strong shoots. A fertiliser high in nitrogen will result in soft, sappy growth which is more prone to attack from pests and diseases.

DISEASES LIKE BLACKSPOT, RUST AND MILDEW are more of a problem in summer, the first two especially if the weather has been damp. Mildew tends to appear when the weather is drier. To minimise the spread of diseases, gather up and burn all infected leaves that have fallen to the ground. Never put them on the compost heap, as this may spread the spores of the disease around the garden. If you spray for blackspot, use a recommended fungicide, but do it early in the season before the disease has got a hold. Once blackspot is established, spraying is useless.

Rust disease, the symptoms of which appear as black spores on the undersides of the leaves, is more prevalent on plants that are deficient in potash, so feeding with a rose fertiliser, which is high in potash, will help to reduce the problem.

Mildew will attack plants that are under stress due to lack of water. Control mildew by keeping plants well watered, and spray with an approved fungicide if it is persistent.

SHRUBS GROWING IN CONTAINERS should be watered regularly and fed once a week with a high-potash fertiliser. Watering may have to be done twice a day in very hot weather.

PRUNING AND TRAINING

CUT LAVENDER FOR DRYING just as you would everlasting flowers (see Annuals and Bedding).

PRUNE EARLY-SUMMER-FLOWERING SHRUBS such as philadelphus and weigela if not done last month (see June).

REMOVE UNWANTED GROWTH FROM THE BASE OR TRUNKS OF TREES AND SHRUBS. Many trees and

Removing suckers Use a knife or secateurs to remove unwanted shoots flush with the trunk.

shrubs often produce a mass of shoots at the base of the plant. One of the most common groups of plants with this habit are the *Sorbus* species, such as rowan and mountain ash. These shoots need to be cut away cleanly to prevent them sapping all the strength of the plant. At the same time, remove any shoots which have grown with plain green leaves on variegated plants.

PROPAGATION

TAKE SEMI-RIPE CUTTINGS FROM SHRUBS. Semi-ripe cuttings are taken from growth made in the current year once the stems have started to become woody at the base. It's an easy and successful way to take cuttings, increasing your stock of plants quickly.

Remove shoots about 10cm (4in) long with a sliver or heel of older bark from the main stem, or just trim them below a leaf joint. Trim the tail of the heel off, if there is one. Remove the lower leaves. Pinch out the tip of the cutting if growth is very soft. Dip the whole of the cutting in a fungicide solution wearing protective gloves. Then dip the base of the cutting in hormone rooting solution. Put the cuttings around the edge of a pot containing peat-free compost mixed with an equal amount of vermiculite. Put a polythene bag over the pot to create a humid atmosphere, and put the pot in a shady part of the garden – in a cold frame, or below a sheltered wall. The cuttings will root in about six to eight weeks, when they can be potted up and grown on.

TAKE CUTTINGS FROM HYDRANGEAS. These showy garden shrubs, a delight in late summer, can be propagated easily. Remove non-flowering shoots 8–10cm (3–4in) long, cutting just above a bud. Remove the lower leaves and trim the base of the cutting with a sharp knife. There is no need to trim the cutting immediately below a leaf joint, as the cuttings will root perfectly well if cut between buds. Hydrangeas have quite large leaves, so to reduce water loss from them, cut the leaves across in half (see p.105 for illustrations). Put into a pot of cuttings compost and cover with a polythene bag and stand in a shady corner. The cuttings will root in about four weeks, when they can be potted up.

TAKE CONIFER CUTTINGS. After trimming your conifer hedge (see overleaf), many of the trimmings can be made into cuttings if you want to increase the number of plants to make another hedge. Pick out some healthy shoots with sideshoots that are 5–8cm (2–3in) long, and just becoming woody at their base where they join the main stem. Tear them off the larger shoot with a heel of older wood, and treat them in exactly the same way as for semi-ripe cuttings of shrubs (left).

TREES *continued*

POT UP OR PLANT OUT softwood cuttings taken earlier which have now rooted, watering them well before and after. If you have space, line them out in a corner of the vegetable garden where they can grow on during the summer, forming excellent plants by autumn. Otherwise pot them into individual pots, but don't let them dry out.

HEDGES

TRIM CONIFER HEDGES TO KEEP THEM UNDER CONTROL. Conifer hedges have received quite a bad press in recent years, due mainly to the notoriety of × *Cupressocyparis leylandii.* This is an excellent hedging plant, but as with all hedges it needs regular trimming to keep it under control. Admittedly it does grow extremely fast, putting on 60–90cm (2–3ft) of growth in most years. As with all other conifer hedges, it needs trimming once a year, or even twice (see October), to keep it in order. If you start doing this when the conifers are small, long before they reach the height and width you require, you will build up a good, thick layer of leafy growth over the entire surface of the hedge.

Cross-section, conifer hedge Leafy growth is only produced on the outer part of the plants.

CLIMBERS

TAKE CUTTINGS FROM CLEMATIS. Clematis are very easy to propagate from cuttings at this time of year. Some people have difficulty in layering them (pegging stems into the ground), and this is an easier method. Clematis cuttings are taken as internodal cuttings; that is, the cuts are made between the leaf joints, and not immediately below a leaf. Take a strong main stem and cut it into sections, cutting midway between the leaf joints, or nodes. Trim the stem below the node so that 2–5cm (1–2in) remains, and trim the stem above the node to 1cm (½in) long. Dip the base (that is, the longer ends) of the cuttings in hormone rooting solution and put in pots containing cuttings compost. Cover the cuttings with thin polythene held off the foliage and tucked under the pot. Put in a shady frame or in a shady spot outside, and they will root in six to eight weeks. Pot them up and grow on.

PRUNE WISTERIA by cutting back all the whippy growths made during the summer to within five or six buds of the main stems. This encourages the formation of flower buds for flowering next year. These shoots are shortened again in winter (see January).

TRY AIR-LAYERING CLIMBING PLANTS LIKE clematis and akebia. This is a fascinating way of making new plants. Select a main shoot and make a cut at a sharp angle into the stem, without cutting it completely. Wrap a little sphagnum moss around the cut and hold it in place with clear polythene, tied at the top and the bottom. When a good root system has formed in a few weeks, remove the young plant from the parent and pot up.

PERENNIALS

DIVIDING IRISES

❶ Lift the clump of old, knobbly rhizomes and cut off small, healthy, young pieces that each have a clump of leaves attached.

❷ Pull off any dead foliage, then with a sharp knife, cut straight across the fan of leaves.

❸ Replant the small divisions in a sunny spot, 8–15cm (4–6in) apart, with the rhizome just below the soil surface.

DIVIDE BEARDED AND OTHER RHIZOMATOUS IRISES after the flowers are over. After several years these irises, which form thick, fleshy rhizomes, tend to lose vigour and need to be divided up. It's also a good opportunity to clear weeds from within iris clumps, as these are notoriously difficult to get out – unless you lift and clean up the plants, a spot weedkiller is usually the only answer, using a sheet of card or paper to protect the iris leaves completely from contact.

Once the flowers are over, lift the clump carefully with a fork and then separate out the younger pieces from around the outside of the clump (see left). Cut off the younger pieces with a sharp knife. The older pieces can be thrown away. Cut off faded leaves, and cut across the remaining foliage about 15cm (6in) from the root, leaving a fan shape of trimmed leaves. This helps reduce water loss from the leaves and stops the wind catching the tall foliage like a sail and blowing the plant over.

Replant in groups of three, five or more and water them in thoroughly. Irises must not be planted too deeply; on an exposed site, it may help to pin down the rhizomes with hoops of galvanized wire, removing these when the plants have developed their own anchoring roots.

DISBUD DAHLIAS if you want larger blooms, and support the flowering stems with canes or stakes. If you've joined a local gardening society (and I can't recommend doing this highly enough) then dahlias are one of the best plants with which to enter the cut-throat world of showing. Any club organising a show will issue its own strict rules on how show flowers are presented, and for dahlias, this nearly always means growing single, large blooms on long, sturdy stems. Rules for flower arrangements may not be so precise, but some stunning dahlias always make a good centrepiece for a display.

All disbudding means is removing some of the sidebuds at the apex of the stems, leaving the larger bud in the middle to flower. Remove sideshoots lower down the stem too, to get those long stems. Dahlias are normally supported with stakes, as there is a fair weight of top growth on the plants. Use one stake at planting time, and later put three or four canes around the plants as well, and tie twine around all the supports. This way the whole plant will be supported.

WHILE BORDERS ARE IN FULL BLOOM it is a good idea to have a wander round the garden and look carefully at the display and decide which plants look out of place – perhaps colours clash – and which just haven't performed very well. Look out too for those overgrown plants that may need dividing during the autumn and winter. Dividing them may rejuvenate them, giving them a new lease of life. Take a notepad or gardening diary with you and note down all the things that need to be done, because by the autumn, if you have a memory like mine, you'll have forgotten everything.

CONTINUE TO CUT BACK FADED FLOWERS on perennials if seed is not required. This will encourage new growth and more flowers later in the summer.

Plants like Oriental poppies and hardy geraniums can be cut back to ground level with a pair of shears, as described in June, and taller perennials like delphiniums should have their faded flower spikes cut back, to encourage new shoots that, hopefully, will produce more flowers later in the summer. Aquilegias can have the old flowering stems removed if seed is not required from the plants. All the old growth can be put on the compost heap. Give the plants a feed and a good watering if the weather is dry.

HARVEST SEED FROM PERENNIALS. Many perennials will be finishing flowering now, and if they haven't been cut off, seed pods will be developing. A lot of seedheads will become ripe towards the end of the month, and must be gathered before they open up and scatter the seeds. You will have to be vigilant if you want to catch them.

Seeds are best collected on a dry, sunny day when there will be less chance of rot getting in to them. When collecting the seeds, put the heads or pods into paper bags with the name of the plant written on them. If the seeds are ripe and are beginning to come out of the seedhead, close the top of the bag and shake it to get all of the seeds out. If you cut off one corner of the bag, you should be able to trickle the seeds out onto a sheet of paper, keeping most of the debris in the bag. If the heads aren't quite open, lay them out on a sheet of paper in a dry place until they begin to shed the seeds.

Carefully separate the seeds from any dirt and chaff using an old kitchen sieve, or by very gently blowing over them. The heavier seeds should stay in place while the chaff is blown away, but do it carefully or the whole lot will disappear.

Put the seeds into paper envelopes, seal them, and write the name of the plant on them. Store the seeds somewhere cool and dry, the ideal place being in an air-tight container on the bottom shelf of the refrigerator.

LAYER PINKS AND CARNATIONS. Border pinks and carnations are delightful cottage garden plants to have in the borders. After three or four years they can become a bit straggly, but they

are easy to propagate. You can layer them by pegging stems into the ground, so that roots form on the stems and become new young plantlets. This can be a bit fiddly, and sometimes not as successful as taking cuttings or "pipings", as they are called (see June). However, the advantage of layering is that you need less space to grow on cuttings and young plants in pots, as the layers can be transplanted directly into

LAYERING PINKS

① Find a shoot that can be bent to touch the ground, and remove all but the top few leaves.

② Wound the stems to stimulate root formation, by nicking the shoot with a very sharp knife at a leaf joint.

③ Use hoops or staples of galvanized wire to peg the shoot into the ground at the point where you have wounded it.

their new site as soon as they have formed good roots, or even left in place until next spring, if you prefer. Some gardeners layer a few stems as a matter of course each summer, just to see what happens. It doesn't take long, and although the results can be a bit hit and miss, you should get at least a new plant or two. If you don't have particularly light soil, you can increase your chances of success by mixing a little sand into the soil where you are going to peg your layer.

HERBACEOUS PERENNIALS IN GENERAL, and late-flowering ones like Michaelmas daisies (asters) and chrysanthemums in particular, will benefit from a sprinkling of a general organic fertiliser now to give a boost to their growth for the rest of the summer. Hoe or lightly rake it in, and if the weather is dry, water it in as well.

ALPINES

SAVE SEEDS FROM ALPINES in exactly the same way as described for herbaceous perennials. The main difference between sowing alpines and most herbaceous perennials is that alpines require a period of cold weather to break the seeds' dormancy, so they have to be left outside or in an unheated cold frame for the winter.

However, seeds of some alpines only remain viable (able to germinate) for a relatively short time and these have to be sown now, straight after harvesting. These include primulas, cyclamen, androsaces, dionysias and meconopsis. Other seeds can be kept for sowing later (see December). If you are not sure of the correct time for sowing a

PERENNIALS *contd*

particular variety of seed, sow some as soon as the seed is ripe, or in the autumn, and then sow some in late winter or spring. This way you cover each period and should have some success. Note down which seeds germinate best at which time for future seed sowing.

This technique of sowing two batches of seeds to ensure germination applies to other plants – shrubs, trees and perennials – too.

SPOT-TREAT ANY PERENNIAL WEEDS that appear among alpines. If perennial weeds grow between or even up through alpines they can be difficult to uproot without disturbing the plants, and impossible to spray with weedkiller, but all is not lost if this happens. There are some weedkillers on the market which come ready-prepared in the form of a gel with a small brush built into the lid of the container. It is an easy matter to brush the weedkiller onto the foliage of the weed, using a piece of cardboard as a shield to protect the alpine plant, and kill the weeds.

SOME ALPINES WITH A CARPETING HABIT can die off in the centre and look horrible. This problem can be remedied by infilling the centre of the plant with gritty alpine compost. This will encourage the plant to regrow, filling in the bare patch.

BULBS

BULBS WHICH WERE HEELED IN in trenches for the foliage to die back can be dug up and stored until they are required for planting in the autumn. The main point is to make sure the bulbs are thoroughly dry and free from any diseased material for the winter, so that they do not rot in store. Remove all the dead foliage and flowering stems if they are still on the bulbs. Inspect the bulbs for any signs of disease or rotting, and remove and discard any that are affected. Lay the bulbs out in a single layer to dry off completely for a few days, either in a greenhouse or in a garage or spare room, and then store in boxes or trays in a cool dry, airy place.

PLANT AUTUMN-FLOWERING BULBS NOW. These bulbs will flower through September, October and, if the weather is reasonable, into November. The flowers appear without foliage, because the leaves have died down during the

Crocus kotschyanus *The cup-shaped flowers appear without leaves in autumn.*

summer. The leaves will appear in the spring. Bulbs to choose are autumn-flowering crocus: *Crocus speciosus* with blue-purple and white flowers, *C. kotschyanus* with lilac-pink flowers, and *C. sativus*, with dark-veined lilac flowers. Plant them in full sun to a depth of 10cm (4in).

Nerines are wonderful plants from the warmer climes of South Africa; very eyecatching indeed. Like colchicums, the flowers appear before the leaves, with tall stems bearing up to nine blooms with pink curling petals. As they come from a warm country they will need a warm, sunny, sheltered spot, preferably at the base of a south-facing wall or fence, and well-drained soil. From the point of view of hardiness, *Nerine bowdenii* is the most widely known and easiest to grow, but even this will need some protection in colder areas. In northern parts and very exposed, chilly gardens it may be best to grow nerines in a cold greenhouse or conservatory. As with all bulbs, the general rule when it comes to depth of planting is to plant the bulb to at least twice its own depth. If you have a heavy clay soil, put a layer of coarse sand or grit in the bottom of the hole and sit the bulbs directly on this. It will help to improve the drainage.

LILIES SHOULD BE LOOKING GORGEOUS NOW, but one note of caution: when lilies are in pots on the patio, it's particularly easy to brush against the flowers inadvertently. If you're wearing light-coloured clothes, the pollen on the large stamens can cause stains which can be difficult to get out. You can cut the stamens off to prevent this, as florists often do.

ANNUALS & BEDDING

CUT FLOWERS TO DRY

① Cut everlasting flowers such as statice (*Limonium*) just as the flowers start to open. Cut low down to get the full length of stem.

② Tie the flowers in small bunches and hang them upside-down in an airy place, out of full sun which will bleach the colour.

CUT AND DRY EVERLASTING FLOWERS. Flowers of plants like statice, bracteantha and rhodanthe can be cut for drying and used for decorative displays in the home during the winter.

They have to be picked just before they reach their peak, which is when they are almost fully open. They will open slightly more as they dry out. Tie them in bunches and hang them up in an airy place to dry out. Don't try to speed up the drying process by putting the flowers in a warm place, as they will shrivel up.

FINISH PLANTING OUT SUMMER BEDDING PLANTS in baskets, containers and borders. Gaps in the borders can be filled with larger plants grown yourself or bought from the garden centre. The sooner this job is done the better, as the plants will have time to settle in and flower for the rest of the summer.

MAINTAIN ANNUALS AND TENDER PERENNIALS to keep the display going well into the autumn. Deadhead old flowers regularly to prevent the plants setting seed unless, of course, you want to collect seeds from some plants. Do bear in mind, though, that hybrid plants such as "F1 hybrids" will not come true to type from seed.

Plants like pansies and petunias tend to get straggly at this time of year, and picking off individual spent flowers from these plants can be tedious. An easy way to deadhead them is to cut them back with secateurs or a pair of shears. Cut them back quite hard, give a quick tonic with a high-potash fertiliser and new growth will soon be produced with flowers later in the summer.

CONTINUE TO WATER PLANTS IF THE WEATHER IS DRY. Give a good soaking once a week rather than a little each day. Regular feeding with a high-

potash fertiliser will also help to prolong the flowering period. Hoe between plants, if they've not grown into each other, to keep down weeds.

TRANSPLANT BIENNIAL SEEDLINGS SOWN IN MAY AND JUNE. Seedlings of wallflowers, forget-me-nots (*Myosotis*), bellis, Canterbury bells (*Campanula medium*) and ornamental kales and cabbages can be transplanted to nursery rows, there to grow into larger plants before planting in their flowering positions in the autumn when the summer bedding has finished. Water the seedlings an hour or so beforehand, and lift them carefully with a small hand fork. Replant about 15cm (6in) apart in rows in a corner, an unused spot in the vegetable garden being ideal. Water the seedlings well after transplanting to settle them in. One tip – wallflowers tend to have one main or tap root with only a few fibrous roots, so to encourage more fibrous roots to grow, cut back the thicker tap root when transplanting them.

Water the young plants regularly, keep them weeded throughout the summer by regularly hoeing between the plants, and they should make fine plants to put in their flowering positions in autumn.

DISBUD TUBEROUS BEGONIAS growing in pots or as bedding. These large-flowered begonias produce three flower buds at the top of the stems. The large central bud is the male flower, and it is this one we want to keep for its doubleness – its crowded frilly petals. The smaller buds either side of this one are the less showy, single female flowers and these need to be removed to get a reasonable-sized double flower.

CONTAINERS

Watering lance These handy hose attachments make watering hanging baskets less of a chore.

CONTINUE MAINTAINING CONTAINERS to extend the colourful display well into autumn. Water and feed the containers regularly. Watering may have to be done twice a day during very hot spells of weather. Containers will still need plenty of water even when it rains. The mass of roots inside the container and the foliage on top make rain penetration almost impossible, and so watering with a watering can or hose is the only answer. Deadhead the plants regularly to keep the plants looking good and prevent them from setting seeds.

Plants crammed together in containers can sometimes begin to look a bit straggly towards late summer, and it is a good idea to go over your containers occasionally, pruning off any straggly shoots and any that are crowding out other plants too much. You can always make some cuttings from the material you cut off.

PONDS

TOP UP PONDS IN HOT WEATHER. As last month, keep an eye on the water level in ponds, particularly if you have fish. Water can evaporate from the pond at an alarming rate during hot spells. Top up with a hose as often as necessary.

KEEP A WATCH ON FISH, because if the water is still and the level drops they may be starved of oxygen. Fish in difficulties will rise to the surface and gulp for air, just as we would. Spray the pond with a jet of water to put some oxygen into the water. It may be worth installing a small feature such as a small waterfall or a fountain, to keep the water moving and oxygen levels high.

OXYGENATING PLANTS IN THE POND will have to be thinned as they can take over the pond completely. Pull them out with a rake and leave by the side of the pond to dry out, and to allow any wildlife hiding in them to escape back into the pond. They can be added to the compost heap.

THINNING OXYGENATORS

1 Thick, smothering weed needs to be thinned to keep the pond healthy. A rake is ideal to remove it.

2 With the weed thinned, other plants and aquatic life will be better off, and the pond looks less neglected.

VEGETABLES & HERBS *continued*

WATCH OUT FOR THE TOMATO PROBLEMS blossom end rot and ghost spot. The symptoms of blossom end rot appear as a sunken brown patch on the fruit at the furthest end from the flower stalk. It is caused by a lack of calcium, which is in turn caused by a lack of water. It only needs the plant to be short of water for a very brief time for this to happen; you may hardly notice the plant wilting. The way to prevent blossom end rot is to water the plants regularly and evenly, never allowing them to dry out.

Watering tomatoes regularly will also prevent splitting. This often happens after a dry spell if the plants are suddenly given a lot of water, the upsurge in water causing the skins of the fruits to split.

Ghost spot appears as small spots on the fruits, surrounded by a lighter ring. This fungal disease can usually be avoided by taking care not to splash the fruits with water when damping down or watering.

BEGIN TO EARTH UP CELERY growing in trenches. By now the stems should be about 30cm (1ft) high, and will be ready for the first stages of blanching. The blanching process (excluding light from the stems) makes the stems more succulent. To prevent soil getting into the centre of the plant and causing rot to set in, make a collar from a sheet of newspaper to go around the plant and tie it in place, leaving the tuft of foliage at the top exposed. The soil can now be gradually filled in from either side of the trench using a draw hoe. Self-blanching celery does not need earthing up, and can be left to grow in its blocks.

WATCH OUT FOR POTATO AND TOMATO BLIGHT. The symptoms of blight appear as yellow-brown patches on the leaves, eventually turning the leaves black when they die off. The only cure is to cut off the top growth on potatoes and burn it (although the tubers can be left in the soil to harvest), and burn all affected tomato plants. Unaffected plants can be sprayed with mancozeb or a copper fungicide as a preventative measure to avoid further spread to other plants.

WATER RUNNER BEANS REGULARLY at the roots to help the flowers set and form pods. Many gardeners also recommend spraying the flowers with water each day. Adding a small handful of hydrated lime to a full two-gallon watering can and applying this along the row of runner beans at the base of the plants will also help the flowers to set and produce more pods. Always wear gloves and a face mask when handling lime, as it can be harmful if ingested.

STOP CLIMBING BEANS when they reach the tops of their supports – that is, pinch out the tip of the leading shoot. This will encourage the plants to make more sideshoots lower down, and therefore more beans will be produced. Be sure to pick beans regularly, because if the pods are left on the plants too long they become tough and stringy and are not very palatable. But perhaps more important is that the more you pick them, the more beans you will get throughout the summer because plants will continue cropping for longer. Of course, if you are exhibiting runner beans you will want pods that are as

straight and long as possible. The longest pods are achieved by growing show varieties such as 'Enorma'.

PROTECT SUMMER CAULIFLOWERS by bending or snapping leaves over the flower heads. If left exposed to the light the curds will begin to open up quickly. Keeping them in the dark by breaking leaves over them will protect them from the light, keep them white and lengthen the time before they begin to open up.

ENDIVES CAN BE BLANCHED to turn the foliage white and make it more palatable. The easiest way to do this is to cover each plant with a plate or large upturned pot, making sure you cover up any drainage holes in the bottom of pots so the plants are in total darkness. They should be ready to harvest after about ten days of blanching.

BLANCHING ENDIVE

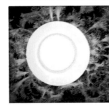

1 Put an upturned plate over the heart of the plant to exclude the light.

2 In a week or two, the inner leaves will have become pale and sweet to eat.

Drying herbs
The woodier herbs such as sage and rosemary keep their pungent flavours well when dried.

HERBS

PICK HERBS REGULARLY to maintain a supply of fresh, young shoots. It's almost like pruning the plant: the more you pick, the more young shoots, with the best flavour for cooking, will be produced. If herbs are not picked regularly they tend to become rather spindly. But if they have been neglected they can be brought back to bushiness again. Most herbs will benefit from being trimmed over occasionally with a pair of garden shears. This will encourage a flush of new growth.

PICK AND DRY HERBS. Sage, rosemary and thyme can be cut now and hung up to dry. Do this in an airy place outdoors, such as a shed or garage, where the herbs will be protected from the rain. A lot of people hang them up in the kitchen to dry, but here they can get covered in dust and grease from cooking, and this makes them less appealing to use, as well as damaging their flavour. Another easy way to store herbs is to freeze them; greener, softer herbs like parsley and chives can be cut up small and put into ice cube trays. Fill with water, put in the ice-making compartment of the fridge and use them as required. Often, you can simply add the ice cube to the dish you are cooking.

FRUIT

TAKE CUTTINGS FROM HERBS such as lemon verbena, sage and thyme – all the herbs that tend to become woody near the ground. To increase success, dip the bases of the cuttings in hormone rooting solution. The cuttings should root in four to six weeks, when they can be potted up individually. They can sit outside in a shady corner over the summer, provided that you remember to water regularly, and planted in autumn or overwintered in a cold frame.

TAKING HERB CUTTINGS

1 Remove the tips of shoots and trim below a leaf joint to make cuttings 5–8cm (2–3in) long.

2 Put them in pots of peat-free compost mixed with an equal amount of vermiculite.

3 Cover with polythene and put in a shady place in good light but out of direct sunlight.

4 When the cuttings have rooted, pot each up into its own individual pot.

Freezing raspberries Lay them out in trays to freeze individually, then store in plastic bags.

PICKING AND STORING

SUMMER-FRUITING RASPBERRIES should ripen this month. If you have a surplus, they freeze very well, either singly as above or, to save freezer space, cooked gently to reduce to a puree.

BLACKCURRANT BUSHES CAN BE PARTIALLY PRUNED, if you like, as the crop is harvested, so you can take some whole branches into the kitchen and pick the fruits off with ease. Remove about one-third of the bush each year low down to encourage strong new shoots from the base of the plants. Pruning blackcurrants is a compromise between cutting out old wood and leaving enough new wood for fruiting the following year. It is inevitable that some new growth will be pruned out. See December for more details.

RED AND WHITE CURRANTS are harvested by pulling or snipping entire, long fruit clusters from the plant. Don't strip the berries off individually until you have them indoors.

PRUNING AND TRAINING

SUMMER-PRUNE RED AND WHITE CURRANTS AND GOOSEBERRIES late in the month. All sideshoots made this year should be trimmed back to three or four buds from their point of growth. Any crossing shoots and those growing into the middle of the bush can be removed at the same time. This pruning allows air to circulate more freely around the bushes, lets more light in to ripen the fruits and reduces the incidence of disease; it also encourages the formation of fruit buds for fruiting next year.

PRUNE SUMMER-FRUITING RASPBERRIES after all of the fruit has been picked. The old fruited canes are easily identifiable as they should have been tied to the supporting wires. If not, the wood of these canes is more brown in colour, there will be the remains of fruit clusters and the leaves tend to look a bit tatty by this time of year. By contrast, the younger canes that have been produced during the summer will have fresh green foliage and the stems will still be green. First untie the old canes from the supporting wires and cut them out to ground level. The new canes can now be tied in, spacing them about 10cm (4in) apart. Only tie in good, strong canes; any weak ones should be pruned out completely. Any canes growing far out from the rows should be dug up or they will continue to creep outwards.

CONTINUE TRAINING NEW CANES of blackberries and other hybrid berries. Most of the hybrid berries have vicious thorns, and if you don't tie them in regularly they will become quite a

Summer-fruiting raspberries Prune out the fruited canes by cutting them at ground level.

problem getting tangled up in other plants. There are some thornless hybrid berries as well as the blackberry variety 'Oregon Thornless', which are better for family gardens – although it can mean that little fingers get to your crop before you do. As with raspberries, tie the new canes to the supports with twine, on the opposite side to the fruiting canes already there. There are many complicated ways of training hybrid berries but this is the easiest way: fruiting canes to one side of the support, and new canes to the other, to form a fan shape.

CONTINUE TRAINING FAN-TRAINED FRUITS. Remove any unwanted shoots that spoil the shape of the fan. Any shoots growing directly towards the wall or fence should also be pruned out. Young shoots growing at the base of each of this year's fruiting shoots should be retained and tied in. These will be used as replacements for the current year's growth when these are pruned out after fruiting, and will fruit next year.

FRUIT *continued*

AT THE END OF THE MONTH begin summer-pruning trained apples and pears. See August.

LOOKING AFTER CROPS

RIPENING FRUIT OF PEACHES AND NECTARINES will need protecting from birds and wasps. Trees trained against walls or fences are relatively easy to protect, by draping horticultural fleece or fine mesh netting over them. Make sure it is secured to the wall and that there are no gaps where birds can get in and be caught up. Free-standing trees are more difficult to protect, but fleece draped over them will give some protection, particularly if it can be secured at ground level.

THIN OUT FRUIT ON APPLES AND PEARS. Once the "June drop" is over (fruit trees naturally shed some fruit in June), it is safe to thin out any other fruits not required. Remove any very small, damaged or diseased fruits in each cluster. To get apples and pears of a reasonable size, thin the remaining fruits to leave one fruit every 10cm (4in) apart. It may seem disappointing to remove a lot of fruit from the tree, but the resulting crops in the autumn will be of far superior quality than if a lot of fruits are left on the tree.

SUPPORT HEAVILY LADEN FRUIT TREE BRANCHES. The weight of fruit on trees can be quite considerable at this time of year, and it makes sense to support the branches of some trees. The branches of plums in particular are very brittle and will break very easily. A stake with a 'V'-shaped notch in the end can be put under any vulnerable-looking

SUPPORTING FRUIT TREES

With small trees, it may be worth holding the branches up by lashing a cane to the stake and creating a "maypole" effect with loops of twine.

Young plums are often trained to have drooping or "festooned" branches which hold a heavy crop better, by arching and tying them down when young.

fruiting branch to prop it up. Smaller shoots on some trees can be tied up to a cane lashed to the tree's stake, or just to a more mature branch, to support the weight of the crop if it is necessary.

INSPECT APPLES FOR woolly aphids and spray with a suitable insecticide. Woolly aphids appear as tight clusters at the tips of shoots, and if a large colony builds up then the young tips, where growth should be made, can become distorted. Aphids of all kinds can also spread virus diseases around, and so they should be controlled. Spray only in the late evening, when there are fewer pollinating and other beneficial insects around. Light infestations can be controlled by squashing the aphids by hand, so do this if you can. Even some of the so-called organic insecticides will harm not only pests, but also beneficial wildlife too.

REMOVE OLD FOLIAGE FROM STRAWBERRIES once fruiting has finished. Old leaves become diseased and are of little use to the plants. Remove them by going over the plants with a pair of shears (see right). Any straw which was put around the plants to keep the fruits from being spoiled should be removed too. Lightly fork over the soil between the plants and take out any weeds. The plants will soon produce new foliage over the next few weeks. The old leaves and straw can be consigned to the compost heap.

PLANNING AHEAD

PREPARE THE GROUND FOR NEW STRAWBERRY PLANTS. After three years, the yield from strawberry plants tends to decline, and the plants sometimes get virus disease. So it is better to replace plants after three seasons of cropping. If the old plants have shown any signs of virus, buy in new plants from reputable fruit nurseries, where you will be able to get healthy new stock which is certified to be free of virus.

Choose a new patch to plant the new strawberries. Prepare the ground well, incorporating plenty of organic matter to improve the soil structure and retain moisture in the soil.

STRAWBERRIES AFTER CROPPING

① After the last fruits have been picked, trim all the leaves off the plants with shears and put them on the compost heap.

② Remove straw mulches or strawberry mats, clear all debris from the crowns of the plants, and weed and gently fork over the soil.

UNDER COVER

KEEP THE GREENHOUSE AND CONSERVATORY WELL VENTILATED in hot weather. Ventilators can be left open almost all of the time now, to help avoid great fluctuations in temperature. Damping down paths regularly with water will also help to reduce the temperature.

Be on the lookout for birds getting inside. Even though the doors and ventilators may be wide open, they often find it difficult to see the way out, and will fly against the windows. To avoid this, put netting over doors and over ventilator openings.

Towards the end of the month there may be the occasional colder night when it is advisable to close the doors and ventilators.

GLASSHOUSE AND HOUSE PLANTS

DISBUD TUBEROUS BEGONIAS. These large-flowered begonias produce three flower buds at the top of the stems. The large central bud is the male double flower, which is the most spectacular. The smaller buds either side of this one are less showy, single female flowers and these can be removed to improve the quality of the double flower.

START TAKING FUCHSIA CUTTINGS. Root them in exactly the same way as you would do for pelargonium cuttings (see August, Annuals & Bedding). When the cuttings have rooted, pot them on.

TRAIN STANDARD FUCHSIAS FROM CUTTINGS. Growing standards is a very attractive way of growing these delightful plants, as the flowers are held

TRAINING A STANDARD FUCHSIA

1 Choose a cutting with a strong, definite vertical main stem, and very carefully remove all sideshoots.

2 Insert a cane and train the main stem up it, again pinching out any sideshoots while as young as possible.

3 When the main stem reaches 1–1.2m (3–4ft), 30cm (12in) or so taller than you want the clear stem to be, pinch out the tip.

4 Let sideshoots and their sideshoots develop on the top third of the main stem, pinching their tips out meticulously every time they have 3 or 4 pairs of leaves.

5 Stop pinching when the head is well-formed to allow flowering. Pinch off any shoots on the clear portion of stem.

higher up and can be appreciated more readily. If you keep your greenhouse or conservatory heated over winter, then the young plants will continue to grow year-round, although growth will inevitably slow during winter – not

because the plants are not warm enough, but because plant growth is very closely linked to day-length, shutting down as the nights draw in.

Cuttings that have naturally developed with a single, definite, sturdy

main stem are the best material to start with. As the cuttings grow, tie them to a cane regularly to keep the stem straight. Remove any sideshoots as they develop from the leaf axils. Pot the young plant on into progressively larger pots as it

UNDER COVER *continued*

Pelargonium 'Ann Hoystead' Take cuttings
from the showy regal pelargoniums now.

grows and keep it growing slowly over
the winter in cool but frost-free
conditions, watering very sparingly. In
spring, growth will pick up again. Once
the plant has reached the height you
want, which is purely a matter of
personal preference, pinch out the
growing tip. The resulting sideshoots
that develop can be pinched out
themselves when they have made three
or four pairs of leaves. Do this another
couple of times and you will develop a
good bushy head to the plant which
will, in summer, be covered in flowers.
Leaves on the clear stem should drop
naturally, but remove any shoots that
develop.

**TAKE CUTTINGS FROM REGAL
PELARGONIUMS.** These showy plants
can be propagated by cuttings from now
through the rest of the summer. Select
non-flowering shoots about 10cm (4in)

long and cut them from the plant.
Remove the lower leaves, leaving just
two or three leaves at the tip of the
cutting. In addition, remove the little
scale-like structures at the base of the
leaf stalks (known as stipules), as these
may rot. They are particularly prominent
on pelargoniums. Trim the cuttings just
below a leaf joint, so that each is about
8cm (3in) long. Dip the ends in
hormone rooting solution and put into
pots containing cutting compost. There
is no need to cover them with
polythene. Stand the pots on a well-lit
bench or windowsill, but out of direct
sunlight. The cuttings will take four
weeks to root, when they can be potted
up to grow on.

PRICK OUT SEEDLINGS of plants
sown earlier for winter-flowering pot
plants, such as cinerarias and
calceolarias. Prick out the seedlings
when they are large enough to handle.
This can be a tricky job with
calceolarias, as the seedlings are small,
yet cannot be left in the seed tray too
long. Either prick out into trays spacing
the seedlings about 5cm (2in) apart or
pot them up individually into small
pots. More seed of these plants can be
sown now to give a succession of
flowers through the winter and into
spring on plants that are kept in the
warmth. Sow in trays or pots of seed
compost, and water the container before
sowing. Seeds of cinerarias and
calceolarias are very small, and can be
sown on the surface of the compost and
left uncovered. You may find it easier to
sow them by first mixing a little silver
sand with the seeds. This makes it a little
easier to see where you have sown the
seeds, and helps distribute them evenly.

CROPS UNDER GLASS
**CONTINUE TO MAINTAIN INDOOR
FRUITS AND VEGETABLES.** Tomatoes
need to have any sideshoots which grow
from the leaf axils removed. Remove
them before they get too large to
minimise the shock to the plant. Keep
feeding all crops under cover with a
high-potash feed, applied weekly, and
water regularly – every evening if
possible now that the fruits are swelling.
Aubergine and pepper plants may
benefit from some support now that the
fruits are forming. Like tomatoes,
their stems are thick but fleshy, and
can snap easily.

START REMOVING FOLIAGE from
tomatoes around the end of the month.
This will allow more light to get to the

ripening tomatoes and will also allow
better circulation of air, reducing the
incidence of diseases like mildew and
botrytis. Start removing the older leaves
at the bottom of the plants, some of
which may be going yellow by now
anyway, especially around the first truss
of tomatoes which will be starting to
ripen by now. Don't remove too many
all at once as this may be quite a shock
to the plant.

**WATCH OUT FOR TOMATO
DISORDERS** like blossom end rot and
ghost spot (see Vegetables & Herbs for
symptoms and control).

REMOVE SOME LEAVES from grape
vines where they are preventing sun
falling on the fruits.

Remove tomato leaves
Start at the base of the
plant where the foliage
may already be
yellowing, to allow more
sun on the fruits.

PLANT A SUMMER BORDER

HERBACEOUS PERENNIALS are terrific plants to have in the garden: they flower for weeks and are very easy to look after. Generally, taller ones should be positioned near the back of the border with shorter plants towards the front. However, slight variations here and there, with slightly taller plants nearer the front or middle of the border, will give variation, making the display more interesting to look at. All the plants here are not fussy as to soil type as long as it is reasonably fertile and there is good drainage, and enjoy full sun, though they will tolerate light, part–day shade. Several need protection in winter, but they will reward your care with a splendid show all summer long.

BACK OF BORDER, LEFT TO RIGHT
1. 3 × *Monarda* 'Croftway Pink' ♔
2. 3 × *Canna* 'Rosemond Coles'
3. 3 × *Romneya coulteri* ♔
4. 3 × *Lobelia tupa*

MIDDLE OF BORDER, LEFT TO RIGHT
5. 3 × *Hemerocallis* 'Green Flutter' ♔
6. 3 × *Phlox paniculata* 'Windsor' ♔
7. 3 × *Iris ensata* ♔
8. 2 × *Euryops pectinatus* ♔

FRONT OF BORDER, LEFT TO RIGHT
9. 4 × *Salvia patens* ♔
10. 1 × *Cordyline australis* ♔
11. 3 × *Penstemon* 'Chester Scarlet'
12. 6 × *Gazania* Chansonette Series
13. 3 × *Eucomis bicolor*
14. 3 × *Phygelius aequalis* 'Yellow Trumpet' ♔

Monarda 'Croftway Pink'
Clump-forming hardy perennial; divide in spring when mature.

Canna 'Rosemond Coles'
Overwinter under cover and plunge the pots in the ground in summer.

Romneya coulteri
The tree poppy, sometimes difficult to establish but then grows with vigour.

Hemerocallis 'Green Flutter'
Hardy, clump-forming perennial with a long succession of flowers.

Phlox paniculata 'Windsor'
Floriferous hardy perennial; deadhead regularly for more flowers.

Salvia patens
Erect, tuberous perennial. Take indoors for winter or overwinter cuttings.

Eucomis bicolor
The pineapple lily, a striking summer bulb of borderline hardiness.

Phygelius aequalis 'Yellow Trumpet'
Small, upright shrub, vulnerable to frost damage but can be cut hard back.

BORDER SIZE: APPROX 2M x 1.5M (6FT x 5FT)

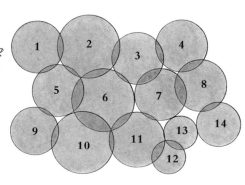

AUGUST

The garden in **August**

August is traditionally the month for a well-earned break, but whether you're going away or just planning to put your feet up at home, make sure that the garden can cope with the summer heat.

THIS IS TRADITIONALLY THE HOLIDAY MONTH, but we mustn't forget the garden before we go away. Some preparation done beforehand will pay dividends when we come back. It's so easy to leave the garden, hoping it will take care of itself while we're away, but at this time of year it can so quickly become overgrown, and there's a risk of returning to find weeds everywhere and much of the hard work you put in earlier in the year wasted.

Try to keep ahead with all the routine jobs, such as deadheading, weeding and watering, that have to be done. The lawn may need trimming if there has been a lot of rain and it is growing fast, but don't cut it shorter than you would normally do as this will only encourage it to grow even faster while you are away. Plants growing inside will need special attention. If you can, ask a neighbour or friend to call in and water indoor plants. If this cannot be arranged, then put as many plants as possible outside in a cool, shady corner of the garden. Even better, if you can, is to plunge the pots in the ground; this way they will not dry out as quickly as when the containers are fully exposed to the sun.

Automatic watering and ventilating systems for greenhouses and conservatories are not overly

Colour under cover ▷
Glasshouse plants will be giving their best for you now, so organise some care for them if you're going away.

expensive to buy from garden centres or specialist firms. Some are controlled by a small computer. There are similar systems that can be set up to water plants in containers outdoors as well, and these are invaluable if you have a patio or courtyard garden, or even a roof terrace or balcony, and rely very heavily on pots and baskets filled with plants. These systems are no more complicated to operate than your average central heating system, and can save you a lot of time even when you're not on holiday – and you can go away at any time at a moment's notice, knowing that your precious plants won't go short of water.

Home and dry

If you're not jetting off to some far-flung corner of the globe then take time to relax and enjoy the fruits of your labour earlier in the year. But make time too for some light summer maintenance in the garden to keep it looking good. As in July, early mornings and evenings are often the most comfortable and pleasant times to work.

The weather in August is often hot and sultry. In a prolonged dry spell, take care to conserve as much water as you can, as many regions will have restrictions on the use of sprinklers which seem to be enforced as soon as we get a glimpse of sunshine

WEATHER WATCH

August temperatures are similar to July, often with hot, sultry days occasionally interspersed with thundery showers. Daily minimum temperatures are usually around 11–13°C in the south, and 8–10°C in the north. Maximum temperatures can, of course, be more than double this on bright sunny days. High ground will always be slightly cooler, and coastal areas are kept fresher by sea breezes.

There are very few gales in any parts of the country now, but there can be strong winds in coastal areas, especially in the north and west. Up to 0.5 days of gales may be experienced in the western isles of Scotland and parts of north-west England may have up to 0.4 days of gales.

Generally August is slightly duller than July, with more marked differences in the number of sunshine hours up and down the country – northern parts getting around 140 hours and southern parts on average 190 hours of direct sun. The amount of sunshine will always vary according to the locality, height above sea level and proximity to the coast, and the local topography.

The amount of rainfall this month will vary considerably depending on where you are. The south coast will typically receive around 50mm of rain this month; inland regions can experience higher rainfall, at around 60mm, due to the higher frequency of thunderstorms as clouds break over higher ground. In the Midlands, for example, thunderstorms occur on average on 15 days a year, but in the west and north this is reduced to around 8 days a year.

There is generally no snow anywhere in the country save on the highest mountains, where patches linger in pockets for most of the year.

for a few days. There are ways to economise on the use of mains water – by using washing-up water on the soil around plants, for instance. This will do them no harm at all. Bath water, as long as you haven't used lashings of bath oil, can also be syphoned out of the bath, either directly onto the borders or into buckets. The most needy plants – it can't be said often enough – are those in pots and hanging baskets, and also trees and shrubs which were planted the previous winter and which are still getting their roots established in the soil. Fruiting vegetables such as tomatoes are also thirsty for water now, as they need a regular supply to help their fruits swell.

△ **Bedding bonanza**
Summer bedding plants like these petunias and nicotianas, planted out in June, take only a few weeks to reach their peak, provided that you did not let the young plants become dry and stressed.

◁ **Sitting in the sun**
Frogs must be able to retreat to the cool of the water in summer, so keep an eye on water levels in ponds and top up when necessary.

Topping up water features

Keep an eye on the level of water in ponds during prolonged dry spells, as the water can evaporate at an alarming rate in these conditions. Oxygen levels in the water will also become low in still, hot conditions, so top up the pond regularly and if you can, spray water on the surface to increase the oxygen levels. This is particularly important if you have fish in the pond, but all aquatic life will feel the

△ **Container displays**

Every corner of patios and courtyards can be packed with colour at this time of year, with tender plants and summer-flowering bulbs complementing those that are permanently on display.

benefit. Oxygenating plants also help keep the water clear and aerated, but at this time of year you are more likely to find that they are becoming overgrown and need thinning, rather than not having enough.

One way to ensure that pond water remains well oxygenated for fish is to install a small fountain to move the water around and refresh it. The low, bubble-type fountains we see so often today are by far the best for water conservation; fine sprays will evaporate quickly and increase water loss. You will need to run electricity outside, usually through a low-voltage transformer, to power the pump. Always consult a professional if you are not confident about installing electrical equipment outdoors, especially in water. You could, as an alternative, investigate self-contained solar-powered fountains. Although these were expensive when they first appeared on the market, prices are now more reasonable.

Weeding wisely

Keep up with the weeding in all parts of the garden. Weeds not only compete for space in the borders, but also use up valuable moisture in the ground. The best tool for weeding is the Dutch hoe, which is used with a pushing and pulling motion. The technique is to slice off the tops of the weeds just below the surface of the soil, and leave them on the surface to dry out in the sun. A dry sunny day is the best for this job. It's well worth doing, as it not only keeps the garden looking good, but by maintaining a loose, crumbly layer on the surface of the soil, you are also preventing the ground from cracking in hot weather, and therefore conserving moisture in the deeper layers of soil.

Saving seeds

Watch out around now for seeds ripening on plants in the garden. Growing plants from seeds collected

△ *Yucca gloriosa* **in flower**

The spiky leaf rosettes of yuccas make them superb architectural plants at any time of year, but their drama is doubled when these superb flower spikes appear.

from your own garden is one of the most rewarding aspects of gardening. You will have to be vigilant, though; seed pods or heads may not look ready, but you can be sure that as soon as your back is turned the seeds will pop out and spread themselves over the border. This is no bad thing, of course, as many plants will freely seed themselves around the garden. But if there are some plants you particularly want seed from, then watch them carefully. Seed heads are usually ripe when they begin to turn brown; this is the time to cut them off and drop into paper bags, to be sorted and stored later on.

Savour the end of summer

This is the last month of summer, and though it's hard to believe with the abundance of flowers, fruits and foliage around us, plant growth really starts to slow down from the end of August onwards. So you can complete summer pruning of fruit trees and wisterias, and trimming of hedges this month, without fear of too much regrowth – although fast-growing conifers may well need a final going over in the autumn to keep them under control. You can also look forward to spending less time weeding from the end of the month onwards as germination also slows down.

And if you want an even sharper reminder that the seasons are about to change, remember that however hot and sultry the weather is right now, this is the month to start forcing pots of bulbs to flower at Christmas!

▽ **Cottage garden classics**
Runner beans and sweet peas are key to the informal, nostalgic garden style, but both will need picking regularly while you are away on holiday. If pods and seeds are left to ripen, then the plant, having accomplished its "mission", will start to deteriorate, with leaves yellowing and growth slowing down. Picking encourages fresh growth, flowers and crops, and keeps plants looking good.

AUGUST
AT A GLANCE

- Make sure birds and other wildlife have fresh water, and keep ponds topped up.
- Water plants that need it regularly.
- Collect ripening seed from plants you wish to propagate.
- Trim hedges.
- Prune rambling roses after flowering.
- Trim lavender after the flowers have faded.
- Layer rhododendrons, pinks and clematis.
- Protect dahlias and chrysanthemums from earwigs.
- Feed and water all plants in containers.
- Take cuttings from tender perennials such as pelargoniums and fuchsias.
- Mow less frequently if the weather is hot and dry.
- Lift and dry onions.
- Cut and dry herbs for winter use.
- Prop up heavily laden branches of fruit trees.
- Summer-prune gooseberries and redcurrants.
- Water and feed tomatoes regularly, and remove yellowing leaves.
- Plant new strawberry plants, and keep them well watered.
- Harvest the first apples and pears.
- Start potted cyclamen and freesias into growth.

! LAST CHANCE
- Finish summer-pruning apples and pears, and other trained fruit trees.
- Complete summer pruning of wisteria.
- Plant colchicums for autumn flowering.

★ GET AHEAD
- Force hyacinths for Christmas.
- Start planting spring bulbs, especially daffodils.
- Prepare ground for making new lawns.
- Divide perennials toward the end of the month.
- Sow parsley and pot up herbs for later use.

Cosmos atrosanguineus • Perennial with chocolate-scented flowers *(see p.312)*

Osteospermum jucundum ♀ • Sun-loving perennial with silvery leaves *(see p.337)*

***Hydrangea paniculata* 'Grandiflora'** ♀ • Huge flower clusters; a lovely shrub for shade *(see p.325)*

***Buddleja davidii* 'Fascinating'** • Shrub with enormous wildlife appeal *(see p.301)*

Begonia x tuberhybrida • Tender perennial with huge, blowsy flowers *(see p.300)*

***Solenostemon* 'Brightness'** • Try bedding out these glasshouse favourites *(see p.353)*

Phygelius x *rectus* **'Salmon Leap'** ♧ • Slightly tender shrub for a sunny, sheltered spot *(see p.340)*

Aconitum **'Bressingham Spire'** ♧ • Lovely perennial, but toxic; site with care in a family garden *(see p.296)*

Monarda **'Mahogany'** • One of the most popular perennials with bees *(see p.333)*

azania **Chansonette Series** • Half-hardy, low-growing perennial for summer bedding *(see p.321)*

Lobelia **'Bees' Flame'** • Dark-leaved perennial that enjoys damp soil *(see p.330)*

Lavatera **'Barnsley'** ♧ • Reliable shrub, good even in poor dry soil *(see p.329)*

TOP ROW: 'Ascotiensis' ♀ • 'Comtesse de Bouchaud' ♀ • 'Jackmanii' ♀ • 'Paul Farges' MIDDLE ROW: 'Madame Julia Correvon' ♀ • 'Prince Charles' • 'Huldine' • 'Abundance' BOTTOM ROW: 'Hagley Hybrid' • 'Ville de Lyon' • 'Etoile Violette' ♀ • 'Perle d'Azur' ♀ (see pp.308–9)

Nemesia caerulea • Woody-based, slightly tender perennial, good in containers *(see p.334)*

Salvia coccinea **'Lady in Red'** ♀ • Vivid perennial that needs some winter protection *(see p.351)*

Lantana camara • Frost-tender shrubs for multicoloured summer display *(see p.329)*

Amaranthus caudatus • Tender perennial easily grown as an annual *(see p.297)*

Echinacea purpurea **'White Swan'** • Hardy perennial, looks good well into autumn *(see p.316)*

Lathyrus odoratus **'Colin Unwin'** • Brick-red sweet pea, an annual climber *(see p.329)*

Argyranthemum foeniculaceum · Tender sub-shrub that forms a flower-covered bush *(see p.299)*

Rhodochiton atrosanguineus ♀ · Tender climber that can be grown annually for summer *(see p.345)*

Indigofera amblyantha ♀ · Sun-loving shrub with pea-like flowers and elegant foliage *(see p.326)*

Fuchsia 'Auntie Jinks' · A trailing variety of these popular half-hardy shrubs *(see p.320)*

Euryops pectinatus ♀ · Sun-loving half-hardy perennial with cheerful daisy flowers *(see p.319)*

Scabiosa Butterfly Blue · Cottage-garden perennial popular with all flying insects *(see p.352)*

***elargonium* 'Apple Blossom Rosebud'** ♀ • Lovely form of this summer favourite *(see p.339)*

Scaevola aemula • Trailing tender perennial, good in hanging baskets *(see p.352)*

Tropaeolum speciosum ♀ • Exotic-looking climber that prefers an acid soil *(see p.356)*

***Perovskia* 'Blue Spire'** ♀ • Dreamy subshrub with silvery stems and leaves *(see p.340)*

Dierama pulcherrimum • Graceful perennial with wand-like flower spires *(see p.316)*

***Heliotropium* 'Marine'** • Tender shrub, good in dry soil and in pots *(see p.323)*

Crocosmia x crocosmiiflora 'Jackanapes' · Clump-forming, nearly hardy perennial (see *p.313*)

Geranium psilostemon ♀ · Hardy perennial covered in flowers until late in the season (see *p.322*)

Abutilon 'Souvenir de Bonn' ♀ · Spindly sun-loving shrub, good against a wall (see *p.294*)

Verbena 'Showtime' · Tender perennial; a popular bedding and container plant (see *p.357*)

Kniphofia 'Green Jade' · Cool-coloured variant of a fiery perennial (see *p.328*)

Cotinus coggygria ♀ · The smoke bush, with clouds of tiny flowers in summer (see *p.312*)

TOP ROW: 'Stapleford Gem' ♡ • 'Maurice Gibbs' ♡ • 'Apple Blossom' ♡
BOTTOM ROW: 'Burgundy' • 'Alice Hindley' ♡ • 'Chester Scarlet' ♡ *(see p.339)*

WHAT TO DO IN AUGUST

AROUND THE GARDEN

USE WATER WISELY (see July), but make sure that bird baths and other containers that wildlife drink from are topped up.

BE VIGILANT IN WATCHING FOR PESTS AND DISEASES. Warm, dry weather encourages diseases such as mildew (a white powdery coating on stems and leaves). Preventative fungicide sprays can be used, but by ensuring the plants do not come under any stress – for instance, lack of water – the plants will stand up to any problems much better. There will be the usual army of aphids about; these can be kept in check by squashing by hand. If you have a bad infestation of aphids, control them by using a specific pesticide available from garden centres, and spray in the evening when fewer beneficial insects are around.

IN DAMP SUMMERS, SLUG DAMAGE TO PLANTS IN THE GARDEN can be rather dispiriting. The lusher and greener foliage is, the more they like it. But there are ways to combat the onslaught without resorting to pellets. First of all, birds, ground beetles and frogs all eat slugs, so the more they can be encouraged into the garden the better. Put down pieces of slate or wood in the border for the slugs to creep under. They like dark, cool, moist hiding places. These traps can then be turned over, exposing the slugs to any birds in the vicinity – or pick them up and dispose of them. Other traps that work well include beer traps (see April). You could also try inverted hollow grapefruit or orange halves placed about the border, or hollowed-out potatoes – these are often used as decoys by

vegetable gardeners trying to protect a potato crop. Plants that are particularly prone to slug attack can be surrounded with a layer of crushed eggshells or grit. Slugs don't like the coarse surface, and so are less likely to reach the plants.

CONTINUE WEEDING BORDERS REGULARLY, while watching for any self-sown seedlings. It is surprising what you can find. Most hybrids and many cultivars of plants will not reproduce true from seed, but the seedlings that do emerge can throw up all sorts of variations in flower colour, plant growth habit and even leaf colour. You never know when you might discover a winner of a plant in your own back yard.

***Hosta* 'Halcyon'** *Slugs can be the scourge of keen hosta growers all year round.*

TREES & SHRUBS

CONTINUE TO DEADHEAD ROSES (SEE JULY). Remove the fading flowers to prevent plants putting energy into producing seeds. Instead, that energy will go into new growth and more flowers. Even when deadheaded now, modern roses can still produce new shoots that will grow vigorously and flower before the end of the season. It is not uncommon these days, with our milder winters, to see roses blooming into November or even later. Prune back to at least one or two leaves below the base of the flowered shoots, to a healthy, outward-facing bud. You may have to prune harder than this to find a good bud, but don't be afraid to do so. The harder you prune, the more strongly the new shoot will grow.

IT'S TOO LATE NOW TO SPRAY FOR BLACKSPOT ON ROSES. Once it has got a hold, spraying does very little to control it. Rake up any affected leaves, and either burn them or put them in the bin. Don't put them on the compost heap, because the spores may survive there and can then be spread around the garden. Spray with a winter wash (see Fruit, December) when the foliage has all dropped in winter, and then spray with a fungicide regularly through the summer. Better still, grow varieties that are less prone to blackspot. Local rose growers will advise you on the best ones to choose.

PRUNING AND TRAINING

TRIM LAVENDER LIGHTLY. At this time, you want to remove the old flower spikes, which you may well have already done if you like to cut lavender for drying. If not, just go over the plants with a pair of hand shears, cutting off the old flower spikes and about 2.5cm (1in) of the leafy growth at the tips of the shoots. This will encourage side shoots to grow, keeping the plants bushy and compact. Lavender rarely grows again from old wood, and if plants have become old and straggly, it is best to either take cuttings from them, or remove the old plants altogether and buy in new plants. If your soil is on the heavy side with a high clay content, incorporate plenty of coarse grit before planting new lavenders. This will improve drainage, which they will enjoy.

PROPAGATION

CONTINUE TO TAKE SEMI-RIPE CUTTINGS FROM SHRUBS (see July). These cuttings are taken when the bases of the young shoots are beginning to turn woody, or ripen. Take the cuttings in the early part of the day or in the evening when it is cooler.

Almost all of the popular garden shrubs we grow, whether deciduous or evergreen, can be increased by taking these cuttings, although you need patience while they grow to maturity. Plants to try include berberis, buddlejas, box, ceanothus, choisya, cistus, cytisus, ericas, escallonia, hebes, lavenders, philadelphus, potentilla, pyracantha, santolina and viburnums.

Taken now, they will have rooted well before Christmas to make a thoughtful gift for someone who has admired a shrub in your garden (provided they have a garden of their own, that is).

LAYER RHODODENDRONS AND AZALEAS. These plants are difficult to root from cuttings, but they are easy to propagate by layering (see also March for illustrations). Choose a flexible young shoot growing close to the ground, so that it can be bent into the surface of the soil. Remove a few leaves 10-15cm (4-6in) from the tip of the shoot. Wound the shoot at the point that will be buried in the soil by cutting part-way through it, or carefully twisting it until it just begins to crack. Make a small depression in the soil and hold the shoot in place in the depression with a wire hoop. Cover the stem with soil, insert a cane next to the shoot and tie the shoot to the cane so that the tip of the shoot remains upright. To conserve moisture, place a brick or large stone over the stem in the soil. After about a year, the layer should have produced a good root system and it can be cut from the parent and planted out.

HEDGES

TRIM HEDGES. Most hedges can be given their final trim towards the end of the month as they will not grow much after this, although conifers may need another going-over (see October). If you want a level top to the hedge, fix a post at either end and tie twine between them at the required height. Trim the sides of the hedge first, working from the bottom up whether using either a powered hedge trimmer or hand shears. The reason for working upwards is that as you cut, the trimmings will fall away, and you will be better able to see where you are going.

Make the hedge wider at the base and narrower at the top. This way it will stand up to the weather better. The top can be trimmed last using the twine as a guide.

You may have trimmed conifer hedges last month (see July); if not, do it now. It is often recommended that conifer hedges only be trimmed with shears, because powered hedge trimmers bruise the growth. This can happen, but frankly, the damage is so minimal that it doesn't really make any difference at all. Even if they are damaged it soon disappears when the hedge regrows. The key point with conifer hedges is never to let them get beyond the height and width you want, as none will regrow if cut back into hard, old wood. The only exception is yew. It can be cut back to very old wood and will still grow again.

Large-leaved hedges such as spotted laurel (*Aucuba*) cannot be trimmed with shears or hedge trimmers, however, because these would cut through the large leaves, causing the edges to go brown. The way to cut these hedges is with a pair of secateurs. Put posts and string across the top as described for other hedges, and trim the sides first in the same way, starting at the base and working up. It can be a tiresome task, especially if you have a large hedge, but it is well worth the effort as the hedge will look so much better with no browned-off foliage.

CLIMBERS

Rambling roses *Prune the flowered sideshoots hard to encourage more next year.*

PRUNE RAMBLING ROSES AFTER THEY HAVE FLOWERED. Pruning of woody plants, most especially roses, can sometimes be portrayed as being very complicated, and this may make you hesitant when it comes to doing the job. But pruning rambling roses is in fact very easy. All you have to remember is that these roses produce flowers on wood produced the previous year. All side shoots that have flowered can be pruned back to one or two buds from the main stems. Any new, strong growths can be tied in to replace older shoots, and any very old stems can be pruned out to the ground, so encouraging more new shoots from the base of the plant.

PROPAGATE CLEMATIS BY LAYERING (see June for illustrations). Select a shoot growing from near the base of the plant, and lay it on the ground. To encourage the formation of

CLIMBERS *continued*

roots, cut part-way through the stem at each of the leaf joints, being careful not to cut right through the stem. If you want to, you can apply some hormone rooting solution to each cut, but it's not essential. Make some wire hoops, and peg each leaf joint to the surface of the soil. Each can be covered with a little soil if you wish. After a few weeks, roots will begin to form, and new growth will appear from each leaf joint. The new plants can then be separated from the parent plant, potted up individually and grown on.

COMPLETE SUMMER PRUNING OF WISTERIA (see also July), pruning all the long whippy side shoots to five or six buds from the main stems. This will encourage the plant to produce flower buds for next year's flowers. Any growth required for tying in to extend the framework of the plant can be left unpruned.

One of the most common questions put to gardening experts is – why does my wisteria not flower? Lack of correct pruning is often the reason given, which rather puts the blame on the gardener. However, the main reason for wisterias not flowering is that they are not named hybrids and have not been grafted. To see if the plant has been grafted, look at the base of the stem to check that there is a slightly swollen area; the point where the plant was grafted. So always make sure you get a named variety. Often some garden centres and market stalls sell unnamed seedlings which can take many years to flower, if at all.

PERENNIALS

CHRYSANTHEMUMS AND DAHLIAS are terrific plants for displaying a mass of flowers throughout late summer and autumn until the first frosts. They also last well as cut flowers. Dahlias are often referred to as the cut-and-come-again flower, as the more you cut them, the more flowers you get. But they both have one problem, and that is that the flowers are irresistible to earwigs. It can be off-putting, to say the least, to put these flowers in a vase and then find earwigs crawling around the room. The best way to control these pests is to put upturned pots filled with straw up on the top of canes among the plants, or if you can't get straw, shredded-up newspaper. Earwigs love to crawl into dark places during the day. In the morning you can empty the pots of earwigs and dispose of them in any way you see fit.

CUT BACK PERENNIALS THAT HAVE COLLAPSED OR SPREAD over the lawn and other plants in the border. In wet weather a lot of taller-growing perennials, especially achilleas, tend to flop over and smother other, smaller plants. Trim them back from the smaller plants to give the latter a chance to recover and flower. The cut-back plants may also grow again and produce some flowers in the autumn.

You may find that perennials that have spread over the lawn will have killed off the grass in that area. Trim the perennials back off the lawn. Give this bare patch of grass a good watering and a dose of lawn fertiliser, and it will very quickly regrow.

HARDY GERANIUMS which were not cut back earlier should be cut back now

to make them look neater. Again they will produce new growth which may flower again later in the autumn. Feed and water them to encourage growth.

CONTINUE TO PROPAGATE CARNATIONS AND PINKS BY LAYERING (see July). Once the layers produce roots, usually in five to six weeks, they can be separated from the parent plant and planted in their flowering positions. There is no need to use hormone rooting solution as the stems root quite easily. If you find nicking the stems tricky, another method is to very slightly and carefully twist the stem between your fingers until you hear, or rather feel, it just begin to crack, and peg this part of the stem in the soil.

DIVIDE BEARDED AND OTHER RHIZOMATOUS IRISES after flowering has finished, unless you got it done last month (see July).

Ripening geranium seeds The seed pods all too readily spring open to disperse the seeds.

Penstemon cuttings Stem-tip cuttings are an easy way to propagate these attractive perennials.

YOU CAN START DIVIDING PERENNIALS towards the end of the month (see September), provided that drought conditions are not lasting. If the soil is dry, wait, or water the plants really thoroughly both an hour or two before and afterwards.

CONTINUE COLLECTING RIPENING SEEDS OF PERENNIALS (see also July). Collecting and sowing your own seed from the garden is not only a great way of saving money, but is a most satisfying and rewarding aspect of gardening. Collect the seedheads carefully and put them into a paper bag. Go back indoors, and spread the seeds on a sheet of paper, and leave them for a while to dry thoroughly. Separate the chaff from the seeds, and store them in paper envelopes, making sure you write the plant's name on the envelope. Some seeds can be sown straight away as they germinate best if they are fresh (such as meconopsis, cyclamen, *Aconitum* and delphiniums) and kept in a cold frame over winter; other seeds can be stored in a cool dark place until spring. If you're not sure which category a plant falls into, sow half the seeds now and half in the new year and see what happens.

TAKE CUTTINGS OF PENSTEMONS, which do not divide easily like other perennials. Take the cuttings in the same way as for pelargoniums, described in Under Cover this month.

ALPINES

TAKE CUTTINGS OF ALPINES. Many alpines, such as aubrieta, *Phlox douglasii*, *P. subulata* and the dwarf helianthemums, can easily be propagated from cuttings. Take small non-flowering shoot tips about 5cm (2in) long, take off the very lowest leaves, and insert them into gritty compost – equal parts peat-free compost and perlite or vermiculite, with a handful of horticultural grit added to the mixture.

Put the cuttings in a warm propagator, spray them daily with clear water to maintain a humid atmosphere and shade in hot sunny weather, and in five or six weeks they should have rooted. You can generally tell when cuttings have rooted, as they begin to regrow. If you're not sure give the cuttings the gentlest tug; if there is resistance then roots have formed. The cuttings can then be potted up.

CONTINUE TO WEED BETWEEN ALPINES, and top up with fresh grit where it has dispersed. Grit or gravel around the plants not only makes them look terrific; it also stops rain splashing soil onto the plants, keeps down weeds and retains moisture in the soil.

BULBS

PLANT DAFFODILS AND NARCISSI before the end of next month. Daffodils look particularly good when they are planted in drifts, naturalised in grass (see also September). Bear in mind, though, that the grass will have to be left uncut for at least six weeks after the flowers are over, to allow the bulb to build up its flower bud for the following spring. Dwarf varieties also look good in rock gardens or in raised beds, where the flowers can be appreciated more easily.

If you are planting the bulbs in a border where you don't need to lift them, always mark them with a label; you may well forget where they are after the flowers and foliage have died down, and it's all too easy to dig them up again, believe me.

The general rule for depth of planting for any bulb is to plant two to three times its own depth. If you're not sure, it's better to plant a little too deep than too shallowly. If your soil is a heavy clay, add some grit to the planting hole and sit the bulbs on this. Bulb-planting tools make the job of planting large quantities of bulbs much easier. Leave tulip bulbs until late October or November before planting.

PLANT COLCHICUMS (often misleadingly called the autumn crocus). The flowers of this bulb appear before the leaves and it can look rather too startling on its own, so plant it in amongst other plants or naturalise it in grass.

PLANT MADONNA LILIES (*Lilium candidum*). Most lilies are planted from November until the spring, but the madonna lily is best planted this month as it is dormant. It will start into growth next month. The most likely source of these exquisite bulbs is from a bulb specialist by mail order. Most advertise in the gardening press. Plant the bulbs

Lilium candidum The madonna lily, with flowers of purest white, makes a beautiful border plant.

in a warm, sunny spot in well-drained soil. These lily bulbs must not be planted as deep as you would plant other lilies. Cover the bulbs with no more than 2.5–5cm (1–2in) of soil. Always feed them after flowering.

POT PREPARED HYACINTHS and other bulbs such as 'Paper White' narcissi for flowers at Christmas. If you are planting them in bulb bowls which have no drainage holes, use bulb fibre; otherwise, any proprietary potting compost will do. Plant several bulbs in a bowl or pot, close enough so they are almost touching, and cover with compost leaving just the nose of the bulbs uncovered. "Plunge" the containers outside, covering them with compost, or put them in a cool dark place. After six to eight weeks, start inspecting the bulbs and when they have made about 2.5cm (1in) of growth they can be brought inside into cool conditions (see also Under Cover).

CHOOSING DAFFODILS

'Broadway Star'

'Ambergate'

'Cassata'

'Actaea'

'Rip Van Winkle'

'Merlin'

'Jumblie'

'Tahiti'

Forcing hyacinths Plant prepared bulbs in bowls now for flowers at Christmas.

ANNUALS & BEDDING

CONTINUE TO DEADHEAD ANNUALS in borders, to prevent the plants' energies going into producing seeds and extend the flowering period well into autumn. However, no matter how regularly you deadhead, some of the earlier-sown hardy annuals will be over later in the month. These can be cleared away and consigned to the compost heap. Gaps in the borders can be filled with larger plants in pots, either planting them or plunging the pots in the ground to be lifted easily in the autumn.

COLLECT SEEDS FROM HARDY ANNUALS. Seed can be collected from most hardy annuals except the F1 hybrids, which will not come true to type. Often they don't produce any seeds at all. Harvest the seeds on a dry sunny day, into paper bags. Once indoors, tip the seeds onto a sheet of paper and sort out the seeds from the chaff. This can be a tedious job, but it's well worth doing to get clean seeds. Any debris left in with the seeds when they are stored may cause them to rot. An old flour sieve can be useful. Store the seeds in labelled paper envelopes.

Collecting honesty seeds The pretty, papery heads each contain several ripe seeds.

Store in a cool, dry place; an airtight box in the bottom of the fridge is ideal.

THIS IS THE TRADITIONAL MONTH FOR TAKING CUTTINGS from pelargoniums, fuchsias and other tender perennials. They can, of course, be taken at other times from spring through until autumn. But if they are taken later than September, then don't pot them up until the spring.

The cuttings are very easy to take, only those of pelargoniums differing in one or two ways. All cuttings should be removed from the parent plant by cutting off strong, non-flowering shoots just above a bud, leaving a cutting about 10cm (4in) long. Trim the lower leaves off and then trim the cutting immediately below a leaf joint. With all pelargoniums remove the stipules – the little papery flaps – at the base of the leaf stalks. Pelargoniums do not need hormone rooting solution; they root perfectly well without it. All other kinds of cuttings will benefit from being dipped in hormone rooting solution. Insert the cuttings around the edge of small pots containing cuttings compost (half peat-free compost, half perlite or vermiculite), and cover all kinds with polythene except pelargoniums; the fine hairs on the leaves of these will trap moisture and may cause the cuttings to rot. Place the pots on the windowsill or in a shady part of the greenhouse. The cuttings will root in about four weeks, when they can be potted on to overwinter under cover.

SOME HARDY ANNUALS CAN BE SOWN OUTSIDE NOW and next month to overwinter and flower early in the summer next year (see September).

CONTAINERS

CONTINUE WATERING AND FEEDING bedding plants in hanging baskets, tubs and other containers. Watering may have to be done several times a day when the weather is very hot. Feed at least once a week with a high-potash fertiliser to encourage the plants to bloom well into autumn.

REMEMBER ALSO TO FEED PERMANENT PLANTS like shrubs, perennials and trees growing in containers. These need looking after just as much as temporary summer bedding plants. They require regular feeding and watering and again, especially with woody plants, feed with a high-potash fertiliser to encourage ripening of the wood, and not the production of soft, sappy growth which may be damaged during the winter.

MAKE SURE CONTAINERS WILL BE CARED FOR if you are going on holiday. Before you go, group all of the containers together in a shady spot, if you can. This will make it easier for the person watering, as well as benefiting the plants: a more humid atmosphere is maintained around the leaves where plants are clustered together. In normal circumstances this is not to be recommended, as crowded growth encourages diseases. But it's fine for a week or two. Hanging baskets can be taken down and grouped with the others by perching them on buckets or upturned pots. See also Around the Garden, July.

PONDS

KEEP PONDS TOPPED UP WITH WATER during hot spells. Water evaporates very quickly in hot weather. Playing water on the surface of the pond will help to aerate it, especially important if you have fish in the pond. At the same time, look over plants surrounding the pond and remove any fading flowers and yellowing leaves. This not only greatly improves the appearance of the pond and the borders surrounding it, but if leaves fall into the water and are left to rot, this increases the nutrient content of the water, which in turn encourages the growth of algae.

THIN OXYGENATING PLANTS (see July) and remove blanket weed as necessary.

Top up ponds Water levels can fall dramatically, especially if you have taken a break away.

LAWNS

CONTINUE TO MOW THE LAWN regularly, raising the blades if the weather is very hot and dry. The frequency of mowing can also be reduced in hot dry weather, as the grass won't be growing much at all in these conditions.

GRASS CLIPPINGS CAN BE LEFT ON THE LAWN in dry weather. Nobody likes to trail grass clippings into the house, especially when they stick to your shoes in damp weather. But in dry spells, leave the grass box off the mower and the clippings will act as a mulch for the grass, helping to retain moisture in the soil and returning organic matter at the same time.

APPLY A FERTILISER WITH A HIGH PHOSPHATE CONTENT. In late summer it is not advisable to apply a high-nitrogen fertiliser to a lawn, as it will promote vigorous growth which will not stand up to the rigours of the winter. Fertilisers high in phosphates will instead promote root growth, and this will toughen up the grass for the winter ahead. These fertilisers are usually sold as autumn lawn feeds and are readily available.

Apply all fertilisers strictly according to the manufacturer's instructions. A wheeled fertiliser spreader will take the guesswork out of applying the feed, and saves the chore of marking out the area to do it by hand. These wheeled applicators can be hired from your local hire shop.

DON'T WATER UNLESS ABSOLUTELY NECESSARY (see also July). There is no point in watering established lawns, as they will soon recover whenever rain

does come. Grass has remarkable powers of recovery.

NEW LAWNS

CONTINUE TO WATER new lawns regularly.

PREPARE FOR SOWING SEED OR LAYING TURF NEXT MONTH. To create a good lawn from scratch takes a bit of work, but done properly it is well worth the effort and you will be well satisfied with the results. Preparation is the key to success; this has been discussed earlier, but it is worth going over some of the points again, as autumn is a good time for making a new lawn. There is usually more moisture in the ground, heavy autumn dews making a contribution. New lawns need a lot of water. Seed must have water to germinate and grow, and if turf dries out it shrinks, and it's impossible to get rid of the cracks that appear along the joins when this happens. With the warm moist weather of autumn you should not need to water new lawns as frequently as during

Neglected site Hand-clearing weedy ground is a laborious but eventually satisfying business.

late spring and summer, and the grass will establish before the winter sets in, ready to grow away strongly in the spring.

Dig over the area thoroughly, removing every trace of perennial weeds. Make sure all their roots are removed or they will grow again. Mowing keeps broad-leaved perennial weeds down in lawns if you are not too fussy about their appearance, but some cause other problems: nettles, for example, can ruin a lawn as a play area. Leave the soil for a few weeks to allow annual weeds to germinate, and then hoe these off, removing them to the compost heap. Preparing the ground a few weeks before you sow seed or lay turf (see September) will also allow the cultivated soil to settle, making it easier to level.

Applying lawn feed Four pots moved around the lawn can be used to measure square metres by eye.

VEGETABLES & HERBS

SOW GREEN MANURE CROPS on vacant ground. If you find it difficult to obtain enough garden compost or farmyard manure to pile on beds year after year, a good substitute is to grow a green manure crop on ground that is vacant. Rape and mustard are fast-growing crops that can be dug in during the autumn (see October), before the plants begin to flower and they are killed off by frosts. Other green manures can be sown then to overwinter, if you wish. These seeds are easily sown by being broadcast (scattered) over the ground. Just lightly fork over the soil and rake it level, scatter the seeds and carefully rake them into the surface of the soil. This is an easy way to add organic matter to the soil, improve the soil structure and reduce the problem of nutrients being leached from bare ground. By covering the ground with a "living mulch" you also reduce the need to weed.

HARVESTING

KEEP HARVESTING CROPS WHILE THEY ARE STILL YOUNG. Vegetables have a much better flavour when picked

Harvesting courgettes Keep cutting the courgettes when they are young and fresh.

VEGETABLES & HERBS *continued*

young. As they age, the flavour and texture become coarser. If marrows and courgettes are harvested regularly, it encourages the plants to produce more flowers and fruits to continue the crop well into autumn. Summer cabbages should be ready to eat too now; cut them before pests get to them first.

HARVEST BEANS AND FREEZE THEM. There is no doubt that fresh vegetables taken direct from the plant to the kitchen and cooked within a short time have the best flavour of all, but there are times when you get a glut of some crops and can't cope with them all. Freezing is one way round the problem, and most vegetables, including French and runner beans and podded broad beans, can be frozen. No matter how often you seem to pick beans there always seems to be buckets of them towards the end of the season. The perfect way to avoid waste is to freeze them. They will provide a welcome vegetable through the winter.

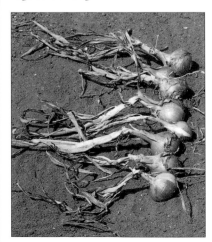

Harvest onions *The bulbs can be left on the soil to dry in prolonged dry, sunny periods.*

HARVEST ONIONS WHEN THE FOLIAGE COLLAPSES, if they weren't ready last month. It is often recommended that you bend over the tops of onions to ripen them, but this happens naturally and there is no need to do it for the plants. Choosing a dry day if you can, get a fork and gently ease the onions out of the soil to break the roots' hold on the ground. Leave the onions on the surface of the ground to dry off. It's important that the onions are properly dry if they are to store well. If the weather turns wet, cover the onions with a sheet of polythene or cloches, or lay them out in a shed or greenhouse.

SOWING AND PLANTING OUTDOORS

SOW JAPANESE ONIONS to harvest in early summer next year. Japanese onions are also available as onion sets. Before sowing seeds or planting sets, rake down the soil and incorporate a general organic fertiliser. For seeds, take out shallow drills 30cm (12in) apart, and water the drills if the soil is dry. Sow the seeds thinly along the drills and cover with dry soil. Thin out to 8-15cm (3-6in) in the spring. In colder areas it may be useful to cover the young plants with cloches during severe winter weather. Japanese onion sets can be planted a little later than seeds, in October or November. Onions of both sets and seeds should be ready to harvest in July the following year, giving an early harvest before other onions are ready.

SOW SOME SALAD CROPS NOW. This is the last month for sowing salad crops outdoors, but it is worth trying a few. Not all of them will mature, but you will at least get some fresh, young salad material in the autumn. Seeds to sow include lettuce, radish, salad onions, red chicory and spinach. It's even worth trying some peas, sowing an early variety such as 'Douce Provence'. You may be lucky with good weather in the autumn. Don't expect to get a great crop, but some fresh peas are always welcome.

CONTINUE TO SOW SPRING CABBAGES at intervals (see also July). Sow the seeds in wetted shallow drills, covering with dry soil. Transplant the seedlings when they are large enough to handle. Plant them 15cm (6in) apart in rows that are 30cm (1ft) apart.

LOOKING AFTER CROPS

CONTINUE WATERING AND WEEDING REGULARLY. The weather can often be very dry in August, and it is important to keep vegetables well watered if they are not to bolt and run to seed and be spoiled. Plants like celery and tomatoes need regular supplies of water, or celery will bolt quickly, and tomatoes will suffer problems such as blossom end rot (dark brown patches on the base of the tomatoes) due to a lack of water. Irregular watering will also cause tomato skins to split; after a dry spell, if they are given a lot of water, the upsurge of sap in the stems causes the skins to rupture.

Weeds rob valuable moisture from the crops we want to grow. They also act as host plants to pests and diseases, so by keeping them down, problems are reduced. And they just make the vegetable garden look untidy too.

KEEP A LOOK OUT FOR PESTS, and where possible use a physical barrier to prevent them getting at crops. A second generation of carrot fly is about now, so make sure vulnerable crops are protected (see May). Crops can be grown under horticultural fleece from sowing to harvesting, as it lets in light and water but protects the plants from insects. Make sure it is tucked into the soil or weighted down securely, or insects will crawl under it. The material doesn't look particularly attractive, but it is effective.

CONTINUE EARTHING UP CELERY (see also July). Blanching makes the rather tough stems more palatable and easier to cook. Draw earth up from either side of the rows until only the foliage is showing. Each time this is done, remember to put a collar of paper round the plant to prevent the soil getting into its heart, causing disease to set in. Self-blanching celery may be left to grow on normally.

MARROWS LEFT TO GROW LARGER FOR STORING over winter are best raised off the ground slightly to expose them to the sun to ripen. This will also help prevent rotting, caused by the fruits sitting on damp earth. Support them on a block of wood or a couple of bricks. At the same time, remove some of the old leaves so that more sunlight can get at the fruits to ripen them. Harvest before the first frosts in autumn.

STOP OUTDOOR TOMATOES when they have produced four trusses of fruit, if this was not done last month. The summer in this country is too short to get more fruits from outdoor-grown plants. Remove any sideshoots growing from the leaf axils. Any old foliage can be removed at the same time. Foliage clustered round the trusses of fruit can be thinned too; this will allow more light to fall on to and ripen the fruits and improve air circulation, thus reducing the risk of diseases such as botrytis getting a hold and spoiling the fruits.

HERBS

MAKE A SOWING OF PARSLEY TO LAST THROUGH THE WINTER. Sow the seeds in shallow drills outside and thin the seedlings to about 15cm (6in) apart when they are large enough to handle. It is worth covering the seeds with fleece to protect them from the second generation of carrot flies which will be around now. Parsley belongs to the same plant family as carrots and is therefore subject to the same range of pests. Cover the young plants with cloches later in the autumn to protect them from the worst of the winter weather. Alternatively, lift a few seedlings and pot them up and grow on in a cool greenhouse or on the windowsill in the kitchen, and you will have a supply of fresh parsley to hand through the winter. See also Under Cover.

POT UP OTHER HERBS SUCH AS CHIVES to grow for use during the winter. Lift a clump of chives from the garden; if it is fairly large, split it into smaller clumps. This way you may get several pieces to pot up. Put each piece into a pot with general multipurpose compost, cut back the old foliage and water them in. Stand on the windowsill or in a cool greenhouse or conservatory

and in a few weeks, you will have a fresh supply of chives.

Other herbs to try in pots include lemon balm and mint.

TAKE SEMI-RIPE CUTTINGS FROM shrubby herbs like bay, hyssop and rosemary and sage (see July).

POT UP CHIVES

① Dig up a clump of chives from the garden with a spade or fork. Shake off the soil.

② Pull the clump apart into sections. Use a knife to help if necessary.

③ Pot up the small clumps individually in small pots, using a peat-free compost.

④ Cut back the leaves to about 5cm (2in), and water thoroughly by standing the pot in a dish or tray of water.

FRUIT

Testing ripeness Cup the fruit in your palm and give it no more than a quarter-twist.

PICKING AND STORING

HARVEST EARLY APPLES AND PEARS. You can tell when the fruit is ready to harvest as there will almost certainly be one or two fruits on the ground. A more reliable way to tell when a fruit is ripe is to cup it in your hand and gently twist. If it is ripe the fruit should part from the tree with its stalk intact with almost no effort at all. If it does not part from the tree, leave it there for a few more days. Early-cropping apples and pears don't store for very long and they are best used soon after picking. Any damaged fruits should be used first if the damage is not too severe, otherwise put them on the compost heap.

LOOKING AFTER CROPS

PAY ATTENTION TO FRUIT TREES trained against walls. The bases of walls can be very dry places indeed, especially

if it is a house wall and there are overhanging eaves. So it is vital that these trees are watered regularly. It's amazing how quickly the soil in these situations dries out. After watering, give the trees a thick mulch of organic matter to help retain the moisture.

PRUNING AND TRAINING

CONTINUE PRUNING SUMMER-FRUITING RASPBERRIES (SEE JULY). Cut out the old fruiting canes and tie in the new canes which have grown this year. Any of these canes that grow beyond the height of the topmost wire of the support can be pruned back to the top wire in the winter. Any thin, weak canes should be pruned out rather than tied in as they will not bear much fruit. The old canes which have been pruned out can be shredded and used as a mulch in other parts of the garden. Shredders can be bought or hired from your local hire shop.

Tying in Secure the new canes of summer-fruiting raspberries, which will fruit next year.

FRUIT *continued*

SUMMER-PRUNE TRAINED FRUIT TREES. Summer pruning of cordon and espalier forms of fruit trees couldn't be easier; try and get it all finished this month.

• Cordon apple and pear trees should have the side growths from the main stem cut back to 8cm (3in). Those shoots which were pruned in the same way last year will have produced side shoots of their own, and these need to

SUMMER PRUNING

❶ The arms of espalier- and fan-trained apples and pears will lose their form if the long, vigorous shoots that are sent upwards in summer are allowed to keep growing.

❷ Cut all of the long, fresh summer shoots back to three or four buds from their point of origin. This will additionally allow more sun to fall on and ripen the fruits.

be pruned back too, to 2.5cm (1in). This encourages the formation of fruit-bearing spurs for fruiting next year. When the leading shoot extending the height of the cordon has reached the limit of the support, prune it in exactly the same way as side growths.

• Espalier and fan-trained trees should be pruned in the same way.

• Trained forms of acid cherries, nectarines and peaches need all the shoots growing from the main branches pruned to 10cm (4in), and side shoots from these pruned to 5cm (2in).

• For fan-trained plums, damsons and sweet cherries, prune back by half all the shoots that have borne fruit.

FINISH OFF SUMMER-PRUNING cordon- and fan-trained gooseberries and redcurrants. See July for details.

PLANTING

PLANT NEW STRAWBERRY PLANTS IN GROUND that was prepared last month, provided that we are not in the middle of a drought: if so, wait until September. If your old plants are healthy and show no signs of virus disease, use some of their runners, or plantlets, which you may have pegged down into pots (see May). But if there are signs of virus, which usually shows up as streaks through the foliage, then start afresh with strawberries from a specialist fruit grower, where you know the stock has been certified as being free from virus. Grow the strawberries on ground that has not grown them for a few years. You can move a strawberry bed in stages – if you have, say, three rows of fruit growing in the vegetable garden, renew one row each year. Plant the new row

to one side of the existing rows and remove the last old row on the other side. Do this each year and you will gradually work your way down the vegetable plot, planting new strawberries in fresh ground each year.

Keep newly planted strawberries well watered. Planting them now enables the plants to build up and get well established before the winter, but if they go short of water this will not happen.

PROPAGATION

STRAWBERRY RUNNERS which were pegged down last month can be cut from the parent plant, either to be planted out (see above) or potted up to be forced inside during the winter to get early fruit in the spring (see Under Glass, January). Pot these plants up into 18cm (7in) pots and leave them outside for the rest of the summer. In autumn, lay the pots on their sides to protect them from winter wet. After Christmas, the pots can be taken inside in stages to provide a succession of fruits when they are scarce and expensive in the shops.

Potted strawberry runner Pot up into a larger pot and leave over the autumn to force in late winter.

UNDER COVER

CHECK GREENHOUSE HEATERS ARE IN WORKING ORDER. Winter may still seem a long way off, but even now the days are beginning to get shorter, and the sooner this job is done the better. It is no good finding out the heater doesn't work on a freezing cold night in autumn. It is better to have any portable heaters, whether gas or electric, sent off for a professional to service. Fixed electric heating pipes can be checked by calling in a qualified electrician, and gas systems should always be checked by an engineer. Paraffin heaters need to have the wicks trimmed or replaced as necessary and then be thoroughly cleaned. Then you will be ready for whatever the winter throws at you.

DAMP DOWN REGULARLY during hot, dry weather. It's been stated many times already, but it is a job that gives a good growing atmosphere to plants and helps to control pests like red spider mite. Soak the floor and under the staging, and you will, almost immediately, feel the atmosphere cooling as the water evaporates. If you can, do this several times a day in hot weather, although it is difficult when you're at work all day. Even if it's done early in the morning and again in the evening it is all to the good.

TOWARDS THE END OF THE MONTH the nights can turn chilly, so it's worth closing ventilators and doors in the evening to maintain a little warmth. But remember to open up again early in the morning.

AT THE END OF THE MONTH, REMOVE SHADING. The days start to

Greenhouse in summer Now that days are shortening, close doors if evenings become chilly.

shorten dramatically at this time, and plants under glass will need all the light they can get. Clean off shading wash with a dry duster, or remove mesh and shake it out and roll it up neatly for storage. If you found these methods unsatisfactory this year, consider investing in roller blinds for next year. It's an ideal time to make enquiries – contractors will be less busy now than in the spring and early summer, when the same idea will occur to a lot of other people.

CONTINUE TAKING CUTTINGS FROM PELARGONIUMS, FUCHSIAS and other tender perennials (see Annuals and Bedding).

GLASSHOUSE AND HOUSE PLANTS

START CYCLAMEN NOW. Those cyclamen that were rested in their pots during the summer can be started into growth now. They may already be under way, and you will be able to see small buds growing. Start watering the plants now, and scrape away some of the

old compost from the surface (being careful not to damage roots), top-dressing with some new potting compost. This will give the plants a good start. Cyclamen don't require a lot of heat, so putting them in a cold frame for the rest of the summer is ideal; then bring them inside early next month. Occasionally they will produce an early flower or two, but these are best removed to allow the plant to build up strength before the main flowering period in the winter.

POT BULBS for flowers at Christmas (see also Bulbs). The end of the month and early September are the latest times to plant prepared hyacinths and other bulbs to flower in time for Christmas. After about six to eight weeks inspect the bulbs, and when they have made about 2.5cm (1in) of growth they can be brought inside to cool conditions. Then, after a few weeks in cool conditions bring them into the warmth to flower in time for Christmas.

START FREESIAS AND LACHENALIAS INTO GROWTH. Freesias are beautifully scented flowers produced on wiry stems, ideal for winter flowering in a cool conservatory or greenhouse. Corms of freesias can be planted from now at intervals over the next few weeks to provide a succession of blooms through the winter. Seven or eight corms can be planted in a 12cm (5in) pot containing multi-purpose compost. Cover the corms with about 2.5cm (1in) of compost. Plunge the pots outside and after about six weeks take the pots inside to flower. Some support may be needed as the stems are tall and slender. After flowering, feed the

plants until the foliage begins to turn yellow, and then rest the corms. Lachenalias, or Cape cowslips, are also good plants for cool greenhouses, grown in the same way as freesias.

CONTINUE TO MAINTAIN HOUSE PLANTS by watering and feeding. Plants with large decorative leaves will really benefit if the foliage is given a wipe over with a damp cloth once in a while. It is amazing how much dust can settle on leaves, reducing the plant's capability to manufacture its food stuffs from sunlight. This process of turning light into energy is called photosynthesis, and is essential for plants to survive. A room in the house is quite dull for plant growth needs – even by a window, as the light is coming only from one side – so it is essential to keep plant foliage clean to make use of all the available light. The plants also look a lot better for it.

CROPS UNDER GLASS

CONTINUE TO REMOVE OLD LEAVES FROM TOMATOES and other greenhouse crops to aid ripening and air

Lachenalias in flower Bulbs of the Cape cowslip can be grown under glass to flower in winter.

circulation. Any yellowing leaves can be removed at the same time, otherwise they will encourage diseases like mildew and botrytis. All these leaves can be put on the compost heap. Tidiness in the greenhouse and conservatory will go a long way to reducing problems with pests and diseases. Insects love to crawl under rotting vegetation, where it is cool and moist. The less chance they have of making a home, the better for your plants.

SOW PARSLEY FOR A WINTER CROP. Sow the seeds in pots or trays, watering the compost before sowing and covering the seeds lightly with compost. Put on the greenhouse bench or on a sunny windowsill. When the seedlings emerge, pot them up individually when they are large enough to handle, and you will have a good crop of parsley to see you through the winter.

SEPTEMBER

The garden in September

By this month we will be gathering in the harvest and autumn colours begin to appear – a hint of the glorious shades to come. There is a distinct chill in the morning air, and northern parts may have their first frosts.

SEPTEMBER CAN OFTEN BE A WONDERFUL MONTH in the garden. The sultry heat of high summer has gone and the air feels fresher. If there is high pressure over the country we may enjoy an Indian summer lasting into October, but those clear sunny days can also mean colder nights. And with heavy dew on the lawn in the mornings, it really is the start of the season of mists and mellow fruitfulness. There are apples, pears, and masses of vegetables to be harvested and stored over the winter months. And after the (relative!) lull in activity in the garden over summer, there suddenly seems to be a lot to get on with.

Hyacinth bulbs ▷
Summer seems to be barely over before thoughts of next spring begin. Buy spring bulbs for the garden early to get the best choice of varieties.

Time to take cover

The effects of the shortening days are now quite noticeable. From now on the climatic differences in the different regions of the country will become more obvious, with the north generally having colder weather and frosts starting early this month. But even in the balmy south, frosts can also start quite early. So it's time to move frost-tender plants indoors.

August and September are the traditional months for taking cuttings from tender perennials such as pelargoniums, fuchsias and argyranthemums. The earlier in the month now this is done the better, as the cuttings will form roots much more quickly before the cooler weather sets in. Normally these cuttings are first inserted round the edge of pots or in seed trays and then potted on when they have rooted, but if taken at this time of year it is better to leave them in their pots or seed trays over winter. The plants will get a better start by being potted on when the days begin to lengthen again.

Some people prefer just to give the old plants shelter over winter – for example, in a cool utility room – and then take cuttings when the plants shoot again in spring. It all depends on what sort of space you have for looking after plants over winter.

Give yourself a treat

If you're forever trying to find space for overwintering plants and pots and trays of cuttings and seedlings, maybe it's time to indulge yourself and choose a greenhouse. It may seem rather odd to advise buying a greenhouse at this time of year, right at the end of summer. But it is, in fact, far better to choose one now, and have it erected and ready, rather than wait until spring and miss out on all the fun you will have raising your own plants. You could make a start right now by sowing a few winter lettuces. Once you have a greenhouse you'll wonder how you ever managed without one.

Plants for a cold greenhouse

It is surprising just what you can grow in even an unheated greenhouse. The most endearing group of plants for growing in a cold glasshouse are alpines. Many will not stand up to our damp winters. It's not the cold that bothers them – after all, they are covered with snow in the mountains – it's the wet that causes them to rot off. A greenhouse with the ventilators and doors open all winter to keep the air circulating is the ideal place to grow alpines.

All the spring-flowering bulbs will flower that little bit earlier if grown inside in pots. Hellebores are terrific too; under cover in pots, the beautiful flowers are not spoiled by rain. Hardy cyclamen also look good under glass, where the beauty of these dainty little plants can be enjoyed to the full.

Winter-flowering shrubs can also be grown in a cold greenhouse, at least in their first year. Shrubs such as *Mahonia* × *media* 'Charity' and *Viburnum* × *bodnantense* 'Dawn' have a terrific scent, and this can be enjoyed to the full under glass. Bring well-grown plants home from a garden centre or nursery, stand them in a corner of the garden, then bring them in during late autumn and the flowers will soon open up, filling the air with fragrance. They can be planted out into the garden on spring.

◁ **Late flower show**
Dahlias and chrysanthemums are reaching their peak, while nasturtiums and hydrangeas continue to flower.

The right greenhouse for you

The choice and size of greenhouse will depend on how deep your pockets are and how big your garden is. All the specialist firms will be able to advise you on the best size for your garden, as well as the best position and aspect. But always try to get the biggest you can. It is amazing just how soon the space will be filled up. Make sure there is good provision for ventilation, with at least one roof ventilator and preferably one in the side. Most manufacturers of good glasshouses will add more ventilators at your request. It's also advisable to have utilities – a power source, or an outside tap – put in at the same time as your greenhouse is built.

The manufacturers will, of course, be able to arrange for your greenhouse to be erected, but there

▽ **Winter pansies**
Plants for winter colour and spring bedding will now be available from garden centres, nurseries and market stalls.

WEATHER WATCH

🌡 **There can be occasional warm days** this month, but on the whole it is cooler in all parts of the country, and the first night frosts can be expected in cold and exposed areas. But the warm autumn days should be relished as the days get shorter and there is less time to work in the garden. Good weather will prolong the flowering display until well into autumn.

🐓 **September can be a windy month,** but after the sultry heat of summer it comes as something of a relief. Gales increase in frequency again as autumn approaches, and more low pressure systems arrive over the country from the Atlantic Ocean: areas most prone to the first autumn gales are the western isles and the west coast. Although most prevailing winds come from the west, the wind direction can change quickly to colder directions like the north and east.

☀ **It is surprising just how much** direct sunshine there can be this month, although this will depend on cloud cover. Parts of the north and west can experience over 100 hours of direct sunshine, and the south and east as much as 150 hours. Days with clear blue sky, bright sunshine and just a hint of a chill in a gentle breeze are a pure delight in autumn.

🌧 **It's not every year we can expect** an Indian summer; the amount of rain falling does generally increase this month. Again, the wettest parts are the north and west sides of the country. The south and east will have the least rain, around 47–51mm falling on average, while the north and west experience anything from 90mm to over 200mm in north-west Scotland.

☁ **Snow rarely falls before** November or December. Only on the high peaks such as Ben Nevis in Scotland does the snow lie on the mountain top all through the summer.

Continuing sunshine ▷

So many of the late summer and autumn-flowering perennials seem to come in warm shades, as if in preparation for the blazing autumn leaf colour that deciduous trees will soon display.

are some that are not so difficult to put up yourself. If you choose this option, then a greenhouse that comes with a base will make the job much easier.

Autumn is a good time of year to start all kinds of garden construction projects, as the weather is not too warm for physical work, nor so cold that you soon get chilled after working hard. Patios and decking are all the rage these days, and now is the time to make such features, before winter sets in and then all too soon the springtime rush makes it difficult to get anything done. Autumn is the season for tidying up the garden, and on p.232 we show you how to make a really cheap and easy compost bin. By using cardboard as insulation, it gives you an opportunity to recycle all those cardboard boxes that accumulate, as well as valuable garden refuse. Make your bin as soon as possible, and it will be ready and in place just when you need it.

Don't forget the plants

Pests and diseases can still be a problem at this time of year, and now is the time to begin clearing up any diseased material in the garden. If it is left lying around, it gives the spores of fungal diseases and other harmful organisms a chance to overwinter in the soil, and thus cause more problems the following year. The same applies to pests: they just love to crawl into a pile of leaves or into the cracks in tree trunks to hibernate over winter. Paradoxically, it is better if you can leave a small corner of the garden untidy for hibernating mammals such as hedgehogs and other beneficial insects. A small pile of leaves makes a perfect home for these friendly creatures. We must do all we can to encourage them, because they are such

allies in the fight against pests in the garden. Some people even put pet food out to entice hedgehogs to stay in the neighbourhood.

Under glass, at this time of year many of the biological controls will become less effective due mainly to the cooler temperatures – most require a minimum of around 10°C (50°F) – and the best thing you can do to prevent pests nestling down in the warmth of the greenhouse or conservatory is to give it a good clean before winter.

Plants to enjoy

There are still plenty of routine jobs in beds and borders, such as deadheading, to be done. At this time of year deadheading is unlikely to extend the flowering performance of plants, but it will make the garden look much tidier, setting off plants such as dahlias and chrysanthemums, which start looking good now. Many asters, those stalwarts of the autumn-flowering border, will be in flower too. They make a stunning show, often well into November if the weather is not too harsh, but some of them are rather prone to attack from mildew. So keep an eye on them and spray with a fungicide before mildew gets a grip. Better still, make sure the stems don't become overcrowded – which encourages mildew – by lifting and dividing the plants every other year to keep them young and vigorous.

◁ **Easy compost bin**

Make a bin this month, and you will have an instant, neat "home" for all the garden debris that needs to be cleared away in autumn. Here it will rot down to make compost, so that you can return all the goodness it contains to your soil.

▽ **Harvested onions**

Now there is dew in the morning and often a dampness in the air as the day draws in. Ensure that onions are dried and stored away somewhere where moisture cannot penetrate.

By September most summer bedding plants are past their best, and spring flowering plants and bulbs can be put in their place. If you haven't sown biennials earlier then there is usually a good selection at garden centres. The sooner they are in and settled the better they will stand up to the winter, and also flower better in the spring.

It may be the end of summer and the days may be drawing in, but in autumn there seems to be a special quality in the light. Early mornings in September can be wonderful, with a clear blue sky and a freshness in the air. Put this together with beautiful autumn-flowering plants and plenty of fruit and vegetables to harvest, and life doesn't get much better.

SEPTEMBER
AT A GLANCE

- Start clearing autumn debris to prevent pests and diseases overwintering.
- Start planting new trees, shrubs, climbers and perennials.
- Move evergreen shrubs.
- Take hardwood cuttings from roses.
- Begin dividing overgrown perennials.
- Support tall late-flowering perennials.
- Stop feeding trees and shrubs in containers.
- Plant spring-flowering bulbs.
- Plant out spring-flowering biennials.
- Lift tender plants and bring them under cover, or take cuttings.
- Plant up containers with spring bedding.
- Sow or turf new lawns.
- Scarify and aerate established lawns.
- Net ponds to keep out autumn leaves.
- Harvest marrows and the last courgettes, and lift maincrop potatoes.
- Plant out spring cabbages.
- Sow winter lettuce.
- Continue to harvest apples and pears, and pick autumn-fruiting raspberries.
- Reduce watering and ventilation in the greenhouse.

! LAST CHANCE
- Force hyacinths for Christmas.
- Plant onion sets.
- Plant new strawberry plants.
- Sow spring cabbages.

★ GET AHEAD
- Start to prune climbing roses when the flowers are over.
- Clean the greenhouse in preparation for winter.
- Dig over heavy clay soil before autumn rains make it less workable.
- Sow hardy annuals to flower next year.

Viburnum opulus 'Compactum' ♀ • Shrub with clustered white flowers, then bright fruits *(see p.358)*

Aster novi-belgii 'Peace' • Michaelmas daisy, a reliable, tall, clump-forming perennial *(see p.299)*

Chrysanthemum 'Carnival Red' • Perennial with scarl flowers on sturdy stems *(see p.305)*

Eryngium x tripartitum ♀ • Prickly perennial with sea-green foliage *(see p.317)*

Solidago 'Goldenmosa' ♀ • Clump-forming perennial, good for cut flowers *(see p.354)*

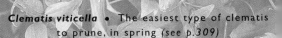

Clematis viticella • The easiest type of clematis to prune, in spring *(see p.309)*

Agapanthus **'Blue Giant'** • Tall bulbous perennial, perfect in a pot *(see p.296)*

Rudbeckia **'Herbstsonne'** • Perennial: the flowerheads still look good when faded *(see p.351)*

Plumbago auriculata • Sprawling shrub for a warm wall or conservatory *(see p.341)*

Sedum spectabile **'Brilliant'** ♀ • Perennial whose flowers are a late treat for wildlife *(see p.353)*

Caryopteris x clandonensis **'Kew Blue'** • Small shrub that enjoys sun and shelter *(see p.303)*

Dahlia **'Bishop of Llandaff'** ♀ • Tender perennial with dark bronze-purple foliage *(see p.314)*

TOP ROW: *Stipa gigantea* ♀ (see p.354) • *Helictotrichon sempervirens* ♀ (p.323) • *Lagurus ovatus* (p.328)
BOTTOM ROW: *Hordeum jubatum* (p.324) • *Hakonechloa macra* 'Aureola' ♀ (p.322) • *Alopecurus pratensis* 'Aureovariegatus' (p.297)

TOP ROW: *Miscanthus sinensis* 'Silberfeder' (p.333) • *Carex pendula* (p.303) • *Arundo donax var. versicolor* (p.299)
BOTTOM ROW: *Carex flagellifera* (p.303) • *Carex oshimensis* 'Evergold' ♀ (p.303) • *Pennisetum alopecuroides* 'Hameln' (p.339)

WHAT TO DO IN SEPTEMBER

AROUND THE GARDEN

BUY OR MAKE A COMPOST BIN FOR ALL THE AUTUMN DEBRIS. It is essential to add plenty of organic matter to the soil to maintain it in good heart. Growing plants intensively, as we tend to do in small gardens, means that a lot of goodness is taken out of the earth in a relatively small area. It is therefore essential to put something back in order to continue to get the best out of the garden. Making your own compost is the ideal way of doing this, and although there are plenty of bins to buy, you can make a simple one yourself (see p.232). It's cheap and easy to construct, and will fit into the smallest corner. Remember to use a good mix of different materials, except woody and diseased material, to make the best compost. If you grow vegetables they will generate quantities of useful composting material.

DAMAGE FROM PESTS AND DISEASES will be slowing down at this time of year, but it is still necessary to be on the lookout to prevent pests overwintering and becoming a problem next year. Clear any debris in borders, consigning it to the compost heap or burning it if it is diseased. Yellowing leaves on plants should be removed as they will encourage mildew and botrytis. Any pests like aphids still around can be dealt with by squashing them. Shoots tips heavily infected with mildew or overwhelmed by aphids can become distorted under the attack. Trim these back to healthy growth and burn the prunings.

TAKE A NOTEBOOK ON RAMBLES AROUND THE GARDEN. Before the summer display is completely over for another year, it is a good idea to have a wander around assessing how plants have performed and deciding whether they need to be moved or removed completely. Sometimes you have to be tough and if a plant just has not come up to expectations, then it has to go. There is no point in spending a lot of time and effort in growing something to find that no matter what you try it just won't grow well.

Perhaps some colours have clashed and plants need to be moved. It can be fascinating thinking up new plant colour themes and contrasts. Don't forget, too, that foliage plays an important part in any display, and dramatic effects can be created by associating different leaf shapes, colours and sizes. Variety and continuity can be created with foliage alone.

CULTIVATING CLAY SOIL. This type of soil can be difficult to cultivate, especially if it has not been worked for several years. Now is a good time to dig it, while the soil is reasonably dry. This will give the winter weather plenty of time to play its part in breaking down lumps of soil, ready for making seed beds or planting out in the spring. Roughly dig the soil, incorporating plenty of organic matter, and leave it rough for the winter. To permanently improve the drainage, dig in, if you can afford it, pea shingle. Combined with the organic matter, this will also raise the level of the soil slightly, making it drain more easily and helping it to warm up faster in spring.

SOW GREEN MANURE CROPS on vacant pieces of ground. See Vegetables & Herbs, August.

TREES & SHRUBS

AUTUMN AND EARLY SPRING (see March for illustrations) are good times to move evergreen shrubs, while the soil is still relatively warm. Dig around the plant as far from the base of the plant as you can and as deep as you can, to take as good a root system as possible. If it's a large shrub you may have to get the help of a friend or family member.

Wrap the roots in hessian or polythene sheeting eased under the rootball to retain moisture. It may be necessary to rock the plant back and forth to work the sheeting under the roots, in which case you will certainly need the help of a friend. Tie the sheet up and move the plant to its new location. Dig a hole big enough to take the root ball without having to cram the roots in. Be sure to plant to the same depth as before. Put the plant in the hole, pull the wrapping out from under the roots and gradually fill in the hole. Work the soil right in and gently firm with your boot as you go. Water in well, and stake the plant if in an exposed place. If there are cold winds it's worth erecting a windbreak of hessian or fine plastic mesh supported on stakes on the windward side of the plant. This will help to reduce evaporation of water from the leaves.

PLANTING

PLANTING CONTAINER-GROWN TREES AND SHRUBS in the autumn is beneficial in several ways. At this time of year the soil is still quite warm and moist, so the roots of the plants can become established before winter sets in and the plants will get off to a flying start in the spring. Because the soil is relatively moist there is no need to pay so much attention to watering in the early stages, saving on water and time. Plant them just as you would container-grown perennials (see right), staking trees in addition (see also January for illustrations). Planting of bare-root plants of deciduous trees and shrubs can start in November through to March.

PROPAGATION

TAKE HARDWOOD CUTTINGS OF ROSES. Roses are normally propagated by budding – grafting a bud of the chosen variety onto a rootstock. This is an easy and quick commercial way of propagating roses. It does, however, have a down side. The rootstock will often throw up suckers which, if left unchecked, will take over the whole bush. Try to remove them when they are still small when they can be torn from the plant easily (see also June). Tearing or pulling them off is better than cutting them out as then they will grow again. It's just like pruning them. But there is a way to produce roses that don't throw up suckers, and that is by taking hardwood cuttings.

Select a shoot of about pencil-thickness and about 30cm (12in) long. Remove the soft growing tip and all but the top three sets of leaves. Trim the base of the cutting immediately below a leaf joint, making the cutting about 23cm (9in) long. Make a slit trench in the ground, and if your soil is heavy clay, put some sharp sand in the bottom of the trench to aid drainage. Set cuttings along the trench to two-thirds of their length, and firm in. The cuttings will root and be ready to transplant to their flowering positions next autumn.

CLIMBERS

PLANT NEW CONTAINER-GROWN CLIMBERS (see Trees & Shrubs).

START PRUNING CLIMBING ROSES when the flowers fade. If they are still going strong, wait until next month. To prune (see below), first remove dead or diseased wood. Then look for new shoots, especially from the base of the plant, for tying in. If there aren't many new basal shoots, prune all the side shoots from the existing framework of branches to two or three buds. If possible, remove entirely any very old stems, pruning them to near ground level. New shoots can be tied in to replace these.

PRUNING CLIMBING ROSES

First remove any dead, damaged and unhealthy-looking stems, and dispose of the prunings.

Tie in shoots that can extend the framework, and prune others back to two or three leaves or buds.

PERENNIALS

PLANTING NEW PERENNIALS

❶ Dig holes for the new plants, and revitalize the soil with garden compost and a handful of bone meal.

❷ Give the plants a good soak an hour or two beforehand, then ease the rootball out of the pot.

❸ If the plant has become tight and congested in its pot, tease out the rootball a little before planting.

❹ Set the plant at the same depth as before, and fill in around it with soil, firming it well in with your fingers.

❺ Water the plant well: half a watering can per plant is not excessive if the weather has been very dry.

❻ Mulch around the plant with garden compost, chipped bark or leafmould to conserve moisture in the soil.

PLANT NEW PERENNIALS. This is a good time of year for planting new perennials. The soil is moist and still warm enough for the plants' roots to become established before the winter sets in. Garden centres should have a good selection of flowering and foliage herbaceous perennials available. It's fun going round deciding what plants to buy, and taking them home. Perennials are generally not dear – and, of course, the plants can be lifted and divided, and cuttings taken, in years to come, so each plant then costs almost nothing.

Choose plants carefully, making sure they are right for your garden and for the position they are intended for. It's a waste of money to buy something just because it is appealing, only to find it struggles or even dies because it was a bad choice. Look for plants with strong healthy growth, with the rootballs showing plenty of roots, but not so packed that the plants are pot-bound. If you don't want to turn the plant out of its pot (though no good nursery should mind you doing this) then at least make sure no roots are thrusting through the drainage holes at the bottom.

Water the plants well before and after planting. If the plants are rather dry when you buy them, plunge them in a bucket of water to ensure the rootball is moist right through.

PERENNIALS *continued*

Dividing perennials If using forks to prise tough clumps apart, push down on the metal hasps that form the lower part of the handle. Then you won't break the handle where the wood joins the hasp.

KEEP COLLECTING SEEDS FROM PERENNIALS as they ripen. Be vigilant, otherwise the seeds will be spread as soon as your back is turned. See July for more details.

CUT DOWN AND DIVIDE PERENNIALS that have finished flowering and are not looking good. Most perennials look rather tatty when the flowers have gone over, and the best thing to do is to cut them down and make the borders look tidier. At the same time, any clumps which are becoming old and bare in the centre should be lifted and divided. Some plants, such as sedums, thrive on being divided every year and others, like peonies, really resent being disturbed. It's very difficult to give generalised advice. There are so many thousands, literally, of perennials now available to gardeners that it is well worth treating yourself to a really good reference book on the subject – or perhaps putting one on your Christmas list this year.

Clumps which need dividing can be lifted with a fork and placed on a sheet of polythene on the lawn. Divide large clumps with two forks back to back pushed into the centre of the clump, pushing them apart. Smaller pieces can be pulled apart by hand. Revitalize the soil with plenty of organic matter and plant the smaller pieces in groups of three, five or more if you have the space.

If you haven't time to divide clumps of herbaceous perennials now, it can be done throughout the autumn and into spring as long as the soil conditions are good enough to work. But if you can't get on with the work, it is a good idea to go out and make notes about the plants to be divided or moved. Sometimes, no matter how expert we like to think we are, some plant associations just don't work. Colour combinations are easy to plan using photographs (though you can still occasionally get not quite the effect you were hoping for), but getting the heights and relative vigour of neighbouring plants right can be more tricky. The one advantage of growing herbaceous perennials is that they are easily moved if this happens and they don't take many years to get established.

TALL-GROWING CLUMPS OF ASTERS will need support or they will be blown down in windy conditions. There are many different ways to support plants. The wire supports available from garden centres are popular and do a good job, but these have to be put in place while the plants are young and can grow through them. The easiest way to provide support now is by using canes and string. Put three

or four canes around the plant and wind string around the canes to enclose all of the stems. If it's done carefully the canes and string will be almost hidden by the foliage of the plant.

ALPINES

ANY PLANTS THAT HAVE OUTGROWN THEIR SPACE can be moved this month. This will give the plants time to settle in before the winter. Water the plants well before transplanting, and lift them carefully, with a good ball of soil around the roots. Plant in the new position to the same depth as before, firm in well and water in to settle the roots. If the weather is dry keep an eye on the plants and water them regularly (perhaps once a week) until they are established. Mulch the plants with grit to help winter rains drain away.

BULBS

CONTINUE PLANTING SPRING-FLOWERING BULBS (SEE ALSO AUGUST). This is the main month for planting most spring-flowering bulbs, with the exception of tulips which prefer being planted later (see November). Buy them early, and you will get the best choice, particularly among sought-after bulbs like the alliums. There are so many more bulbs to choose from than the ubiquitous daffodils and crocuses. Look out for chionodoxas, ornithogalum, scillas, puschkinia and *Iris histrioides*, for example, as well as corms of the many varieties of *Anemone blanda*. Grape hyacinths (*Muscari*) are essentials, too, for

PLANTING BULBS IN GRASS

Planting small bulbs in grass Make H-shaped cuts and lift flaps in the turf, planting beneath.

Planting large bulbs in grass Make individual holes with a planter, spacing the bulbs randomly.

pretty, low-growing clumps of the most vivid blue flowers. Don't forget to put some bulbs in amongst your spring bedding plants for a stunning show in the spring. See below for more choices to grow in pots.

If you have problems with mice taking bulbs (they are particularly fond of crocuses), pegged-down chicken wire can give some protection.

THIS IS THE LATEST MONTH FOR PLANTING bulbs to flower at Christmas (see August). But continue planting spring-flowering bulbs in pots (see also Under Cover).

Dwarf bulbs in pots are particularly appealing, as the beauty of these miniatures can really be appreciated at close quarters. There are plenty of daffodils to choose from, among them *Narcissus tazettus*, with yellow and white scented flowers; 'Jack Snipe', with creamy yellow petals, and 'Minimus' with yellow flowers. Other dwarf bulbs to try include species tulips, such as *Tulipa tarda*; chionodoxas, crocus and dwarf iris.

PLANT BULBS TO NATURALISE IN GRASS (SEE LEFT). Bulbs always look particularly pleasing growing in turf. All bulbs, with the exception of the tiniest alpines, can be used in this way. For smaller bulbs or corms like miniature daffodils and crocus, the easiest way to plant them is to lift a piece of turf and place the bulbs in groups on the soil, replacing the turf afterwards. With larger bulbs like daffodils and tulips, use a bulb planter rather than trying to dig individual holes for each bulb. To get an informal drift of bulbs in grass scatter a handful of bulbs over the area, and plant

CORMLETS FROM GLADIOLI

1 Once the leaves start yellowing, lift the bulb-like corms gently with a trowel. Leave them to dry, and then cut back the foliage.

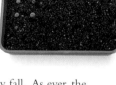

2 Small cormlets can be picked off before the main corms are cleaned and stored.

3 Sow the cormlets in seed trays in spring, covering with a layer of sieved compost.

them where they fall. As ever, the general rule when planting all bulbs is to plant them two to three times their own depth.

TOWARDS THE END OF THE MONTH, LIFT GLADIOLI (see above). When the leaves start to go yellow it is time to lift the corms before frost damages them. Lift them carefully with a fork as the corms are usually surrounded by little cormlets, and these can be saved and grown on if you want

to increase your stock of plants. Leave the old foliage on until it has dried off and then cut it off 5–8cm (2–3in) above the new, main corm that has developed above the remains of the old one. When the corms have dried twist off the old corm and dust the base of the new corm with sulphur to prevent disease getting in, and store in a cool dry place. The cormlets can be separated out and

DIVIDING CROCOSMIAS

1 Once flowers are over and the leaves are fading, lift congested clumps carefully with a fork, trying not to damage the roots.

3 You may need a knife to start separating the clumps; after that, they can be pulled apart into small sections and the leaves cut off.

stored in envelopes with the other corms. These can be "sown" in trays in spring, just like seeds. It doesn't matter which way up they are; they are so small that the shoots will find their own way to the surface.

DIVIDE CROCOSMIAS. Lift and divide overgrown clumps as for perennials (see below).

2 Crocosmias form exceptionally tight, crowded clumps; it may help to lay them down and play a hose over them at first.

4 Lay all of the divisions out, about 15cm (6in) apart, before you plant them – then you won't lose track of where you are.

ANNUALS & BEDDING

SOW HARDY ANNUALS FOR FLOWERING NEXT YEAR. Some hardy annuals can be sown outside now for flowering next year. Sown now, the plants will flower from early May the following year. To sow (for illustrations, see March), rake the soil to a fine tilth, and mark out informal areas with a stick or sand poured out of an empty wine bottle. Take out shallow drills within each marked area, and water them if the soil is dry. Sow the seeds thinly and cover with dry soil. When the seedlings are about 2.5cm (1in) high, thin them out to about 10cm (4in). In spring you may have to thin them again. Look on the back of seed packets for those annuals that can be sown outside in August and September; they include *Calendula officinalis*, *Centaurea cyanus*, *Limnanthes douglasii*, California poppies (*Eschscholzia*) and *Papaver somniferum*.

If your soil is heavy clay there is a risk that the seedlings will rot, because of excessive wet. Sow the seeds in modules and overwinter them in a cold frame, planting them out in the spring.

Clearing bedding Bedding does not have time to root very deeply, and can be raked out.

LIFT TENDER PERENNIALS before autumn frosts begin. Plants like argyranthemums, gazanias, lantanas, osteospermums, pelargoniums and arctotis will have to be lifted and taken under cover for protection, otherwise they will be lost. Give the plants a trim, removing any yellowing leaves and spent flowers; if they are a bit large for the space you've got, don't be afraid to prune them quite hard. If space is really limited, pack them closely into boxes and cover the roots with compost. Otherwise pot them up and keep in a cool but frost-free place over winter – a frost-free greenhouse, a cold frame or a shed, garage or utility room. High temperatures will induce spindly growth to be made, which you don't want. Keep them on the dry side, too, giving just enough water to keep them ticking over until the better weather and longer days of spring. Some of the plants can be kept to be replanted next year just as they are. But others, like pelargoniums, are much better grown from cuttings each year. Cuttings can be taken either now (see August) or in the spring (see March, Under Cover).

PLANT OUT SPRING-FLOWERING BIENNIALS, either bought or transplanted from where you have been growing them in nursery rows through the summer. Clear old summer bedding away when the flowers have gone over. This is the time to incorporate organic matter into the soil if it is needed. Afterwards, rake the soil level, and mark out informal drifts with a stick. Plant groups of each kind of plant in each drift for the best effect. Make sure the crown of each plant is level with the soil, and that you firm them in well.

Water plants in to settle the soil around the roots. If you haven't been able to grow your own biennials, garden centres should have a selection available from now on. Plants to look for are wallflowers, forget-me-nots (*Myosotis*), bellis, canterbury bells (*Campanula medium*), sweet Williams (*Dianthus barbatus*), foxgloves (*Digitalis purpurea*), anchusa, Iceland poppies (*Papaver nudicaule*), ornamental cabbages and winter-flowering pansies.

Remember: don't grow wallflowers and ornamental cabbages in the same piece of ground as last year. They belong to the brassica family (cabbages, Brussels sprouts and their relatives) and like brassica crops, are subject to the disease clubroot (a swelling of the root system) which is very infectious and persists in the soil. Rotate them just as you would brassica crops.

Digitalis purpurea var. *albiflora*   *Bellis perennis*

Erysimum 'Blood Red'   *Anchusa* 'Loddon Royal'

CONTAINERS

CONTINUE TO CARE FOR BEDDING PLANTS by deadheading and feeding to extend the display until the first frosts.

STOP FEEDING PERMANENT PLANTS growing in containers. Plants like shrubs, trees and fruit trees growing in containers will, if fed, produce soft growth now which will be damaged in winter. So stop feeding them with general fertilisers now. One last feed with sulphate of potash, or rock potash if you want to be organic, will benefit them by ripening the wood, making it more able to stand up to the rigours of winter.

MOVE POTS OF TENDER PERENNIALS like fuchsias and pelargoniums under cover, to be kept over winter in a cool frost-free greenhouse or conservatory (see Annuals & Bedding).

ONCE SUMMER BEDDING PLANTS IN CONTAINERS have come to the end of their time they can be cleared out, and spring bedding plants planted in their place (see also Annuals & Bedding).

Remove some of the old compost and put in some fresh, preferably a John Innes potting compost as it will retain more nutrients and, being heavier, will prevent containers blowing over in windy weather. The choice of plants and colour schemes is entirely personal, so let your imagination run riot. If you haven't raised your own spring bedding like wallflowers, forget-me-nots and bellis yourself, garden centres will have a wide range of plants to choose from. Remember to plant bulbs in with the spring bedding too.

PLANT BULBS IN CONTAINERS. For these there is no need to renew the compost when summer bedding has been pulled out, as bulbs will thrive perfectly well in the old compost. The most important time to feed bulbs is after flowering, when they are building up the flower bud to flower the following year. Pack the bulbs in as close as you can, planting them between two and three times their own depth. Use one kind or colour of bulb for each container to make a stunning show in the spring. See Bulbs this month for some suggested varieties.

Planting bulbs in layers Large bulbs at the bottom and small ones at the top will fill out the display.

PONDS

CONGESTED PLANTS IN THE POND CAN BE THINNED OUT. Oxygenating and floating plants can grow so well that they almost take over the pond, so these will need thinning out if there are other plants growing in the water. After removing them, always leave them by the side of the pond for a few days to allow any wildlife in the plants to get back into the pond. While you're at it, poolside plants like irises and astilbes which have finished flowering can also be divided if they are becoming congested.

COVER PONDS WITH NETTING. Done early this will prevent leaves falling into the pond. If leaves accumulate and rot in the pond they give off gases as they decompose, and these can be lethal to fish and other wildlife. Use the finest mesh you can get, otherwise smaller leaves will still get in. Secure it around the edge of the pond with bricks or pegs used for securing horticultural fleece. Pegs can also be made from fencing wire. If any leaves have fallen in the pond already, fish them out before netting.

Repot marginals You will have to slice off roots like these before the plant will come out of its basket.

LAWNS

START MOWING LESS FREQUENTLY as the growth of grass begins to slow down (see also October).

AUTUMN MAINTENANCE. Towards the end of the month, most gardeners start the annual round of work on the lawn to reinvigorate it. If you just have too much to do in the autumn, it can be done in the new year (see January and March).

• **REMOVE THATCH FROM THE LAWN.** Over a period of time, a layer of dead grass and other debris accumulates in any lawn; this is called thatch. If it is left in the lawn over the years it restricts air movement around the grass and can cause problems with surface drainage, encouraging moss and other weeds to colonize the lawn. From late August through the autumn, begin to remove this thatch. It can be done in several ways, the most back-breaking method being to drag it out with a spring-tined rake. Use this tool to rake out the dead grass and moss. It can be very hard work, and it is easier to use a powered scarifier if you have a large lawn. These can be hired, and will remove all the thatch with little effort. Be warned, the lawn will look an absolute mess when scarifying has been done, but it will do it the world of good and will soon recover.

• **THE NEXT JOB TO BE DONE IS AERATION.** Like any other plant, grass needs air, and the surface of the lawn gets very compacted over the summer with constant use and cutting every week. To relieve this compaction, aerate the lawn with a fork pushed into the ground, to a depth of 15cm (6in) at 15-18cm (6-9in) intervals over the whole area. Again, if you have a large lawn, machines can be hired to do this job too. Some of these remove a small core of soil, which is of particular benefit if you have a heavy clay soil.

• **TOP-DRESS IMMEDIATELY AFTER AERATING.** Top-dressing ensures that aerating holes stay open and revitalizes the upper layer of soil. A mix of three parts sieved garden soil, two parts of sharp sand and one part sieved garden compost (or old potting compost, if you have some) is the best top-dressing to use. If your lawn is a bit worn, mix in some grass seed with the top-dressing mix. Spread a 1-2cm (½-1in) layer over the lawn and work it in with a stiff broom or the back of a rake. It will look a bit of a mess for a couple of weeks, but the grass will soon grow through again.

PATCHES OF BROAD-LEAVED WEEDS can be treated with a lawn weedkiller in autumn, or in spring (see May). Make sure you use a selective weedkiller especially formulated for lawns otherwise you will damage the grass. Always use these chemicals stictly according to the manufacturer's instructions.

ESTABLISHED LAWNS CAN BE FED NOW unless you did so last month (see August). Don't use up high-nitrogen feeds you were using earlier; at this time of year, you need one of the low-nitrogen fertilisers sold as autumn lawn feeds in garden centres, as you don't want to encourage soft, sappy growth.

RESEED WORN PATCHES ON THE LAWN. Small bare patches can be easily repaired by sowing seed. Rake out any thatch and then roughen the surface

LAWNS *continued*

slightly with a fork to make a fine tilth, and level it. Put the grass seed in a bucket and mix in an equal quantity of old potting compost or sieved garden compost. Spread this mix evenly over the bare patch and tamp it down with the back of a rake. To encourage quick germination, cover the area with polythene pegged into the ground. Keep the patch watered if it gets dry, and the seed should germinate in two to three weeks. Remove the polythene as soon as the seeds begin to germinate.

NEW LAWNS

SOW GRASS SEED OR LAY TURF. Although grass seed can be sown and turf laid at almost any time of the year, by far the best time is in early autumn. If you have not already prepared the ground (see August), do it as soon as you can now, digging over thoroughly and removing all trace of weeds. After that, preparation up to a certain point is the same whether you are sowing seed or laying turf:
• Roughly level the soil with a rake to break down the lumps.
• Then tread the ground with your weight on your heels, keeping your feet together.
• Rake over the soil and then tread it again, this time shuffling across it at right-angles to the first time. Stand back and squat down to look across the soil surface and spot any hollows and bumps that should be taken out.
• Finally, rake the soil to a fine tilth as if preparing any seedbed.
Now, either sow seed or lay turf:
• Sow grass seed according to the specifications on the packet. If sowing by hand you can mark out the area in square metres with string and canes to make it easier (see April for illustrations). Measuring the amount for each square metre into a small plastic cup once and using this as a guide will save a lot of time, by removing the need to weigh out all the seeds. An even quicker way to sow is to use a fertiliser spreader. The instructions for sowing seeds with these will come with the spreader.
• Lay turf by rolling it out and butting it up close so there are no gaps. Lay it in the same pattern house bricks are laid, so none of the joints line up. This ensures a good bond when the turf knits together. Always work outwards, from boards placed across the turf already laid. Water well, and keep it watered if necessary, but keep off the new turf as much as possible for four or five weeks to allow it to establish.

LAYING TURF

❶ Start from a definite edge, whether defined by a hard surface or a line. Butt the turves up closely together.

❷ Lay the next row with staggered joints. Almost overlap the turves and press them down with your fingers.

❸ Once all of the turves are laid, it is worth going over them tamping down the joints with the back of a rake.

❹ Cut edges as necessary with a hemispherical edging iron. Hosepipe or rope can be used to mark out curves.

❺ Walking backwards, brush up the grass with a stiff broom to stimulate its growth, especially across joints.

❻ Water really thoroughly with cans or a sprinkler, and keep the turf well watered until autumn rains lend a hand.

VEGETABLES & HERBS

Asparagus fern *Female plants will produce these bright berries amongst the ferny foliage.*

CUT DOWN ASPARAGUS FOLIAGE now that it is turning brown. Be careful when doing this, as there are sharp spines on the stems which can give you a nasty scratch. After cutting down the foliage, give the plants a generous mulch of organic matter. This is also a good time to prepare a site for planting new asparagus crowns next spring (see October). If your soil is a heavy clay it is worth ordering some grit to incorporate into the soil to improve drainage, as asparagus likes a well-drained soil.

HARVESTING

HARVEST THE LAST OF THE GLOBE ARTICHOKES, cutting only buds that have not started to open up.

PICK MARROWS, PUMPKINS AND SQUASHES. Leave them in the sun for a couple of weeks, or put them in a greenhouse if the weather is wet, to ripen and dry off before storing them in a cool, dark place. They should keep until well after Christmas. Clear the old plants away as soon as the fruits have been picked, as they will by now almost certainly have been attacked by mildew.

BEGIN LIFTING ROOT VEGETABLES for storing. Vegetables like beetroot, carrots and turnips can be lifted and stored for use over the winter. Parsnips are best left in the ground as they taste better when they have had a bit of frost on them.

To store all the others select only undamaged roots. Any damaged ones should be used straight away and not stored, as they are liable to spread disease through the rest. Lift the roots and twist or cut off the foliage, leaving a few centimetres of stem. Put the roots in boxes between layers of sand or old potting compost. This prevents them drying out too quickly and keeps them in the dark, discouraging them from growing again. Make sure they are in a frost-free place. Inspect them regularly and throw out any showing signs of rotting. Another old-fashioned but effective way to store root vegetables is to make a clamp (see October).

LIFT MAINCROP POTATOES at the end of the month. Lift them on a warm sunny day, and leave them on the surface of the soil for an hour or two to dry out. Again store only undamaged ones, in paper sacks tied at the neck, in a frost-free dark place. Potatoes must be kept dark, otherwise they turn green.

GET ONIONS UNDER COVER Lift and dry any still in the ground (see August), and bring them into a cool, dry storage area before damp autumn weather sets in. In mild autumns especially, if onions are left in the ground after the leaves have gone over, they often start to regrow, and they are then lesss useful in the kitchen and no good for storing.

SOWING AND PLANTING OUTDOORS

SOW A WINTER VARIETY OF LETTUCE. Sow in shallow drills in the usual manner, and cover with cloches. The seeds will germinate quickly, and when the seedlings are large enough to handle, thin them out to about 15cm (6in) apart. Harvest from January onwards. A good old reliable favourite is 'Winter Density'.

PLANT GARLIC. Autumn is the traditional time for planting garlic, as it needs a period of cold weather to grow well. To get good-quality crops buy bulbs specially cultivated for planting. Plant in a sunny site in well-drained soil. On heavy soil, dig in some horticultural grit to aid drainage. Break each bulb into individual cloves, and plant each one 8–10cm (3–4in) apart, with 30cm (1ft) between rows. Plant so that the tips of the cloves are just below soil level.

To get the plants off to a quicker start, plant them in module trays with large cells (see November) and keep these in a cold frame for the winter, or place them at the base of a sheltered wall. The plants can then be put in the ground in the spring.

PLANT OUT SPRING CABBAGES sown last month. These can be planted 15cm (6in) apart in rows 30cm (1ft) apart. Harvest every other plant as spring greens, leaving the others to heart up. Cover the plants with netting or fleece or the pigeons will have them eaten to the ground as soon as your back is turned.

There is still time to sow a fast maturing variety like 'Duncan' or 'Pixie' under cover. To get them off to a good start sow the seeds in modules, so that when it comes to planting them out the roots are not disturbed and the plants will get away without a check to their growth.

PLANT AUTUMN ONION SETS. The sooner these go in and get growing before winter sets in the better. Varieties to look for are 'Radar' and 'Swift'. Plant them 8cm (3in) apart in drills deep enough to just cover the tip of the sets. Apply a general organic fertiliser now and again in spring to boost their growth.

EARTH UP TRENCH-GROWN CELERY for the final time, leaving just a tuft of foliage poking out at the top. Blanching makes the stems more tender. Keep some straw or fleece handy, and throw it over the tops of the plants if severe frost is forecast over winter. Harvest the last of the self-blanching celery before the first frosts.

LAY TOMATO PLANTS ON A LAYER OF STRAW and cover with cloches to speed up ripening. It is rare in our short summers to ripen the whole crop from outdoor tomatoes. By laying the plants down and covering them you can maximise the ripening effect of late sunshine. Any fruits left unripe can be used to make green tomato chutney – or, place them into a drawer and put a banana in with them. The gases given off by the banana help the ripening process.

Outdoor tomatoes *Lay cordon plants down on clean straw and cover with cloches to finish ripening.*

FRUIT

Storing apples
Fruits must be sound and completely dry before storing in polythene bags.

PICKING AND STORING

CONTINUE HARVESTING FRUIT as it ripens. Cooking varieties of apples and pears will not be ready for picking until near the end of the month and into October. Handle all fruits gently, as the skins are easily bruised, which adversely affects their keeping qualities.

Store only those fruits that are unblemished. Fruits showing damage should be used right away, or kept away from the main storage area. Large crops of apples should be individually wrapped in paper (old newspaper is handy for this purpose) and laid on trays in a single layer. Smaller quantities can be stored in polythene bags. Make a few holes in the bags with a skewer to let out gases given off by the fruits that will hasten the ripening process. Pears are best left unwrapped, standing on slatted benches. Pick early dessert pears while they are still hard and let them ripen indoors.

TOWARDS THE MIDDLE AND END OF THE MONTH autumn-fruiting raspberries come into their own. These late-fruiting varieties are delicious, often more concentrated in flavour than their summer counterparts. Once the fruit is picked, leave the canes unpruned until late winter or early spring.

BLACKBERRIES RIPEN IN SUCCESSION over a much longer period than other soft fruits, and if you have only a few plants, it can be frustrating trying to gather enough for a good meal in one go. The trick is to freeze them in small batches until you have gathered enough together – like currants and raspberries, blackberries and hybrid berries freeze very well.

LOOKING AFTER CROPS

AT THE END OF THE MONTH, FIX GREASE BANDS to the trunks of fruit trees (see also October). Many pests like to crawl up the trunks and hibernate or lay their eggs in little cracks and crevices on the branches of the trees. One way of reducing this problem is to use grease bands: waxed paper covered in sticky grease which can be bought from garden centres. They will trap wingless female winter moths and other insects as they make their way up the trunk of the tree.

PROTECT RIPENING FRUITS from birds and wasps, who like the sweet ripening crops just as much as we do. Netting is the only way to keep birds off fruit trees, but it must be well secured to prevent birds from getting trapped in it. Better still, if you can, grow all your fruit in a fruit cage made specially for the purpose. There are many different ones on the market, or you could make your own. Pick up spoiled windfalls and scatter them on bare ground in the vegetable garden or similar for wildlife, being wary of course of wasps when picking them up. Plums are a favourite with butterflies, who love to feed on the sugary juice.

PRUNE OFF MILDEW-INFECTED shoots of apples and pears. Mildew often attacks trees at this time, and once it has got a hold, spraying with a fungicide is next to useless. Fungicides should be used in the early part of the season before the mildew appears as a preventive measure. Now the only remedy is to prune off the infected shoots and burn them or put them in the bin. Don't shred them or put them on the compost heap, or the spores of the mildew will be spread around the garden.

KEEP STRAWBERRIES planted last month well watered.

PRUNING AND TRAINING

FINISH CUTTING OUT FRUITED CANES of summer-fruiting raspberries (see July). Don't get them confused with autumn-fruiting raspberries, which will be ripening this month.

PRUNE BLACKCURRANTS. From now through the winter blackcurrants can be pruned, if you wish. It was in the past the practice to prune blackcurrants as soon as the fruits had been picked. But at that time the plants are still in full leaf, the foliage manufacturing plant foods. Early pruning takes off a lot of leaves, reducing the plants' capacity to manufacture this food; and it is also more difficult to see what you are doing. It is far better to leave the pruning until the leaves have begun to fall in the autumn and in winter when you can see what you are doing more clearly. For pruning see December.

PLANTING

FINISH PLANTING NEW STRAWBERRY PLANTS before the end of the month. This is the latest they can be planted to allow them to become established before winter sets in. The plants must have time to establish and form a good root system to crop successfully the following summer. However, if they go short of water this will not happen and they will not fruit very well next year, so if the weather is dry, they need plentiful watering. Plants under stress from lack of water are also more prone to attack from pests and diseases.

Strawberries are not a permanent crop like other fruits so, if you can, grow them in the vegetable garden where they can be rotated like the other crops. See August for details of planting.

PLANT CONTAINER-GROWN PEACHES AND NECTARINES in a sheltered spot. Planting now in the autumn will give the plants a good chance to become established before winter. Prepare the soil by digging it over and incorporate plenty of farmyard manure or garden compost. Dig out a hole big enough to take the rootball and deep enough to plant it at the depth it is in the container. Make sure the point at which the tree is grafted (a swollen part of the stem near the base of the tree) is above ground level. The rootstock onto which the tree is grafted controls the vigour of the tree. Gently replace the soil in stages, firming as you go. Water in if the soil is dry, and if the tree is being trained against a wall or fence, tie it to its supports.

UNDER GLASS

Cleaning glass After removing shding, give the glass a clean. A palette knife is a useful tool.

REMOVE SHADING (see also August). Clean off shading washes, give blinds a shake or brush before rolling them back, or fold and store any shading curtains. From now on plants under cover need all the light they can get.

CHECK ALL OF THE GLASS AND PUTTYING in the greenhouse to see if any repairs are needed. Replace any broken panes of glass. It is surprising just how much heat can be lost through a crack in a pane of glass, and any pane not fitting close to the framework will also cause a loss of heat.

START PREPARING THE GLASSHOUSE FOR WINTER. Towards the end of the month, but before tender perennials are brought inside for the winter and while things inside are still relatively quiet, take all the plants outside and thoroughly clean the place from top to bottom. Get it done this month, so that if it takes more than one day to do it, the plants can be left outside overnight without much fear of them being harmed by frosts. Make sure you get into every little corner; these are where pests like to hibernate and lay their eggs. A hose down with a forceful jet of water, inside and outside, is ideal

initially; then, wash down with a weak solution of household bleach or one of the proprietary products that can be bought from a garden centre. Then rinse down again. Be sure to cover any electrical power points and remove any appliances. If you can, switch off the power supply completely from the house while you are doing this job. If there are any problems with electricity, call out a professional to see to them before turning it on again.

REDUCE WATERING AND VENTILATION. Now that the nights are getting cooler it is advisable to reduce watering, and to water as early in the day as you can. This will allow the greenhouse to dry out before the cooler evenings, reducing the chances of diseases such as mildew and botrytis getting a hold. Ventilators should be closed now at night. You never know when there might be a slight nip in the air and maybe a frost from now on. Opening the ventilators on mild days to keep the air circulating will go a long way to reducing the problems of disease infection.

BRING IN TENDER PLANTS TO OVERWINTER. Plants like pelargoniums, argyranthemums and lantanas should all be brought inside now (see also Annuals & Bedding). With these plants inside, the greenhouse can seem as packed as it was in the spring, but most will be quite happy under the staging where it is cool. Be careful when watering, giving just enough to keep the plants ticking over until the spring. Inspect them regularly and remove any yellowing or diseased leaves before infection gets a chance to spread.

RAISING PLANTS FOR OUTDOORS

SOW THE LAST SPRING CABBAGES. There is still time to sow fast-maturing spring cabbage varieties like 'Duncan' or 'Pixie'. They are best sown in modules (see also Vegetables & Herbs).

GLASSHOUSE AND HOUSE PLANTS

BRING HOUSEPLANTS INDOORS that have been standing on the patio or on greenhouse shelves for the summer.

CONTINUE PLANTING WINTER- AND SPRING-FLOWERING BULBS IN POTS. You must get prepared hyacinths and other bulbs in before the end of the month if they are to flower at Christmas, but non-prepared hyacinths and plenty of other bulbs will provide a continuity of blooms until spring. Plunge them outside under a heap of compost or leafmould, or put them in cool dark place to form roots. The formation of a good root system first is the key to getting a good display from forced bulbs.

SOW HARDY ANNUALS IN POTS to flower under cover during the spring. You can choose whatever you like, or sow your own seeds collected in the summer. Sow a few seeds thinly in each 12cm (5in) pot and cover them with a thin layer of compost. The seeds will germinate fairly quickly, and can be kept in a cool greenhouse or conservatory over the winter. Don't give them too much warmth, or they will produce a lot of weak growth with the lack of light through the winter. Just keep them watered as necessary and

look forward to a delightful display in the spring. If you sow at two-week intervals, you will have plants in flower for longer.

CROPS UNDER GLASS

PICK TOMATOES, PEPPERS AND AUBERGINES. Continue harvesting tomatoes as they colour up. Removing some of the leaves from around the trusses of fruit will let more light in, hastening the ripening process. This will also increase air circulation around the plants, reducing the possibility of botrytis affecting the ripening fruits. The leaves are removed easily: snap them off by putting your thumb under the leaf stalk close to the main stem and pushing upwards, then give a sharp push down and the leaf will come away cleanly. Feed and water regularly or some fruits may split.

Harvest peppers regularly. They can be harvested green (red peppers are in fact just ripe peppers), so you don't have to worry if they don't all colour up. If you are growing the chilli type of peppers, bear in mind that the riper they get, the hotter they will be. If there are any fruits still to ripen at the end of the month, remove the plants from the pots, shake the soil off the roots and hang them up in a warm place with the fruits still attached to the plant; they will soon ripen.

Aubergines should be picked when the fruits are well coloured but the skin is still taut and shiny. If they are left any longer and the skin begins to wrinkle, they will taste bitter. They are harvested by cutting the stalk at least 2.5cm (1in) away from the fruits. They don't keep for long, so use them quickly.

MAKE A COMPOST BIN

MAKING YOUR OWN GARDEN COMPOST is environmentally friendly, recycling waste to recover all its goodness to give back to the soil, and improves the soil structure no end, making plants grow so much better. There are many different types of container on the market these days, but you don't have to spend a fortune to make good garden compost. This bin costs less than a large container-grown shrub, and is a much more useful long-term investment. You could grow annual climbers up the sides to cheer it up.

YOU WILL NEED: 4 posts, approx. 1.5m (5ft) long • Chicken wire: approx. 1.2m (4ft) wide x 2.5m (8ft) long • Fencing staples • Plenty of cardboard boxes • An old bit of carpet (although you can also buy proprietary "compost duvets")

❶ Set the posts about 75cm (2½ft) apart to make a square. Drive the stakes about 30cm (12in) into the ground, leaving 1.2m (4ft) above ground.

❷ Wrap the chicken wire around the posts, attaching it firmly with plenty of fencing staples to each one.

❸ Continue unwinding the netting until you get to the last post, remembering to leave the front open.

❹ Attach the netting to the last post.

❺ Snip off any excess wire and make sure no sharp edges are left to cause injury.

❻ Flatten the cardboard boxes and put several layers on each side. Slot them in between the posts against the netting to hold them in place.

❼ Gradually layer in garden refuse, using a variety of green material, not woody stuff (unless shredded) or diseased material. If the material is dry, water it well. Even when filled to the top, the composting material soon starts to sink down as it decomposes, enabling you to add more.

8 You can add kitchen refuse, and grass clippings too, but mix these well with other, more fibrous material, or they will rot to a slimy mess.

9 Every time you leave the heap, cover it with an old piece of carpet to keep excess rain off and to help retain the heat which builds up as the material begins to decompose. Make sure the carpet comes down over the edge, and that it stays in place as the heap rots down and decreases in size.

10 In a year or so, the end product will be wonderful garden compost. Renew the cardboard when you empty the bin.

OCTOBER

The garden in October

Autumn colours are at their best this month. Make the most of them as they pass very quickly. And garden birds will be attracted to the bright fruits and berries displayed by your trees and shrubs

OCTOBER CAN BRING A RICHNESS OF COLOUR to the garden, with the multitude of different hues displayed by autumn foliage. The night frosts and clear sunny days which we often get in October bring out the intensity of the colours in the leaves of trees and shrubs. There are many gardens open to the public which are famous for their autumn show, such as Westonbirt Arboretum in Gloucestershire. Some of the colours will take your breath away.

Sharing with friends

Fruits and berries are an added attraction now, not only to us but to the birds as well. Shrubs such as cotoneaster, and trees like the mountain ashes and crab apples are often covered in fruits. But the birds love them so much that often a whole tree can be stripped of berries quite literally overnight. I for one don't feel too aggrieved about sharing with these garden friends – though ask me that again in the spring when they've stripped an unprotected fruit tree of buds! Overall, though, garden birds are a joy, not only when they eat up pests for us, but also when you witness their feeding and bathing antics, and especially when they honour our own green sanctuary by raising their young in it.

Because frosts are quite common now, any tender plants in the borders which you want to keep over winter must now be lifted, potted up, and put into a frost-free greenhouse or conservatory – or if you have room, overwinter cuttings taken from them on the windowsill.

Shortening days

There is less time to garden in the evenings now, so for most people that means most of the work outdoors must be done at the weekends. This leaves little time to get on with things, depending on the size of your garden, of course. With some jobs, the earlier they are done in autumn the better. One such is winter digging, especially if you have heavy clay soil. The more time this type of soil gets for the winter weather to break it down the better, so dig it as early as you can. Don't underestimate the effect wind, rain, frost and snow will have in improving this type of soil. After a winter of pounding by the elements, in spring you will be able to break down the clods easily to make good seed beds. Incorporate as much organic matter as you can into the soil as this will also help to improve the structure of the soil. If you don't have a compost heap of your own

then look in your local directory for riding stables and go along and get a load of horse manure. It's wonderful stuff ,and most riding stables will either charge a very small fee, or be only too glad to see the back of it. It's not as difficult to get these days as many people imagine.

Time for planting

This is a good month to start planting trees, shrubs and herbaceous plants, while the soil is still warm enough for the roots to get a hold before winter sets

WEATHER WATCH

🌡 **There is a significant drop in temperatures** now, with frosts more likely on clear nights. But October can have warm, sunny days too. A still, frosty start to a bright sunny day definitely increases the intensity of autumn leaf colour in deciduous trees.

The number of gales does tend to increase now that we are well into autumn. A pity, in some ways, because high winds blow the leaves off the trees, spoiling the beautiful autumn display. Gales are now most likely in western coastal areas, and will occur on average 3–4 days in the month. Southern and eastern areas generally get off more lightly, with between 0.1 and 1.3 days in the south-west.

☀ **The amount of direct sunshine** is now on the decrease, but there can be some fine days in October. The northern Highlands of Scotland compare favourably with parts of central England: round Wick on the north coast of Scotland the average is 88 hours of sun, and in Nottingham, 86. The south coast always fares better, averaging 107 hours this month.

☁ **October inevitably brings more rain** for all parts of the country, most noticeably in the north and west. The north of England and the central belt of Scotland receive similar amounts of rainfall, ranging from 93mm in north-west England to 115mm in the Glasgow area. The further north you go the more rain falls, with Highland areas getting about 216mm this month month. The driest places are East Anglia and north-east England. In these areas typical October rainfall is 47–67mm.

☁ **Snow does begin to fall this month,** but only on high ground in the north. Northern areas of Scotland and Ireland will have on average 0.1 day of snow on ground above 30m. In the north-east this may increase to 0.3 days on ground above 300m. In these areas, make the best of any good weather this month before winter really sets in.

in. Any plants which are on the borderline of hardiness are better not bought until spring, when they will have a better chance of survival.

You can choose plants that will give you a good show right now – this month, on p.255, we suggest an "instant" autumn planting scheme using a selection of late-blooming plants and attractive ornamental grasses that will not only brighten the garden straight away, but give continuing pleasure every year at this time with bright flowers and interesting foliage.

△ **Autumn scene**
Many ornamental grasses stay looking good well into winter, or even longer. Here the textural effect is highlighted by the bright spots of nerines in flower and a Japanese maple.

Bringing in the harvest

Now is the time to gather in any remaining fruits such as apples and pears before they are damaged by frost. It is easy to tell if a fruit is ripe and ready for picking. Carefully cup the fruit in your hand, and with a gentle upward movement the fruit should part

from the tree easily; if it's not ripe, leave it for a few days, and try again. Only store fruit that is not damaged in any way. Storing damaged or diseased fruit will only encourage diseases to spread through the other fruits more quickly, reducing the time they will keep over the winter.

Elbow grease in the glasshouse

Now is a good time to get the greenhouse and conservatory thoroughly cleaned out before the onset of winter. Most plants can still be left outside for the day, and this will make the process of cleaning much easier. Thoroughly clean the glass inside and out to admit the maximum amount of light in the short days of winter. Scrub down benches with a disinfectant and finally hose the whole place down, paying particular attention to all the corners where pests can lurk and hibernate for the winter.

You may have frost-tender plants that will need some heat at night, so check now to see that all your heaters are in working order. Be careful with electrical heaters; if you are unsure about anything or you suspect there is a problem with your heater, then contact a qualified electrician. And always use an ELCB (earth leakage circuit breaker). This will cut the current in a fraction of a second if there is a problem with the electrical supply – much quicker than a fuse alone would do.

Seedheads to save

Keep on watching out for ripening seeds to propagate, and collect them before they are shed. Dry the seeds off and put them in paper envelopes, storing these in turn in an airtight container, which

◁ **Maple in autumn colour**

The maples, or acers, provide some of the most brilliant foliage tints in autumn, from burning yellows through rich reds to bronze-purple.

◁ **Seeds and fruits**

The fluffy seedheads give clematis its common name of "old man's beard". Both the seeds and these succulent rose hips are a treat for garden birds.

▽ **Pumpkin time**

Whether destined for the table, for show or for Halloween Jack-o'-lanterns, pumpkins benefit from being harvested in advance. Leave them in the sun for a few days to harden, or "cure", the skins and dry off the fleshy stalks.

you can place on the bottom shelf of the fridge. If you're not sure when to sow the seeds you've collected, it's a good idea to sow half of them now, but store the other half and sow those when spring arrives.

Even if you're not on the lookout for seeds to collect, so many plants now have seed heads and pods as beautiful as their flowers. While autumn is a time for tidying up the borders, it's also perfectly possible to clear up at ground level without cutting down the tall stems of plants like achillea and acanthus. If bad weather threatens to knock them down, you can always cut the stems for drying and displaying indoors. But if the weather holds, October can be a lovely month in the garden – so savour it before the onset of winter.

OCTOBER AT A GLANCE

- Rake up fallen leaves, and pile them up to make leafmould.
- Continue clearing up the garden, and burn or bin debris that shows signs of fungal infection.
- Dig over empty areas of soil.
- Finish planting evergreen shrubs.
- Take hardwood cuttings from shrubs and fruit bushes.
- Collect berries from trees and shrubs for seed-sowing.
- Give conifer hedges a last trim if necessary.
- Plant new climbers and perennials.
- Divide overgrown perennials.
- Protect alpines from winter wet.
- Lift and store dahlias, gladioli and summer-flowering bulbs.
- Plant lily and tulip bulbs.
- Tidy ponds and remove pumps for the winter.
- Make new lawns from turf.
- Cut down the dying tops of perennial vegetables.
- Lift and divide rhubarb.
- Fix grease bands to apple and pear tree trunks to catch pests that crawl up them.
- Insulate the greenhouse, and check that greenhouse heaters are in good working order.

! LAST CHANCE
- Sow grass seed.
- Finish planting spring bedding.
- Harvest apples and pears before they are damaged.
- Lift and store tender perennials.
- Lift potatoes and carrots and store them.

★ GET AHEAD
- Prepare the ground for planting bare-rooted stock next month.
- Make early sowings of broad beans for next year.
- Sow sweet peas for next year under cover.

Nerine bowdenii ♀ • Spring-like flowers at the end of the season *(see p.335)*

Sorbus commixta • Deciduous tree with white flowers followed by heavy fruit clusters *(see p.354)*

Rhus typhina ♀ • The stag's horn sumach, a spreading deciduous tree *(see p.347)*

Prunus sargentii ♀ • Flowering cherry tree with fine autumn colour *(see p.343)*

Colchicum cilicicum • Perennial whose funnel-shaped flowers appear before the leaves *(see p.310)*

Physalis alkekengi ♀ • Perennial with fruits enclosed in bright papery cases *(see p.341)*

TOP ROW: *Acer palmatum* 'Bloodgood' ♀ • *Acer palmatum* 'Linearilobum' ♀ • *Acer palmatum* 'Garnet' ♀

BOTTOM ROW: *Acer palmatum* 'Sango-kaku' ♀ • *Acer palmatum* 'Corallinum' ♀ • *Acer palmatum* 'Chitoseyama' ♀ *(see p.295)*

TOP ROW: *Malus pumila* 'Cowichan' • *Malus* 'Butterball' • *Malus* 'Marshall Oyama'
BOTTOM ROW: *Malus* 'Veitch's Scarlet' • *Malus* 'John Downie' ♚ • *Malus x zumi* 'Professor Sprenger' ♚ *(see p.332)*

Parthenocissus tricuspidata ♀ • Self-clinging climber that will creep up any wall *(see p.338)*

Schizostylis coccinea 'Sunrise' ♀ • The kaffir lily, an exotic but hardy perennial *(see p.352)*

Amelanchier lamarckii ♀ • Shrub or small tree with spring and autumn interest *(see p.297)*

Anemone x hybrida 'Max Vogel' • Perennial with pink flowers that fade to white *(see p.298)*

Cotinus 'Grace' ♀ • Smoke bush with brilliant autumn colour *(see p.312)*

Rosa rugosa • Shrub rose with purple-pink flowers and large hips *(see p.351)*

WHAT TO DO IN OCTOBER

AROUND THE GARDEN

PESTS ARE GENERALLY ON THE DECLINE now that the weather is turning cooler, but diseases such as botrytis and mildew are still quite prevalent with the more moist weather in autumn. Practising good garden hygiene will go a long way to avoiding problems. Don't leave a lot of rubbish lying around; either compost it or put it in the bin. Diseased material should be burned or put in the bin, and should never be composted. Clear weeds, as they act as host plants to many pests and diseases.

It's not worth using chemical sprays for mildew and botrytis at this time; they are more effective as a preventative measure early in the year. Plants like courgettes and marrows are particularly prone to both these diseases at this time of year. Burn the infected parts of the plants as they come to the end of their cropping time.

RAKE UP FALLEN LEAVES at regular intervals from the lawn and amongst plants in the borders. If leaves are left in a thick layer on the lawn for even just a few days they will kill off the grass. Fallen leaves left lying over and around plants can encourage slugs and snails.

MAKE A CONTAINER FOR FALLEN LEAVES. It seems to be something of a tradition to burn leaves in the autumn, but this is an awful waste of a valuable commodity. Autumn leaves piled into a heap and left to decompose for a year or two will make the most wonderful organic matter to use as a mulch or a soil conditioner, known as leafmould. Leaves can of course be mixed with other material and put on the compost heap, but if you want leafmould, then

Bin for leaves *This cage is simple to make and will stop piles of leaves being blown about.*

they will need a heap of their own. The best way to do this is by making a container with four stakes and some chicken wire netting. Bang the four posts into the ground to make a square, and nail the netting round the posts to form the container (see above). The netting helps to keep the leaves in one place, looking tidier and stopping them being blown all over the garden again. Larger leaves will take longer to rot down, but after about 18 months to two years you should have good friable leafmould. Use it as a mulch or dig it in to the soil as you would do with garden compost.

If you haven't room to make a wire enclosure for the leaves, or enough leaves to make it worthwhile, then put them into black polythene bags with a few holes punched in them and tie them up. You will have good leafmould in the same length of time.

DRY ATTRACTIVE SEEDHEADS FOR INDOOR DISPLAY. Many plants, such as *Acanthus spinosus*, poppies, achillea, eryngiums and globe artichokes, have

beautiful seedheads which can be cut and dried for decoration in the home over winter. Cut the seedheads off with plenty of stem, and hang them up in an airy place to dry out. It is better to let them dry naturally, rather than try to hasten drying in a warm room.

DIG EMPTY AREAS OF SOIL. Digging sounds like hard work, and so it can be if you do it all day long day after day. But it needn't be like that. By this time of year the soil is moist but not too sticky, and the weather, generally, is not too warm or too cold – perfect for some exercise. The first point to make about digging is not to rush at it. Take it easy and work at a steady but not hectic pace. Work for short periods, perhaps for half an hour at a time, and then take a break or do something else which does not involve bending. Then go back to the digging for another half an hour, and so on.

Use a good spade that is well balanced. Always pick tools up and handle them for a while before buying. If you can afford it, choose a stainless steel spade, as it should last a lifetime with little need for maintenance. Don't lift too much soil at one time as this will only cause backache.

You can sow green manure crops to cover and condition soil that otherwise will be bare over winter (see also Vegetables, August). Green manures that will stand through winter, to be dug in in spring, include winter rye, field beans and tares.

TREES & SHRUBS

CONTINUE TO PLANT container-grown trees and shrubs (see September).

MOVE EVERGREEN SHRUBS (see September, and also March for illustrations). This is still a good time to move evergreens, while the soil retains some warmth. At this time of year there will be less need to water plants that have been moved as there would be in the hot weather of summer. These shrubs can also be moved in spring, for similar reasons. In exposed areas it is worth erecting a wind barrier on the windward side of the transplanted shrub, as winter winds can cause water to evaporate from the leaves. This can cause browning, known as scorch.

Deciduous trees and shrubs should be moved when dormant (see January).

RAKE UP FALLEN LEAVES FROM ROSES to prevent blackspot spores from overwintering in the soil. This is a job that should be done regularly, and the leaves burned or put in the bin. On no account add these leaves to the compost heap, as the heat generated may not be sufficient to kill off the blackspot spores. It is difficult to make a large enough compost heap in a small garden which will generate enough heat to kill off all harmful organisms.

PRUNING AND TRAINING

TALL SHRUBS LIKE LAVATERAS and *Buddleja davidii*, which will be pruned hard in the spring, can be cut back now by about a half their height to neaten up their appearance and, more importantly, to prevent wind rock during the winter. If plants have a lot of top growth to catch the wind, they can

be blown about in windy conditions, rocking them to and fro at the base. When this happens a hole forms in the soil at the base of the plant's stem; water collects here and this can cause the stem to rot. In hard weather the water can freeze, damaging the roots further. Check all newly planted trees, shrubs and hedging plants, and if they are loose, firm them in again carefully, and if necessary provide a stake to hold the plant steady. If your soil is a heavy clay be careful not to firm too heavily, as air will be driven out of the soil and this can be worse for the plant, as it causes the roots to die.

PLANNING AHEAD

PREPARE GROUND FOR PLANTING bare-root trees and shrubs next month. If you want long-lasting plants to give the garden structure, it is worth preparing the ground well to get them off to a flying start. Don't skimp on preparation, as it is not so easy to make up for this after the plants are put in.

If you are planting a whole border of shrubs and trees, dig over the entire area, removing any roots of perennial weeds. Don't leave even tiny portions of roots behind as they will grow again, effectively propagating the weed. Dig in plenty of organic matter. If the soil has not been cultivated before, "double-dig" it. To do this, take out a trench at one end of the area and barrow the soil to the other end. Then break up the soil in the bottom of the trench with a fork, without bringing the poorer subsoil to the surface. Put plenty of organic matter into the trench and mix it in. To make the next trench, throw the soil forward onto the first trench covering the

organic matter. Continue the process until the area has been dug. The soil you barrowed to the end when you began goes in the last trench.

For planting individual trees and shrubs in an existing border, take out a hole big enough to take the roots without cramping them. If required, drive a stake into the hole before planting, so as not to damage the plant's roots. Again fork over the bottom of the hole to break up the subsoil, and mix in organic matter. Plant the tree or shrub to the same depth as before (easily seen by the darker mark low down on the main stem), checking this with a cane placed across the hole. Work soil back in among the roots and gradually fill in, firming with your boot as you go. Then rake the soil level, and water in. Finally, tie the trunk to the stake using an adjustable tree tie.

PROPAGATION

TAKE HARDWOOD CUTTINGS OF DECIDUOUS SHRUBS. Taking hardwood cuttings is an easy and cheap way of propagating your favourite shrubs; if you don't need them yourself, you can give them away to friends. Take out a slit trench by pushing a spade into the soil, and then pushing and pulling the handle to and fro. If your soil is heavy clay, trickle in some sharp (horticultural) sand to improve drainage. Remove shoots of the current season's growth, about 30cm (12in) long. For each, trim off the soft growing tip, and trim the base of the cutting below a bud. Dip the base into hormone rooting solution. Place the cuttings in the trench to about two-thirds of their length (see p.253 for illustrations), and firm in

gently with your boot. Label the row and the cuttings will root and be ready to plant out next autumn.

Plants to try from hardwood cuttings include buddleja, cornus, escallonia, forsythia, leycesteria, philadelphus, roses (see also September) and weigela.

COLLECT BERRIES FROM TREES AND SHRUBS. It's always fascinating to grow your own trees and shrubs from seeds you have collected from the garden. They generally don't need warm conditions to germinate, and in fact most actually need to go through a period of cold weather to break the seed dormancy. This process is called stratification.

First remove the seeds from the berries or fruits. Squashing the berries in an old flour sieve is ideal (see also January for illustrations). Separate the seeds, and if not sowing straight away, dry them off and store in a cool place. Sow the seeds in trays or small pots of multipurpose compost, covering the seeds not with compost, but with grit. Place the container outside in a cold frame, or in a sheltered place covered with a sheet of glass or plastic to keep excessive rain out.

Alternatively the seeds can be stratified, or given a chilling period, artificially. Mix the seed with moistened vermiculite or sharp sand in a plastic bag, and place it in a refrigerator. The length of chilling time varies, but generally up to six weeks will be required. Check the seeds regularly and when you see any signs of germination take them out and sow in trays or pots.

Some trees and shrubs to grow from berries: cotoneasters, *Rosa rugosa*, gaultheria and all sorbus.

TREES & SHRUBS *contd*

POT UP CUTTINGS TAKEN IN SUMMER. A cold frame is ideal for overwintering them, or any light, frost-free place.

HEDGES

TRIM CONIFERS AGAIN IF NECESSARY (see also July). Leyland cypress in particular can regrow after trimming in late summer, but can now be trimmed again for the final time. Be sure not to cut into old wood, as most conifers will not regenerate.

PLANT HEDGES OF EVERGREEN AND DECIDUOUS PLANTS. Evergreen plants for hedging should be put in as soon as possible this month; if this is not possible, wait until spring. Deciduous hedging can be planted all through the winter if soil conditions allow. Prepare a trench 90cm (3ft) wide along the length of the proposed hedge (see also January). Dig in generous amounts of organic matter, and add a dressing of bonemeal, according to the instructions on the pack. Peg out a line along the trench to plant to. Deciduous hedging such as beech is usually planted at around 45cm (18in) apart, and conifers about 90cm (3ft) apart. Plant firmly to the same depth as they were previously planted, and water them in well if the soil is dry.

If you live in an exposed part of the country, protect conifers with a screen of plastic mesh stapled or nailed between strong posts for the first year after planting. Make sure all new hedges are watered regularly during their first year while they get established, and feed them with an organic fertiliser in the spring.

CLIMBERS

PRUNE CLIMBING ROSES (see September) and get them tied in before autumn gales pick up. Rose stems are stiff compared to those of other climbers, and can be snapped by high winds. Clear up all fallen leaves around them carefully, and also any leaves that ramblers have dropped. Rose leaves can harbour diseases such as blackspot: it is safer to bin them rather than putting them on the compost heap.

PLANT CONTAINER-GROWN CLIMBERS, provided that they are hardy plants that will stand up to their first winter when young. All are planted in the same way as container-grown trees and shrubs, then tied into their support to get going. Dig a deep hole and work some organic matter into the bottom – leafmould and a sprinkle of bonemeal is ideal, as it will condition the soil without adding too much nitrogen at this time of year.

Climbers should be planted with the surface of the root ball level with the surface of the soil, with the exception of clematis.

Most clematis varieties are rather prone to a disease called clematis wilt. It is noticeable when a plant suddenly begins to wilt for no apparent reason. To overcome this problem it is advisable to plant clematis deeper than is normally suggested for most plants, with part of the stems below the surface of the soil. Plant so that the top of the root ball is up to 15cm (6in) below soil level.

If the plant is then affected by wilt, cut it down completely. The portion of stem below ground will have unaffected buds that may send up new shoots from the base of the plant, so giving a better chance of survival.

PLANTING A CLEMATIS

① Set the plant at an angle, leaning it in towards the support you have chosen, with the top of the rootball 10–15cm (4–6in) below ground level. Use a cane as a gauge if needed.

② Backfill the hole and firm the plant in, then cover the root area to keep the roots cool, which clematis enjoy. Here, terracotta roof tiles have been overlapped around the plant.

PERENNIALS

CUT BACK PERENNIALS THAT HAVE FINISHED FLOWERING. This will make the garden look much tidier, and discourage diseases from attacking old growth. If on some plants the flowers have finished but the foliage is still quite green and attractive, leave it until it is really blackened by the frosts. Cutting everything down can leave unsightly gaps in the borders, and this should be avoided until as late in the autumn as possible. Any soft growth cut down, such as that of hardy geraniums, can be consigned to the compost heap. Other growth which is semi-woody will take longer to break down on its own. But the process can be speeded up by shredding the material, rather than burning it, which is the more usual practice. Shredded material can be added to the compost heap to rot down further, or used as a mulch on the borders in spring.

PLANT NEW HERBACEOUS PERENNIALS while the soil is still warm and moist (see September). Prepare the soil well by incorporating plenty of organic matter and adding some bonemeal. There is a wide range of perennials to choose from nowadays, and very attractive displays can be made for little financial outlay. Perennials will last for many years if they are propagated regularly, by dividing them up and replanting, collecting seed and sowing it (with seed you may not necessarily get exactly the same plant; there will always be a slight variation) and by taking cuttings and growing them on.

Perennials always look best when they are planted in groups of three or more plants, but if your budget is limited, buy one of each of the varieties you want, and then propagate them yourself using whichever methods are most appropriate, so building up the numbers over two or three years.

LIFT AND DIVIDE OVERGROWN CLUMPS OF PERENNIALS. Older clumps are easily spotted, as all the young vigorous growth is towards the outside of the clump and the centre is bare. Dividing can be done from now through until spring as long as soil conditions allow. If the soil is so wet that it sticks to your boots, then keep off it; likewise later on if it is frozen. Late-flowering perennials like asters (Michaelmas daisies) are best left until the spring before being divided.

Lift the clumps and separate larger ones with two forks pushed into the centre of the clump back to back, pushing the handles apart to separate the roots (see September). Smaller pieces can be separated out by hand. Replant the new pieces after revitalizing the soil with organic matter. Water in well after planting.

DAHLIA TUBERS will have to be lifted and stored now. Cut the plants from their supports, and cut the stems back to about 10cm (4in) from ground level. Label each plant before you lift it and forget which variety it is. Use a garden fork to dig carefully around the plant so as not to damage the tubers underground. Shake off as much of the old soil as you can; you can also hose or rinse off the tubers to get rid of the last of the soil. The stems of dahlias are hollow, and if moisture collects at the base of the stems while the tubers are in store it will cause them to rot. So the

LIFTING & STORING DAHLIAS

① Cut down all of the top growth from the plants (here blackened by an early frost). Lift the tubers and shake or rinse off all soil.

② Stand them upside-down in wooden trays in a cool, dry place so that they dry off thoroughly.

③ Store them for winter in boxes of dry, peat-free compost. To save space, they can be packed more tightly. Make sure the stem is above the surface and space out in spring.

tubers and stems must be turned upside down, and left like this for a couple of weeks in a cool, dry place to allow any moisture to drain from the stems. After that, box up the tubers in peat-free compost, making sure the crowns of the tubers (the point where the stems meet the tubers) are not buried in compost. Small embryo buds are located here, and if they are buried in compost they may rot off. You can cover the surface of the compost with something loose and dry, like bark chippings, as an extra precaution. Keep them in a cool frost-free place over winter. They can be started back into growth in the spring (see February) and will provide cuttings to increase your stock before they are planted out.

ALPINES

CLEAR LEAVES FROM AROUND ALPINES. Leaves collecting in amongst alpines will tend to encourage rots and other diseases to affect the plants. Pick out all leaves from around the plants at regular intervals during the autumn. Plants that are particularly susceptible to rotting are those with grey woolly foliage, but it's best to keep all plants clear of leaves if you can. A layer of leaves on plants will also exclude any light, making the plants turn yellow and eventually killing them. Don't let leaves lie on top of any plants for any length of time.

PROTECT ALPINES FROM WET. This is the time of year when alpines will appreciate some protection from the wet weather we have during our winters. It's not the cold alpine plants mind – they come from high

mountainous regions of the world where they may be covered in snow for most of the winter – but the damp. This is why some alpines are grown in alpine houses, where there is no heat in the winter, and plenty of ventilation. Proper alpine houses have extra ventilators fitted to keep a good through-flow of air at all times, but an ordinary unheated greenhouse will make a perfectly good home for alpines, or even a cold frame.

Of course not all alpines have to be grown in an alpine house, and those growing outside can be protected from the rain quite easily by using a cloche, with the ends left open for ventilation, or a piece of glass or rigid clear plastic supported on bricks. Weight the sheet down with more bricks to prevent it being lifted off by winds. If you have a raised alpine bed, then with a little improvisation you can make a mini-greenhouse with open sides to protect the plants through the winter.

Protecting alpines *Frames with the lids propped up all winter make good homes for alpines.*

BULBS

PLANT TULIP BULBS towards the end of this month and next month (see November). Tulips are more prone to disease than other bulbs and for this reason they are planted later. As with other bulbs, the depth of planting for tulips is about twice to three times their own depth. On heavy clay soils, put a layer of grit in the bottom of the hole and sit the bulbs on this. Tulips also look good naturalized in grass with other bulbs and wild flowers, as in a wild flower meadow.

LIFT AND STORE GLADIOLI if this wasn't done last month (see September).

LIFT AND STORE TENDER SUMMER-FLOWERING BULBS. In sheltered gardens and warm regions, slightly tender bulbs like galtonias may survive *in situ*, but in cold areas bulbs such as these and eucomis, and certainly tigridias, should be lifted, dried and stored in pots or boxes of dry sand. Lift, clean up and dry the bulbs just as you would spring-flowering bulbs.

Forced hyacinths *Once bulbs have formed roots and made some growth, bring them into the light.*

CANNAS MUST BE LIFTED by early next month wherever you are. These have a thick, fleshy root rather than a true bulb, and can be treated as for any tender perennial (see Annuals & Bedding, September): trimmed, cleaned up and potted into peat-free compost, and stored somewhere cool and dry.

FINISH PLANTING ALL SPRING-FLOWERING BULBS now before winter sets in. The bulbs will start to grow now, sending out roots into the soil. Planting them late just means they will flower that bit later than others – perhaps no bad thing to give continuity.

EXAMINE BULBS BEING FORCED in darkness to see if any top growth is being made. If so, bring them into the light in a cool place. But first knock them out of their containers to see how good a root system has been made. If there are not many roots put them back in the dark for a few more weeks.

PLANT LILY BULBS THIS AND NEXT MONTH. Plant them in well-prepared soil in sun or partial shade. If your soil is heavy, sit the bulbs on a layer of coarse grit to aid drainage. Plant the bulbs at two and a half times their own depth.

Lilies can also be grown in pots to make graceful summer patio plants. Some are powerfully scented too. The bulbs can be planted in pots, in ordinary multipurpose compost and again on a layer of grit, from now until late winter. Leva the pots outside to allow a good root system to form. When new growth has been made, you can take some pots inside, and the lilies will flower early, in spring. After flowering these bulbs can be planted in the garden.

ANNUALS & BEDDING

Tender plants to bring in under cover without delay: from left to right, Argyranthemum *'Mary Wootton',* Osteospermum *'Nairobi Purple' and* Arctotis fastuosa *'Zulu Prince'.*

FINISH LIFTING TENDER PERENNIALS to protect them from frost (see September). If you don't have anywhere suitable to keep them, cuttings can still be taken (see August). Those taken earlier may need potting up now, but don't pot up any cuttings you take now until the spring.

HALF-HARDY FUCHSIAS need a rest period over winter and should be potted up if necessary and taken under cover, either storing them with other tender perennials, or keeping them on benches in gently heated glasshouses or cool rooms. The leaves will still drop off now, but these plants will start into growth and produce the earliest shoots for cuttings. The plants should be kept cool and on the dry side, but don't let them dry out completely. Give just enough water from time to time to keep them alive. It's difficult to say how often plants kept over winter should be watered, as it depends on how warm the plants are kept. It really is a matter of experience and practice.

FINISH PLANTING SPRING BEDDING PLANTS this month (see also Containers). It is important to get this job done, especially if you have a heavy clay soil, before the soil cools down too much. In some parts of the country summer bedding plants may still be flowering, but you will have to take the bull by the horns and get them out if you want to get spring bedding in. On light, sandy soils you may get away with planting spring bedding later, as these soils warm up quicker in the spring. If planting late, add a little fertiliser high in phosphates like bonemeal, seaweed meal or hop manure to the soil rather than a general feed. This encourages root growth, which is what we want at this time of year. Soft growth made now will be more easily damaged during winter.

SOW OVERWINTERING HARDY ANNUALS OUTSIDE if this was not done last month (see September). There is still time to do this in milder parts of the country, as soon as possible.

CONTAINERS

CONTINUE PLANTING CONTAINERS with spring bedding plants and bulbs to get a worthwhile display in the spring. The sooner this job is completed, the sooner the plants will establish before the winter sets in.

DON'T FORGET PERENNIALS AND SHRUBS FOR WINTER COLOUR. You don't have to limit your choice of plants for containers to bedding plants. Many evergreen shrubs will provide colour and interest year round. Variegated shrubs are particularly good value, and will brighten up a dull corner at any time of the year. Look out for *Euonymus japonicus* 'Marieke' and 'Aureopictus'. There are also varieties of variegated box, and dwarf conifers in a wide variety of shapes and colours. Other plants to brighten containers through winter include hardy cyclamen and heathers, which also have a wide range of foliage hues. Winter-flowering pansies will give a bright, cheerful display from now until early summer.

Winter evergreens *Trailing ivies add the perfect touch to container plantings.*

PONDS

Netting a pond *Stop autumn leaves falling into the pond, as they will rot and foul the water.*

REDUCE FEEDING OF FISH. Now the days are getting shorter fish are becoming less active, so feeding should be reduced. Any food not eaten by the fish will just decompose in the water, and apart from being a waste of food, large amounts of rotting food in the water may cause harm to the fish.

REMOVE TENDER FLOATING PLANTS like the water hyacinth as these will be killed by the first frosts. Keep them in a bucket of water in a light, frost-proof place for the winter.

PONDS CAN BE TIDIED UP before the onset of winter. Any fallen leaves in the water should be fished out, and any yellowing leaves from plants like waterlilies can be removed at the same time. The dead growth on marginal plants can be cut back too. Remove any blanket weed and thin out oxygenating plants, remembering to leave the portions removed by the side of the pond for a few days so any wildlife hiding in the clumps can return to the water.

PUT A NET OVER THE POND to prevent leaves falling in and sinking to the bottom (see also September). Use as fine a mesh as you can get, otherwise smaller leaves will still find their way in. Make the net secure around the edge of the pond to ensure small birds don't get caught up in it. Bricks are ideal for securing the netting, or make some wire hoops to hold it in place in the soil.

UNLESS AN INDIAN SUMMER is allowing you to continue the enjoyment of your water feature, remove submersible pumps and lighting systems from the pond and store them over the winter (see November).

LAWNS

REDUCE FREQUENCY OF MOWING. Established lawns should be mown less frequently now as growth slows down. Also, raise the height of the cutting blades. Grass which is cut too short over the winter will not stand up to the poorer weather conditions, and will be more likely to become infested with moss and weeds, because it is weaker.

RAKE OUT THATCH, AERATE AND TOP-DRESS LAWNS (see September for details). This autumn overhaul will make a tremendous difference to the lawn after a summer of hard use. For large lawns, powered machines can be bought or hired to help with all of these jobs.

RESEED ANY BARE OR WORN PATCHES (see August).

NEW LAWNS

MAKE NEW LAWNS (see September). Turf can be laid at almost any time of the year as long as the soil is not frozen or waterlogged. There is still time to sow grass seed if it is done early in the month. The soil is still reasonably warm and moist, and germination should be fairly quick. If you have doubts about the weather and the area sown is not too big, cover it with polythene; this will encourage even more rapid germination. Remove the polythene as soon as seedlings come through.

NEW LAWNS MADE EARLIER may need cutting, but again, don't cut them too short. About 2.5cm (1in) is the closest to cut newly sown lawns and newly laid turf for the last cut before winter.

VEGETABLES & HERBS

Cut down Jerusalem artichokes In autumn the plants will slump and die off.

CUT DOWN THE TOPS OF JERUSALEM ARTICHOKES. It is the swollen roots, rather like potatoes, of these plants that are eaten. The tops can grow to over 2m (6ft), making this an excellent plant to use for screening ugly structures like the shed or the compost heap in summer; occasionally they produce quite attractive yellow flowers. But by this time of year, the plants will be dying back and just look a mess. Cut them down to ground level. Shred the old stems and use them for mulching borders, or mix in with other garden compost. Although good as a screen, Jerusalem artichokes can be invasive, so keep a check on them and harvest the swollen roots regularly in the autumn. As with potatoes, even the smallest tuber left in the ground will regrow.

CUT DOWN ASPARAGUS FERN now that it has turned yellow, if you didn't do it last month. Be aware that there are small sharp spines on asparagus stems and they can give you a nasty cut, so wear gloves when pruning them. After cutting down the foliage, top-dress over the crowns with garden compost or well-rotted farmyard manure.

EMPTY COMPOST BINS of well-rotted compost and use it for mulching and digging in to improve the soil. Well-made garden compost will do the soil a power of good, and using it up will free the compost bin for more material; it may take a little longer to rot down at this time of year but should be ready to use in the spring. If you haven't got much compost, it is better to give enough to a smaller area, rather than trying to spread it too thinly over all of the ground. This would really just be a waste of good compost. With a good crop rotation system going you should plan to incorporate organic matter into at least a third of the vegetable garden each year.

AS SOON AS GROUND IS CLEARED, DIG IT OVER IF NECESSARY. The sooner soil cultivation in the vegetable garden can be done the better (though of course no-dig deep beds will not need it). Heavy clay soils in particular will benefit from being broken up and exposed to winter weather conditions for as long as possible. Rains, snow and frost all play a vital part in breaking down soil particles, enabling us to make good seed and planting beds in the spring. Dig for short periods at a time, and do other jobs inbetween to prevent damage to your back.

The easiest way to dig a large area of the vegetable garden is to take out a trench at one end of the plot and barrow the soil to the other end. Put organic matter into the bottom of the trench. Then take out the next trench with your spade and throw the soil forward into the first one, covering the organic matter. Do this over the whole area and fill in the last trench with the soil taken out at the start.

DIG IN GREEN MANURE CROPS sown earlier in the autumn. Green manure crops are a good substitute for well-rotted garden compost or farmyard manure if you cannot get a good supply of organic matter. They will condition the soil and some, like clover and field beans, also "fix" nitrogen for use by the plants that follow. To dig them in, take out a trench as described above, and skim the surface of the neighbouring soil, scraping the tops of the plants into the bottom of the trench. Throw the soil containing the roots forward into this first trench to cover them, making the next trench in the process. Repeat until the job's done. You can also sow green manures now to overwinter (see Around the Garden).

COVER SOME GROUND WITH POLYTHENE to keep the worst of the rain off. From now onwards we can expect more rain, and later in the winter, snow. To enable us to get on with preparing the soil in the new year it really does help to cover at least part of it; then you can get up to date with cultivating before the busy seed sowing and planting season in the spring. Hold the polythene in place with bricks or long pieces of wood. Weeds will tend to grow under the polythene in milder weather, but these can be easily removed if they are caught before they get too big. It is surprising just how much water will be kept off the land by covering it, and how early you can start planting and sowing by replacing the polythene sheeting with cloches in late winter and early spring.

HARVESTING AND STORING

PICK THE LAST OF THE RUNNER BEANS. No matter how quickly you pick runner beans there comes a point when they seem never-ending. If they are not too big they can be frozen; overgrown pods can be composted, as they will be old and stringy. If you want to collect your own seed, leave some pods on the old plants until they turn brown. Otherwise, cut the plants from their supports and compost them, but leave the roots in the ground. Runner beans, like broad beans and peas, return valuable nitrogen to the soil and this is a resource which should not be wasted. In the crop rotation system, beans can be followed by leafy crops such as brassicas which have a high demand for nitrogen. By doing this, less nitrogen will have to be applied to the soil in the form of synthetic feeds.

FINISH LIFTING MAINCROP POTATOES. Leave them on the surface of the soil for a couple of hours to dry out. If it is a damp day, put them in a cold frame or a greenhouse to dry. They must be dry before putting them into storage. Store only undamaged potatoes, using those that are damaged first. Store them in paper or hessian sacks ensuring no light gets to them, which will turn them green. Storing in polythene bags will make the potatoes sweat, and this will encourage rotting. Any potatoes that are turning green should be discarded.

CONTINUE LIFTING CARROTS AND BEETROOT for storing. As with potatoes, only store sound produce. Any that is damaged, however slightly, should be used first and not stored. Store these crops in boxes in layers separated with moist sand or old potting compost. Store all root crops in a cool, dark and frost-free place. Check through all the stored produce at regular intervals during winter. If any are showing signs of rotting discard them.

MAKE A CLAMP TO STORE ROOT VEGETABLES. This is an old method of storing root crops, but it is ideal if you haven't got much room indoors for storage. You will have to get some straw, but that is not too difficult. Put a thick layer of straw on the ground and start

Storage clamp *You can mix root crops, or make a clamp for each crop to keep track of supplies.*

laying the dry roots on it. Build up the crops in a cone shape, tapering towards the top. Next put a layer of straw round the mound of roots, building it up to the top and making sure it goes right over the top. Next start covering the straw with soil, digging it from around the mound and again building it up to the top until the entire mound is covered, except at the very tip. Here you must leave some straw poking out, so as to let some air in. Potatoes, carrots, swedes, turnips and beetroot will keep in this clamp all through the winter.

SOWING AND PLANTING OUTDOORS

PLANT OUT SPRING CABBAGES if this was not done last month (see September). This is the latest month for planting spring cabbages, and the sooner the better. Remember to net the plants or the birds will have the lot overnight.

PLANT GARLIC IF YOU DIDN'T DO IT LAST MONTH. If the soil is too wet to plant outside then grow the cloves in modules and plant out in late winter or early spring. Put one clove in each cell, with the tip of each clove just sticking out of the compost. They don't need any warmth, so keep them in a well-ventilated cold frame or outside under the shelter of a wall, just to keep the heaviest of the rain off them.

FINISH PLANTING AUTUMN ONION SETS (SEE ALSO SEPTEMBER). Plant them 8cm (3in) apart in well prepared soil. Japanese onion sets can also be planted, a little later than seeds are sown, in October or November. Japanese onions from both sets and

seeds should be ready to harvest in June the following year, giving an early harvest before other onions are ready.

SOW BROAD BEANS OUTSIDE and cover with cloches in colder parts of the country. Take out a shallow trench about 5cm (2in) deep with a spade, or a draw or onion hoe. The seeds are quite large, and can be spaced at intervals of 15cm (6in). Cover with soil and tamp it down with the back of a rake. Cover with a cloche or fleece, principally to stop mice digging them up.

The seeds will germinate fairly quickly and then grow slowly through the winter, producing a crop of succulent beans in early summer the following year.

LOOKING AFTER CROPS

EARTH UP CELERY for the last time, if not done last month. Leave just a tuft of foliage at the top uncovered. If hard frost is forecast keep some straw or fleece handy to cover the plants. Straw can be held in place with chicken wire or plastic netting pegged into the ground; fleece is easily kept in place with a few bricks. Start harvesting the celery as and when necessary.

REMOVE YELLOWING LEAVES FROM BRUSSELS SPROUTS and other winter brassicas such as cabbages, cauliflowers and broccoli. Old yellowing leaves are of no use to the plants; they will just encourage diseases such as botrytis and grey mould to invade, reducing the overall crop yield. Removing these leaves and putting them on the compost heap also makes the garden look a lot tidier.

PLANNING AHEAD

PREPARE A BED FOR PLANTING ASPARAGUS IN THE SPRING. Asparagus likes well-prepared soil enriched with plenty of organic matter, but at the same time drainage must be good. Drainage can be improved permanently, especially on heavy soils, by incorporating pea shingle at the same time as digging in the organic matter. This will raise the level of the proposed asparagus bed, but this is no bad thing as a raised bed will also help to improve drainage.

If your soil is very heavy clay, which asparagus really doesn't thrive on, there is still a way of growing it; in high raised beds with strong sides to retain the soil. Make sturdy wooden surrounds with planks and posts, about 60cm (2ft) deep and as long and wide as you want, but 1.2m × 1.2m (4 × 4ft) is a good size. Make up a compost mix to fill the beds, ideally of equal parts garden compost and grit; if you don't have enough compost, you will have to buy in bagged products.

BEAT THE SEASONS

FORCE CHICORY. Even if you haven't got a greenhouse, you can organise supplies of home-grown winter salad stuff. Chicory such as Witloof which has been growing through the summer can be lifted in batches and forced for a succession of pointed, tight-leaved "chicons". The roots can be potted up (see overleaf) in old potting compost, which is quite good enough for forcing. Cover the pot with another upturned pot, ensuring you cover any drainage holes in the upturned pot. To get the best chicons, place the pots

VEGETABLES & HERBS *continued*

FORCING CHICORY

1 Dig up plants of varieties of chicory recommended for forcing that were grown from seed over the summer (see May).

2 Trim the leaves and tip, and put three to five roots in a 20cm (8in) pot of old potting compost, and cover.

3 The chicory should be ready for using three or four weeks after potting up, so take a look under the cover then.

somewhere with a minimum temperature of 10°C (50°F).

FORCE SEAKALE. This perennial plant can be forced from now until January, the blanched stems making an unusual vegetable. Cut the plants right down, cut off any yellowing leaves and clear debris from around the base. In cold areas put a 10cm (4in) layer of straw over the crowns of the plants to act as insulation. Now cover the plants with a bucket or a large pot, making sure you cover any drainage holes in the base of the pot to exclude all light. The stems will be ready to harvest in about three months.

HERBS

LIFT PARSLEY AND MINT for winter use. A few pots of herbs will provide you with valuable additions to winter meals. Dig up a few roots of each and remove any yellowing leaves. Pot each piece in small pots of compost, water them in and stand on a bright windowsill in the kitchen. You will then have fresh herbs at your fingertips all through the winter – much tastier than dried or frozen ones.

BASIL OUTDOORS will not survive now. If grown in pots, you could bring it into a greenhouse or conservatory – or, harvest all the leaves and freeze in ice cube trays topped up with water.

Forcing seakale Excluding light produces the pale, blanched young stems that are eaten.

FRUIT

PICKING AND STORING

FINISH PICKING MAINCROP APPLES. Varieties like 'Spartan' and 'Sunset' and the cookers will be ready for harvesting around now. Pick when they are ripe and only store sound fruit (see September for details). Damaged fruit can be used straight after picking, if it is ripe. If fruits are ripe they should part from the tree with very little effort. If they don't, leave them on the tree for a little longer. If stored properly they will last for most of the winter. Apples can be eaten straight from store, but pears may need a few days in a warm room to ripen fully.

LOOKING AFTER CROPS

CLEAN UP STRAWBERRY BEDS. Remove any yellowing foliage and old runners which were overlooked and generally weed the area to tidy it up and lessen the risk of pest and disease problems next year. Any older plants showing signs of virus infection (stunting or mottling of the foliage) should be taken out and put in the bin. New plants can be bought in and planted in the spring. Young plants put in during the spring should not be cropped in the first summer as they need time to build up a crown to produce good crops in subsequent years.

KEEP NEWLY PLANTED STRAWBERRIES WELL WATERED. Planting strawberries now enables them to get well established before winter so that the plants develop well, but if they go short of water this will not happen and they will not fruit very well next year. Plants under stress from lack of water are also more prone to problems.

Winter moth damage These pests of apple and pear trees can be foiled with grease bands.

FIX GREASE BANDS TO APPLE AND PEAR TREES to prevent pests such as winter moth crawling up the trunks (see September). Fix bands around stakes, too, if they offer an alternative route into the tree for the pests.

SPRAY PEACHES AND NECTARINES against peach leaf curl. Trees that were sprayed with copper fungicide earlier in the year to prevent peach leaf curl need another application now, just as the leaves begin to fall. When the leaves have fallen, covering the trees with polythene supported on a wooden framework will also reduce the incidence of peach leaf curl disease, as its spores are carried in rain.

PRUNING AND TRAINING

PRUNE BLACKCURRANTS. These can be pruned now if you want to get the job done. But it is better to wait until winter as you will be able to see what you are doing much better with no foliage on the plants. For how to prune, see December.

Pruning blackberries *Untie all the fruited canes and cut them to the ground.*

BLACKBERRIES AND HYBRID BERRY FRUITS

BLACKBERRIES AND HYBRID BERRY FRUITS such as loganberries should be pruned after the fruit has been harvested. Cut out all the old fruited canes and tie in the new ones. It is easier to cope with training these fruits if the new canes are tied all to one side of the support, then the canes which will grow next year and fruit the following one can be trained to the other side, so forming a fan shape.

PLANNING AHEAD

ORDER NEW FRUIT TREES. This is a good time to look through specialist fruit nursery catalogues and choose new fruit trees. Ordering bare-root trees to plant in the dormant season (November to March) is a cheaper way of buying these trees and bushes, which can be expensive when container-grown. The sooner you order the trees the better the chance of getting all the varieties you want. There will be a wide selection of varieties available, all on different types of rootstock. What this means is that the top part of the tree that bears the fruit has been grafted at a very early stage

onto the roots of a different tree. The chosen rootstock will affect the vigour, and thus the eventual size, of your fruit tree, and also the age at which it bears fruit. Various rootstocks are available and each one gives a different size of tree. Good catalogues will give you plenty of information about the rootstocks they use, and how large trees will eventually grow.

Small gardens demand trees grown on dwarfing rootstocks. For instance, rootstock M9 has a dwarfing effect, and produces a small tree, no more than about 3m (10ft) high. Very dwarf fruit trees can also be obtained for growing in pots on the patio, or even on a balcony, so there is no need to be without some kind of fruit tree no matter how small your garden.

Take a look, too, at some of the pre-trained fan and cordon fruits that are increasingly on offer these days. With modern gardens getting smaller, an ideal solution, if you want to have fruit, is to train it against walls and fences. Most

Order new fruit trees *Dwarf trees like these pear pyramids are perfect in small gardens.*

fruit trees can be trained in a variety of ways. With these methods of training you can fit in several varieties of fruit tree in a small space.

PREPARE THE GROUND FOR NEW FRUIT TREES. It's a very good idea to do this in advance if you don't know exactly when your trees will arrive. You can also choose a mild, dry day to do your digging. If you're planting several trees together, dig over the whole area incorporating plenty of organic matter. If just one or two trees are being planted, prepare generously sized individual holes to accommodate the roots without cramming them in. Break up the bottom of the hole to loosen the subsoil, without bringing any subsoil to the surface. Put plenty of muck in the hole and work it into the bottom of the hole. Unless you ordered them with the trees, buy low stakes and tree ties now so you have them to hand when planting.

PROPAGATION

TAKE HARDWOOD CUTTINGS OF BLACKCURRANTS, RED AND WHITE CURRANTS AND GOOSEBERRIES. The preparation of the cuttings for all of these plants is exactly the same. Take shoots around 30cm (12in) long, cutting just above a bud on the parent plant. Remove the top 5cm (2in) of softer growth at the tip of the cutting, and trim the base just below a bud. Dip the base in hormone rooting solution. Make a slit trench by pushing a spade into the ground and then pushing the handle back and forth. If your soil is a heavy clay, trickle some sharp sand into the bottom of the trench, and then line out

GOOSEBERRY CUTTINGS

1 Line out the cuttings along the trench to two-thirds of their depth, and then carefully firm them in.

2 Next autumn, lift the cuttings and rub out any leaf buds, and replant. This helps retain a single main stem.

3 The young plants can be lifted and put into their fruiting postions the following winter.

the cuttings (see above). If blackcurrants have shown any signs of reversion virus or big bud mite (see April) then don't propagate from them.

The new plants will be have rooted by next autumn, but you can leave them for another year before moving to their permanent positions, as they will not fruit when young.

UNDER COVER

THOROUGHLY CLEAN the glasshouse or conservatory if you didn't do so last month (see September).

CONTINUE VENTILATING ON WARM DAYS, but close down the vents in mid-afternoon to conserve some heat. It is important to keep the air circulating indoors to keep diseases such as mildew and botrytis at bay, as they flourish in warm, moist, still conditions.

BUY BUBBLE POLYTHENE to insulate the greenhouse or conservatory. To heat a greenhouse or conservatory these days is an expensive business, and you can do a lot to keep those bills down by lining the structure with bubble polythene. This acts in the same way as double glazing, and although it may cut down on some of the light getting in, it is well worth installing it for the warmth it keeps in. It can be taken down again in the spring, as it is not the most attractive material to look at throughout the summer.

TAKE MORE CARE WITH WATERING at this time of year. With the shorter days and cooler temperatures, watering has to be done with much more care now. If diseases like botrytis are not to thrive, it is better to get any watering done early in the day, so that the place has a chance to dry out before nightfall. Watering in early morning is preferable, without splashing too much water around on the staging and paths. Try to avoid getting water on the plants' leaves too, as this can also take some time to dry out. Most plant growth will have slowed down now, so only water plants when you can see they really need it. An exception are the potted azaleas available in garden centres from autumn until late winter. These plants must be kept moist and never allowed to dry out.

CHECK PLANTS OVER REGULARLY, and remove any yellowing leaves and fading flowers. Don't leave these lying around as they will encourage diseases to set in and attack your cherished plants. A look around the greenhouse once a week is quite a pleasant job when the weather is bad outside. It also gives you an opportunity to spot pests that may be lurking, and deal with them quickly and easily. It is surprising how many pests will overwinter in warm conditions inside.

RAISING PLANTS FOR OUTDOORS

SOW SWEET PEAS FOR NEXT SPRING. With the luxury of space in a greenhouse, you can get ahead and sow sweet peas now, though a cool, light windowsill will accommodate a few pots too. Sow as you would in spring (see January), but sowing five or six seeds to a 12cm (5in) pot rather than using long tubes, and the young plants can be potted up individually in spring.

GLASSHOUSE AND HOUSE PLANTS

CITRUS FRUIT TREES and any other tender shrubs in pots, such as bay and oleander, which have been outside for the summer should be brought in now. Keep them in cool but frost-free conditions, opening ventilators or a window whenever the weather is mild to give them some fresh air. Feeding and watering will have to be done carefully, as citrus trees will be coming into flower. Some will already have fruits on them as well, and these should ripen over the winter. The scent from citrus flowers is terrific and they are well worth growing for their flowers alone, never mind the bonus of a few fruits.

LIFT A FEW HERBACEOUS PERENNIALS for some early flowers inside. Naturally early-flowering plants like hellebores, doronicum and pulmonarias can be potted up and they will flower even earlier. You can do this when dividing them (see Perennials). Pot them in pots containing John Innes or other soil-based compost, and water them in. Stand them outside for now, and bring them in from January onwards. They make unusual pot plants and can be planted out afterwards in the garden.

CROPS UNDER GLASS

CLEAR OUT OLD TOMATO, aubergine and pepper plants and all their debris as they finish cropping. Any green tomatoes can be brought indoors to ripen on the windowsill, clearing the space so you can give the greenhouse a clean before winter.

GROW RADISHES, MUSTARD AND CRESS FOR WINTER SALADS IN GROWBAGS used previously for tomatoes and other crops. Some lettuces (see below) will also do well. Give them a liquid feed regularly, as the previous plants will have used up the nutrients in the compost. It is a good way of making full use of these growbags. And when these crops have finished, the compost can be used again, to improve the soil in the garden. Don't however, add the compost from tomato growbags to beds where you will be growing potatoes or outdoor tomatoes next year, as diseases common to both (they belong to the same family) may be passed on.

SOW A FEW WINTER LETTUCES in a cold greenhouse, or grow a few in pots on the kitchen windowsill. Sow the seeds in small pots or trays. and place in a propagator, maintaining a temperature of 16°C (61°F). The seeds will germinate in a few days, when they can be either potted up in small pots of peat-free compost, or planted in the border soil of a greenhouse or in used growbags (see also above). Water the lettuces carefully as they are very prone to botrytis and rotting off. Always err on the cautious side when watering in the winter. The lettuces will be ready to harvest in early spring. Varieties to try are 'All the Year Round' and 'Winter Density'.

PLANT AN AUTUMN BORDER

THIS BORDER IS DESIGNED to prolong the display given by herbaceous perennials well into autumn. All of these plants are easy to grow and will tolerate a wide range of soil types. They are also equally happy growing in full sun or partial shade. As with summer flowering-perennials (see July, p.187) plant the shorter ones to the front and larger ones to the back. Lift and divide them every three or four years to keep them healthy. If you haven't room for the complete autumn–flowering border, try and fit some of these lovely plants in amongst others. If the weather is reasonable they should flower well into November, shortening the dreary months of winter.

BACK OF BORDER, LEFT TO RIGHT
1. 3 × *Crocosmia* 'Jenny Bloom'
2. 3 × *Aster amellus* 'King George' ♚
3. 3 × *Aster novae-angliae* 'Rosa Sieger'
4. 3 × *Rudbeckia fulgida* var. *deamii*

MIDDLE OF BORDER, LEFT TO RIGHT
5. 3 × *Chrysanthemum* Nicole
6. 3 × *Sedum* 'Autumn Joy'
7. 3 × *Carex comans* bronze form
8. 3 × *Helenium* Pipsqueak
9. 3 × *Aster novi-belgii* 'Jenny'

FRONT OF BORDER, LEFT TO RIGHT
10. 3 × *Chrysanthemum* Robin
11. 3 × *Houttuynia cordata*
12. 3 × *Milium effusum* 'Aureum'
13. 3 × *Heuchera* 'Chocolate Ruffles'
14. 3 × *Erica gracilis*

Crocosmia 'Jenny Bloom'
Clump-forming perennial with strap-shaped leaves. Enjoys a winter mulch.

Aster amellus 'King George'
A classic lavender-blue aster, with large, yellow-centred flowers.

Carex comans bronze form
A lovely fine grass, with no formal name yet but very widely available.

Aster novi-belgii 'Jenny'
Vivid Michaelmas daisy, or New York aster; divide every three years.

Chrysanthemum Robin
Easy, hardy chrysanthemum, free-flowering without any pinching out.

Milium effusum 'Aureum'
Semi-evergreen grass; the golden colour is intensified in part-shade.

Heuchera 'Chocolate Ruffles'
Perennial with pink flowers in spring, but chiefly grown for its rich foliage.

Erica gracilis
Low-growing, evergreen, late-flowering heather. Not for very cold areas.

BORDER SIZE: APPROX 2M × 1.5M (6FT × 5FT)

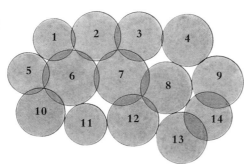

NOVEMBER

The garden in November

November can be a damp, raw month. Flowers may be scarce in the garden but there are many berries, evergreen foliage and trees with decorative bark to add interest on the dullest of days.

By this month there is still some colour in the garden, especially from the asters – or Michaelmas daisies – if the weather has been reasonable. Nerines will also be in flower, and if you are lucky, there will still be a few roses to pick and take into the house. And there may still be some late autumn foliage colour. The main period for autumn colour is usually in October, but due to seasonal variations the peak of the autumn display can vary by several weeks from year to year. So there are may well be gardens to visit where you can still enjoy some late autumn colour.

Where leaves have fallen, clear them up. A blanket of sodden leaves on lawns and around the bases of plants will do no good at all, and wet leaves on paths and steps are a real safety hazard. Fallen leaves will rot down into a really good soil conditioner – leafmould – in time, so heap them up, or make a chicken wire container for them to stop them blowing about. If you don't have enough leaves to make a good pile, then either put them on the compost, or stuff them into a plastic rubbish bag with some holes pierced in it. If you choose the latter option, then remember that the leaves must be wet to rot down, so either bag them on a damp day or pour in some water.

△ *Chrysanthemum* **Shelley**
The fantastic hardy chrysanthemums now available flower until very late and can be left out in the garden all winter.

An end and a beginning

Some of the more exposed northerly parts of the country may experience wintry spells now, while other more sheltered parts will often be quite mild right through the month. Snowfalls in November seem quite rare, and any snow that does fall usually clears as quickly as it came down. There can often be beautiful days in November, but there's no doubt that it can sometimes be a dreary month weatherwise. Before the real winter weather sets in we must take advantage of any good spells to crack on with the work if we are not to fall behind in the spring. Many people regard this as the end of the gardening season, but it is really the beginning. Work done now can save a lot of time and effort when spring comes around.

Revamp the veg plot

The earlier any winter digging is done the better, as this will allow rain, snow and frost to break down the clods of soil, improving its structure and making it much easier to cultivate in the spring. One major project, which if done now will save you lots of work not only next spring but in many years to come, is to convert your vegetable plot to the deep bed system. This is a way of growing vegetables that acknowledges the "no-dig" approach to gardening, popular with many organic gardeners. The theory is that if you cultivate and improve the soil once, really thoroughly, you will encourage a population of soil-dwelling creatures, especially earthworms, that in subsequent years will take a mulch of organic matter down into the soil for you, aided and abetted by the ongoing processes of planting and harvesting. So

△ **November frosts**

Early morning sunshine increases the chance of frost damage on plants. The rapid rise in heat thaws frozen plant tissues much too quickly, rupturing cell walls and leaving foliage limp.

there's no need for digging and turning to interfere with the soil's structure and, because beds are made small, there's never a need to tread on the soil and compact it. You'll have to sacrifice some of your plot to create more paths from which you can work and weed, but on the other hand, you'll find that with this system you can plant much more closely, so it shouldn't affect yields.

You can make beds long and narrow, or, as we suggest on p.272, create a checkerboard effect with small, square beds intersected by paths, a design that lends itself to the attractive, formal "potager" style of kitchen gardening, which really shows off the ornamental potential of many crops. We use June's herb garden (see p.156) as a centrepiece.

WEATHER WATCH

Some November days can be damp and raw, especially with low cloud cover. Frosts can be quite frequent at night, especially when it is calm and clear. Cold winds, especially those from the east, will make it feel much colder than it really is.

Gales increase this month, now that we're in the middle of autumn. In England, most hit the south-west, with on average 2 days of gales being driven in from the Atlantic. Inland it's generally calmer, but eastern coastal areas can turn very cold when the wind comes from mainland Europe. However the worst gales are suffered on the west sides of Scotland and Ireland – up to 5 days of gales in some parts.

If we're lucky and no depressions head our way from the Atlantic, November can be bright and pleasant. The amount of sunshine will be considerably reduced compared with summer for all parts of the country, but it is all the more welcome. The south-west comes off best, averaging over 107 hours of sunshine this month; the north of England gets 85–90hrs, and Scotland will average 80 up to 100 hours in some favoured places.

Rainfall is on the increase, and November can be a soggy month. The wettest parts of the country are the Highlands of Scotland, and Ireland. Here rainfall can be as much as 267mm, compared to eastern parts of England where it can be as little as 47mm. Get on with soil cultivation as soon as the weather permits, and cover some ground with polythene sheeting to protect it from the wet.

Snow is definitely on the agenda now in north-eastern parts. Braemar in Aberdeenshire can expect on average 5 days of snow on the ground. Other parts of the country may see some snow, but it is rare, and can range from none at all in the south to 1.7 days in the central belt of Scotland.

△ **Leafy landscape**

Autumn gales will leave a carpet of leaves on the lawn, which need sweeping or raking up. Gather them together and let them compost down into leafmould, a fine soil conditioner.

Routine tasks

Tidying borders by clearing away old stems and dead foliage and lightly forking over the ground around plants will transform the appearance of the garden, making it neat for the rest of the winter. Leave a few plants like *Sedum spectabile* and ornamental grasses such as *Carex pendula* and miscanthus uncut, as frost on these plants looks terrific.

During all this clearing up you will inevitably generate a lot of material, most of which can be composted, but some of the woody and semi-woody material will take a long time to rot down. The usual way to get rid of this woody material is to have a bonfire, but although a fire can be cheery and satisfying, it's a terrible waste of material which can be recycled in the garden. Therefore if you can, invest in a garden shredder. There are many different makes available, powered by petrol or electricity. These machines will shred up all woody material into fine pieces which can then be used as a mulch – or, they can be mixed with other composted material to make the best compost you'll ever have. And, of course, these machines can also be hired if you don't want to buy one.

Planting and transplanting

November is a good time to plant new trees, shrubs and roses. And if you have been walking round the garden with notebook in hand earlier in the year, making notes of any changes to be made, then this is a good month to move plants, because there is still some warmth in the soil left from the summer. Larger plants are best moved first, with as much soil around the roots as possible. And if they are large trees or shrubs, remember to stake them again if you garden in an exposed place. Water plants well after moving them and mulch with a thick layer of organic matter; remember to keep watering them well throughout the next season.

Stars among the sleepers

This is the month when most plants become dormant and everything, as far as plant growth goes, shuts down for the winter; but there are some plants which begin to flower around now and carry their blooms throughout the winter months. Plants such as *Viburnum × bodnantense* will produce exquisite pink flowers from as early as October right through the season. The flowers borne by this shrub are also powerfully and sweetly scented, and will fill the air around them with fragrance even on the coldest and dullest November days. The winter-flowering

△ **Cut down dead stems**

Now is the time to trim off unsightly dead stems from many perennials, and clear the remains of the last annuals. Clear debris so that it cannot harbour pests and diseases near your plants .

◁ **Winter warmers**

The rich brown tones of sedum seedheads give pleasure right through the winter. Once their thick, succulent stems dry out, they are robust enough to withstand all but the strongest winter winds.

▽ **Hungry squirrel**

If your garden is visited by squirrels, then any gardening you do at this time of year is likely to turn up caches of nuts. Putting up a squirrel feeder can distract them from taking food put out for the birds.

autumn cherry, *Prunus subhirtella* 'Autumnalis' produces its white blossom intermittently throughout the winter. For a change in colour try the pink-flowering variety, 'Autumnalis Rosea'.

Ordering early

When the weather makes it difficult to do any work outside, having a look through seed catalogues is not just a pleasurable occupation for a dank autumn day. If you get your seed order in early, you are less likely to be disappointed, because the seed companies often quickly run out of popular lines of seeds. This applies especially to any plants highlighted at flower shows, on TV programmes, and in the gardening magazines earlier in the year. And you'll get your seeds earlier too, and can therefore get a head start in the spring.

NOVEMBER
AT A GLANCE

- Tidy the garden for winter.
- Clear out bird boxes, and put food out for birds.
- Don't have a bonfire without checking the heap for hibernating creatures.
- Press on with winter digging.
- Clean or chuck old pots and trays.
- Plant bare-rooted trees and shrubs and new roses.
- Protect tender and newly planted shrubs from frost and wind.
- Plant tulip bulbs.
- Get the lawnmower serviced and sharpened.
- Protect alpines from winter rains.
- Keep off the lawn in frosty weather.
- Insulate pots left out for the winter.
- Install pond and greenhouse heaters.
- Heel in a winter supply of leeks by the back door.
- Plant fruit trees and bushes.
- Lift and divide rhubarb crowns.
- Winter-prune fruit trees and bushes.
- Insulate the greenhouse.

! LAST CHANCE

- Protect tender plants from winter weather.
- Lift and store dahlias.
- Start off hippeastrum (amaryllis) bulbs to flower at Christmas.
- Plant out spring bedding.
- Plant garlic.

★ GET AHEAD

- Order seed catalogues.
- Begin any winter-pruning of deciduous trees and shrubs, including renovation of hedges.
- Prune glasshouse vines.

Cimicifuga simplex 'White Pearl' • Autumn-flowering herbaceous perennial (see p.305)

Vitis coignetiae ♀ • Clinging, very vigorous climber, at its finest in autumn (see p.359)

Libertia ixioides • Slightly tender perennial with brown-edged white flowers (see p.329)

Pyracantha 'Golden Charmer' • Spiny shrub ideal for wall training (see p.344)

Lonicera fragrantissima • Shrubby honeysuckle with richly scented flowers (see p.330)

Euonymus alatus ♀ • Dense, bushy deciduous shrub with bright fruits and leaves (see p.318)

Chelone obliqua • Herbaceous perennial that enjoys heavy damp soil (see p.304)

***Chrysanthemum* 'Glowing Lynn'** • Hardy perennial; can be left in the garden all winter (see p.305)

***Cortaderia selloana* 'Sunningdale Silver'** ♔ • Pampas grass, an old favourite back in vogue (see p.311)

***Clematis* Golden Tiara** • One of the last clematis of the year to flower (see p.309)

Rosa moyesii • Shrub rose with distinctive bullet-shaped hips (see p.350)

Iris foetidissima ♔ • The stinking iris, with insignificant flowers but vivid fruits (see p.326)

WHAT TO DO IN

NOVEMBER

AROUND THE GARDEN

Clear up for winter *Wash and dry any used pots, and organise pots and trays on clean shelves.*

THERE WILL BE FEW PESTS AROUND NOW, but it is best to be on your guard as some will be hiding away in corners. The best way to avoid problems is to practise good hygiene, and this includes keeping sheds and equipment clean and tidy as well as the borders. Any dirty pots and seed trays kicking about should be thrown out or, better, recycled: washed in a weak solution of a garden disinfectant and stored away for the winter. Clean the ends of stakes and canes before storing them for the winter as pests often lurk there.

ORDER SEED CATALOGUES if you haven't done so already. The sooner you do this and get your seed orders off, the more likely you are to get all the varieties you want before they are sold out. It's exciting to plan what you are going to grow in the coming season, and the catalogues are usually full of new varieties every year to tempt you.

CLEAN OUT BIRD BOXES of old nesting material which can harbour parasites. Clearing them out will encourage birds to nest in them again

next year. Do this job as soon as possible, as birds will soon be looking for winter roosts in which to keep warm. If they are already familiar with a box by spring, they are much more likely to select it as a nesting site.

IF YOU ARE PLANNING A BONFIRE, check the rubbish to be burned beforehand to see if any hedgehogs or toads are hibernating in it. If there are, leave them in peace, taking away some of the heap to burn elsewhere if you must but leaving the creatures some debris undisturbed. Do all you can to encourage these creatures, as they are great allies in controlling pests.

PROTECT YOUNG PLANTS from rabbits. Rabbits can do an enormous amount of damage in the garden, but a few simple precautions will prevent some of it. Surrounding young plants with chicken wire netting will give them some protection. Tree trunks can be surrounded similarly, or there are special rabbit guards which wrap directly around the trunk of the tree to stop rabbits eating the bark. If you can afford it, putting chicken wire around the perimeter of the garden, sinking it at least 15cm (6in) into the ground, is the best deterrent of all, but it can be expensive. Bend another few inches at the base of the netting in the trench outwards, making an L-shape, to prevent the rabbits from digging down and then under it.

CONTINUE TO GATHER UP FALLEN LEAVES. This job can be made much easier by using a vacuum, either bought from the garden centre or hired from your local hire shop. There are both

electric and petrol-driven models available. Some have a blowing facility so leaves can be easily be blown out from around the base of plants.

CONTINUE SOWING GREEN MANURE CROPS on bare ground (see also October), especially in the vegetable garden. Winter rye can be sown well into November. These crops can be dug in during the spring and they will return valuable organic matter to the soil, improving the soil structure and its organic content.

REPAIR FENCES, PERGOLAS AND TRELLISES. This is a good time of year to repair any of these structures if necessary. There is less plant growth on them now, with the leaves mostly gone, and that makes it easier to see what you are doing, and to untie or cut back the plants and get on with the repairs.

COLD FRAMES are endlessly useful unheated, but they can also be insulated for warmth and even heated, either with small heaters or electric heating cables on the base and around the sides on the inside. To install any electrical wiring, especially outdoors, call in a qualified electrician to do the job.

Bubble polythene can be used to insulate the top of the frame and polystyrene slabs cut to size for the sides. Insulation alone will help to keep out several degrees of frost, enabling some tender plants to be overwintered there if space in the greenhouse or conservatory is limited. More protection can be given on very cold nights by covering the cold frame with a piece of old carpet or another sheet of polystyrene held in place with bricks.

TREES & SHRUBS

PROTECT TENDER AND NEWLY PLANTED TREES AND SHRUBS from frosts and cold winds. Bitter winds damage foliage by dehydrating it, and strong winds in freezing temperatures can cause more harm to plants than a severe frost on its own. Use a wind-break made from netting supported by posts. Evergreen shrubs and hedging plants are more prone to wind damage than deciduous ones, so these are the more important ones to protect. Smaller shrubs and newly planted ones can be protected from frost by packing straw or bracken round them, and holding it in place with netting. Polythene can also be used for temporary protection, but it must not touch the foliage of evergreen plants as any moisture condensing out on the polythene will freeze and damage the foliage. Support the polythene by nailing it onto a framework of canes or wooden battens.

CHECK TREE TIES AND STAKES. These should be checked on a regular basis to see that the stakes are sound and that ties are not cutting into the trunks of the plants; if so, they will eventually strangle the plant as the trunk expands outwards over the years.

CLEAR ANY SNOW OFF CONIFERS AND OTHER SHRUBS. Heavy snow lying on branches will weigh them down, spoiling the shape of the plants. Although it looks very pretty, shake the snow off the plants as soon as you can to avoid branches being broken under the weight of snow. It is surprising just how heavy a layer of snow can be.

PLANTING

AT THIS TIME OF YEAR bare-rooted stock of most deciduous trees and shrubs will become available, and can be planted throughout the dormant season (that is, from now until at the latest, March), whenever soil conditions allow. They are cheaper than container-grown plants, but do take a look at the root systems before you buy to ensure that they have been lifted with care and are not dried-up. Make sure they are well wrapped before transporting them, and plant as soon as possible. If the plants arrive by post, phone the supplier straight away if the plants do not seem satisfactory, to arrange an exchange.

To plant (see right and also January for illustrations), prepare the ground well, incorporating plenty of organic matter. Dig a hole large enough to take the root system without cramping the roots. Put a stake in first for trees and tall shrubs, on the windward side so the plant is blown away from the stake (this prevents rubbing). Then plant the tree or shrub to the same depth as it was planted before at the nursery (easily seen by the darker part of the stem near the roots), fill in the hole and firm in gently with your boot.

Make sure all newly planted trees and shrubs are well staked and tied. After spending a lot of money on trees this is a job worth doing well. The stake should come at most about a third of the way up the trunk, and often even shorter stakes are recommended. The only exception is when staking top-grafted standards such as dwarf weeping trees, when the stake should reach the graft point. But for all other trees, a low stake allows the top of the tree to flex in the wind, strengthening the trunk.

Make sure the tree is secured to the stake using a plastic tree tie. Check on the tree as it grows and loosen ties as the trunk expands.

Container-grown trees and shrubs can

PLANTING BARE-ROOTED ROSES

● Remove any damaged growth and spindly shoots, and any stems crossing the centre of the plant. Trim off any damaged roots.

● Dig a generous hole so as not to cramp the root system. If you haven't prepared the soil beforehand, incorporate organic matter into the hole and add a small handful of bonemeal.

● Place the rose in the hole with the roots well spread out. Lay a cane across the hole to check that the graft union will be below soil level.

● Fill in the hole by gradually working soil in around the roots with your hands, and pressing down firmly. Lightly tread the soil and water well.

also be planted all through the year. The soil will require the same thorough preparation as for bare-root trees and shrubs. If container-grown plants look a little pot-bound – that is, there is a solid mass of roots when they are knocked out of the container – it is a good idea to tease out some roots, otherwise they will continue to grow round in circles, forming a weak root system.

PLANT NEW ROSES (SEE LEFT). Bare-root roses should be available from this month through to March. They are slightly cheaper than container-grown plants and they do establish better. For roses to give of their best, thorough preparation of the soil is essential. Cultivate as large an area as you can or dig as large a hole as possible and work in plenty of organic matter.

Never allow the roots to dry out, and if the roses have just arrived by mail order and the roots are dry, put them in a bucket of water for a couple of hours. Plant the rose deep enough so that the point at which it was grafted (the joint between the stems and roots) is about 5cm (2in) below ground level. Work soil in amongst the roots well and firm with your boot as you go. To finish, mulch the surface with well-rotted garden compost or manure.

If you are considering planting new roses to replace old ones, you may have problems. New roses planted in soil that has grown roses for a number of years are prone to a disease known as rose sickness. If you must plant new roses in this situation, then take out as much of the old soil as possible and replace it with fresh soil from another part of the garden which has not grown roses before.

TREES & SHRUBS *continued*

Staking trees These angled stakes give support low down where it is needed, and can be inserted without damaging the rootball of container-grown plants.

PRUNING AND TRAINING

BEGIN WINTER PRUNING DECIDUOUS TREES AND SHRUBS (SEE ALSO DECEMBER). Don't prune, however, if nothing needs doing, however satisfying a job it is hacking away at woody growth. Unnecessary pruning weakens growth, and the fewer wounds you can make on a plant the better, as each is a potential entry point for disease. Ornamental cherries (*Prunus* species) are susceptible to the same disease, silverleaf, that is so dangerous to plum and cherry trees if pruned in winter, and it may be wiser to delay pruning of any ornamental cherries that need it until the summer. Some trees, most particularly walnuts, "bleed" or exude an enormous amount of sap whenever they are pruned, too, so any unnecessary cuts are dangerous.

However, on most deciduous trees, dead, diseased and damaged wood should be removed now, as although the pruning will create wounds these are, on balance, less risky than leaving the unhealthy wood on the plant. Any further cuts you make will probably be more cosmetic, intended to improve the shape of the plant, but consider the effect carefully before removing anything substantial – it's not only the effect of removing growth that you must envisage, but also the direction in which the new growth that will come from the point of pruning will grow.

PROPAGATION

CONTINUE SOWING SEEDS OF BERRIED SHRUBS AND TREES (see October).

HARDWOOD CUTTINGS TAKEN LAST AUTUMN should have rooted by now, and these can be lifted and planted in their permanent positions. Hardwood cuttings are a cheap and easy way to propagate plants as they don't require any special conditions, being happy outside completely unprotected. There is still plenty of time to take more hardwood cuttings. See October.

HEDGES

CONTINUE PLANTING HEDGING PLANTS. See October.

CARRY OUT RENOVATION OF DECIDUOUS HEDGES. From now until spring major renovation in the form of hard pruning can be carried out on deciduous hedges. For more details see December. Evergreen hedges should be left until spring.

CLIMBERS

Tying in for winter Make sure all whippy shoots are well secured before winter winds pick up.

TIE IN LONG, WHIPPY SHOOTS of climbers and wall shrubs to prevent them being blown about and possibly damaged in bad weather. If there doesn't seem to be a suitable gap in the framework to secure the shoot to, prune it back to five or six buds.

CONTINUE PLANTING new climbers as for other container-grown woody plants (see Trees & Shrubs).

PERENNIALS

Lily-of-the-valley rhizome Dig up small sections like this and plant as many as you can to each pot.

POT UP SOME LILY-OF-THE-VALLEY rhizomes to force them into flower early. A cool, frost-free greenhouse or conservatory will allow the plants to grow at their own pace, but if you want to hurry them on a bit give them warmer conditions. The plants can be put back in the garden after flowering and will flower again the following year.

PROTECT KNIPHOFIAS (RED-HOT POKERS) FROM FROST. In colder parts of the country kniphofias may not be reliably hardy, especially when young, but they can easily be given some protection. Gather up the foliage and tie it together quite firmly. This will protect the crown of the plant, so if the foliage is damaged by hard frosts the crown should be unaffected. Protect

Protecting slightly tender plants A blanketing mulch of leafmould can be sufficient.

other slightly tender herbaceous plants like penstemons too (see also Around the Garden). Bracken or straw placed over the plants and held in place with netting, or a layer of a dry loose mulch such as leafmould or bark chippings, will give a good degree of protection from hard frosts. Check the plants from time to time through the winter to ensure no diseases have set in.

CLEAR LEAVES THAT HAVE ACCUMULATED on top of clumps of perennials. If the leaves are left there for any length of time the plants will suffer through lack of light, and the dark moist conditions will attract slugs and snails. Don't burn the fallen leaves; either add them to the compost heap or make a separate leaf heap to make leafmould (see October).

TAKE ROOT CUTTINGS of perennials from now until late winter. For details see January.

IF DAHLIAS HAVE NOT YET BEEN LIFTED do so when the foliage has been blackened by frost (see October).

Cutting bamboo canes Use loppers and wear gloves, as some types can give you a nasty cut.

Cutting back perennials Cut down and clear growth as soon as it loses its ornamental value.

Dry and pack them into boxes, and fill in with old potting compost, leaving the crown uncovered, and keep them in a frost-free place. Cuttings can be taken from the tubers in the spring.

CONTINUE LIFTING AND DIVIDING herbaceous perennials as the weather and soil conditions allow. The earlier this is done in the month the better, as the newly divided plants will have time to settle in before the harsher winter weather.

CUT BACK ORNAMENTAL GRASSES and bamboos. Those that are not ornamental in winter are best cut back now as they can often look messy in winter. Some bamboos, if their canes are thick enough, can be cut, cleaned up and stored and used for supporting plants next season.

THE ROUTINE JOB OF CUTTING DOWN OLD GROWTH can continue, but if you live in colder parts it may be better to leave some of the old growths

on now to provide protection for the plants in severe weather. Some of the more attractive or architectural dead stems can look quite stunning when covered with frost or snow.

HELLEBORUS NIGER, **THE CHRISTMAS ROSE**, rarely actually flowers in time for Christmas, but it can be encouraged to flower a little earlier if you cover it with a cloche. Covering it will also help prevent the flowers being splashed with soil in heavy winter rain. Also, you could try lifting one or two plants and potting them up, and forcing them in gentle heat or just in a cold greenhouse. Then the full beauty of the flowers can be enjoyed without having to go out in the cold.

ALPINES

CONTINUE TO REMOVE FALLEN LEAVES FROM AROUND ALPINES. If the leaves are left they will keep light off the plants and encourage slugs and snails. At the same time clear any weeds growing in between the plants, and give the rock garden a general tidy-up before winter.

COVER VULNERABLE ALPINES to protect the crowns of the plants from the rain (see October), or take alpines in pots under cover. Plants that are most susceptible to winter wet are those with grey, woolly leaves, such as erinus, lewisias and edelweiss.

BULBS

CONTINUE PLANTING LILIES UNTIL THE SPRING (SEE OCTOBER).

REMEMBER TO EXAMINE BULBS BEING FORCED for early flowering. When they have made about 2.5cm (1in) of growth, move them into a cool greenhouse or cold frame. A cool windowsill is also ideal. When hyacinths and narcissi such as 'Paper White' and 'Soliel d'Or' begin to form flower buds, bring them into warmer conditions to flower in time for Christmas.

CONTINUE TO CHECK stored bulbs, corms and tubers. Any that are showing signs of rotting should be thrown away. If only small parts of the bulb, corm or tuber are affected you may get away with cutting out the infected part with a sharp knife and dusting the cut surface with flowers of sulphur, but keep them separate from the others in store just in case any infection is spread.

PROTECT SLIGHTLY TENDER BULBS left in the ground, such as nerines and agapanthus, with a thick mulch of garden compost. If possible grow them in a sheltered part of the garden, at the base of a south-facing wall or fence.

IF YOU WANT HIPPEASTRUMS (AMARYLLIS) IN FLOWER AT CHRISTMAS, start them into growth at the beginning of the month. Pot up and water the bulbs, and put in a warm place to get them going quickly. Some people start them off in an airing cupboard, but check them regularly if you do this as they grow so rapidly that they may be a couple of feet tall before you know it. Over a radiator (a place most houseplants hate) is also ideal.

BULBS *continued*

PLANT TULIPS THIS MONTH. By planting tulips late, after all the other spring-flowering bulbs are in, there is a better chance of preventing the bulbs being infected with the fungal disease, tulip fire. Try to get them in before the end of the month.

Tulips flower better in a sunny situation, and if your soil is heavy clay, lighten it by digging in coarse grit. You can of course grow tulips in pots as well as other spring-flowering bulbs. One advantage of growing them in pots is that they can be planted, pot and all, in any part of the garden lacking colour in the spring, and then are easily lifted out again when the flowers are over. Plant tulips in borders and pots just as you would other bulbs, at two to three times their own depth. Plant the bulbs on a layer of coarse grit to prevent them rotting off. It is always better to plant tulips a little more deeply than too near the surface.

CHOOSING TULIPS

'Keizerskroon'

'Dreaming Maid'

Tulipa whittallii

'Dreamboat'

'Carnaval de Nice'

'Fringed Beauty'

ANNUALS & BEDDING

PROTECT SEEDLINGS OF HARDY ANNUALS. Keep an eye on the weather forecast and if it turns very cold, protect those hardy annuals sown earlier in the autumn. Cover them with cloches, or have some horticultural fleece handy to throw over the plants. It would be rare indeed for these plants to be killed by frost, but it does no harm to have some protection to hand for really severe weather.

TUBEROUS BEGONIAS that were bedded out for the summer should be lifted and brought inside before the frost gets at them. Allow them to dry out under a greenhouse bench or other frost-free place. Once the old stems have parted from the tubers, clean these up and store them in boxes in a cool place.

FINISH PLANTING SPRING BEDDING PLANTS. If the planting of wallflowers, forget-me-nots, bellis and sweet Williams has not been completed by now, get it done as soon as possible so that the plants have a little time to become established before the winter sets in.

CONTAINERS

Insulate pots Even if the plant is hardy, the root system exposed above ground may be vulnerable.

INSULATE POTS THAT ARE TOO LARGE TO TAKE INDOORS. The roots of plants growing in containers outside are more prone to frost damage than plants growing in the open ground, and they need some protection from hard frosts. Insulate them by wrapping bubble polythene or hessian sacking around the pots. Tie up the leaves of plants like cordylines to protect the growing tip from excess winter wet, which will rot it, and wrap in fleece. Containers can be moved together for mutual protection. Modern plastic or terracotta containers are generally frost-proof, but older terracotta pots may not be, so even if empty, wrap them or take indoors for the winter. Ensure containers are lifted off the ground slightly to improve drainage. There are decorative "feet" available from garden centres for this purpose.

FINISH PLANTING CONTAINERS with spring-bedding plants.

PONDS

REMOVE SUBMERSIBLE PUMPS and lights if this was not done last month. Clean pump filters and dry them off before storing them. If there are any problems, send them off to be repaired or replace them. Check that the cabling is in good condition too. If you have any doubts about the safety of outdoor cables or other electrical connections, call in an electrician. Water and electricity don't mix.

If you have a power source to your pond, you might consider visiting an aquatic centre and looking at one of the low-voltage pond heaters that can be connected to the pump's electricity source. These are especially valuable if you keep fish in your pond, as you never need worry that the pond will freeze over and deprive them of oxygen. Have it installed before the really cold weather sets in, so that the heater is ready to be turned on when icy weather is forecast.

CONTINUE TO CUT DOWN plants growing around the pond and in the shallows. Old growth and leaves falling in the pond will rot and give off gases that are toxic to fish, so get debris out of the water as soon as possible.

Low-voltage pump *Remove these from ponds now and clean and check them before putting away.*

LAWNS

KEEP OFF THE LAWN IN WET WEATHER. If you have to go over the lawn when it is extremely wet to reach borders, then put down some planks to walk on, but ideally try to keep off it altogether. Don't walk on the lawn when it is frosted, either (see also December).

IN DRY WEATHER, RAKE UP FALLEN LEAVES on the lawn. Don't burn or bin these – they can be used to make leafmould, an excellent soil conditioner, mulch and ingredient in potting composts. To make leafmould, see Around the Garden in October.

SEND THE LAWN MOWER AWAY for sharpening and servicing. All machines do a far better job if maintained properly. Service agents are relatively quiet at this time of year. A lot of people leave it until the last moment in spring to have mowers serviced, and this causes a rush. Don't forget, though, to give the lawn an occasional light trim through the winter to keep it looking neat. Just take the tops off, and don't do it if the lawn is very wet or frozen.

NEW LAWNS

CONTINUE TO DIG OVER AREAS FOR NEW LAWNS, AND TO LAY TURF (see September) on prepared ground when the soil is not excessively wet or frozen. This month may be the last chance to lay turf in the current year, as the weather may turn bad next month. The one advantage of laying turf at this time of the year is that it won't dry out. Always work from boards when laying turf so as not to compact the soil in places and make the lawn uneven.

VEGETABLES & HERBS

PRESS ON WITH WINTER DIGGING as the weather allows. The soil should not be so wet that it sticks to your boots when you walk on it. You can cover ground with polythene sheeting to keep off the worst of the rain. Pull it back on a fine day to dig, and cover the soil again when you are finished.

CHECK ALL STORED CROPS for signs of disease. It is better to do this regularly so any rotting doesn't get a chance to spread. It's a good job to do when it is too wet to work outside.

HARVESTING

LIFT PARSNIPS. Parsnips taste better when they have had a touch of frost on them, but they can be lifted and stored in the same way as carrots. Pack them in boxes of sand and they will keep through the winter. An alternative, if you haven't much room for storing crops, is to heap them up outside the back door and cover them with a thick layer of straw. Hold this in place with some netting pegged into the ground.

HEEL IN A SUPPLY OF LEEKS BY THE BACK DOOR. Severe frosts will make it impossible to dig up crops for the kitchen, so lift a supply and re-bury them horizontally with the tops sticking out, close to the house in a sheltered part of the garden.

BEGIN HARVESTING BRUSSELS SPROUTS. Start harvesting from the bottom of the plant upwards, as the largest sprouts form at the base of the plant first. Very tall plants which look as if they may blow over in high winds can be staked and tied to a cane.

SOWING AND PLANTING OUTDOORS

FINISH PLANTING GARLIC by the end of the month. The sooner it is in, the better it will grow. If the weather is too wet to plant outside, start the cloves off in modular trays, and overwinter these in a cold frame.

BROAD BEANS AND PEAS can still be sown outside this month, covered with cloches, but the difference between the cropping times of these and sowings made in the spring is negligible. These sowings will, however, be greatly appreciated by all the mice in the neighbourhood, so make sure the cloches are firmly in place and the ends closed properly so there are no gaps.

To make some cheap, improvised cloches (see also p.45), get a length of polythene and some galvanized fencing wire. Cut the wire to make hoops and stick these, at intervals, into the ground. Stretch the polythene over the hoops and bury it in the soil at both ends. These cloches will also be useful for protecting crops sown and planted early in the spring.

Planting garlic in modules *Choose a tray with large cells to accommodate the chunky cloves.*

VEGETABLES *continued*

LOOKING AFTER CROPS

NET ALL BRASSICAS if you haven't done this by now. As the weather gets colder and there is less food around, pigeons will be increasingly attracted to the winter crops in your garden. There are many different types of bird scarer on the market, but by far the best way to protect the crops is by covering them. Make sure traditional netting is properly secured at ground level so that small birds don't get caught up in it; a safer alternative for birds is the very fine mesh sheeting used as a barrier to pests like carrot fly, or even spare pieces of horticultural fleece. Whatever you use as a cover, you must hold it up off the plants with cane supports or the birds will peck through it. Remember to shake it after a heavy fall of snow, or the weight may bring supports down or rip the netting, making it useless.

PROTECT THE CURDS OF CAULIFLOWERS to keep them white and delay the time when the flowers will open up. The inner leaves can be tied or snapped and bent over the curd.

BEAT THE SEASONS

FORCE CHICORY AND SEAKALE (see October).

HERBS

TERRACOTTA POTS CONTAINING HERBS may have to be wrapped with insulating material (see Containers) if the pots cannot be moved indoors.

LIFT CLUMPS OF CHIVES and grow them in pots on a windowsill (see October).

FRUIT

PICKING AND STORING

CHECK FRUITS IN STORE REGULARLY and remove any showing signs of deterioration. Use them in the kitchen or, if too far gone, throw them out for the birds or put them on the compost heap.

PRUNING AND TRAINING

START WINTER PRUNING ESTABLISHED APPLE AND PEAR TREES. Winter pruning of established trees consists mainly of pruning back the leaders of branches by about one-third. Long side shoots can be pruned to two or three buds to form fruiting spurs on spur-bearing trees. Tip-bearing apples produce fruiting buds on spurs and on the tips of branches, so only limited spur-pruning is required. Short shoots made during the summer, of about 23cm (9in) or less, should be left unpruned and longer shoots can be spur-pruned to prevent congestion. The leading shoots of the branches can be tipped, pruning off the top three or four buds, to encourage them to produce more side shoots. In addition to this pruning, any older branches which are

Pruning an apple bush *Shorten strong young stems to a few buds to encourage fruiting spurs.*

Crossing branches *Always remove one of two branches that rub together, or the chafing will create an entry point for disease.*

crossing and rubbing against one another should be cut out completely to prevent damage and to keep the centre of the tree fairly open. This will allow air to circulate more freely, so reducing the risk of diseases affecting the trees.

PRUNE GOOSEBERRIES AND REDCURRANTS in a similar way to apples and pears. The intention with pruning young bushes is to build up a framework of four or five main branches, each with plenty of fruiting spurs to produce a lot of succulent fruits.

On established frameworks, any shoots not summer-pruned in late summer should be pruned back to two or three buds from the previous year's growth. Leading shoots (those extending the length of main branches) can be pruned by one-third to half depending on their vigour. Any crossing, dead or diseased wood can be cut out at the same time. Aim to open up the centre of the bush, allowing free circulation of air which will reduce the incidence of diseases.

BLACKCURRANTS are pruned in a slightly different way (see January). These produce shoots from the base of

the plant, and you will have to cut out some of the older shoots to ground level every year to stimulate new shoots from the base. Aim to remove about a third of the bush each year. It is inevitable that you will remove young, current year's growth when pruning, but it is necessary to encourage those new shoots from the base.

CUT OUT THE FRUITED CANES of blackberries and hybrid berries such as tayberries and loganberries. For details see October.

MULCH ALL PRUNED FRUIT WITH A LAYER OF ORGANIC MATTER. After pruning mulch fruit to retain moisture and revitalize the soil. Mulching will also help prevent weed seeds germinating and competing for the nutrients in the soil. Any kind of organic matter is suitable as a mulch, as long as it is unlikely to hold any diseases that could infect the fruit plants.

PLANTING

PLANT FRUIT TREES AND BUSHES whenever the soil is not frozen or too wet. Bare-root trees and bushes are planted during the dormant season, from now until March. Container-grown plants can be planted at any time of the year. Make sure the ground has been well prepared by incorporating plenty of organic matter in the form of garden compost or well-rotted farmyard manure. If just one or two trees are being planted the preparation can be done at planting time. Dig a generous hole to accommodate the roots without cramping them. Break up the bottom of the hole to loosen the subsoil, without bringing any subsoil to the surface. Add plenty of organic matter, ideally well-rotted farmyard manure, and work it into the bottom of the hole. Fruit trees on dwarfing rootstocks will need staking for most of their lives, so make sure you put in a good stout stake at planting time, hammering the stake in first before planting the tree, so as not to harm the root system.

The planting technique is exactly the same as for all trees and shrubs, with the fruits always being planted at the same depth as they were growing previously (with the exception of blackcurrants – see below). One point to bear in mind with grafted fruit trees is that the point of grafting (a swollen part low down on the main stem) should always be kept above ground level. Otherwise the variety part of the tree (the upper part which produces the fruit and was grafted onto the rootstock) will begin to root into the soil, and so any control over the vigour of the tree will be lost. So, never plant deeply: be sure to put the tree in at the same level as it was planted before. The darker mark on the stem is the indicator of its previous planting depth. Gradually fill in, working the soil between the roots and firm gently with your boot. Level off and water in thoroughly, and finally tie to the stake with an adjustable tree tie. Then mulch with a thick layer of organic matter. Garden compost or well-rotted manure is ideal; straw is also good in sheltered spots.

BLACKCURRANTS ARE A SLIGHT EXCEPTION to the planting rules above in that they should be set lower in the planting hole, with 8–10cm (3–4in) of stem below ground level. This encourages new growth from the base of the plant. The newly planted bushes should then be pruned to 10cm (4in) from the ground to produce strong growth for future fruiting.

PRUNE NEWLY PLANTED YOUNG APPLE AND PEAR BUSHES AND TREES. Trees bought when they are three years old or more, especially those already partly trained to grow as fans, espaliers and cordons, should not need pruning, but young trees to be grown freestanding will benefit from pruning to form a good shape and framework of branches. Any crossing branches or those which make the tree look misshapen should be pruned out first. What you do then depends on the age of the tree you have bought.
• Maiden (one-year-old) trees should have the main stem pruned back to about 75cm (30in) from the ground, cutting to a bud. This will encourage branches to form lower down the tree.
• For a two-year-old tree, prune the resulting side shoots to about half of their length. These will form the primary branches. Cut the main stem back to the topmost side shoot, and this will help to keep the centre of the tree open.
• In the third year, prune the leaders selected to form the main branches by about half again, cutting to a bud facing in the direction you wish the branch to extend (usually upwards and outwards). Any sub-laterals (side shoots) growing from these branches should be pruned to one or two buds to form fruiting spurs. In the fourth year formative pruning should be finished and the tree will be cropping.

LOOKING AFTER CROPS

PUT GREASE BANDS on the trunks of fruit trees if this was not done last month (see October).

PROPAGATION

PROPAGATE RHUBARB. Lift a large root and split it into smaller pieces, with each piece having at least one bud. Plant the divided portions 90cm (3ft) apart in soil that has been well enriched with plenty of organic matter.

YOUNG STRAWBERRY RUNNERS that were potted up for forcing and left outside should be put on their sides to prevent them from getting too wet. Alternatively put them in a cold frame, but keep it well ventilated so as not to start them into growth too early.

TAKE HARDWOOD CUTTINGS OF redcurrants, whitecurrants, blackcurrants and gooseberries (see October).

TAKE CUTTINGS FROM VINES. Now is a good time to propagate vines, from eye cuttings. Make each cutting about 3cm (1⅛in) long, with each having one bud or "eye". On the opposite side to the eye, make a shallow sloping cut just underneath the bud and dip the cut part into hormone rooting solution. Then put the cutting horizontally, with the bud facing upwards, into a small pot of cutting compost, lightly covered. Keep in a propagator at a temperature of 24°C (75°F) until roots have formed. After the roots have formed, gradually accustom the young plant to cooler conditions, and plant in the greenhouse or outside in the spring.

UNDER COVER

SOME HEATING WILL BE REQUIRED NOW if you are keeping frost-tender plants inside. The most convenient heaters are thermostatically controlled electric ones, although there are gas and paraffin heaters as well. The type you buy will be a matter of personal choice. Bear in mind that with paraffin heaters, you must keep them clean and trim the wicks regularly, otherwise they will give off harmful fumes. Also, with gas and paraffin heaters, always keep a ventilator open a crack to prevent the build-up of harmful gases and to keep the air drier. These heaters cause condensation, so increasing the humidity inside. Heating large greenhouses can be quite expensive. To save on heating bills:
• Separate off a smaller part of the greenhouse with a curtain of bubble plastic used for insulation, and heat only that smaller area.
• Insulate the whole greenhouse with bubble plastic to reduce the heating costs. On aluminium greenhouses, the polythene can be fixed to the framework using special clips made for the purpose. With wooden greenhouses fix the polythene with drawing pins.
• If your greenhouse or conservatory has glass to the ground, the lower half of the greenhouse can be insulated not only with bubble plastic, but also with sheets of polystyrene. This is a great insulator; large sheets can be bought relatively cheaply and cut to size to fit your requirements.

VENTILATE WHENEVER POSSIBLE. It may seem odd to be advising opening ventilators at this time of year, especially after talking about insulating to conserve heat. But it is vital to keep air circulating, especially in late autumn,

UNDER COVER *continued*

and even in winter when the weather is reasonably mild. A good circulation of air, without causing draughts to affect the plants, is vital to keep down diseases such as botrytis, which thrive in moist, still conditions. Be sure to close the ventilators in the early afternoon to conserve that precious heat.

CLEAN POTS AND SEED TRAYS. If this job is done now and over next month it will save a lot of rushing around trying to find clean containers for seed-sowing and taking cuttings in spring. Also, trays left lying around with bits of dead plants and old compost in them will harbour all sorts of pests and diseases, making propagation, which should be one of the most fascinating and enjoyable aspects of gardening, less successful. Using clean containers is an important step towards success in propagating plants.

WATER ALL PLANTS MORE CAREFULLY NOW. With shorter days and cooler temperatures, plant growth will, generally, be slowing down. So it is important to be more careful with watering. Wait until plants look as if they really need watering. The best way to tell if a plant needs water is to lift it; if it feels light, it needs water, and the heavier it feels, the less water will be required. It may take a little practice to get the feel of different weights, but it will come with experience.

GLASSHOUSE AND HOUSE PLANTS

POT UP SOME LILY-OF-THE-VALLEY rhizomes (see Perennials) for an unusual and fragrant houseplant.

CHECK BULBS being forced for Christmas for growth (see Bulbs).

SOW CYCLAMEN NOW to give the plants a long growing period before flowering, not this coming Christmas, but the following one, giving them 14 months to make good plants with plenty of flowers. Soak the seeds prior to sowing to soften the seed coat, then sow in a pot or tray filled with seed compost and cover them lightly with compost or vermiculite. A temperature of 12-15°C (54-60°F) is required for germination. When the seedlings are large enough to handle, prick them out into small pots and water in well, avoiding getting water on the foliage. A winter temperature of 10°C (50°F) will have to be maintained to keep the young plants growing. A final potting into a 12-15cm (5-6in) pot will be required in the summer. The plants can be stood outside for the summer once the threat of frost has gone, usually about the beginning of June in most parts of the country. Feed and water the plants regularly through the summer. Bring them inside again in September.

CROPS UNDER GLASS

BEGIN PRUNING INDOOR VINES by cutting all the fruited shoots back to one or two buds from the main stem (see also Fruit, December). Vines can be pruned from now through to late winter, but those under glass are best pruned early to admit light for other plants under cover. Cuttings can be made from the prunings (see Fruit).

DEEP BEDS FOR VEGETABLES

DEEP BEDS CAN BE ANY LENGTH, as long as they are no more than about 1.2m (4ft) wide, so that they can be tended from each side without treading on them. However, here we suggest a design using square beds intersected by paths that makes a really good-looking, as well as productive, kitchen garden, combining potager-style traditional formality with an up-to-date, labour-saving way of growing crops.

The design uses the herb garden featured on pp.156–7 as a centrepiece, and all of the vegetable beds are built in exactly the same way, except that the soil beneath will benefit from being dug and turned thoroughly before the top layer of soil and compost, or soil-based John Innes-type compost, is added. However, this is the last time you will dig these beds. The soil will sink and settle over time, making room for a good top-dressing of well-rotted manure or garden compost and a feed with an organic fertiliser every winter – and that's it!

Remember to rotate crops around the beds just as you would in allotment-style rows (see right). Path materials are up to you. Beaten earth is serviceable (and free), although it can become muddy. A thick layer of straw with planks laid on top for the wheelbarrow is traditional and clean. Old, mucky straw can go onto the compost heap in spring.

Having cultivated the ground first, make each square bed exactly as for the one used to create the herb garden on pages 156–7.

Space plants on deep beds equally each way.

CROP ROTATION

Move crops to different beds each year on [a] year rotation (right). Crops that do not fall [in] traditional rotation groups, such as salad le[aves,] sweetcorn, and also potatoes and tomatoe[s, as] long as ground has not been recently man[ured,] can replace any crop in any year (do not f[ollow] potatoes with tomatoes or vice versa). Strawberries and perennial vegetables cou[ld] also occupy beds on a longer-term basis.

BED 1
Beetroot and carrots

BED 2
Turnips and celeriac, and a wigwam of
runner beans

BED 3
Kohl rabi and parsnips

BED 4
Brussels sprouts and broccoli, with a
wigwam of peas and sweet peas

BED 5 (CENTRAL BED)
Herb feature (see June, p.156)

BED 6
Lettuce and radishes, with a wigwam of
peas and sweet peas

BED 7
Onions, shallots and salad onions

BED 8
Cabbages and cauliflowers, with a
wigwam of runner beans

BED 9
Dwarf runner beans and broad beans

Year 1	1, 2.	3, 4.	6, 7.	8, 9.
Year 2	8, 9.	1, 2.	3, 4.	6, 7.
Year 3	6, 7.	8, 9.	1, 2.	3, 4.
Year 4	3, 4.	6, 7.	8, 9.	1, 2.
Year 5	1, 2.	3, 4.	6, 7.	8, 9.

ALL BEDS ARE 1.2M (4FT) x 1.2M (4FT)

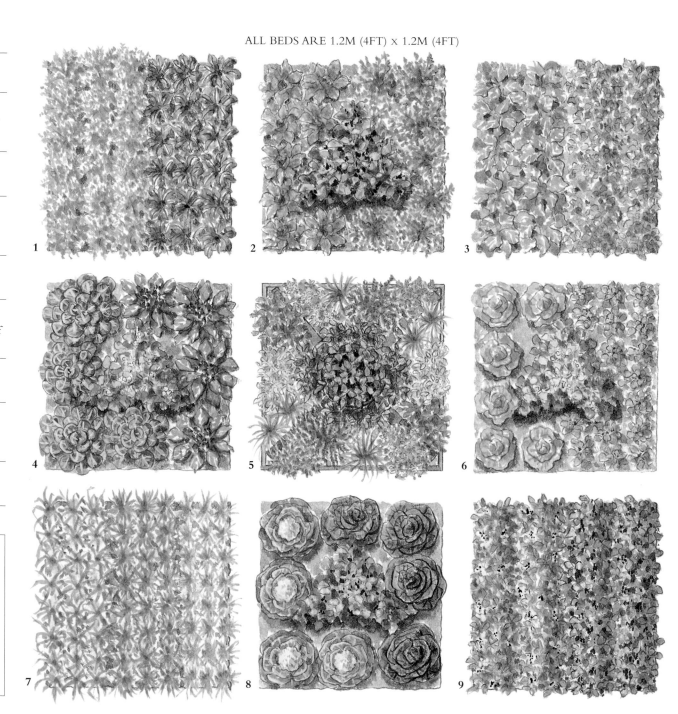

DECEMBER

The garden in December

Any sunshine there is in December will be weak, but sunny days can be quite pleasant, and if you wrap up well, you can have a good day in the garden, digging or catching up with other clearing-up jobs.

D ECEMBER CAN BE A WONDERFUL MONTH in the garden. The days may be short but on the whole the weather is usually not too bad, with wonderfully clear, frosty, sunny days when it can be a pleasure to be out. It really is much better for you than snoozing in front of the fire! Make the most of these days as they may be few and far between.

Plants can look charming with a covering of snow on them, and the bare stems of trees and shrubs can be transformed with a silvering from a sharp frost. On the other hand, heavy falls of snow will damage trees and shrubs so it will have to be knocked off before it causes any harm.

Ivy in winter ▷
Mature ivy stems become bushy, rather than clinging, and left untrimmed will provide a cosy haven for wildlife. The black fruits borne in winter are a valuable food for birds.

The winter scene

It's not a completely bleak month for colour in the garden. Plants like the winter-flowering heathers and *Jasminum nudiflorum* should be in flower throughout the month. *Hamamelis mollis* and *Iris unguicularis* are others which can be relied on to cheer up December days in the garden. There should still be berries on trees and shrubs, too, if the birds haven't eaten them all during spells of bad weather.

There is still plenty to do outside, although the pace of work will be more gentle now. There is no need for the urgency with which things have to be done in the spring and summer. With borders tidied up, it is an ideal opportunity to give borderline-hardy plants such as penstemons protection against hard frosts. As the years go by and our winters become milder, and nurseries select and breed more robust cultivars, many plants, including penstemons, that were once always lifted for winter protection now stay happily outdoors all year round. But they are not immune to the harshest weather, so it is well worth covering them as winter enters its coldest phase. The easiest way of doing this is by covering the plants

with a cloche, and many ornamental cloches are available today in either glass or plastic. More utilitarian cloches can be made with plastic sheeting stretched over wire frames. Alternatively, use horticultural fleece or a layer of straw held in place with pegged-down netting.

Winter-pruning of fruit trees is a satisfying job to be undertaken now. And it's a good time to do any major pruning of ornamental deciduous trees and shrubs, not only because the plants are now in their dormant period, but also, with the leaves now off the plants, it's much easier to see what you are doing. It's also much easier to identify dead and diseased wood, which can then be cut out. Of course, shrubs such as the dogwoods (*Cornus*) and willows grown for their ornamental bark should be left until spring. If you prune them now you will lose the colourful stems, the very reason why they are grown.

Company in the garden

Winter digging can continue this month whenever weather conditions allow; that is, when the soil is not excessively wet or frozen. Whilst digging you will most likely be accompanied by a robin, eagerly waiting for a worm or other insects to be uncovered by your work. They can be too friendly at times, getting so close that you may fear trampling on them. But it's certainly a reminder to remember garden birds now that the weather is getting harsher. A varied selection of food put out regularly from now on will help see birds through the winter, and keep them in the neighbourhood of your garden, rather than trying their luck elsewhere.

▽ **Tapestry of colour**
Heathers of all kinds, whether in flower now or displaying intense leaf colour, are such a boon for winter interest, and make superb low-maintenance, ground-hugging plantings.

WEATHER WATCH

Although there can be a few relatively mild December days, it's a cold month and there's no getting away from it. One exceptionally bitter Christmas in my home town near Glasgow the temperature fell to -19°C for several days. With sharp frosts and driving winds, some days the temperature will rarely get above freezing. However the cold can be beneficial in the garden, by killng off pests and diseases.

Definitely a windy month, with bitingly cold winds at times. But it can be calm, especially in frosty weather. The most intense gales are likely in western coastal areas close to the Atlantic Ocean as weather depressions are driven across from America. Northern areas can expect from 2 to 5 days on average of gale force winds. Southern areas experience from 0.7 to 2 days of gales.

The north of the country comes off worst in the sunshine stakes this month: only 13 hrs in the far north, up to about 50 hrs in the north-east. Southern parts can expect up to 54 hours of direct sunshine.

It can be quite wet this month too, with all areas seeing an increase in rainfall. All coastal areas can be wet, as well as hilly areas like the Highlands of Scotland. Here you can expect around 275mm of rain, whereas in the south the average is 53mm. Keep off the soil when it is sodden, or you will do more harm than good.

There is an increased chance of snow this month, but rarely does it last, or lie on the ground, for long. We may hope for a white Christmas, but it rarely happens these days. A good covering of snow can turn the garden into a winter wonderland, but do be aware that it can also damage plants. The weight of snow on trees and shrubs can break the branches, so shake it off before the damage occurs.

If you have decided to replant part of the garden, you can do much to encourage birds by including plants that will attract them to your plot. All the berrying trees and shrubs will attract birds, and if you have room, a mixed, informal hedgerow of flowering and fruiting trees and shrubs will give them both sustenance and shelter. Bare-rooted mixed hedging plants will be available all through the winter, and can be planted whenever weather conditions are good enough for digging. It's also a good time for taking hardwood cuttings of trees and shrubs, for an even more economical option. A small water feature will also attract birds, as they love to drink and, in summer, bathe in shallow water, and this could also form part of your plans for spring.

Conserving warmth
Inside there will be a lot to do if you haven't yet cleaned out the greenhouse or conservatory. After doing this, insulate with plastic bubble polythene to reduce the cost of heating. Quite a dramatic reduction in costs can be achieved by insulation, and it will enable you to get your plants off to a good start early in the new year.

If you don't have a greenhouse, and simply don't have room for one, you should at least have a cold frame. You'll be surprised at how much more scope it will give you for propagating and sheltering plants. This month we set out instructions for making a frame (see p.290). Painted or stained in one of the new garden shades, it will be as ornamental as it is useful in the garden, so go on and treat yourself, or a friend – a well-built cold frame has got to be high up on any keen gardener's Christmas list!

Plants for winter display
Garden centres are now packed with winter-flowering pot plants, and there will be a wide variety to choose from. In very cold weather, make sure the plants are properly wrapped when you buy them, as even a short period exposed to the cold can affect the growth and flowering of these plants. A good selection includes azaleas, poinsettias, winter cyclamen and *Solanum capsicastrum* (the winter cherry). These will fill your home with colour over the holiday period. Remember that these are living decorations, and all will last longer given a little care and attention.

Another way to have colour in the home at this time is by cutting shoots from winter-flowering shrubs and putting them in water, and in the warmth of the greenhouse, conservatory or home the flowers will open up. If you can do this early in December the flowers will open in time for Christmas.

Armchair gardening
If the weather is just too bad to do any work outside then it is a good idea to plan ahead and consider the plants you want to grow and the features to be created in your garden for next year. It's a pleasant occupation, leafing through seed and plant catalogues

◁ **Make a cold frame**
Making your own cold frame will save you a fortune when you look at the prices of the better kinds available. You'll soon wonder how you managed without one.

▽ **Birch bark**
As the last leaves fall from deciduous trees, white-barked birches come into their own, shining out on even the dullest days and spectacular when snow covers the ground.

by the fireside. Getting orders off early will ensure that you get the plants you want before the nursery runs out of them. There are many specialist plant nurseries around the country, and most of them produce catalogues. These can be a mine of information, and you will often come across some little treasures. Vegetable seed catalogues are also a fine source of inspiration. With memories still fresh of the crops that did and didn't do well this year for you, all of the information that the best brochures give on the strengths and weaknesses of the various cultivars will probably have you planning next year's menus, never mind plantings, well in advance.

DECEMBER
AT A GLANCE

- Prune woody ornamental plants and fruit trees and bushes, and shred the prunings if possible.
- Feed birds in cold weather, and do not allow ponds, water features and bird baths to freeze over.
- Continue winter digging, incorporating organic matter into the soil.
- Clean paths, and repair sheds and fences.
- Spray fruit trees and also roses with a tar oil winter wash.
- Shake snow off trees, shrubs and hedges.
- Prune ornamental vines and grape vines.
- Continue taking hardwood cuttings.
- Sow seed of alpine plants.
- Repair lawns if weather conditions allow.
- Lift and heel in celery for winter supplies.
- Earth up tall Brussels sprout stems to support them.
- Water plants overwintering under cover sparingly now that they are dormant, to avoid the risk of overwatering and rotting.
- Take care of pot plants to get the best of their winter display.

! LAST CHANCE
- Protect plants and pots vulnerable to frost damage.
- Insulate garden taps and exposed pipes.
- Prune tall bush roses to guard against wind rock.
- Bring in Christmas bulbs for flowering.

★ GET AHEAD
- Sow pelargonium seeds under cover for next year's plants.
- Sow some early crops under cover for the first plants to put out in the new year.

Mahonia **x** *media* **'Charity'** ♀ • Evergreen shrub with honey-scented flowers *(see p.332)*

Viburnum **x** *bodnantense* **'Dawn'** ♀ • Beautifully scented flowers on bare winter branches *(see p.357)*

Ilex aquifolium **'Handsworth New Silver'** ♀ • Variegate female holly bearing bright berries *(see p.325)*

Hippeastrum **'Apple Blossom'** • One of the most spectacular bulbs to grow as a houseplant *(see p.324)*

Elaeagnus **x** *ebbingei* **'Gilt Edge'** ♀ • Variegated evergreen shrub for a splash of colour *(see p.316)*

Salix **x** *rubens* **'Basfordiana'** ♀ • Prune this willow hard each year for bright stems *(see p.351)*

Rhododendron **'Inga'** • Compact azalea, ideal as
a winter pot plant *(see p.346)*

Cotoneaster frigidus **'Fructu Luteo'** • Yellow-berried
shrub popular with birds *(see p.313)*

Clematis armandii **'Apple Blossom'** • Evergreen
clematis with scented winter flowers *(see p.306)*

Jasminum nudiflorum ♀ • A straggly but welcome
winter-flowering climber *(see p.327)*

Cyclamen coum ♀ • Perennial that can be grown in pots
for an indoor display *(see p.314)*

Aucuba japonica **'Variegata'** • Hedging stalwart
puts on a winter show *(see p.300)*

WHAT TO DO IN DECEMBER

AROUND THE GARDEN

THERE ARE FEW PESTS AROUND in the garden now. But it always pays to be vigilant, as the milder winters we now seem to be having lead to many pests surviving the winter when they would normally be killed off during cold weather. Practising good garden hygiene will go a long way to reducing problems in spring and summer. Clear away any debris or fallen leaves around plants, where problems could lurk. Any diseased material should be either burned or put in the bin.

For those of us these days who want to garden in a more natural way, there is a slight paradox in advice about clearing the garden. To encourage beneficial wildlife into the garden to eat the pests we don't want, we must provide places where they can hibernate for the winter. Hedgehogs, for instance, like a nice heap of leaves to winter in, so leave the odd pile in an out-of-the-way corner of the garden. Ladybirds, so good at controlling aphids, hibernate in all sorts of little crevices. They have been known to come out of the masonry of old stone-built houses where the stone is a bit flaky. So do please bear this in mind when you are clearing up, and leave a few safe havens where these creatures can rest undisturbed.

FEED BIRDS IN COLD WEATHER. Birds are terrific allies in the garden, even though they try to eat the fruit grown for our consumption. It is very hard for them to find food when the ground is frozen or there is a thick layer of snow. So make sure you put something out for them regularly. It's better to get special bird food for them than to leave out household scraps, as seed and nut mixtures provide a better diet for the birds – and cooked food especially can attract vermin. Do also leave a shallow dish of water out, and thaw it with warm water as necessary; dehydration can be as harmful for birds as hunger.

CONTINUE RAKING UP ANY FALLEN LEAVES. Be aware that creatures like hedgehogs may be sleeping beneath, so use your hands or garden "grippers" to pick up piles, not a fork. If you come across a hedgehog, leave it undisturbed until spring.

ANY PLANTS, whether deciduous trees, shrubs and climbers or herbaceous perennials, can be moved if they are growing in the wrong place or have become too big for their current position, provided that soil conditions permit – that is, that the ground is not frozen or waterlogged. Always take as big a rootball as you can cope with when lifting larger plants, or get a friend to help if it's too much for one person. Remember to revitalize the soil both where the plant is taken from and in the new position. Stake tall plants to prevent wind rock, and provide a windbreak shelter to protect from cold winds if necessary.

PROTECT PLANTS VULNERABLE TO FROST if you haven't done so before, as the year is now entering its coldest phase. Take in under cover any plants that have been overlooked. Plants *in situ* like penstemons will benefit from a layer of protection, particularly in colder parts of the country. Herbaceous perennials are very easy to protect now that plants have died back – though it won't harm them even if they are in leaf. Just put a thick layer of straw or bracken over the crown of the plant, and hold it in position with some wire netting held in place with pegs stuck into the ground. Taller shrubs can be "lagged" with straw held in place with hessian or sacking. Don't use plastic as even when plants are dormant they still need to breathe.

WINTER IS PRUNING TIME for ornamental and fruiting woody plants. If you have not done so before, consider shredding the prunings rather than burning them. Shreddings make a terrific mulch, or can be added to the compost heap to rot down mixed with greener material. If your garden is mostly laid to shrubs and lawn, so there isn't much bulky material for the compost heap in summer, keep a pile of shreddings to mix in with grass clippings in the summer months. These need plenty of air in them if they are to rot down properly, and not form a slimy,

Protect plants vulnerable to frost *This cosy swaddling will protect the plant over winter.*

stinking mess. Don't shred any diseased material as the disease will be spread around the garden. There are many different makes of shredder on the market, and they can be hired too. But if you don't want to go to the bother yourself, some local authorities now have shredding machines at their domestic refuse collection points, so take the prunings there where they will be recycled to do some good.

WRAP INSULATION AROUND OUTSIDE TAPS. As ice forms, water expands and this can easily burst pipes, which could affect the water supply to the house. You can insulate taps by binding them in several layers of hessian, or there are nowadays products on the market especially for insulating outside taps. If at all possible, turn off the supply to outside taps during the winter, and this way you will avoid any possibility of burst pipes.

TREAT TIMBER OF SHEDS AND FENCES WITH PRESERVATIVE. It's a good job to do at this time of year, when there is less work in the rest of the garden. Often the weather in December can be fairly dry, allowing painting jobs to be done. There are many different types of timber preservative on the market, in a wide range of colours. Be sure to read the instructions and check if any are harmful to plants. It may be the case that you will have to untie any climbing plants on fences to put the preservative on. Creosote is an old-established timber preservative and still very good. But one word of caution – make sure that you get 100% creosote; other types of creosote contain toxins which are

harmful to plants. It doesn't mean that you can splash 100% creosote onto your plants, but it is safer.

CONTINUE WINTER DIGGING of new planting areas and empty vegetable beds for as long as the weather permits. If the soil is so wet that it sticks to your boots then keep off it until it dries out a bit. If you have to walk on the soil when it's wet, use planks to get across. Trodden soil is compacted by your weight and, especially if the soil is a heavy clay, the air will be driven out of it; when it does eventually dry out it will set as hard as concrete. To prevent excessive wet in the soil, especially if you have to get on with the work, cover at least part of the ground with polythene to keep off the worst of the rain. When you want to work the soil, pull it back, and when you're finished cover it up again.

ORDER OR BUY MANURE from farms and riding stables for digging in if you didn't do it in the autumn. The sooner all winter digging is done the better. If you're digging manure in straight away, make sure you get well-rotted stuff, but you can stack fresher manure to rot down (see also Make a Hot Bed, in Vegetables & Herbs), or add it gradually to other composting material to make the most wonderful mix for digging into the soil. Even in towns, it's not as difficult to get as most people think. Just look for local riding stables in the business directory. Most cities and towns now have riding stables on their outskirts. Some may charge a nominal amount for the manure but most will be only too glad to see the back of the stuff.

Order manure *Well-rotted farmyard or stable manure will revitalize your soil.*

CLEAN MOSS AND LICHEN FROM PATHS. Paths can become treacherous at this time of year when they get wet. There are many proprietary path and patio cleaners on the market today, and all are easy to use. Just mix them according to the instructions and water onto the area to be cleaned. Using a solution of household bleach will get the job done just as well. Water on the solution, leave for a few minutes and then scrub the moss and lichen off. On large areas, a power washer will do the job much more easily. These can be hired quite cheaply, and certainly make light work of this necessary chore. You will be amazed at the difference it makes to any stonework or woodwork being blasted clean.

MAKE A COLD FRAME (see p.290). Even in this quiet month, there are at least half-a-dozen uses for a cold frame listed in the pages that follow. Once you've discovered how useful a frame can be, you'll be knocking up a second one.

TREES & SHRUBS

EARLY IN DECEMBER cut a few shoots from winter-flowering shrubs like *Viburnum* × *bodnantense* and *Prunus* × *subhirtella* 'Autumnalis'. Put the shoots in water and keep them in a cool place indoors. Soon the buds will begin to open, and the beautifully scented flowers can be added to holiday decorations.

HOLLY TREES WITH THEIR RED BERRIES are very attractive at this time of year, and they provide excellent Christmas decorations for the home. But birds love to eat the berries just as much as we like to look at them. While we mustn't begrudge birds their food in harsh winter weather, it is wise to cover at least part of a holly tree with some netting to save some of the berries for the Christmas festivities. Make sure the netting is secured as firmly as possible so that birds don't get caught up in it.

CHECK NEWLY PLANTED TREES AND SHRUBS, including roses, to see if they have been loosened by winds or lifted by frost. When this happens, gaps form around the roots, causing them to dry out because they are not in close contact with the soil. If you see cracks around the plant, gently firm in with your feet. Be careful on heavy clay soils not to tread too heavily, or all the air will be driven out of the soil.

PUT A WINDBREAK AROUND NEWLY PLANTED EVERGREENS. Strong cold winds can have a devastating effect on recently planted leafy shrubs. Plants are continuously losing water from their leaves (this is known as transpiration) and the rate of water loss increases with high winds passing over the surface of the leaves –

TREES & SHRUBS *continued*

just as a windy day dries washing more quickly. The edges of the leaves dry out faster than the plant can replace the water, and so cells die off. It's known as wind scorch. To reduce damage, erect a shelter around the plants. It can be made from any material stretched between posts, from hessian sacking to polythene, or fine net mesh made specially for the purpose. If you haven't got enough to go right round the plant, make sure it is at least on the windward side.

YOU CAN SPRAY ROSES with a winter wash, as with fruit trees (see Fruit this month), to kill off any blackspot spores on the plants and in the soil. First, clear away all old foliage on and around the roses as the spores can be transferred from the leaves to the soil. Spray the soil around the bushes as well as the roses themselves.

SHAKE SNOW OFF TREES AND SHRUBS. It is rare that we get a lot of snow in December, but it is best to be aware that although plants look terrific with a layer of snow on them, it can be a considerable weight and will easily bring down a branch or two. As long as the layer of snow hasn't frozen hard, brush it off as soon as possible and the damage will be slight.

Conifers planted as specimen trees, where the shape of the plant is all-important, can be protected, if not too large, by tying thin wire or strong string around them, preventing the branches opening up when the snow falls on them. Don't worry about snow laying over low plants: it actually gives them protection against cold, blanketing them from frost.

CUTTING OFF A LOW BRANCH

1 First reduce the weight of the branch so that the final cut is easier to make cleanly. To prevent downward tearing, make an undercut.

2 Supporting the weight of the branch, cut downwards straight through it about 5cm (2in) beyond the undercut.

3 Now cut back the stub cleanly, cutting just beyond the swollen ring or "branch collar" where it meets the trunk.

PRUNING AND TRAINING

PRUNE DECIDUOUS TREES AND SHRUBS FOR HEALTH AND TO SHAPE. Have a look at all of the deciduous trees and shrubs in your garden to see if any need attention to improve the health or shape of the plant. At this time of year, with no leaves in the way, it is easier to see what you are doing. You will need a good pair of secateurs, a pair of loppers and a pruning saw for cutting off larger branches. Chainsaws can be hired from

local hire shops, but unless you are familiar with these machines they are best left to the experts; they can be extremely dangerous in inexperienced hands. Likewise, on no account saw through large branches, or branches high up in a tree, yourself. These are jobs for a trained tree surgeon. And check with your local council before doing any pruning on old established trees to make sure they do not have a tree preservation order on them.

• First remove any dead or diseased wood and any crossing branches that are rubbing together, cutting out whole shoots to a joint whenever possible rather than just tipping them back.

• If the plant is taking up too much room in a smaller garden then it can be trimmed. The main point to remember is that the harder you prune, the stronger will be the resulting growth, so when restricting size, light pruning will have a much more satisfactory effect than hacking away. Don't just give freestanding plants an all-over "haircut", as when trimming a hedge. Try to open up the centre of the plant to allow air to circulate and reduce the amount of shadow cast on lower-growing plants in the border.

• Take your time when pruning. Stand back and look at the plant often and consider what effect removing a branch

Check woody plants for diseases
Coral spot is a fungal disease that must be cut out completely.

PRUNE TALL ROSES

Before pruning
The stiff branches catch the wind like a sail, and can loosen the plant.

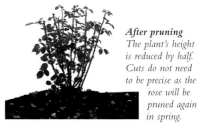

After pruning
The plant's height is reduced by half. Cuts do not need to be precise as the rose will be pruned again in spring.

will have on the appearance of the plant before making the cut. You can't stick a branch back on once it's been pruned off.

• Most woody material can be put through a shredder to make a mulch for borders. Any diseased material should be put in the bin, taken to the local household waste tip or burned. Composting it will more than likely spread the disease.

• Feed after pruning, preferably with an organic fertiliser, and mulch with organic matter.

• Most plants will tend to produce a mass of young shoots from the points where they were pruned. Keep an eye on this regrowth through spring and summer and remove shoots while they are still young.

PRUNE TALL BUSH ROSES BY HALF TO PREVENT WIND ROCK (see left). If plants are rocked about by wind a hole will form at the base of the plant where water will collect and cause the roots to rot. In frosty weather the water may freeze, resulting in further damage to the root system.

PLANTING

CONTINUE PLANTING TREES, SHRUBS AND CLIMBERS. As long as the soil is not frozen or waterlogged, press on with planting, as weather conditions can change quickly and short days mean there is less time to work in the garden. Heel in plants if soil conditions are not suitable for planting (see January). Plants will keep for quite a long time if planted temporarily in a corner of the garden.

PROPAGATION

CONTINUE TAKING HARDWOOD CUTTINGS (see October, and also Climbers, right).

HEDGES

BRUSH ANY HEAVY SNOW OFF evergreen hedges before the weight of it splays out branches.

PRUNE OVERGROWN DECIDUOUS HEDGES like beech and hornbeam. No matter how often we trim hedges through the summer, they imperceptibly creep outwards, taking up more space and becoming more difficult to cut.

Now, while the plants are dormant, is a good time to reduce the hedge to a manageable size. On an old established hedge you may need loppers or a pruning saw to cut some of the larger branches.

Cut back the sides until the hedge is no more than 45-60cm (18-24in) wide at the top, tapering it so that the bottom of the hedge is wider. This shaping will protect the hedge from damage by heavy snowfalls. The top can be trimmed to whatever height you want. To get the top level, you may need to put up a line at the height required.

TAKING HARDWOOD CUTTINGS (see October, and also Climbers, right) is an ideal way of producing quantities of hedging plants for free. The cuttings will have rooted by next winter, when they can be dug up and planted in their permanent positions.

Or, grow a deciduous hedge from hardwood cuttings *in situ*. Prepare a trench along the line of the proposed hedge as the planting area, and line out cuttings along it, about 30cm (1ft) apart. Put a few more in at the end of the row as spares in case some of the cuttings don't root. And there you will have, eventually, the cheapest hedge in the world.

CLIMBERS

BRUSH SNOW OFF dense evergreen climbers and wall shrubs; when snow accumulates on these it can not only break stems but also puts strain on ties and supports.

EARLY IN DECEMBER cut a few shoots from winter jasmine. Put the shoots in water and keep them in a cool place indoors. Soon the buds will begin to open and the beautifully scented flowers can be used to add to the Christmas decorations.

ORNAMENTAL VINES can be pruned now to keep them from completely taking over the garden. Vines can produce growths up to 3m (10ft) or more in one season, and over several years, if they are not pruned, you will end up in a mess. Thin out overcrowded shoots, and then prune sideshoots to two buds from the main stems kept as a framework.

TAKE HARDWOOD CUTTINGS OF DECIDUOUS CLIMBERS. Remove strong woody shoots about 30cm (1ft) long from the plant, cutting just above a bud. Trim the base to just below a bud, and cut off the tip just above a bud to leave a section of stem about 22.5cm (9in) long. Dip the cut end into hormone rooting solution. Make a slit trench in a corner of the garden with a spade, to the depth of the spade. On heavy clay soils put some grit in the base of the trench to improve drainage. Put the cuttings in to two-thirds their depth, and carefully firm in with your boot. The cuttings will have rooted by next winter, when they can be dug up and planted in their permanent positions.

PERENNIALS

CONTINUE TO CUT DOWN DEAD GROWTH on herbaceous perennials, and generally weed and tidy borders. The sooner this is done, the less work there will be left in the busy spring period. But robust stems with seed heads, as on sedums, can be left uncut until the spring, as you will find they are beautiful when wrapped in a layer of frost: a lovely sight, especially on a sunny, clear morning.

DURING REASONABLE PERIODS OF WEATHER when the ground is not frozen or excessively wet, you can continue to lift and divide herbaceous perennials (see November).

ROOT CUTTINGS of perennials can be taken through the winter. For details see January.

ALPINES

CONTINUE TO CLEAR FALLEN LEAVES FROM THE ROCK GARDEN. Most alpine plants will suffer if left covered with a damp layer of leaves for any length of time. So it is important to remove them regularly, as soon as possible. In their native mountainous regions, alpines are usually protected by a blanket of snow, which actually keeps them relatively dry. The snow generally melts quickly and the plants are then exposed to the fresh alpine air.

SOW ALPINE SEEDS. This may seem an odd time to do this, but in the wild alpine seeds have to go through a period of cold weather to break the seed's dormancy. This can be imitated at home by sowing the seeds in a pot and standing the pot outside to let the seeds

PERENNIALS *contd*

freeze from time to time, with a sheet of glass over the pot to protect them from excessive wet. The seeds will germinate in the spring. You can sow them later, in warmer months, but then you will have to put the seeds in the fridge for six to eight weeks before sowing to break dormancy.

Sow the seeds in pots containing alpine compost, consisting of equal parts loam, sharp grit and peat-free compost. Water the compost before sowing and sow the seeds thinly on the surface. Cover them with horticultural grit. This will reduce the problem of algae growing on the compost, as the seeds can take some time to germinate. They may also germinate at different times. Don't throw away the pots until you have the number of plants you require. Grow the plants on in the same type of compost. Alpines don't need a lot of fertiliser, so little feeding is necessary.

COVERING ALPINE SEEDS

1 Cover the seeds when sown with a layer of clean, fine grit.

2 The grit will allow water to drain away from the crown of the young plant, which is prone to rot in the wet.

BULBS

CHECK BULBS, CORMS AND TUBERS IN STORE for signs of disease. Diseases such as botrytis and rotting can quickly spread through bulbs and tubers kept in store through the winter. If any diseases do start to show, remove the affected bulb or tuber – or if only part of it is affected, cut out the diseased portion and dust the cut surface with flowers of sulphur. This should prevent the disease spreading further.

HIPPEASTRUM BULBS make popular Christmas gifts. If you want to pot one up as a present, or if you are given one yourself, simply set them so that the nose of the bulb is just at the surface of the compost, in a pot large enough to take the bulb comfortably. Place them somewhere cool and light to grow, or you can force them a little (see November) for faster results.

BRING BULBS BEING FORCED FOR CHRISTMAS INTO LIGHT AND WARMTH. Bulbs like prepared hyacinths and daffodils which were plunged outside in the autumn, and then brought into cool conditions a few weeks ago, can be brought into the warmth to encourage them into flower in time for the Christmas festivities. Hyacinths are a particular favourite as they fill the room with their scent.

BULBS THAT HAVE BEEN PLUNGED for forcing into flower in spring should also be inspected regularly. Check to see if they need watering. Don't overwater, especially if the bulbs are growing in bulb bowls that have no drainage holes, or rot will set in.

When the bulbs have made about 2.5–5cm (1–2in) of growth they should

Pot up hippeastrums Set these large bulbs in a pot just large enough to hold them comfortably.

be taken indoors to a cool greenhouse or conservatory, or placed on the windowsill of a cool room. A few weeks later the bulbs can be moved to a warmer room to flower and fill the room with winter cheer. Too much warmth too early causes them to grow thin and straggly, and they don't then produce the best flowers. Turn them regularly to make sure they grow up straight. Tall narcissi often benefit from some support; a few twiggy sticks, especially bare stems of twisted hazel or willow, look attractive.

CONTINUE TO POT UP LILIES for a succession of blooms. Put four or five bulbs into an 18cm (7in) pot containing coir compost, covering the bulbs with about 10cm (4in) of compost. Water them in and wait for the stunning flowers in spring.

ANNUALS & BEDDING

GET SEED CATALOGUES and plan border designs and colour schemes for next year. Even on a cold winter's day, you can dream of the summer to come. The earlier you can order seeds, the less likely it is that they will be late in arriving. Seed companies get very busy in the spring, when they get a rush of orders, because people leave it to the last moment to think about seeds. You'll also have more chance of getting the varieties you want if you order early. It's always exciting to try a few new varieties each year.

SOW PELARGONIUM SEEDS THIS MONTH. It may seem early to be starting seeds into growth, but these bedding plants do need a relatively long growing period to flower the first year after sowing. The ideal way to start off the seeds is in a propagator. This cuts down the on the cost of having to heat a whole greenhouse. Place the propagator on the windowsill to get the maximum amount of light during the short days of winter. A temperature of 18°C (65°F) is needed for the seeds to germinate successfully. The seeds can be sown in small pots of peat-free compost, watering the compost before sowing. Lightly cover them with sieved compost or vermiculite and place in the propagator. Pot up the seedlings into larger pots when they are large enough to handle. If you haven't got the room to germinate your own seeds, then you can order seedlings or young plants ("plug plants") from seedsmen for delivery in spring, so reducing the expense and time needed to grow the plants at home. But do send off for them quickly as they are very popular, and are usually sold out fast.

CONTAINERS

Clear out debris *Don't leave fallen leaves trapped around the stems of container plants.*

PERMANENT PLANTS IN CONTAINERS should be checked over regularly and any debris cleared out. Fallen leaves can get in around the base of plants in containers, encouraging disease and also giving pests somewhere to hibernate, as well as making the plants look untidy.

MOVE POTS OF BORDERLINE HARDY PLANTS inside if this was not done earlier. It is rare, in fact, that we get very severe weather in December, but there can often be quite sharp frosts this month. Move plants into an unheated or cool greenhouse or conservatory. Very little heat is required, otherwise the plants will tend to put on growth which will be straggly due to the lack of light. Water the plants carefully, giving them just enough to keep them alive. Don't overdo it as the plants may be killed off. Whenever possible ensure there is plenty of air circulating around the plants. Open the ventilators on reasonably mild days. Damp, still air encourages diseases such as botrytis to set in.

PONDS

INSTALL A POND HEATER to prevent the whole surface of the pond freezing in cold weather. They are easy to install, plugging in to where the pump was, and cheap to run. It is important not to let the pond freeze over for long periods particularly if you have fish. If the pond stays frozen over, the pond and fish will be starved of oxygen. If you haven't got a pond heater and the pond freezes, over put a pan of hot water on the ice and this will melt a hole. A small ball can be floated on the surface of the water to keep an area clear, and also to absorb the pressure of the ice so that it does not damage the sides of the pond (see also January).

LAWNS

KEEP OFF THE LAWN if it is frosted or very wet. If you walk on the lawn when it is frozen, then when it thaws yellow patches will appear where you have been treading, and the grass will have been damaged. If you have to go on the lawn for any reason when it is frozen or sodden, put down some planks to walk on.

REPAIR LAWNS WITH TURVES (see right). Any worn areas of the lawn can be returfed now, working from boards to disperse your weight if the ground is very wet. Leave the turf a little higher than the surrounding lawn to allow it to settle. If you can't get hold of a small quantity of turf, or at least one that in any way resembles your own, the trick is to swap the damaged part with a sound patch taken from somewhere where the damaged one will be less noticeable – just as one can covertly move stained carpet tiles around.

Damaged patches on the edges of neat lawns should always be repaired by returfing, not sowing, to give the required clean, firm edge, and here as well, turves can be swapped around. See March for illustrations.

RAKE UP ANY FALLEN LEAVES left lying on the lawn. If they are left the grass will die off due to lack of light, and diseases may set in due to a lack of air circulation. If a lawn has been neglected under a layer of leaves for any length of time, spiking the lawn after clearing the leaves will help to improve aeration again, especially to the roots.

NEW LAWNS

IF WEATHER CONDITIONS ALLOW – that is, the soil is not sodden or frozen – you may continue to prepare ground and lay turf.

REPAIRING A DAMAGED PATCH

❶ Cut cleanly around the damaged patch and undercut it with a spade so that you can lift it away cleanly. Fork over the soil lightly to fluff it up, and then rake it even and water well.

❷ Try and use a new turf that is slightly larger than the hole, so that you really have to shoehorn it in with an edging tool. This way the joins disappear quickly. Water regularly.

VEGETABLES & HERBS

COVER BARE BEDS with polythene to protect the soil from winter rain. This will allow you to dig in the new year without being held up by bad weather.

MAKE A HOTBED FROM FRESH HORSE MANURE. This is a Victorian idea, but still perfectly valid today. It makes good use of horse manure piled up to rot down. There is a lot of heat given off by manure as it breaks down, and this can be harnessed to produce some early crops. Fresh horse manure is not as difficult to obtain as most people think. There are many riding stables in towns or on the edges of cities and towns these days and all too often they are glad to be rid of it. Some places may ask a modest price, but it is well worth it. You will almost certainly have to transport it home yourself, unless you live close to the stables.

A hotbed can be made as a free-standing heap, but the heat will be retained better in a container – a wooden compost bin is ideal. Pile it in until it is mounded slightly above the topmost timbers. Then cap the manure with a soil mix of 7 parts loam, 3 parts spent mushroom compost and two parts coarse grit. Mix it well and spread a good layer on top of the heap.

Put a cold frame on top and leave for about a week to allow the temperature to build up. It is surprising just how hot it gets – stick a cane into the heap and then pull it out after a few days, and you'll see just how much heat is being generated. In two or three weeks when it has cooled a little, you can sow lettuces, carrots, radishes and turnips and spinach for early crops. Once these crops have finished, you can grow trailing tomatoes, cucumbers or even

melons on the heap. At the end of the season you will left with a fine pile of well-rotted manure to dig into the soil.

HARVESTING

KEEP HARVESTING WINTER CROPS. Sprouts and parsnips (see November) are essentials for those festive meals.

LIFT CELERY as required. If severe weather is forecast, it is worth lifting some and heeling it in in a sheltered part of the garden – by the back door is ideal, as it will then stay fresh and be handy for the kitchen. Plants left in the ground can be protected from severe frost by covering the tops with a thick layer of straw or bracken, held in place with chicken wire and wire hoops pushed into the ground.

LOOKING AFTER CROPS

EARTH UP SPRING CABBAGES and other winter brassicas to give them better anchorage in strong winds. Tall-growing Brussels sprouts are particularly prone to being blown over. It may also

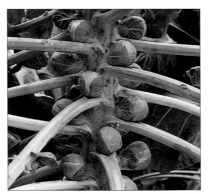

Brussels sprouts *Always harvest sprouts from the base of the stem upwards.*

be necessary to put in canes and tie the plants to them. Remove yellowing leaves regularly, as these encourage fungal diseases. Spring cabbages are normally planted in the autumn at a distance of about 15cm (6in) apart. During the winter, cut every other one as winter greens, leaving the others to grow on and heart up in the spring.

SOWING INDOORS

SOW SOME EARLY CROPS. If you have space, you could sow a few pots or module trays of lettuce, summer cabbages and cauliflowers, radishes, round varieties of carrots, spinach, salad onions and turnips. These seeds don't require high temperatures to germinate; about 13°C (55°F) is adequate, so a windowsill is fine if you don't have a propagator. If you sow in pots or seed trays you will need to prick the seedlings out, spacing them about 2.5cm (1in) apart into another tray. Grow the young plants on in good light, watering regularly. They will be ready to put out under cloches or horticultural fleece in February for the very earliest crops.

BEAT THE SEASONS

FORCE CHICORY AND SEAKALE (see October).

HERBS

BAY TREES GROWN IN POTS should be taken indoors if cold weather is forecast, or moved to the most sheltered part of the garden.

FORCE MINT FOR WINTER SPRIGS (see January).

FRUIT

PICKING AND STORING

KEEP INSPECTING STORED FRUIT for signs of rotting. Any that are showing signs of rot should be thrown out onto the lawn or vegetable garden for the birds to feed on. It will be a welcome treat for them in harsh weather.

LOOKING AFTER CROPS

CHECK APPLE AND PEAR TREES FOR SIGNS OF CANKER. See January's fruit section.

CHECK TREE STAKES AND TIES ARE SOUND. Tree ties can easily break after a few years, so it is as well to check them regularly. Also bear in mind that as a tree grows the stem expands, making the tree tie tighter around the trunk. So on your regular inspection tours check that ties are not too tight or they will strangle your trees.

SPRAY FRUIT TREES AND BUSHES WITH A WINTER WASH. Many pest and disease problems can be reduced if fruit is given an annual tar oil winter wash, which destroys overwintering eggs of many pests. It has to be done when the plants are completely dormant, as the spray will harm any green foliage it comes into contact with. If the trees are growing in grass or there are other plants under the trees, it is worth covering them with a sheet of polythene, otherwise they will be harmed by the spray. Be sure to spray thoroughly, getting into all the little cracks and crevices on the tree. These are the places where the pests love to hibernate. The product you need is readily available from garden centres.

Follow the instructions with care, and be sure to wear gloves and old or protective clothing. Spray on a still day to minimise drift.

PRUNING AND TRAINING

WINTER-PRUNE APPLE AND PEAR TREES (see November).

FINISH PRUNING currants and gooseberries through the winter (see November).

PRUNE GRAPE VINES (SEE BELOW). Vines must only be pruned when dormant as they will "bleed" sap copiously if cut when in growth, which weakens the plant. All the laterals (side shoots made in one season) should be pruned back to two or three buds, leaving you with long, stumpy main stems, which you can also cut back in length if overgrown. You may feel that you are being a bit ruthless pruning so hard, but vines produce a lot of extremely vigorous growth and if this is not kept in check you'll end up in an awful mess. The new shoots that grow from the stumpy stems will grow long and bear fruit all in one season next year. You can make some of the prunings into cuttings (see November).

PLANTING

PLANT FRUIT TREES AND BUSHES (see November) whenever the soil is not frozen or too wet.

PROPAGATION

TAKE HARDWOOD CUTTINGS OF redcurrants, whitecurrants, blackcurrants and gooseberries (see October). All are taken in exactly the same way.

Pruning vines *First cut all of the fruited shoots back to two or three buds from the main stem.*

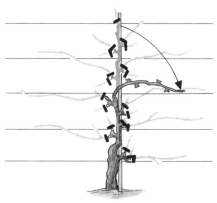

Completing grape vine pruning
Untie all of the fruited shoots, once pruned, and remove them. Cut all small, unfruited shoots back to one or two buds. Finally, untie the top portion of the main stem and retie it horizontally along a wire. This encourages more fruiting sideshoots to form. In spring, it can be retied upright.

UNDER COVER

TIDY PLANTS IN THE GREENHOUSE AND CONSERVATORY regularly, removing yellowing and fallen leaves and fading flowers. The warm, moist atmosphere and short days are perfect breeding conditions for moulds and other fungal diseases. Any dead plant material left lying around will encourage them.

CHECK GREENHOUSE HEATERS are working efficiently. If not, take them to a service agent or call in an electrician.

WATER ALL PLANTS CAREFULLY as their growth is reduced to a minimum, unless they are flowering plants like cyclamen and indoor azaleas. Do all watering in the early part of the day if at all possible. This will give the greenhouse or conservatory time to dry out before nightfall. Cooler damp conditions overnight are the perfect breeding ground for diseases such as botrytis (grey mould). Try to ventilate for an hour or two on mild days to keep air circulating, for exactly the same reason.

RAISING PLANTS FOR OUTDOORS

SOW PELARGONIUM SEEDS. See Annuals & Bedding.

GLASSHOUSE AND HOUSE PLANTS

KEEP HOUSEPLANTS IN GOOD LIGHT. During the short days of winter plants need all the light they can get, especially houseplants that get light from only one side. Keep them at as bright a window as you can and turn them every few days so they don't grow to one side as they stretch for the light. If you can move them to a heated conservatory or greenhouse for the midwinter period, so much the better. Clean the leaves of large foliage plants like rubber plants, as dust gathers on these regularly, reducing the amount of light getting to the leaf surfaces.

POT PLANTS MAKE POPULAR PRESENTS, but often they don't last for very long. Some of them are quite expensive and with a few points borne in mind they will last a long time. They all need slightly differing conditions to get the best out of them.

The ever popular winter-flowering *Cyclamen persicum* needs a cool room and good light. When watering, try not to splash the corm and the foliage with water. It is best watered from below, standing the pot in a shallow saucer for a while.

Poinsettias with their spectacular red, pink or white bracts are actually a type of euphorbia native to warm countries, where they make tall trees. They therefore need quite warm rooms and should be kept moist, but they dislike being waterlogged, so be careful when watering them.

Azaleas are pretty flowers which last a long time. They do need cool conditions and should never be allowed to dry out – not even slightly. Keep them well watered all the time. Give them good light and a cool place and they will flower for weeks.

CROPS UNDER GLASS

PRUNE GRAPE VINES UNDER GLASS. See November, and also Fruit this month.

MAKE A COLD FRAME

A COLD FRAME ACTS AS A SORT OF HALFWAY-HOUSE between the warmer climate in a greenhouse or conservatory and the great outdoors. It is most useful for hardening off bedding before planting out in early summer, and for germinating seed, rooting cuttings and overwintering plants that need a little protection.

YOU WILL NEED: 12 lengths of 100mm tongue-and-groove floorboard: six 120mm long (3 for the front; 3 for the back), and six 600mm long (3 for each side) • 4 lengths of roofing lath: two 300mm long for the back support, and two 250mm long for the front supports • A piece of clear rigid plastic 1200mm × 630mm • For the lid's frame, 4 lengths of 40mm x 20mm planed timber, two 1200mm long and two 550mm long • 4 angle brackets, 20mm wide • 2 hinges • 1 clasp • Screws and nails • 10 rubber washers • Wood glue

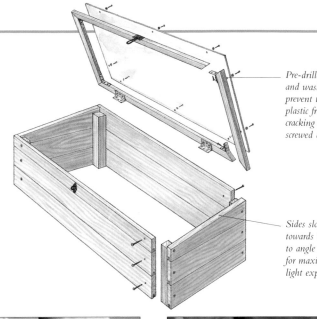

Pre-drilled holes and washers prevent the rigid plastic from cracking when screwed down

Sides slope down towards the front to angle the lid for maximum light exposure

MAKING THE BOX

① Mark the top board of each side to form a slope from back to front. Run the diagonal from the top right-hand corner to the half-way point on the left-hand end.

② Plane off the tongue from the top back board. Cut the top front board in half lengthwise, so that it is 50mm wide.

③ Put wood glue in all the grooves of the boards.

④ Fiit the boards together (see diagram above) to make the four side panels of the box.

⑤ Screw the support battens for the back to the inside rear of each of the side panels, then screw the shorter uprights to the inside front of each of the side panels.

⑥ You will need someone to hold the front and back panels upright and steady as you offer up the first side panel that will join them. Affix by screwing through the back and front sections into the support battens on the side (see diagram). Repeat to complete the box shape.

⑦ Paint the box with a non-toxic wood preservative. Allow to dry.

MAKING THE LID

8 Join the four lengths of planed timber together to make the frame for the lid, using the four angle brackets. Paint the frame and leave to dry.

13 You can pack a lot into a small cold frame.

9 Place the sheet of clear plastic over the frame and pre-drill screw holes to prevent the plastic from splitting.

10 Screw the plastic to the lid using the washers.

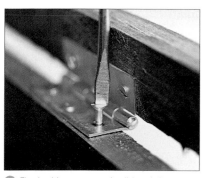

11 Fix the hinges on to the lid and then secure them to the frame base at the back.

12 Fix the clasp to the front of the box.

14 The complete cold frame in use in early summer, filled to bursting with bedding.

A-Z PLANT DIRECTORY

A-Z PLANT

DIRECTORY

This directory gives siting and growing information for all of the "Star Plants" featured month by month throughout the book, arranged here in A–Z order for ease of reference. We also recommend other good species and cultivars, and suggest "Perfect Partners" to look out for, to help you plan planting schemes and groupings.

H = Height; remember that trees and shrubs may take many years to reach the height given.

S = Spread: to obtain planting distances between two different plants, add the spreads together and divide by 2.

♔ = The plant holds the RHS Award of Garden Merit, given to plants that perform reliably well, are generally not difficult to grow, and should be widely available.

A

Abelia '**Edward Goucher**' ♔

Abutilon '**Souvenir de Bonn**' ♔

ABELIA

A moderately vigorous, semi-evergreen shrub with arching branches.
H 1.5m (5ft), S 2.5m (8ft).

SEASONAL HIGHLIGHTS
Bears a mass of trumpet-shaped, lilac-pink flowers from summer to autumn.

VALUE AT OTHER TIMES
The glossy, dark green leaves are bronzed when young.

IDEAL SITE
Excellent in a shrub border.

CULTIVATION
Best in fertile, well-drained soil in full sun, but tolerates light, dappled shade. Protect from cold winds. Prune after flowering. Deadhead and shorten to a strong bud any shoots that spoil the outline.

ALSO RECOMMENDED
Abelia × *grandiflora* ♔

PERFECT PARTNERS
Abelia triflora, taller with fragrant white flowers; *Jasminum humile*, evergreen shrub with yellow flowers from spring to autumn.

ABUTILON, INDIAN MALLOW

Evergreen shrub or small tree.
H 3m (10ft), S 2-3m (6-10ft)

SEASONAL HIGHLIGHTS
From spring to autumn, it has hanging, bowl-shaped orange flowers with darker veins.

VALUE AT OTHER TIMES
Pale green leaves with creamy white margins all year.

IDEAL SITE
A sunny border, warm wall, or conservatory.

CULTIVATION
Under glass, grow in loam-based compost (e.g. John Innes No. 2). Grow in fertile, well-drained soil outdoors. It is best in a sheltered spot in full sun, but will tolerate dappled shade. Bring indoors for the winter in cold areas, as it will not tolerate frost.

ALSO RECOMMENDED
Abutilon megapotamicum ♔ with plain green leaves and yellow and red flowers.

PERFECT PARTNERS
All kinds of summer bedding.

ACER PALMATUM

'Bloodgood' ♔
H & S 5m (15ft)

'Chitoseyama' ♔
H 2m (6ft), S 3m (10ft)

'Corallinum'
H 2m (6ft), S 3m (10ft)

'Garnet' ♔
H 2m (6ft), S 3m (10ft)

'Sango-kaku' ♔
H 2m (6ft), S 3m (10ft)

'Linearilobum' ♔
H 2m (6ft), S 3m (10ft)

JAPANESE MAPLES

Acer palmatum cultivars are deciduous, mostly mound-forming shrubs or small trees with lobed or finely cut leaves.

SEASONAL HIGHLIGHTS
All are valued for their habit and vibrant autumn colours.

VALUE AT OTHER TIMES
Most have small, beautifully tinted spring flowers and winged fruits in autumn.

IDEAL SITE
A sheltered shrub border, or in decorative containers.

CULTIVATION
Grow in full sun, or dappled shade, in leafy, moist but well-drained soil. Mulch annually in autumn. Shelter from cold winds and spring frosts, which may damage new growth.

RECOMMENDED CULTIVARS
'Bloodgood' has red-purple leaves that turn scarlet in autumn; 'Chitoseyama' has crimson-green leaves with red-purple autumn colour; 'Corallinum' has red-pink young leaves that are green in summer, then red, orange and yellow in autumn; 'Garnet' has finely cut, red-purple leaves; 'Sango-kaku' has coral-red shoots and orange-yellow young leaves that turn yellow in autumn; 'Linearilobum' has deeply cut leaves that turn yellow in autumn.

PERFECT PARTNERS
Conifers and heathers.

Acer pensylvanicum
'Erythrocladum' ♔

MOOSEWOOD, STRIPED MAPLE

A deciduous tree with an upright habit of growth.
H 12m (40ft), S 10m (30ft).

SEASONAL HIGHLIGHTS
The bark on young shoots is a striking, brilliant coral-pink in winter, fading to orange-red with greyish-white stripes at maturity.

VALUE AT OTHER TIMES
In spring, clusters of yellow-green flowers hang beneath fresh green leaves, which turn yellow in autumn.

IDEAL SITE
Use as a specimen, or grow in a woodland garden.

CULTIVATION
Thrives in any fertile, well-drained soil in sun or dappled shade. Provide shelter from cold winds and late frosts.

ALSO RECOMMENDED
Acer platanoides 'Crimson King' ♔ has leaves of the deepest red-purple.

PERFECT PARTNERS
Conifers and heathers.

Achillea **'Fanal'**

ACHILLEA, YARROW

A moderately vigorous, clump-forming, herbaceous perennial with fragrant leaves.
H 75cm (30in), S 60cm (24in).

SEASONAL HIGHLIGHTS
Throughout summer, it bears flat heads of bright red flowers with yellow centres.

VALUE AT OTHER TIMES
The flowers fade with age, but can be dried for winter flower arrangements.

IDEAL SITE
A sunny mixed or herbaceous border.

CULTIVATION
It prefers an open site in sun, but tolerates light, dappled shade. Grow in moist, but well-drained soil. Lift and divide every three or four years to maintain vigour.

ALSO RECOMMENDED
A. millefolium 'Cerise Queen' has heads of magenta-pink flowers with white centres.

PERFECT PARTNERS
Phlox, hemerocallis.

A

Aconitum 'Bressingham Spire' ♀

Agapanthus 'Blue Giant'

Alcea rosea Chater's Double Group

Alchemilla mollis ♀

A. hollandicum ♀
(*syn. A. aflatunense*)

MONKSHOOD, ACONITE

A clump-forming, herbaceous perennial of upright growth. All parts are toxic if ingested.
H to 1m (3ft), S 30cm (1ft)

SEASONAL HIGHLIGHTS
Bears tall, tapered spires of deep violet-blue flowers from midsummer to autumn.

VALUE AT OTHER TIMES
It has pretty, glossy, dark green foliage from spring to autumn.

IDEAL SITE
A mixed or herbaceous border.

CULTIVATION
Best grown in partial shade, but tolerates full sun. Grow in moist, fertile soil enriched with organic matter. Divide the plants every three or four years in spring or autumn.

ALSO RECOMMENDED
Aconitum carmichaelii 'Arendsii' has branched spires of clear blue flowers in autumn.

PERFECT PARTNERS
Aconitum 'Ivorine', with ivory white flowers in late spring and early summer.

AGAPANTHUS, AFRICAN BLUE LILY

A clump-forming herbaceous perennial of upright habit.
H 1.2m (4ft), S 60cm (2ft)

SEASONAL HIGHLIGHTS
Has rounded clusters of bell-shaped, rich blue flowers from mid- to late summer.

VALUE AT OTHER TIMES
Large, strap-shaped, deep green leaves.

IDEAL SITE
A sunny border, or a tall, shapely container.

CULTIVATION
Best in sun, but will tolerate light, dappled shade. Grow in moist but well-drained soil. In cold areas, mulch in winter to protect fleshy roots from frost.

ALSO RECOMMENDED
Agapanthus campanulatus has pale to dark blue, occasionally white flowers, from mid- to late summer.

PERFECT PARTNERS
The strap-shaped foliage contrasts well with the bold, rounded leaves of hostas.

HOLLYHOCK

A short-lived perennial of vigorous, upright growth.
H to 2.5m (8ft), S 60cm (2ft)

SEASONAL HIGHLIGHTS
In summer, it bears peony-like flowers, ranging from white, yellow, apricot and red to lavender and purple. They attract butterflies and bees.

VALUE AT OTHER TIMES
Attractive leaves for most of the year.

IDEAL SITE
The back of a sunny border, especially in cottage gardens.

CULTIVATION
Flowers best in sun, but tolerates dappled shade. Grow in any fertile, well-drained soil. Stake in exposed sites. Treat as annuals or biennials to limit hollyhock rust.

ALSO RECOMMENDED
Alcea rosea 'Nigra', with single, chocolate-maroon flowers.

PERFECT PARTNERS
Other tall herbaceous plants like delphiniums.

ALCHEMILLA, LADY'S MANTLE

A vigorous, clump-forming, herbaceous perennial.
H 60cm (24in), S 75cm (30in)

SEASONAL HIGHLIGHTS
Bears loose clusters of tiny greenish-yellow flowers from early summer to autumn.

VALUE AT OTHER TIMES
The hairy, soft green leaves look especially good spangled with droplets of rain or dew.

IDEAL SITE
The front of an herbaceous border, or in paving crevices.

CULTIVATION
Thrives in sun or partial shade. Grow in any moist, humus rich soil. Deadhead after flowering, or it will seed itself all over the garden.

ALSO RECOMMENDED
A. alpina is similar but lower-growing and mat-forming.

PERFECT PARTNERS
It associates well with most other herbaceous perennials but looks especially good with penstemons.

ALLIUM, ORNAMENTAL ONION

A moderately vigorous, bulbous perennial.
H 1m (3ft), S 10cm (4in).

SEASONAL HIGHLIGHTS
In summer, it produces dense, rounded heads of many star-shaped, purplish-pink flowers.

VALUE AT OTHER TIMES
The attractive seedheads of autumn can be dried for flower arrangements.

IDEAL SITE
The perfect highlight in a sunny mixed border.

CULTIVATION
Ideally grow in full sun, but will tolerate light shade. Grow in any fertile, well-drained soil. Plant bulbs 5–10cm (2–4in) deep in autumn.

ALSO RECOMMENDED
A. caeruleum has intense, bright blue flowers.

PERFECT PARTNERS
Excellent with hemerocallis and achilleas, providing good contrasts of form and colour.

Alopecurus pratensis 'Aureovariegatus'

Alstroemeria 'Orange Glory' ♀

Amaranthus caudatus

Amelanchier lamarckii ♀ *in spring and autumn*

FOXTAIL GRASS

A spreading perennial grass.
H 1.2m (4ft), S 40cm (16in),
often more, but not invasive.

SEASONAL HIGHLIGHTS
It produces dense, cylindrical
heads of pale green to purple
flowers from mid-spring to
midsummer.

VALUE AT OTHER TIMES
Has narrow green leaves that
are striped rich yellow and
arranged in basal tufts.

IDEAL SITE
A sunny mixed border or
wild garden.

CULTIVATION
Best in full sun, but it will
tolerate light shade. Grow in
fertile, well-drained soil. Cut
back to ground level in spring
for the freshest coloured
foliage in summer.

ALSO RECOMMENDED
A. lanatus has silver-grey leaves.

PERFECT PARTNERS
Hakonechloa macra 'Aureola' ♀
and *Carex elata* 'Aurea' ♀ for
contrasting golden foliage.

ALSTROEMERIA, PERUVIAN LILY

An upright, moderately
vigorous, herbaceous perennial.
H 1m (3ft), S 60cm (2ft)

SEASONAL HIGHLIGHTS
For many weeks in summer,
it bears showy, orange-yellow
flowers with darker speckles.
They are excellent for cutting.

VALUE AT OTHER TIMES
It has grey-green foliage.

IDEAL SITE
A mixed border, or one
devoted to flowers for cutting.

CULTIVATION
Ideally, grow in full sun; it
tolerates light shade. Plant
carefully in late summer or
early autumn in any moist
but well-drained soil; the
fleshy roots are fragile and
resent disturbance. In cold
areas, apply a dry winter mulch.

ALSO RECOMMENDED
A. hookeri, pale pink flowers;
A. 'Parigo Charm' in salmon.

PERFECT PARTNERS
Roses, sunflowers and tall
border phlox.

LOVE-LIES-BLEEDING, TASSEL FLOWER

A vigorous, bushy, upright
perennial, usually grown as a
frost-tender annual.
H 1–1.5m (3–5ft),
S 45–75cm (18–30in).

SEASONAL HIGHLIGHTS
From summer to autumn, it
produces long, hanging tassels
of crimson-purple flowers.

VALUE AT OTHER TIMES
Lush leaves with red or
purple stems. Flowers are
good for dried arrangements.

IDEAL SITE
An annual or cutting border.

CULTIVATION
Grow in full sun in humus-
rich soil in a sheltered spot. It
tolerates poor soils. Sow seeds
under glass in early spring
and plant out when the threat
of frost has passed.

ALSO RECOMMENDED
A caudatus 'Viridis' has green
flowers that fade to cream.

PERFECT PARTNERS
Grow amidst annual bedding
as a dot plant.

AMELANCHIER, SNOWY MESPILUS, JUNEBERRY

A moderately vigorous,
deciduous shrub or small tree,
with upright, branching stems.
H 10m (30ft), S 12m (40ft)

SEASONAL HIGHLIGHTS
In mid-spring, a profusion of
star-shaped white flowers are
borne in hanging clusters all
along the branches.

VALUE AT OTHER TIMES
The young leaves are bronzed
as they unfold, turning to
green in summer and then to
blazing shades of orange and
red in the autumn.

IDEAL SITE
Use in a sunny shrub border,
in an open glade in a
woodland garden, or as a
specimen plant.

CULTIVATION
It will tolerate light, dappled
shade, but autumn colour and
flowering are best in full sun.
Grow in lime-free (acid) soil
that is moist but well-drained
and enriched with plenty of

organic matter. It generally
needs pruning only to
shorten wayward branches,
but it tolerates hard pruning
and old, neglected specimens
can be rejuvenated by cutting
out overcrowded and
intertwined stems.

ALSO RECOMMENDED
A. × *grandiflora* 'Ballerina' ♀ is
smaller, but similar, and has
arching clusters of white
flowers in mid-spring.

PERFECT PARTNERS
To extend the period of
interest through midsummer,
combine with a late, large-
flowered clematis, such as
'Ville de Lyon', with bright
carmine-red flowers, or
'Rouge Cardinal' with velvety
crimson flowers. Any
moderately vigorous clematis
that is pruned back to strong
buds at the base in early
spring is ideal for twining
through supporting shrubs.

A

Anemone blanda 'Violet Star'

Anemone x *hybrida* 'Max Vogel'

Antirrhinum majus 'Trumpet Serenade'

Aquilegia vulgaris 'Nora Barlow' ♀

Arctotis x *hybrida* 'Red Devil'

ANEMONE, MOUNTAIN WINDFLOWER

A moderately vigorous, spreading, tuberous perennial. H & S to 15cm (6in).

SEASONAL HIGHLIGHTS
In spring, it produces clear amethyst flowers with a white reverse to the petals.

VALUE AT OTHER TIMES
The dark green leaves are pretty but fade away during summer dormancy.

IDEAL SITE
Excellent when naturalized in turf or woodland and good at the front of a border.

CULTIVATION
Plant tubers 5–8cm (2–3in) deep in autumn, in humus-rich, well-drained soil, in sun or dappled shade.

ALSO RECOMMENDED
A. blanda 'White Splendour' ♀ has large, white flowers that are pink on the reverse.

PERFECT PARTNERS
Create a spring tapestry of bloom with dwarf narcissus and crocus.

JAPANESE ANEMONE

A vigorous, spreading, herbaceous perennial of upright growth.
H 1.2–1.5m (4–5ft), S indefinite.

SEASONAL HIGHLIGHTS
From late summer until late autumn, it bears single, light pink flowers that become paler as the flower ages.

VALUE AT OTHER TIMES
The lobed, dark green leaves make good ground cover.

IDEAL SITE
A mixed or herbaceous border, or woodland garden.

CULTIVATION
Prefers a moist, humus-rich soil and thrives in sun or dappled shade. It is invasive, but easily controlled by digging out unwanted pieces.

ALSO RECOMMENDED
A. × *hybrida* 'Honorine Jobert' ♀ has white flowers.

PERFECT PARTNERS
Use with roses and other perennials. It looks good in an open woodland glade.

SNAPDRAGON

A bushy, upright, moderately vigorous perennial that is grown as an annual.
H & S 30cm (12in).

SEASONAL HIGHLIGHTS
From summer to autumn, it bears spikes of open trumpet-shaped, bicoloured flowers in a mixture of pastel shades.

VALUE AT OTHER TIMES
Has attractive, lance-shaped semi-glossy leaves.

IDEAL SITE
Good for bedding, containers and for childrens' plots.

CULTIVATION
Best in full sun, but it tolerates light shade and thrives in any fertile soil. Sow seeds in late winter under glass. Set out when risk of frost has passed.

ALSO RECOMMENDED
A. majus 'Jamaican Mist' is early and long-flowering in a range of pastel colours.

PERFECT PARTNERS
Snapdragons associate well with a wide range of annual bedding plants.

AQUILEGIA, GRANNY'S BONNET, COLUMBINE

A robust, upright, moderately vigorous perennial.
H 90cm (36in), S 45cm (18in).

SEASONAL HIGHLIGHTS
From late spring to early summer, it bears pompon-like flowers with narrow, spurless petals in pale green and red.

VALUE AT OTHER TIMES
Has pretty, dark greyish green foliage in spring and summer.

IDEAL SITE
A sunny border, especially in a cottage garden.

CULTIVATION
Grow in full sun or light shade, in any fertile, moisture-retentive soil. Increase is easy by division in spring, or seed sown in spring or autumn and self-sown seedlings come fairly true to type.

ALSO RECOMMENDED
A. alpina is shorter with clear blue flowers.

PERFECT PARTNERS
Roses, lupins, delphiniums and other perennials.

ARCTOTIS, AFRICAN DAISY

Moderately vigorous, semi-erect perennial that is grown as a half-hardy annual.
H 45–50cm (18–20in), S 30cm (12in)

SEASONAL HIGHLIGHTS
Throughout summer, it bears dark-centred, red flowerheads.

VALUE AT OTHER TIMES
Felted, silvery green leaves are good for foliage contrasts.

IDEAL SITE
Sunny banks and borders, gravel gardens and containers.

CULTIVATION
Grow in sun, in well-drained soil. Will tolerate light, part-day shade. Sow seed under glass in early spring and set young plants out when risk of frost has passed.

ALSO RECOMMENDED
A. × *hybrida* 'African Sunshine' has orange-yellow flowerheads.

PERFECT PARTNERS
Gazanias and other sun-loving, annual bedding plants.

Argyranthemum foeniculaceum

Artemisia alba 'Canescens' ⚆

Arundo donax var. *versicolor*

Aster novi-belgii 'Peace'

Astilbe 'Bronce Elegans' ⚆

ARGYRANTHEMUM, MARGUERITE

A compact, fairly vigorous subshrub, evergreen but frost-tender.
H & S to 80cm (32in).

SEASONAL HIGHLIGHTS
It bears single, white, daisy-like flowerheads with yellow centres, continuously from summer to autumn.

VALUE AT OTHER TIMES
Fine, blue-grey leaves all year.

IDEAL SITE
Sunny borders and containers.

CULTIVATION
Prefers full sun, but tolerates light shade. Grow in well-drained soil. Pinch out stem tips to keep plants bushy and deadhead regularly. In cold areas, overwinter under glass.

ALSO RECOMMENDED
A. frutescens is similar, with less finely cut leaves.

PERFECT PARTNERS
A. 'Jamaica Primrose' ⚆ with primrose yellow flowerheads; *A.* 'Vancouver' with pink, anemone-centred blooms.

ARTEMISIA, WHITE SAGE

A vigorous, bushy, semi-evergreen perennial.
H 45cm (18in), S 30cm (12in)

SEASONAL HIGHLIGHTS
It is grown mainly for its beautiful, aromatic, silver-grey leaves that are very finely cut.

VALUE AT OTHER TIMES
In late summer, it bears yellow-brown flowerheads, but most gardeners prefer to remove them.

IDEAL SITE
A hot, sunny border or gravel garden.

CULTIVATION
Grow in any well-drained soil in sun or light, part-day shade. Dig coarse grit into heavy clay soils to improve drainage.

ALSO RECOMMENDED
A. arborescens has finely dissected, silver-white leaves.

PERFECT PARTNERS
Argyranthemums and bold foliage plants, like irises and yuccas, contrast well with the fine foliage of artemisias.

GIANT REED

A vigorous, half-hardy, perennial grass.
H 1.8m (6ft), S 60cm (24in)

SEASONAL HIGHLIGHTS
The arching, white-striped leaves are attractive all summer.

VALUE AT OTHER TIMES
In late summer, it bears dense heads of creamy spikelets.

IDEAL SITE
At the back of a border, or in containers in a conservatory.

CULTIVATION
Any well-drained soil is suitable and it tolerates light shade, but grows best in sun in reliably moist soil. Protect from cold winds and hard frost. Cut to the base in spring for the best coloured foliage.

ALSO RECOMMENDED
A. donax is taller, hardier and has plain, bluish-green leaves.

PERFECT PARTNERS
Pennisetum villosum, with feathery, pale buff-purple flowerheads; *Stipa gigantea* ⚆, very tall with airy, glistening, golden spikelets.

ASTER, MICHAELMAS DAISY

An upright, moderately vigorous, herbaceous perennial.
H 1.2m (4ft), S 90cm (36in).

SEASONAL HIGHLIGHTS
From late summer to mid-autumn, it bears masses of single, yellow-centred, mauve flowerheads, 7cm (3in) across.

VALUE AT OTHER TIMES
Attractive lance-shaped leaves.

IDEAL SITE
Indispensable in a late summer and autumn border.

CULTIVATION
Grow in sun or light shade. Well-cultivated, moisture-retentive soil, full of organic matter, is best. Divide every three or four years. Cut down the old stems after flowering.

ALSO RECOMMENDED
A. amellus 'Sonia' is shorter with pale pink flowerheads.

PERFECT PARTNERS
Rudbeckias and sedums, which also bring useful late colour to the garden in late summer and autumn.

ASTILBE

A moderately vigorous, clump-forming herbaceous perennial of upright growth.
H 30cm (12in), S 25cm (10in)

SEASONAL HIGHLIGHTS
In late summer, it produces plumes of red-pink flowers.

VALUE AT OTHER TIMES
The red-stemmed, dark green leaves are good ground cover.

IDEAL SITE
A bog garden, waterside plantings, or a shady border.

CULTIVATION
Best grown in boggy soil in sun, but will tolerate slightly drier conditions in partial shade. Cut down old foliage in late autumn. Divide every three to four years.

ALSO RECOMMENDED
A. 'Aphrodite' has sprays of red flowers and bronze leaves.

PERFECT PARTNERS
Hemerocallis, ferns and grasses, such as squirreltail grass (*Hordeum jubatum*) with silky, beige flowerheads.

A

Astrantia major

Aubrieta 'J.S. Baker'

Aucuba japonica 'Variegata'

B

Begonia x *tuberhybrida*

Bellis perennis Tasso Series

ASTRANTIA, MASTERWORT

A moderately vigorous, upright herbaceous perennial. H 30–90cm (12–36in), S 45cm (18in)

SEASONAL HIGHLIGHTS
In early and midsummer, it bears heads of tiny green, pink, or purplish-red flowers surrounded by white bracts.

VALUE AT OTHER TIMES
The flowerheads can be used for dried arrangements.

IDEAL SITE
A mixed or herbaceous border, especially in cottage gardens.

CULTIVATION
Ideally, grow in full sun, but it will tolerate light shade. Plant in a humus-rich soil that doesn't dry out. Cut down dead stems when flowering is over. This plant self-seeds quite prolifically.

ALSO RECOMMENDED
A. major subsp. *involucrata* has green-tipped white bracts.

PERFECT PARTNERS
Astilbes, rudbeckias, asters.

AUBRETIA

A spreading, mat-forming perennial of dense, moderately vigorous growth. H 5cm (2in), S 60cm (24in)

SEASONAL HIGHLIGHTS
In spring, it produces single, white-eyed, purple flowers in profusion.

VALUE AT OTHER TIMES
The greyish-green leaves form dense ground cover.

IDEAL SITE
A rock garden, drystone wall, sunny bank, or border front.

CULTIVATION
Grow in well-drained, preferably neutral to alkaline soil, enriched with organic matter. Cut back hard after flowering to maintain neat, compact plants.

ALSO RECOMMENDED
A. 'Joy' has double mauve flowers.

PERFECT PARTNERS
Aurinia saxatilis, with yellow flowers, and most arabis, which have flowers in white, or shades of pink.

SPOTTED LAUREL

A vigorous, evergreen shrub of dense, bushy growth. H & S to 3m (10ft).

SEASONAL HIGHLIGHTS
Attractively variegated foliage all year round.

VALUE AT OTHER TIMES
Upright clusters of small red flowers appear in mid-spring; on female plants, like this cultivar, they are followed by bright red berries.

IDEAL SITE
Grows almost anywhere, but good in dark, shady corners, in containers, or as hedging.

CULTIVATION
Exceptionally tolerant of a range of difficult sites, from deep, dry shade to coastal cliffs. It grows in any but waterlogged soil. Prune, or trim hedges, in spring. Very tolerant of hard pruning.

ALSO RECOMMENDED
A. japonica 'Crotonifolia' ♥ has yellow-speckled leaves.

PERFECT PARTNERS
Potentillas, rhododendrons.

TUBEROUS BEGONIA

Tuberous, moderately vigorous, frost-tender perennials that die down in winter. H & S 23cm (9in).

SEASONAL HIGHLIGHTS
Throughout summer, they bear showy, mostly double flowers, in vibrant shades of red, pink, white, and yellow. Upright and trailing cultivars are available.

VALUE AT OTHER TIMES
Large, glossy leaves.

IDEAL SITE
Bedding and containers.

CULTIVATION
Best in full sun but tolerant of partial shade. Grow in fertile, moist but well-drained soil. Bring into growth in warmth in early spring. Plant when the threat of frost has passed. Lift in autumn and store dry.

ALSO RECOMMENDED
B. semperflorens cultivars are compact, with masses of small flowers throughout summer.

PERFECT PARTNERS
Petunias and asters.

BELLIS, DOUBLE DAISY

Moderately vigorous, rosette-forming perennial, usually grown as a biennial. H & S 5–20cm (2–8in).

SEASONAL HIGHLIGHTS
From late winter until late summer, bears double daisy flowers in red, pink or white.

VALUE AT OTHER TIMES
Attractive spoon-shaped, semi-glossy, dark green leaves.

IDEAL SITE
Bedding, border edging and containers.

CULTIVATION
Grow in any fertile, well-drained soil, in sun or light shade. Sow seeds outside in early summer or indoors in early spring. Deadhead to encourage more flowers and prevent self seeding.

ALSO RECOMMENDED
B. perennis 'Pomponette' ♥ has double flowers with quilled petals.

PERFECT PARTNERS
Tulips, wallflowers and forget-me-nots.

Berberis darwinii

Bergenia 'Sunningdale'

Betula papyrifera

Borago officinalis

Buddleja davidii 'Fascinating'

BERBERIS

A vigorous, spiny, evergreen shrub of dense, arching growth.
H & S 1.5m (5ft)

SEASONAL HIGHLIGHTS
In mid to late spring, it bears hanging clusters of deep orange flowers.

VALUE AT OTHER TIMES
Small, blue-black fruits appear in autumn and glossy, spiny, dark green leaves last all year.

IDEAL SITE
Shrub borders and hedging.

CULTIVATION
Easily grown in sun or partial shade, in any fertile, well-drained soil. After flowering, trim hedges, or prune single specimens lightly to shape.

ALSO RECOMMENDED
B. buxifolia is taller with deep orange-yellow flowers.

PERFECT PARTNERS
B. thunbergii 'Rose Glow' ♀, deciduous with red-purple leaves flecked with white; hardy fuchsias, *Elaeagnus*.

BERGENIA, ELEPHANT'S EARS

Clump-forming herbaceous perennial.
H 30–45cm (12–18in),
S 45–60cm (18–24in)

SEASONAL HIGHLIGHTS
Rich lilac-magenta flowers on red stems appear in early and mid-spring.

VALUE AT OTHER TIMES.
Bold, glossy dark green leaves that turn copper-red in winter.

IDEAL SITE
Front of a border, containers, in a woodland garden.

CULTIVATION
Best in sun in well-drained soil enriched with plenty of organic matter, but tolerant of partial shade and poor soils. Lift and divide every three to five years to maintain vigour.

ALSO RECOMMENDED
B. 'Ballawley' ♀ has crimson flowers and bronze-purple winter leaves.

PERFECT PARTNERS
Roses, hostas, fuchsias and other herbaceous perennials.

PAPER BIRCH, CANOE BIRCH

A deciduous, fairly vigorous tree of conical outline.
H 20m (70ft) or more,
S 10m (30ft)

SEASONAL HIGHLIGHTS
The peeling white bark reveals pale orange-brown bark beneath and is beautiful when leafless in winter.

VALUE AT OTHER TIMES
Dark green leaves turn yellow and orange in autumn. Long yellow catkins appear in spring.

IDEAL SITE
A fine specimen, especially in damp soils by streams or pools.

CULTIVATION
Grow in fertile, humus-rich soil in sun or dappled shade. In winter, prune out lowest branches when very small to create a clear trunk.

ALSO RECOMMENDED
B. pendula 'Youngii' ♀ is dome-shaped and weeping.

PERFECT PARTNERS
Rowans (*Sorbus*), willows (*Salix*) and conifers.

BORAGE

A very vigorous, branching annual, used as a culinary herb.
H 60cm (24in), S 45cm (18in)

SEASONAL HIGHLIGHTS
Throughout summer, it bears bright blue, star-shaped flowers.

VALUE AT OTHER TIMES
Mounds of white-bristly, matt green leaves and hairy stems.

IDEAL SITE
Herb gardens, dry, sunny sites.

CULTIVATION
Best in sun, in well-drained soil, but tolerates light shade. On heavy clay soils, dig in plenty of coarse grit to improve the drainage. Self-seeds freely.

ALSO RECOMMENDED
B. pygmaea is mat-forming and bears hanging, clear blue, bell-shaped flowers.

PERFECT PARTNERS
Mints, sage (*Salvia officinalis*), and feverfew (*Tanacetum parthenium*).

BUTTERFLY BUSH

A vigorous, deciduous shrub with arching branches.
H 3m (10ft), S 5m (15ft)

SEASONAL HIGHLIGHTS
From summer to autumn, it bears dense, arching spires of lilac-pink flowers.

VALUE AT OTHER TIMES
Attractive mid-green to grey-green foliage. It is excellent for attracting butterflies.

IDEAL SITE
Shrub or mixed borders and wildlife gardens.

CULTIVATION
It tolerates dappled shade but flowers best, and attracts more butterflies, in full sun. Grow in any fertile, well-drained soil, rich in organic matter. Prune back the previous year's growth to a woody framework in early spring.

ALSO RECOMMENDED
B. davidii 'White Profusion' ♀ has white flowers.

PERFECT PARTNERS
Hypericum, berberis, and tree peonies.

B

C

Buddleja globosa ♔

Caltha palustris ♔

Camassia cusickii 'Zwanenburg'

Camellia × *williamsii* 'Anticipation' ♔

Campanula lactiflora

ORANGE BALL TREE

Vigorous, deciduous or semi-evergreen shrub.
H & S 5m (15ft)

SEASONAL HIGHLIGHTS
In early summer, it bears rounded clusters of fragrant, orange-yellow flowers.

VALUE AT OTHER TIMES
The dark green, deeply veined leaves are handsome.

IDEAL SITE
A shrub or mixed border.

CULTIVATION
Best grown in sun, in any fertile garden soil enriched with organic matter. It will tolerate light shade. Keep pruning to a minimum, but when mature, occasionally remove some of the oldest flowered shoots at the base, after flowering.

ALSO RECOMMENDED
B. × *weyeriana* 'Sungold' ♔ has dark orange-yellow flowers.

PERFECT PARTNERS
Hypericum, berberis and tree peonies.

KINGCUP, MARSH MARIGOLD

A vigorous, creeping, rhizomatous perennial.
H 40cm (16in), S 45cm (18in)

SEASONAL HIGHLIGHTS
In spring, it bears glossy, yellow, cup-shaped flowers, often with a second flush of bloom later in the year.

VALUE AT OTHER TIMES
The heart-shaped leaves are attractive for most of the year.

IDEAL SITE
A bog garden, at the waterside, or in a damp border.

CULTIVATION
Best in full sun but tolerates light shade. Grow in boggy, permanently moist soil at the water's edge, or in planting baskets, in water to 23cm (9in) deep.

ALSO RECOMMENDED
C. palustris 'Flore Pleno' ♔ has double flowers.

PERFECT PARTNERS
Water lilies, *Mimulus luteus*, *M. ringens*.

CAMASSIA

An upright, moderately vigorous, bulbous perennial.
H 60–80cm (24–32in), S 10cm (4in)

SEASONAL HIGHLIGHTS
In late spring, it bears spires of starry, deep blue flowers.

VALUE AT OTHER TIMES
The grass-like leaves are ornamentally insignificant.

IDEAL SITE
An herbaceous border or wildflower meadow.

CULTIVATION
Plant bulbs 10cm (4in) deep in autumn. Flowers best in full sun but tolerates light shade. Grow in deep, fertile, moisture-retentive soil. Mulch in winter in cold, frosty areas.

ALSO RECOMMENDED
C. cusickii has pale to deep steely blue flowers.

PERFECT PARTNERS
Alliums (ornamental onions), cowslips (*Primula veris*).

CAMELLIA

A moderately vigorous, evergreen shrub of narrowly upright growth.
H 4m (12ft), S 2m (6ft)

SEASONAL HIGHLIGHTS
The beautiful, peony-like crimson flowers appear from mid-winter to mid-spring.

VALUE AT OTHER TIMES
The lustrous, dark green foliage is delightful all year.

IDEAL SITE
Shrub borders, woodland gardens and containers.

CULTIVATION
Thrives in sun or dappled shade, but needs shade from early morning sun, which may damage flowers in frosty weather. Grow in humus-rich, lime-free (acid) soil, or in ericaceous compost in pots. Trim lightly to shape after flowering, if necessary.

ALSO RECOMMENDED
C. × *williamsii* 'Donation' ♔ has semi-double, pink flowers.

PERFECT PARTNERS
Rhododendrons and azaleas.

MILKY BELLFLOWER

A moderately vigorous, upright herbaceous perennial.
H 1.2–1.5m (4–5ft), S 60cm (24in)

SEASONAL HIGHLIGHTS
Clusters of bell-shaped flowers from early summer to early autumn are white to pale blue, lilac-blue or violet.

VALUE AT OTHER TIMES
Attractive leaves from early spring to late summer.

IDEAL SITE
A mixed or herbaceous border, or woodland garden.

CULTIVATION
Thrives in sun, but flower colour is better preserved in light shade. Grow in fertile, well-drained, neutral to alkaline soil. It may need staking in exposed gardens.

ALSO RECOMMENDED
C. lactiflora 'Prichard's Variety' ♔ has violet-blue flowers.

PERFECT PARTNERS
Roses, *C. lactiflora* 'Loddon Anna' ♔ with lilac-pink flowers, *C.* 'Elizabeth', cream flowers.

Carex flagellifera

Carex oshimensis 'Evergold' ♀

Carex pendula

Caryopteris x *clandonensis* 'Kew Blue'

Centaurea hypoleuca 'John Coutts'

NEW ZEALAND SEDGE
A moderately vigorous, tuft-forming, arching sedge.
H 1.1m (3½ft), S 90cm (3ft)

SEASONAL HIGHLIGHTS
Grass-like, reddish-brown leaves all year.

VALUE AT OTHER TIMES
Tall stems bear light brown flower spikes in summer.

IDEAL SITE
A mixed border, gravel plantings or containers.

CULTIVATION
Grow in sun or partial shade. in any soil that is not too wet or too dry. In cold areas, protect with a winter mulch.

ALSO RECOMMENDED
C. siderosticha 'Variegata' has pink-flushed, pale green and white striped leaves.

PERFECT PARTNERS
Use *C. oshimensis* 'Evergold' ♀, or *Hakonechloa macra* 'Aureola' ♀ for contrasting shades of green and gold.

GOLDEN SEDGE
A vigorous, evergreen, mound-forming sedge.
H 30cm (12in), S 35cm (14in)

SEASONAL HIGHLIGHTS
The arching, dark green leaves have a central creamy white stripe and remain attractive all year round.

VALUE AT OTHER TIMES
In mid to late spring, tall spikes of brown flowers appear.

IDEAL SITE
A mixed border, gravel plantings or containers.

CULTIVATION
Thrives in sun or partial shade. A fertile, moist but well-drained soil is required.

ALSO RECOMMENDED
C. elata 'Aurea' ♀ has rich yellow leaves.

PERFECT PARTNERS
Polystichum setiferum (soft shield fern) and hostas form good foliage contrasts.

WEEPING SEDGE
A vigorous, clump-forming, evergreen sedge.
H 1.4m (4½ft), S 1.5m (5ft)

SEASONAL HIGHLIGHTS
In late spring and early summer, arching stems bear catkin-like, dark brown flower spikes that are erect at first, then droop with age.

VALUE AT OTHER TIMES
Shiny mid-green leaves that are blue-green beneath.

IDEAL SITE
Poolsides, damp borders and woodland gardens.

CULTIVATION
Grow in sun or partial shade. Plant in moist, fertile soil.

ALSO RECOMMENDED
C. grayi (mace sedge) is shorter; its green flower spikes give rise to spiky seedheads.

PERFECT PARTNERS
Use hostas to form a broad-leaved contrast to the narrow leaves of the sedge.

CARYOPTERIS
A moderately vigorous, arching, deciduous shrub.
H 1m (3ft), S 1.5m (5ft)

SEASONAL HIGHLIGHTS
From late summer to early autumn, it bears spires of deep blue flowers.

VALUE AT OTHER TIMES
The dark grey-green leaves are silvery beneath.

IDEAL SITE
A mixed or shrub border, gravel plantings, hot, dry sites.

CULTIVATION
It flowers best in full sun but tolerates light dappled shade. Prefers light, fertile, well-drained soil. In areas with cold winters and cool summers, plant against a warm, sheltered wall. In early spring, cut back to a permanent woody framework.

ALSO RECOMMENDED
C. × *clandonensis* 'Worcester Gold' has golden foliage and lavender-blue flowers.

PERFECT PARTNERS
Lavatera, fuchsias, potentillas.

KNAPWEED, CORNFLOWER
A vigorous, spreading, clump-forming herbaceous perennial.
H 60cm (24in), S 45cm (18in)

SEASONAL HIGHLIGHTS
In summer, it bears fragrant, deep rose-pink flowers that attract bees and butterflies.

VALUE AT OTHER TIMES
The divided, grey-green leaves are grey-white beneath.

IDEAL SITE
An herbaceous border, especially in a cottage garden.

CULTIVATION
Grow this drought-tolerant plant in full sun in any well-drained soil. Regular dead-heading results in more flowers later in the season. Divide every three to four years to maintain vigour.

ALSO RECOMMENDED
C. dealbata 'Steenbergii' has carmine-pink flowerheads.

PERFECT PARTNERS
C. macrocephala, Lythrum, border phlox and other herbaceous perennials.

C

Chaenomeles speciosa
'Phylis Moore'

Chaenomeles **x** *superba*
'Knap Hill Scarlet' ♀

Chelone obliqua

Chimonanthus praecox

Chionodoxa forbesii **'Pink Giant'**

FLOWERING QUINCE, JAPONICA
A vigorous, deciduous shrub with wide-spreading branches. H 2.5m (8ft), S to 5m (15ft)
SEASONAL HIGHLIGHTS
In spring, before and with the new leaves, it bears large clusters of semi-double, almond-pink flowers.
VALUE AT OTHER TIMES
Aromatic yellow fruits appear in autumn; they can be cooked in jellies or preserves.
IDEAL SITE
Shrub borders, sunny or shaded walls and hedging.
CULTIVATION
Grow in any fertile, well-drained soil in sun or partial shade. After flowering, shorten flowered shoots to strong buds. When mature, take out 1 in 5 of the oldest shoots.
ALSO RECOMMENDED
C. speciosa 'Moerloosei' ♀ has apple-blossom-pink flowers.
PERFECT PARTNERS
Forsythia, pyracantha and *Ribes sanguineum* (flowering currant).

FLOWERING QUINCE, JAPONICA
A vigorous, rounded, spiny-stemmed, deciduous shrub. H 1.5m (5ft), S 2m (6ft)
SEASONAL HIGHLIGHTS
From spring to summer, it bears clusters of large, scarlet flowers with golden anthers.
VALUE AT OTHER TIMES
Later in autumn, it produces golden yellow fruits.
IDEAL SITE
Shrub borders, sunny or shaded walls and hedging.
CULTIVATION
Grow in any fertile, well-drained soil in sun or partial shade. After flowering, shorten flowered shoots to strong buds. When mature, take out 1 in 5 of the oldest shoots.
ALSO RECOMMENDED
C. x *superba* 'Nicoline' ♀ has large, often semi-double, scarlet flowers.
PERFECT PARTNERS
Forsythia, pyracantha and *Ribes sanguineum* (flowering currant).

TURTLEHEAD
A vigorous, upright, herbaceous perennial. H 40–60cm (16–24in), S 30cm (12in).
SEASONAL HIGHLIGHTS
From late summer to mid autumn, it bears dark pink or purple flowers with yellow beards on the lower lip.
VALUE AT OTHER TIMES
It has attractive, lance-shaped boldly veined leaves.
IDEAL SITE
Mixed or herbaceous borders, bog gardens.
CULTIVATION
Grow in full sun or partial shade. A deep fertile soil which retains moisture is ideal. Mulch well in spring before growth begins. Will tolerate heavy clay soils.
ALSO RECOMMENDED
C. lyonii is similar but taller.
PERFECT PARTNERS
Coreopsis verticillata, Crocosmia 'Lady Hamilton'.

WINTERSWEET
A spreading, moderately vigorous, deciduous shrub. H 4m (12ft), S 3m (10ft)
SEASONAL HIGHLIGHTS
On bare winter shoots, it bears nodding, very fragrant, soft yellow flowers.
VALUE AT OTHER TIMES
The leaves are rather coarse, but this shrub is an ideal host for late-flowering clematis.
IDEAL SITE
As a specimen, in a shrub border, against a warm wall.
CULTIVATION
Grow in full sun or partial shade. Grow in any fertile soil. Prune after flowering, removing misplaced shoots to maintain a good shape.
ALSO RECOMMENDED
C. praecox 'Grandiflorus' ♀ has larger, deeper yellow flowers.
PERFECT PARTNERS
Jasminum nudiflorum ♀ (winter jasmine), *Mahonia* × *media* 'Charity' ♀; both have yellow flowers in winter.

GLORY OF THE SNOW
A moderately vigorous, bulbous perennial. H 10–20cm (4–8in), S 3cm (1¼in)
SEASONAL HIGHLIGHTS
In early spring, it bears spikes of starry, white-centred, pink flowers.
VALUE AT OTHER TIMES
Dies back after flowering.
IDEAL SITE
A rock garden, raised bed, beneath shrubs, in containers.
CULTIVATION
Plant in autumn 8cm (3in) deep. Grow in any well-drained soil in sun or dappled shade. Lift and separate the bulbs after four to five years if they become congested.
ALSO RECOMMENDED
C. forbesii has white-eyed, blue flowers.
PERFECT PARTNERS
Grow as a carpet beneath a forsythia, with dwarf daffodils.

Choisya 'Aztec Pearl' ♀

Chrysanthemum 'Carnival Red'

Chrysanthemum 'Glowing Lynn'

Cimicifuga simplex 'White Pearl'

Cistus × *cyprius* ♀

MEXICAN ORANGE BLOSSOM

A bushy, fairly vigorous, evergreen shrub.
H & S to 2.5m (8ft)

SEASONAL HIGHLIGHTS
In both late spring and late summer, it bears clusters of pink-tinted white flowers, often with a few in autumn.

VALUE AT OTHER TIMES
Beautiful, aromatic leaves, divided into narrow, glossy dark green leaflets.

IDEAL SITE
A shrub border, or against a warm or lightly shaded wall.

CULTIVATION
It flowers best in sun but will tolerate partial shade. Grow in any good garden soil. Trim after flowering in spring to improve the second flowering.

ALSO RECOMMENDED
C. ternata ♀ has broader leaves and white flowers.

PERFECT PARTNERS
C. ternata Sundance ('Lich') ♀ has golden foliage if grown in sun, but seldom flowers.

CHRYSANTHEMUM

A bushy, upright, moderately vigorous herbaceous perennial.
H & S 45cm (18in) or more

SEASONAL HIGHLIGHTS
In late summer and early autumn, it bears sprays of small, double red flowers; they are excellent for cutting.

VALUE AT OTHER TIMES
Aromatic dark green leaves.

IDEAL SITE
Borders and containers.

CULTIVATION
Grow in full sun in fertile, well-drained soil. Plant out in late spring and pinch out the growing tips to encourage plentiful flowers. Except in very cold areas, it can be left outdoors in winter; protect the crown with a deep dry mulch. Bring potted plants under glass for winter.

ALSO RECOMMENDED
C. 'Bronze Faerie' has pompon-like bronze flowers.

PERFECT PARTNERS
Aster novi-belgii (Michaelmas daisies), dahlias, rudbeckias.

CHRYSANTHEMUM

A bushy, upright, moderately vigorous herbaceous perennial.
H & S 45cm (18in) or more

SEASONAL HIGHLIGHTS
It bears masses of double, red–bronze flowers in late summer and autumn. They make excellent cut flowers.

VALUE AT OTHER TIMES
Aromatic dark green leaves.

IDEAL SITE
Borders and containers.

CULTIVATION
Grow in full sun in fertile, well-drained soil. Plant out in late spring and pinch out the growing tips to encourage plentiful flowers. Except in very cold areas, it can be left outdoors in winter; protect the crown with a deep dry mulch. Bring potted plants under glass for winter.

ALSO RECOMMENDED
C. 'Peach Margaret' has sprays of pale salmon pink flowers.

PERFECT PARTNERS
Aster novi-belgii (Michaelmas daisies), dahlias, rudbeckias.

CIMICIFUGA, BUGBANE

A robust, upright, herbaceous perennial.
H 60–90cm (24–36in), S 60cm (24in)

SEASONAL HIGHLIGHTS
From early to mid-autumn, it bears spires of white flowers that open from green buds.

VALUE AT OTHER TIMES
The divided, pale green leaves form dense, weed-smothering ground cover.

IDEAL SITE
Damp borders and woodland gardens.

CULTIVATION
Grow in moist, fertile, humus-rich soil in partial shade. May need staking in exposed gardens.

ALSO RECOMMENDED
C. simplex var. *simplex* 'Brunette' has purplish brown foliage and purple-tinted white flowers.

PERFECT PARTNERS
Aster 'Violet Queen', *Salvia* × *superba*.

ROCK ROSE, SUN ROSE

A moderately vigorous, bushy evergreen shrub.
H & S to 1.5m (5ft)

SEASONAL HIGHLIGHTS
During summer, it bears clusters of white flowers with crimson blotches at the bases of the petals.

VALUE AT OTHER TIMES
Forms a neat mound of rather sticky, dark green leaves with wavy margins.

IDEAL SITE
Sunny banks, borders, hot, dry sites and containers.

CULTIVATION
Tolerant of poor and alkaline soils. Grow in well-drained soil in full sun. Set out new plants in spring when the risk of frost has passed. Pinch out stem tips to keep the plant bushy, but don't prune hard.

ALSO RECOMMENDED
C. × *dansereaui* 'Decumbens' is low and spreading with red-blotched white flowers.

PERFECT PARTNERS
Roses and lavenders.

C

Clarkia amoena

Clematis alpina 'Frances Rivis' ♛

Clematis armandii 'Apple Blossom'

Clematis cirrhosa 'Freckles' ♛

Clematis macropetala 'Markham's Pink' ♛

SATIN FLOWER

A moderately vigorous, upright, hardy annual.
H 75cm (30in), S 30cm (12in)

SEASONAL HIGHLIGHTS
Throughout summer, it bears clusters of satin-textured, lilac to red-pink flowers.

VALUE AT OTHER TIMES
Of no real value at other times. They last for only the summer.

IDEAL SITE
Annual borders and containers.

CULTIVATION
Best in sun in slightly acid, moist but well-drained soil, but tolerates light shade. Rich soils encourage leafy growth at the expense of flowers. Sow seeds in the flowering site in spring or autumn. Protect late-sown seedlings with cloches overwinter.

ALSO RECOMMENDED
C. amoena 'Sybil Sherwood' has salmon-pink flowers.

PERFECT PARTNERS
A wide range of hardy annuals.

ALPINE CLEMATIS

A vigorous, deciduous, twining climber.
H 2–3m (6–10ft), S 1.5m (5ft)

SEASONAL HIGHLIGHTS
In spring or early summer, it bears hanging, blue flowers with slightly twisted petals.

VALUE AT OTHER TIMES
Has attractive foliage all summer and fluffy seedheads in late summer and autumn.

IDEAL SITE
Walls, trellis, or scrambling through late-flowering shrubs.

CULTIVATION
Tolerates sun or dappled shade, but the roots should be shaded. Grow in fertile, well-drained soil enriched with plenty of organic matter. After flowering, remove dead or damaged shoots and shorten others to confine to bounds.

ALSO RECOMMENDED
C. alpina 'Pink Flamingo' has pale pink flowers.

PERFECT PARTNERS
Sturdy shrubs, like *Buddleja globosa* or *Phlomis fruticosa*.

CLEMATIS

A vigorous, slightly frost-tender, evergreen climber.
H 3–5m (10–15ft), S 2–3m (6–10ft)

SEASONAL HIGHLIGHTS
In early spring, it bears fragrant, pink-tinted white flowers with pink undersides.

VALUE AT OTHER TIMES
Has attractive foliage all year.

IDEAL SITE
A sheltered wall, through shrubs and trees, or, in cold areas, as a conservatory plant.

CULTIVATION
Grow in sun or dappled shade in fertile, humus-rich, well-drained soil, with the roots in shade. After flowering, remove dead or damaged shoots and shorten others to confine to bounds. Use a fertile, loam-based compost for pot-grown plants and enjoy the scent at close quarters.

ALSO RECOMMENDED
C. armandii has white flowers.

PERFECT PARTNERS
Camellias make good hosts.

WINTER-FLOWERING CLEMATIS

A vigorous, slightly frost-tender, evergreen climber.
H 2.5–3m (8–10ft), S 1.5m (5ft)

SEASONAL HIGHLIGHTS
In late winter and early spring, it bears creamy-white, red-speckled flowers.

VALUE AT OTHER TIMES
Has bronzed leaves all year and silky seedheads in summer.

IDEAL SITE
A sheltered wall, or through shrubs and trees.

CULTIVATION
Grow in sun or dappled shade in fertile, humus-rich, well-drained soil, with the roots in shade. Protect from cold wind. After flowering, remove dead or damaged shoots; shorten others to confine to bounds.

ALSO RECOMMENDED
C. cirrhosa var. *balearica* has fragrant, red-brown speckled, cream flowers.

PERFECT PARTNERS
Large mahonias make good host shrubs.

CLEMATIS

A vigorous, deciduous climber.
H 2–3m (6–10ft), S 1.5m (5ft)

SEASONAL HIGHLIGHTS
From spring to early summer, it bears soft sugar-pink flowers.

VALUE AT OTHER TIMES
Pale green foliage and silver seedheads in summer.

IDEAL SITE
Prefers sun, but will tolerate dappled shade.

CULTIVATION
Grow in sun or dappled shade in fertile, well-drained soil, enriched with organic matter. Site with the roots in shade. After flowering, remove dead or damaged shoots and shorten others to confine to allotted space.

ALSO RECOMMENDED
C. macropetala 'White Swan' has white flowers with creamy-white centres.

PERFECT PARTNERS
Forsythias, larger philadelphus and lilacs are excellent host shrubs.

Clematis montana f.
grandiflora ♀

CLEMATIS

A very vigorous, deciduous
climber.
H 10m (30ft), S 4m (12ft)

SEASONAL HIGHLIGHTS

Single white flowers with
cream anthers are produced
for about four weeks in late
spring and early summer.

VALUE AT OTHER TIMES

Attractive foliage all summer.

IDEAL SITE

A wall, fence or large tree.

CULTIVATION

Grow in sun or dappled shade
in fertile, well-drained soil,
enriched with organic matter.
Site with the roots in shade.
After flowering, remove dead
or damaged shoots and
shorten others to confine to
allotted space.

ALSO RECOMMENDED

C. *montana* 'Elizabeth' ♀ has
scented, pale pink flowers.

PERFECT PARTNERS

Conifers, old fruit trees and
beech (*Fagus sylvatica*) are
good hosts; they must be
vigorous to carry the weight.

EARLY, LARGE, SINGLE-FLOWERED CLEMATIS

Clematis 'Fireworks' ♀
H 2.5m (8ft), S 1m (3ft)

Clematis 'Guernsey Cream'
H 2.5m (8ft), S 1m (3ft)

Clematis 'Lasurstern' ♀
H 2.5m (8ft), S 1m (3ft)

Clematis 'Marie Boisselot' ♀
H 3m (10ft), S 1m (3ft)

Clematis 'Nelly Moser' ♀
H 2–3m (6–10ft), S 1m (3ft)

Clematis 'Niobe' ♀
H 2–3m (6–10ft), S 1m (3ft)

Clematis 'The President' ♀
H 2–3m (6–10ft), S 1m (3ft)

Clematis Vino ('Poulvo')
H 2–3m (6–10ft), S 1m (3ft)

LARGE-FLOWERED HYBRID CLEMATIS

These vigorous, deciduous
clematis bloom in late spring
and early summer, often with
a second flush later in summer.

IDEAL SITE:

Walls, trellis, arbours, pergolas;
over shrubs, trees or hedges.

CULTIVATION

Grow in fertile, well-drained
soil enriched with well-rotted
organic matter. They flower
best with top-growth in sun
and roots in shade, but darker
colours bleach in sun, so these
are better in partial shade.
Plant with 10–15cm (4–6in)
of stem below soil level to
reduce danger of clematis
wilt. Shade the roots with
stone slabs or with nearby
plants. In spring, before
growth begins, cut out
twiggy, dead or damaged
growth and trim remaining
shoots back to strong buds.

RECOMMENDED CULTIVARS

C. 'Fireworks' ♀, blue-violet
with a central red-purple bar,
in early and late summer.
C. 'Guernsey Cream', creamy
yellow in early summer and
smaller and creamy white, in
late summer.
C. 'Marie Boisselot' ♀, white
flowers almost continuously
from early to late summer.
C. 'Nelly Moser' ♀, pinkish
mauve flowers with darker
central bands, in early and late
summer.
C. 'Niobe' ♀, free-flowering
with velvety deep red flowers
through most of the summer.
C. 'Lasurstern' ♀, blue flowers
with cream anthers, in early
summer.
C. 'The President' ♀, rich
purple with silver undersides,
in early and late summer.
*C.*Vino (syn. 'Poulvo'), purplish
wine-red with yellow anthers,
in early summer.

C

EARLY DOUBLE CLEMATIS

C. 'Duchess of Edinburgh'
H 2.5m (8ft), S 1m (3ft)

C. 'Multi Blue'
H 2.5m (8ft), S 1m (3ft)

C. 'Proteus'
H 2.5–3m (8–10ft), S 1m (3ft)

C. 'Vyvyan Pennell' ♥
H 2–3m (6–10ft), S 1m (3ft)

DOUBLE CLEMATIS

The large, early-flowering clematis include several that bear sumptuous double flowers in late spring and early summer. Most produce a second flush of blooms. Grow and prune as for the other large, early-flowering sorts (*see previous page*).

RECOMMENDED CULTIVARS:
C. 'Duchess of Edinburgh' has double white flowers with yellow anthers; outer petals are green-tinted, especially in cool seasons. Not vigorous. *C.* 'Multi Blue' has double blue flowers with upstanding central petals in early summer. *C.* 'Proteus' has double, mauve-pink flowers in early summer and paler, single ones from midsummer onwards. *C.* 'Vyvyan Pennell' ♥ has double flowers with a central cluster of lavender-blue petals; later flowers are single.

LATE-FLOWERING CLEMATIS

C. 'Abundance'
H 3m (10ft), S 1m (3ft)

C. 'Ascotiensis' ♥
H 3–4m (10–12ft) S 1m (3ft)

C. 'Comtesse de Bouchaud'
♥ H 2–3m (6–10ft), S 1m (3ft)

C. 'Huldine'
H 3–5m (10–15ft) S (2m (6ft)

C. 'Jackmanii' ♥
H 3m (10ft), S 1m (3ft)

C. 'Madame Julia Correvon'
♥ H 3m (10ft), S 1.5m (5ft)

C. 'Perle d'Azur' ♥
H 3m (10ft), S 1m (3ft)

C. 'Prince Charles'
H 3m (10ft), S 1m (3ft)

C. 'Ville de Lyon'
H 2–3m (6–10ft), S 1m (3ft)

LATE-FLOWERING CLEMATIS

C. 'Etoile Violette' ♛
H 3–5m (10–15ft), S 1.5m (5ft)

C. 'Paul Farges'
H 7–9m (21–28ft), S 3m (10ft)

C. viticella
H 2–4m (6–12ft), S 1.5m (5ft)

C. 'Hagley Hybrid'
H 2m (6ft), S 1m (3ft)

LATE-FLOWERING CLEMATIS

The late-flowering clematis include large- and small-flowered cultivars, as well as species, that extend the flowering season from mid-summer well into autumn.

CULTIVATION

Late-flowering clematis are grown as for early-flowered clematis (*see previous page*) but are pruned differently, since they flower on the current season's shoots. Simply cut back all of the previous year's stems to strong buds 23–45cm (9–18in) above the ground, just as the buds begin to break in spring. If some of the new shoots are trimmed lightly when they reach 30–50cm (12–20in) long, they flower later and extend the season.

RECOMMENDED CULTIVARS

C. 'Abundance' bears wine-red flowers freely from midsummer to late autumn. C. 'Ascotiensis' ♛ bears rich violet-blue flowers from mid- to late summer, often well into autumn. C. 'Comtesse de Bouchaud' ♛ bears its large, single, bright mauve-pink flowers from late summer onwards. C. 'Etoile Violette' ♛ has violet-purple flowers with contrasting yellow anthers. They are small but borne freely from midsummer to late autumn. C. 'Hagley Hybrid' has large single flowers with incurved, pinkish mauve sepals and red anthers, from midsummer on. They retain their colour better in semi-shade. C. 'Huldine' has cupped flowers that are white, mauve beneath and with a boss of creamy anthers. They appear from midsummer onwards. C. 'Jackmanii' ♛ is vigorous and reliable, with large, velvety, dark purple flowers with light greenish-brown anthers. They appear in mid- to late summer. C. 'Mme Julia Correvon' ♛ produces large, bright wine-red flowers with yellow anthers from midsummer until late autumn. C. 'Paul Farges' is very vigorous and bears star-shaped white flowers with a prominent boss of creamy anthers from midsummer on. C. 'Perle d'Azur' ♛ has distinctive, azure-blue flowers with creamy anthers, borne very freely from midsummer until autumn. C. 'Prince Charles' has large flowers of an unusual shade of soft blue with a hint of grey, in mid- to late summer. C. 'Ville de Lyon' bears bright carmine-red flowers with darker margins and yellow anthers in midsummer. C. viticella is a slender but tough species and bears nodding, open bell-shaped flowers in colours ranging from blue to purple and red, from midsummer into autumn.

PERFECT PARTNERS

Since many of this group bloom well in autumn, with luck, the last of their flowers will complement autumn colours of shrubs like amelanchier, or the late flowers of hydrangeas. The creamy and white-flowered ones, like 'Huldine', look especially good with purple-leaved shrubs like *Cotinus coggygria* 'Royal Purple' ♛ or C. 'Grace' ♛. Grey-leaved plants, like *Pyrus salicifolia* 'Pendula' ♛ are ideal hosts for those with flowers of deep purple or wine-red.

***Clematis* Golden Tiara**

LATE-FLOWERING CLEMATIS

Vigorous deciduous climber.
H & S 2–3m (6–10ft)

SEASONAL HIGHLIGHTS

From late summer until autumn, it produces open lantern-flowers in bright golden yellow, followed by fluffy seedheads that persist into early winter.

VALUE AT OTHER TIMES

Attractive foliage all through the summer.

IDEAL SITE

Walls and fences of any aspect; climbing through deciduous trees.

CULTIVATION

Grow in moderately fertile soil enriched with organic matter. Plant deeply and shade the roots. Prune to 30cm (12in) from the ground in spring.

ALSO RECOMMENDED

C. 'Bill Mackenzie', similar if a litte more vigorous.

PERFECT PARTNERS

Clematis flammula, flowering in white at the same time; amelanchiers and crab apples.

C

Cleome hassleriana 'Colour Fountain'

CLEOME, SPIDER FLOWER
A vigorous, half-hardy annual. H 1.2m (4ft), S 45cm (18in)
SEASONAL HIGHLIGHTS
Throughout summer, it bears dense heads of scented flowers with delicate petals, in shades of pink, violet-pink, or white.
VALUE AT OTHER TIMES
Pretty, divided leaves of fresh green.
IDEAL SITE
An annual or cutting border, or to fill seasonal gaps in an herbaceous borders.
CULTIVATION
Best in sun but tolerates light dappled shade. Grow in light, free-draining soil. Sow seeds under glass in warmth in spring and plant out when the threat of frost has passed. Cut or deadhead regularly to prolong the flowering period.
ALSO RECOMMENDED
C. hassleriana has white, pink or purple flowers.
PERFECT PARTNERS
Clarkias and rudbeckias.

Colchicum cilicicum

AUTUMN CROCUS, NAKED LADIES
Upright, low-growing, cormous perennials. H 10cm (4in), S 8cm (3in)
SEASONAL HIGHLIGHTS
In autumn, it bears funnel-shaped, purplish-pink flowers. They appear before the leaves.
VALUE AT OTHER TIMES
The leaves are not ornamentally significant.
IDEAL SITE
Beneath deciduous shrubs or naturalized in grass.
CULTIVATION
Best in an open site in full sun, but will tolerate light shade. Plant corms 10cm (4in) deep in late summer or early autumn, in fertile, well-drained soil. If grown in grass, allow the foliage to die down naturally before mowing.
ALSO RECOMMENDED
C. autumnale has lavender-pink flowers.
PERFECT PARTNERS
Hydrangeas, *Viburnum* × *bodnantense* 'Deben' ♥.

Convallaria majalis ♥

LILY-OF-THE-VALLEY
A vigorous, spreading, upright perennial with fleshy roots. H 23cm (9in), S 30cm (12in)
SEASONAL HIGHLIGHTS
In late spring, arching stems of small, nodding, waxy white flowers appear. They are strongly scented.
VALUE AT OTHER TIMES
The attractive leaves make dense ground cover.
IDEAL SITE
A shady border, woodland garden, or in containers, especially for forcing.
CULTIVATION
Tolerates deep or partial shade. Grow in damp, leafy, fertile soil. A top-dressing of leafmould in autumn is beneficial. Pot some up in autumn and grow under glass for a scented display indoors.
ALSO RECOMMENDED
C. majalis 'Flore Pleno' has double flowers.
PERFECT PARTNERS
Azaleas, dwarf rhododendrons and narcissus.

C. alba 'Aurea' ♥
H & S 3m (10ft)

C. alba 'Sibirica' ♥
H & S 3m (10ft)

C. alba 'Elegantissima' ♥
H & S 3m (10ft)

C. sanguinea 'Winter Beauty'
H 3m (10ft), S 2.5m (8ft)

C. stolonifera 'Flaviramea' ♥
H 2m (6ft), S 4m (12ft)

C. stolonifera 'Kelseyi'
H 75cm (30in), S 1.5m (5ft)

DOGWOODS

The dogwood includes several vigorous, deciduous shrubs that are valued for their brightly coloured leafless stems that bring interest to the winter garden.

VALUE AT OTHER TIMES

They bear clusters of white flowers in spring and white or blue-black fruit in autumn.

IDEAL SITE

A shrub border, winter garden or beside pools and streams.

CULTIVATION

Grow in any moderately fertile soil. Tolerate shade but stems colour best in sun. For the best effect, prune the stems back to the base each year in early spring.

RECOMMENDED CULTIVARS

C. alba 'Aurea' ♥ has yellow leaves, and red winter stems. *C. alba* 'Sibirica' ♥ has glossy, bright red winter stems. *C. alba* 'Elegantissima' ♥ has grey-green, cream-margined leaves and red winter stems. *C. sanguinea* 'Winter Beauty' has bright orange-yellow and red winter shoots. *C. stolonifera* 'Flaviramea' ♥ has bright yellow-green shoots. *C. stolonifera* 'Kelseyi' is compact with red-tipped, yellow-green shoots.

PERFECT PARTNERS

Winter-flowering heathers; *Rubus cockburnianus* and *R. biflorus* with white winter stems.

Cornus mas ♥

CORNELIAN CHERRY

Spreading, moderately vigorous, deciduous shrub or small tree.
H & S 5m (15ft)

SEASONAL HIGHLIGHTS

In late winter, it bears small but profuse clusters of yellow flowers on bare branches.

VALUE AT OTHER TIMES

The dark green leaves turn red-purple in autumn. It sometimes produces small bright red fruits in autumn.

IDEAL SITE

Winter garden, shrub borders, or as a specimen.

CULTIVATION

Any fertile, well-drained soil, including chalky ones. Best in an open sunny site, but will tolerate light shade. Keep pruning to a minimum.

ALSO RECOMMENDED

C. mas 'Variegata' ♥ has white-margined leaves.

PERFECT PARTNERS

Chimonanthus praecox, *Viburnum* × *bodnantense* 'Dawn' ♥.

Cortaderia selloana
'Sunningdale Silver' ♥

PAMPAS GRASS

A vigorous perennial grass.
H 3m (10ft) or more,
S 2.5m (8ft)

SEASONAL HIGHLIGHTS

In late summer and autumn, it sends up feathery, silvery white flower plumes that are very weather resistant.

VALUE AT OTHER TIMES

Clumps of arching bluish-green leaves all year round.

IDEAL SITE

As a specimen, at the back of a border, in woodland gardens.

CULTIVATION

It prefers an open, sunny site, but tolerates dappled shade. Grow in fertile, well-drained soil. In late winter or early spring, carefully cut or comb out old foliage; the leaves have viciously sharp edges.

ALSO RECOMMENDED

C. selloana 'Albolineata' has yellow-margined leaves.

PERFECT PARTNERS

Stipa gigantea, *Arundo donax* var. *versicolor*.

Corydalis flexuosa

CORYDALIS, FUMEWORT

A slowly spreading, summer-dormant herbaceous perennial.
H 30cm (12in),
S 20cm (8in) or more

SEASONAL HIGHLIGHTS

From late spring to summer, it produces dense clusters of slender-tubed, brilliant blue flowers with white throats.

VALUE AT OTHER TIMES

Fern-like, bluish-green leaves. Dies back after flowering.

IDEAL SITE

Shady borders, rock gardens, and woodland gardens.

CULTIVATION

Grow in a cool site in partial or dappled shade, in a humus-rich, fertile, moist but well-drained soil.

ALSO RECOMMENDED

C. fumariifolia has azure-blue, sometimes purple, flowers.

PERFECT PARTNERS

C. lutea, with yellow flowers.

Corylopsis glabrescens

CORYLOPSIS

A moderately vigorous, deciduous shrub of open, spreading habit.
H & S to 5m (15ft)

SEASONAL HIGHLIGHTS

In mid-spring, it produces hanging tassels of fragrant, pale yellow flowers.

VALUE AT OTHER TIMES

It has oval leaves that are pale to dark green on top and blue-green beneath.

IDEAL SITE

Shady shrub borders, woodland gardens.

CULTIVATION

Grow in partial or dappled shade. It prefers well-drained, humus-rich, acid soil, but will tolerate deep soils over chalk. Prune out or shorten badly placed shoots after flowering.

ALSO RECOMMENDED

C. pauciflora has cowslip-scented, pale yellow flowers; it does not tolerate chalky soils.

PERFECT PARTNERS

Corylus avellana 'Contorta', magnolias, *Salix lanata*.

C

Corylus avellana 'Contorta' ♟

Cosmos atrosanguineus

Cosmos bipinnatus
Sensation Series

Cotinus coggygria ♟

Cotinus 'Grace' ♟

CORKSCREW HAZEL

A fairly vigorous, deciduous shrub with twisted shoots.
H & S to 5m (15ft)

SEASONAL HIGHLIGHTS
The twisted shoots look good in winter, especially when snow-covered. Yellow catkins hang from bare branches in late winter or early spring.

VALUE AT OTHER TIMES
The heart-shaped, wrinkled leaves are also twisted.

IDEAL SITE
As a specimen or at the back of a shrub border.

CULTIVATION
Thrives in any good garden soil in sun or partial shade. Remove any suckers which grow from the base and carefully prune out any misplaced shoots in winter.

ALSO RECOMMENDED
C. maxima 'Purpurea' ♟ has purple leaves and purple-tinted catkins.

PERFECT PARTNERS
Magnolias, *Salix lanata*.

CHOCOLATE COSMOS

A spreading, herbaceous perennial with tuberous roots.
H 75cm (30in), S 45cm (18in)

SEASONAL HIGHLIGHTS
From midsummer to autumn, velvety, dark maroon flowers open to release an elusive, dark-chocolate fragrance.

VALUE AT OTHER TIMES
Clumps of divided, fresh green foliage.

IDEAL SITE
Warm, sheltered borders.

CULTIVATION
Grow in fertile, well-drained soil in full sun. Deadhead regularly to prolong flowering. In cold areas, lift tubers before the first frosts and store in a dry, frost-free place.

ALSO RECOMMENDED
C. bipinnatus is a tall annual, with white, pink or crimson flowers of similar form.

PERFECT PARTNERS
Achilleas, border phlox. Grey foliage and bright flowers form a good contrast to the flowers of *C. atrosanguineus*.

ANNUAL COSMOS

A vigorous, erect, freely branching, half-hardy annual.
H to 90cm (36in),
S to 45cm (18in)

SEASONAL HIGHLIGHTS
Large pink or white flowers are produced freely through summer and autumn. They are good for cutting.

VALUE AT OTHER TIMES
Has feathery foliage all summer.

IDEAL SITE
Annual and cutting borders, or as gap-fillers in mixed or herbaceous borders.

CULTIVATION
Best in full sun, but tolerates dappled shade. Grow in any well-drained, moderately fertile soil. Sow seeds under glass in early spring, or in the flowering site in late spring. Deadhead regularly.

ALSO RECOMMENDED
C. bipinnatus Sonata Series are dwarf and good in containers.

PERFECT PARTNERS
Clarkia, *Chrysanthemum carinatum*.

COTINUS, SMOKE BUSH

Vigorous, mound-forming deciduous shrub.
H & S 5m (15ft)

SEASONAL HIGHLIGHTS
Plumes of tiny buff-purple flowers become smoky grey by late summer, giving rise to the common name.

VALUE AT OTHER TIMES
The oval green leaves turn yellow to orange and finally flaming red in autumn.

IDEAL SITE
As a specimen, or in a mixed or shrub border.

CULTIVATION
Grow in any moderately fertile, moist but well-drained soil. For larger, brighter coloured foliage, prune back hard in spring, but allow the plant to become established before doing so.

ALSO RECOMMENDED
C. coggygria 'Royal Purple' ♟ has dark red-purple foliage and vivid red autumn colour.

PERFECT PARTNERS
Berberis, escallonias, weigelas.

COTINUS, SMOKE BUSH

A vigorous, deciduous shrub or small tree.
H 6m (20ft), S 5m (15ft)

SEASONAL HIGHLIGHTS
A haze of tiny purple-pink flowers appear in summer giving the plant the common name of smoke bush.

VALUE AT OTHER TIMES
Oval purple leaves that turn a brilliant translucent red in late autumn.

IDEAL SITE
As a specimen, or in a mixed or shrub border.

CULTIVATION
Grow in any moderately fertile, moist but well-drained soil. To get larger, brighter coloured foliage, prune all shoots back hard in spring. but let plants become well-established before doing so.

ALSO RECOMMENDED
C. coggygria 'Notcutt's Variety' has wine-red foliage.

PERFECT PARTNERS
Berberis, escallonias, weigelas.

Cotoneaster frigidus 'Fructu Luteo'

Crambe cordifolia ♀

Crataegus laevigata 'Rosea Flore Pleno' ♀

Crocosmia x *crocosmiiflora* 'Jackanapes'

Crocus tommasinianus ♀

COTONEASTER

A moderately vigorous, erect then spreading, deciduous tree or large shrub.
H & S to 10m (30ft)

SEASONAL HIGHLIGHTS
Large clusters of tiny white flowers appear in summer followed by creamy yellow fruits in autumn. The flowers attract bees; fruits are eaten by birds in hard winters.

VALUE AT OTHER TIMES
Has peeling bark.

IDEAL SITE
At the back of a shrub border, or as a specimen.

CULTIVATION
Tolerates almost any soil including dry ones, but best in moderately fertile, well-drained soil in full sun. Prune lightly to shape in winter, if necessary.

ALSO RECOMMENDED
C. franchettii is semi-evergreen with bright orange-red fruits.

PERFECT PARTNERS
C. horizontalis, shrubby potentillas, ceanothus.

CRAMBE

A vigorous, clump-forming herbaceous perennial.
H 2.5m (8ft), S to 1.5m (5ft)

SEASONAL HIGHLIGHTS
In early to midsummer, tall strong stems arise bearing clouds of honey-scented white flowers.

VALUE AT OTHER TIMES
Forms a mound of glossy, puckered, dark green leaves that die down in late summer.

IDEAL SITE
At the back of a mixed or herbaceous border.

CULTIVATION
Grow in deep, fertile soil in full sun. Will tolerate partial shade. Shelter from strong winds. Is best increased by root cuttings in winter.

ALSO RECOMMENDED
C. maritima is shorter with blue-grey, puckered, twisted and wrinkled leaves and white flowers.

PERFECT PARTNERS
Old garden roses, philadelphus.

MIDLAND HAWTHORN, MAY

A very hardy, deciduous tree with a rounded crown.
H & S to 8m (25ft)

SEASONAL HIGHLIGHTS
Clusters of double pink flowers appear in late spring.

VALUE AT OTHER TIMES
Red fruits (haws) are produced in autumn.

IDEAL SITE
As a specimen, especially in small gardens, or as hedging.

CULTIVATION
Tolerates sun and partial shade and a wide variety of soils. Needs minimal pruning to maintain the shape and to cut out dead or damaged wood in winter.

ALSO RECOMMENDED
C. laevigata 'Paul's Scarlet' ♀ has double, deep pink flowers.

PERFECT PARTNERS
Acers, fastigiate beech (*Fagus sylvatica* 'Dawyck' ♀), tulip tree (*Liriodendron tulipifera* ♀).

MONTBRETIA

A moderately vigorous, upright cormous perennial.
H 40–60cm (16–24in),
S 8cm (3in)

SEASONAL HIGHLIGHTS
In late summer, it produces arching sprays of orange-red and yellow flowers.

VALUE AT OTHER TIMES
Handsome, sword-shaped leaves for most of the year.

IDEAL SITE
Mixed or herbaceous borders.

CULTIVATION
Ideally grow in full sun, but it will tolerate partial shade. Plant the corms 8-10cm (3-4in) deep in fertile soil. On heavy clay, plant on a layer of coarse grit. Lift and divide every three or four years, in spring.

ALSO RECOMMENDED
C. 'Emberglow' has dark red flowers in summer.

PERFECT PARTNERS
C. 'Golden Fleece', with lemon-yellow flowers, asters, rudbeckias.

EARLY CROCUS

A robust, cormous perennial.
H 10cm (4in), S 2.5cm (1in)

SEASONAL HIGHLIGHTS
In late winter or early spring, slender, goblet-shaped flowers appear. They come in white, lilac and red-purple, often with silvery overtones.

VALUE AT OTHER TIMES
No real value at other times.

IDEAL SITE
Naturalize in turf, in borders, rock and woodland gardens.

CULTIVATION
Best in full sun but will tolerate dappled shade. Grow in fertile, well-drained soil. Plant corms in the autumn, 8–10cm (3–4in) deep.

ALSO RECOMMENDED
C. tommasinianus f. *albus* has starry white flowers with golden anthers.

PERFECT PARTNERS
Snowdrops (*Galanthus*) and winter aconites (*Eranthis hyemalis* ♀).

C

D

Crocus vernus 'Pickwick'

Cyclamen coum ♀

C. coum Pewter Group ♀

Cytisus x *praecox* 'Warminster' ♀

Dahlia 'Bishop of Llandaff' ♀

DUTCH CROCUS

Robust, cormous perennial. H 12cm (5in), S 5cm (2in)
SEASONAL HIGHLIGHTS
From early to late spring, it produces white flowers, striped pale and dark lilac, with dark purple bases.
VALUE AT OTHER TIMES
No real value at other times.
IDEAL SITE
Naturalized in turf, in borders, rock and woodland gardens and in containers.
CULTIVATION
Grow in sun or light dappled shade, in fertile, well-drained soil. Plant corms in autumn, 8–10cm (3–4in) deep.
ALSO RECOMMENDED
C. vernus 'Remembrance' has glossy violet flowers.
PERFECT PARTNERS
Snowdrops (*Galanthus*), winter aconites (*Eranthis hyemalis* ♀), narcissi.

HARDY CYCLAMEN

Hardy cyclamen are spreading and low-growing perennials that grow from underground tubers. There are several species that flower in late summer, or in autumn and winter, providing carpets of colour when most other plants have faded. Some flower before the leaves and others with them, but all have a delicacy that belies their tough constitution. Most self-seed freely, forming extensive colonies with time.
IDEAL SITE
Naturalized in turf, in shady borders, beneath shrubs and trees, including conifers.
CULTIVATION
Grow in moderately fertile well-drained soil, ideally beneath a canopy of trees or shrubs to protect them from excessive summer rain when dormant. *C. purpurascens* needs soil that does not dry out and prefers alkaline soils. Plant tubers 3–5cm (1¼-2in) deep

in autumn, or in early spring for *C. purpurascens*. Plants can be bought in flower and planted directly if the soil is not frozen or too wet. Give a deep, dry mulch of leafmould as the leaves wither.
RECOMMENDED CYCLAMEN
C. coum bears neat little blooms in white and shades of pink or carmine-red, in winter or early spring, above shiny, deep green leaves that are often marked with silver.
C. coum Pewter Group ♀ has completely silvered leaves. H 8cm (3in), S 10cm (4in)
C. hederifolium ♀ has small flowers in shades of white or pink in mid- to late autumn. Rounded, dark grey-green leaves, often patterned with silver, appear after the flowers. H 13cm (5in), S 15cm (6in)
C. purpurascens ♀ bears sweetly scented, pale to deep carmine-red flowers in mid- to late summer, with the shiny, dark green leaves. H & S 10cm (4in)

WARMINSTER BROOM

A moderately vigorous, arching evergreen shrub. H1.2m (4ft), S 1.5m (5ft)
SEASONAL HIGHLIGHTS
In mid and late spring, each stem is wreathed in pea-like, creamy-yellow flowers.
VALUE AT OTHER TIMES
Arching wand-like shoots bear small dark green leaves.
IDEAL SITE
Shrub borders, sunny banks, hot, dry sites.
CULTIVATION
Grow in a moderately fertile, well-drained soil in full sun. Tolerates poor acid soils and deep soils over chalk. After flowering, cut back the flowered shoots to buds lower down green young wood. Don't cut into old wood.
ALSO RECOMMENDED
C. nigricans bears yellow flowers in late summer.
PERFECT PARTNERS
Choisyas, camellias, and other broad-leaved evergreens.

DAHLIA

A vigorous, tuberous, frost-tender perennial. H 1.1m (3½ft), S 45cm (18in).
SEASONAL HIGHLIGHTS
From late summer until late autumn, it produces peony-like, semi-double, velvety glowing red flowers.
VALUE AT OTHER TIMES
It also has very attractive dark red, almost black leaves.
IDEAL SITE
Bedding, and mixed borders.
CULTIVATION
Best in full sun. Dahlias are gross feeders and need a fertile, well-drained soil enriched with well-rotted organic matter. Set out in early summer when all risk of frost has passed. Lift tubers when the foliage has been blackened by autumn frosts. Store in a cool dry place.
ALSO RECOMMENDED
D. 'Alloway Cottage' has soft yellow flowers.
PERFECT PARTNERS
Chrysanthemums.

Daphne mezereum

Delphinium **Black Knight Group**

Dianthus 'Little Jock'

Diascia barberae **'Blackthorn Apricot'** ♀

Dicentra spectabilis ♀

DAPHNE, MEZEREON

An upright, deciduous shrub. All parts are highly toxic. H 1.2m (4ft), S 1m (3ft)

SEASONAL HIGHLIGHTS
From late winter until early spring, it produces clusters of pink to purplish-pink flowers, on bare branches.

VALUE AT OTHER TIMES
Fleshy red fruits in summer.

IDEAL SITE
Shrub borders and woodland gardens.

CULTIVATION
Grow in sun or partial shade. Prefers a slightly alkaline, humus-rich, moist but well-drained soil. Mulch to keep the roots cool. Prune only to take out dead or damaged wood, after flowering.

ALSO RECOMMENDED
D. mezereum 'Bowles' Variety' has white flowers with yellow fruit to follow.

PERFECT PARTNERS
Mahonias, *Viburnum* × *bodnantense* 'Dawn' ♀.

DELPHINIUM

A moderately vigorous, upright, herbaceous perennial. H 1.7m (5½ft), S 75cm (30in)

SEASONAL HIGHLIGHTS
From early to midsummer, it bears long spikes of black-eyed, deep purple flowers.

VALUE AT OTHER TIMES
Has attractive, deeply lobed, mid- to light green foliage.

IDEAL SITE
A sunny border, especially in cottage gardens.

CULTIVATION
Grow in full sun in fertile, well-drained soil enriched with plenty of organic matter. Needs staking in exposed gardens. Cut back in autumn when foliage has withered.

ALSO RECOMMENDED
D. 'Emily Hawkins' has semi-double, lilac flowers.

PERFECT PARTNERS
Achilleas, lupins, oriental poppies (*Papaver orientalis*).

ALPINE PINK

A low-growing, cushion-forming, evergreen perennial. H & S 10cm (4in)

SEASONAL HIGHLIGHTS
In summer, it bears clove-scented, double, pale pink flowers with a maroon eye and fringed petals, just above the foliage.

VALUE AT OTHER TIMES
Neat mounds of grey-green foliage all year.

IDEAL SITE
Rock gardens, troughs and other containers.

CULTIVATION
Prefers an open, sunny spot, in sharply drained, gritty, slightly alkaline soil. On clay soils, dig in plenty of grit. Good drainage is essential.

ALSO RECOMMENDED
D. alpinus 'Joan's Blood' ♀ has deep magenta-pink flowers with crimson centres.

PERFECT PARTNERS
Aurinia saxatilis, *Saponaria caespitosa*, alpine phlox, thymes.

DIASCIA

A moderately spreading, mat-forming, evergreen or semi-evergreen perennial. H 25cm (10in), S 50cm (20in)

SEASONAL HIGHLIGHTS
From summer until autumn, it bears a profusion of apricot flowers in loose spikes.

VALUE AT OTHER TIMES
The mats of heart-shaped, mid-green foliage are present for most of the year.

IDEAL SITE
A sunny bank or border, in a rock garden, or raised bed.

CULTIVATION
Grow in full sun in fertile, moist but well-drained soil. Deadhead regularly to induce more flowers. May not survive very cold, wet winters. Take stem cuttings in summer and overwinter young plants under glass.

ALSO RECOMMENDED
D. rigescens ♀ is trailing with deep pink flowers.

PERFECT PARTNERS
Veronica prostrata, *V. spicata*.

BLEEDING HEART, DUTCHMAN'S BREECHES

A vigorous, clump-forming, herbaceous perennial. H 1.2m (4ft), S 45cm (18in)

SEASONAL HIGHLIGHTS
In late spring and early summer, arching stems bear hanging, heart-shaped flowers with rose-pink outer petals and white inner ones.

VALUE AT OTHER TIMES
Ferny, pale green leaves.

IDEAL SITE
Shady borders and woodland gardens.

CULTIVATION
Best in partial shade, but will tolerate part-day sun, if soils are reliably moist. Grow in damp, fertile, preferably neutral to slightly alkaline soil. Divide every three or four years to maintain vigour.

ALSO RECOMMENDED
D. spectabilis f. *alba* bears white flowers over longer periods.

PERFECT PARTNERS
Bold foliage plants like hostas.

D

Dierama pulcherrimum

Digitalis x *mertonensis* ♀

Doronicum x *excelsum* 'Harpur Crewe'

E

Echinacea purpurea 'White Swan'

Elaeagnus x *ebbingei* 'Gilt Edge' ♀

ANGEL'S FISHING ROD

A vigorous, upright, evergreen, cormous perennial.
H 1–1.5m (3–5ft)
S 60cm (24in)

SEASONAL HIGHLIGHTS
In summer, it produces tall stems bearing bell-shaped, pale to deep magenta-pink flowers on very slender stalks.

VALUE AT OTHER TIMES
Grass-like, grey-green leaves for most of the year.

IDEAL SITE
At the front of a sunny border, or by a pool.

CULTIVATION
Best in full sun in leafy, fertile, well-drained soil. Keep well watered in dry weather. Plant corms 5–7cm (2–3in) deep in spring. Divide every three or four years. Divisions may take a season to flower.

ALSO RECOMMENDED
D. 'Miranda' is shorter with bright pink flowers.

PERFECT PARTNERS
Acanthus, penstemons, salvias.

PERENNIAL FOXGLOVE

An upright, fairly vigorous herbaceous perennial.
H 90cm (36in), S 30cm (12in)

SEASONAL HIGHLIGHTS
Tall spires of tubular, pinkish-buff flowers rise above the foliage in spring and early summer. They attract bees.

VALUE AT OTHER TIMES
Mounds of crinkled, deeply veined, dark green leaves.

IDEAL SITE
Woodland gardens or mixed and herbaceous borders.

CULTIVATION
Prefers partial shade and humus-rich soils, but tolerates most aspects and soils if not too wet or dry. Deadhead after flowering; it self-seeds but seedlings are variable.

ALSO RECOMMENDED
D. grandiflora ♀ has brown-veined, pale yellow flowers.

PERFECT PARTNERS
D. obscura, with yellow flowers; dicentras.

DORONICUM, LEOPARD'S BANE

A vigorous, upright and bushy herbaceous perennial.
H & S to 60cm (24in).

SEASONAL HIGHLIGHTS
In spring, branched stems each bear 3-4 golden yellow, daisy-like flowers.

VALUE AT OTHER TIMES
Has attractive, soft green, hairy, heart-shaped leaves.

IDEAL SITE
Shady borders or naturalized in woodland.

CULTIVATION
Best in partial or dappled shade but tolerates a more open aspect if soils are not too dry. Grow in a fertile, moisture-retentive soil. Lift and divide every four to five years to maintain vigour.

ALSO RECOMMENDED
D. columnae 'Miss Mason' has large, bright yellow flowers.

PERFECT PARTNERS
Narcissus, pulmonarias, Polyanthus primulas.

ECHINACEA, CONEFLOWER

A vigorous, upright, clump-forming herbaceous perennial.
H 60cm (24in), S 45cm (18in)

SEASONAL HIGHLIGHTS
From midsummer until early autumn, it bears large, single white flowers with orange-brown centres.

VALUE AT OTHER TIMES
Has clumps of narrow, roughly hairy basal leaves.

IDEAL SITE
Late summer borders.

CULTIVATION
Best in full sun, but tolerates light, part-day shade. Grow in fertile, humus-rich, well-drained soil. Cut back the flowering stems as the blooms fade to encourage a second flush of flowers.

ALSO RECOMMENDED
E. purpurea 'Robert Bloom' has mauve-crimson flowers with orange-brown centres.

PERFECT PARTNERS
Achilleas, chrysanthemums, border phlox.

ELAEAGNUS

A dense, bushy, moderately vigorous evergreen shrub.
H & S to 4m (12ft)

SEASONAL HIGHLIGHTS
All year round, it has lustrous dark leaves with gleaming, creamy yellow margins.

VALUE AT OTHER TIMES
The autumn flowers are fragrant but insignificant.

IDEAL SITE
Shrub borders and hedges.

CULTIVATION
The leaves colour best in sun, but it tolerates dappled shade. Grow in any fertile soil that is not too dry or wet; it does not thrive on shallow, chalky soils. Prune lightly to shape in mid- to late spring; cut out shoots with all-green leaves.

ALSO RECOMMENDED
E. pungens 'Frederici' has yellow-centred, shining green leaves, and is slow-growing.

PERFECT PARTNERS
Dark-leaved shrubs like hollies (*Ilex*), escallonias and *Viburnum tinus*.

Epimedium **x** *warleyense*

Eranthis hyemalis ♀

Erica carnea '**Springwood White**' ♀

Erica **x** *darleyensis* '**Arthur Johnson**' ♀

Eryngium **x** *tripartitum* ♀

BISHOP'S MITRE, BARRENWORT

A vigorous, clump-forming, evergreen perennial.
H 50cm (20in), S 75cm (30in)

SEASONAL HIGHLIGHTS
From mid to late spring, it bears sprays of nodding, yellow and orange-red flowers.

VALUE AT OTHER TIMES
The leaves are tinted red in spring and autumn and form good ground cover.

IDEAL SITE
Shady mixed borders and woodland gardens.

CULTIVATION
Best in partial shade, but tolerates some sun if soil is moist. Grow in fertile, moist but well-drained soil. Shelter from cold winds. Cut back old foliage in late winter to get the best flowering display.

ALSO RECOMMENDED
E. 'Versicolor' has dark red and yellow flowers.

PERFECT PARTNERS
E. × *perralchicum* ♀ (bright yellow flowers); dwarf narcissi.

WINTER ACONITE

A vigorous perennial with small, knobbly tubers.
H 5–8cm (2–3in), S 5cm (2in)

SEASONAL HIGHLIGHTS
In late winter and early spring, bright yellow flowers appear above a ruff of dissected, bright green leaves.

VALUE AT OTHER TIMES
No great value at other times. The foliage dies back after flowering.

IDEAL SITE
Beneath deciduous trees and shrubs or naturalized in grass.

CULTIVATION
Grow in full sun, in any fertile soil that isn't very dry in summer. . Plant tubers 5cm (2in) deep in autumn, or, buy plants "in-the-green" and plant when the soil is not too wet or frozen.

ALSO RECOMMENDED
E. pinnatifida has white flowers.

PERFECT PARTNERS
Snowdrops, crocus, hardy cyclamen.

WINTER HEATH

A vigorous, spreading, slightly trailing evergreen shrub.
H 15cm (6in), S 45cm (18in)

SEASONAL HIGHLIGHTS
From winter to mid-spring, it is covered with small, dense spires of white flowers.

VALUE AT OTHER TIMES
Bright green foliage makes good ground cover all year.

IDEAL SITE
Rock gardens, especially with dwarf conifers.

CULTIVATION
Best in an open, sunny site in well-drained acid soil; it will tolerate slightly alkaline soils. After flowering, trim off the old flowers with shears and top-dress with leafmould, garden compost or similar.

ALSO RECOMMENDED
E. carnea 'Springwood Pink' has rose-pink flowers.

PERFECT PARTNERS
Dwarf conifers and dwarf rhododendrons, shrubby potentillas and gaultherias.

DARLEY DALE HEATH

A dense, bushy, vigorous evergreen shrub.
H 1m (3ft), S 75cm (30in)

SEASONAL HIGHLIGHTS
From mid-winter until spring it bears long, dense spikes of mauve-pink flowers.

VALUE AT OTHER TIMES
Young foliage has cream and pink tips in spring; it makes good ground cover all year.

IDEAL SITE
Rock gardens, especially with dwarf conifers.

CULTIVATION
Best in an open, sunny site in well-drained acid soil; it will tolerate slightly alkaline soils. After flowering, trim with shears and top-dress with leafmould or garden compost.

ALSO RECOMMENDED
E. x *darleyensis* 'Darley Dale' has cream-tipped leaves in spring and shell-pink flowers.

PERFECT PARTNERS
Dwarf conifers and dwarf rhododendrons, shrubby potentillas and gaultherias.

SEA HOLLY

An upright, clump-forming herbaceous perennial.
H 60–90cm (24–36in), S 50cm (20in)

SEASONAL HIGHLIGHTS
From midsummer until early autumn, it bears branching stems of violet-blue flowers with narrow, grey-blue bracts; they are good for drying.

VALUE AT OTHER TIMES
Basal clumps of shiny, slightly spiny, dark green leaves.

IDEAL SITE
Sunny borders, seaside and gravel gardens.

CULTIVATION
Grow in full sun in poor, dry gritty soil. It may need protection from excessive winter wet, especially in cold or exposed gardens.

ALSO RECOMMENDED
E. giganteum ♀ is a taller, self-seeding biennial with steel-blue flowers and silver bracts.

PERFECT PARTNERS
Yucca gloriosa ♀, *Y. filamentosa* ♀.

E

Erysimum cheiri **Bedder Series**

Erythronium 'Pagoda' ♀

Eschscholzia californica ♀

Euonymus alatus ♀

Euonymus fortunei 'Silver Queen' ♀

WALLFLOWER

Upright, bushy, compact perennials grown as biennials.
H 30cm (12in), S 23cm (9in)

SEASONAL HIGHLIGHTS
Over long periods in spring, bear short spikes of sweetly scented, golden yellow, orange or scarlet-red flowers.

VALUE AT OTHER TIMES
They are usually discarded after flowering.

IDEAL SITE
Spring bedding or containers.

CULTIVATION
Grow in sun in well-drained, poor to moderately fertile, well-drained soil. Rich soils encourage leafy growth with fewer flowers. Sow seed in a seedbed in late spring or early summer. Prick out into a nursery bed. Plant in the flowering sites in the autumn.

ALSO RECOMMENDED
E. cheiri 'Blood Red' has luminous, deep red flowers.

PERFECT PARTNERS
Forget-me-nots (*Myosotis*), tulips, polyanthus primulas.

TROUT LILY, PAGODA FLOWER

Upright, vigorous, clump-forming, bulbous perennial.
H 15–35cm (6–14in), S 10cm (4in)

SEASONAL HIGHLIGHTS
In spring, it bears heads of nodding, brown-marked, sulphur-yellow flowers.

VALUE AT OTHER TIMES
Has bronze-mottled leaves that die down in summer.

IDEAL SITE
Beneath deciduous shrubs, rock and woodland gardens, or naturalized in turf.

CULTIVATION
Grow in partial shade in fertile, reliably moist, humus-rich soil. Plant bulbs 10cm (4in) deep in autumn. Do not let bulbs dry out before planting, or when dormant.

ALSO RECOMMENDED
E. revolutum ♀ has lilac-pink flowers and brown-mottled, dark green leaves.

PERFECT PARTNERS
Crocus and narcissus.

CALIFORNIA POPPY

A moderately vigorous, mat-forming hardy annual.
H 30cm (12in), S 15cm (6in)

SEASONAL HIGHLIGHTS
From summer to autumn, it bears satiny orange, yellow, white or red flowers.

VALUE AT OTHER TIMES
The flowers are followed by long, curving seed pods.

IDEAL SITE
Annual borders, dry, sunny banks, gravel gardens.

CULTIVATION
Grow in poor, well-drained soil in full sun. Sow the seeds outdoors in early spring and thin out to about 15cm (6in) when the seedlings are large enough to handle. Deadhead regularly to prolong the flowering period.

ALSO RECOMMENDED
E. caespitosa is dwarf, with scented, bright yellow flowers.

PERFECT PARTNERS
Shirley poppies (*Papaver rhoeas* Shirley Series).

WINGED SPINDLE

A dense, bushy, vigorous deciduous shrub.
H 2m (6ft), S 3m (10ft)

SEASONAL HIGHLIGHTS
The leaves turn brilliant crimson in autumn, setting off the red-purple fruits that split to reveal orange seeds.

VALUE AT OTHER TIMES
The stems have corky "wings" and the dark green leaves are attractive all summer.

IDEAL SITE
A mixed or shrub border.

CULTIVATION
Autumn colour is best in full sun, but it will tolerate partial shade. Grow in any well-drained soil. Prune in winter, if necessary, to shape and to remove any wayward, or dead and damaged shoots.

ALSO RECOMMENDED
E. alatus 'Compactus' is similar but smaller and more dense.

PERFECT PARTNERS
E. fortunei 'Emerald 'n' Gold' ♀, with gold and green leaves.

EUONYMUS

A very hardy, vigorous, bushy, mounded, evergreen shrub.
H 2.5m (8ft), S 1.5m (5ft); H to 6m (20ft) if climbing

SEASONAL HIGHLIGHTS
The shiny green leaves with white, often pink-flushed margins make good ground cover all year round.

VALUE AT OTHER TIMES
Tiny, greenish white flowers in summer, followed by pink fruits with orange seeds.

IDEAL SITE
Mixed or herbaceous borders, walls and containers.

CULTIVATION
Foliage colour is best in full sun, but it tolerates light shade. Grow in any well-drained soil. Trim in mid- to late spring; remove any all-green shoots as soon as seen.

ALSO RECOMMENDED
E. fortunei 'Emerald Gaiety' ♀ has white-variegated leaves.

PERFECT PARTNERS
E. europaeus 'Red Cascade' ♀ has red autumn leaves and fruit.

F

Euphorbia **x** *martinii* ♀

Euphorbia polychroma ♀

Euryops pectinatus ♀

Exochorda **x** *macrantha* 'The Bride' ♀

Forsythia **x** *intermedia*

EUPHORBIA, SPURGE
Upright, moderately vigorous, herbaceous perennial.
H & S 1m (3ft)
SEASONAL HIGHLIGHTS
From spring to midsummer, it bears heads of clustered, yellow-green flowers with dark red nectar glands.
VALUE AT OTHER TIMES
Red stems and narrow green leaves that are often purple-tinged when young.
IDEAL SITE
Mixed or herbaceous borders.
CULTIVATION
Best in full sun, but tolerant of light, dappled shade. Grow in a light, well-drained soil enriched with organic matter. On clay soils, dig in some grit to improve drainage.
ALSO RECOMMENDED
E. mellifera is evergreen and much taller, with honey-scented, red-brown flowers.
PERFECT PARTNERS
The broad glossy leaves of bear's breeches (*Acanthus*).

EUPHORBIA, SPURGE
A vigorous, bushy, clump-forming, herbaceous perennial.
H 40cm (16in), S 60cm (24in)
SEASONAL HIGHLIGHTS
From mid-spring to midsummer, it bears long-lasting, bright yellow-green flowers at the stem tips.
VALUE AT OTHER TIMES
Forms a dense mound of dark green, sometimes purple-tinted, leaves.
IDEAL SITE
Herbaceous borders and decorative containers.
CULTIVATION
Best in full sun, but tolerant of light, dappled shade. Grow in a light, well-drained soil enriched with organic matter.
ALSO RECOMMENDED
E. rigida has thick, arching stems with grey-green leaves and yellow flowers in spring and early summer.
PERFECT PARTNERS
Stachys byzantina 'Primrose Heron'.

SOUTH AFRICAN DAISY
An upright, bushy, vigorous, half-hardy evergreen perennial.
H & S 1m (3ft)
SEASONAL HIGHLIGHTS
From early summer to mid-autumn, it bears bright yellow, daisy-like flowers.
VALUE AT OTHER TIMES
It has grey-hairy fern-like foliage all year round.
IDEAL SITE
As a filler in herbaceous borders, or in decorative pots.
CULTIVATION
Grow in full sun, in sharply drained, moderately fertile soil. Trim after flowering to keep compact. Take stem cuttings in summer; over-winter young plants and potted plants under glass.
ALSO RECOMMENDED
E. acraeus ♀ is more compact and cold-tolerant, with yellow flowers and silver-grey leaves.
PERFECT PARTNERS
Penstemons, osteospermums.

EXOCHORDA, PEARL BUSH
A vigorous, mound-forming, deciduous shrub.
H 2m (6ft), S 3m (10ft)
SEASONAL HIGHLIGHTS
In late spring and early summer, the arching stems are wreathed in white flowers.
VALUE AT OTHER TIMES
Has attractive, light green leaves from spring to autumn.
IDEAL SITE
A shrub or mixed border.
CULTIVATION
Grow in full sun or partial shade, in any fertile, well-drained soil. Will tolerate shallow, chalky soils. Shorten flowered shoots to strong buds after flowering.
ALSO RECOMMENDED
E. racemosa is taller, with upright clusters of white flowers in late spring.
PERFECT PARTNERS
Camellias as a dark-leaved backdrop; *Magnolia stellata* ♀.

FORSYTHIA
A vigorous, strongly upright, deciduous shrub.
H & S to 1.5m (5ft)
SEASONAL HIGHLIGHTS
In spring, it bears bright, deep yellow flowers all along the bare branches.
VALUE AT OTHER TIMES
Undistinguished in summer, but a good host for clematis.
IDEAL SITE
Shrub and mixed borders, or as informal hedging.
CULTIVATION
Thrives in any fertile soil in sun or light dappled shade. sufficient. Shorten flowered shoots to strong buds after flowering; when established, cut out one in four of the oldest stems to encourage new growth from the base.
ALSO RECOMMENDED
F. × *intermedia* 'Lynwood' ♀ has rich yellow flowers in great profusion.
PERFECT PARTNERS
Create a blue carpet beneath forsythias with *Scilla siberica*.

F

Freesia 'Imperial Red'

Fremontodendron 'California Glory' ♔

Fritillaria imperialis

Fritillaria meleagris ♔

Fuchsia 'Auntie Jinks'

FREESIA

An upright, half-hardy, bulbous perennial.
H 40cm (16in), S 5cm (2in)

SEASONAL HIGHLIGHTS
Bears scented, pinkish-red, creamy-throated flowers from late winter to spring.

VALUE AT OTHER TIMES
Is grown only for its flowers.

IDEAL SITE
A cool greenhouse or conservatory; prepared bulbs are summer-flowering and can be grown outdoors.

CULTIVATION
Plant bulbs in pots of loamy compost with added grit, in autumn. Keep temperature below 13°C (55°F). Give a balanced liquid feed weekly when the flower buds appear. Dry off after flowering and rest for the summer.

ALSO RECOMMENDED
F. 'Oberon' with lemon-yellow and red flowers.

PERFECT PARTNERS
Cinerarias (*Pericallis*), paper white narcissus (*N. papyraceus*).

FLANNEL BUSH

A vigorous, upright then spreading, evergreen shrub
H 6m (20ft), S 4m (12ft)

SEASONAL HIGHLIGHTS
A long succession of saucer-shaped, deep yellow flowers appear from late spring to mid-autumn.

VALUE AT OTHER TIMES
The lobed, dark green leaves have tawny down beneath.

IDEAL SITE
A warm, sunny, sheltered wall.

CULTIVATION
Grow in fertile, well-drained soil. Protect from cold winds. To wall-train, tie in the main stems to a support of wires or trellis. Keep pruning to a minimum; just shorten outward-growing shoots on wall-trained plants after the first flush of bloom, and trim out damaged or dead wood.

ALSO RECOMMENDED
F. 'Pacific Sunset' has yellow flowers with pointed petals.

PERFECT PARTNERS
Clematis 'Ascotiensis'.

CROWN IMPERIAL

A robust, strongly upright, bulbous perennial.
H to 1.5m (5ft),
S 25–30cm (10–12in)

SEASONAL HIGHLIGHTS
In late spring or early summer, at the tips of stout stems, bears large, nodding, orange, yellow or red flowers crowned by leafy bracts.

VALUE AT OTHER TIMES
Of no real value at other times.

IDEAL SITE
A sunny border or raised bed.

CULTIVATION
Grow in full sun in fertile, well-drained soil. Plant bulbs in autumn, at four times their own depth, setting on a layer of sharp sand to improve drainage. The bulbs will rot in wet soils.

ALSO RECOMMENDED
F. imperialis 'Lutea' has bright yellow flowers.

PERFECT PARTNERS
Mid-season and late-flowering tulips.

SNAKE'S HEAD FRITILLARY

An upright, slender bulbous perennial.
H 30cm (1ft), S 5–8cm (2–3in)

SEASONAL HIGHLIGHTS
In spring, it bears hanging, bell-shaped flowers in delicate, chequered shades of pink, purple or white.

VALUE AT OTHER TIMES
No real value at other times.

IDEAL SITE
In a rock garden, or naturalized in turf.

CULTIVATION
Grow in fertile, humus-rich, moisture-retentive soil. Plant the bulbs in autumn at two to three times their own depth and the same distance apart. If grown in grass, delay the first mowing until the leaves have faded naturally.

ALSO RECOMMENDED
F. acmopetala ♔ has pale green, maroon-marked flowers.

PERFECT PARTNERS
Narcissus, camassias.

FUCHSIA

A trailing, moderately vigorous, half-hardy shrub.
H 15–20cm (6–8in),
S 20–40cm (8–16in)

SEASONAL HIGHLIGHTS
From early summer until late autumn, it bears masses of single flowers with pink-red tubes, cerise-margined white sepals and purple corollas.

VALUE AT OTHER TIMES
Of no value during winter.

IDEAL SITE
Containers, including hanging baskets, or mixed borders.

CULTIVATION
Tolerates sun or light shade. Grow in fertile, well-drained soil or potting mix. Plant out when the threat of frost has passed. Bring indoors for the winter. Deadhead regularly. Cut back hard in spring.

ALSO RECOMMENDED
F. 'Celia Smedley' ♔ has pink and currant-red flowers.

PERFECT PARTNERS
Argyranthemums, osteospermums, pelargoniums.

G

Galanthus plicatus subsp. *byzantinus* ♀

Garrya elliptica

Gazania Chansonette Series

Genista aetnensis ♀

Geranium himalayense

SNOWDROP

A vigorous perennial bulb.
H 20cm (8in), S 8cm (3in)

SEASONAL HIGHLIGHTS
In late winter or early spring, it bears nodding, honey-scented, white flowers with green markings on the inner petals.

VALUE AT OTHER TIMES
Of no value at other times.

IDEAL SITE
Woodland gardens, beneath trees and shrubs, or naturalized in turf.

CULTIVATION
Grow in dappled shade in any fertile garden soil that does not dry out in summer. Lift and divide the bulbs when congested, after flowering but before the leaves have faded. May self-seed.

ALSO RECOMMENDED
G. nivalis ♀ has white flowers with a V-shaped green mark on each petal.

PERFECT PARTNERS
Winter aconites (*Eranthis hyemalis*), hardy cyclamen.

GARRYA, SILK TASSEL BUSH

A dense, vigorous, bushy evergreen shrub.
H & S 4m (12ft)

SEASONAL HIGHLIGHTS
From midwinter to early spring, it bears swags of silky, hanging, grey-green catkins.

VALUE AT OTHER TIMES
Glossy, wavy-margined, dark greyish-green leaves all year.

IDEAL SITE
Shrub or mixed borders, and shady walls.

CULTIVATION
Grow in any fertile, well-drained soil in sun or partial shade. Shelter from cold wind. After flowering, shorten any shoots that spoil the shape, or grow away from, or in to the wall, if wall-trained.

ALSO RECOMMENDED
G. elliptica 'James Roof' ♀ has dark sea-green leaves and very long catkins.

PERFECT PARTNERS
Jasminum nudiflorum ♀, *Mahonia* × *media* 'Charity' ♀.

GAZANIA

Vigorous, half-hardy perennial often grown as an annual.
H 20cm (8in), S 25cm (10in)

SEASONAL HIGHLIGHTS
Throughout summer, it bears daisy-like, dark-zoned flower heads in bronze, orange, rose-pink, salmon-pink or red.

VALUE AT OTHER TIMES
The glossy, dark green leaves have silky white hair beneath.

IDEAL SITE
Bedding, containers, hot, sunny borders, seaside gardens.

CULTIVATION
Sow seeds in warmth in spring and plant out young plants when the risk of frost has passed. Grow in full sun in light, well-drained soil. Deadhead regularly to prolong flowering.

ALSO RECOMMENDED
Gazania Daybreak Series has white, yellow, orange and pink flowers.

PERFECT PARTNERS
Pelargoniums, French marigolds.

MOUNT ETNA BROOM

A vigorous, deciduous shrub or small tree with upright, then weeping shoots.
H & S to 8m (25ft)

SEASONAL HIGHLIGHTS
Fragrant, yellow, pea-like flowers are borne at the stem tips in mid- to late summer.

VALUE AT OTHER TIMES
The weeping shoots are bright green and give an evergreen appearance.

IDEAL SITE
Sunny walls, banks or borders.

CULTIVATION
Grow in full sun in light, poor, very well-drained soil. After flowering, shorten flowered shoots to strong buds on green wood; don't cut into old wood.

ALSO RECOMMENDED
G. hispanica is dense, spiny and much smaller with golden yellow flowers in late spring and early summer.

PERFECT PARTNERS
Cytisus nigricans.

HARDY GERANIUM, HIMALAYAN CRANESBILL

A vigorous, mound-forming herbaceous perennial.
H 30–45cm (12–18in), S 60cm (24in)

SEASONAL HIGHLIGHTS
In early summer, it bears a profusion of white-centred, violet-blue to deep blue flowers, and then blooms sporadically into autumn.

VALUE AT OTHER TIMES
The lobed, soft green leaves colour well in autumn.

IDEAL SITE
Mixed or herbaceous borders.

CULTIVATION
Grow in any fertile, well-drained soil, in sun or partial shade. Trim after the first flush of flowers to encourage more in the autumn. Divide every three or four years in spring.

ALSO RECOMMENDED
G. endressii ♀ has silvery pink flowers all summer.

PERFECT PARTNERS
Achilleas, hemerocallis, border phlox.

G

Geranium psilostemon ♀

HARDY GERANIUM, ARMENIAN CRANESBILL
A vigorous, clump-forming herbaceous perennial.
H 60–120cm (2–4ft),
S 60cm (24in)
SEASONAL HIGHLIGHTS
From early until late summer, it bears sprays of upturned, brilliant magenta flowers with black centres and veins.
VALUE AT OTHER TIMES
The leaves are tinted crimson in spring and red in autumn; they make good ground cover.
IDEAL SITE
Mixed or herbaceous borders, especially in cottage gardens.
CULTIVATION
Grow in sun or light shade, in in any fertile soil. Deadhead regularly to encourage continuous blooming.
ALSO RECOMMENDED
G. 'Ann Folkard' is similar but more spreading.
PERFECT PARTNERS
Achilleas, border phlox, hemerocallis.

Geum 'Borisii'

GEUM, AVENS
A vigorous, clump-forming, herbaceous perennial.
H 30–50cm (12–20in),
S 30cm (12in)
SEASONAL HIGHLIGHTS
From late spring to late summer, it bears long-stemmed clusters of bright, brick-red flowers with a boss of golden yellow stamens.
VALUE AT OTHER TIMES
Basal mounds of divided, fresh green leaves.
IDEAL SITE
The front of sunny, mixed or herbaceous borders, especially in cottage gardens.
CULTIVATION
Grow in any fertile, well-drained soil in full sun or light, part-day shade. Lift and divide the plants every three or four years to rejuvenate.
ALSO RECOMMENDED
G. 'Red Wings' has semi-double, scarlet flowers.
PERFECT PARTNERS
G. 'Lady Stratheden' ♀ with yellow flowers.

Gunnera manicata ♀

GUNNERA
A massive, very vigorous, herbaceous perennial.
H 2.5m (8ft), S 3–4m (10–12ft)
SEASONAL HIGHLIGHTS
The enormous, prominently veined, bright green leaves have red-prickly stems and reach 2m (6ft) long.
VALUE AT OTHER TIMES
In summer, it bears fat spikes of tiny greenish-red flowers, followed by orange-red fruit.
IDEAL SITE
Pool- and streamsides, damp borders.
CULTIVATION
Grow in sun or partial shade in deep, permanently moist soil enriched with plenty of organic matter. In cold areas, protect the crown in winter with a deep dry mulch of straw or leafmould.
ALSO RECOMMENDED
G. tinctoria is similar but more compact.
PERFECT PARTNERS
Iris sibirica, Rheum palmatum 'Atrosanguineum'.

H

Hakonechloa macra 'Aureola' ♀

HAKONECHLOA
A spreading, mound-forming, deciduous grass.
H 35cm (14in), S 40cm (16in)
SEASONAL HIGHLIGHTS
The narrow, arching leaves, striped bright yellow and green, are present for much of the year. Pale green flower spikes appear from late summer to autumn.
VALUE AT OTHER TIMES
Leaves turn red in autumn and often persist into winter.
IDEAL SITE
The front of a border, in containers, in rock gardens, or woodland gardens.
CULTIVATION
Grow in full sun, or for the best leaf colours, in partial shade. Grow in fertile, moist, but well-drained soil.
ALSO RECOMMENDED
Carex elata 'Aurea' ♀, with golden, grass-like leaves.
PERFECT PARTNERS
Miscanthus sinensis 'Gracillimus' has blue-green leaves that turn bronze in autumn.

Hamamelis x *intermedia* 'Arnold Promise' ♀

WITCH HAZEL
Slow-growing, deciduous shrub of vase-shaped outline.
H & S to 4m (12ft)
SEASONAL HIGHLIGHTS
Bare branches are spangled with fragrant, spidery, yellow flowers in early to mid-winter.
VALUE AT OTHER TIMES
The leaves turn yellow before falling in autumn.
IDEAL SITE
A woodland garden, as a specimen, in a shady border.
CULTIVATION
Needs a fertile, humus-rich, moisture-retentive, neutral to acid soil and a sheltered spot in sun or partial shade. Keep pruning to a minimum, but remove crossing or damaged shoots after flowering.
ALSO RECOMMENDED
H. × *intermedia* 'Jelena' ♀ has coppery orange flowers.
PERFECT PARTNERS
Mahonias, *Viburnum* × *bodnantense* 'Dawn' ♀.

Hebe 'Gauntlettii'

Helianthemum 'Raspberry Ripple'

Helianthus annuus 'Teddy Bear'

Helictotrichon sempervirens ♔

Heliotropium 'Marine' ♔

HEBE

A bushy, upright, fast-growing, half-hardy evergreen shrub.
H & S to 1m (3ft)

SEASONAL HIGHLIGHTS
From late summer until late autumn, it bears hanging clusters of small pink flowers.

VALUE AT OTHER TIMES
Has glossy rich-green leaves.

IDEAL SITE
Sunny mixed or shrub borders, decorative containers.

CULTIVATION
Grow in fertile, well-drained, neutral to alkaline soil in sun or dappled shade. Shelter from cold winds. It may not survive outdoors in very cold areas; bring pot-grown plants into a cold greenhouse for the winter. Trim lightly to shape in spring.

ALSO RECOMMENDED
H. 'Great Orme' ♔ is hardier, with bright pink flowers.

PERFECT PARTNERS
Bamboos, cotoneasters, shrubby potentillas.

ROCK ROSE, SUN ROSE

A spreading, low-growing, evergreen shrub.
H 20cm (8in), S 30cm (12in)

SEASONAL HIGHLIGHTS
The white flowers, irregularly marked with raspberry-pink, appear over long periods from late spring to midsummer.

VALUE AT OTHER TIMES
Dark greyish-green leaves.

IDEAL SITE/WILL TOLERATE
Sunny banks, borders and raised beds, hot, dry sites.

CULTIVATION
Grow in full sun, in well-drained, neutral to alkaline soil that is not too fertile. Too rich a soil produces fewer flowers and soft growth that is more susceptible to cold damage. After flowering, trim back flowered shoots to strong young growth.

ALSO RECOMMENDED
H. 'Rhodanthe Carneum' ♔ has flesh-pink flowers.

PERFECT PARTNERS
Alpine pinks, *Phlox subulata*.

SUNFLOWER

A vigorous, upright, hardy annual.
H 90cm (3ft), S 30cm (12in)

SEASONAL HIGHLIGHTS
In summer, it bears large, double, shaggy golden yellow flowerheads, 13cm (5in) wide.

VALUE AT OTHER TIMES
Is discarded after flowering.

IDEAL SITE
Sunny annual borders; is good for childrens' plots.

CULTIVATION
Grow in full sun in fertile, well-drained soil, in a warm sheltered site for most prolific flowering. Sow seeds under glass in small pots in early spring, or in the flowering site in late spring.

ALSO RECOMMENDED
H. annuus 'Sun Spot' is shorter, with larger, bright yellow flowerheads.

PERFECT PARTNERS
Dahlias, chrysanthemums.

BLUE OAT GRASS

A mounded, evergreen perennial grass.
H to 1.4m (4½ft), S 60cm (2ft)

SEASONAL HIGHLIGHTS
In early and midsummer, stiff, upright stems bear airy, straw-coloured, purple-flushed flowering spikes.

VALUE AT OTHER TIMES
Spiky mounds of grey-blue leaves all year.

IDEAL SITE
The front of a border, a rock garden, or gravel garden.

CULTIVATION
The leaves colour best in full sun, but it tolerates light dappled shade. Grow in poor, well-drained, preferably alkaline soil. Remove dead leaves and old flower spikelets in spring. Divide in spring.

ALSO RECOMMENDED
Leymus arenarius, a grass with bright blue-grey leaves.

PERFECT PARTNERS
Purple sage (*Salvia officinalis* 'Pupurascens' ♔), and grey-leaved *Helichrysum splendidum*.

HELIOTROPE, CHERRY PIE

A bushy, upright, frost-tender, evergreen shrub, usually grown as an annual.
H to 1.2m (4ft),
S 35–40cm (12–18in)

SEASONAL HIGHLIGHTS
Over long periods in summer, it bears dense heads of sweetly scented, deep violet-blue flowers; they attract butterflies and bees.

VALUE AT OTHER TIMES
It has wrinkled, dark green, purple-tinted leaves.

IDEAL SITE
Bedding and containers.

CULTIVATION
Grow in any fertile, moist but well-drained soil in sun or partial shade. Sow seeds under glass in spring and plant out when the threat of frost has passed.

ALSO RECOMMENDED
H. 'Chatsworth' ♔ has deep purple, very fragrant flowers.

PERFECT PARTNERS
African and French marigolds.

H

Helleborus niger **'Potter's Wheel'**

HELLEBORE, CHRISTMAS ROSE

A robust, upright perennial. H 30cm (12in), S 45cm (18in)

SEASONAL HIGHLIGHTS
From winter to early spring, it bears bowl-shaped white flowers with green "eyes".

VALUE AT OTHER TIMES
Leathery, dark green leaves on purple-marked stems.

IDEAL SITE
Shady borders, or naturalized in woodland gardens.

CULTIVATION
Grows best in dappled shade, but tolerates a more open aspect if soil doesn't dry out. Grow in fertile, preferably heavy, neutral to alkaline soil. Will tolerate clay soils. Trim away old leaves before flowers emerge for the best display.

ALSO RECOMMENDED
H. purpurascens has purplish or slate-grey flowers that are pink-flushed pale green inside.

PERFECT PARTNERS
Ferns, snowdrops (*Galanthus*), winter aconites (*Eranthis*).

Helleborus orientalis

HELLEBORE, LENTEN ROSE

A vigorous, upright, evergreen perennial. H & S 45cm (18in)

SEASONAL HIGHLIGHTS
From mid-winter to spring, it bears stout-stemmed, white or creamy green flowers that flush pink with age.

VALUE AT OTHER TIMES
Leathery, divided, deep green basal leaves persist all year.

IDEAL SITE
Mixed or herbaceous borders, woodland gardens.

CULTIVATION
Grows best in dappled shade, but tolerates sun if the soil is reliably moist. Grow in any good garden soil. Tolerates clay soils. Trim away old leaves before flowers emerge to display them at their best.

ALSO RECOMMENDED
H. orientalis subsp. *guttatus* has creamy white flowers spotted maroon within.

PERFECT PARTNERS
Ferns, snowdrops (*Galanthus*), winter aconites (*Eranthis*).

Hemerocallis **'Gentle Shepherd'**

HEMEROCALLIS, DAYLILY

A moderately vigorous, semi-evergreen perennial. H 65cm (26in), S 1.2m (4ft)

SEASONAL HIGHLIGHTS
The ivory-white flowers with green throats appear over long periods in midsummer.

VALUE AT OTHER TIMES
The slender, arching green leaves often persist through winter and make good ground cover.

IDEAL SITE
Sunny borders, gravel gardens.

CULTIVATION
Prefers full sun, but tolerates light, dappled shade. Grow in fertile, moist but well-drained soil. Mulch in autumn. Divide every three or four years, in spring, to maintain vigour.

ALSO RECOMMENDED
H. 'Chorus Line' has bright pink, yellow-marked flowers with dark green throats.

PERFECT PARTNERS
Achilleas, border phlox, monardas.

Hippeastrum **'Apple Blossom'**

AMARYLLIS

A robust, bulbous perennial. H 30–50cm (12–20in), S 30cm (12in)

SEASONAL HIGHLIGHTS
In winter, it bears large, white, funnel-shaped flowers with pink-flushed petal tips.

VALUE AT OTHER TIMES
Has little value at other times.

IDEAL SITE
In a well-lit spot in the home, or in a warm conservatory.

CULTIVATION
Plant the bulbs in autumn, with "neck and shoulders" above soil level. Water little until growth is well underway then water freely and feed every two weeks with a balanced liquid fertilizer. After flowering gradually reduce watering as the leaves begin to die down.

ALSO RECOMMENDED
H. 'Picotee' has white flowers with red-rimmed petals.

PERFECT PARTNERS
Early, forced narcissus, such as *N. papyraceus*, and hyacinths.

Hordeum jubatum

SQUIRREL TAIL GRASS

A moderately vigorous, annual or perennial grass. H 50cm (20in), S 30cm (12in)

SEASONAL HIGHLIGHTS
In early and midsummer, erect stems bear nodding heads of silky, long-bristled, pale green spikelets. They are flushed red or purple and turn buff as they age.

VALUE AT OTHER TIMES
Has tufts of narrow, light green leaves. The flowerheads are good for drying.

IDEAL SITE
A wild garden or an annual, mixed or herbaceous border.

CULTIVATION
Prefers full sun, but will tolerate light, dappled shade. Grow in any well-drained soil.

ALSO RECOMMENDED
Stipa tenuissima has narrow, feathery, buff-coloured flowerheads in summer.

PERFECT PARTNERS
Stipa gigantea, Lagurus ovatus (hare's tail grass).

Hyacinthoides non-scripta

BLUEBELL
A vigorous, clump-forming perennial bulb.
H 20–40cm (8–16in),
S 8cm (3in)
SEASONAL HIGHLIGHTS
In spring, sturdy stems bear nodding, sweetly scented, violet-blue flowers amid glossy, dark green strap-shaped leaves.
VALUE AT OTHER TIMES
Dies back in summer.
IDEAL SITE
Woodland gardens and shady borders.
CULTIVATION
Grow in dappled shade, in any fertile soil that does not dry out in summer. Plant the bulbs 8cm (3in) deep in autumn. May self-seed to form extensive colonies.
ALSO RECOMMENDED
H. hispanica (Spanish bluebell) is taller, with unscented blue flowers.
PERFECT PARTNERS
Erythronium 'Pagoda', *Fritillaria cirrhosa*.

Hyacinthus orientalis 'City of Haarlem' ♀

HYACINTH
A vigorous, upright bulb.
H 20–30cm (8–12in),
S 8cm (3in)
SEASONAL HIGHLIGHTS
In late spring, sturdy stems arise bearing dense spikes of highly scented, soft primrose-yellow flowers.
VALUE AT OTHER TIMES
Of no value at other times.
IDEAL SITE
Spring bedding, pots indoors.
CULTIVATION
Best in full sun. Plant bulbs in autumn, 10cm (4in) deep, in fertile, well-drained soil. Use prepared bulbs for winter flowers indoors. Plant in bowls of bulb fibre with the tip of the bulb exposed. Keep in a cool, dark place for six weeks. When shoots are about 2.5cm (1in) long, bring into light and warmth.
ALSO RECOMMENDED
H. orientalis 'Jan Bos' has cerise-red flowers.
PERFECT PARTNERS
Narcissus, tulips.

Hydrangea paniculata 'Grandiflora' ♀

HYDRANGEA
A vigorous, deciduous shrub.
H 3–7m (10–22ft),
S 2.5m (8ft)
SEASONAL HIGHLIGHTS
In late summer and early autumn, it produces large, conical heads of white flowers that flush pink with age.
VALUE AT OTHER TIMES
Handsome dark green leaves. Flowers are good for drying.
IDEAL SITE
A shrub or mixed border or a woodland garden.
CULTIVATION
Grow in fertile, humus-rich, moisture-retentive soil in partial shade or sun. Shelter from cold, dry winds. Needs minimal pruning, but for larger flowers, in late winter, cut back all sideshoots to within 5–8cm (2–3in) of the main stems.
ALSO RECOMMENDED
H. paniculata 'Floribunda' ♀ has narrower flowerheads.
PERFECT PARTNERS
Hypericums, hostas.

Ilex aquifolium 'Handsworth New Silver' ♀

ENGLISH HOLLY
A dense, vigorous, evergreen shrub of columnar outline.
H 8m (25ft), S 5m (15ft)
SEASONAL HIGHLIGHTS
Bright red berries in winter.
VALUE AT OTHER TIMES
All year, its dark purple stems bear glossy dark green leaves with spiny cream margins.
IDEAL SITE
In a shrub border, woodland garden, or as a specimen.
CULTIVATION
Full sun produces the best variegation, but it tolerates dappled shade. Grow in any fertile, well-drained soil. Prune to shape, if necessary, in early spring.
ALSO RECOMMENDED
I. x *altaclerensis* 'Lawsoniana' ♀ gold-and-green leaves and red-brown berries.
PERFECT PARTNERS
Mahonia x *media* 'Charity' ♀, *Viburnum* x *bodnantense* 'Dawn' ♀.

Impatiens Super Elfin Series

BUSY LIZZIE
Compact, frost-tender perennials grown as annuals.
H & S to 25cm (10in)
SEASONAL HIGHLIGHTS
Throughout summer, bears a mass of flat, spurred flowers in violet, orange, lipstick-pink, red and various pastel shades.
VALUE AT OTHER TIMES
Can be grown as a pot plant to flower through the winter.
IDEAL SITE
Summer bedding, containers.
CULTIVATION
Sow seeds in warmth in early spring. Plant out when the threat of frost has passed, into moisture-retentive, fertile soil in partial or dappled shade.
ALSO RECOMMENDED
I. walleriana 'Starbright' has red, orange, rose-pink and violet-blue flowers, each with a central white star.
PERFECT PARTNERS
Pelargoniums, Semperflorens begonias.

Indigofera amblyantha ♧

Ipomoea tricolor 'Heavenly Blue'

Iris danfordiae

Iris foetidissima ♧

Iris germanica ♧

INDIGOFERA
A vigorous, deciduous shrub with arching branches.
H 2m (6ft), S 2.5m (8ft)

SEASONAL HIGHLIGHTS
From early summer until early autumn, it bears slender, upright clusters of pale pink, pea-like flowers.

VALUE AT OTHER TIMES
From spring to autumn, it has elegant bright green leaves.

IDEAL SITE
A shrub border, or as a specimen on a warm wall.

CULTIVATION
Grow in full sun in fertile, moist but well-drained soil. In late winter or early spring, trim overlong, badly placed, or damaged shoots. In very cold areas, if severely damaged by cold, prune all stems back hard to a woody framework.

ALSO RECOMMENDED
I. heterantha has purplish-pink flowers and grey-green leaves.

PERFECT PARTNERS
Kalmia latifolia (on acid soils), escallonias.

MORNING GLORY
A vigorous, twining, frost-tender annual climber.
H to 4m (12ft), S 15cm (6in)

SEASONAL HIGHLIGHTS
From summer until autumn, it bears white-throated, funnel-shaped, deep sky-blue flowers.

VALUE AT OTHER TIMES
It has heart-shaped, bright green leaves. It is usually discarded after flowering.

IDEAL SITE
Train through shrubs, on poles and pyramids, or in decorative containers.

CULTIVATION
Prefers a warm, sheltered site, in moderately fertile well-drained soil. It needs sun but with shade from strong midday sun. Sow seeds in spring at 18°C (64°F); grow on in warmth and set out when risk of frost has passed.

ALSO RECOMMENDED
I. lobata has narrowly tubular, red and yellow flowers.

PERFECT PARTNERS
Tropaeolum peregrinum.

DWARF IRIS
A small, sturdy perennial bulb.
H10–15cm(4–6in), S 5cm (2in)

SEASONAL HIGHLIGHTS
Solitary yellow flowers with greenish-yellow markings appear in late winter and early spring amid a sheaf of narrow greyish-green leaves.

VALUE AT OTHER TIMES
No real value at other times.

IDEAL SITE
Rock gardens, raised beds, troughs, beneath deciduous shrubs.

CULTIVATION
Best in full sun. Plant bulbs at twice their own depth in late summer or early autumn in well-drained soil. Add coarse grit to heavy clay soils to improve drainage.

ALSO RECOMMENDED
I. histrioides 'Major' ♧ has deep blue flowers.

PERFECT PARTNERS
Snowdrops (*Galanthus nivalis* ♧), winter aconites, (*Eranthis hyemalis* ♧), winter-flowering heaths (*Erica carnea*).

STINKING IRIS, STINKING GLADWYN
A vigorous, rhizomatous evergreen perennial.
H & S 30–90cm (1–3ft)

SEASONAL HIGHLIGHTS
In early summer, it bears subtly coloured dull purple flowers suffused with yellow.

VALUE AT OTHER TIMES
In autumn, the seed pods split to reveal bead-like scarlet seeds. The strap-shaped dark green leaves give off an unpleasant scent if crushed.

IDEAL SITE
Dry, shady borders.

CULTIVATION
Grow in any well-drained soil in sun or shade.

ALSO RECOMMENDED
I. foetidissima var. *citrina* has lemon-yellow flowers.

PERFECT PARTNERS
Lily turf (*Liriope muscari*), with sheaves of strap-shaped leaves and spikes of bead-like violet-mauve flowers in autumn.

BEARDED IRIS
A vigorous, rhizomatous perennial.
Height 60–120cm (2–4ft), S 30cm (12in)

SEASONAL HIGHLIGHTS
In late spring or early summer, upright stems bear blue-violet flowers with yellow beards.

VALUE AT OTHER TIMES
Fans of sword-shaped, grey-green leaves.

IDEAL SITE
Mixed or herbaceous borders, especially in cottage gardens.

CULTIVATION
Grow in full sun or light, part-day shade in any moderately fertile well-drained soil.

ALSO RECOMMENDED
I. germanica 'Florentina' has scented white flowers.

PERFECT PARTNERS
The broad foliage of acanthus and hostas; *Centaurea montana.*

J

Iris 'Harmony'

Iris 'Katharine Hodgkin' ♀

Iris unguicularis ♀

Jasminum mesnyi ♀

Jasminum nudiflorum ♀

DWARF IRIS

A small, sturdy perennial bulb.
H 10–15cm (4–6in),
S 5cm (2in)

SEASONAL HIGHLIGHTS
Yellow-marked, royal-blue flowers appear in late winter amid a sheaf of narrow leaves.

VALUE AT OTHER TIMES
No real value at other times.

IDEAL SITE
Rock gardens, troughs or other containers, or beneath deciduous shrubs.

CULTIVATION
Best in full sun. Plant bulbs at twice their own depth in late summer or early autumn in well-drained soil. Add coarse grit to heavy clay soils to improve drainage.

ALSO RECOMMENDED
I. 'Joyce' has deep sky-blue flowers.

PERFECT PARTNERS
Snowdrops (*Galanthus nivalis* ♀), winter aconites, (*Eranthis hyemalis* ♀), *Erica carnea* 'Springwood White' ♀.

DWARF IRIS

A small but vigorous, bulbous perennial.
H 12cm (5in), S 5cm (1in)

SEASONAL HIGHLIGHTS
In late winter, it bears pale blue flowers, delicately patterned in blue and yellow.

VALUE AT OTHER TIMES
No real value at other times.

IDEAL SITE
Rock gardens, troughs or other containers, or beneath deciduous shrubs.

CULTIVATION
Best in full sun. Plant bulbs at twice their own depth in late summer or early autumn in well-drained soil. Add coarse grit to heavy clay soils to improve drainage.

ALSO RECOMMENDED
I. 'Natascha' has very pale blue-grey flowers.

PERFECT PARTNERS
Snowdrops (*Galanthus nivalis* ♀), winter aconites, (*Eranthis hyemalis* ♀), winter heaths (*Erica carnea*).

ALGERIAN IRIS

A vigorous, rhizomatous, evergreen perennial.
H 30cm (12in), S 5cm (2in)

SEASONAL HIGHLIGHTS
In late winter and early spring, it bears scented, pale lavender to deep violet, yellow-marked flowers with contrasting veins.

VALUE AT OTHER TIMES
Has tough, grass-like leaves throughout the year.

IDEAL SITE
Sunny borders, or at the base of a warm wall.

CULTIVATION
Grow in full sun in poor to moderately fertile, very freely draining, neutral to alkaline soil in a sheltered spot. Once planted, leave undisturbed; they flower with increasing freedom as they settle in.

ALSO RECOMMENDED
I. unguicularis 'Alba' has yellow-marked cream flowers.

PERFECT PARTNERS
Interplant with autumn-flowering *Nerine bowdenii.*

PRIMROSE JASMINE

A vigorous, scrambling, half-hardy evergreen shrub.
H 2.5m (8ft), S 3m (10ft)

SEASONAL HIGHLIGHTS
In early spring and early summer, it bears fragrant, bright yellow flowers.

VALUE AT OTHER TIMES
The divided, glossy, deep green leaves persist all year.

IDEAL SITE
A warm, sheltered wall in mild areas, or a conservatory.

CULTIVATION
Grow in full sun, in fertile, well-drained soil or potting compost. Tie in shoots to a support as growth proceeds. After flowering, thin out the oldest flowered shoots and shorten the remainder to strong buds.

ALSO RECOMMENDED
J. humile is similar but hardier.

PERFECT PARTNERS
J. officinale 'Argenteovariegatum' ♀ has grey-green leaves with creamy white margins and very fragrant white flowers.

WINTER JASMINE

A vigorous, very hardy, deciduous, scrambling shrub.
H & S to 3m (10ft)

SEASONAL HIGHLIGHTS
In winter and early spring, it bears masses of bright yellow flowers on bare branches.

VALUE AT OTHER TIMES
The green shoots and dark green leaves persist for most of the year.

IDEAL SITE
Tied in to supports on a sunny or lightly shaded wall, or sprawling over a sunny bank.

CULTIVATION
Grow in any fertile garden soil. After flowering, cut back flowered shoots to strong buds. Every three or four years, take out some of the oldest growths at the base.

ALSO RECOMMENDED
J. officinale ♀ bears fragrant white flowers from summer to autumn.

PERFECT PARTNERS
Daphne mezereum, Garrya elliptica.

K

L

Kerria japonica 'Picta'

Kniphofia 'Green Jade'

Laburnum × *watereri* 'Vossii' ♥

Lachenalia aloides 'Nelsonii'

Lagurus ovatus

KERRIA
An upright, moderately vigorous, deciduous shrub.
H 1.5m (5ft), S 2m (6ft)
SEASONAL HIGHLIGHTS
In mid and late spring, it bears golden yellow flowers.
VALUE AT OTHER TIMES
It has grey-green leaves with margins of creamy white.
IDEAL SITE
A mixed or shrub border.
CULTIVATION
Grow in sun or partial shade, in any well-drained soil enriched with organic matter. After flowering, cut back flowered shoots to strong sideshoots or buds.
ALSO RECOMMENDED
K. japonica 'Pleniflora' ♥ is more vigorous with pompon-like, double yellow flowers.
PERFECT PARTNERS
Purple-leaved berberis; *Ribes sanguineum* 'Pulborough Scarlet' (flowering currant).

RED-HOT POKER
A vigorous, clump-forming evergreen perennial.
H 1.5m (5ft),
S 60–75 cm (24–30in)
SEASONAL HIGHLIGHTS
In late summer and early autumn, it bears tall spikes of green flowers that fade to cream and then white. They are attractive to bees.
VALUE AT OTHER TIMES
Has broad, grass-like, greyish green leaves all year.
IDEAL SITE
Mixed or herbaceous borders, gravel gardens.
CULTIVATION
Grow in full sun in light, fertile, humus-rich, well-drained soil. Protect the crowns, of young plants especially, with a dry mulch.
ALSO RECOMMENDED
K. 'Prince Igor' has deep orange-red flowers.
PERFECT PARTNERS
Hemerocallis, *Knautia macedonica*.

LABURNUM, GOLDEN RAIN
A vigorous, deciduous tree with a spreading crown.
H & S to 8m (25ft)
SEASONAL HIGHLIGHTS
In late spring and early summer, it produces long, hanging chains of golden yellow flowers.
VALUE AT OTHER TIMES
It has lustrous, dark green leaves from spring to autumn.
IDEAL SITE
As a specimen or trained over a pergola.
CULTIVATION
Grow in full sun in any moderately fertile soil. Prune in late winter to remove dead and damaged wood and badly placed shoots.
ALSO RECOMMENDED
L. anagyroides is similar with shorter flower clusters.
PERFECT PARTNERS
Crataegus laevigata 'Rosea Flore Pleno', rhododendrons and azaleas (on acid soils).

LACHENALIA, CAPE COWSLIP
A vigorous, frost-tender perennial bulb. H 30-40cm (12-16in), S 5cm (2in)
SEASONAL HIGHLIGHTS
In winter or early spring, it produces dark-stemmed spikes of hanging, tubular, golden yellow flowers.
VALUE AT OTHER TIMES
It has clumps of strap-shaped, smooth green leaves.
IDEAL SITE
As a houseplant or in a greenhouse or conservatory.
CULTIVATION
Plant bulbs 10cm (4in) deep in autumn, in fertile potting compost. Grow in full light and water moderately when in growth. Reduce watering as the leaves fade and rest in dry conditions in summer.
ALSO RECOMMENDED
L. aloides has tubular yellow flowers with scarlet tips.
PERFECT PARTNERS
Cyclamen persicum (but not in the same pot).

HARE'S TAIL GRASS
Upright, tufted, moderately vigorous annual grass.
H 50cm (20in), S 30cm (12in)
SEASONAL HIGHLIGHTS
Throughout summer, it has dense heads of softly hairy, purple-tinted, pale green flower spikelets that age to creamy white.
VALUE AT OTHER TIMES
The flowerheads can be dried and used for arrangements indoors throughout the year.
IDEAL SITE
A mixed or annual border.
CULTIVATION
Grow in full sun in light, well-drained soil. Sow the seeds in the flowering site in spring, or in containers in a cold frame in autumn.
ALSO RECOMMENDED
Hordeum jubatum has long-bristled, silky flowerheads.
PERFECT PARTNERS
Carex elata 'Aurea' ♥.

Lantana camara cultivars

Lathyrus odoratus 'Colin Unwin'

Lavandula angustifolia 'Munstead'

Lavatera 'Barnsley' ♀

Libertia ixioides

LANTANA

Vigorous, frost-tender, evergreen shrubs, often grown as annual summer bedding.
H & S 1–2m (3–6ft)

SEASONAL HIGHLIGHTS
From late spring to autumn, they bear rounded heads of small white, yellow, salmon-pink, red or purple flowers.

VALUE AT OTHER TIMES
The prickly stems bear finely wrinkled, deep green leaves.

IDEAL SITE
As bedding, or in containers for patios and conservatories.

CULTIVATION
Grow in full sun in fertile, moist but well-drained soil. Sow seeds in warmth in spring. Plant out when the risk of frost has passed. Bring patio plants under glass in autumn. Prune back shoots to strong buds in late winter.

ALSO RECOMMENDED
L. camara 'Snow White' has pure white flowers.

PERFECT PARTNERS
Petunias and clarkias.

SWEET PEA

A hardy, vigorous annual that climbs with twining tendrils.
H 2.5m (8ft), S 45cm (18in)

SEASONAL HIGHLIGHTS
From early to midsummer, it bears frilled, soft red flowers; many more cultivars asre available, with usually fragrant flowers in white, red, pink or blue. Flowers are good for cutting.

IDEAL SITE
In mixed borders or cottage gardens, on poles or wigwams.

CULTIVATION
Grow in sun in fertile, well-drained soil enriched with plenty of organic matter. Sow seeds in under glass in late autumn or late winter, or in the flowering site in spring.

ALSO RECOMMENDED
"Old-fashioned" sweet peas have small but intensely fragrant flowers.

PERFECT PARTNERS
Grow with lavenders and pinks, or with runner beans in the kitchen garden.

LAVENDER

A compact, evergreen shrub.
H 45cm (18in), S 60cm (24in)

SEASONAL HIGHLIGHTS
From mid- to late summer, it bears long-stemmed, very fragrant, blue-purple flowers.

VALUE AT OTHER TIMES
It has aromatic, narrow, grey-green leaves.

IDEAL SITE
Sunny, mixed or herbaceous borders, in containers on a patio, in gravel gardens, as low hedging.

CULTIVATION
Grow in full sun in any moderately fertile, well-drained soil. On heavy clay incorporate plenty of grit to improve drainage. In mid-spring, cut back the previous year's growth by about 5cm (2in) to strong pairs of buds. Don't cut into old wood.

ALSO RECOMMENDED
L. angustifolia 'Loddon Pink' has soft pink flowers.

PERFECT PARTNERS
Roses, cistus.

LAVATERA, MALLOW

A very vigorous, bushy, semi-evergreen shrub.
H & S to 2m (6ft)

SEASONAL HIGHLIGHTS
Throughout summer, it produces open funnel-shaped, red-eyed, white flowers that flush soft pink with age.

VALUE AT OTHER TIMES
It has attractive lobed, grey-green leaves.

IDEAL SITE
A sunny shrub or mixed border, or as a specimen.

CULTIVATION
Prefers an open, sunny site. Grow in any reasonably fertile, well-drained soil. Shelter from cold winds in exposed gardens. In spring, cut back hard to good buds low down on the shrub and apply a balanced fertilizer.

ALSO RECOMMENDED
L. cashmiriana has clear rose-pink flowers.

PERFECT PARTNERS
Escallonias, lavenders, roses.

LIBERTIA

An upright, moderately vigorous evergreen perennial.
H & S to 60cm (24in)

SEASONAL HIGHLIGHTS
In late spring and early summer, slender stems arise bearing dense clusters of small white flowers.

VALUE AT OTHER TIMES
Clusters of orange-brown seeds follow the flowers and the narrow, leathery, dark green leaves turn orange-brown in autumn.

IDEAL SITE
A sunny mixed border.

CULTIVATION
Grow in moist, but well-drained soil in full sun. Protect with a dry mulch in winter, especially in cold areas.

ALSO RECOMMENDED
L. grandiflora is similar but taller with white flowers.

PERFECT PARTNERS
Asphodelus albus, Scilla peruviana.

L

Lilium 'Sun Ray'

Lobelia 'Bees' Flame'

Lobelia erinus 'Crystal Palace'

Lonicera fragrantissima

Lonicera x *heckrottii*

LILY

A vigorous, perennial bulb.
H 1m (3ft), S 15cm (6in)
SEASONAL HIGHLIGHTS
From early to midsummer, it bears bowl-shaped glossy yellow flowers with brown dots on the petals.
VALUE AT OTHER TIMES
No value at other times.
IDEAL SITE
Sunny borders and in containers on a patio.
CULTIVATION
Grow in sun but shade the roots from hot sun. Best in fertile, well-drained soil enriched with leafmould or well-rotted organic matter. Plant the bulbs in autumn at twice their own depth. On clay soils, plant on a layer of grit.
ALSO RECOMMENDED
L. 'Sterling Star' has scented, brown-speckled, cream-flushed white flowers.
PERFECT PARTNERS
Looks good with peonies, poppies and roses.

PERENNIAL LOBELIA

A vigorous, clump-forming, perennial of upright growth.
H 75cm (30in), S 30cm (12in)
SEASONAL HIGHLIGHTS
In mid- and late summer, it produces long spires of bright crimson flowers.
VALUE AT OTHER TIMES
It has attractive red-purple stems and leaves all summer.
IDEAL SITE
A damp mixed border or by a pool- or streamside.
CULTIVATION
Best in an open, sunny site in moist, fertile soil. Divide every three or four years to maintain vigour.
ALSO RECOMMENDED
L. × *gerardii* 'Vedrariensis' has violet-purple flowers.
PERFECT PARTNERS
Ligularia przewalskii, border phlox and *Achillea ptarmica*.

LOBELIA

A dense, compact herbaceous perennial grown as a half-hardy annual.
H & S 10cm (4in)
SEASONAL HIGHLIGHTS
From summer to autumn, it produces masses of dark blue, flowers above mounds of dark green foliage.
VALUE AT OTHER TIMES
Is discarded after flowering.
IDEAL SITE
Bedding, border edging and containers, including window boxes and hanging baskets.
CULTIVATION
Prefers an open, sunny site but will tolerate light dappled shade. Grow in any fertile, moisture-retentive soil. Sow seeds in late winter. Plant out when risk of frost has passed.
ALSO RECOMMENDED
L. erinus Cascade Series are trailing, with carmine-red, pink, blue or white flowers.
PERFECT PARTNERS
Alyssum (*Lobularia maritima*), begonias, marigolds.

WINTER-FLOWERING HONEYSUCKLE

Bushy, spreading, moderately vigorous, semi-evergreen shrub.
H 2m (6ft), S 3m (10ft)
SEASONAL HIGHLIGHTS
In winter and early spring, it bears very fragrant flowers.
VALUE AT OTHER TIMES
It has dark green leaves that are blue-green beneath.
IDEAL SITE
A shrub border, or against a warm wall; it flowers more freely in warmth with shelter.
CULTIVATION
Grow in any fertile, well-drained soil in sun or light shade. After flowering, prune back flowered shoots to strong buds or shoots lower down the stems.
ALSO RECOMMENDED
L. × *standishii* is similar and flowers from late autumn to early spring.
PERFECT PARTNERS
J. nudiflorum; use a clematis like *C.* 'Ernest Markham' for interest in summer.

HONEYSUCKLE

A vigorous, semi-evergreen, twining climber.
H 5m (15ft), S 3m (10ft)
SEASONAL HIGHLIGHTS
From mid- to late summer, it bears clusters of fragrant coral-pink flowers that are orange-yellow within.
VALUE AT OTHER TIMES
Has dark green leaves with blue-green undersides and sometimes bears glossy red berries in autumn.
IDEAL SITE
A wall, fence or trellis.
CULTIVATION
Grow in any fertile, moist but well-drained soil. In early spring, shorten shoots to strong buds or shoots lower down the stems.
ALSO RECOMMENDED
L. periclymenum 'Graham Thomas' ♥ has yellow flowers.
PERFECT PARTNERS
Clematis 'Huldine', *C.* 'Ville de Lyon'.

M

Lonicera x *purpusii*

Lupinus 'The Page'

Lychnis chalcedonica ♀

Lysichiton americanus ♀

Magnolia stellata ♀

WINTER-FLOWERING HONEYSUCKLE

A moderately vigorous, semi-evergreen or deciduous shrub. H 2m (6ft), S 2.5m (8ft)

SEASONAL HIGHLIGHTS
In winter and early spring, it bears small clusters of very fragrant white flowers with conspicuous yellow anthers.

VALUE AT OTHER TIMES
It has purple shoots and dark green leaves for the summer.

IDEAL SITE
A shrub border, or against a warm wall; it flowers most freely in warmth with shelter.

CULTIVATION
Grow in any fertile, well-drained soil in sun or dappled shade. After flowering, cut back flowered shoots to strong buds, but only to confine to bounds.

ALSO RECOMMENDED
L. × *purpusii* 'Winter Beauty' ♀ is very free-flowering.

PERFECT PARTNERS
Daphne mezereum, mahonias, sarcococca.

LUPIN

A vigorous, clump-forming herbaceous perennial. H 90cm (36in), S 75cm (30in)

SEASONAL HIGHLIGHTS
It produces dense spires of pea-like, carmine-red flowers in early and midsummer.

VALUE AT OTHER TIMES
Cut back after the first flush for a few more flowers later in summer. The attractive foliage fades after flowering.

IDEAL SITE
A mixed or herbaceous border, cottage gardens.

CULTIVATION
Grow in light, fertile, well-drained, preferably slightly acid soil in sun; it tolerates part-day shade. Take basal cuttings in mid-spring; lupins are often short-lived.

ALSO RECOMMENDED
L. 'Chandelier' has bright yellow flowers.

PERFECT PARTNERS
Delphiniums, Oriental poppies (*Papaver orientalis*), pyrethrums.

MALTESE CROSS

A moderately vigorous, herbaceous perennial. H 0.9–1.2m (3-4ft), S 30cm (12in)

SEASONAL HIGHLIGHTS
In early and midsummer, it produces rounded clusters of cross-shaped scarlet flowers at the tips of upright stems.

VALUE AT OTHER TIMES
Has basal clumps of bright green leaves.

IDEAL SITE
A mixed or herbaceous border.

CULTIVATION
Grow in any fertile, moist but well-drained soil in sun or light shade. Provide support. Deadhead to prolong flowering. Divide in spring or autumn. Self-seeds freely.

ALSO RECOMMENDED
L. coronaria has grey leaves and magenta flowers.

PERFECT PARTNERS
Aquilegias, lupins, Oriental poppies (*Papaver orientalis*).

SKUNK CABBAGE

A very vigorous, spreading herbaceous perennial. H 1m (3ft), S 1.2m (4ft)

SEASONAL HIGHLIGHTS
In early spring, before the leaves appear, it bears club-like spikes of tiny green flowers surrounded by large, glossy yellow spathes.

VALUE AT OTHER TIMES
The large, paddle-shaped leathery green leaves elongate after flowering.

IDEAL SITE
Pool- or streamsides.

CULTIVATION
Grow in full sun or light dappled shade in moist, fertile, humus-rich soil. Allow plenty of room for the leaves to grow.

ALSO RECOMMENDED
L. camtschatcensis ♀ has creamy-white flower spathes.

PERFECT PARTNERS
Caltha palustris.

STAR MAGNOLIA

Compact, bushy, slow-growing, deciduous shrub. H 3m (9ft), S 4m (12ft)

SEASONAL HIGHLIGHTS
In early and mid-spring, the silky buds open to star-shaped, white flowers.

VALUE AT OTHER TIMES
Has a neat habit and attractive leaves for the summer.

IDEAL SITE
As a specimen, or in a shrub or mixed border.

CULTIVATION
Grow in moist but well-drained, fertile, humus-rich soil in sun or dappled shade. It tolerates slightly acid and slightly alkaline soils. Shelter from cold winds and late frosts, which may damage the flowers. Little or no pruning is required.

ALSO RECOMMENDED
M. stellata 'Waterlily' has larger, double white flowers.

PERFECT PARTNERS
Camellias, flowering quince (*Chaenomeles*).

M

Mahonia **x** *media* **'Charity'** ♈

MAHONIA
An upright, bushy, vigorous evergreen shrub.
H to 5m (15ft), S 4m (12ft)

SEASONAL HIGHLIGHTS
From late autumn to early spring, it bears long spikes of fragrant, deep yellow flowers.

VALUE AT OTHER TIMES
During the rest of the year, it has attractive, glossy dark-green, sharply toothed leaves.

IDEAL SITE
In a shrub border, woodland garden, or as a specimen.

CULTIVATION
Grow in moist but well-drained, humus-rich soil, in partial shade or in sun if soils are reliably moist. It needs little pruning; if it becomes leggy or outgrows its allotted space, prune after flowering.

ALSO RECOMMENDED
M. repens 'Rotundifolia' is shorter and spreading with dark yellow flowers in spring.

PERFECT PARTNERS
Viburnum tinus, Daphne mezereum.

MALUS

Malus **'Butterball'**
H & S 8m (25ft)

Malus **'Marshall Oyama'**
H 8m (25ft), S 6m (20ft)

Malus **'Evereste'** ♈
H 7m (22ft), 6m (20ft)

Malus **'John Downie'** ♈
H 10m (30ft), 6m (20ft)

Malus **x** *hartwigii* **'Katherine'**
♈ H & S 6m (20ft)

Malus **x** *moerlandsii* **'Liset'**
H & S 6m (20ft)

Malus pumila **'Cowichan'**
H & S 8m (25ft)

Malus **x** *zumi* **'Professor Sprenger'** ♈ H & S 7m (22ft)

Malus **'Royalty'**
H & S 8m (25ft)

Malus **'Veitch's Scarlet'**
H & S 8m (25ft)

Malus transitoria ♈
H 8m (25ft), S 10m (30ft)

Malus toringo
H 2.5m (8ft), S 3m (10ft)

CRAB APPLES

Deciduous, mostly vigorous small trees that are ideal as specimens for smaller gardens.

SEASONAL HIGHLIGHTS
In spring, they bear masses of blossom ranging from white to pink and purplish reds.

VALUE AT OTHER TIMES
In autumn, they bear crab apples in colours ranging from yellow to red; the leaves turn yellow and orange too.

CULTIVATION
Grow in any fertile, well-drained soil in sun; they tolerate light shade, but purple-leaved variants are best in sun. Prune in winter to remove misplaced shoots or dead or damaged wood.

RECOMMENDED CULTIVARS
Clockwise from top left:
'Butterball' has pink-flushed white flowers; 'Cowichan' has rose-pink flowers; 'Evereste' has red-flushed orange fruit; 'John Downie' has white flowers; 'Katherine' has small, red-flushed yellow fruit; 'Liset' has purple-red fruit; 'Marshall Oyama' has pink-flushed white flowers; 'Professor Sprenger' has white flowers; 'Royalty' has flowers of crimson-purple; 'Veitch's Scarlet' has white flowers; *M. transitoria* has pea-like, yellow fruit; *M. toringo* has small, red or yellow fruit.

Matthiola **Brompton Group**

BROMPTON STOCKS

Vigorous, bushy, woody-based perennials grown as annuals or biennials.
H 45cm (18in), S 30cm (12in)

SEASONAL HIGHLIGHTS
From late spring to summer, they bear densely packed spikes of scented, single or double flowers in pink, red, purple, yellow and white. They are excellent cut flowers.

VALUE AT OTHER TIMES
No real value at other times.

IDEAL SITE
Cottage gardens, cutting borders and mixed borders.

CULTIVATION
Grow in full sun in fertile, well-drained soil. Sow seeds in warmth in spring and set out when the risk of frost has passed. For larger, earlier flowers sow in autumn and overwinter in a cold frame.

ALSO RECOMMENDED
M. 'Giant Excelsior Column' has tall spires of double flowers.

PERFECT PARTNERS
China asters, border carnations.

Miscanthus sinensis **'Silberfeder'**

MISCANTHUS

Vigorous, upright, deciduous perennial grass.
H 2.5m (8ft), S 1.2m (4ft)

SEASONAL HIGHLIGHTS
It has silvery, pinkish-brown flowerheads in early to mid-autumn; these and the dry leaves persist through winter.

VALUE AT OTHER TIMES
Has arching blue-green leaves.

IDEAL SITE
Mixed or herbaceous borders.

CULTIVATION
Grow in any fertile, moist but well-drained soil in full sun; it tolerates light shade. Cut old growth to the ground in spring. Divide congested clumps in spring.

ALSO RECOMMENDED
M. sinensis 'Zebrinus' ♀ has green leaves horizontally banded with yellow.

PERFECT PARTNERS
Stipa gigantea, Glyceria maxima 'Variegata'.

Monarda **'Mahogany'**

MONARDA, BERGAMOT, BEE BALM

A vigorous, clump-forming, herbaceous perennial.
H 90cm (36in), S 45cm (18in)

SEASONAL HIGHLIGHTS
From midsummer until autumn, it bears whorls of wine-red flowers at the stem tips. The flowers attract bees.

VALUE AT OTHER TIMES
Has aromatic, red-veined, dark green leaves.

IDEAL SITE
A mixed or herbaceous border, or herb garden.

CULTIVATION
Best in sun, but will tolerate light, dappled shade. Grow in any fertile, well-drained soil that doesn't dry out in summer. Divide overcrowded clumps in spring.

ALSO RECOMMENDED
M. 'Cambridge Scarlet' ♀ has scarlet-red flowers.

PERFECT PARTNERS
Achilleas, border phlox, sunflowers (*Helianthus*).

Muscari armeniacum ♀

MUSCARI, GRAPE HYACINTH

A vigorous, bulbous perennial.
H 20cm (8in), S 5cm (2in)

SEASONAL HIGHLIGHTS
In spring, it produces spikes of tubular, bright blue flowers with white mouths.

VALUE AT OTHER TIMES
Of no value at other times.

IDEAL SITE
A rock garden, the front of a mixed or herbaceous border, in containers.

CULTIVATION
Grow in full sun in any well-drained, moderately fertile soil. Plant bulbs, 10cm (4in) deep, in autumn. Lift to divide congested clumps as the leaves fade in summer.

ALSO RECOMMENDED
M. botryoides f. *album* has fragrant white flowers.

PERFECT PARTNERS
Erythroniums, crocus.

N

Narcissus **'Cheerfulness'** ♔

Narcissus cyclamineus ♔

Narcissus **'Dutch Master'** ♔

Nemesia caerulea

Nemesia strumosa **'KLM'**

DOUBLE NARCISSUS

Robust, bulbous perennial.
H 40cm (16in), S 8cm (3in)

SEASONAL HIGHLIGHTS
In mid-spring, each stem produces several sweetly scented, double white flowers with clustered, creamy-white segments at the centre.

VALUE AT OTHER TIMES
Of no value at other times.

IDEAL SITE
Borders, and containers indoors and outside.

CULTIVATION
Grow in sun or light, dappled shade. Plant the bulbs in autumn at twice their own depth, in any fertile, well-drained soil. If flowering declines and bulbs are congested, allow the foliage to die down naturally and lift and divide the clumps.

ALSO RECOMMENDED
N. 'Yellow Cheerfulness' has golden yellow flowers.

PERFECT PARTNERS
Forsythia, doronicums, crocus.

WILD NARCISSUS

A vigorous, perennial bulb.
H 15–20cm (6–8in),
S 2.5cm (1in)

SEASONAL HIGHLIGHTS
In early spring, it bears nodding, golden yellow flowers with backswept petals.

VALUE AT OTHER TIMES
Of no value at other times.

IDEAL SITE
Naturalized in turf or in rock or woodland gardens.

CULTIVATION
Grow in sun or dappled shade in any moderately fertile, well-drained soil. Plant bulbs in autumn at twice their own depth. If grown in turf, allow foliage to fade naturally before mowing.

ALSO RECOMMENDED
N. 'Jumblie' has similar but larger flowers with golden orange cups.

PERFECT PARTNERS
Crocus, chionodoxas.

TRUMPET DAFFODIL

A vigorous perennial bulb.
H 35cm (14in), S 8cm (3in)

SEASONAL HIGHLIGHTS
In mid-spring, it bears large golden yellow flowers, with short, slightly frilled trumpets.

VALUE AT OTHER TIMES
Can be grown in pots to flower earlier indoors.

IDEAL SITE
Naturalized in grass, in borders, or containers.

CULTIVATION
Grow in sun or dappled shade in fertile, well-drained soil. Plant bulbs in autumn at twice their own depth. For forcing, plant in pots and plunge in a cold frame for about 8 weeks or until shoots appear. Bring into a cool greenhouse, and take indoors as flower buds begin to open.

ALSO RECOMMENDED
N. 'Little Beauty' is shorter with creamy-white, yellow-cupped flowers.

PERFECT PARTNERS
Crocus, chionodoxas.

PERENNIAL NEMESIA

A vigorous, bushy, woody-based perennial.
H 60cm (24in), S 30cm (12in)

SEASONAL HIGHLIGHTS
Clusters of yellow-throated, pink, pale blue, lavender-blue or white flowers appear from early summer to autumn.

VALUE AT OTHER TIMES
It has dark green leaves.

IDEAL SITE
Borders, raised beds and decorative containers.

CULTIVATION
Grow in a sheltered site in full sun in moderately fertile, well-drained soil. It may not survive very cold winters. If pot-grown, it can be brought into a greenhouse in autumn. Otherwise, take stem cuttings in summer and overwinter young plants under glass.

ALSO RECOMMENDED
N. caerulea 'Innocence' ♔ has white flowers.

PERFECT PARTNERS
Argyranthemums, osteospermums.

ANNUAL NEMESIA

Bushy, free-flowering annual.
H 18–30cm (7–12in),
S 10–15cm (4–6in).

SEASONAL HIGHLIGHTS
Bears bicoloured, blue and white flowers with pink throats and yellow beards, from mid- to late summer.

VALUE AT OTHER TIMES
Can be grown as an early spring-flowering houseplant.

IDEAL SITE
Bedding, hanging baskets and other containers.

CULTIVATION
Grow in full sun or light dappled shade in any moderately fertile, well-drained soil. Sow seeds in warmth in spring and plant out when the risk of frost has passed. Or sow in autumn and overwinter under glass for early flowers indoors.

ALSO RECOMMENDED
N. strumosa 'Prince of Orange' has orange flowers.

PERFECT PARTNERS
Clarkias and petunias.

Nepeta **x** *faassenii*

Nerine bowdenii ♔

Nicotiana **x** *sanderae*
Starship Series

Nicotiana sylvestris ♔

Nigella damascena
'Miss Jekyll' ♔

CATMINT, CATNIP

A vigorous, clump-forming, herbaceous perennial.
H & S 45cm (18in)

SEASONAL HIGHLIGHTS
From early summer to early autumn, it bears fragrant, pale lavender-blue flowers with darker purple spots. Attracts bees, moths and butterflies.

VALUE AT OTHER TIMES
It also has wrinkled, hairy, aromatic, grey-green leaves.

IDEAL SITE
Mixed or herbaceous borders, cottage and wildlife gardens.

CULTIVATION
Grow in any fertile, well-drained soil. Trim hard after the first flush of flowers to keep plants tidy and encourage more flowers. Rejuvenate old plants by dividing in spring or autumn.

ALSO RECOMMENDED
N. sibirica is taller with blue to lavender-blue flowers.

PERFECT PARTNERS
Alchemillas, lavenders, roses.

NERINE

A moderately vigorous, perennial bulb.
H 45cm (18in), S 8cm (3in)

SEASONAL HIGHLIGHTS
In autumn, it bears rounded heads of funnel-shaped, faintly scented pink flowers. The strap-shaped leaves emerge after flowering.

VALUE AT OTHER TIMES
Of no value at other times.

IDEAL SITE
At the base of a warm sunny wall, or in raised beds.

CULTIVATION
Grow in full sun in sharply drained soil in a warm, sheltered site. Provide a dry winter mulch in cold areas. Plant in summer with the nose (tip) of the bulb just at soil level.

ALSO RECOMMENDED
N. bowdenii f. *alba* has white, often pink-flushed flowers

PERFECT PARTNERS
Schizostylis, Scilla scilloides.

TOBACCO PLANT

Upright, bushy, moderately vigorous, half-hardy annuals.
H 30cm (12in), S 10cm (4in)

SEASONAL HIGHLIGHTS
From summer until autumn, bears a profusion of pink, red, rose-pink, white or lime-green flowers.

VALUE AT OTHER TIMES
Of no value at other times.

IDEAL SITE
Annual and mixed borders, decorative containers.

CULTIVATION
Grow in full sun or light, dappled shade in any fertile, well-drained soil. Sow seeds under glass in early spring and plant out when the danger of frost has passed.

ALSO RECOMMENDED
N. Domino Series 'Salmon Pink' is compact with upturned salmon-pink flowers.

PERFECT PARTNERS
Pelargoniums, petunias, asters.

TOBACCO PLANT

A vigorous biennial or short-lived perennial.
H 1.5m (5ft), S 60cm (2ft)

SEASONAL HIGHLIGHTS
It bears loose heads of white, trumpet-shaped flowers that are very fragrant when they open in the evening.

VALUE AT OTHER TIMES
It has a basal rosette of large, dark green leaves.

IDEAL SITE
Mixed or herbaceous borders, or woodland gardens.

CULTIVATION
Grow in light, dappled shade in any fertile, moist but well-drained soil. Tolerates full sun in reliably moist soils. Sow seeds in under glass in early spring. Plant out when the threat of frost has passed. Provide a deep winter mulch in cold areas.

ALSO RECOMMENDED
N. 'Lime Green' ♔ is annual with lime-green flowers.

PERFECT PARTNERS
Eremurus, roses.

LOVE-IN-A-MIST

A vigorous annual.
H 50cm (20in), S 23cm (9in)

SEASONAL HIGHLIGHTS
During summer, it produces sky-blue flowers, surrounded by a ruff of slender leaves.

VALUE AT OTHER TIMES
It has finely divided, feathery foliage. The seedpods can be dried for indoor arrangements.

IDEAL SITE
Annual borders, cutting borders, cottage gardens.

CULTIVATION
Grow in full sun in any moderately fertile, well-drained soil. Sow seeds in the flowering site in spring and thin seedlings to 23cm (9in) apart. May also be sown in autumn for earlier flowers. Protect with cloches in areas with very cold wet winters.

ALSO RECOMMENDED
N. hispanica 'Curiosity' has scented, dark-eyed, bright blue flowers.

PERFECT PARTNERS
Clarkias and calendulas.

NYMPHAEA

Nymphaea 'Firecrest'

Nymphaea 'Laydekeri Fulgens'

Nymphaea 'Marliacea Albida'

Nymphaea 'Marliacea Chromatella' ♔

Nymphaea 'Odorata Sulphurea Grandiflora'

Nymphaea 'René Gérard'

Nymphaea 'Rose Arey'

Nymphaea 'Vésuve'

Nymphaea alba

Nymphaea capensis

Nymphaea Pearl of the Pool

Nymphaea tetragona 'Helvola'

WATERLILIES
These submerged aquatic perennials mostly have a spread of 0.9–2.2m (3–7ft), depending on cultivar; *N. tetragona* 'Helvola', only 25–40cm (10–16in) across, can be grown in very small pools.

SEASONAL HIGHLIGHTS
In summer, they bear large single or double flowers in white and shades of pink, red or yellow. There are frost-tender species, like *N. capensis*, with fragrant, pale blue flowers, that are grown in indoor pools in cold areas.

VALUE AT OTHER TIMES
The large, flat leaves float on the water's surface, providing shelter for fish and helping shade out algal growth. Most are glossy dark green, but several, like 'Marliacea Chromatella', have attractive bronze or purple markings.

IDEAL SITE
Pools with still water.

CULTIVATION
Grow in full sun. Plant in aquatic planting baskets of loamy soil and cover the surface with pea gravel to prevent the soil muddying the water. Remove yellowing leaves through the summer. Lift and divide when leaves become crowded and thrust out of the water.

PERFECT PARTNERS
Mimulus, Typha latifolia.

O

Oenothera fruticosa
'Fyrverkeri' ♀

EVENING PRIMROSE, SUNDROPS

An upright, vigorous, herbaceous perennial.
H 30–90cm (12–36in),
S 30cm (12in)

SEASONAL HIGHLIGHTS
From late spring until late summer, cupped yellow flowers open from red buds.

VALUE AT OTHER TIMES
It has red-tinted stems and maroon-flushed leaves.

IDEAL SITE
Mixed or herbaceous borders.

CULTIVATION
Easily grown in moderately fertile, moist but well-drained soil in full sun.

ALSO RECOMMENDED
O. macrocarpa ♀ is trailing with golden yellow flowers.

PERFECT PARTNERS
Coreopsis verticillata, border phlox, *Lychnis chalcedonica*.

Osteospermum jucundum ♀

OSTEOSPERMUM

A vigorous, clump-forming evergreen perennial.
H 10–50cm (4–20in),
S 50–90cm (20–36in)

SEASONAL HIGHLIGHTS
From late spring to autumn, it bears mauve-pink to magenta, daisy-like flowerheads.

VALUE AT OTHER TIMES
The dense mat of grey-green leaves are good ground cover.

IDEAL SITE
Beds and borders, especially in hot, dry sites.

CULTIVATION
Grow in sun in any well-drained soil. Deadhead regularly to prolong flowering. May not survive cold wet winters, so take stem cuttings in late summer; overwinter young plants under glass.

ALSO RECOMMENDED
O. 'Buttermilk' ♀ bears primrose-yellow flowers with a bronze reverse.

PERFECT PARTNERS
Argyranthemums, pyrethrums, chrysanthemums.

P

PEONIES

Paeonia lactiflora **'Bowl of Beauty'** ♀

Paeonia lactiflora **'Laura Dessert'** ♀

Paeonia lactiflora **'Sarah Bernhardt'** ♀

Paeonia lactiflora **'Ballerina'**

HERBACEOUS PEONIES

Vigorous, long-lived, herbaceous perennials.

SEASONAL HIGHLIGHTS
From early to midsummer, they bear very showy, bowl-shaped, single or double flowers in white and shades of red and pink.

VALUE AT OTHER TIMES
The dark green or greyish-green leaves often colour well in autumn.

IDEAL SITE
Mixed or herbaceous borders, especially in cottage gardens.

CULTIVATION
Best in full sun, but tolerant of dappled shade for part of the day. Grow in deep, fertile, moist but well-drained soil that is enriched with plentiful organic matter. The large-flowered sorts may need unobtrusive, grow-through supports, especially in exposed gardens.

Paeonia lactiflora **'Kelway's Supreme'**

RECOMMENDED CULTIVARS
P. lactiflora 'Ballerina' has large, double pink flowers.
H & S 90–100cm (36–39in)
P. lactiflora 'Bowl of Beauty' has very large, carmine-red flowers with a central boss of narrow, creamy-white petals.
H & S 80–100cm (32–39in)
P. lactiflora 'Kelway's Supreme' bears fragrant, semi-double pale pink flowers.
H & S 90–100cm (36–39in)
P. lactiflora 'Laura Dessert' has scented, double flowers with pale pink outer petals and creamy-yellow inner ones.
H & S 70–75cm (30–32in)
P. lactiflora 'Sarah Bernhardt' produces very large, double, rose-pink flowers with a silvery sheen.
H & S 90–100cm (36–39in)

PERFECT PARTNERS
Hostas, Oriental poppies (*Papaver orientalis*), roses.

P

Paeonia mlokosewitschii ♇

Paeonia officinalis 'Rubra Plena' ♇

Papaver orientale 'Cedric Morris' ♇

Papaver rhoeas Shirley Series

Parthenocissus tricuspidata ♇

CAUCASIAN PEONY

A vigorous, clump-forming herbaceous perennial.
H & S 65–90cm (26–36in)

SEASONAL HIGHLIGHTS
In late spring and early summer, it bears single, bowl-shaped, lemon-yellow flowers.

VALUE AT OTHER TIMES
The bluish-green leaves are heavily suffused with red-purple as they emerge.

IDEAL SITE
Mixed or herbaceous borders.

CULTIVATION
Grow in full sun or part-day shade in deep, fertile, moist but well-drained soil enriched with organic matter. Shelter from strong winds.

ALSO RECOMMENDED
P. emodii has nodding, pure white flowers in late spring.

PERFECT PARTNERS
Aquilegia alpina, Polemonium carneum.

COMMON PEONY

A vigorous, clump-forming herbaceous perennial.
H & S 70–75cm (30–32in)

SEASONAL HIGHLIGHTS
In early and midsummer, it bears large, double, satin-textured, rich crimson flowers.

VALUE AT OTHER TIMES
Deep green, divided leaves.

IDEAL SITE
Mixed or herbaceous borders, especially in cottage gardens.

CULTIVATION
Grow in full sun or part-day shade in deep, fertile, moist but well-drained soil enriched with organic matter. Provide a grow-through support in exposed gardens.

ALSO RECOMMENDED
P. officinalis 'Rosea Superba Plena' has large, double, rose-pink flowers.

PERFECT PARTNERS
Lavenders, roses, campanulas.

ORIENTAL POPPY

A vigorous, clump-forming, herbaceous perennial.
H 45–90cm (18–36in),
S 60–90cm (24–36in)

SEASONAL HIGHLIGHTS
From late spring to midsummer, it bears bowl-shaped, satiny, soft pink flowers with frilled petals, each with a black basal mark.

VALUE AT OTHER TIMES
The bristly, jagged leaves die back soon after flowering.

IDEAL SITE
Mixed or herbaceous borders, especially in cottage gardens.

CULTIVATION
Grow in full sun, in deep, fertile, well-drained soil. Cut back hard after flowering, to produce fresh foliage and a few later flowers.

ALSO RECOMMENDED
P. orientalis 'Beauty of Livermere' ♇ has large, glossy, scarlet-crimson flowers.

PERFECT PARTNERS
Lupins, hemerocallis.

SHIRLEY POPPY

Vigorous, free-flowering hardy annuals.
H 90cm (36in), S 30cm (12in)

SEASONAL HIGHLIGHTS
During summer, bears bowl-shaped, single or semi-double flowers in white and shades of yellow, pink, orange and red.

VALUE AT OTHER TIMES
They have hairy stems with downy, light-green leaves.

IDEAL SITE
Annual and mixed borders, especially in cottage gardens.

CULTIVATION
Grow in sun in any poor to moderately fertile, well-drained soil. Sow seeds in spring in the flowering site. Self-seeds freely, but seedlings are variable.

ALSO RECOMMENDED
P. somniferum 'Paeony Flowered' has large, double, frilly flowers in white and shades of red, pink and purple.

PERFECT PARTNERS
Clarkias, escholschzias, nigellas.

BOSTON IVY

A very vigorous, deciduous, self-clinging climber.
H & S to 20m (70ft)

SEASONAL HIGHLIGHTS
The leaves turn brilliant red and deep purple in autumn.

VALUE AT OTHER TIMES
Has lobed, bright green leaves from spring onwards.

IDEAL SITE
Large walls, fences, or growing through large trees.

CULTIVATION
Grow in any fertile, well-drained soil in sun or shade. Guide young plants into the support until they cling for themselves. Prune in late winter, if necessary, to confine to bounds.

ALSO RECOMMENDED
P. henryana ♇ has dark green, often pink-flushed leaves with silver veins; they turn bright red in autumn.

PERFECT PARTNERS
Jasminum nudiflorum, late-flowering clematis.

Pelargonium 'Apple
Blossom Rosebud' ♀

ZONAL PELARGONIUM, "GERANIUM"

Frost-tender, evergreen,
fleshy-stemmed perennial.
H 40cm (16in), S 25cm (10in)

SEASONAL HIGHLIGHTS
From summer to autumn, it
bears large clusters of white
flowers with pink margins.

VALUE AT OTHER TIMES
Rounded, pale green leaves.

IDEAL SITE
Containers on a patio, or in
the home or conservatory.

CULTIVATION
Grow in fertile, well-drained
soil or compost in full sun.
Set out when risk of frost has
passed. Give a high-potash
fertilizer weekly. Deadhead
regularly. Take stem cuttings
during spring or summer and
overwinter under glass.

ALSO RECOMMENDED
P. Horizon Series are seed-
raised and good for bedding;
they have flowers in white,
and shades of pink and red.

PERFECT PARTNERS
Annual lobelias, fuchsias.

Pennisetum alopecuroides
'Hameln'

FOUNTAIN GRASS

A vigorous, clump-forming
evergreen grass.
H & S 1.2m (4ft)

SEASONAL HIGHLIGHTS
In summer and autumn, it
bears cylindrical, feathery,
greenish-white flowerheads
that mature to pale grey.

VALUE AT OTHER TIMES
The dark green leaves turn
golden yellow in autumn. The
flowerheads can be dried for
indoor flower arrangements.

IDEAL SITE
Mixed or herbaceous borders.

CULTIVATION
Grow in light, well-drained
soil in full sun. Cut back dead
top growth in spring. Plant
and divide overcrowded
clumps in late spring.

ALSO RECOMMENDED
P. villosum is shorter and
deciduous, with feathery, pale
green then purple flowerheads.

PERFECT PARTNERS
Lagurus ovatus, Stipa gigantea.

PENSTEMON

'Alice Hindley' ♀
H 90cm (3ft), S 45cm (18in)

'Burgundy'
H 90cm (3ft), S 45cm (18in)

'Maurice Gibbs' ♀
H 75cm (30in), S 45cm (18in)

'Apple Blossom' ♀
H & S 45–60cm (18–24in)

'Chester Scarlet' ♀
H 60cm (2ft), S 45cm (18in)

'Stapleford Gem' ♀
H 60cm (2ft), S 45cm (18in)

PENSTEMONS

Vigorous, frost-hardy,
evergreen or semi-evergreen
perennials of upright growth.

SEASONAL HIGHLIGHTS
From summer to late
autumn, they bear bell-
shaped, foxglove-like flowers
in white and shades of red,
pink, lilac and maroon.

VALUE AT OTHER TIMES
Form dense clumps of fresh
green leaves.

IDEAL SITE
Mixed or herbaceous borders.

CULTIVATION
Best in sun, but tolerant of
dappled, part-day shade. Grow
in fertile, well-drained soil.
Incorporate grit into heavy
clay soil. Dead-head regularly.
May not survive cold wet
winters, so take stem cuttings
in late summer and
overwinter under glass.

RECOMMENDED CULTIVARS
'Alice Hindley' has lilac-blue
flowers; 'Apple Blossom' has
white-throated, pink flowers;
'Burgundy' has wine-red
flowers; 'Chester Scarlet' has
large scarlet flowers; 'Maurice
Gibbs' bears white-throated,
cerise-pink blooms;
'Stapleford Gem' has large,
lilac-purple flowers suffused
with pink and white within.

PERFECT PARTNERS
Achilleas, border phlox, hardy
geraniums, *Phygelius.*

P

Perovskia **'Blue Spire'** ♀

Petunia **Million Bells Pink**

Philadelphus microphyllus

Phlox paniculata **'Eva Cullum'**

Phygelius **x** *rectus* **'Salmon Leap'** ♀

PEROVSKIA, RUSSIAN SAGE

A moderately vigorous, deciduous subshrub.
H 1.2m (4ft), S 1m (3ft)

SEASONAL HIGHLIGHTS
In late summer and early autumn, it bears tall spires of violet-blue flowers.

VALUE AT OTHER TIMES
It has grey-white stems and silver-grey leaves.

IDEAL SITE
Sunny borders, especially in hot, dry sites, chalky soils, or seaside gardens.

CULTIVATION
Grow in poor to moderately fertile, well-drained soil in full sun. In early spring, cut back all shoots to within 30cm (12in) of the ground.

ALSO RECOMMENDED
P. 'Hybrida' has dark lavender-blue flowers.

PERFECT PARTNERS
Roses, hardy fuchsias, lavenders.

PETUNIA

Vigorous, half-hardy perennials grown as annuals.
H & S to 30cm (12in)

SEASONAL HIGHLIGHTS
From early summer until late autumn, bears masses of small, trumpet-shaped, bright magenta-pink flowers.

VALUE AT OTHER TIMES
Cuttings can be taken and plants grown inside to flower in winter and early spring.

IDEAL SITE
Bedding and containers, including hanging baskets.

CULTIVATION
Grow in full sun in light, well-drained soil. Shelter from strong winds. This cultivar is usually sold as "plugs" or young plants.

ALSO RECOMMENDED
P. Surfinia Series are vigorous with large, white, pink, red, magenta or violet-blue flowers.

PERFECT PARTNERS
Pelargoniums, fuchsias, annual lobelias and nasturtiums (*Tropaeolum majus*).

PHILADELPHUS, MOCK ORANGE

A vigorous, deciduous shrub.
H & S to 1m (3ft)

SEASONAL HIGHLIGHTS
In early and midsummer, it bears single, very fragrant, pure white flowers.

VALUE AT OTHER TIMES
It has peeling, dark chestnut-brown bark and glossy leaves.

IDEAL SITE
A mixed or shrub border.

CULTIVATION
Grow in full sun or light, dappled shade, in any moderately fertile, well-drained soil. After flowering, shorten flowered shoots to strong buds. When mature, cut back one in five of the oldest stems at the base.

ALSO RECOMMENDED
P. 'Buckley's Quill' is taller, with scented, very double white flowers packed with quill-like petals.

PERFECT PARTNERS
Jasminum humile, shrubby potentillas, roses.

BORDER PHLOX

A vigorous, strongly upright herbaceous perennial.
H 1.2m (4ft), S to 1m (3ft)

SEASONAL HIGHLIGHTS
From summer to mid-autumn, it bears bright, deep-pink flowers with darker pink centres and a heady scent. Excellent for cutting.

VALUE AT OTHER TIMES
Fresh green leaves from spring onwards.

IDEAL SITE
Mixed or herbaceous borders.

CULTIVATION
Grow in fertile, moist soil in sun or light dappled shade. Divide every 3–4 years in autumn or spring to maintain vigour. Take basal cuttings in spring, or root cuttings in autumn or winter.

ALSO RECOMMENDED
P. paniculata 'Windsor' ♀ has purple-eyed, red-pink flowers.

PERFECT PARTNERS
Roses, penstemons, hardy geraniums.

PHYGELIUS

A vigorous, suckering, upright evergreen shrub.
H 1.2m (4ft), S 1.5m (5ft)

SEASONAL HIGHLIGHTS
Throughout summer and into autumn, it produces curving tubular orange flowers that hang from slender stalks.

VALUE AT OTHER TIMES
Glossy dark green leaves look good for most of the year.

IDEAL SITE
A shrub or mixed border, or against a sunny wall.

CULTIVATION
Grow in sun in fertile, moist but well-drained soil. Dead-head regularly. Give a deep winter mulch in cold areas. Needs little pruning; cut back frost-damaged growth to strong buds in spring, to the base if necessary.

ALSO RECOMMENDED
P. aequalis 'Yellow Trumpet' has creamy yellow flowers.

PERFECT PARTNERS
Hardy geraniums, hemerocallis, penstemons.

Physalis alkekengi ♀

Pieris 'Flamingo'

Plumbago auriculata

Polemonium carneum

Potentilla fruticosa **Princess** ('Blink')

CHINESE LANTERNS

A vigorous, rhizomatous, herbaceous perennial.
H 60–75cm (2–2½ft), S 90cm (3ft)

SEASONAL HIGHLIGHTS
Nodding, bell-shaped, creamy white flowers in midsummer.

VALUE AT OTHER TIMES
In late summer and autumn, inflated, papery red lanterns enclose orange-red fruits. They can be used in dried flower arrangements.

IDEAL SITE
Mixed or herbaceous borders.

CULTIVATION
Grow in full sun in any well-drained soil. Cut stems for drying just as the lanterns begin to colour.

ALSO RECOMMENDED
P. alkekengii var. *franchetii* is similar with smaller flowers.

PERFECT PARTNERS
Lychnis chalcedonica.

PIERIS

A dense, bushy, moderately vigorous evergreen shrub.
H to 4m (12ft), S 3m (10ft)

SEASONAL HIGHLIGHTS
In late winter and spring, it bears hanging clusters of urn-shaped, dark flamingo-pink flowers that open from dark red buds.

VALUE AT OTHER TIMES
The glossy green leaves are attractive all year round.

IDEAL SITE
Shrub borders, as specimens, in woodland gardens.

CULTIVATION
Grow in leafy, moist but well-drained, acid (lime-free) soil in sun or dappled shade. Shelter from cold dry winds. Keep pruning to a minimum.

ALSO RECOMMENDED
P. japonica 'White Cascade' bears long clusters of white flowers over long periods.

PERFECT PARTNERS
Winter heaths (*Erica carnea* cultivars), rhododendrons and azaleas.

PLUMBAGO, CAPE LEADWORT

A frost-tender, scrambling or climbing evergreen shrub.
H 3–6m (10–20ft), S 1–3m (3-10ft)

SEASONAL HIGHLIGHTS
From summer until late autumn, it bears long-tubed, sky-blue flowers in dense clusters at the stem tips.

VALUE AT OTHER TIMES
The smooth, often bluish-green tinged leaves look good for most of the year.

IDEAL SITE
Greenhouse or conservatory.

CULTIVATION
Grow in fertile free-draining potting compost in full sun. Tie stems in to a support as growth proceeds. Prune all sideshoots to within 3–4 buds of the main stems in spring.

ALSO RECOMMENDED
P. indica is shrubby with rose-pink flowers in winter.

PERFECT PARTNERS
Jasminum mesnyi, J. polyanthum.

JACOB'S LADDER

A moderately vigorous, bushy herbaceous perennial.
H 10–40cm (4–16in), S 20cm (8in)

SEASONAL HIGHLIGHTS
In early summer, it bears loose clusters of shallowly bell-shaped, pale pink, yellow, occasionally dark purple or lavender flowers.

VALUE AT OTHER TIMES
It has attractive divided leaves.

IDEAL SITE
Herbaceous or mixed borders and rock gardens.

CULTIVATION
Grow in full sun or light, dappled shade in any fertile, well-drained soil. Add grit to heavy clay soils to improve drainage. Deadhead regularly to encourage more flowers.

ALSO RECOMMENDED
P. caeruleum is taller with lavender-blue flowers.

PERFECT PARTNERS
Tradescantia 'Purple Dome'. *Erigeron* 'Serenity', *Potentilla atrosanguinea*.

SHRUBBY POTENTILLA

A compact but vigorous, deciduous shrub.
H 60cm (2ft), S to 1m (3ft).

SEASONAL HIGHLIGHTS
From late spring until mid-autumn, it produces saucer-shaped, pale pink flowers that fade to white.

VALUE AT OTHER TIMES
It has dense, dark green leaves that make good ground cover.

IDEAL SITE
Mixed or shrub borders, containers, as low hedging.

CULTIVATION
Prefers full sun but tolerates light, dappled shade. Grow in poor to moderately fertile, well-drained soil. In early spring, cut back all stems to within 2.5cm (1in) of the old growth. The easiest way is to use a pair of shears.

ALSO RECOMMENDED
P. fruticosa 'Elizabeth' ♀ has bright yellow flowers.

PERFECT PARTNERS
Philadelphus microphyllus, hypericums.

P

Primula denticulata ♀

Primula **Gold-laced Group**

Primula **'Miss Indigo'**

Prunus avium **'Plena'** ♀

Prunus **'Amanogawa'** ♀

Prunus **'Kanzan'** ♀

DRUMSTICK PRIMULA
A vigorous, rosette-forming herbaceous perennial.
H & S to 45cm (18in)
SEASONAL HIGHLIGHTS
In mid-spring and early summer, stout stems bear dense, spherical clusters of purple, yellow-eyed flowers.
VALUE AT OTHER TIMES
It has handsome rosettes of mid-green leaves that are white-mealy beneath.
IDEAL SITE
Rock gardens, at the front of beds and borders.
CULTIVATION
Grow in sun or dappled shade in moist, fertile soil. Divide every three to four years in autumn or spring.
ALSO RECOMMENDED
P. florindae ♀ is taller with clusters of fragrant, bell-shaped, sulphur-yellow flowers.
PERFECT PARTNERS
Euphorbia polychroma, Welsh poppy *(Meconopsis cambrica).*

POLYANTHUS PRIMULA
A rosette-forming evergreen or semi-evergreen perennial.
H 25cm (10in), S 30cm
SEASONAL HIGHLIGHTS
In mid- to late spring, it produces clusters of velvety mahogany-red flowers, each petal having a gold margin.
VALUE AT OTHER TIMES
The rosettes of mid-green leaves are tinged with red.
IDEAL SITE
Borders, bedding, containers, rock garden or alpine house.
CULTIVATION
Grow in moist, fertile, humus-rich, neutral to acid soil. Under glass, grow in pots of loam-based potting compost (e.g. John Innes No. 2).
ALSO RECOMMENDED
P. 'Blossom' has gold-centred, crimson flowers.
PERFECT PARTNERS
Sweet violets *(Viola odorata),* and violas.

PRIMULA
Vigorous, evergreen or semi-evergreen perennial.
H 20cm (8in), S 35cm (14in).
SEASONAL HIGHLIGHTS
From late winter to late spring, it produces clusters of double, indigo-purple flowers with creamy white tips.
VALUE AT OTHER TIMES
Has rosettes of wrinkled, bright green leaves for most of the year.
IDEAL SITE
Shady borders, bedding, containers.
CULTIVATION
Grow in dappled shade in damp, fertile, humus-rich soil. Divide after flowering to maintain vigour.
ALSO RECOMMENDED
P. vulgaris 'Marie Crousse' has double violet flowers.
PERFECT PARTNERS
Sweet violets *(Viola odorata),* and violas, pulmonarias.

GEAN, WILD CHERRY
A vigorous, deciduous tree with a wide-spreading crown.
H & S 12m (40ft)
SEASONAL HIGHLIGHTS
In mid-spring, it bears hanging clusters of double white flowers.
VALUE AT OTHER TIMES
The leaves are bronze when they emerge and turn red, yellow and orange in autumn.
IDEAL SITE
Perfect as a specimen tree.
CULTIVATION
Grow in any moist, but well-drained soil. Needs minimal pruning; remove badly placed or crossing branches in winter, or in midsummer if silverleaf disease is a problem in your area.
ALSO RECOMMENDED
P. avium ♀ has single flowers.
PERFECT PARTNERS
Crab apples *(Malus),* laburnums.

Prunus **'Spire'** ♀

CHERRIES

'Kiku-shidare-zakura'
(syn. 'Cheal's Weeping') ♥

Prunus 'Shirotae'
(syn. 'Mount Fuji') ♥

Prunus 'Ukon' ♥

JAPANESE CHERRIES

Vigorous, free-flowering deciduous trees.
H 10–12m (30–40ft),
S 8–10m (25–30ft)

SEASONAL HIGHLIGHTS
They bear a profusion of fragrant blossom in spring.

VALUE AT OTHER TIMES
Most have fine autumn colour.

IDEAL SITE
All of the recommended cultivars are beautiful specimen trees.

CULTIVATION
Grow in any moist, but well-drained soil. Need minimal pruning; remove badly placed or crossing branches in winter, or in midsummer if silverleaf disease is a problem in your area.

RECOMMENDED CULTIVARS
'Amanogawa' is narrowly upright with semi-double, pale pink flowers; 'Kanzan' is vase-shaped with double, deep pink flowers; 'Kiku-shidare-zakura' is weeping, with double, bright pink flowers; 'Shirotae' is arching and spreading with single or semi-double white flowers; 'Spire' is vase-shaped with single, pale pink flowers; 'Ukon' is vigorous and spreading with pink-flushed, creamy-white flowers.

PERFECT PARTNERS
Crab apples (*Malus*), laburnum, amelanchier.

Prunus padus 'Watereri' ♥

BIRD CHERRY

A vigorous, deciduous tree with a spreading crown.
H 15m (50ft), S 10m (30ft)

SEASONAL HIGHLIGHTS
In late spring, it bears long, slender spires of many small, fragrant white flowers.

VALUE AT OTHER TIMES
The dark green leaves turn red and yellow in autumn. In mid- to late summer, it bears small, black cherries that attract birds into the garden.

IDEAL SITE
As a specimen, or in woodland gardens.

CULTIVATION
Grow in any moist, but well-drained soil. Needs minimal pruning; remove badly placed or crossing branches in winter, or in midsummer if silverleaf disease is a problem in your area.

ALSO RECOMMENDED
P. padus 'Colorata' ♥ has red-purple leaves and pink flowers.

PERFECT PARTNERS
Crab apples (*Malus*).

Prunus sargentii ♥ *in spring and autumn*

SARGENT'S CHERRY

A vigorous, deciduous tree with a wide-spreading crown.
H to 20m (60ft),
S 15m (50ft)

SEASONAL HIGHLIGHTS
In early to mid-spring, it bears hanging clusters of large, single, bowl-shaped flowers of soft pale pink.

VALUE AT OTHER TIMES
The bark is a shining dark chestnut brown. The elliptical leaves have long, tapering tips and are bronze-red as they emerge with the flowers. Small, glossy crimson fruits (cherries) follow the flowers and attract birds into the garden. This is one of the finest cherries for autumn colour, and is usually one of the first trees to colour in autumn. The leaves turn to brilliant shades of rich orange and red.

IDEAL SITE
A beautiful specimen tree, it also thrives in woodland gardens.

CULTIVATION
Grow in any moist, but well-drained soil. It needs minimal pruning; remove badly placed or crossing branches in winter, or in midsummer if silverleaf disease is a problem in your area.

ALSO RECOMMENDED
P. sargentii 'Columnare' is a narrowly upright form that reaches 3m (10ft) tall.

PERFECT PARTNERS
Crab apples (*Malus*), laburnum and amelanchier, with underplantings of crocus, narcissi and daffodils.

P

Prunus serrula ♀

Prunus x *subhirtella*
'Autumnalis Rosea' ♀

Pulmonaria angustifolia
subsp. *azurea*

Pulsatilla vulgaris ♀

Pyracantha 'Golden
Charmer'

TIBETAN CHERRY
A moderately vigorous,
rounded, deciduous tree.
H & S 10m (30ft)
SEASONAL HIGHLIGHTS
In late spring, it bears small,
single, bowl-shaped white
flowers.
VALUE AT OTHER TIMES
The polished mahogany bark
is beautiful throughout the
year. The leaves turn yellow
in autumn.
IDEAL SITE
A perfect specimen tree for
small gardens.
CULTIVATION
Grow in fertile, moist but
well-drained soil in sun or
light dappled shade. It needs
minimal pruning (in late
summer); when young,
remove sideshoots from the
trunk when very small to
display the bark at its best.
ALSO RECOMMENDED
P. maackii has coppery bark.
PERFECT PARTNERS
Betula papyrifera, crocus and
colchicums.

HIGAN OR ROSEBUD CHERRY
A moderately vigorous,
spreading, deciduous tree.
H & S 8m (25ft)
SEASONAL HIGHLIGHTS
From late autumn to spring,
it bears small, semi-double,
pale pink flowers.
VALUE AT OTHER TIMES
Leaves are bronzed when
young and yellow in autumn.
IDEAL SITE
A perfect specimen tree for
small gardens.
CULTIVATION
Grow in fertile, moist but
well-drained soil in sun or
light dappled shade. It needs
minimal pruning, in late
summer, to remove damaged
or badly placed shoots.
ALSO RECOMMENDED
P. autumnalis 'Pendula Rosea'
♀ has weeping branches and
rose-pink flowers.
PERFECT PARTNERS
Underplant with crocus (for
spring) and colchicums (for
autumn).

BLUE COWSLIP, LUNGWORT
A vigorous, spreading,
herbaceous perennial.
H 25cm (10in), S 45cm (18in)
SEASONAL HIGHLIGHTS
From early to late spring, it
bears funnel-shaped, bright
blue flowers, tinted red in bud.
VALUE AT OTHER TIMES
It has smooth, unspotted,
glistening dark green leaves
that make good ground cover.
IDEAL SITE
Shady borders and wild or
woodland gardens.
CULTIVATION
Grow in deep or dappled
shade, in damp, humus-rich
soil. Cut back after flowering
for a fresh crop of new leaves.
Divide every three to four
years to maintain vigour.
ALSO RECOMMENDED
P. rubra 'Redstart' has coral-
red flowers from mid-winter
to spring.
PERFECT PARTNERS
Narcissus, crocus, doronicums
and primroses.

PASQUE FLOWER
A clump-forming, moderately
vigorous herbaceous perennial.
H 10–20cm (4–8in),
S 20cm (8in)
SEASONAL HIGHLIGHTS
Nodding, bell-shaped, silky-
hairy flowers in shades of
purple, or occasionally white,
appear in spring.
VALUE AT OTHER TIMES
The finely divided, hairy
leaves grow taller after
flowering. Silky, silvery
seedheads follow the flowers.
IDEAL SITE
A rock garden or raised bed.
CULTIVATION
Grow in fertile, gritty, sharply
drained soil in sun. It thrives
on shallow chalky soils.
Protect from excessive winter
wet. Pulsatillas dislike being
disturbed, so choose the site
with care.
ALSO RECOMMENDED
P. alpina has white flowers.
PERFECT PARTNERS
Dwarf tulips, *Aubrieta*, scillas.

PYRACANTHA, FIRETHORN
A vigorous, bushy, spiny
evergreen shrub.
H & S to 3m (10ft)
SEASONAL HIGHLIGHTS
Has bright orange berries
from autumn through winter.
VALUE AT OTHER TIMES
Clusters of small white flowers
in early summer; glossy, bright
green leaves all year.
IDEAL SITE
Sunny or shady walls; as a
specimen or as hedging.
CULTIVATION
Grow in any fertile, well-
drained soil. Trim hedging in
summer. On wall-trained
plants, shorten outward- and
inward-growing shoots in
mid-spring. Trim sideshoots
to 2–3 leaves after flowering
to expose the berries.
ALSO RECOMMENDED
P. 'Orange Glow' *k* has dark
orange-red berries.
PERFECT PARTNERS
Jasminum nudiflorum, *Garrya
elliptica*.

R

Pyrus salicifolia 'Pendula' ♀

WEEPING PEAR

A vigorous, weeping, deciduous tree.
H 5m (15ft), S 4m (12ft)

SEASONAL HIGHLIGHTS
Creamy white flowers in spring, followed by small, hard, unpalatable green pears.

VALUE AT OTHER TIMES
The stiffly weeping branches bear willow-like, grey-hairy leaves from spring to autumn.

IDEAL SITE
A fine specimen tree for small gardens.

CULTIVATION
Grow in sun in any fertile soil. It needs little pruning other than routine removal of any dead, damaged, or crossing growth in winter.

ALSO RECOMMENDED
P. ussuriensis is taller with large clusters of white flowers in spring and green leaves that turn red-bronze in autumn.

PERFECT PARTNERS
Betula pendula 'Youngii', crab apples (*Malus*) or rowans (*Sorbus*).

Rhodochiton atrosanguineus ♀

RHODOCHITON

A frost-tender, herbaceous perennial climber.
H 3m (10ft), S 75cm (30in)

SEASONAL HIGHLIGHTS
From summer to autumn, it bears hanging, tubular, deep red-purple flowers with a "skirt" of rose-pink calyces.

VALUE AT OTHER TIMES
It has attractive, heart-shaped rich green leaves.

IDEAL SITE
A warm wall, conservatory, containers, hanging baskets.

CULTIVATION
Grow in sun or light shade, in humus-rich, moist but well-drained soil or potting compost. Trim in summer, if necessary, to keep it within bounds. Bring under glass for the winter.

ALSO RECOMMENDED
This is the only species in common cultivation.

PERFECT PARTNERS
Annual lobelias (in hanging baskets); twining through sweet peas (*Lathyrus odoratus*).

RHODODENDRONS & AZALEAS

Rhododendron 'Beauty of Littleworth' ♀

Rhododendron 'Golden Torch' ♀

Rhododendron 'Halfdan Lem'

EVERGREEN RHODODENDRONS

With over 500 species and thousands of cultivars, rhododendrons are extremely variable, ranging from tiny alpine shrubs to huge, tree-like species. The best way to discover the ones you like is to visit gardens with good, clearly labelled collections.

SEASONAL HIGHLIGHTS
Most bear spectacular flowers between early spring and early summer, but there are winter- and late summer-flowering sorts too.

VALUE AT OTHER TIMES
Lustrous, usually dark green leaves persist all year, but are often particularly beautiful as they emerge after flowering.

IDEAL SITE
Shrub borders and woodland gardens. If you garden on limy soil, grow them in large containers filled with lime-free (ericaceous) compost.

CULTIVATION
All rhododendrons and azaleas must have an acid (lime-free), moist but well-drained, leafy, humus-rich soil. Grow in light, dappled shade with shelter from cold, dry winds. Plant with the top of the root ball no deeper than it was in the pot; rhododendrons are shallow-rooting and will not tolerate deep planting. Keep pruning

Rhododendron cinnabarinum subsp. *xanthocodon*

to a minimum; shorten any overlong shoots that spoil the shape after flowering. Dead-head carefully, so as not to damage the new leaves that emerge beneath the flowers.

RECOMMENDED
R. 'Beauty of Littleworth' has large dark green leaves and huge trusses of fragrant white flowers in late spring.
H & S 4m (12ft)
R. 'Golden Torch' has trusses of soft yellow flowers that open from pink buds in late spring and early summer.
H & S 1.5m (5ft)
R. 'Halfdan Lem' has rounded trusses of dark-spotted red flowers in mid- to late spring.
H & S 2.5m (8ft)
R. cinnabarinum subsp. *xanthocodon* has loose trusses of waxy, tubular, rich yellow flowers in mid-spring and early summer.
H 6m (20ft), S 2m (6ft)

R

RHODODENDRONS & AZALEAS

Rhododendron 'Freya'

Rhododendron 'Strawberry Ice' ♥

Rhododendron 'Inga'

R. 'Vuyk's Scarlet' ♥

R. yakushimanum

DECIDUOUS AZALEAS

Azaleas are a sub-section of the genus *Rhododendron* that have smaller leaves and bear profuse trusses of small, often vividly coloured flowers in spring or early summer. Many of the deciduous azaleas also have brilliant autumn colour.

IDEAL SITE

Rock and woodland gardens, shrub borders and containers.

CULTIVATION

Grow in acid (lime-free), moist but well-drained, leafy, humus-rich soil in dappled shade or sun. Deciduous azaleas are more tolerant of open sites in sun than evergreen rhododendrons, but are best sited so that they do not receive early morning sun, as this will exacerbate damage to the flowers in frosty weather. Plant with the top of the root ball no deeper than it was in the pot; they will not tolerate deep

planting. Keep pruning to a minimum; just shorten any overlong shoots that spoil the shape, after flowering. Dead-head carefully, if practical.

RECOMMENDED

R. 'Freya' is a compact shrub with small leaves bearing dense trusses of small, funnel-shaped "hose-in–hose" flowers (one flower within another) in late spring and early summer. They are fragrant, pink-flushed salmon-orange. It enjoys full sun. H & S 1.5m (5ft)

R. 'Strawberry Ice' is bushy and compact with rounded trusses of widely funnel-shaped flowers in late spring. They are a soft flesh-pink with darker veins and deeper pink at the petal margins. H & S 2m (6ft)

INDICA AZALEA

A compact, frost-tender, evergreen shrub. H & S 50cm (20in)

SEASONAL HIGHLIGHTS

In winter, it bears funnel-shaped, pink flowers with white margins to the slightly frilled petals.

VALUE AT OTHER TIMES

Small, glossy, dark green leaves throughout the year.

IDEAL SITE

Use as a houseplant.

CULTIVATION

Grow in pots of lime-free (ericaceous) compost in bright light, but shaded from direct sun. Keep just moist and mist daily until the flower buds show colour. Keep the temperature no higher than 13–16°C (55–61°F). Re-pot after flowering. Plunge them in a shaded cold frame for the summer and keep them cool and moist. Bring back indoors in early winter.

EVERGREEN AZALEA

A hardy evergreen shrub. H 75cm (30in), S 1.2m (4ft)

SEASONAL HIGHLIGHTS

In mid-spring, is covered in funnel-shaped, scarlet flowers with frilled petals. Plants in pots flower earlier if brought into a cool greenhouse at the end of autumn.

VALUE AT OTHER TIMES

Glossy, dark leaves all year.

IDEAL SITE

Shrub borders, rock gardens and woodland gardens, pots.

CULTIVATION

Grow in acid, moist but well-drained, humus-rich soil, or in large pots in ericaceous compost, in dappled shade or full sun. Shelter from cold, dry winds. Trim shoots that spoil the form after flowering.

ALSO RECOMMENDED

R. 'Vuyk's Rosy Red' has deep rose-pink flowers.

PERFECT PARTNERS

Japanese maples; smoke bush.

RHODODENDRON

A very hardy, vigorous, evergreen shrub. H to 2m (6ft)

SEASONAL HIGHLIGHTS

In mid-spring, it bears trusses of funnel-shaped flowers that open from deep pink buds and fade gradually to white.

VALUE AT OTHER TIMES

The glossy, dark green leaves are clothed in dense tawny down when young.

IDEAL SITE

Shrub borders, woodland gardens.

CULTIVATION

Grow in acid (lime-free), moist but well-drained, leafy, humus-rich soil in dappled shade or full sun. Shelter from cold, dry winds. Trim any shoots that spoil the shape and deadhead after flowering.

ALSO RECOMMENDED

R. yakushimanum 'Ken Janeck' has white flowers, lined with pink-purple and green spots.

Rhus typhina ♈

Ribes sanguineum

STAG'S HORN SUMACH

A vigorous, suckering, deciduous shrub or small tree.
H 5m (15ft), S 6m (20ft)

SEASONAL HIGHLIGHTS
In summer, it bears spires of yellow-green flowers that give rise, on female plants, to dense clusters of hairy, deep crimson-red fruits.

VALUE AT OTHER TIMES
In autumn, the divided leaves turn brilliant orange-red.

IDEAL SITE
Mixed and shrub borders, or as a specimen.

CULTIVATION
Gives the best autumn colour in sun, but tolerates light shade. Grow in any moist but well-drained soil. Can be pruned hard in spring to within two or three buds of the base for larger, lusher leaves.

ALSO RECOMMENDED
R. glabra has smooth shoots and glossy blue-green leaves.

PERFECT PARTNERS
Cotoneaster frigidus 'Cornubia', *Cotinus* 'Grace'.

FLOWERING CURRANT

A vigorous, deciduous shrub.
H & S to 2m (6ft)

SEASONAL HIGHLIGHTS
In spring, it bears hanging clusters of tiny, deep pinkish-red flowers.

VALUE AT OTHER TIMES
It has dense, aromatic, dark green foliage from spring to autumn. Flowers are followed by small, blue-black fruits.

IDEAL SITE
A mixed or shrub border, or as informal hedging.

CULTIVATION
Grow in full sun or light, dappled shade in any fertile soil. Prune flowered shoots back to strong buds, or shoots lower down the shrub, after flowering, to keep compact and bushy. Trim hedging after flowering.

ALSO RECOMMENDED
R. odoratum has fragrant yellow flowers.

PERFECT PARTNERS
Forsythias, *Chaenomeles* × *superba* 'Rowallane'.

BUSH ROSES

Amber Queen ('Harroony')

Blue Moon ('Tannacht')

'Crimson Glory'

Hannah Gordon ('Korweiso')

HYBRID TEA AND FLORIBUNDA ROSES
The hybrid tea or large-flowered roses are upright, freely branching bushes bearing large, usually double flowers, either singly or in small clusters in several flushes from spring to autumn. The floribundas, or cluster-flowered roses, bear smaller, single to fully double flowers in large clusters from summer to autumn. Many are richly scented and are excellent as cut flowers.

VALUE AT OTHER TIMES
All have attractive dark green leaves from spring to autumn.

IDEAL SITE
Rose beds, mixed and shrub borders, or as informal hedges.

CULTIVATION
Grow in full sun in deep, fertile, moist but well-drained soil. They thrive in heavy clay soils that have been enriched with plenty of well-rotted organic matter. Apply a balanced fertiliser and mulch in late winter or early spring. Prune large-flowered roses in late winter or early spring, cutting the main stems back to strong, outward-facing buds, 20–25cm (8–10in) above the ground. Reduce sideshoots to 2–3 buds. For cluster-flowered roses, prune back main stems to 25–45cm (10–18in) above ground and shorten sideshoots to 2–3 buds. Deadhead regularly to encourage more flowers.

RECOMMENDED
Amber Queen has clusters of very fragrant, cupped, fully double, amber-yellow flowers.
H 50cm (20in), S 60cm (24in)
Blue Moon has large, high-centred, double flowers of soft lilac-mauve.
H 1m (3ft), S 70cm (28in)
'Crimson Glory' bears large, fully double flowers of velvety dark crimson with a strong fragrance.
H & S 60cm (2ft)
Hannah Gordon bears clusters of cupped, double pale pink blooms with darker pink petal margins.
H 80cm (32in), S 65cm (26in)

PERFECT PARTNERS
Lavenders, rock roses (*Cistus*), *Anemone* × *hybrida*.

R

Anna Ford ♀

Chinatown ♀

Eglantyne ('Ausmark')

Will Shakespeare 2000 ('Ausromeo')

Graham Thomas ('Ausmas')

'Königin von Danemark' ♀

PATIO ROSES

These dwarf, cluster-flowered roses make compact, deciduous shrubs. From summer to autumn, they bear clusters of rounded, single to fully double flowers. They have abundant, glossy, dark green leaves. Anna Ford has urn-shaped, semi-double, orange-red flowers.
H 45cm (18in), S40cm (16in)

IDEAL SITE
In containers, in mixed borders, as border edging.

CULTIVATION
Grow in fertile, well-drained soil in full sun. Prune in the dormant season, as for floribunda roses. Cut back the main stems and sideshoots by no more than a third to a half of their length.

ALSO RECOMMENDED
Queen Mother has semi-double, clear pink flowers.

PERFECT PARTNERS
Lavenders and pinks.

MODERN SHRUB ROSES

Diverse in size, habit and flower form, modern shrubs are vigorous, deciduous, and flower freely from summer to autumn. They bear single to fully double flowers in few- to many-flowered clusters and are often beautifully scented. Chinatown has double, pink-flushed yellow flowers.
H 1.2m (4ft), S 1m (3ft)

IDEAL SITE
Shrub and mixed borders, as hedges, or as specimen plants.

CULTIVATION
Grow as for bush roses (*see previous page*). Prune only to for health and to reduce overcrowding. Every 3–4 years, cut an older stem or two to the base of the plant.

ALSO RECOMMENDED
'Buff Beauty' has fragrant, double, apricot-buff flowers.

PERFECT PARTNERS
Lavenders, cistus, *Anemone × hybrida*.

ENGLISH ROSES

A group of modern shrub roses that have been bred to combine the shapes, colours and scents of the Old garden roses with the vigour, disease-resistance and repeat-flowering virtues of the modern shrubs. They are graceful, deciduous or semi-evergreen shrubs and flower almost continuously from early summer to autumn. Many are exquisitely scented.

IDEAL SITE
Mixed and shrub borders, and as specimens.

CULTIVATION
Grow as for bush roses (*see previous page*). Prune as for floribunda bush roses (see previous page) but much more lightly, to maintain the shrub's stature.

RECOMMENDED
Eglantyne has strongly scented, cupped, fully double flowers of clear pale pink.
H 1.2m (5ft), S 1.5m (5ft)
Will Shakespeare 2000 has fully double, fragrant flowers of velvety crimson.
H 1.2m (5ft), S 1.5m (5ft)
Graham Thomas has cupped, fully double, yellow flowers with a fruity scent.
H 1.2m (5ft), S 1.5m (5ft)

PERFECT PARTNERS
Lavenders, pinks and border phlox go well with most roses.

OLD GARDEN ROSE (ALBA)

Vigorous shrub of arching growth with grey-green leaves.
H 1.5m (5ft), S 1.2m (4ft)

SEASONAL HIGHLIGHTS
Flowers profusely over long periods in midsummer, bearing fully double, intensely fragrant, pink flowers with a green eye.

IDEAL SITE
In mixed or shrub borders or as specimens.

CULTIVATION
Grow as for bush roses (*see previous page*). Albas tolerate shade better than most roses. To encourage bushy growth, after flowering, reduce main stems by a third of their height and sideshoots by two-thirds.

ALSO RECOMMENDED
'Alba Semiplena' ♀ has flat, semi-double white flowers.

PERFECT PARTNERS
Lavenders, cistus, *Anemone × hybrida*.

CLIMBING ROSES

'William Lobb' ♀

OLD GARDEN ROSE (MOSS)

Vigorous, upright or arching shrub with dark green leaves. H & S 2m (6ft)

SEASONAL HIGHLIGHTS

In midsummer, bears fully double, intensely fragrant red-purple flowers that fade with lavender-grey tints, on thorny shoots with dense, mossy growth on the stem tips.

IDEAL SITE

Beds and borders.

CULTIVATION

Grow as for bush roses (*see previous page*). To encourage bushy growth, after flowering, reduce main stems by a third of their height and sideshoots by two-thirds.

ALSO RECOMMENDED

'Nuits de Young', shorter, with dense brown-green moss and deep maroon flowers.

PERFECT PARTNERS

Lavanders, cistus, *Anemone ×
hybrida*.

***Rosa gallica* var. *officinalis*
'Versicolor'** ♀

OLD GARDEN ROSE (GALLICA), ROSA MUNDI

Dense, vigorous, thorny, free-branching shrub. H 80cm (32in), S to 1m (3ft)

SEASONAL HIGHLIGHTS

In midsummer, bears scented, semi-double, pale pink flowers striped with darker pink in small clusters.

IDEAL SITE

Beds, borders and as hedging.

CULTIVATION

Grow as for bush roses (*see previous page*). To encourage bushy growth, after flowering, cut back any overlong shoots by up to one third and sideshoots by two-thirds.

ALSO RECOMMENDED

'Charles de Mills' has very fragrant, fully double, deep mulberry-pink flowers.

PERFECT PARTNERS

Lavanders, cistus, *Anemone ×
hybrida*.

'Climbing Iceberg' ♀

Danse du Feu

Handel ('Macha')

Compassion ♀

Golden Showers ♀

High Hopes ('Haryup')

CLIMBING ROSES

Deciduous, thorny, stiff-stemmed climbing shrubs.

SEASONAL HIGHLIGHTS

They bear single to fully double, often fragrant flowers, singly or in clusters, from summer to autumn.

IDEAL SITE

On pillars, walls, or fences.

CULTIVATION

Grow as for bush roses (*see p. xxx*). In the first two years after planting, trim sideshoots only, to 2–4 buds. Tie in the stems to wires; aim to bend them as nearly horizontal as possible for maximum flower production. In subsequent years, shorten main shoots to fit the space and prune the sideshoots back to 3–4 buds.

RECOMMENDED

'Climbing Iceberg' has scented, double white flowers. H & S 3m (10ft)
Compassion has fragrant, double, apricot-pink flowers. H 3m (10ft), S 2.5m (8ft)
Danse du Feu has double scarlet flowers. .
H & S 2.5m (8ft)
Golden Showers has large, fragrant, double yellow blooms. H 3m (10ft), S 2.5m (8ft)
Handel has double white with pink petal margins. H 3m (10ft), S 2.2m (7ft)
High Hopes has double, scented, rose-pink flowers. H 4m (12ft), S 2.5m (8ft)

R

CLIMBING AND RAMBLING ROSES

'Noisette Carnée'

'Albertine' ♔

'American Pillar'

'Bobbie James' ♔

'Francois Juranville' ♔

'Goldfinch'

CLIMBING OLD GARDEN ROSE (NOISETTE)
A moderately vigorous climber, with smooth stems.
H 2–4m (6–12ft),
S 2–2.5m (6–8ft)
SEASONAL HIGHLIGHTS
From summer until autumn, it bears sprays of cupped, double, pale pink flowers with a spicy fragrance.
IDEAL SITE
A warm, sheltered wall.
CULTIVATION
The noisettes need more warmth and shelter than most climbers to flower and repeat well, otherwise grow as for bush roses and prune as for climbers.
ALSO RECOMMENDED
R. 'Mme Alfred Carrière' ♔, with tea-scented, fully double creamy-white flowers.
R. 'Gloire de Dijon' ♔ with fully double, quartered, fragrant, creamy buff flowers.

RAMBLING ROSES
Very vigorous, deciduous or semi-evergreen climbers with long, flexible, thorny stems.
SEASONAL HIGHLIGHTS
Unlike climbers, ramblers bloom only once in summer. They bear single to fully double, often scented flowers, usually in many-flowered clusters. They have more or less glossy, pale to dark green leaves with small leaflets.

IDEAL SITE
Pergolas, arbours and arches, and growing through large old trees.
CULTIVATION
Grow as for bush roses (*see p. 333*). Most will tolerate light dappled shade. After planting, guide and tie stems into the support. In the first two years, prune only to reduce the sideshoots to 2–4 buds after flowering. In the third year, shorten sideshoots as before and cut out one in three of the flowered stems at the base to stimulate vigorous new growth from the base.
RECOMMENDED
'Albertine' has double, soft salmon-pink flowers.
H 5m (15ft), S 4m (12ft)
'American Pillar' bears single, white-eyed, carmine-red flowers.
H 5m (15ft), S 4m (12ft)
'Bobbie James' has sprays of semi-double, scented, creamy-white flowers.
H 10m (30ft), S 6m (20ft)
'Francois Juranville' bears apple-scented, pompon-like, pale salmon-pink blooms.
H 6m (20ft), S 5m (15ft)
'Goldfinch' has fragrant, rosette-shaped, deep yellow flowers that fade to cream.
H 2.5m (8ft), S 2m (6ft)
PERFECT PARTNERS
Use late-flowering clematis to extend the interest.

Rosa moyesii

WILD OR SPECIES ROSE
A vigorous, upright, open deciduous shrub with long, arching branches.
H to 4m (12ft), S 3m (10ft)
SEASONAL HIGHLIGHTS
Single, cupped, sealing-wax red flowers in summer, very attractive to honey bees.
VALUE AT OTHER TIMES
In autumn, it produces large, crimson, flask-shaped hips.
IDEAL SITE
Grow as a specimen.
CULTIVATION
Grow in any fertile, moist but well-drained soil in sun or light dappled shade. Every 3–4 years, in winter, cut one or two old shoots to the ground. Overlong, wayward shoots can be shortened at any time.
ALSO RECOMMENDED
R. moyesii 'Geranium' ♔ is more compact with brighter, cherry-red flowers.
PERFECT PARTNERS
Clematis florida 'Sieboldii'.
Tropaeolum speciosum.

S

Rosa rugosa

Rudbeckia 'Herbstsonne'

Salix caprea 'Kilmarnock' ♥

Salix x *rubens* 'Basfordiana' ♥

Salvia coccinea 'Lady in Red' ♥

HEDGEHOG ROSE
A vigorous, deciduous shrub of dense, prickly growth.
H & S 1–2.5m (3–8ft)
SEASONAL HIGHLIGHTS
In summer, it bears single, spicily fragrant, magenta to carmine-red or white flowers with a boss of yellow stamens.
VALUE AT OTHER TIMES
Each flower produces a large, round, bright tomato-red hip and flowers and hips are present at the same time.
IDEAL SITE
In a border, or as an informal hedge; thrives in coastal sites.
CULTIVATION
Grow in any fertile, moist but well-drained soil in sun or light dappled shade. Every three or four years, in winter, cut out one or two old shoots to the ground. Shorten wayward shoots at any time.
ALSO RECOMMENDED
R. rugosa var. *alba* ♥ has clove-scented, white flowers.
PERFECT PARTNERS
Tropaeolum speciosum.

RUDBECKIA, CONEFLOWER
Vigorous, clump-forming, herbaceous perennial.
H to 2m (6ft), S 90cm (36in)
SEASONAL HIGHLIGHTS
From midsummer until early autumn, it bears daisy-like, bright yellow flowerheads with cone-shaped centres.
VALUE AT OTHER TIMES
It has attractive, prominently veined, glossy green leaves.
IDEAL SITE
Mixed or herbaceous borders, or naturalized in woodland.
CULTIVATION
Best in full sun, but tolerates light, dappled shade. Grow in a fertile, preferably heavy soil. After three or four years, lift and divide in spring or autumn to rejuvenate.
ALSO RECOMMENDED
R. laciniata 'Goldquelle' ♥ is shorter, with double, lemon yellow flowers.
PERFECT PARTNERS
Sedum spectabile, Aster novi-belgii (Michaelmas daisies).

KILMARNOCK WILLOW
A top-grafted, stiffly weeping, deciduous tree.
H 1.5–2m (5-6ft), S 2m (6ft)
SEASONAL HIGHLIGHTS
In mid and late spring, it produces grey male catkins, studded with yellow anthers, on bare shoots.
VALUE AT OTHER TIMES
Forms a dense umbrella of stout, yellow-brown stems and narrow dark green leaves that are grey-green beneath.
IDEAL SITE
As a specimen, or in large containers.
CULTIVATION
Grow in full sun or light shade, in any moist but well-drained soil. Prune annually between late autumn and early spring to thin out congested shoots.
ALSO RECOMMENDED
S. exigua is taller and upright with narrow, silvery leaves.
PERFECT PARTNERS
Betula pendula 'Youngii', *Corylopsis glabrescens.*

WILLOW
Vigorous, upright, deciduous tree; pruned regularly, it makes a twiggy shrub.
H 15m (50ft), S 10m (30ft)
SEASONAL HIGHLIGHTS
It has bright orange-yellow young shoots in winter.
VALUE AT OTHER TIMES
In spring, it bears slender, yellow catkins with the emerging, narrow grey-green leaves that become glossy, bright green in summer.
IDEAL SITE
In a shrub border, or by the water's edge.
CULTIVATION
Grow in any moist but well-drained soil. Cut all stems back hard each or, for catkins, every other year in early spring, to the ground or to a short trunk. Young shoots have the best colour.
ALSO RECOMMENDED
S. daphnoides 'Aglaia' ♥ has glossy mahogany-red shoots.
PERFECT PARTNERS
Corylopsis, dogwoods.

SALVIA
An upright, bushy, half-hardy perennial, often grown as an annual. H 40cm (16in), S 30cm (12in)
SEASONAL HIGHLIGHTS
From summer to autumn, it bears slender open spikes of luminous red flowers.
VALUE AT OTHER TIMES
It has heart-shaped, toothed and veined, dark green leaves.
IDEAL SITE
Bedding, borders and containers.
CULTIVATION
Grow in full sun in any moderately fertile, well-drained soil. May not survive cold, wet winters, so take softwood cuttings in spring or summer and overwinter young plants under glass.
ALSO RECOMMENDED
S. patens 'Cambridge Blue' ♥ has pale blue flowers.
PERFECT PARTNERS
Osteospermums and argyranthemums.

S

Santolina chamaecyparissus **'Lemon Queen'**

COTTON LAVENDER

A vigorous, evergreen shrub. H & S 60cm (2ft)

SEASONAL HIGHLIGHTS

From mid- to late summer, it bears pompon-like, lemon-yellow flowerheads.

VALUE AT OTHER TIMES

It has white-woolly young shoots that carry slender, finely divided leaves with a wonderful sharp fragrance.

IDEAL SITE

Mixed or herbaceous borders.

CULTIVATION

Best in full sun, but will tolerate light, part-day shade. Grow in any moderately fertile, well-drained soil. On heavy clay soils, dig in coarse grit to improve drainage. In early spring, trim over plants with shears to keep them bushy and compact.

ALSO RECOMMENDED

S. pinnata subsp. *neapolitana* 'Sulphurea' is slightly taller.

PERFECT PARTNERS

Salvia officinalis 'Tricolor'.

Sarcococca hookeriana **var. humilis**

CHRISTMAS BOX, SWEET BOX

A moderately vigorous, suckering evergreen shrub. H 60cm (2ft), S to 1m (3ft)

SEASONAL HIGHLIGHTS

In winter, it bears clusters of tiny, honey-scented, pink-tinted white flowers, followed by round, dark blue fruits.

VALUE AT OTHER TIMES

The glossy, dark green leaves make good ground cover.

IDEAL SITE

In a woodland garden or shrub border, or as low, informal hedging.

CULTIVATION

Grow in fertile, moist but well-drained soil in deep or partial shade, or in sun if soils remain moist. Needs little pruning. Dig out suckers at the margins of the clump if it encroaches on other plants.

ALSO RECOMMENDED

S. confusa ♔ is taller but similar.

PERFECT PARTNERS

Helleborus niger, *Viburnum × bodnantense* 'Dawn', *V. tinus*.

Scabiosa **Butterfly Blue**

SCABIOUS, PINCUSHION FLOWER

A clump-forming, spreading herbaceous perennial. H & S 40cm (16in)

SEASONAL HIGHLIGHTS

From mid- to late summer, it bears wiry-stemmed, lavender-blue flowers that attract butterflies and bees.

VALUE AT OTHER TIMES

It has divided, grey-green basal leaves.

IDEAL SITE

A mixed or herbaceous border, especially in cottage gardens; wildlife gardens.

CULTIVATION

Grow in any moderately fertile, well-drained soil in full sun, or light part-day shade.

ALSO RECOMMENDED

S. caucasica 'Miss Willmott' ♔ has white flowerheads.

PERFECT PARTNERS

Lavenders, pinks (*Dianthus*) and herbaceous potentillas, such as 'Yellow Queen'.

Scaevola aemula

FAIRY FAN-FLOWER

A tufted, frost-tender, evergreen perennial, grown as an annual in cold areas. H & S to 50cm (20in)

SEASONAL HIGHLIGHTS

Throughout summer, it bears leafy, trailing spikes of small, fan-shaped, purple-blue or blue flowers.

VALUE AT OTHER TIMES

Is discarded after flowering.

IDEAL SITE

Containers, hanging baskets.

CULTIVATION

Grow in full sun or light, dappled shade, in any moist but well-drained, fairly fertile soil or potting compost. Take stem cuttings in spring or summer and overwinter under glass, or sow seed in warmth in spring. Set out when risk of frost has passed.

ALSO RECOMMENDED

S. 'Mauve Clusters' has lilac-mauve flowers.

PERFECT PARTNERS

Fuchsias, pelargoniums, French marigolds (*Tagetes*).

Schizostylis coccinea **'Sunrise'** ♔

KAFFIR LILY

A vigorous, evergreen, rhizomatous perennial. H 60cm (24in), S 30cm (12in)

SEASONAL HIGHLIGHTS

From late summer to early winter, it bears spikes of glossy, salmon-pink flowers. They are good for cutting.

VALUE AT OTHER TIMES

The narrowly sword-shaped, bright green leaves persist for most of the year.

IDEAL SITE

Mixed or herbaceous borders, or in containers.

CULTIVATION

Grow in a fertile, moist but well-drained soil. Shelter from cold winds. It benefits from an organic mulch in winter, especially in very cold areas.

ALSO RECOMMENDED

S. coccinea 'Major' ♔ has glossy scarlet flowers.

PERFECT PARTNERS

Asters (Michaelmas daisies), *Sedum spectabile*, rudbeckias.

Scilla siberica **'Spring Beauty'**

Sedum spectabile **'Brilliant'** ♔

Skimmia japonica

Solanum crispum **'Glasnevin'** ♔

Solenostemon **'Brightness'**

SCILLA, SQUILL
A slender, perennial bulb.
H 20cm (8in), S 5cm (2in)
SEASONAL HIGHLIGHTS
In spring, it bears loose spikes of small, nodding, deep blue flowers amid narrow, strap-shaped, shining green leaves.
VALUE AT OTHER TIMES
Of no value at other times.
IDEAL SITE
A rock garden, at the front of a mixed border, in containers.
CULTIVATION
Grow in full sun or light, dappled shade, in any fertile, humus-rich soil. Plant the bulbs in autumn at twice their own depth.
ALSO RECOMMENDED
S. peruviana f. *alba* is taller with white flowers.
PERFECT PARTNERS
Grow with chionodoxas and *Anemone blanda* cultivars beneath forsythias.

SEDUM, ICE PLANT
A vigorous, clump-forming, herbaceous perennial.
H & S 45cm (18in)
SEASONAL HIGHLIGHTS
From late summer until late autumn, it bears large, flat heads of many tiny, star-shaped, bright pink flowers. It's an excellent plant for attracting butterflies.
VALUE AT OTHER TIMES
The fleshy, slightly scalloped, grey-green leaves are handsome throughout spring and summer.
IDEAL SITE
Mixed or herbaceous borders; is good in hot, dry sites.
CULTIVATION
Grow in fertile, well-drained, preferably neutral to slightly alkaline soil in sun. Divide in spring, every three or four years to maintain vigour.
ALSO RECOMMENDED
S. spectabile 'Iceberg' has pale green leaves and white flowers.
PERFECT PARTNERS
Asters, rudbeckias, *Schizostylis*.

SKIMMIA
A vigorous, dome-shaped, evergreen shrub.
H to 5m (15ft), S 1.5m (5ft)
SEASONAL HIGHLIGHTS
In winter, it produces dense clusters of pink buds that open in mid- to late to reveal scented white flowers.
VALUE AT OTHER TIMES
It has slightly aromatic, glossy dark green leaves all year. Female plants bear red berries, if male and female plants are grown together.
IDEAL SITE
A shrub or mixed border.
CULTIVATION
Grow in dappled or deep shade, in any fertile, humus-rich soil. It needs little, if any pruning other than to shape, if necessary, after flowering.
ALSO RECOMMENDED
S. japonica 'Bronze Knight' is shorter, male, and has dark, bronze-red buds in winter.
PERFECT PARTNERS
Gaultherias, winter heaths (*Erica carnea*).

CHILEAN POTATO TREE
A very vigorous, evergreen or semi-evergreen, scrambling shrub or climber.
H & S to 6m (20ft)
SEASONAL HIGHLIGHTS
Throughout summer, it bears fragrant, deep purple-blue flowers at the stem tips, followed by pale yellow fruit.
VALUE AT OTHER TIMES
It has handsome dark green leaves for most of the year.
IDEAL SITE
On a warm, sunny wall.
CULTIVATION
Grow in full sun, or light, part-day shade, in neutral to slightly alkaline, fertile, well-drained soil. After flowering, shorten sideshoots to three or four buds.
ALSO RECOMMENDED
S. jasminoides 'Album' ♔ has white flowers.
PERFECT PARTNERS
Clematis 'Pagoda'; climbing or rambling roses.

COLEUS
A bushy, fast-growing, frost-tender perennial, often grown as a foliage annual.
H 45cm (18in), S 30cm (12in)
SEASONAL HIGHLIGHTS
All year it has rust-red leaves, edged with pale green.
IDEAL SITE
As a houseplant, or outdoors as bedding or in containers.
CULTIVATION
Grow in a sheltered, sunny site, in fertile, moist but well-drained soil or potting mix. Sow seed in warmth in early spring and plant out when the risk of frost has passed. Pinch out shoot tips to promote bushiness, and also any flowers to preserve good leaf colour and condition. Take stem cuttings in summer.
ALSO RECOMMENDED
S. scutellarioides Wizard Series has leaves patterned in green, red, cream, yellow and purple.
PERFECT PARTNERS
French marigolds (*Tagetes*), pelargoniums.

Solidago '**Goldenmosa**' ♀

Sorbus commixta

Spiraea '**Arguta**'

Stipa gigantea ♀

'**Charles Joly**' ♀

'**Katherine Havemeyer**' ♀

'**Président Grévy**'

GOLDENROD

A vigorous, bushy, herbaceous perennial.
H 75cm (30in), S 45cm (18in)

SEASONAL HIGHLIGHTS
In late summer and early autumn, it bears feathery, conical plumes of yellow-stalked, bright yellow flowers.

VALUE AT OTHER TIMES
It has wrinkled, mid-green leaves. The flowers are good for cutting.

IDEAL SITE
An herbaceous border, or wild garden.

CULTIVATION
Grow in full sun in any poor to moderately fertile soil. Every three or four years, lift and divide in spring or autumn to maintain vigour. Cut off the flowers as they fade to prevent them seeding.

ALSO RECOMMENDED
S. 'Golden Wings' is taller, with horizontally spreading plumes of golden-yellow.

PERFECT PARTNERS
Rudbeckias, *Sedum spectabile*.

SORBUS, ROWAN

A vigorous, broadly conical, deciduous tree.
H 10m (30ft), S 7m (22ft)

SEASONAL HIGHLIGHTS
In late spring, it bears broad heads of tiny white flowers.

VALUE AT OTHER TIMES
In autumn, clusters of orange-red berries festoon the branches, and the divided leaves turn yellow to red and purple. The berries attract birds into the garden.

IDEAL SITE
A beautiful specimen tree.

CULTIVATION
Grow in any fertile, moist but well-drained, neutral to acid soil. Little pruning is necessary except to remove any crossing or damaged branches in winter.

ALSO RECOMMENDED
S. *sargentiana* ♀ is similar, with many small, bright red berries.

PERFECT PARTNERS
Maples (acers) and birches (*Betula*).

BRIDAL WREATH

A vigorous, deciduous shrub with arching branches.
H & S 2.5m (8ft)

SEASONAL HIGHLIGHTS
In spring, clusters of tiny, bright white flowers wreathe the branches.

VALUE AT OTHER TIMES
It has attractive leaves of fresh, bright green.

IDEAL SITE
A mixed or shrub border.

CULTIVATION
Best in full sun, but tolerates light, part-day shade. Grow in any fertile, moist but well-drained soil. After flowering cut back the flowered shoots to strong buds. Every three or four years, cut out one in three of the oldest flowered stems to the base to encourage strong, new growth.

ALSO RECOMMENDED
S. *japonica* 'Little Princess' is compact, with pink flowers.

PERFECT PARTNERS
Chaenomeles × *superba* 'Nicoline', *Cytisus* × *praecox*.

GOLDEN OATS, GIANT FEATHER GRASS

A vigorous, evergreen or semi-evergreen perennial grass.
H 2.5m (8ft), S 1.2m (4ft)

SEASONAL HIGHLIGHTS
In summer, tall arching stems bear open flowerheads of silvery, purple-green spikelets that turn gold as they ripen.

VALUE AT OTHER TIMES
It forms arching clumps of narrow green leaves.

IDEAL SITE
A fabulous specimen, border or container plant.

CULTIVATION
Grow in full sun in any moderately fertile soil. It tolerates light shade and heavy clay soils. Cut down the old growth in spring.

ALSO RECOMMENDED
S. *tenuissima* is shorter with filament-like leaves and feather-fine flowerheads.

PERFECT PARTNERS
Hakonechloa macra 'Aureola', *Carex pendula*.

T

SYRINGA VULGARIS

'Charles X'

'Madame Lemoine' ♡

'Primrose'

LILACS
Vigorous, deciduous shrubs or small trees.
H & S 7m (22ft)

SEASONAL HIGHLIGHTS
In late spring and early summer, they bear dense, conical clusters of intensely fragrant flowers.

VALUE AT OTHER TIMES
They have heart-shaped, dark green leaves from spring to late autumn.

IDEAL SITE
In a shrub border, or as specimens.

CULTIVATION
Grow in any fertile, neutral to alkaline soil. Deadhead young plants, cutting back to strong buds lower down on the shrub. If necessary, prune to shape after flowering.

RECOMMENDED
'Charles Joly' has double, dark purple flowers.
'Charles X' has single, purple-red flowers.
'Katherine Havemeyer' has double, lavender-blue flowers, that are purple in bud.
'Madame Lemoine' has double white blooms.
'Président Grévy' has large spires of double, lilac-blue flowers with red-violet buds.
'Primrose' has soft, primrose yellow flowers.

PERFECT PARTNERS
Hawthorn (*Crataegus*) and laburnums.

Tagetes 'Naughty Marietta'

FRENCH MARIGOLD
A compact, bushy, vigorous, half-hardy annual.
H & S 30–40cm (12–16in)

SEASONAL HIGHLIGHTS
From early to late summer, deep yellow flowerheads with maroon-red marks emerge atop the dark green leaves.

VALUE AT OTHER TIMES
They are consigned to the compost heap after flowering.

IDEAL SITE
Bedding, border edging and containers.

CULTIVATION
Grow in sun in moderately fertile, well-drained soil. Sow seeds in warmth under glass in spring and set out when risk of frost has passed; or sow in the flowering site in late spring. Deadhead regularly to prolong the flowering period.

ALSO RECOMMENDED
T. 'Tangerine Gem' has deep orange flowers.

PERFECT PARTNERS
Pelargoniums, annual lobelias, fuchsias.

Tamarix tetrandra ♡

TAMARISK
A vigorous, open, deciduous shrub or small tree.
H & S 3m (10ft)

SEASONAL HIGHLIGHTS
In mid- to late spring, it bears short spikes of many tiny, pale dusky pink flowers all along the arching branches.

VALUE AT OTHER TIMES
It has purple-brown shoots and small, needle- or scale-like green leaves.

IDEAL SITE
In a shrub border, or as a specimen; it does especially well in coastal gardens.

CULTIVATION
Grow in full sun, in moist but well-drained soil. Shelter from cold, dry winds. It is resistant to strong winds in coastal areas. After flowering, shorten flowered shoots to strong buds lower down the shoots.

ALSO RECOMMENDED
T. ramosissima 'Pink Cascade' has pink flowers in late summer.

PERFECT PARTNERS
Syringa, *Spiraea* 'Arguta'.

Thunbergia alata

BLACK-EYED SUSAN
A frost-tender, evergreen perennial climber, grown as an annual in cold areas.
H 2.5m (8ft), S 45cm (18in)

SEASONAL HIGHLIGHTS
From summer to autumn, the twining stems bear single, orange or yellow, occasionally creamy-white flowers; some have chocolate-purple centres.

VALUE AT OTHER TIMES
It has pretty heart-shaped, toothed, mid-green leaves.

IDEAL SITE
In containers, on supporting wigwams or poles.

CULTIVATION
Grow in sun in any moist but well-drained soil. Sow the seeds in spring in heat; plant in containers and grow on in warmth. Set out when the weather is warm and settled. Take stem cuttings in summer and overwinter under glass.

ALSO RECOMMENDED
T. gregorii has orange flowers.

PERFECT PARTNERS
Ipomoea tricolor.

T

Trollius **x** *cultorum* 'Earliest of All'

Tropaeolum majus 'Empress of India'

Tropaeolum speciosum ♀

Tulipa 'Spring Green' ♀

Tulipa tarda ♀

GLOBEFLOWER

A moderately vigorous, clump-forming herbaceous perennial.
H 50cm (20in), S 40cm (16in)

SEASONAL HIGHLIGHTS
The bowl-shaped, shining, clear yellow flowers arise on strong stems from mid-spring to midsummer.

VALUE AT OTHER TIMES
It has basal mounds of lobed, toothed, glossy green leaves.

IDEAL SITE
Bog gardens and stream- or poolsides, damp borders or meadow gardens.

CULTIVATION
Best in full sun, but tolerant of partial shade. Grow in reliably moist, deep, fertile soil. Lift and divide the plants every three or four years to rejuvenate them.

ALSO RECOMMENDED
T. × *cultorum* 'Alabaster' has pale creamy-yellow flowers.

PERFECT PARTNERS
Caltha palustris, Lysichiton americanus, Darmera peltata.

NASTURTIUM

A bushy, compact, vigorous, hardy annual.
H 30cm (10in), S 45cm (18in)

SEASONAL HIGHLIGHTS
From early summer to autumn, it bears funnel-shaped, spurred, semi-double, rich scarlet flowers.

VALUE AT OTHER TIMES
It has rounded, bluish-green, purple-tinted leaves in summer. Both leaves and flowers are edible.

IDEAL SITE
Annual beds and borders, containers, hanging baskets.

CULTIVATION
Grow in full sun, in poor, moist but well-drained soil; rich soils promote leafy growth at the expense of flowers. Sow seeds in the flowering site in mid-spring, or in early spring under glass for earlier flowers.

ALSO RECOMMENDED
T. 'Peach Melba' has red-marked, creamy-yellow flowers.

PERFECT PARTNERS
Calendulas, clarkias.

FLAME CREEPER

A moderately vigorous, herbaceous perennial climber.
H & S to 3m (10ft) or more.

SEASONAL HIGHLIGHTS
From summer to autumn, the slender stems form swags of long-spurred, vermilion flowers.

VALUE AT OTHER TIMES
It has very attractive, lobed, bright green leaves.

IDEAL SITE
Grow through dark-leaved shrubs or hedges, like yew, or with creamy-flowered roses.

CULTIVATION
Grow in moist, reasonably fertile, preferably slightly acid soil, with its roots in cool shade and head in sun. It can be difficult to establish, as the long fleshy white roots are fragile; plant carefully.

ALSO RECOMMENDED
T. tuberosum is a frost-tender, tuberous perennial with orange and yellow flowers.

PERFECT PARTNERS
T. peregrinum, a yellow-flowered annual.

VIRIDIFLORA TULIP

A moderately vigorous, bulbous perennial.
H 40cm (16in), S 8cm (3in)

SEASONAL HIGHLIGHTS
In late spring, it produces very elegant, green-feathered, ivory-white flowers.

VALUE AT OTHER TIMES
Of little value at other times.

IDEAL SITE
Bedding, borders and decorative containers.

CULTIVATION
Grow in full sun, in any moderately fertile, well-drained soil. Add coarse grit to heavy clay soils. Plant bulbs 10–15cm (4–6in) deep in late autumn. Lift bulbs once the leaves fade and ripen in a cool greenhouse.

ALSO RECOMMENDED
T. 'Queen of Night' has glossy, dark maroon-purple flowers in late spring.

PERFECT PARTNERS
Wallflowers (*Erysimum*), polyanthus primulas, winter-flowering pansies.

SPECIES TULIP

A vigorous, perennial bulb.
H to 15cm (6in), S 5cm (2in)

SEASONAL HIGHLIGHTS
In early and mid-spring, it produces open, starry, greenish-white flowers that are yellow inside.

VALUE AT OTHER TIMES
Of no value at other times.

IDEAL SITE
Rock gardens, borders and containers.

CULTIVATION
Best in full sun, but it will tolerate light, part-day shade. Grow in any poor to moderately fertile, well-drained soil. Add coarse grit to heavy clay soils. Plant the bulbs at twice their own depth in late autumn.

ALSO RECOMMENDED
T. turkestanica ♀ has starry white flowers.

PERFECT PARTNERS
Scillas and chionodoxas.

V

***Verbascum* 'Cotswold Queen'**

***Verbena* 'Showtime'**

***Verbena bonariensis* ♥**

***Veronica gentianoides* ♥**

***Viburnum* x *bodnantense* 'Dawn' ♥**

VERBASCUM, MULLEIN
An upright, moderately vigorous perennial.
H 1.2m (4ft), S 30cm (12in)
SEASONAL HIGHLIGHTS
From early until late summer, erect spires bear saucer-shaped yellow flowers with red-purple centres.
VALUE AT OTHER TIMES
It has striking basal rosettes of wrinkled, grey-green leaves.
IDEAL SITE
Sunny banks and borders.
CULTIVATION
Best in full sun in poor, well-drained, preferably slightly alkaline soil. Too rich a soil produces soft, floppy stems that then need staking. May be short-lived, so divide in spring or autumn, or take root cuttings in winter.
ALSO RECOMMENDED
V. chaixii f. *album* has white flowers with mauve centres.
PERFECT PARTNERS
Delphiniums, monkshood, border phlox.

BEDDING VERBENA
Bushy, half-hardy perennial grown as an annual.
H & S 25cm (10in)
SEASONAL HIGHLIGHTS
From summer until autumn, it produces masses of flowers in shades of rose-pink to magenta, scarlet or white, some with white centres. The toothed, dark green leaves form dense, neat mounds.
VALUE AT OTHER TIMES
Discard after flowering.
IDEAL SITE
Annual borders, edging, containers or hanging baskets.
CULTIVATION
Grow in sun, in well-drained, not-too-fertile soil or potting compost. Sow seeds in early spring in warmth. Plant out when the risk of frost is past.
ALSO RECOMMENDED
V. 'Peaches and Cream', with pale orange-pink to apricot-yellow flowers.
PERFECT PARTNERS
Clarkias, busy lizzies (*Impatiens*), pelargoniums.

VERBENA
A vigorous, frost-hardy, clump-forming perennial.
H to 2m (6ft), S 45cm (18in)
SEASONAL HIGHLIGHTS
From midsummer to autumn, wiry, branching stems bear heads of lilac-purple flowers.
VALUE AT OTHER TIMES
It has attractive, toothed, dark green basal leaves.
IDEAL SITE
Mixed or herbaceous borders, gravel gardens, especially in hot dry sites.
CULTIVATION
Grow in any moderately fertile soil in full sun. It may not survive cold wet winters, so provide a dry winter mulch. Take stem-tip cuttings in late summer. Overwinter young plants under glass.
ALSO RECOMMENDED
V. corymbosa is more densely clump-forming, with red-purple flowers.
PERFECT PARTNERS
Verbascums, *Cynara cardunculus*, *Ferula communis*.

VERONICA, SPEEDWELL
A moderately vigorous, mat-forming herbaceous perennial.
H & S to 45cm (18in)
SEASONAL HIGHLIGHTS
In early summer, it produces upright stems of shallowly cupped, pale blue flowers.
VALUE AT OTHER TIMES
It has attractive basal rosettes of slightly scalloped, glossy, dark green leaves.
IDEAL SITE
At the front of a border, or in a rock garden.
CULTIVATION
Best in full sun, but tolerates light, part-day shade. Grow in moderately fertile, well-drained soil. Plants begin to lose vigour after two or three years, so divide in autumn or spring to rejuvenate.
ALSO RECOMMENDED
V. longifolia is much taller, with lilac-blue flowers.
PERFECT PARTNERS
Lavenders, hardy geraniums.

VIBURNUM
A sturdy, upright, vigorous deciduous shrub.
H 3m (10ft), S to 2m (6ft)
SEASONAL HIGHLIGHTS
From late autumn to early spring, it bears small, rounded clusters of fragrant pink flowers, on bare branches.
VALUE AT OTHER TIMES
It has deeply pleated, bright green leaves that are bronze when young.
IDEAL SITE
Shrub borders, woodland gardens, or informal hedging.
CULTIVATION
It thrives in any reasonably fertile, well-drained soil in sun or dappled shade. It needs little pruning other than to shorten any shoots that spoil the shape and to thin out congested shoots on mature plants. Prune after flowering.
ALSO RECOMMENDED
V. farreri ♥ has white, often pink-flushed winter flowers.
PERFECT PARTNERS
Mahonias, sarcococcas.

V

Viburnum x *juddii* ♥

Viburnum opulus
'Compactum' ♥

Viburnum plicatum
'Mariesii' ♥

Viburnum sargentii
'Onondaga' ♥

Viburnum tinus

VIBURNUM

A rounded, deciduous shrub.
H 1.2m (4ft), S 1.2m (4ft).

SEASONAL HIGHLIGHTS
In mid- to late spring, it bears
rounded clusters of fragrant,
pink-tinted, white flowers
that open from pink buds.

VALUE AT OTHER TIMES
In autumn, the dark green
leaves turn dark red.

IDEAL SITE
A mixed or shrub border.

CULTIVATION
Grow in full sun. It will
tolerate partial shade. Grow in
any reasonably fertile, well-
drained soil. After flowering,
shorten any shoots that spoil
the outline.

ALSO RECOMMENDED
V. carlesii is similar but taller
and has red fruits in autumn.

PERFECT PARTNERS
Daphne retusa, Prunus tenella.

GUELDER ROSE

A sturdy but slow-growing
deciduous shrub.
H & S to 1.5m (5ft)

SEASONAL HIGHLIGHTS
In late spring and early
summer, it produces showy,
flat, "lacecap" clusters of white
flowers at the stem tips.

VALUE AT OTHER TIMES
In autumn, the glossy, bright-
red fruits nestle among the
bright red autumn leaves.

IDEAL SITE
Shrub borders, woodland
gardens, or informal hedging.

CULTIVATION
It thrives in any reasonably
fertile, well-drained soil in
sun or dappled shade. It needs
little pruning other than to
shorten any shoots that spoil
the shape after flowering.

ALSO RECOMMENDED
V. opulus 'Xanthocarpum' ♥
has yellow fruits.

PERFECT PARTNERS
*Ceratostigma willmottianum,
Lonicera* x *purpusii.*

JAPANESE SNOWBALL
TREE

A vigorous, spreading,
deciduous shrub with
distinctively tiered branches.
H & S to 4m (12ft)

SEASONAL HIGHLIGHTS
In late spring, it produces flat
"lacecap" white flowerheads.

VALUE AT OTHER TIMES
It has heart-shaped leaves that
turn red-purple in autumn.

IDEAL SITE
Shrub and mixed borders,
woodland gardens.

CULTIVATION
Grow in any reasonably
fertile, well-drained soil in
sun or partial shade. After
flowering, lightly prune any
shoots that spoil the outline
of the shrub.

ALSO RECOMMENDED
V. plicatum; both the shrub and
the flowerheads are more
rounded in shape.

PERFECT PARTNERS
Osmanthus delavayi.

VIBURNUM

A bushy, moderately vigorous,
deciduous shrub.
H 3m (10ft), S 2m (6ft)

SEASONAL HIGHLIGHTS
In late spring, it bears flat,
"lacecap" heads of pink-
flushed, white flowers.

VALUE AT OTHER TIMES
The maple-like leaves are
purple-bronze in spring,
green in summer and dark
red-purple in autumn.

IDEAL SITE
Shrub and mixed borders,
woodland gardens.

CULTIVATION
Grow in any reasonably
fertile, well-drained soil in
sun or partial shade. After
flowering, lightly prune any
shoots that spoil the outline
of the shrub.

ALSO RECOMMENDED
V. sieboldii is taller, with open
clusters of small white flowers
in late spring and pink fruit.

PERFECT PARTNERS
Mahonias, *Daphne mezereum,*
sarcococcas.

LAURUSTINUS

A dense, moderately vigorous,
evergreen shrub.
H & S to 3m (10ft)

SEASONAL HIGHLIGHTS
Over long periods in winter
and spring, it bears flattened
clusters of white flowers.

VALUE AT OTHER TIMES
The glossy, dark green leaves
are attractive all year.

IDEAL SITE
In shrub borders or as
informal hedging.

CULTIVATION
Grow in sun or partial shade
in any fertile, moist but well-
drained soil. Trim hedging
after flowering and, on free-
standing specimens, shorten
any overlong shoots that spoil
the outline.

ALSO RECOMMENDED
V. rhytidophyllum is very tall,
with deeply veined, leathery,
dark green leaves.

PERFECT PARTNERS
Forsythias, mahonias, *Rubus
thibetanus.*

W

Z

Vinca minor

Vitis coignetiae ♥

Weigela 'Looymansii Aurea'

Wisteria floribunda 'Multijuga' ♥

Zinnia elegans 'Dasher Scarlet'

LESSER PERIWINKLE
A dense, vigorous, trailing evergreen shrub.
H to 20cm (8in), S indefinite
SEASONAL HIGHLIGHTS
From spring until autumn, it bears blue-violet, occasionally pale blue, red-purple, or white flowers.
VALUE AT OTHER TIMES
The attractive lance-shaped, glossy, dark green leaves make excellent ground cover.
IDEAL SITE
Shady or sunny banks and borders or woodland gardens.
CULTIVATION
Grow in any but the driest soil in partial or deep shade. In sun, the soil needs to be reliably moist. Prune as hard as necessary to keep it within bounds.
ALSO RECOMMENDED
V. major 'Variegata' ♥ spreads rampantly and has larger, cream-variegated leaves.
PERFECT PARTNERS
Euonymous fortunei 'Emerald 'n' Gold'.

ORNAMENTAL VINE
A vigorous, deciduous climber.
H 15m (50ft), S indefinite
SEASONAL HIGHLIGHTS
Undoubtedly at its best in the autumn when the large, heart-shaped leaves turn gold then brilliant red and purple.
VALUE AT OTHER TIMES
The deep green, spring and summer leaves are wrinkled and deeply veined with thick brown felt beneath.
IDEAL SITE
On large walls, through tall trees, to disguise unsightly garden structures.
CULTIVATION
Grow in sun or partial shade in well-drained, preferably neutral to slightly alkaline soil. Prune in winter and again in summer, as needed, to confine to allotted space.
ALSO RECOMMENDED
V. vinifera 'Purpurea' ♥ has purple leaves (red in autumn).
PERFECT PARTNERS
Parthenocissus thompsonii, Tropaeolum tuberosum.

WEIGELIA
A slow-growing, arching, deciduous shrub.
H & S to 1.5m (5ft)
SEASONAL HIGHLIGHTS
In late spring and early summer, it bears bell-shaped flowers that are pale pink with a darker pink reverse.
VALUE AT OTHER TIMES
It has golden-yellow leaves from spring to autumn.
IDEAL SITE
Sunny, mixed or shrub borders.
CULTIVATION
Grow in full sun or light, dappled shade in any fertile, well-drained soil. Shorten flowered shoots to strong buds after flowering. Every three or four years, take out about one in four of the oldest shoots at the base to encourage new growth.
ALSO RECOMMENDED
W. florida 'Variegata' ♥ has white-edged, grey-green leaves.
PERFECT PARTNERS
Shrubby potentillas, philadelphus, *Spiraea japonica.*

JAPANESE WISTERIA
A very vigorous, deciduous twining climber.
H & S 9m (28ft) or more
SEASONAL HIGHLIGHTS
In early summer, it bears hanging chains of fragrant, pea-like, lilac-blue flowers.
VALUE AT OTHER TIMES
It has attractive, fresh green leaves from spring to autumn.
IDEAL SITE
Walls, arbours, pergolas, trees.
CULTIVATION
Grow in sun in any fertile, well-drained soil. Avoid east-facing walls; early sun will exacerbate damage to frosted flower buds. Train main stems on to supporting wires. In summer, cut back the leafy sideshoots to 5–6 buds from the main stems, and again in winter, shortening them to 2–3 buds.
ALSO RECOMMENDED
W. sinensis 'Alba' ♥ has chains of white flowers.
PERFECT PARTNERS
Late-flowering clematis.

ZINNIA
Bushy, half-hardy annual.
H & S 30cm (12in)
SEASONAL HIGHLIGHTS
From early summer to autumn, it bears semi-double heads of scarlet, weatherproof flowers above dense mounds of pale to mid-green leaves.
VALUE AT OTHER TIMES
Is discarded after flowering.
IDEAL SITE
Bedding and edging, containers, window boxes.
CULTIVATION
Grow in sun, in any moderately fertile, well-drained soil. Sow seeds in warmth in early spring. For a longer succession of blooms, sow some in the flowering site in late spring. Deadhead regularly to keep more flowers coming.
ALSO RECOMMENDED
Z. haageana 'Orange Star' has orange flowerheads.
PERFECT PARTNERS
French marigolds, tuberous begonias, nemesias.

index

water hyacinth 124, 150, 249
waterfalls, oxygenating ponds 99, 124, 179
watering 144, 160
    automatic trickle irrigation systems 174
    bedding plants 148
    brassicas 181
    containers 23, 123–4, 179, 206
    fruit 74, 129–30, 154
    greenhouses 28, 76, 254
    hanging baskets 123–4, *179*
    lawns 150, 160, 180, 207
    newly planted trees and shrubs 120
    pot plants 154
    seephose 148, 174, 180
    sprinklers 148
    strawberries 252
    vegetables 101, 155, 180, 208
    water butts 19, 136, 174
    water-retentive crystals 70
    in winter 248, 272, 289
waterlilies 124, *167*, 336, *336*
    autumn clearance 249
    dividing 97, *97*
weather
    climate change 136
    January 11
    February 35
    March 57
    April 83
    May 111
    June 135

    July 161
    August 191
    September 215
    October 237
    November 259
    December 277
weedkillers
    for lawns 126, 227
    in rock gardens 68
    spot-treating with 178
weeds
    in alpine beds 178, 205
    around fruit 102
    hoeing 73, 120, 128, 144, 180, 192
    in lawns 45, 99, 126, 207
    mulching beds 58, 64, 120
    perennial weeds 144, 178
    in ponds 124, *124*, 150, *150*
    in rock gardens 68
    seedlings 18, 58
    in vegetable gardens 208
weeping pear 345
weeping sedge 303
Weigela 359
    pruning 145, 175
    florida 'Variegata' 359
    'Looymansii Aurea' *141*, *359*
Westonbirt Arboretum, Gloucestershire 236
white sage 299
whitecurrants
    cuttings 253, 271, 289
    harvesting 183

    pruning 27, 183
    training 103
whitefly 18, 103–4, 131, 155
wigwams, sweet peas 69, *69*
wildflower meadows *135*
wildlife
    drinking water 18, 174, 202, 278, 282
    pest control 92
    in ponds 44, *135*, 174
willow *see Salix*
wind
    scorch 94, 284
    supporting trees and shrubs 10, 265
    wind rock 48, 245, 283, 285
windbreaks
    evergreens 283–4
    moving shrubs 222
    protecting trees and shrubs 19, 265
windflower, mountain 298
windowsills, light boxes *52–3*
winged spindle *see Euonymus*
winter aconite *see Eranthis*
winter heath 317
winter jasmine 285, 327
winter moth 230, *252*
winter purslane 181, *181*
winter rye 264
winter wash
    fruit trees 26–7, 48, 288–9
    roses 202, 284
wintersweet *see Chimonanthus*
wire, supporting climbers *66*

Wisteria 359
    failure to flower 204
    layering 146
    pruning 21, *21*, 176, 204
    floribunda 'Multijuga' *116*, *359*
    sinensis 'Alba' 359
witch hazel *see Hamamelis*
witloof chicory, sowing 127, 152
wood, preservatives 283
wood pigeons 152, 181
woolly aphids 184
worm casts 24, 45

y

yarrow *see Achillea*
"Yellow Book", garden visiting 112
yew
    pruning 41
    trimming hedges 203
Yucca gloriosa 192

z

Zantedeschia aethiopica 98
Zinnia 359
    sowing 77
    elegans 'Dasher Scarlet' *168*, *359*
    haageana 'Orange Star' 359
zonal pelargonium 339

acknowledgements

AUTHOR'S ACKNOWLEDGEMENTS
I wish to express my heartfelt thanks to all of the people involved with this book project, for without their help and encouragement I would never have finished it. Firstly I must thank the publisher, Dorling Kindersley, and the Royal Horticultural Society for having faith in me and allowing the project to go ahead. Individually I must thank David Lamb, Louise Abbott, Alison Lotinga, Anna Kruger, Lee Griffiths and Viv Watton. They have all been very professional, excellent company and I have learned a lot from all of them. Thanks to all the team at the RHS too for their editorial input. And to anyone not mentioned my apologies and special thanks.

I would also like to thank Lin Hawthorne for editing the Plant Directory. Other people to thank include Mr Chris Ayton for information on Yoder chrysanthemums from Littlehampton in West Sussex and The Met Office in Bracknell, Berkshire for the meteorological facts and figures used to help compile the Weather Watch for each month.

I also wish to express special thanks to Lynda Hamilton for the use of her garden as a setting for some of the monthly projects.

Lastly, but by no means least, my thanks to Steve Hamilton for taking the photographs for each of the monthly projects. He showed extreme patience, especially considering my carpentry skills!

PUBLISHER'S ACKNOWLEDGEMENTS
Dorling Kindersley would like to thank Susanne Mitchell, Karen Wilson, Barbara Haynes, Andrew Halstead and Chris Prior of the Royal Horticultural Society; Lin Hawthorne for editorial assistance, and Murdo Culver for technical assistance.

Index
Hilary Bird

PICTURE CREDITS
Commissioned Photography
Steve Hamilton

Illustrations
Karen Gavin, pages 30, 78, 187bl, 255bl, 272/273, 290; Gill Tomblin, pages 187br, 255br.

Dorling Kindersley photographs
Peter Anderson, Clive Boursnell, Deni Bown, Jonathan Buckley, Andrew Butler, Andy Crawford, Eric Crichton, Christine M. Douglas, John Fielding, Neil Fletcher, John Glover, Jerry Harpur, Stephen Hayward, C. Andrew Henley, Jacqui Hurst 3, 5br, 135tl, 193, 217br, 239br; Dave King, Andrew Lawson, Howard Rice, Bob Rundle, Richard Surman, Kim Taylor/Jane Burton, Juliette Wade, Matthew Ward, Steven Wooster, Jerry Young.

The publishers would also like to thank the following for their kind permission to reproduce their photographs:
(Key: t=top, c=centre, b=bottom, f=far, r=right, l=left)

David Austin Roses:
170cr, bfr, br, bl, cfl, 348tc, tfr, c, 349tl, tfl.
A-Z Botanical Collection:
J.Borg 263br, 327tfl; Ron Chapman 114bl, 342tfl; Anthony Cooper 11, 280br, 351tr; Ian Gowland 39tl, 306tr; R.Greenwood 281br, 300tc; Ray Lacey 141tc, 296tr; Jiri Loun 221br, 339tl; Mrs Monks 218tr, 234, 305tl; Adrian Thomas 168bc, 315tl; H.Thomson 63bl, 319tfr.
Gillian Beckett:
86tl, 119tc, 243tr, 297tr, tfr, 342tfr.
Corbis UK Ltd:
Eric Crichton 278; Tony Hamblin/Frank Lane Picture Agency 34.

Eric Crichton Photos:
36, 86bc, 139tl, tfr, 168bl, 240bl, 274, 306tl, 313tl, 343tfr, 355tr, 357tc.
Garden Picture Library:
Mark Bolton 214; Mark Boulton 17tr, 310bfr; Brian Carter 173tc, 356tl; Ron Evans 13b, 194bc, 300tr; Christopher Fairweather 255c; John Glover 15tfr, 295tr; Neil Holmes 39bl, 304tfl; Lamontagne 115bc, 345bc; Zara McCalmont 17bc, 310cr; Howard Rice 37bl, 60bc, 351tc; Friedrich Strauss 169tr, 340tl; Bridgitte Thomas 89br, 332tr; Didier Willery 132, 262tl, 305tr; Paul Windsor 136.
Garden and Wildlife Matters:
59bc, 84l, 90br, 114tc, 116bc, 134, 142br, 166tl, 166tc, 192l, 243br, 262tr, 263bl, 277, 281tr, 283, 305tfl, 306tc, 309tr, 328c, 329tfr, 347tl, 351tfl, 353tr, 358tc; Nancy Rothwell 16tc, 327tc; Steffie Shields 62bl, 116tl, 343tr, 356tfr; Debi Wagner Stock Pics 266b.
Image Bank:
Grant V. Faint 111t; Steve Satushek 80.
Living Colour/Jacques Amands:
61bc, 334tc.
Nature Photographers:
Paul Sterry 135tc, 191b.
Clive Nichols:
8, 57, 85, 191t; Bassibones Farm, Bucks 108; Dower House, Glocs 32; Lady Farm, Somerset 292; Rupert Golby(Chelsea 95) 163t; Leeds City Council (Chelsea 98) 162; Wollerton Old Hall, Shropshire 10.
Photos Horticultural:
14tr, 16tl, 17tc, 38br, 60tl, 63tl, bc, 82, 91tc, 111b, 113, 116bl, 117tl, 119br, 140cr, 142bl, 164tc, 168tr, 174, 197br, 198tr, 200br, 216, 218br, 237, 240tr, 241tc, 255tl, 255tr, 255cr, 255cfr, 260l, 263bc, 276, 280tl, 295bl, 296tl, 296tl, 297tl, 298tr, 302tc, 304tl, tr, 307cl, 309, 310tr, 312tfr, 316tc, 317tr, 320tfl, 326tfl, 329tl, tc, 332tfl, 347tfl, 350tr, 356tr, 358tr, tfl, 359tfr.
Gettyone stone:
Chris Everard 188; Mark Douet 1, 236.